RETIREMENT
PLACES
R·A·T·E·D

RETIREMENT PLACES R·A·T·E·D

DAVID SAVAGEAU

Macmillan • USA

Acknowledgments

This revision of *Retirement Places Rated* could not have been done without the insights and criticisms of hundreds of readers.

I'm indebted once more to the people at Macmillan General Reference and Travel—particularly the very patient Leanne Coupe—for energy, humor, and encouragement every step of the way.

Thanks also to: Bob Fraser and Bob Fulton, PHH Technology Services; and Paul LoBue, Mapping Specialists Ltd.

Finally, special thanks are due Woods and Poole Economics, Inc., of Washington, D.C., for their population, income, and employment forecasts. The use of this information, and the conclusions drawn from it, are solely the responsibility of the author.

Publisher's Note

This book contains information gathered from many sources. It is published for general reference and not as a substitute for independent verification by users when circumstances warrant. Although care and diligence have been used in its preparation, the Publisher does not guarantee the accuracy of the information. The interpretation of the data and the views expressed are the author's and not necessarily those of Macmillan Travel.

Macmillan Travel
A Simon & Schuster Macmillan Company
15 Columbus Circle
New York, NY 10023

ISBN 0-02-860055-X
Library of Congress Catalog Card No.: 90-7714

Printed in the United States of America

10 9 8 7 6 5 4 3 2 1

Fourth Edition

CONTENTS

••

*I*NTRODUCTION

··

When you arrive at that certain age and bid goodbye to the job, will you stay where you are? "The best place to retire," advises Dr. Robert Butler, former head of the National Institute on Aging, "is the neighborhood where you spent your life."

Now that's a dash of common sense. People do have more power, independence, and plain practical knowledge in the place where they're living than they might ever have in a distant, unfamiliar location.

Statistics bear this out. For all the hype about moving away, the number of older adults who actually settle each year in another state after they retire wouldn't crowd the route for the Cotton Bowl parade. Most of us are inclined to stay where we are.

There's more to it than convenience. The psychic connection that comes with raising children, working at a job, and paying off a mortgage in one place may be missed in a new one. When you move you can take the philodendron, the oak blanket chest, the canoe, and the car, but you can't pack a deep sense of place.

Perhaps for you, relocation is unthinkable. You've known your neighbors for years, your doctor knows you, you don't need to look up the bank's phone number, ask for directions to a discount hardware store, or scratch your head for the name of the one person in city hall who can get the sewer fixed. What you may

ultimately want is "R and R" in familiar territory, not an agenda that takes high energy and risk just to sink new roots.

If all this is true, stay put. But possibly—just possibly—there is someplace in this country where you might prosper more than where you now live. And possibly, too, it is a lack of information that keeps you from taking a look.

RETIREMENT PLACES RATED

For more than a dozen years, this book has profiled hundreds of retirement spots throughout the country. This new edition takes the same approach as all of its predecessors and has been thoroughly updated, revised, and expanded.

Retirement Places Rated is meant for those who are planning for retirement and are weighing the pros and cons of moving or staying. It is a guide offering facts about 183 carefully chosen places that have attracted a large number of retired persons who make interstate moves.

It is more than a collection of interesting and useful information about places, however. It also grades these places on the basis of seven factors that influence the quality of retirement life: money matters, climate, job

SEVENTEEN REGIONS

In addition to the places in this book, you'll see references to broadly defined *regions* where places might be grouped. Few of the regions match the political boundaries shown in a road atlas; most embrace parts of more than one state, and some states are apportioned among more than one region.

California Coast
Carmel–Monterey–Pebble Beach, CA
Laguna Beach–Dana Point, CA
San Diego, CA
San Luis Obispo, CA
Santa Barbara, CA
Santa Rosa–Sonoma, CA

Desert Southwest
Cottonwood–Verde Valley, AZ
Hesperia–Apple
  Valley–Victorville, CA
Kingman, AZ
Lake Havasu City, AZ
Las Vegas, NV
Pahrump Valley, NV
Palm Springs–Coachella Valley, CA
Payson, AZ
Phoenix–Mesa–Scottsdale, AZ
Prescott–Prescott Valley, AZ
Riviera–Bullhead City, AZ
St. George–Zion, UT
Sedona, AZ
Silver City, NM
Tucson, AZ
Wickenburg, AZ
Yuma, AZ

Florida Interior
Brooksville–Spring Hill, FL
Gainesville, FL
Inverness, FL
Kissimmee–St. Cloud, FL
Lakeland–Winter Haven, FL
Leesburg–Lady Lake, FL
Ocala, FL
Sebring–Avon Park, FL

Gulf Coast
Bay St. Louis–Pass Christian, MS
Bradenton, FL
Fairhope–Gulf Shores, AL
Fort Myers–Cape Coral, FL
Naples, FL
New Port Richey, FL
Panama City, FL
Port Charlotte–Punta Gorda, FL
Rockport–Aransas Pass, TX
St. Petersburg–Clearwater, FL
Sarasota, FL
Western St. Tammany Parish, LA

Hawaii
Kauai, HI
Maui, HI

Inner South
Aiken, SC
Athens, GA
Crossville, TN
Guntersville, AL
Kentucky Lake, KY
Lake Martin, AL
Madison, MS
Oxford, MS
Southern Pines–Pinehurst, NC
Thomasville, GA

Mid-Atlantic Metro Belt
Annapolis, MD
Chapel Hill, NC
Charles Town–Harpers
  Ferry–Shepherdstown, WV
Charlottesville, VA
East End Long Island, NY
Easton–St. Michaels–Oxford, MD

Fredericksburg–Spotsylvania, VA
Lower Cape May, NJ
Northern Neck, VA
Ocean City, MD
Pike County, PA
Rehoboth Bay–Indian River Bay,
  DE
State College, PA
Toms River–Barnegat Bay, NJ
Virginia Beach, VA
Williamsburg, VA

New England
Amherst–Northampton, MA
Bar Harbor, ME
Burlington, VT
Camden, ME
Cape Cod, MA
Hanover, NH
Lake Winnipesaukee, NH
Litchfield Hills, CT
St. Jay–Northeast Kingdom,
  VT
Southern Berkshire County,
  MA
Woodstock, VT
York Beaches, ME

North Woods
Charlevoix–Boyne City–East
  Jordan, MI
Eagle River, WI
Houghton Lake, MI
Northern Door Peninsula, WI
Oscoda–Tawas–Huron
  Shore, MI
Petoskey–Harbor Springs, MI
Traverse City, MI

outlook, available services, housing, leisure, and personal safety.

Retirement Places Rated doesn't treat later life as a kind of autumn or a second career, turning point, third age, or transformation. The book simply gives you the facts you need to start evaluating other locations where you might live.

After using the book, your hunch that you'll never find a better place than your own hometown might well be confirmed. On the other hand, given the variety offered throughout the country, what are the odds the place where you happen to live is the right one for you?

WHERE ARE THESE PLACES?

If you were asked, in a kind of geographic word-association test, to name the states that spring to mind when you hear the word retirement, you might well tick off the big ones in the Sun Belt: Arizona, California, Florida, Georgia, Nevada, New Mexico, North Carolina, South Carolina, and Texas.

You'd be right, of course. In the generations since the end of World War II, these attracted most of the older adults who packed up and moved to another state. Several of their large cities—Phoenix, San Diego, Fort Myers, Albuquerque, Las Vegas, Asheville, Charleston, and San Antonio—are as synonymous with retirement as any in the country.

But states above the Sun Belt deserve a place in retirement geography. Oregon and Washington are drawing thousands of equity-rich Californians. The 160-mile stretch of New Jersey's sandy Atlantic coastline from Cape May up to Monmouth owes a good part of its economic rebound to older newcomers moving in from New York and Philadelphia. Catalogs mailed out by coastal Maine real estate brokers to retirementplanning Washingtonians are getting fatter and slicker. Meanwhile, the requests for relocation packets from Floridians are an amazement to chambers of commerce in the northern Rockies.

It's no secret that places in every part of the country benefit from older adults moving into them. Roughly

SEVENTEEN REGIONS *(continued)*

Ozarks and Ouachitas
Beaver Lake, AR
Branson, MO
Fayetteville, AR
Hot Springs, AR
Lake of the Cherokees, OK
Lake of the Ozarks, MO
Norfork Lake, AR
Table Rock Lake, MO

Pacific Northwest
Bellingham, WA
Bend, OR
Brookings–Gold Beach, OR
Florence, OR
Grants Pass, OR
Medford–Ashland, OR
Newport–Lincoln City, OR
Port Angeles–Seqium, WA
Port Townsend, WA
San Juan Islands, WA
Whidbey Island, WA

Rio Grande Country
Alamogordo, NM
Albuquerque, NM
Alpine–Big Bend, TX
Las Cruces, NM
Mission–McAllen–Alamo, TX
Ruidoso, NM
Santa Fe, NM
Taos, NM

Rocky Mountain
Chewelah, WA
Coeur d'Alene, ID
Colorado Springs, CO
Delta–Cedaredge, CO

Durango, CO
Fort Collins–Loveland, CO
Grand Junction, CO
Hamilton–Bitterroot Valley, MT
Kalispell–Flathead Valley, MT
Ketchum–Sun Valley, ID
McCall–Cascade–Payette Valley, ID
Montrose, CO
Pagosa Springs, CO
Polson–Mission Valley, MT
Sandpoint–Priest River, ID
Wenatchee, WA

South Atlantic Coast
Beaufort, SC
Boca Raton–Delray Beach, FL
Charleston Sea Islands, SC
Conway, SC
Dare Outer Banks, NC
Daytona Beach, FL
Edenton, NC
Hilton Head Island, SC
Key West–Key Largo–Marathon, FL
Melbourne, FL
Myrtle Beach–North Myrtle Beach, SC
New Bern, NC
Pompano Beach, FL
St. Augustine, FL
St. Simons–Jekyll Islands, GA
Savannah, GA
Southport–Brunswick Islands, NC
Vero Beach–Sebastian, FL

Southern Highlands
Asheville, NC

Blairsville, GA
Boone–Blowing Rock, NC
Brevard, NC
Clayton, GA
Clemson–Pendleton District, SC
Hendersonville–East Flat Rock, NC
Hiawassee, GA
Maryville, TN
Smith Mountain Lake, VA
Tryon, NC
Winchester, VA

Tahoe Basin and the Other California
Amador County, CA
Carson City–Carson Valley, NV
Grass Valley–Nevada City, CA
Oakhurst–Coarsegold, CA
Paradise–Magalia, CA
Placerville–Shingle Springs, CA
Redding, CA
Reno–Sparks, NV
Sonora–Groveland–Twain Harte, CA

Texas Interior
Austin, TX
Cedar Creek Lake, TX
Fredericksburg, TX
Kerrville, TX
Lake Buchanan–Lake LBJ, TX
Lake Conroe, TX
Lake Granbury, TX
Lake Livingston, TX
New Braunfels, TX
San Antonio, TX
Wimberly, TX

---

every tenth older adult is a newcomer in one out of five of the country's 3,142 counties. If these locations were to be daubed in red on a blank map of the United States, the nation would look as if it had measles.

They are found along rural roads within commuting distance of big cities. They are in the midst of forested federal lands. They are positioned along rocky ocean coastlines, in river valleys, around lakes, on mountain slopes, and in desert crossroads with striking distant vistas.

To identify likely places from among the hundreds of possibilities, *Retirement Places Rated* uses several criteria. The place should have a 1995 area population greater than 10,000. A smaller population may signal a lower level of human services. Moreover, the place should be growing. Between 1990 and 1995, the U.S. population grew 5 percent; the retirement places profiled here together grew 11 percent.

In addition, the place should be attractive to older adults. In almost all of the retirement places in this book, there is a much greater number of persons 60 to 65 years

of age today than there were persons 50 to 55 years of age a decade ago. This simple demographic exercise indicates the place is drawing older newcomers.

The place should be relatively safe. The U.S. annual average crime rate, for example, is 5,759 per 100,000 people. In seven out of ten of the places profiled here, it's much less.

The place should be affordable, too. The money it takes to live in nine out of 10 of the places included in this book is less than the U.S. average estimated costs for a newly retired household.

The place should have natural endowments. Most of the places included here are blessed either with large areas of federal recreation land, state recreation land, large areas of inland water, or an ocean coastline. Several have all four.

Based on personal visits, the advice of experts, and recommendations from hundreds of older adults, *Retirement Places Rated* profiles 183 places. One hundred and sixteen are found in the 14 Sun Belt states. Retirement relocation is largely a march to low-cost living and

Bellingham
Port Angeles-Sequim · San Juan Islands
Port Townsend · Whidbey Island
WA
Wenatchee · Chewelah · Sandpoint-Priest River
Kalispell-Flathead Valley
Polson-Mission Valley
Coeur d'Alene
MT ND
OR
Newport-Lincoln City · Hamilton-Bitterroot Valley
Florence
Bend
SD
Brookings-Gold Beach · McCall-Cascade-Payette Valley
Grants Pass
Medford-Ashland · WY
Ketchum-Sun Valley
CA
NV UT ID
Redding
NE
Paradise-Magalia
Grass Valley-Nevada City · Reno-Sparks
Santa Rosa-Sonoma · Carson City-Carson Valley
Placerville-Shingle Springs
Amador County
Sonora-Groveland-Twain Harte
CO
Fort Collins-Loveland
Oakhurst-Coarsegold · Grand Junction
Carmel-Monterey-Pebble Beach · Delta-Cedaredge · Colorado Springs
Montrose
St. George-Zion
San Luis Obispo · Durango
Pahrump Valley · Las Vegas · Pagosa Springs
AZ NM
KS
Santa Barbara · Riviera-Bullhead City · Taos
Hesperia-Apple Valley-Victorville · Kingman · Santa Fe
Lake Of The Cherokees
Sedona
Palm Springs-Coachella Valley · Lake Havasu City · Cottonwood-Verde Valley · Albuquerque · OK
Laguna Beach-Dana Point · Prescott-Prescott Valley · TX
Payson
Wickenburg
San Diego · Silver City · Ruidoso
Yuma · Phoenix-Mesa-Scottsdale · Alamogordo
Tucson · Las Cruces
Lake Granbury · Cedar Creek Lake
Lake Livingston
Alpine-Big Bend
HI
Lake Buchanan-Lake LBJ · Austin · Lake Conroe
Kauai · Fredericksburg · Wimberly-San Marcos
Kerrville · New Braunfels
San Antonio
Maui
Rockport-Aransas Pass
Mission-McAllen-Alamo

Copyright © 1995 by Places Rated Partnership

183 Retirement Places

MN

WI

Eagle River

Petoskey-Harbor Springs
Charlevoix-Boyne City-East Jordan
Northern Door Peninsula
Traverse City
Oscoda-Tawas-Huron Shore
Houghton Lake

IA

MI

ME

St. Jay-Northeast Kingdom
Burlington
Woodstock
Lake Winnipesaukee
Hanover
Amherst-Northampton
Southern Berkshire County
VT
NH
York Beaches
Bar Harbor
Camden
Cape Cod
MA
CT
Litchfield Hills
RI
East End Long Island

IL

MO

IN   OH

NY
PA
NJ

State College
Pike County
Toms River-Barnegat Bay

Charles Town-Harpers Ferry-Shepherdstown
Winchester
Fredericksburg-Spotsylvania
Annapolis
MD
DE
Lower Cape May
Rehoboth Bay-Indian River Bay
Easton-St. Michaels-Oxford
Ocean City

KY   WV

Charlottesville
Northern Neck
Williamsburg
Virginia Beach
Edenton

VA

Smith Mountain Lake
Dare Outer Banks

Lake of the Ozarks

Table Rock Lake
Branson
Beaver Lake
Norfork Lake
Fayetteville

Kentucky Lake

Boone-Blowing Rock
Chapel Hill
New Bern

Crossville
Maryville
Asheville
Hendersonville-East Flat Rock
Brevard
Tryon
Clayton
Blairsville
Hiawassee

Southern Pines-Pinehurst
Clemson-Pendleton District
Conway
Southport-Brunswick Islands
NC
Myrtle Beach

TN

MS   AL

Oxford
Guntersville

GA

Athens
Aiken
SC

Hot Springs

AR

LA

Lake Martin

Madison

Charleston Sea Islands
Beaufort
Savannah
Hilton Head Island
St. Simons-Jekyll Islands

Thomasville

Fairhope-Gulf Shores
Bay St. Louis-Pass Christian
Western St. Tammany Parish
Panama City
FL

Gainesville
Ocala
Inverness
Brooksville-Spring Hill
Lakeland-Winter Haven
New Port Richey
St. Petersburg-Clearwater
Port Charlotte-Punta Gorda
Fort Myers-Cape Coral
Naples

St. Augustine
Daytona Beach
Leesburg-Lady Lake
Kissimmee-St. Cloud
Melbourne
Sebring-Avon Park
Vero Beach-Sebastian
Bradenton
Sarasota
Boca Raton-Delray Beach
Pompano Beach

Key West-Key Largo-Marathon

Population

- ● 250,000 and over
- ◉ 100,000 to 249,000
- ⊙ 30,000 to 99,000
- ○ less than 29,999

The Last Move

An odd statistic from AT&T market researchers says we change our address 11 times in a lifetime. The common reasons are job changes or job transfers, shifts out of rental housing into home ownership, moves up to larger homes, and divorce.

Is retirement still another reason? Not at all. Each year, fewer than half a million persons between the ages of 55 and 65 pack up and relocate to another state. Another million and a half simply trade the big family house for a smaller place within the same city. Consider your own options. You might:

- Stay at your present address. Forty-seven out of 50 persons between 55 and 65 do.
- Stay close to town but sell or rent your home and move into an apartment, condominium, or smaller home. One in 27 older adults takes this route.
- Move out of town to another part of the state to occupy a vacation home year-round, perhaps. Just one in 70 older adults does this.
- Move to another state. Among 94 older adults, only one of them will take this course.
- Move out of the country. The longest shot of all, just one of 432 older adults does this, and most who do are returning to their native country.

Clearly, hometown turf beats the distant happy valley. Even if you're not thrilled with your current location, you still have to decide whether moving is the key to a more satisfying later life. The anecdotes of people who moved, became disillusioned, and later moved or returned home aren't uncommon.

A basic rule for successful relocation says the day-to-day attractions of a destination must be much, much stronger than the day-to-day attractions of home, and a corollary requires that hometown attractions be overshadowed by hometown liabilities.

Surburban Spots

Not every place in this book is in the sticks. Most are within major media markets and 13 are found in the surburban counties of metro areas with more than one million people.

Dallas—Cedar Creek Lake

Fort Worth–Arlington—Lake Granbury

Houston—Lake Conroe

Jacksonville—St. Augustine

New Orleans—Western St. Tammany Parish

Orlando—Kissimmee–St. Cloud and Leesburg–Lady Lake

Sacramento—Placerville–Shingle Springs

San Antonio—New Braunfels

Seattle—Whidbey Island

Tampa–St. Petersburg—New Port Richey

Washington, DC—Charles Town–Harpers Ferry–Shepherdstown and Fredricksburg–Spotsylvania

Population Growth

Fastest-Growing Places	Increase, 1990–1995
Riviera–Bullhead City, AZ	46.0%
Brooksville–Spring Hill, FL	41.9
St. George–Zion, UT	41.4
Lake Havasu City, AZ	40.2
Cottonwood–Verde Valley, AZ	30.0
New Port Richey, FL	29.0
Amador County, CA	28.3
Kissimmmee–St. Cloud, FL	28.1
Pahrump Valley, NV	28.0
Grass Valley–Nevada City, CA	27.5

Source: Woods & Poole Economics, Inc., population forecasts, and Places Rated Partnership estimates.

milder winters, that much is certain. Because there is a growing counterstream to attractive places outside this region, 67 of these are profiled. In all, 38 states are represented.

Although this selection of places does not by any means include every desirable destination, it does include many of the country's best, and it does represent the variety many persons are choosing for retirement.

A WORD ABOUT PLACE NAMES

None of the 183 places profiled here coincide with the corporate limits of towns or cities. For good reason, most of them are counties. Thanks to the car, the space you can cover on a typical day has expanded since the nostalgic era when Main Street truly was the noisy, exciting center of things. Now people likely live in one town, work in another, visit friends in still another, shop at a mall miles away, and escape to open country—all within an easy drive.

It is no different in retirement places. Metropolitan San Diego not only takes in the country's 6th largest city, it also includes Chula Vista, Oceanside, Escondido, El Cajon, and other suburban places, and the desert east of the Cuyamaca Mountains to boot.

Several retirement destinations in this book take in more than one county. Kentucky Lake encompasses Calloway and Marshall counties in western Kentucky's Purchase area. Burlington includes urban Chittenden and tiny Grand Isle on the Vermont shore of Lake Champlain.

County names can ring a bell with travelers. Hawaii's Maui, Wisconsin's Door, and New Jersey's Cape May are three such places. Other counties—Santa Fe in New Mexico, Yuma in Arizona, and San Luis Obispo on the California coast—have the same name as their well-known seats of government. In these instances, it's natural to call the retirement place by its county name.

But county names aren't usually tossed about in discourse. Washington County, Arkansas, is one of 31 counties honoring the first president of the United States. The name draws a blank to Texans, Louisianans, Missourians, and Oklahomans (neighboring states that have their own Washington County). Fayetteville, home of the University of Arkansas and the seat of Washington County, is better recognized by everyone.

Another case is Barnstable County, Massachusetts, which includes all of Cape Cod from Buzzards Bay out old U.S. 6 on the famous sandy spit of land to Province-

town. Centuries ago, Cape Cod elbowed Barnstable County aside in popular New England usage.

Sometimes the name given a retirement place is that of the one or two biggest population centers; thus North Carolina's Orange County becomes Chapel Hill, and Florida's Charlotte County becomes Port Charlotte–Punta Gorda. In other instances, the name of a town may be paired with a well-known natural feature; Polson–Mission Valley identifies Lake County, Montana; likewise, New Jersey's Ocean County becomes Toms River–Barnegat Bay.

The following chart names the 183 places as they are used throughout *Retirement Places Rated* and shows their component counties.

183 Retirement Places

Places and Component Counties	1990 Population	1995 Population	Growth, 1990–1995	Places and Component Counties	1990 Population	1995 Population	Growth, 1990–1995
Aiken, SC Aiken county	121,920	138,330	13.5%	**Bradenton, FL** Manatee county	212,700	258,390	21.5
Alamogordo, NM Otero county	51,960	52,370	0.8	**Branson, MO** Taney county	25,720	30,140	17.2
Albuquerque, NM Bernalillo county	482,250	522,210	8.3	**Brevard, NC** Transylvania county	25,540	26,440	3.5
Alpine–Big Bend, TX Brewster county	8,640	8,550	−1.0	**Brookings–Gold Beach, OR** Curry county	19,390	20,760	7.1
Amador County, CA Amador county	30,260	38,810	28.3	**Brooksville–Spring Hill, FL** part of Hernando county	102,140	144,900	41.9
Amherst–Northampton, MA Hampshire county	146,580	154,230	5.2	**Burlington, VT** Chittenden and Grand Isle counties	137,180	148,020	7.9
Annapolis, MD part of Anne Arundel county	154,280	168,330	9.1	**Camden, ME** Knox county	36,390	38,500	5.8
Asheville, NC Buncombe county	175,430	189,820	8.2	**Cape Cod, MA** Barnstable county	186,800	195,040	4.4
Athens, GA Clarke county	87,600	90,390	3.2	**Carmel–Monterey–Pebble Beach, CA** part of Monterey county	129,880	135,970	4.7
Austin, TX Travis county	579,900	661,560	14.1	**Carson City–Carson Valley, NV** Carson City independent city and Douglas county	68,810	75,040	9.1
Bar Harbor, ME Hancock county	47,040	49,530	5.3	**Cedar Creek Lake, TX** Henderson county	58,630	61,790	5.4
Bay St. Louis–Pass Christian, MS parts of Hancock and Harrison counties	58,580	60,920	4.0	**Chapel Hill, NC** Orange county	94,200	104,860	11.3
Beaufort, SC part of Beaufort county	52,330	55,560	6.2	**Charles Town–Harpers Ferry–Shepherdstown, WV** Jefferson county	36,070	38,620	7.1
Beaver Lake, AR Carroll county	18,730	21,940	17.1	**Charleston Sea Islands, SC** Charleston county	296,850	304,390	2.5
Bellingham, WA Whatcom county	128,770	146,170	13.5	**Charlevoix–Boyne City–East Jordan, MI** Charlevoix county	21,540	23,060	7.1
Bend, OR Deschutes county	76,010	89,520	17.8	**Charlottesville, VA** Albemarle county and Charlottesville independent city	108,510	117,000	7.8
Blairsville, GA Union county	12,060	14,100	16.9				
Boca Raton–Delray Beach, FL part of Palm Beach county	390,100	468,120	19.5				
Boone–Blowing Rock, NC Watauga county	36,980	42,960	16.2				

Places and Component Counties	1990 Population	1995 Population	Growth, 1990–1995
Chewelah, WA part of Stevens county	10,680	11,200	4.9
Clayton, GA Rabun county	11,680	12,740	9.1
Clemson–Pendleton District, SC parts of Anderson, Oconee, and Pickens counties	110,850	121,380	9.5
Coeur d'Alene, ID Kootenai county	70,610	81,310	15.2
Colorado Springs, CO El Paso county	398,360	431,970	8.4
Conway, SC part of Horry county	37,340	42,560	17.4
Cottonwood–Verde Valley, AZ part of Yavapai county	24,970	32,460	27.1
Crossville, TN Cumberland county	34,980	38,940	11.3
Dare Outer Banks, NC Dare county	22,790	27,920	22.5
Daytona Beach, FL Volusia county	373,000	408,560	9.5
Delta–Cedaredge, CO Delta county	21,110	21,830	3.4
Durango, CO La Plata county	32,510	34,880	7.3
Eagle River, WI Vilas county	17,790	19,640	10.4
East End Long Island, NY part of Suffolk county	52,050	53,610	3.0
Easton–St. Michaels–Oxford, MD Talbot county	30,700	32,080	4.5
Edenton, NC Chowan county	13,540	14,020	3.5
Fairhope–Gulf Shores, AL Baldwin county	99,060	115,350	16.4
Fayetteville, AR Washington county	113,940	122,750	7.7
Florence, OR part of Lane county	17,300	18,050	4.3
Fort Collins–Loveland, CO Larimer county	187,300	212,470	13.4
Fort Myers–Cape Coral, FL Lee county	337,360	414,070	22.7
Fredericksburg, TX Gillespie county	17,260	18,680	8.2
Fredericksburg–Spotsylvania, VA Fredericksburg independent city and Spotsylvania county	76,920	94,600	23.0
Gainesville, FL Alachua county	182,430	197,190	8.1
Grand Junction, CO Mesa county	93,780	100,750	7.4
Grants Pass, OR Josephine county	63,060	67,950	7.8
Grass Valley–Nevada City, CA Nevada county	79,100	100,840	27.5

Places and Component Counties	1990 Population	1995 Population	Growth, 1990–1995
Guntersville, AL Marshall county	70,990	79,340	11.8
Hamilton–Bitterroot Valley, MT Ravalli county	25,240	27,230	7.9
Hanover, NH Grafton county	74,960	80,840	7.8
Hendersonville–East Flat Rock, NC Henderson county	69,570	74,370	6.9
Hesperia–Apple Valley–Victorville, CA part of San Bernardino county	170,710	203,560	19.2
Hiawassee, GA Towns county	6,780	7,000	3.2
Hilton Head Island, SC part of Beaufort county	30,890	35,210	11.6
Hot Springs, AR Garland county	73,670	76,860	4.3
Houghton Lake, MI Roscommon county	19,890	21,160	6.4
Inverness, FL Citrus county	94,230	114,060	21.0
Kalispell–Flathead Valley, MT Flathead county	59,550	67,410	13.2
Kauai, HI Kauai county	51,990	63,580	22.3
Kentucky Lake, KY Calloway and Marshall counties	57,990	61,300	5.4
Kerrville, TX Kerr county	36,420	42,120	15.7
Ketchum–Sun Valley, ID Blaine county	13,680	15,150	10.7
Key West–Key Largo–Marathon, FL Monroe county	78,200	89,110	14.0
Kingman, AZ part of Mohave county	32,000	38,560	20.5
Kissimmee–St. Cloud, FL Osceola county	109,070	139,720	28.1
Laguna Beach–Dana Point, CA part of Orange county	147,800	158,300	7.1
Lake Buchanan–Lake LBJ, TX Burnet and Llano counties	34,360	36,390	5.3
Lake Conroe, TX part of Montgomery county	184,310	217,720	18.1
Lake Granbury, TX Hood county	29,260	33,800	15.5
Lake Havasu City, AZ part of Mohave county	26,720	37,450	40.2
Lake Livingston, TX parts of Polk, San Jacinto, and Trinity counties	58,820	64,740	13.3
Lake Martin, AL Tallapoosa county	38,930	40,750	4.7
Lake of the Cherokees, OK Delaware county	28,180	29,760	5.6

Places and Component Counties	1990 Population	1995 Population	Growth, 1990–1995
Lake of the Ozarks, MO Camden county	27,590	30,630	11.0
Lake Winnipesaukee, NH parts of Belknap and Carroll counties	84,580	87,400	6.7
Lakeland–Winter Haven, FL Polk county	406,830	424,770	4.4
Las Cruces, NM Dona Ana county	136,390	152,120	11.5
Las Vegas, NV Clark county	754,390	920,070	22.0
Leesburg–Lady Lake, FL Lake county	153,260	194,340	26.8
Litchfield Hills, CT part of Litchfield county	28,190	30,250	7.3
Lower Cape May, NJ part of Cape May county	60,870	62,500	2.7
Madison, MS Madison county	54,180	59,830	10.4
Maryville, TN Blount county	86,490	95,390	10.3
Maui, HI Maui county	102,110	126,210	23.6
McCall–Cascade–Payette Valley, ID Valley county	6,220	7,860	26.4
Medford–Ashland, OR Jackson county	147,260	159,240	8.1
Melbourne, FL part of Brevard county	219,940	241,730	9.9
Mission–McAllen–Alamo, TX Hidalgo county	386,330	457,210	18.3
Montrose, CO Montrose county	24,560	26,560	8.1
Myrtle Beach–North Myrtle Beach, SC part of Horry county	61,270	74,750	22.0
Naples, FL Collier county	153,550	192,450	25.3
New Bern, NC Craven county	81,790	84,890	3.8
New Braunfels, TX Comal county	52,110	60,780	16.6
New Port Richey, FL part of Pasco county	191,550	247,150	29.3
Newport–Lincoln City, OR Lincoln county	39,110	40,900	4.6
Norfork Lake, AR Baxter county	31,310	34,580	10.4
Northern Door Peninsula, WI part of Door county	8,200	8,720	6.4
Northern Neck, VA Lancaster and Northumberland counties	21,490	22,170	3.2
Oakhurst–Coarsegold, CA Madera county	89,040	103,420	16.2
Ocala, FL Marion county	196,340	219,630	11.9
Ocean City, MD Worcester county	35,300	39,480	11.8

Places and Component Counties	1990 Population	1995 Population	Growth, 1990–1995
Oscoda–Tawas–Huron Shore, MI Iosco county	30,310	31,560	4.1
Oxford, MS Lafayette county	31,880	33,850	6.2
Pagosa Springs, CO Archuleta county	5,390	6,080	12.8
Pahrump Valley, NV part of Nye county	7,440	9,520	28.1
Palm Springs–Coachella Valley, CA part of Riverside county	225,480	259,570	15.1
Panama City, FL Bay county	127,650	136,320	6.8
Paradise–Magalia, CA part of Butte county	36,480	40,100	9.9
Payson, AZ part of Gila county	13,440	15,050	12.4
Petoskey–Harbor Springs, MI Emmet county	25,160	28,920	14.9
Phoenix–Mesa–Scottsdale, AZ part of Maricopa county	2,130,570	2,371,510	11.3
Pike County, PA Pike county	28,460	31,570	10.9
Placerville–Shingle Springs, CA El Dorado county	127,380	144,040	13.1
Polson–Mission Valley, MT Lake county	21,180	22,560	6.5
Pompano Beach, FL part of Broward county	599,620	657,180	9.6
Port Angeles–Seqium, WA Clallam county	56,850	63,460	11.6
Port Charlotte–Punta Gorda, FL Charlotte county	112,060	140,660	25.5
Port Townsend, WA Jefferson county	20,380	24,270	19.1
Prescott–Prescott Valley, AZ part of Yavapai county	52,430	65,500	24.9
Redding, CA Shasta county	148,380	172,580	16.3
Rehoboth Bay–Indian River Bay, DE Sussex county	113,860	120,490	5.8
Reno–Sparks, NV Washoe county	256,260	282,550	10.3
Riviera–Bullhead City, AZ part of Mohave county	30,640	44,730	45.9
Rockport–Aransas Pass, TX Aransas county	18,030	18,900	4.8
Ruidoso, NM Lincoln county	12,330	13,010	5.5
St. Augustine, FL St. Johns county	84,530	94,800	12.1
St. George–Zion, UT Washington county	49,340	69,760	41.4
St. Jay–Northeast Kingdom, VT Caledonia county	27,880	28,750	3.1

Places and Component Counties	1990 Population	1995 Population	Growth, 1990–1995
St. Petersburg–Clearwater, FL Pinellas county	854,160	900,000	5.4
St. Simons–Jekyll Islands, GA part of Glynn county	14,050	14,580	3.8
San Antonio, TX Bexar county	1,188,730	1,277,180	7.4
San Diego, CA San Diego county	2,508,880	2,736,460	9.1
San Juan Islands, WA San Juan county	10,160	11,620	14.4
San Luis Obispo, CA San Luis Obispo county	217,350	236,780	8.9
Sandpoint–Priest River, ID Bonner county	26,910	29,970	11.4
Santa Barbara, CA part of Santa Barbara county	370,430	383,650	3.6
Santa Fe, NM Santa Fe county	99,450	114,820	15.5
Santa Rosa–Sonoma, CA Sonoma county	389,790	435,440	11.7
Sarasota, FL Sarasota county	279,160	299,340	7.2
Savannah, GA Chatham county	217,690	231,210	6.2
Sebring–Avon Park, FL Highlands county	68,760	73,420	6.8
Sedona, AZ parts of Coconino and Yavapai counties	13,210	14,830	12.3
Silver City, NM Grant county	27,730	29,860	7.7
Smith Mountain Lake, VA parts of Bedford and Franklin counties	85,780	93,370	8.9
Sonora–Groveland–Twain Harte, CA Tuolumne county	48,760	58,140	19.2
Southern Berkshire County, MA part of Berkshire county	31,880	31,560	−0.9
Southern Pines–Pinehurst, NC Moore county	59,280	64,080	8.1
Southport–Brunswick Islands, NC Brunswick county	51,260	62,730	22.4
State College, PA Centre county	123,950	131,460	6.1
Table Rock Lake, MO Stone county	19,220	21,470	11.7
Taos, NM Taos county	23,230	25,100	8.0
Thomasville, GA Thomas county	39,060	39,570	1.3
Toms River–Barnegat Bay, NJ Ocean county	434,170	453,950	4.6
Traverse City, MI Grand Traverse county	64,560	76,930	19.2
Tryon, NC Polk county	14,440	15,010	3.9
Tucson, AZ Pima county	668,570	755,690	13.0
Vero Beach–Sebastian, FL Indian River county	90,600	109,690	21.1
Virginia Beach, VA Virginia Beach independent city	394,750	417,280	5.7
Wenatchee, WA Chelan county	52,410	57,660	10.0
Western St. Tammany Parish, LA part of St. Tammany parish	72,400	81,080	11.7
Whidbey Island, WA Island county	60,700	68,470	12.8
Wickenburg, AZ part of Maricopa county	7,920	8,910	12.3
Williamsburg, VA James City county and Williamsburg independent city	46,670	51,340	10.0
Wimberly–San Marcos, TX Hays county	65,740	72,400	10.1
Winchester, VA Frederick county and Winchester independent city	67,950	77,750	14.4
Woodstock, VT Windsor county	54,090	56,890	5.2
York Beaches, ME York county	164,670	169,210	2.8
Yuma, AZ Yuma county	121,550	131,300	8.0

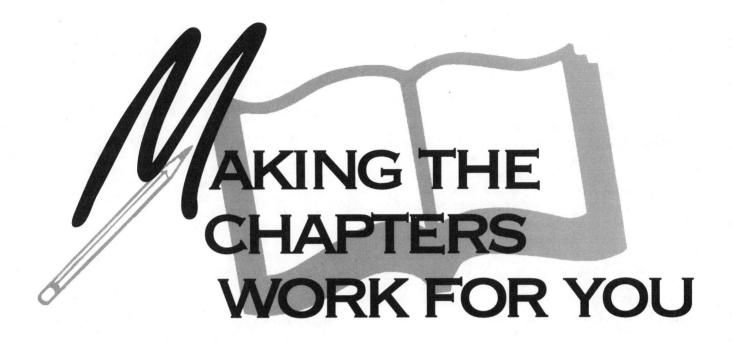

MAKING THE CHAPTERS WORK FOR YOU

There are three points of view on rating places. The first says that defining what's good for all people at all times is not only unfair, it's impossible and shouldn't be tried at all. Another view says you can but shouldn't because measuring a touchy thing like "liveability" pits cities and towns against each other and leads to wrong conclusions. The third point of view says do it as long as you make clear what your statistical yardsticks are and go on to use them consistently.

Although the first and second positions may be valid, *Retirement Places Rated* sides with the third.

RATING PLACES: AN OLD AMERICAN TRADITION

It may seem the height of effrontery, this business of judging places from best to worst with numbers. After all, how can intangible things like friendliness and optimism be measured with statistics? Yet *numeracy* is almost as strong a national character trait as *literacy*. When it comes to picking a new place to live, we've been digesting numbers for a long, long time.

To sell colonists on settling in Maryland rather than in Virginia, 17th-century boosters assembled figures showing heavier livestock, more plentiful game, and

lower mortality from summer diseases and Indian attacks.

California for Health, Wealth, and Residence, just one volume in a library of post–Civil War guides touting the West's superior quality of life, gathered data to show the climate along the southern Pacific coast to be the world's best. Not so, countered the Union Pacific Railroad's land office in 1871; settlers will find the most "genial and healthy seasons" in western Kansas.

In our own century, the statistical nets were flung even wider. "There are plenty of Americans who regard Kansas as almost barbaric," noted H. L. Mencken back in 1931, "just as there are other Americans who shudder whenever they think of Arkansas, Ohio, Indiana, Oklahoma, Texas, or California."

Mencken wrote these words in his *American Mercury* magazine to introduce his formula for measuring the progress of civilization in each of the states. He mixed the number of Boy Scouts and *Atlantic Monthly* subscribers with lynchings and pellagra cases, added a dash of *Who's Who* listings along with rates for divorce and murder, threw in figures for rainfall and gasoline consumption, and found that, hands down, Mississippi was the worst American state. Few were surprised by his finding since Mencken didn't like the South anyway. Massachusetts, a state he did like, came out best.

But the Bay State was demoted in 1978 when Chase Econometrics, an economic consulting firm, rated it the worst state for retirement. And the best state according to the Chase forecasters? Utah.

Rating Retirement Places: One Way

Retirement Places Rated is more useful than any system that just looks at states. When it comes to finding your own spot for retirement, you would do well to ignore the shopworn truisms about states and the track records in attracting older adults.

Thinking of Florida as a destination still means having to make a choice from among thousands of cities, towns, and unincorporated places from Escambia County farm country in the panhandle all the way down some 900 miles to Key West. People don't retire to states, they retire to specific places.

Moreover, statewide averages hide local realities. For some persons, there may be a world of difference between Alamogordo and Santa Fe in New Mexico and these differences may be more important in retirement than the differences between California and Florida.

Certainly this book is more objective than the hearsay that travelers share at an interstate highway rest stop or at an airport gate. Each of the 183 places is rated by seven factors that most persons planning for retirement deem highly important.

- **Money Matters** looks at typical personal incomes and taxes, and it also measures the costs for items such as food and health care.
- **Housing** also looks at costs, including property taxes, utility bills, and average sales prices, and it also notes whether condominiums, mobile homes, and rental apartments are available.
- **Climate** reviews winter discomfort factors such as wind chill and rates summer discomfort factors such as humidity and dampness. Psychological factors such as cloudiness, darkness, and fog also receive scrutiny.
- **Personal Safety** measures the annual rate of violent and property crimes in each place and looks also at the latest local five-year trends, whether up, down, or flat.
- **Services** evaluates the supply of health care, public transportation, and continuing education amenities in each place.
- **Working** compares the local prospects for jobs in three basic industries most promising to older adults: finance, insurance, and real estate; retail trade; and services.
- **Leisure Living** counts recreational and cultural assets such as public golf courses, good restaurants, symphony orchestras and opera companies, and lakes and national parks and state recreation areas.

FINDING YOUR WAY IN THE CHAPTERS

Each of the chapters in *Retirement Places Rated* has four parts:

- The **Introduction** gives basic information on the chapter's topic, peppered with facts and figures to help you evaluate places.
- **Grading** explains how the places are rated. Here, several places are selected as "grading examples" to show why one finishes better than another.
- The **Place Profiles** are capsule comparisons, arranged alphabetically by place, covering all the elements used in the ratings. Here you can see differences among places at a glance.
- The **Et Cetera** section expands on topics mentioned in the introduction and also has essays on related subjects. These range all the way from state-by-state college tuition breaks for older adults to state-by-state tax treatment of retirement income and tactics for avoiding property crime.

The last chapter, "Putting It All Together," averages the grades to identify America's best all-around retirement places, discusses differing lifestyles, and describes the strengths and weaknesses of a particular area.

You may fault *Retirement Places Rated*'s criteria. Admittedly, this book's measurements for health care, public transportation, continuing education, and the performing arts favor big places over small ones. On the other hand, the ratings for personal safety and costs of living favor small places over big ones. The standards for warm, occasionally hot climates and outdoor recreation assets are certainly not everyone's. But they have nothing to do with population size.

Rating Retirement Places: Your Way

At the end of this book, in the chapter entitled "Putting It All Together," money matters, housing, climate, personal safety, community services, working, and leisure living get equal weight to identify retirement places with across-the-board strengths.

You may not agree with this system. You may give more weight to personal safety than to good fishing spots. For you, a place where fixed income goes further might be more important than an abundance of physicians, an ocean coastline, or a busy performing arts calendar. To identify which factors are more important and which factors are less, you might want to take stock of your own preferences.

YOUR PREFERENCE INVENTORY

The following Preference Inventory has 63 pairs of statements. For each pair, decide which statement is more important to you when judging a retirement place. Even if both statements are equally important or neither is important, select one anyway. If you can't decide quickly, pass up the item but return to it after you complete the rest of the inventory.

Don't worry about being consistent. The paired statements aren't repeated. There aren't any right or wrong answers, only those that are best for you. Although the inventory takes about 15 minutes to finish, there is no time limit. You may want to ask your spouse or a friend to use one of the extra preference profiles on the last page of this chapter. Comparing your Preference Inventory with another person's can be an interesting exercise.

Preference Inventory

Directions

For each numbered item, decide which of the two statements is more important to you when choosing a place to retire. Mark the box next to that statement. Be sure to make a choice for all of the items.

1. A. ☐ The costs of living,

    or

  B. ☐ Historic homes in an area.

2. C. ☐ The duration of the winter,

    or

  D. ☐ The odds of being a crime victim.

3. E. ☐ Opportunities for taking college courses,

    or

  F. ☐ Opportunities for volunteer work.

4. A. ☐ How far Social Security benefits will stretch,

    or

  G. ☐ Public golf courses.

5. B. ☐ Adults-only housing developments,

    or

  C. ☐ How hot is summer and how cold is winter.

6. D. ☐ Local burglaries and holdups,

    or

  E. ☐ Medical specialists and accredited hospitals.

7. F. ☐ Five-year forecast for jobs in an area,

    or

  G. ☐ Nearby national parks and forests.

8. A. ☐ Typical household incomes in an area,

    or

  C. ☐ Elevation, humidity, and temperatures.

9. B. ☐ The number of rental apartments in an area,

    or

  D. ☐ How free an area is from criminal activity.

10. C. ☐ A mild, four-season climate,

    or

  E. ☐ Academic programs at local colleges.

11. D. ☐ The local crime rate,

    or

  F. ☐ Variety of volunteer opportunities.

12. E. ☐ Local library acquisition budgets,

    or

  G. ☐ Ocean coastlines and inland lakes.

13. A. ☐ The bite state and local taxes might take,

    or

  F. ☐ Retired Senior Volunteer programs.

14. B. ☐ Nearby life-care residences,

    or

  G. ☐ Symphonies, operas, and theaters.

15. C. ☐ Annual temperature extremes,

    or

  F. ☐ Service Corps of Retired Executives programs.

16. A. ☐ Where the living is inexpensive,

    or

  D. ☐ The odds of being burglarized.

17. B. ☐ Mobile-home parks in an area,

     or

    E. ☐ Health care and public transportation.

18. C. ☐ The length of the growing season,

     or

    G. ☐ Camping, fishing, and hiking.

19. D. ☐ The property crime rate,

     or

    G. ☐ Theater, symphony, and opera seasons.

20. A. ☐ State and local taxes,

     or

    E. ☐ The variety of local college courses.

21. B. ☐ New housing developments in an area,

     or

    F. ☐ Self-employment opportunities.

22. A. ☐ Places where fixed incomes go further,

     or

    B. ☐ Typical property taxes in an area.

23. C. ☐ The number of rainy and snowy days,

     or

    D. ☐ Violent and property crime rates.

24. E. ☐ Accredited short-term, acute-care hospitals,

     or

    F. ☐ Outlook for part-time employment.

25. A. ☐ Tax bites and health-care costs in an area,

     or

    G. ☐ Golf, movies, and good restaurants.

26. B. ☐ Local prices of housing,

     or

    C. ☐ The number of clear and cloudy days.

27. D. ☐ The area's criminal activity,

     or

    E. ☐ Public transit alternatives to the car.

28. F. ☐ Job opportunities in the tourist trade,

     or

    G. ☐ The area's fine arts calendar.

29. A. ☐ The costs of living index,

     or

    C. ☐ The number of thunderstorms in a year.

30. B. ☐ The area's condominium market,

     or

    D. ☐ Local burglaries, robberies, and assaults.

31. C. ☐ Humidity, elevation, and wind speed,

     or

    E. ☐ Public library branches and collections.

32. D. ☐ How safe the area is from violent crime,

     or

    F. ☐ Forecasted employment growth in retail trade.

33. E. ☐ Access to specialized medical care,

     or

    G. ☐ Night life.

34. A. ☐ Where physician fees are low,

     or

    F. ☐ Opportunities for work in the service sector.

35. B. ☐ Typical utility bills in an area,

     or

    G. ☐ Boating, fishing, and swimming.

36. C. ☐ Annual amounts of rain and snow,

     or

    F. ☐ Forecasted employment growth.

37. A. ☐ Where a fixed income will stretch further,

     or

    D. ☐ The area's criminal activity.

38. B. ☐ Taxes on residential property,

     or

    E. ☐ Continuing education at local colleges.

39. C. ☐ How cold the winters are,

     or

    G. ☐ Access to skiing and the great outdoors.

40. D. ☐ Burglary and robbery rates,

     or

    G. ☐ The local performing arts calendar.

41. A. ☐ Making retirement income stretch further,

or

E. ☐ The area's supply of public transportation.

42. B. ☐ Planned retirement communities in an area,

or

F. ☐ Forecasted job growth.

43. A. ☐ Local physician fees,

or

B. ☐ Historic neighborhoods in an area.

44. C. ☐ The area's number of foggy and rainy days,

or

D. ☐ Its number of burglaries and auto thefts.

45. E. ☐ Specialized medical care,

or

F. ☐ Local unemployment potential.

46. A. ☐ State and local tax bites,

or

G. ☐ Cross-country skiing.

47. B. ☐ An area's rental housing market,

or

C. ☐ A mild, four-season climate.

48. D. ☐ Crime-free neighborhoods,

or

E. ☐ Local medical specialists.

49. F. ☐ Job opportunities in real estate and insurance,

or

G. ☐ An area's good restaurants.

50. A. ☐ The bills for heating and cooling a home,

or

C. ☐ January wind chills and July humidities.

51. B. ☐ Newly built housing,

or

D. ☐ Neighborhood crime-watch programs.

52. C. ☐ The potential for cloudy days,

or

E. ☐ Public libraries and bus routes.

53. F. ☐ Seasonal jobs in the tourist season,

or

D. ☐ An area's crime rate.

54. E. ☐ An area's emergency medical services,

or

G. ☐ Good restaurants and first-run movie theaters.

55. A. ☐ Local tax breaks,

or

F. ☐ An area's unemployment rate.

56. B. ☐ Mobile-home parks,

or

G. ☐ Nearby wildlife refuges and national parks.

57. C. ☐ How hot the summers are,

or

F. ☐ Competition for part-time or seasonal work.

58. A. ☐ Launching a part-time business,

or

D. ☐ Crime-free neighborhoods.

59. B. ☐ The typical age of an area's housing stock,

or

E. ☐ The quality of municipal services.

60. C. ☐ Threat of tornadoes and hurricanes,

or

G. ☐ Ocean coastlines and inland lakes.

61. D. ☐ Local auto-theft rates,

or

G. ☐ Local night life.

62. A. ☐ The cost of utilities,

or

E. ☐ The supply of physician specialists.

63. B. ☐ Historic neighborhoods,

or

F. ☐ Local unemployment rates.

Source: Adapted from "The Prospering Test," courtesy Thomas F. Bowman, Ph.D; George Giuliani, Ph.D; and M. Ronald Minge, Ph.D.

Plotting Your Preference Profile

It is important that you make a choice for each of the 63 items. Have you left any unchecked? If not, you're ready to draw your Preference Profile.

First Step. Count all the marks you've made in the boxes next to the letter A. Then enter the number of "A" statements on the line next to the words "Money Matters" on your Preference Profile. In the same way, count the number of statements for each of the other letters. Enter their totals in their respective places on your Preference Profile.

Second Step. Now plot your totals on the blank chart. Place a dot on the appropriate line for each of the numbers and connect the dots to form a line graph of your results (see the Sample Preference Profile).

Analyzing Your Preference Profile

Each of the seven factors in your Preference Profile—money matters, housing, climate, personal safety, community services, working after retirement, and recreation—is not only a major concern when finding a likely place to retire; it also has a complete chapter in this book. The purpose of the Preference Inventory is to help you decide the relative importance of each of the chapters to you personally.

If your scores are high for one or two of these factors, you may want to give extra attention to the chapters covering them. Likewise, if your scores are low for any of the seven, you may not need to give as much consideration to them as you would the ones with high scores. Bear in mind that the inventory *orders* your preferences in a hierarchy, that each of the factors has some importance to you, and that none should be entirely ignored.

Sample Preference Profile

A. Money Matters _12_
B. Housing _8_
C. Climate _12_
D. Personal Safety _6_
E. Services _7_
F. Working _4_
G. Leisure Living _14_

Your Preference Profiles

A. Money Matters _____
B. Housing _____
C. Climate _____
D. Personal Safety _____
E. Services _____
F. Working _____
G. Leisure Living _____

	0	1	2	3	4	5	6	7	8	9	10	11	12	13	14	15	16	17	18
A. Money Matters																			
B. Housing																			
C. Climate																			
D. Personal Safety																			
E. Services																			
F. Working																			
G. Leisure Living																			

	0	1	2	3	4	5	6	7	8	9	10	11	12	13	14	15	16	17	18
A. Money Matters																			
B. Housing																			
C. Climate																			
D. Personal Safety																			
E. Services																			
F. Working																			
G. Leisure Living																			

MONEY MATTERS

Some people say high prices are a sign of the best places because expensive places are more desirable. Say again?

Explain that to people who've fled costly New York for Florida, pricey California for Nevada, or even middle-money Florida for the lower-cost Carolinas.

Because of windowed envelopes—interest, dividends, annuities, pensions, and Social Security checks —that can be sent to a forwarding address, you needn't remain rooted in an unaffordable place. The best economic reason you'll need for leaving home is the potential savings you'll find living somewhere else.

RETIREMENT INCOME: GETTING IT

"Money's no problem," an accountant with wit will tell you. "Lack of money . . . now *that's* a problem." Can you afford to stop working? More to the point, can you swing retirement where you're living now—or might there be somewhere else where you can do it more easily?

Lack of enough money causes many people to cling to unsatisfying jobs. For those who do retire, it crimps plans for travel or for life in a sunny, clean-air place where the bass fishing is good. It indefinitely defers the dream of a small part-time business, the book you've been meaning to write, the boat you want to build.

In retirement there isn't one source of income but many. Apart from Social Security, there is a multitude of annuities, Individual Retirement Accounts (IRAs) and Keogh Plans, thousands of government-employee plans (federal civil service, military, state, and municipal) and nearly a million private pension plans, each of which has different rules for age of eligibility, years of service required, payouts, and how spouses are covered.

For most, the main income sources—in descending dollar amounts—are Social Security benefits, private pensions, and asset income. More and more persons also count on earnings from a job or self-employment.

Social Security

Social Security is money paid out by the federal government at the end of each month to persons who paid into the system during their working years.

While determining benefits is complex, in general, annual earnings up to the year of eligibility for retirement are averaged and adjusted for inflation to derive an Average Index of Monthly Earnings (AIME). A benefit formula is then applied to the AIME to determine your Primary Insurance Amount (PIA). The percent of the PIA that you actually get depends on when you retire.

Currently, you are eligible for 100 percent of your PIA when you turn 65, the "normal" retirement age

Replacing Income: Part One

A rule circulating in retirement planning states: "If your retirement income is 70 to 75 percent of what it was in the last year of work, you'll hardly notice a change in your standard of living." The rule holds for households with job incomes between $45,000 and $70,000.

To keep up your standard of living after you retire, you'll need roughly the following:

Dollar Amount	Percent of Job Income	Job Income
$13,400	90%	$15,000
$17,000	85	$20,000
$20,400	82	$25,000
$23,700	79	$30,000
$30,700	77	$40,000
$36,600	73	$50,000
$42,800	71	$60,000
$48,800	70	$70,000
$54,400	68	$80,000
$59,000	66	$90,000

Income figures are pretax amounts. The percentage "replacement rates" do not reflect the impact of future inflation.

Where the Money Comes From

Of every 100 couples over 65 in the United States . . .	receive a median income of . . .	annually from . . .
93	$11,656	Social Security
79	$2,482	Interest, dividends, rents, and royalties
42	$8,219	Private pensions
31	$9,398	Earnings
20	$11,838	Government pensions

Source: Social Security Administration, *Income of the Population 55 and Over,* 1994.

defined by the Social Security program almost 60 years ago. The normal age will gradually rise to 67 over the next several decades.

Reduced benefits equal to 80 percent of your PIA are available at age 62. For every month after age 62 you put off claiming your benefits, the 20 percent early retirement penalty is reduced by 0.56 percent (or 6.67 percent a year) so that your full PIA is earned at 65. If you stay on the job after 65, you receive a delayed retirement credit of 3 percent a year. If you work and put off claiming Social Security benefits until you're 68, for instance, you would receive benefits equal to 109 percent of your PIA.

The maximum monthly check comes to $1,199 for a single worker, $1,799 for a couple with one dependent spouse, and $2,398 for a couple when both spouses are eligible. These amounts assume the worker made maximum contributions and retires at 65. The average amount mailed out each month to a couple is much less—$1,047, or $12,564 a year.

Pensions

Everyone working in government contributes to a pension. Just half of all workers in the private sector are covered by an employer pension plan, however. And only half of these will ever see the money because of vesting requirements. Not for nothing are persons getting benefits from their old employer called "the pension elite."

Unlike the Social Security system to which workers contribute no matter how many different jobs they hold, private pensions are the equivalent of a corporate loyalty test—at least for the standard eight or 10 years of service

required before an employee is vested and shares in a pension fund.

Unlike Social Security, too, most employer pension plans don't have a cost-of-living escalator clause. The typical amount from a private pension is $8,500 for a married couple age 62 to 65 that is eligible for payments. While the amount isn't paltry, it isn't lavish, either. According to a recent study from the Social Security Administration, just seven out of 100 couples with private pensions can rely on them for at least half their income.

Assets

Dividends from stock investments you've made over the years; rents from real estate you own; royalties from your invention, song, computer software, book, or oil well; and interest from IRAs, Keogh Plans, CDs, passbook savings accounts, and loans are examples of asset income.

Like private pensions and earnings from a job, income from assets supplements Social Security for a more comfortable later life. Nearly eight out of every 10 households over 65 count on money from these sources.

Earnings

Once you start collecting Social Security and private pension checks, there's almost nothing you can do to dramatically increase their amounts. If they aren't enough, the surest way of boosting your income is to get a job. The options run all the way from an eight-hour-a-day, 50-week-a-year new career to part-time or seasonal work.

Though savings, investments, and pension income don't affect the amount of your Social Security check, there is a ceiling on how much you can make on the job and still collect Social Security benefits. If you're under 65 and you make more than $680 a month, your benefits will be reduced by $1 for every $2 you're earning over the ceiling. If you're between 65 and 69 and you're making more than $940 a month, your benefits will be cut by $1 for every $3 you're paid over the ceiling. After age 70, these reductions no longer apply.

Scraping by on $58,160 a Year

One simple way to judge whether you can stop work, take the money, and run to another part of the country is to compare your income with incomes in other places.

The average household income in the United States before taxes is $58,160. Among the locations profiled in *Retirement Places Rated*, the highest is $82,500 out on Long Island's East End and the lowest is $32,400 in Kingman, Arizona.

Households can be a family, a husband and wife, a group of unrelated people, or even a single person. Average amounts tend to be high because most households aren't retired and count on wages and salaries from more than one member. Still, the figures are useful for making comparisons.

"Replacement Rates"

Get used to the idea of never living comfortably on Social Security. If you are a $61,200-a-year worker retiring at 65 with maximum earnings in "covered employment" (a job in which Social Security is deducted from wages) each year since 1951, you can expect $14,388 a year. Even though Social Security increases with inflation, the money comes way short of what you were pulling down at work.

One indicator of how far your Social Security benefits, pension, and asset income will go is the rate at which it would replace different household incomes around the country.

In locations in Rio Grande Country, the Ozarks and Ouachitas and the Southern Highlands, your income might go a lot further in replacing local household incomes than it would back home in, say, New York, Denver, or Altoona.

Retired persons who move tend to quit richer areas with high costs for places with more modest incomes. They are in search of spots where their own money can be stretched. In short, where costs are lower.

RETIREMENT INCOME: TAXING IT

Though you've chucked the tie and briefcase and bid good-bye to the commuting hassles that go with working full-time, you won't be completely immune from paying taxes in spite of the many tax breaks coming along when you turn 65.

Although your tax bracket will be lower after you leave work, federal income taxes may still hit you with the same impact whether you surface in Bellingham, Ocala, or San Antonio. But state and local taxes can differ tremendously.

Should you move only to one of the handful of no-income-tax states and ignore the alternatives? That might be a mistake. It's better to broaden your search to include other states with two characteristics: (1) a favorable tax treatment of retirement income (see the State Income Tax Profiles later on in this chapter) and (2) lower living costs.

Replacing Income: Part Two

Just as you want to come close to your on-the-job earnings with your retirement income, you might want to move to where your retirement income comes close to or exceeds average household income.

Lowest

Kingman, AZ	$32,400
Boone–Blowing Rock, NC	$34,000
Lake of the Cherokees, OK	$34,000
Payson, AZ	$34,700
Hiawassee, GA	$34,700

Highest

East End Long Island, NY	$82,500
Laguna Beach–Dana Point, CA	$81,400
Litchfield Hills, CT	$74,900
Santa Barbara, CA	$74,000
Hilton Head Island, SC	$72,700

Source: Woods & Poole Economics, Inc., household income forecasts.

RETIREMENT INCOME: SPENDING IT

Back to household incomes. Do they reflect local prices? For the most part, they do indeed. A Bureau of Labor Statistics study showed that two-thirds of the difference in incomes between, say, Traverse City and Tucson indicates their different costs of living. The rest is due to different employers, worker skills, and prevailing wages.

If you're thinking of moving, consider how far your income would stretch elsewhere. Household incomes in different places provide the first clue. Comparing actual costs completes the picture.

Local Costs of Living

It's a "black hole," the *Wall Street Journal* noted on just what everyone means by cost of living. The government's monthly Consumer Price Index (CPI) offers no help. It reports price inflation, but quotes no prices. While the CPI has gone up eightfold since the start of World War II, it offers no insights on the money you'd need to get by in Santa Barbara versus a small town in the Ozarks.

A few years ago, a group of experts appointed by the Department of Labor to look into better ways to measure cost differences between places threw in the towel. Given the infinite range of consumer tastes and household tactics for saving a dollar, they noted, the few ways to pin down why life in one place is more expensive than in another is to focus on the weather's effect on clothing costs and household utility bills. Then look at taxes.

Taxes certainly do make a difference. But clothing and home energy bills? Not that much. According to one retailer, the price difference between cotton and synthetic wardrobes in the Sun Belt and woolen and down-filled Frost Belt clothing amounts to less than 1 percent of a household's annual budget. As for the comparative costs of keeping warm in the North Woods winter and staying cool in the Florida Interior, often the only difference is the season during which local residents pay most of their bill.

One firm that counsels transferred employees uses the 80/20 rule. In its experience, 80 percent of the difference in living costs between where you've come from and where you're going comes down to two items: housing and taxes. The other 20 percent comes from hundreds of things such as spin-balancing the wheels on your car, a six-pack of beer, soap flakes, greens fees for a weekend round of golf, and a shampoo, trim, and blow-dry at a salon.

The Budget

To measure what it costs to live in each place, *Retirement Places Rated* prices items in an age 65, $38,500-a-year couple's budget. To produce an overall index, these items are weighted by their share in the budget using government surveys on spending.

Making mortgage payments and paying property taxes based on local *Housing* is the biggest item. It claims 22.6 percent. Local average and up-market home prices, plus typical property taxes, are detailed in the Housing chapter.

Where the real estate broker touts location, location, location, you might answer rent, rent, rent. While it adds nothing to your net worth, renting permits you to avoid most of the cost differences among places and gives you flexibility. Good rental markets include large college towns and large, seasonal resorts.

If you're like most older newcomers, you'll eventually end up owning. Property taxes, on average, will account for 4 percent of your household budget for as long as you own, unless you settle in a state (1) with low effective tax rates or (2) generous homestead exemptions for older people with no income qualifications or (3) both. Bear in mind, too, that taxes tend to be much lower when the property lies beyond the corporate limits of cities and towns.

Transportation, at 17.3 percent, is next. Since there is a national market for cars, meaning you can buy one anywhere for a similar price, the cost of purchasing one doesn't vary much by location. What does vary are taxes, insurance, title and registration fees, and gasoline excise taxes.

Thirteen percent of the budget goes for *Food,* which includes groceries *and* dining out. While prices for prepared foods don't vary enough to hit differing budgets around the country with differing effect, prices for fresh fruits, vegetables, and dairy products do. In spots

with agricultural economies, farmers' markets and road-side stands on the back of pickup trucks are a money saver.

Utilities includes electricity, piped-in natural gas and fuel oil, and claims 7 percent of a household's expenses. Unlike packaged groceries, monthly utility bills vary widely around the country. Climate determines how much money will be needed to keep interiors comfortable. Geography, too, plays a part in the choice of fuel and the distance from the fuel source.

Health Care expenses claim 5.8 percent and will require more and more of your income each year as you get older. True, basic Medicare covers hospital bills after you turn 65, but it won't cover things like an outpatient diagnostic visit, a prescription painkiller, or a splint for a broken thumb. Most important, it doesn't cover physicians fees.

To measure costs in each place, *Retirement Places Rated* looks at the amounts Medicare permits five doctors to charge their older patients for specific services. They are:

- Family practitioner—office outpatient visit
- Internist—electrocardiogram, complete
- Psychiatrist—psychotherapy, 75–80 minutes
- Orthopedic surgeon—open reduction of dislocation
- Ophthalmologist—eye exam

Charges for a semiprivate room in the area's largest acute-care hospital are also part of this factor.

Recreation covers everything from a health club membership, weekday play at 18-hole public or semiprivate golf course, overnight camping at a state park, and movie tickets. It claims 5.4 percent. Like the dining out part of the food budget, enjoying yourself can be a controllable expense. Costs at large resorts are highest.

Finally, state income and state and local sales *Taxes* exact 1.9 percent and 1 percent, respectively.

A Caution

Let's admit here that pricing living costs for all people for all the time is impossible. The number of unique items that fill a shopping cart trundled by a household for a year is close to a thousand. Some trade at Walmart and others at convenience stores, some by mail-order and others at Price Club, BJ's Wholesale, and Burlington Coat Factory. Having said that, *Retirement Places Rated* nevertheless makes a reasonable attempt at averages.

GRADING: Money Matters

Will your income stretch farther in the Rio Grande Country than in the Desert Southwest? Do prices really vary tremendously among different places, or can sharp-pencil budgeting and bargain-price shopping keep your head above water anywhere you choose to live?

To help you compare each place's differences, *Retirement Places Rated* looks at several factors: (1) state and local sales and income tax indexes for a hypothetical couple, and (2) cost indexes for food, housing, utilities, health care, transportation, and recreation against U.S. average figures. An index of 95 for health care, for example, means 5 percent less costly than the U.S. average. An index of 110 for transportation, for another example, means 10 percent more expensive than the U.S. average.

The indexes are then weighted by their percent share in the couple's budget. The utilities index, for example, is weighted at 7 percent, the health care index at 5.8 percent, and so on. The result is then scaled against a standard where living costs that are 25 percent below the national average get a perfect 100 and living costs double the national average get a 0.

RANKINGS: Money Matters

To grade places for costs of living, eight items are indexed against a national average: (1) *state income taxes*, (2) *state and local sales taxes*, (3) *home mortgage payments and property taxes*, (4) *utilities*, (5) *health care*, (6) *transportation*, (7) *food*, and (8) *recreation*.

The resulting indexes are then weighted by how important they are in a retired household, and then scaled against a standard where three-fourths of the national average gets a perfect 100 and twice the national average gets a 0.

Grades are rounded two decimal places. Locations with tie grades get the same rank and are listed alphabetically.

Retirement Places from First to Last

Rank	Grade	Rank	Grade	Rank	Grade
1. Hamilton–Bitterroot Valley, MT	97.12	24. Beaver Lake, AR	93.21	47. Ocala, FL	89.88
2. Thomasville, GA	97.04	25. Clemson–Pendleton District, SC	93.04	49. Las Cruces, NM	89.75
3. Delta–Cedaredge, CO	96.59			50. Coeur d'Alene, ID	89.68
4. Guntersville, AL	96.18	26. Conway, SC	92.93	51. Inverness, FL	89.60
5. Mission–McAllen–Alamo, TX	95.97	27. Alpine–Big Bend, TX	92.78	52. Pagosa Springs, CO	89.56
		28. Norfork Lake, AR	92.76	53. Charlevoix–Boyne City–East Jordan, MI	89.36
6. Lake of the Cherokees, OK	95.81	29. Table Rock Lake, MO	92.61	54. Fredericksburg, TX	89.30
7. Chewelah, WA	95.73	30. Newport–Lincoln City, OR	92.49	55. Daytona Beach, FL	89.09
8. Lake Martin, AL	95.69				
9. Kentucky Lake, KY	95.63	31. Aiken, SC	92.34	56. Kingman, AZ	88.76
10. Crossville, TN	95.62	32. Hiawassee, GA	92.01	57. Smith Mountain Lake, VA	88.56
		33. Wenatchee, WA	91.99	58. Lake of the Ozarks, MO	88.43
11. Blairsville, GA	95.37	34. Medford–Ashland, OR	91.87	59. Colorado Springs, CO	88.41
12. Florence, OR	94.98	35. Grand Junction, CO	91.83	60. Bay St. Louis–Pass Christian, MS	88.28
13. Silver City, NM	94.51				
14. Polson–Mission Valley, MT	94.44	36. Cedar Creek Lake, TX	91.68	61. Charles Town–Harpers Ferry–Shepherdstown, WV	88.13
15. Lake Livingston, TX	94.18	37. Sebring–Avon Park, FL	91.36		
		38. Fayetteville, AR	91.14	62. San Antonio, TX	88.12
16. Branson, MO	94.15	39. New Port Richey, FL	91.02	63. Brooksville–Spring Hill, FL	87.97
17. Maryville, TN	94.14	40. Panama City, FL	90.77	64. Fort Collins–Loveland, CO	87.84
18. Oscoda–Tawas–Huron Shore, MI	94.00	41. Clayton, GA	90.71	65. Sandpoint–Priest River, ID	87.82
19. Montrose, CO	93.86	42. Brookings–Gold Beach, OR	90.58		
20. Kalispell–Flathead Valley, MT	93.68	43. Grants Pass, OR	90.47	66. Kerrville, TX	87.57
		44. Madison, MS	90.05	67. Western St. Tammany Parish, LA	87.51
21. Oxford, MS	93.60	45. Lakeland–Winter Haven, FL	89.98		
22. Houghton Lake, MI	93.33			68. Bend, OR	87.40
23. Alamogordo, NM	93.23	46. Fairhope–Gulf Shores, AL	89.96		
		47. Gainesville, FL	89.88		

Rank	Grade
69. St. Jay–Northeast Kingdom, VT	86.97
70. Hot Springs, AR	86.87
71. Leesburg–Lady Lake, FL	86.82
72. Traverse City, MI	86.81
73. Port Angeles–Seqium, WA	86.72
74. Charleston Sea Islands, SC	86.70
74. Cottonwood–Verde Valley, AZ	86.70
74. Durango, CO	86.70
77. Ruidoso, NM	86.55
78. Pahrump Valley, NV	86.23
79. Lake Granbury, TX	86.10
80. Lake Buchanan–Lake LBJ, TX	86.06
81. Rockport–Aransas Pass, TX	85.91
82. Athens, GA	85.69
83. State College, PA	85.67
84. Port Townsend, WA	85.62
85. New Braunfels, TX	85.56
86. Edenton, NC	85.55
87. Winchester, VA	85.29
88. Kissimmee–St. Cloud, FL	85.10
89. Petoskey–Harbor Springs, MI	85.07
90. St. Petersburg–Clearwater, FL	85.05
91. Bellingham, WA	84.80
92. Beaufort, SC	84.71
93. Yuma, AZ	84.25
94. Wimberly–San Marcos, TX	84.22
95. Savannah, GA	84.14
96. Melbourne, FL	84.04
97. Taos, NM	84.03
98. Bradenton, FL	83.82
99. Port Charlotte–Punta Gorda, FL	83.74
100. Hendersonville–East Flat Rock, NC	83.65
101. McCall–Cascade–Payette Valley, ID	83.39
102. Lake Conroe, TX	83.19
103. Asheville, NC	83.15
104. Albuquerque, NM	83.12
105. New Bern, NC	82.75
106. Eagle River, WI	82.50
107. Tryon, NC	82.43

Rank	Grade
108. Rehoboth Bay–Indian River Bay, DE	82.42
109. Southport–Brunswick Islands, NC	82.37
110. Lake Havasu City, AZ	81.85
111. Whidbey Island, WA	81.84
112. Wickenburg, AZ	81.45
113. Payson, AZ	81.42
113. St. Augustine, FL	81.42
115. Brevard, NC	81.19
116. Tucson, AZ	80.77
117. Las Vegas, NV	80.69
118. Ocean City, MD	80.45
119. Austin, TX	80.27
119. Oakhurst–Coarsegold, CA	80.27
121. Prescott–Prescott Valley, AZ	80.24
122. Myrtle Beach, SC	79.77
123. Camden, ME	79.58
124. Sarasota, FL	79.52
125. Fort Myers–Cape Coral, FL	79.15
126. Boone–Blowing Rock, NC	78.75
127. Virginia Beach, VA	78.29
128. Vero Beach–Sebastian, FL	78.01
129. St. George–Zion, UT	77.91
130. Northern Door Peninsula, WI	77.80
131. Fredericksburg–Spotsylvania, VA	77.62
132. Redding, CA	77.40
133. Bar Harbor, ME	77.30
134. Pompano Beach, FL	77.24
135. Northern Neck, VA	77.12
136. Paradise–Magalia, CA	77.10
137. Hanover, NH	77.04
138. Southern Pines–Pinehurst, NC	76.97
139. Lake Winnipesaukee, NH	76.71
140. Phoenix–Mesa–Scottsdale, AZ	76.50
141. Reno–Sparks, NV	76.36
142. Carson City–Carson Valley, NV	76.29
142. Riviera–Bullhead City, AZ	76.29
144. Amador County, CA	76.03
145. York Beaches, ME	75.74
146. Sonora–Groveland–Twain Harte, CA	75.55
147. Pike County, PA	75.52

Rank	Grade
148. Burlington, VT	74.80
149. Dare Outer Banks, NC	74.62
150. Woodstock, VT	74.48
151. Charlottesville, VA	73.47
152. Williamsburg, VA	73.17
153. Santa Fe, NM	72.61
154. Chapel Hill, NC	72.37
155. Hesperia–Apple Valley–Victorville, CA	71.84
156. Boca Raton–Delray Beach, FL	71.32
157. Amherst–Northampton, MA	70.86
158. Southern Berkshire County, MA	70.01
159. Placerville–Shingle Springs, CA	67.95
160. Easton–St. Michaels–Oxford, MD	67.36
161. Lower Cape May, NJ	67.15
162. Naples, FL	66.71
163. Sedona, AZ	66.69
164. Toms River–Barnegat Bay, NJ	66.56
165. Ketchum–Sun Valley, ID	66.30
166. Grass Valley–Nevada City, CA	65.63
167. St. Simons–Jekyll Islands, GA	65.44
168. San Juan Islands, WA	62.72
169. Annapolis, MD	61.96
170. Kauai, HI	61.26
171. Palm Springs–Coachella Valley, CA	61.00
172. Cape Cod, MA	57.86
173. San Diego, CA	57.34
174. Key West–Key Largo–Marathon, FL	57.03
175. Maui, HI	56.03
176. Litchfield Hills, CT	54.00
177. Santa Rosa–Sonoma, CA	53.47
178. Hilton Head Island, SC	52.46
179. San Luis Obispo, CA	51.36
180. Santa Barbara, CA	43.91
181. East End Long Island, NY	38.09
182. Carmel–Monterey–Pebble Beach, CA	27.82
183. Laguna Beach–Dana Point, CA	27.22

PLACE PROFILES: Money Matters

The pages that follow highlight the factors used to grade each place: state and local tax indexes, plus cost indexes for housing, utilities, health care, transportation, food, and recreation—all against U.S. average expenses for a hypothetical couple, age 65, with a gross income of $38,500.

The column next to each location name shows its household income. The next column shows the state

income tax index above the state and local sales tax index for the couple, who file joint returns. Their income consists of $14,564 in Social Security benefits for a worker and dependent spouse, the worker's $16,820 private pension, and $7,116 in interest from CDs and corporate bonds.

The next three columns show indexes grouped by: (1) Housing above Utilities, (2) Health Care above

Transportation, and (3) Food above Recreation, according to the column headings at the top of the page.

The data come principally from Places Rated Partnership tax and consumer price surveys at the end of 1994. In addition, a number of sources were used. These include: Advisory Commission on Intergovernmental Relations, *Significant Features of Fiscal Federalism* (state income and sales tax rates), 1994; American Automobile Association, *Digest of Motor Laws* (state motor vehicle license, registration fees, and gasoline excise taxes), 1994; American Hospital Association, *Hospital Statistics* (semiprivate room costs by state), 1994; Commerce Clearing House, *State Tax Guide* (state income and sales tax rates), 1994; Macmillan Travel Publishing, *Mobil Travel Guide* (state park fees, dining out costs), 1994; Minnesota Revenue Department, *Comparison of Individual Income Tax Burdens by State*, 1992 and forthcoming

1995; Health Insurance Association of America, *Source Book of Health Insurance Data* (Medicare and semiprivate hospital room rates by state), 1994; Sports Directories, Inc., *National Golf Course Directory* (public golf course fees), 1994; U.S. Department of Labor, Bureau of Labor Statistics, unpublished data, *Consumer Expenditure Survey* (budget expense weights), 1994, and *Consumer Price Index*, final quarter 1994; U.S. Department of Health and Human Services, Health Care Financing Administration, unpublished medical procedures costs and geographic adjustment factors, 1994; U.S. General Services Administration, *Federal Travel Directory* (local *per diems* for food away from home), monthly, 1994; and Woods & Poole Economics, Inc., unpublished household income data, 1994.

A check mark (✓) preceding a place's name indicates it is one of the top 18 places for money matters.

	Typical Household Income	Income Taxes Sales Taxes	Housing Utilities	Health Care Transportation	Food Recreation	Grade
UNITED STATES	**$58,160**	**$690** **$320**	**$12,950** **$1,336**	**$1,863** **$5,558**	**$4,240** **$1,734**	**80**
Aiken, SC	$53,800	47 151	63 103	91 96	100 70	92
Alamogordo, NM	$40,800	132 187	52 115	94 86	101 75	93
Albuquerque, NM	$54,000	132 184	80 117	95 86	112 99	83
Alpine–Big Bend, TX	$36,000	0 150	51 111	97 103	98 97	93
Amador County, CA	$46,700	70 132	114 99	104 108	98 90	76
Amherst–Northampton, MA	$54,200	212 91	126 110	106 98	101 96	71
Annapolis, MD	$71,700	186 91	174 78	103 98	109 83	62
Asheville, NC	$49,200	190 183	71 114	92 108	102 82	83
Athens, GA	$44,300	39 153	80 120	99 96	104 80	86
Austin, TX	$54,400	0 145	97 119	99 103	109 83	80
Bar Harbor, ME	$54,900	114 109	90 117	93 102	109 144	77
Bay St. Louis–Pass Christian, MS	$41,900	34 216	61 99	94 101	106 118	88
Beaufort, SC	$48,500	47 155	84 85	91 96	107 122	85
Beaver Lake, AR	$41,800	129 197	49 112	88 97	100 65	93
Bellingham, WA	$49,700	0 142	97 34	99 107	103 112	85
Bend, OR	$50,200	201 0	78 79	97 81	103 128	87
✓ Blairsville, GA	$36,100	39 151	58 72	95 91	100 97	95
Boca Raton–Delray Beach, FL	$73,800	0 109	127 117	106 108	107 97	71
Boone–Blowing Rock, NC	$34,000	190 182	75 114	92 108	101 144	79

	Typical Household Income	Income Taxes / Sales Taxes	Housing / Utilities	Health Care / Transportation	Food / Recreation	Grade
UNITED STATES	$58,160	$690 $320	$12,950 $1,336	$1,863 $5,558	$4,240 $1,734	80
Bradenton, FL	$50,700	0 127	81 110	98 108	101 105	84
✓ Branson, MO	$45,900	109 224	54 75	90 92	107 79	94
Brevard, NC	$42,800	190 181	76 77	92 108	100 150	81
Brookings–Gold Beach, OR	$41,000	201 0	87 38	97 81	98 104	91
Brooksville–Spring Hill, FL	$37,400	0 109	66 109	98 108	97 111	88
Burlington, VT	$60,700	119 91	118 113	94 96	103 102	75
Camden, ME	$51,800	114 109	98 117	98 102	103 78	80
Cape Cod, MA	$65,300	212 91	170 105	106 98	104 135	58
Carmel–Monterey–Pebble Beach, CA	$68,800	70 132	268 101	107 108	110 241	28
Carson City–Carson Valley, NV	$66,500	0 123	116 92	103 103	115 90	76
Cedar Creek Lake, TX	$36,700	0 150	63 105	95 103	97 80	92
Chapel Hill, NC	$56,500	190 190	116 86	92 108	112 87	72
Charles Town–Harpers Ferry–Shepherdstown, WV	$44,900	78 182	81 84	93 97	101 71	88
Charleston Sea Islands, SC	$43,500	47 186	87 82	91 96	107 74	87
Charlevoix–Boyne City–East Jordan, MI	$50,900	77 109	64 130	102 91	103 75	89
Charlottesville, VA	$59,000	116 142	110 123	97 101	111 97	73
✓ Chewelah, WA	$43,100	0 136	49 78	96 107	98 84	96
Clayton, GA	$36,400	39 151	74 81	95 91	100 97	91
Clemson–Pendleton District, SC	$46,100	47 151	64 80	91 96	100 86	93
Coeur d'Alene, ID	$47,500	170 153	72 51	97 97	103 84	90
Colorado Springs, CO	$52,700	52 116	79 88	98 99	101 75	88
Conway, SC	$38,400	47 151	61 89	91 96	100 89	93
Cottonwood–Verde Valley, AZ	$34,900	90 109	72 119	100 101	97 85	87
✓ Crossville, TN	$38,600	40 249	51 55	92 97	100 111	96
Dare Outer Banks, NC	$42,300	190 186	111 82	92 108	107 91	75
Daytona Beach, FL	$43,600	0 109	70 96	99 108	101 84	89
✓ Delta–Cedaredge, CO	$36,500	52 145	47 87	97 99	97 77	97
Durango, CO	$47,900	52 127	81 85	97 99	110 82	87
Eagle River, WI	$42,000	192 100	73 123	94 104	101 103	83

	Typical Household Income	Income Taxes / Sales Taxes	Housing / Utilities	Health Care / Transportation	Food / Recreation	Grade
UNITED STATES	$58,160	$690 / $320	$12,950 / $1,336	$1,863 / $5,558	$4,240 / $1,734	80
East End Long Island, NY	$82,500	70 / 200	224 / 122	115 / 116	114 / 160	38
Easton–St. Michaels– Oxford, MD	$71,500	186 / 91	149 / 78	97 / 98	103 / 114	67
Edenton, NC	$40,800	190 / 182	68 / 89	92 / 108	101 / 91	86
Fairhope–Gulf Shores, AL	$45,700	91 / 245	63 / 89	96 / 93	103 / 94	90
Fayetteville, AR	$46,800	129 / 198	55 / 116	88 / 97	102 / 65	91
✓ Florence, OR	$47,000	201 / 0	68 / 37	97 / 81	98 / 111	95
Fort Collins–Loveland, CO	$52,000	52 / 109	82 / 86	98 / 99	103 / 72	88
Fort Myers–Cape Coral, FL	$51,900	0 / 109	93 / 104	99 / 108	109 / 123	79
Fredericksburg, TX	$50,400	0 / 150	70 / 116	99 / 103	100 / 64	89
Fredericksburg– Spotsylvania, VA	$53,800	116 / 140	103 / 79	96 / 101	108 / 122	78
Gainesville, FL	$46,200	0 / 109	65 / 95	100 / 108	100 / 93	90
Grand Junction, CO	$44,700	52 / 141	61 / 94	97 / 99	103 / 77	92
Grants Pass, OR	$40,700	201 / 0	74 / 49	97 / 81	101 / 138	90
Grass Valley–Nevada City, CA	$51,500	70 / 132	151 / 85	104 / 108	101 / 126	66
✓ Guntersville, AL	$44,100	91 / 212	47 / 77	93 / 93	101 / 88	96
✓ Hamilton–Bitterroot Valley, MT	$39,400	106 / 0	58 / 73	88 / 86	98 / 92	97
Hanover, NH	$58,000	15 / 0	113 / 119	100 / 79	109 / 160	77
Hendersonville–East Flat Rock, NC	$48,000	190 / 181	82 / 78	92 / 108	100 / 81	84
Hesperia–Apple Valley– Victorville, CA	$58,800	70 / 132	107 / 154	105 / 108	109 / 93	72
Hiawassee, GA	$34,700	39 / 151	72 / 72	95 / 91	100 / 97	92
Hilton Head Island, SC	$72,700	47 / 158	189 / 85	91 / 96	112 / 220	52
Hot Springs, AR	$44,800	129 / 183	55 / 112	88 / 97	103 / 146	87
Houghton Lake, MI	$39,100	77 / 109	50 / 135	102 / 91	97 / 78	93
Inverness, FL	$37,600	0 / 109	65 / 109	98 / 108	97 / 88	90
Kalispell–Flathead Valley, MT	$46,200	106 / 0	68 / 83	88 / 86	101 / 93	94
Kauai, HI	$59,400	86 / 126	173 / 122	107 / 92	112 / 75	61
✓ Kentucky Lake, KY	$44,300	190 / 109	49 / 65	90 / 98	98 / 80	96
Kerrville, TX	$52,800	0 / 141	80 / 102	99 / 103	103 / 65	88
Ketchum–Sun Valley, ID	$64,700	170 / 162	159 / 40	90 / 97	118 / 106	66

	Typical Household Income	Income Taxes Sales Taxes	Housing Utilities	Health Care Transportation	Food Recreation	Grade
UNITED STATES	**$58,160**	**$690** **$320**	**$12,950** **$1,336**	**$1,863** **$5,558**	**$4,240** **$1,734**	**80**
Key West–Key Largo–Marathon, FL	$49,700	0 127	157 141	98 108	115 173	57
Kingman, AZ	$32,400	90 118	58 147	99 101	97 69	89
Kissimmee–St. Cloud, FL	$55,600	0 127	71 112	98 108	103 118	85
Laguna Beach–Dana Point, CA	$81,400	70 132	289 100	113 108	115 142	27
Lake Buchanan–Lake LBJ, TX	$50,400	0 150	78 100	99 103	103 98	86
Lake Conroe, TX	$55,200	0 141	83 107	104 103	103 112	83
Lake Granbury, TX	$56,700	0 150	81 104	97 103	97 100	86
Lake Havasu City, AZ	$39,600	90 127	84 150	99 101	100 69	82
✓ Lake Livingston, TX	$38,500	0 150	49 103	97 103	97 97	94
✓ Lake Martin, AL	$44,000	91 212	44 79	96 93	101 101	96
✓ Lake of the Cherokees, OK	$34,000	145 242	49 77	91 87	100 84	96
Lake of the Ozarks, MO	$42,700	109 147	71 73	90 92	107 117	88
Lake Winnipesaukee, NH	$64,600	15 0	128 119	100 79	103 117	77
Lakeland–Winter Haven, FL	$44,700	0 109	61 101	98 108	101 99	90
Las Cruces, NM	$40,000	132 195	64 108	94 86	106 83	90
Las Vegas, NV	$57,000	0 127	95 96	103 103	115 98	81
Leesburg–Lady Lake, FL	$45,000	0 127	68 109	98 108	97 118	87
Litchfield Hills, CT	$74,900	95 109	186 120	110 104	115 103	54
Lower Cape May, NJ	$66,500	55 109	119 105	102 107	109 201	67
Madison, MS	$48,000	34 210	66 105	94 102	98 74	90
✓ Maryville, TN	$45,700	40 250	59 69	93 97	101 80	94
Maui, HI	$65,600	86 126	185 133	107 93	112 98	56
McCall–Cascade–Payette Valley, ID	$48,300	170 155	82 100	90 97	107 86	83
Medford–Ashland, OR	$47,000	201 0	77 48	97 81	103 96	92
Melbourne, FL	$52,300	0 109	84 109	100 108	101 92	84
✓ Mission–McAllen–Alamo, TX	$38,000	0 150	44 123	91 103	97 64	96
Montrose, CO	$41,900	52 127	56 87	97 99	97 90	94
Myrtle Beach, SC	$46,900	47 155	95 80	91 96	107 168	80
Naples, FL	$72,700	0 109	147 115	98 108	108 100	67

	Typical Household Income	Income Taxes / Sales Taxes	Housing / Utilities	Health Care / Transportation	Food / Recreation	Grade
UNITED STATES	**$58,160**	**$690** / **$320**	**$12,950** / **$1,336**	**$1,863** / **$5,558**	**$4,240** / **$1,734**	**80**
New Bern, NC	$41,500	190 / 183	70 / 97	92 / 108	103 / 112	83
New Braunfels, TX	$61,100	0 / 150	85 / 110	99 / 103	103 / 65	86
New Port Richey, FL	$36,400	0 / 109	58 / 111	98 / 108	101 / 79	91
Newport–Lincoln City, OR	$46,700	201 / 0	72 / 38	97 / 81	103 / 123	92
Norfork Lake, AR	$40,800	129 / 197	49 / 95	88 / 97	100 / 97	93
Northern Door Peninsula, WI	$52,000	192 / 100	98 / 114	94 / 104	101 / 90	78
Northern Neck, VA	$64,200	116 / 137	105 / 82	96 / 101	102 / 135	77
Oakhurst–Coarsegold, CA	$52,300	70 / 132	84 / 139	98 / 108	101 / 90	80
Ocala, FL	$40,200	0 / 109	61 / 109	100 / 108	101 / 89	90
Ocean City, MD	$53,500	186 / 91	96 / 79	97 / 98	109 / 98	80
✓ Oscoda–Tawas–Huron Shore, MI	$40,800	77 / 109	49 / 132	102 / 91	97 / 72	94
Oxford, MS	$35,800	34 / 212	53 / 88	94 / 101	101 / 86	94
Pagosa Springs, CO	$35,500	52 / 127	74 / 82	97 / 99	102 / 82	90
Pahrump Valley, NV	$45,000	0 / 127	73 / 91	103 / 103	103 / 131	86
Palm Springs–Coachella Valley, CA	$61,000	70 / 132	132 / 165	105 / 108	109 / 159	61
Panama City, FL	$44,500	0 / 127	62 / 105	98 / 108	101 / 72	91
Paradise–Magalia, CA	$45,000	70 / 132	97 / 140	103 / 108	106 / 74	77
Payson, AZ	$34,700	90 / 109	81 / 136	99 / 101	97 / 115	81
Petoskey–Harbor Springs, MI	$58,400	77 / 109	82 / 128	102 / 91	103 / 80	85
Phoenix–Mesa–Scottsdale, AZ	$55,200	90 / 122	89 / 161	103 / 101	109 / 98	77
Pike County, PA	$60,100	86 / 109	119 / 92	93 / 102	103 / 102	76
Placerville–Shingle Springs, CA	$63,600	70 / 132	150 / 97	103 / 108	101 / 74	68
✓ Polson–Mission Valley, MT	$39,900	106 / 0	68 / 72	88 / 86	98 / 98	94
Pompano Beach, FL	$62,400	0 / 109	101 / 117	106 / 108	107 / 107	77
Port Angeles–Seqium, WA	$47,600	0 / 144	91 / 34	98 / 107	103 / 103	87
Port Charlotte–Punta Gorda, FL	$44,400	0 / 109	80 / 115	98 / 108	103 / 102	84
Port Townsend, WA	$46,400	0 / 144	98 / 34	98 / 107	101 / 103	86
Prescott–Prescott Valley, AZ	$42,700	90 / 109	88 / 141	99 / 101	103 / 86	80
Redding, CA	$50,000	70 / 132	89 / 149	104 / 108	105 / 90	77

	Typical Household Income	Income Taxes / Sales Taxes	Housing / Utilities	Health Care / Transportation	Food / Recreation	Grade
UNITED STATES	$58,160	$690 / $320	$12,950 / $1,336	$1,863 / $5,558	$4,240 / $1,734	80
Rehoboth Bay–Indian River Bay, DE	$53,600	213 / 0	89 / 102	102 / 91	101 / 101	82
Reno–Sparks, NV	$64,100	0 / 127	118 / 93	103 / 103	103 / 108	76
Riviera–Bullhead City, AZ	$36,400	90 / 127	105 / 150	99 / 101	97 / 82	76
Rockport–Aransas Pass, TX	$41,400	0 / 150	72 / 128	96 / 103	103 / 97	86
Ruidoso, NM	$42,700	132 / 213	69 / 106	94 / 86	109 / 108	87
St. Augustine, FL	$56,900	0 / 109	95 / 94	100 / 108	103 / 102	81
St. George–Zion, UT	$40,900	254 / 182	91 / 70	101 / 104	106 / 116	78
St. Jay–Northeast Kingdom, VT	$45,600	119 / 91	69 / 113	94 / 96	101 / 104	87
St. Petersburg–Clearwater, FL	$56,400	0 / 127	80 / 104	98 / 108	101 / 99	85
St. Simons–Jekyll Islands, GA	$54,700	39 / 153	160 / 91	97 / 96	104 / 130	65
San Antonio, TX	$50,000	0 / 141	68 / 121	97 / 103	103 / 82	88
San Diego, CA	$63,000	70 / 132	191 / 77	105 / 108	110 / 86	57
San Juan Islands, WA	$65,000	0 / 136	173 / 94	99 / 107	98 / 109	63
San Luis Obispo, CA	$55,000	70 / 132	205 / 106	106 / 108	110 / 93	51
Sandpoint–Priest River, ID	$41,900	170 / 151	68 / 100	89 / 97	101 / 86	88
Santa Barbara, CA	$74,000	70 / 132	239 / 92	107 / 108	107 / 103	44
Santa Fe, NM	$54,000	132 / 194	119 / 103	95 / 86	112 / 134	73
Santa Rosa–Sonoma, CA	$66,600	70 / 132	194 / 124	105 / 108	107 / 86	53
Sarasota, FL	$65,000	0 / 127	100 / 112	98 / 108	103 / 92	80
Savannah, GA	$53,800	39 / 155	78 / 105	97 / 96	107 / 128	84
Sebring–Avon Park, FL	$43,800	0 / 127	56 / 112	99 / 108	97 / 86	91
Sedona, AZ	$66,600	90 / 111	155 / 116	99 / 101	103 / 69	67
✓ Silver City, NM	$40,200	132 / 193	48 / 110	94 / 86	100 / 76	95
Smith Mountain Lake, VA	$50,000	116 / 136	70 / 77	91 / 101	100 / 101	89
Sonora–Groveland–Twain Harte, CA	$44,800	70 / 132	118 / 98	97 / 108	98 / 90	76
Southern Berkshire County, MA	$57,400	212 / 91	134 / 105	106 / 98	101 / 86	70
Southern Pines–Pinehurst, NC	$53,000	190 / 190	89 / 91	92 / 108	112 / 115	77
Southport–Brunswick Islands, NC	$36,600	190 / 183	74 / 90	92 / 108	103 / 111	82
State College, PA	$49,400	86 / 109	70 / 114	95 / 102	103 / 103	86

	Typical Household Income	Income Taxes / Sales Taxes	Housing / Utilities	Health Care / Transportation	Food / Recreation	Grade
UNITED STATES	**$58,160**	**$690** $320	**$12,950** $1,336	**$1,863** $5,558	**$4,240** $1,734	**80**
Table Rock Lake, MO	$42,400	109 177	55 97	90 92	106 81	93
Taos, NM	$36,100	132 211	73 113	94 86	107 132	84
✓ Thomasville, GA	$47,000	39 151	51 97	96 91	100 65	97
Toms River–Barnegat Bay, NJ	$60,900	55 109	129 160	105 107	103 109	67
Traverse City, MI	$52,500	77 109	74 132	102 91	103 76	87
Tryon, NC	$55,800	190 181	73 78	92 108	100 137	82
Tucson, AZ	$45,600	90 127	80 146	101 101	103 98	81
Vero Beach–Sebastian, FL	$62,600	0 127	104 114	99 108	101 101	78
Virginia Beach, VA	$54,200	116 142	105 79	96 101	111 94	78
Wenatchee, WA	$54,400	0 144	72 43	97 107	98 97	92
Western St. Tammany Parish, LA	$55,700	28 245	81 98	98 91	104 74	88
Whidbey Island, WA	$48,900	0 144	109 35	104 107	104 105	82
Wickenburg, AZ	$44,200	90 109	84 138	100 101	97 102	81
Williamsburg, VA	$52,800	116 142	81 79	96 101	111 285	73
Wimberly–San Marcos, TX	$45,400	0 150	87 110	99 103	97 98	84
Winchester, VA	$50,400	116 136	86 73	91 101	100 96	85
Woodstock, VT	$52,000	119 91	96 113	94 96	106 194	74
York Beaches, ME	$49,600	114 109	112 107	98 102	103 99	76
Yuma, AZ	$44,400	90 118	62 173	100 101	100 89	84

 ET CETERA: Money Matters

Question: Where in America can you find rock-bottom property taxes, no personal income tax on any of your retirement income, no sales tax on the basics you'll need like food and medicine, no inheritance taxes for your heirs to pay, and a minimum of nickel-and-dime fees for licensing a car or for taking out a fishing license?

Answer: Dream on. The ideal tax haven would have to have the low property taxes of Louisiana, Alaska's forgiveness of taxes on personal income, and the absence of sales taxes as in Oregon. Unfortunately, you just can't find all these tax breaks together in any one state.

The ways states raise revenue differ dramatically. Sales taxes, excise taxes, license taxes, income taxes, intangibles taxes, property taxes, estate taxes, and inheritance taxes are just some of the forms their levies take. Depending on where you live, you may encounter all or only a few.

STATE RETIREMENT INCOME TAX PROFILES

Between 1980 and 1991 state tax collections increased 168 percent, outrunning the 92 percent rise in federal taxes and the 66 percent rise in inflation. Today, some state and local taxes can total almost half the size of the federal tax bite.

When federal income taxes were enacted in 1914, two states—Mississippi and Wisconsin—were already collecting income taxes of their own. It was only during the 1920s and 1930s that the majority of states began to raise cash by tapping personal incomes. Today 41 states impose the tax. Two—New Hampshire and Tennessee—apply it only to income from interest and dividends. Seven—Alaska, Florida, Nevada, South Dakota, Texas, Washington, and Wyoming—don't tax income at all.

Of the 41 states with a broad-based income tax, 35 base the taxes on federal returns, typically taking a portion of what you pay the IRS or using your federal adjusted gross income or taxable income as the starting point for their own computation. However, these states take differing views on income from Social Security, government pensions, and private employer pensions.

The following descriptions of how states tax income include specific features regarding their treatment of retirement income. The best way to learn what your income taxes will be in a new state is to write for its *resident* income tax form and instructions, fill it out, and compare the bottom line with that of your current state. (Addresses and taxpayer assistance telephone numbers are in "Relocation Resources" at the end of this book.) Of course, you should always consult a tax advisor for help with complex tax issues.

Personal Exemptions and Standard Deductions. Most states specify amounts for taxpayers and each of their dependents that can be used as an offset in determining taxable income. And most of these also specify additional amounts for persons over 65.

Medical and Dental Deductions. Most states treat health care expenses as having already been deducted from federal returns. North Dakota and Oregon grant full deductions for this major retirement expense. Four states in the Great Lakes—Illinois, Indiana, Michigan, and Ohio—do not permit itemized deductions at all.

Federal Taxes Aren't Deductible Everywhere. Of the 41 states with broad-based income taxes, 12 allow taxpayers to deduct federal income taxes. Is this an advantage? It is if you're deciding between two states with similar tax rates, but only one of them allows you to deduct. In the latter case, your effective tax rate would be less. This makes a big difference to high-income households.

Social Security Exemption. Twenty-six states fully exempt Social Security. The others tax this form of retirement income if it is subject to the federal income tax. In the following state tax profiles, Railroad Retirement benefits and Social Security benefits are treated the same. Missouri is the only exception to this rule.

Public Pension Exemption. Because of legal challenges in recent years, pensions paid by federal, state, and local governments are treated identically in most states. For example, a state-government pension cannot be taxed more favorably than a federal-government pension. Eleven states fully exempt public pensions.

Private Pension Exemption. States typically exempt only defined-benefit, or qualified plans, that is, pensions that provide a specific amount to a retired employee based on years of employment and compensation received.

Be Aware of Source Taxes. Eleven states apply a "source tax" to the pension income of nonresidents. If you worked and earned a pension in one of them, you will be required to pay tax on your pension benefits to that state even if you no longer live there. You won't be taxed twice on the same income. Credits against taxes paid to the state of residence eliminate that possibility. Reciprocity agreements between states determine which state receives the payment.

Taxing the Necessities

You'll pay sales tax on groceries in . . .

Alabama	Mississippi	Tennessee
Arkansas	Missouri	Utah
Georgia	New Mexico	Virginia
Hawaii	North Carolina	West Virginia
Idaho	Oklahoma	Wyoming
Kansas	South Carolina	
Louisiana	South Dakota	

And sales tax on medicine in . . .

Louisiana	New Mexico

But no sales tax on clothing in . . .

Connecticut	New Jersey
Massachusetts	Pennsylvania
Minnesota	Rhode Island

And no sales tax, period, in . . .

Alaska	New Hampshire
Delaware	Oregon
Montana	

Source: Commerce Clearing House, *State Tax Guide.*
Taxes are paid by all taxpayers, not just those of retirement age.

State Sales Tax Rates

	Percent
Alabama*	4%
Arizona*	5
Arkansas*	4.5
California*	6
Colorado*	3
Connecticut	6
Florida*	6
Georgia*	4
Hawaii*	4
Idaho	5
Illinois*	6.25
Indiana	5
Iowa*	5
Kansas*	4.9
Kentucky*	6
Louisiana*	4
Maine	6
Maryland	5
Massachusetts	5
Michigan	6
Minnesota*	6
Mississippi	7
Missouri*	4.225
Nebraska*	5
Nevada*	6.5
New Jersey	6
New Mexico	5
New York*	4
North Carolina*	4
North Dakota	5
Ohio*	5
Oklahoma*	4.5
Pennsylvania*	6
Rhode Island	7
South Carolina*	5
South Dakota*	4
Tennessee*	6
Texas*	6.25
Utah*	5
Vermont	4
Virginia*	3.5
Washington*	6.5
West Virginia	6
Wisconsin*	5
Wyoming*	4

Source: Commerce Clearing House, *State Tax Guide*.

*Indicates state permits local additions to its base tax rate. All other states have a single tax rate.

State Treatment of Death Taxes

	Pickup Only	Estate and Pickup	Inheritance and Pickup
Alabama	•		
Alaska	•		
Arizona	•		
Arkansas	•		
California	•		
Colorado	•		
Connecticut*			•
Delaware			•
District of Columbia	•		
Florida	•		
Georgia	•		
Hawaii	•		
Idaho	•		
Illinois	•		
Indiana*			•
Iowa*			•
Kansas*			•
Kentucky*			•
Louisiana*			•
Maine	•		
Maryland*			•
Massachusetts*		•	
Michigan	•		
Minnesota	•		
Mississippi		•	
Missouri	•		
Montana*			•
Nebraska*			•
Nevada	•		
New Hampshire*			•
New Jersey*			•
New Mexico	•		
New York		•	
North Carolina*			•
North Dakota	•		
Ohio*		•	
Oklahoma*		•	
Oregon	•		
Pennsylvania			•
Rhode Island	•		
South Carolina	•		
South Dakota*			•
Tennessee*			•
Texas	•		
Utah	•		
Vermont	•		
Virginia	•		
Washington	•		
West Virginia	•		
Wisconsin	•		
Wyoming	•		

Source: Commerce Clearing House, *State Tax Guide*.
*Indicates transfers to spouse are exempt.

Five states—Connecticut, Massachusetts, Minnesota, Vermont, and Wisconsin—apply the tax only to unqualified retirement plans. Louisiana and New York exempt public pensions. California, Iowa, Kansas, and Oregon apply the tax broadly. Arizona, Colorado, and North Dakota laws permit taxing pension incomes of nonresidents, but these states do not impose the tax.

ALABAMA

PERSONAL INCOME TAX RATES

Single or Married Separate Return		Married Joint Return	
Taxable Income	**Rate**	**Taxable Income**	**Rate**
First $500	2%	First $1,000	2%
Next $2,500	4%	Next $5,000	4%
Over $3,000	5%	Over $6,000	5%

FEATURES

Personal Exemptions or Credits.............................$1,500 single, $3,000 married joint return,
                                                          $300 each dependent
Standard Deduction......................................$2,000 single, $4,000 married joint return
Medical and Dental Deduction..............................Limited to excess of 4% of adjusted gross income
Federal Income Tax Deduction..............................Full
Public Pension Exclusion.................................Full
Private Pension Exclusion................................Full
Social Security Exemption................................Full

ALASKA

The personal income tax was repealed in 1979.

ARIZONA

PERSONAL INCOME TAX RATES

Single or Married Separate Return		Married Joint Return	
Taxable Income	**Rate**	**Taxable Income**	**Rate**
First $10,000	3.25%	First $20,000	3.25%
$10,001–$25,000	4.0%	$20,001–$50,000	4.0%
$25,001–$50,000	5.05%	$50,001–$100,000	5.05%
$50,001–$150,000	6.4%	$100,001–$300,000	6.4%
Over $150,001	6.9%	Over $300,001	6.9%

FEATURES

Personal Exemptions or Credits
   All taxpayers ....$2,100 single, $4,200 married joint return
                                                          $2,300 each dependent
   Additional for older adults ....$2,100, 65 or older
Standard Deduction......................................$3,500 single, $7,000 married joint return
Medical and Dental Deduction..............................Limited to excess of 4% of adjusted gross income
Federal Income Tax Deduction..............................None
Public Pension Exclusion.................................$2,500
Private Pension Exclusion................................None
Social Security Exemption................................Full

State law authorizes tax on pension income of nonresidents. Tax is not imposed.

ARKANSAS

PERSONAL INCOME TAX RATES

All Taxpayers			
Taxable Income	**Rate**	**Taxable Income**	**Rate**
First $2,999	1.0%	Next $6,000	4.5%
Next $3,000	2.5%	Next $10,000	6.0%
Next $3,000	3.5%	$25,000 or over	7.0%

FEATURES

Personal Exemptions or Credits
   All taxpayers ....$20 credit, single; $40 credit, married
                                                          $20 credit, each dependent
   Additional...$20 credit, 65 or older
Standard Deduction......................................10% of gross income to maximum of $1,000
Medical and Dental Deduction..............................Federal amount
Federal Income Tax Deduction..............................None
Public Pension Exclusion.................................$6,000
Private Pension Exclusion................................$6,000
Social Security Exemption................................Full

CALIFORNIA

PERSONAL INCOME TAX RATES

Single or Married Separate Return		Married Joint Return	
Taxable Income	**Rate**	**Taxable Income**	**Rate**
First $4,666	1.0%	First $9,332	1.0%
$4,666–$11,059	2.0%	$9,332–$22,118	2.0%
$11,059–$17,633	4.0%	$22,118–$34,006	4.0%
$17,633–$24,228	6.0%	$34,006–$48,456	6.0%
$24,228–$30,620	8.0%	$48,456–$61,240	8.0%
$30,620–$106,190	9.3%	$61,240–$212,380	9.3%
$106,190–$212,380	10.0%	$212,380–$424,760	10.0%
Over $212,380	11.0%	Over $424,760	11.0%

FEATURES

Personal Exemptions or Credits

All taxpayers . . . . . $65 credit, single
$1308 credit, married joint return
$65 credit, each dependent

Additional. . . . . $65 credit, 65 or older
Standard Deduction. . . . . $2,431 single, $4,862 married joint return
Medical and Dental Deduction . . . . . Federal amount
Federal Income Tax Deduction. . . . . None
Public Pension Exclusion. . . . . $40 credit, military
Private Pension Exclusion . . . . . None
Social Security Exemption . . . . . Full

State law authorizes tax on pension income of nonresidents. State withholds a 7% income tax on payments to nonresidents.

COLORADO

PERSONAL INCOME TAX RATES
All Taxpayers
5% of Federal Taxable Income

FEATURES

Personal Exemptions or Credits. . . . . None
Standard Deduction. . . . . None
Medical and Dental Deduction . . . . . Federal amount
Federal Income Tax Deduction. . . . . None
Public Pension Exclusion. . . . . $20,000 for persons 55 and older
Private Pension Exclusion . . . . . $20,000 for persons 55 and older
Social Security Exemption . . . . . Federal amount

State law authorizes tax on pension income of nonresidents. Tax is not imposed.

CONNECTICUT

PERSONAL INCOME TAX RATES
All Taxpayers
Flat Rate of 4.5%

FEATURES

Personal Exemptions or Credits

All taxpayers . . . . . Up to $12,000 single
Up to $19,000 head of household
Up to $24,000 married joint return

Standard Deduction. . . . . None
Medical and Dental Deduction . . . . . None
Federal Income Tax Deduction. . . . . None
Public Pension Exclusion. . . . . None
Private Pension Exclusion . . . . . None
Social Security Exemption . . . . . None

State law authorizes tax on pension income of nonresidents. Tax applies to nonqualified deferred compensation only.

DELAWARE

PERSONAL INCOME TAX RATES

All Taxpayers			
Taxable Income	**Rate**	**Taxable Income**	**Rate**
$2,000–$5,000	3.2%	$25,000–$35,000	7.0%
$5,000–$10,000	5.0%	$35,000–$40,000	7.6%
$10,000–$20,000	6.0%	Over $40,000	7.7%
$20,000–$25,000	6.6%		

DELAWARE   *(continued)*
FEATURES
Personal Exemptions or Credits
   All taxpayers . . . . $1,250, each exemption allowed on federal return
   Additional. . . . . $1,250, 65 or older
Standard Deduction. . . . . $1,300 single, $1,600 married joint return
        additional $1,000, 65 or older
Medical and Dental Deduction . . . . Federal amount
Federal Income Tax Deduction. . . . . None
Public Pension Exclusion. . . . . $2,000 for persons under 60
        $3,000 for persons 60 or older
Private Pension Exclusion . . . . $2,000 for persons under 60
        $3,000 for persons 60 or older
Social Security Exemption. . . . . Full

DISTRICT OF COLUMBIA
PERSONAL INCOME TAX RATES
All Taxpayers

Taxable Income	Rate
First $10,000	6.0%
$10,000–$20,000	8.0%
Over $20,000	9.5%

FEATURES
Personal Exemptions or Credits
   All taxpayers . . . . $1,370, each exemption allowed on federal return
   Additional. . . . . $1,370, 65 or older
Standard Deduction. . . . . $1,000 married separate return
        $2,000 single and married joint return
Medical and Dental Deduction . . . . Federal amount
Federal Income Tax Deduction. . . . . None
Public Pension Exclusion. . . . . $3,000 for persons 62 or older
Private Pension Exclusion . . . . None
Social Security Exemption. . . . . Full

FLORDIA

The state does not tax personal income.

GEORGIA
PERSONAL INCOME TAX RATES

Single or Married Separate Return		Married Joint Return	
Taxable Income	Rate	Taxable Income	Rate
First $750	1.0%	First $1,000	1.0%
$750–$2,250	2.0%	$1,000–$3,000	2.0%
$2,250–$3,750	3.0%	$3,000–$5,000	3.0%
$3,750–$5,250	4.0%	$5,000–$7,000	4.0%
$5,250–$7,000	5.0%	$7,000–$10,000	5.0%
Over $7,000	6.0%	Over 10,000	6.0%

FEATURES
Personal Exemptions or Credits. . . . . $1,500 single, $3,000 married joint return
        $2,500 each dependent
Standard Deduction. . . . . $2,300 single, $3,000 married joint return
        $700 additional, taxpayer over 65
        $700 additional, spouse over 65
Medical and Dental Deduction . . . . Federal amount
Federal Income Tax Deduction. . . . . None
Public Pension Exclusion. . . . . $12,000 for persons 62 or older
Private Pension Exclusion . . . . $12,000 for persons 62 or older
Social Security Exemption. . . . . Full

HAWAII

PERSONAL INCOME TAX RATES

Single or Married Separate Return		Married Joint Return	
Taxable Income	**Rate**	**Taxable Income**	**Rate**
First $1,500	2.0%	First $3,000	2.0%
$1,500–$2,500	4.0%	$3,000–$5,000	4.0%
$2,500–$3,500	6.0%	$5,000–$7,000	6.0%
3,500–$5,500	7.25%	$7,000–$11,000	7.25%
5,500–$10,500	8.0%	$11,000–$21,000	8.0%
10,500–$15,500	8.75%	$21,000–$31,000	8.75%
15,500–$20,500	9.5%	$31,000–$41,000	9.5%
Over $20,500	10.0%	Over $41,000	10.0%

FEATURES

Personal Exemptions or Credits
  All taxpayers . . . . $1,040, each individual
  Additional . . . . $1,040, taxpayer or spouse over 65
Standard Deduction . . . . $1,500 single, $1,900 married joint return
Medical and Dental Deduction . . . . Federal amount
Federal Income Tax Deduction . . . . None
Public Pension Exclusion . . . . Full
Private Pension Exclusion . . . . Full
Social Security Exemption . . . . Full

IDAHO

PERSONAL INCOME TAX RATES

Single or Married Separate Return		Married Joint Return	
Taxable Income	**Rate**	**Taxable Income**	**Rate**
First $1,000	2.0%	First $2,000	2.0%
$1,000–$2,000	4.0%	$2,000–$4,000	4.0%
$2,000–$3,000	4.5%	$4,000–$6,000	4.5%
$3,000–$4,000	5.5%	$6,000–$8,000	5.5%
$4,000–$5,000	6.5%	$8,000–$10,000	6.5%
$5,000–$7,500	7.5%	$10,000–$15,000	7.5%
$7,500–$20,000	7.8%	$15,000–$40,000	7.8%
Over $20,000	8.2%	Over $40,000	8.2%

FEATURES

Personal Exemptions or Credits . . . . Federal amount
Standard Deduction . . . . Federal amount
Medical and Dental Deduction . . . . Federal amount
Federal Income Tax Deduction . . . . None
Public Pension Exclusion . . . . Federal amount, except federal and military which exclude -
  $13,536 military, 65 or older, single return
  $20,304 military, 65 or older, joint return
Private Pension Exclusion . . . . None
Social Security Exemption . . . . Full

ILLINOIS

PERSONAL INCOME TAX RATES
All Taxpayers
Flat Rate of 3%

FEATURES

Personal Exemptions or Credits
  All taxpayers . . . . $1,000 personal
  $1,000 each additional federal exemption
  Additional . . . . $1,000 taxpayer or spouse 65 or older
Standard Deduction . . . . None
Medical and Dental Deduction . . . . None
Federal Income Tax Deduction . . . . None
Public Pension Exclusion . . . . Full
Private Pension Exclusion . . . . Full
Social Security Exemption . . . . Full

INDIANA

PERSONAL INCOME TAX RATES
All Taxpayers
Flat Rate of 3.4%

FEATURES
Personal Exemptions or Credits
All taxpayers	$1,000 individual
	$1,000 each dependent
Additional	$1,000 taxpayer or spouse 65 or older
Standard Deduction	None
Medical and Dental Deduction	None
Federal Income Tax Deduction	None
Public Pension Exclusion	$2,000 for federal over 62 and military over 60
Private Pension Exclusion	None
Social Security Exemption	Full

IOWA

PERSONAL INCOME TAX RATES

All Taxpayers

Taxable Income	Rate	Taxable Income	Rate
First $1,060	0.4%	$15,900–$21,200	7.2%
$1,060–2,120	0.8%	$21,200–$31,800	7.55%
$2,120–$4,240	2.7%	$31,800–$47,700	8.8%
$4,240–$9,540	5.0%	Over $47,700	9.98%
$9,540–$15,900	6.8%		

FEATURES
Personal Exemptions or Credits
All taxpayers	$20 credit, single
	$40 credit, married joint return
	$15 credit, each dependent
Additional	$20 credit, 65 or older
Standard Deduction	$1,330 single, $3,270 married joint return
Medical and Dental Deduction	Federal amount
Federal Income Tax Deduction	Full
Public Pension Exclusion	None
Private Pension Exclusion	None
Social Security Exemption	Federal amount

State law authorizes tax on pension income of nonresidents. Tax is imposed.

KANSAS

PERSONAL INCOME TAX RATES

Single or Married Separate Return	Rate	Married Joint Return	Rate
First $20,000	4.4%	First $30,000	3.5%
$20,000–$30,000	7.5%	$30,001–$60,000	6.25%
Over 30,000	7.75%	Over 60,000	6.45%

FEATURES
Personal Exemptions or Credits	$2,000 each exemption
Standard Deduction	$3,000 single, $5,000 married joint return
Medical and Dental Deduction	Federal amount
Federal Income Tax Deduction	None
Public Pension Exclusion	Full
Private Pension Exclusion	None
Social Security Exemption	Federal amount

State law authorizes tax on pension income of nonresidents. Tax is imposed.

KENTUCKY

PERSONAL INCOME TAX RATES

All Taxpayers

Taxable Income	Rate	Taxable Income	Rate
First $3,000	2.0%	$5,000–$8,000	5.0%
$3,000–$4,000	3.0%	Over $8,000	6.0%
$4,000–$5,000	4.0%		

KENTUCKY *(continued)*

FEATURES

Personal Exemptions or Credits	
All taxpayers	$20 credit, each exemption
Additional	$40 credit, 65 or older
Standard Deduction	$650 single, $650 married joint return
Medical and Dental Deduction	Federal amount
Federal Income Tax Deduction	None
Public Pension Exclusion	Full
Private Pension Exclusion	None
Social Security Exemption	Full

LOUISIANA

PERSONAL INCOME TAX RATES

Single or Married Filing Separately		Married Joint Return	
Taxable Income	**Rate**	**Taxable Income**	**Rate**
First $10,000	2.0%	First $20,000	2.0%
$10,001–$50,000	4.0%	$20,001–$100,000	4.0%
Over $50,000	6.0%	Over $100,000	6.0%

FEATURES

Personal Exemptions or Credits	
All taxpayers	$4,500 single, married separate return
	$9,000 married joint return, head of household
	$1,000 each dependent
Additional	$1,000, 65 or older
Standard Deduction	Combined with personal exemptions
Medical and Dental Deduction	Federal amount
Federal Income Tax Deduction	Partial to Full
Public Pension Exclusion	Full
Private Pension Exclusion	$6,000, 65 and older
Social Security Exemption	Full

State law authorizes tax on private pension income of nonresidents. Tax is imposed.

MAINE

PERSONAL INCOME TAX RATES

Single or Married Filing Separately		Married Joint Return	
Taxable Income	**Rate**	**Taxable Income**	**Rate**
First $4,150	2.0%	First $8,250	2.0%
$4,150–8,249	4.5%	$8,250–$16,499	4.5%
$8,250–$16,499	7.0%	$16,500–$32,999	7.0%
Over $16,500	8.5%	Over $33,000	8.5%

FEATURES

Personal Exemptions or Credits	$2,100 each federal exemption
Standard Deduction	$3,800 single, $6,350 married joint return
	additional $950, single over 65
	additional $750, one spouse over 65
	additional $1,500, both spouses over 65
Medical and Dental Deduction	Federal amount
Federal Income Tax Deduction	None
Public Pension Exclusion	None
Private Pension Exclusion	None
Social Security Exemption	Full

MARYLAND

PERSONAL INCOME TAX RATES

Single or Married Filing Separately		Married Joint Return	
Taxable Income	**Rate**	**Taxable Income**	**Rate**
First $1,000	2.0%	First $1,000	2.0%
$1,001–$2,000	3.0%	$1,001–$2,000	3.0%
$2,001–$3,000	4.0%	$2,001–$3,000	4.0%
$3,001–$100,000	5.0%	$3,001–$150,000	5.0%
Over $100,000	6.0%	Over $150,000	6.0%

MARYLAND *(continued)*
FEATURES
Personal Exemptions or Credits
All taxpayers	$1,200 each personal and dependent exemption
Additional.	$1,000 personal, 65 or older
	$1,200 dependent, 65 or older
Standard Deduction.	$1,500 or 15% of Maryland adjusted gross income to maximum of $3,000 for single returns; $2,000 to $4,000 married joint return
Medical and Dental Deduction	Federal amount
Federal Income Tax Deduction.	None
Public Pension Exclusion.	Partial, 65 or older
Private Pension Exclusion	Partial, 65 or older
Social Security Exemption	Full

MASSACHUSETTS
PERSONAL INCOME TAX RATES
All Taxpayers
Taxable Income	Rate
Earned and Business Income, In-State Interest	5.95%
Capital Gains	6.00%
Out-of-State Interest, Dividends	12.00%

FEATURES
Personal Exemptions or Credits
All taxpayers	$2,200 single, $4,400 married joint return
	$1,000 each dependent
Additional.	$700, 65 or older
Standard Deduction.	None
Medical and Dental Deduction	Federal amount
Federal Income Tax Deduction.	None
Public Pension Exclusion.	Full
Private Pension Exclusion	None
Social Security Exemption	Full

State law authorizes tax on pension income of nonresidents. Tax applies to nonqualified deferred compensation only.

MICHIGAN
PERSONAL INCOME TAX RATES
All Taxpayers
Flat Rate of 4.4%

FEATURES
Personal Exemptions or Credits
All taxpayers	$2,100 each federal exemption
Additional.	$2,100 each federal exemption, 65 or older
Standard Deduction.	None
Medical and Dental Deduction	None
Federal Income Tax Deduction.	None
Public Pension Exclusion.	Full
Private Pension Exclusion	$30,000 single, $60,000 married joint return
Social Security Exemption	Full

MINNESOTA
PERSONAL INCOME TAX RATES
Single Return		Married Joint Return	
Taxable Income	Rate	Taxable Income	Rate
First $15,230	6.0%	First $22,260	6.0%
$15,230–$50,030	8.0%	$22,260–$88,460	8.0%
Over $50,030	8.5%	Over 88,460	8.5%

MINNESOTA *(continued)*

FEATURES
Personal Exemptions or Credits............................ Federal amount
Standard Deduction...................................... Federal amount
Medical and Dental Deduction .... Federal amount plus full amount of medical insurance premiums
for self-employed in excess of that included in federal amount
Federal Income Tax Deduction............................ None
Public Pension Exclusion................................ None
Private Pension Exclusion .... None
Social Security Exemption............................... Full
Other .... Residents 65 or older filing single returns may exclude a
maximum of $8,000; residents 65 or older filing married joint
returns may exclude a maximum of $15,000; in both cases, the
amount is reduced as income rises.

State law authorizes tax on pension income of nonresidents. Tax applies to nonqualified deferred compensation only.

MISSISSIPPI

PERSONAL INCOME TAX RATES
All Taxpayers

Taxable Income	Rate
First 5,000	3.0%
$5,000–$10,000	4.0%
Over $10,000	5.0%

FEATURES
Personal Exemptions or Credits
   All taxpayers .... $6,000 single, $9,500 married joint return
$1,500 each dependent
   Additional.. $1,500 65 or older
Standard Deduction..................................... $2,300 single, $3,400 married joint return
Medical and Dental Deduction .... Partial
Federal Income Tax Deduction............................ None
Public Pension Exclusion................................ Full
Private Pension Exclusion .... Full
Social Security Exemption............................... Full

---

MISSOURI

PERSONAL INCOME TAX RATES

	All Taxpayers			
Taxable Income	Rate	Taxable Income		Rate
First $1,000	1.5%	$5,001–$6,000		4.0%
$1,001–$2,000	2.0%	$6,001–$7,000		4.5%
$2,001–$3,000	2.5%	$7,001–$8,000		5.0%
$3,001–$4,000	3.0%	$8,001–$9,000		5.5%
$4,001–$5,000	3.5%	Over $9,000		6.0%

FEATURES
Personal Exemptions or Credits........................... $1,200 taxpayer and spouse
$400 each dependent
Standard Deduction..................................... Federal amount
Medical and Dental Deduction .... Federal amount
Federal Income Tax Deduction............................ Full
Public Pension Exclusion................................ $6,000, single and income less than $25,000 exclusive of Social
Security
$6,000, married and income less than $32,000 exclusive of Social
Security
Private Pension Exclusion .... None
Social Security Exemption............................... Federal amount
Railroad Retirement Exemption .... Full

MONTANA

PERSONAL INCOME TAX RATES

Taxable Income	**All Taxpayers** Rate	Taxable Income	Rate
First $1,700	2.0%	$14,000–$17,500	7.0%
$1,700–$3,500	3.0%	$17,500–$24,400	8.0%
$3,500–$7,000	4.0%	$24,400–$34,900	9.0%
$7,000–$10,500	5.0%	$34,900–$61,100	10.0%
$10,500–$14,000	6.0%	Over $61,100	11.0%

FEATURES

Personal Exemptions or Credits
  All taxpayers . . . . $1,400 each exemption
  Additional. . . . . $1,400 each 65 or older
Standard Deduction. . . . . $2,620 single, $5,240 married joint return
Medical and Dental Deduction . . . . Federal amount
Federal Income Tax Deduction . . . . Full
Public Pension Exclusion. . . . . $3,600 maximum, depending on income
Private Pension Exclusion . . . . $3,600 maximum, depending on income
Social Security Exemption . . . . Federal amount

NEBRASKA

PERSONAL INCOME TAX RATES

Single or Married Filing Separately Taxable Income	Rate	**Married Joint Return** Taxable Income	Rate
First $2,400	2.62%	First $4,000	2.62%
$2,400–$17,000	3.65%	$4,000–$30,000	3.65%
$17,000–$26,500	5.24%	$30,000–$46,750	5.24%
Over $26,500	6.99%	Over $46,750	6.99%

FEATURES

Personal Exemptions or Credits. . . . . $65 credit, each federal exemption
Standard Deduction. . . . . Federal amount
Medical and Dental Deduction . . . . Federal amount
Federal Income Tax Deduction. . . . . None
Public Pension Exclusion. . . . . None
Private Pension Exclusion . . . . None
Social Security Exemption . . . . Federal amount

NEVADA

The state does not tax personal income.

NEW HAMPSHIRE

PERSONAL INCOME TAX RATES

All Taxpayers

5.0% tax only on interest and dividends. Exceptions include interest from bonds issued by the state and its cities and towns, and interest paid by New Hampshire and Vermont banks.

FEATURES

Personal Exemptions or Credits
  All taxpayers . . . . $1,200 each taxpayer
  Additional. . . . . $1,200 65 or older

NEW JERSEY

PERSONAL INCOME TAX RATES

Single or Married Filing Separately Taxable Income	Rate	**Married Joint Return** Taxable Income	Rate
First $20,000	1.9%	First $20,000	1.9%
$20,000–$35,000	2.375%	$20,000–$50,000	2.375%
$35,000–$40,000	4.75%	$50,000–$70,000	3.325%
$40,000–$75,000	6.175%	$70,000–$80,000	4.75%
Over $75,000	6.65%	$80,000–$150,000	6.175%
		Over $150,000	6.65%

NEW JERSEY *(continued)*

FEATURES

Personal Exemptions or Credits

All taxpayers . . . . $1,000 single, $2,000 married joint return
$1,500 each dependent

Additional. . . . . $1,000 65 or older, taxpayer or spouse

Standard Deduction. . . . . None

Medical and Dental Deduction . . . . Limited to excess of 2% of gross income

Federal Income Tax Deduction . . . . None

Public Pension Exclusion . . . . $7,500 single
$5,000 married filing separately
$10,000 married joint return

Private Pension Exclusion . . . . $7,500 single
$5,000 married filing separately
$10,000 married joint return

Social Security Exemption . . . . Full

NEW MEXICO

PERSONAL INCOME TAX RATES

Single or Married Filing Separately		Married Joint Return	
Taxable Income	**Rate**	**Taxable Income**	**Rate**
First $5,500	1.7%	First $8,000	2.2%
$5,501–$11,000	3.0%	$8,001–16,000	3.2%
$11,001–$16,000	4.7%	$16,001–$24,000	4.7%
$16,001–$26,000	6.0%	$24,001–$36,000	6.0%
$26,001–$31,200	7.1%	$36,001–$48,000	7.1%
$31,201–$41,600	7.9%	$48,001–$64,000	7.9%
Over $41,600	8.5%	Over $64,000	8.5%

FEATURES

Personal Exemptions or Credits

All taxpayers . . . . Federal amount

Additional. . . . . Maximum $8,000, 65 or older, depending on income

Standard Deduction. . . . . Federal amount

Medical and Dental Deduction . . . . Credit of 3% of unreimbursed prescription drug expenses to maximum of $150 per individual or $300 per return

Federal Income Tax Deduction . . . . None

Public Pension Exclusion . . . . None

Private Pension Exclusion . . . . None

Social Security Exemption . . . . Federal amount

NEW YORK

PERSONAL INCOME TAX RATES

Single or Married Filing Separately		Married Joint Return	
Taxable Income	**Rate**	**Taxable Income**	**Rate**
First $6,500	4.55%	First $13,000	4.55%
$6,500–$9,500	5.55%	$13,000–$19,000	5.55%
$9,500–$12,500	6.55%	$19,000–$25,000	6.55%
Over $12,500	7.50%	Over $25,000	7.50%

FEATURES

Personal Exemptions or Credits. . . . . $1,000 each dependent

Standard Deduction. . . . . $6,300 single, $10,200 married joint return

Medical and Dental Deduction . . . . Federal amount

Federal Income Tax Deduction . . . . None

Public Pension Exclusion . . . . Full

Private Pension Exclusion . . . . $20,000 for 591/2 or older

Social Security Exemption . . . . Full

State law authorizes tax on private pension income of nonresidents. Tax is imposed.

NORTH CAROLINA

PERSONAL INCOME TAX RATES

Single or Married Filing Separately		Married Joint Return	
Taxable Income	Rate	Taxable Income	Rate
First $12,750	6.00%	First $21,250	6.00%
Next $47,250	7.00%	Next $78,750	7.00%
Over $60,000	7.75%	Over $100,000	7.75%

FEATURES

Personal Exemptions or Credits. . . . . Federal amount
Standard Deduction. . . . . $3,000 single, $5,000 married joint return
Medical and Dental Deduction . . . . Federal amount
Federal Income Tax Deduction. . . . . None
Public Pension Exclusion. . . . . $4,000 per taxpayer; $4,000 maximum if taxpayer receives both
   public and private pensions
Private Pension Exclusion . . . . $2,000 per taxpayer; $4,000 maximum if taxpayer receives both
   public and private pensions
Social Security Exemption. . . . . Full

NORTH DAKOTA

PERSONAL INCOME TAX RATES

All Taxpayers			
Taxable Income	Rate	Taxable Income	Rate
First $3,000	2.67%	$15,000–$25,000	8.00%
$3,000–$5,000	4.00%	$25,000–$35,000	9.33%
$5,000–$8,000	5.33%	$35,000–$50,000	10.67%
$8,000–$15,000	6.67%	Over $50,000	12.00%

OPTIONAL

Taxpayers may forgo state adjustments to federal taxable income and pay 14% of federal tax liability.

FEATURES

Personal Exemptions or Credits. . . . . Federal amount plus -
   $300 married joint return
   $300 single return, head of household
Standard Deduction. . . . . Federal amount
Medical and Dental Deduction . . . . Full
Federal Income Tax Deduction. . . . . Full
Public Pension Exclusion. . . . . $5,000, less Social Security benefits, for federal pensions
   $5,000, less Social Security benefits, for
   North Dakota public safety pensions
Private Pension Exclusion . . . . None
Social Security Exemption. . . . . Federal amount

State law authorizes tax on pension income of nonresidents. Tax is not imposed.

OHIO

PERSONAL INCOME TAX RATES

All Taxpayers			
Taxable Income	Rate	Taxable Income	Rate
First $5,000	0.743%	$40,000–$80,000	5.201%
$5,000–$10,000	1.486%	$80,000–$100,000	5.943%
$10,000–$15,000	2.972%	$100,000–$200,000	6.9000%
$15,000–$20,000	3.715%	Over $200,000	7.500%
$20,000–$40,000	4.457%		

FEATURES

Personal Exemptions or Credits
  All taxpayers . . . . $650 taxpayer, spouse, each dependent
  Additional. . . . . $50 credit, taxpayer over 65
Standard Deduction. . . . . None
Medical and Dental Deduction . . . . None
Federal Income Tax Deduction. . . . . None
Public Pension Exclusion. . . . . $200 maximum credit, based on income
Private Pension Exclusion . . . . $200 maximum credit, based on income
Social Security Exemption. . . . . Full

OKLAHOMA

PERSONAL INCOME TAX RATES

Single or Married Filing Separately		Married Joint Return	
Taxable Income	**Rate**	**Taxable Income**	**Rate**
First $1000	0.5%	First $2,000	0.5%
Next $1,500	1.0%	Next $3,000	1.0%
Next $1,250	2.0%	Next $2,500	2.0%
Next $1,150	3.0%	Next $2,300	3.0%
Next $1,300	4.0%	Next $2,400	4.0%
Next $1,500	5.0%	Next $2,800	5.0%
Next $2,300	6.0%	Next $6,000	6.0%
Over $10,000	7.0%	Over $21,000	7.0%

FEATURES

Personal Exemptions or Credits
- All taxpayers . . . . $1,000 each taxpayer
- Additional. . . . . $1,000 65 or older, depending on federal adjusted gross income

Standard Deduction. . . . . $1,000 to $2,000 for single and joint returns
$500 to $1,000 for married filing separately

Medical and Dental Deduction . . . . Federal amount
Federal Income Tax Deduction. . . . . Full, but higher rates apply to the remaining taxable income
Public Pension Exclusion. $5,500
Private Pension Exclusion . . . . None
Social Security Exemption. . . . . Federal amount

OREGON

PERSONAL INCOME TAX RATES

Single or Married Filing Separately		Married Joint Return	
Taxable Income	**Rate**	**Taxable Income**	**Rate**
First $2,050	5.0%	First $4,100	5.0%
$2,050–$5,150	7.0%	$4,100–$10,300	7.0%
Over $5,150	9.0%	Over $10,300	9.0%

FEATURES

Personal Exemptions or Credits
- All taxpayers . . . . $113 credit, each federal exemption
- Additional. . . . . Credit equal to 40% of federal credit

Standard Deduction. . . . . $1,800 single, $3,000 married joint return
additional $1,200, single return over 65
additional $2,000, joint return over 65

Medical and Dental Deduction . . . . Full only for age 59 or older, if itemized
Federal Income Tax Deduction. . . . . $3,000 ($1,500 if married filing separately)
Public Pension Exclusion. . . . . Up to 9% for persons age 59 or older with household income
under $45,000 (married joint return) or household income under
$22,500 (other filing status)

Private Pension Exclusion . . . . Identical to public pension exclusion
Social Security Exemption. . . . . Full

State law authorizes tax on pension income of nonresidents. State withholds a maximum 10% income tax on retirement plan distributions.

PENNSYLVANIA

PERSONAL INCOME TAX RATES

All Taxpayers
Flat Rate of 2.8%

FEATURES

Personal Exemptions or Credits. . . . . None
Standard Deduction. . . . . None
Medical and Dental Deduction . . . . None
Federal Income Tax Deduction. . . . . None
Public Pension Exclusion. . . . . Full
Private Pension Exclusion . . . . Full
Social Security Exemption. . . . . Full

RHODE ISLAND

PERSONAL INCOME TAX RATES

All Taxpayers
27.5% of federal income tax liability

RHODE ISLAND *(continued)*

FEATURES

Personal Exemptions or Credits	Federal amount
Standard Deduction	Federal amount
Medical and Dental Deduction	Federal amount
Federal Income Tax Deduction	None
Public Pension Exclusion	None
Private Pension Exclusion	None
Social Security Exemption	Federal amount

SOUTH CAROLINA

PERSONAL INCOME TAX RATES

All Taxpayers

Taxable Income	Rate	Taxable Income	Rate
First $2,170	2.5%	$6,510–$8,680	5.0%
$2,170–$4,340	3.0%	$8,680–$10,850	6.0%
$4,340–$6,510	4.0%	Over $10,850	7.0%

FEATURES

Personal Exemptions or Credits	Federal amount
Standard Deduction	Federal amount
Medical and Dental Deduction	Federal amount
Federal Income Tax Deduction	None
Public Pension Exclusion	$3,000 for persons under 65 / $10,000 for persons over 65
Private Pension Exclusion	$3,000 for persons under 65 / $10,000 for persons over 65
Social Security Exemption	Full

SOUTH DAKOTA

The state does not tax personal income.

TENNESSEE

PERSONAL INCOME TAX RATES

All Taxpayers

6.0% on income from stock dividends and interest from bonds and other obligations. Exceptions include federal obligations, and instruments of indebtedness issued to Tennesee banks.

FEATURES

Personal Exemptions or Credits. . . . . $1,250 single, $2,500 married joint return

TEXAS

The state does not tax personal income.

UTAH

PERSONAL INCOME TAX RATES

Single or Married Filing Separately		Married Joint Return	
Taxable Income	Rate	Taxable Income	Rate
First $750	2.55%	First $1,500	2.55%
$750–$1,500	3.5%	$1,500–$3,000	3.5%
$1,500–$2,250	4.4%	$3,000–$4,500	4.4%
$2,251–$3,000	5.35%	$4,500–$6,000	5.35%
$3,000–$3,750	6.25%	$6,000–$7,500	6.25%
Over $3,750	7.2%	Over $7,500	7.2%

UTAH *(continued)*

FEATURES

Personal Exemptions or Credits	75% of federal amount
Standard Deduction	Federal amount
Medical and Dental Deduction	Federal amount
Federal Income Tax Deduction	50% deductible
Public Pension Exclusion	$7,500 maximum, reduced as income rises
Private Pension Exclusion	$7,500 maximum, reduced as income rises
Social Security Exemption	Federal amount

VERMONT

PERSONAL INCOME TAX RATES
All Taxpayers
25.0% of federal tax liability

FEATURES

Personal Exemptions or Credits	Federal amount
Standard Deduction	Federal amount
Medical and Dental Deduction	Federal amount
Federal Income Tax Deduction	None
Public Pension Exclusion	None
Private Pension Exclusion	None
Social Security Exemption	Federal amount

State law authorizes tax on pension income of nonresidents. Tax applies to nonqualified deferred compensation only.

VIRGINIA

PERSONAL INCOME TAX RATES
All Taxpayers

Taxable Income	Rate
First $3,000	2.0%
$3,000–$5,000	3.0%
$5,000–$17,000	5.0%
Over $17,000	5.75%

FEATURES

Personal Exemptions or Credits	
All taxpayers	$800 each federal exemption
Additional	$800 each person 65 or older
Standard Deduction	$3,000 single, $5,000 married joint return
Medical and Dental Deduction	Partial
Federal Income Tax Deduction	None
Public Pension Exclusion	None
Private Pension Exclusion	None
Social Security Exemption	Full
Other	Residents 62 to 64 may exclude up to $6,497 of income from any source; residents 65 or older may exclude up to $12,994 from any source. These exclusions are reduced by the amount of Social Security benefits the taxpayer receives.

WASHINGTON

The state does not tax personal income.

WEST VIRGINIA

PERSONAL INCOME TAX RATES

Single or Married Filing Separately		Married Joint Return	
Taxable Income	Rate	Taxable Income	Rate
First $10,000	3.0%	First $5,000	3.0%
$10,000–$25,000	4.0%	$5,000–$12,500	4.0%
$25,000–$40,000	4.5%	$12,500–$20,000	4.5%
$40,000–$60,000	6.0%	$20,000–$30,000	6.0%
Over $60,000	6.5%	Over $30,000	6.5%

WEST VIRGINIA   *(continued)*

FEATURES

Personal Exemptions or Credits	$2,000 each federal exemption
Standard Deduction	None
Medical and Dental Deduction	None
Federal Income Tax Deduction	None
Public Pension Exclusion	$2,000; public safety pensions fully exempt
Private Pension Exclusion	None
Social Security Exemption	Federal amount
Other	Each person over 65 may exclude up to $8,000 of income included in federal adjusted income, including pensions deductions.

WISCONSIN

PERSONAL INCOME TAX RATES

Single or Married Filing Separately		Married Joint Return	
Taxable Income	**Rate**	**Taxable Income**	**Rate**
First $7,500	4.90%	First $10,000	4.90%
$7,500–$15,000	6.55%	$10,000–$20,000	6.55%
Over $15,000	6.93%	Over $20,000	6.93%

FEATURES

Personal Exemptions or Credits	
All taxpayers	$50 credit, each dependent on federal return
Additional	$25 credit, each taxpayer and spouse over 65
Standard Deduction	Maximum $5,200 single, reduced as income rises Maximum $8,900 married joint return, reduced as income rises
Medical and Dental Deduction	5% credit for expenses in excess of standard deduction
Federal Income Tax Deduction	None
Public Pension Exclusion	Federal and benefits from specified Wisconsin retirement systems
Private Pension Exclusion	None
Social Security Exemption	Federal amount

State law authorizes tax on pension income of nonresidents. Tax applies to nonqualified deferred compensation only.

WYOMING

The state does not tax personal income.

STATE/LOCAL SALES TAXES

Sometimes called "retail taxes" or consumption taxes, sales taxes are collected on the purchase of goods at the store level. After property taxes, sales taxes account for the largest source of revenue for state and local governments. Unlike property taxes, however, since 1991 they haven't been deductible from your federal tax return.

Nationally, the median sales tax is 5 percent. If you're living in Mississippi or Rhode Island, you're paying the nation's highest state rate, 7 percent. But combined state and local sales taxes, in the 31 states that allow it, can top 8 percent.

Alaska, Delaware, Montana, New Hampshire, and Oregon collect no sales taxes at all. To a retired couple, this could mean saving $300 to $600 a year. But you can avoid much of that cost in states where food, medicine, and clothing are exempt.

STATE DEATH TAXES

Most persons need never worry about federal estate taxes. The law lets you leave as much as you wish to your spouse and up to an additional $600,000 to other heirs tax-free. In some states, however, inheritances valued at $100 can be hit by death taxes. Depending on where you live, there are three kinds: a "pickup" tax, an inheritance tax, or an estate tax. (See table on page 33.)

The pickup tax doesn't cost you or your heirs anything. It picks up for the state some of the money that the estate would otherwise pay to the federal government. It is the only death tax in 30 states. If you live in any of them, you won't have to worry about the pickup tax unless your estate is subject to the federal tax.

The inheritance tax, applicable in 16 states, may amount to a good deal of money depending on who the heirs are and how much they get. Property left to a spouse, however, is tax-free in 14 of these states.

The estate tax is used in five states. The amount they collect is determined solely by the size of the estate. Mississippi allows a $600,000 exemption; the exemption in Massachusetts is only $200,000. The relationship of the heirs to the person who left the estate has no bearing unless the heir is a surviving spouse.

HOUSING

"You can't get too much housing," real estate salespeople say with one hand on the steering wheel and the other on their listings as they drive prospective buyers about for a windshield tour of neighborhoods.

True enough, you never need the space until you don't have it, and there are still tax and investment advantages to owning a home on your own piece of ground. But when you retire, you've probably got too much housing indeed.

The condition is called "overhousing," and it crops up when your children leave home and scatter like tumbleweeds in the wind. Bedrooms are full of furniture but closed off. The creaking and settling once heard at night when everything was still are now heard all the time. And those bills for property taxes, insurance, and upkeep on the family's sentimental shrine are as high as they ever were, and still have to be paid.

Overhousing isn't just an empty-nester syndrome. If you plan to see the country, thinking about a vacant house and its yard running to weeds will dampen any good time. Your home is likely your biggest asset now. Might its market value, which has appreciated over the years, be turned into cash and put to better use?

Certainly developers, investors, and marketers think so. "Move over, baby boomers," *Builder*, a construction trade magazine, announces. "Make way for your elders, who will constitute housing's hottest market for the rest of the century." If you're 55 to 65, you're now part of the "go-go" market for active adults-only housing developments. If you're 65 to 75, you're a "go-slow" customer for newfangled congregate housing. And if you're over 75, stop worrying; "no-go" continuing-care facilities are springing up everywhere.

While these types of housing are attracting customers, the seven alternatives for more independent living are the same and as plentiful as they ever were for older adults: buying a smaller house, condominium, or mobile home; or renting an apartment, smaller home, condominium, or mobile home.

TYPICAL HOUSING CHOICES . . .

If the burdens of overhousing lead you to put the old ark up for sale, heed the advice of other retired persons and scale down your housing needs when you scout for another address. Buying down to smaller, less expensive shelter not only leaves you with more income—it leaves you with more leisure time.

If you're thinking of buying down in a distant place, it helps to know in advance what kinds of typical housing choices there are, and since most relocating retired people end up buying a single-family house, how much that would cost.

Newer Homes in Retirement Places

In some retirement places, more than one-fifth of the single-family housing stock has been built over the latest five years.

Place	New Homes	Value
St. George–Zion, UT	35%	$79,700
Las Vegas, NV	30	67,600
Lake Havasu City, AZ	28	82,300
Kissimmee–St. Cloud, FL	27	80,600
San Juan Islands, WA	25	91,800
Madison, MS	22	81,900
Port Townsend, WA	22	63,500
Bend, OR	21	104,400
Leesburg–Lady Lake, FL	21	65,100

Source: Census Bureau, *Housing Permits and Construction Contracts,* 1990–1994; Places Rated Partnership estimates. Value is the average construction costs, including permits, labor, materials, design fees, and contractor's profit, exclusive of house lot.

Condominiums

You'll search in vain for a condo in 23 retirement places. In 12 others, they are a major part of the housing mix. In the following places this kind of housing is more likely to be rented or seasonally occupied by their owners than anywhere else.

Place	Percent of Housing Units
Naples, FL	37%
Ocean City, MD	34
Ketchum–Sun Valley, ID	29
Maui, HI	24
Sarasota, FL	22
Vero Beach–Sebastian, FL	20
Fort Myers–Cape Coral, FL	19
St. Petersburg–Clearwater, FL	18
Bradenton, FL	16
Boca Raton, FL	15
St. Augustine, FL	15
St. George–Zion, UT	15

Source: U.S. Bureau of the Census; Places Rated estimates.

Single Houses

Older adults are no different from everyone else in the kind of roof they prefer overhead. The common detached house is the overwhelming favorite.

If you open the front door of this typical American home, you'll find yourself in a structure that has a single-level, 1,800-square-foot floor plan enclosing six rooms (three bedrooms, one bath, a living room, and a complete kitchen); an insulated attic and storm windows to conserve the heat from the gas-fired, warm-air furnace; and no basement. This house is kept cool during hot spells by a central air-conditioning unit. It is also connected to city water and sewerage lines.

So much for the national composite. Among the 73 million single houses in the United States, a buyer can choose from Cape Cods, Cape Annes and Queen Annes, mountain A-frames, American and Dutch colonials, desert adobes, cabins of peeled pine log, Greek revivals, Puget Sounds, cat-slides, saltboxes, exotic glass solaria, futuristic earth berms, Victorians, plantation cottages, ubiquitous split-levels, and California bungalows.

But in retirement places, the number of single homes you'll actually find among the other options—apartments, condominiums, and mobile homes—varies considerably.

Condominiums

Condominium was an obscure Latin word before a new legal form of housing tenure was imported from Puerto Rico to the U.S. mainland in 1960. Under the arrangement, you could own outright an apartment, townhome, or single house in a multiple-unit development. As an owner, you were subject to property taxes and could sell, lease, bequeath, and furnish that legally described cube of air space independently of other unit owners.

What's more, you owned the elevators, heating plant, streets, parking spaces, garden landscaping, ten-nis courts, swimming pool, lights, and walkways in common with the rest of the development's residents.

Most condo owners are people younger than 35 who are making their way out of the rental market and people older than 65 who want to unload large houses for smaller ones. While the construction boom has subsided in some sections of the country, the fact that the number of condos grew from zero in 1960 to 5 million today vouches for their appeal.

Though condominium housing ranges all the way from units in oceanfront high-rises in Myrtle Beach to row townhouse developments in Prescott and even mobile-home parks in south Florida, most are either one-family (nearly all attached, such as townhomes) or in small low-rise buildings with fewer than 15 units.

California and Florida account for 37 percent of all condos in this country. In several of their real estate markets, in San Diego and in Sarasota, for instance, and in resorts like Ocean City and Maui, condos outnumber single homes in the "for sale" market. In more rural places, they play no part in the housing mix.

Mobile Homes

From western deserts to southern pinewoods, drive the country roads long enough and you'll meet up with a "wide load" convoy trucking halves of a Double Wide mobile home to its new owner's lot.

They are a big part of the Sun Belt housing mix. Last year, half of all newly built mobile homes were shipped in eight states: California, Florida, Georgia, Louisiana, North Carolina, Oklahoma, South Carolina, and Texas. You won't find a mobile-home park in Hawaii, the less rural parts of New England, and larger cities where the high cost of land offsets any savings from buying a mobile home.

<table>
<tr><td colspan="2">

Trailer Life

A popular Sun Belt housing option, *manufactured housing*—as the mobile-home industry prefers to call it—shelters one in 18 people in the United States.
</td></tr>
</table>

Place	Percent of Housing Units
Kingman, AZ	42%
Yuma, AZ	38
Leesburg–Lady Lake, FL	36
Southport–Brunswick Islands, NC	36
Lake Granbury, TX	35
Brookings–Gold Beach, OR	33
Cedar Creek Lake, TX	33
Inverness, FL	31
Ocala, FL	31

Source: U.S. Bureau of the Census; Places Rated estimates.

Apartments

Almost one in five housing units in this country is an apartment in a building with five or more units. Except in larger cities and college towns, this kind of lifestyle isn't nearly as common in most retirement places.

Place	Percent of Housing Units
Austin, TX	25%
Las Vegas, NV	24
San Diego, CA	23
Athens, GA	22
Burlington, VT	22
Chapel Hill, NC	21
Reno–Sparks, NV	21
State College, PA	21
Gainesville, FL	20

Source: U.S. Bureau of the Census; Places Rated estimates.

Their big plus is that they are the cheapest kind of housing you can buy. That they are affordable doesn't mean mobile homes resemble the drafty, 300-square-foot trailers that housed defense workers during World War II or the larger cheapjack units built during the 1950s and parked in enclaves beyond the railroad tracks.

Mobile homes now average 14 feet by 70 feet, offering nearly 1,000 square feet of living space. A 70-foot-long Double Wide can enclose three bedrooms, two ceramic-tiled baths, a living room, a dining room, and a full kitchen. These mobile homes are typically marketed complete: appliances, furniture, draperies, and carpeting are included in the price, as are the built-in plumbing, heating, air-conditioning, and electrical systems.

Outside, owners landscape with grass, trees, and shrubberies. When carports, porches, sheds, patios, and pitched shake roofs are added to the basic structures, even sharp-eyed tax assessors mistake them for conventional houses.

The only time the mobile home is mobile is when it leaves the factory and is trucked in one or more sections to a concrete foundation on the owner's property or at one of 24,000 trailer parks in the country. When it gets there, the wheels, axle, and towing tongue are taken off.

After that, the only element that hints of its origins as a trailer is the welded I-beam chassis, which becomes hidden structural reinforcement once the unit is winched onto the concrete pad and plumbed. When it's in place, the mobile home becomes more or less permanent; no more than 3 percent of them will ever be jacked up and rolled off to a new site.

Renting an Apartment

It does happen. One day you're out with a real estate broker scouting for a condo or small home and you spot an immaculate, stately old building near downtown with flowers in front and no sign but one: AN APARTMENT FOR RENT. The next day you're a tenant.

Unlike younger newcomers who usually rent after relocating, most retired persons buy. But renting may be smart for the short term; it allows you to remain flexible, since you need not stay in an apartment beyond the term of the lease if you decide to buy or to relocate to a different place.

Renting is also cheaper. Rents haven't gone up as fast as the costs of owning. Other pluses: you don't need to come up with a large down payment; taxes, insurance, repairs, and sometimes utilities are the landlord's headaches. What's more, vacancy rates are predicted to climb as more and more renters buy. In some overbuilt Sun Belt places—Austin and Phoenix, for example—landlords are offering month-to-month arrangements or leases with a short period of free rent.

Don't be put off by the image of impersonal blocks of large, high-rise tower complexes near a place's central business district. Only one out of 50 apartments is in a building of 13 stories or more, and only one out of 10 is in a building higher than three stories. Make note: apartments make up a large chunk of housing, not only in bigger places, but in smaller places dominated by state universities.

. . . AND TYPICAL HOUSING PRICES

If you sell your home, you'll likely realize enough cash to buy another home, perhaps a smaller one. Or you might buy a mobile home or condo. You might even rent, investing the money from the sale of your old home to provide retirement income. Of course, if you decide to buy, what you buy and where you buy it greatly influences the price you pay.

Nationally, prices are lowest for mobile homes, rise for resale condos, move higher for resale detached homes, higher still for new condos, and then peak for new homes.

The price difference between a mobile home and a site-built house is almost entirely due to labor costs. It takes a small builder's crew 60 to 90 days to erect a typical three-bedroom tract house. A mobile home takes 80 to 100 hours at the factory. In 1994, when the average square-foot cost of building a conventional home was $65, exclusive of land, the cost of manufacturing a mobile home was $35 per square foot.

If you want to strike a compromise between small-scale living and the satisfaction of owning your own address, consider the condominium form of ownership. In a new condominium, you'll have less interior space to look after (1,250 square feet, on average, versus 1,800 square feet for a new single home). Moreover, the tax advantages of ownership are yours at a lower cost (on average, new condos cost 10 to 15 percent less than new single homes).

How Much Can You Afford?

According to the 10/25 rule in mortgage lending, a household that puts down 10 percent on a home can finance the rest if no more than 25 percent of their gross income covers the principal and interest. At an average mortgage rate of 8.5 percent, for example, you'd need a gross income of $35,000 to handle the $720 monthly principal and interest on a $100,000 house.

That's one way of looking at it. A far simpler way is to recall the long-standing rule of thumb handed down from parents to children which states that, if you buy a house that costs much more than two and a half times your gross income, you're headed for trouble. For example, if your gross annual income is $35,000, the price range of houses to shop for is $87,500 to $90,000; if your income is $50,000, you can afford a house costing between $125,000 and $130,000.

Based on either rule, can local households afford a typical home in each retirement place? In two-thirds of these places, yes.

PROPERTY TAX SHOPPING

Just because you're getting older doesn't mean tax assessors take notice and graciously lower your tax bill. Property tax relief, in the states that offer it to older adults, usually comes after specific income tests. The only state where persons over 65 can completely forget their property taxes is Alaska (a state, incidentally, with the lowest proportion of people over 65). Why not shop for favorable property taxes the way corporations do when they plan moves?

In recent years, homeowners who organized to fight confiscatory property taxes likened them to a ransom they were forced to pay to save their homes from the assessor's auction block. Using this analogy, New Yorkers buy their homes back every 53 years, since their state's average residential property tax rate is 1.9 percent of a home's fair market value. In Louisiana, the ransom period is 249 years because of an extremely low average rate of 0.401 percent. The difference in these figures

Property Tax Bills

Lowest to Highest	Bill
Lake Martin, AL	$267
Guntersville, AL	286
Fairhope–Gulf Shores, AL	403
Western St. Tammany Parish, LA	421
Crossville, TN	465
183 Places Average	*1,429*
Laguna Beach–Dana Point, CA	3,441
Lake Winnipesaukee, NH	3,661
East End Long Island, NY	3,839
Cape Cod, MA	3,843
Lower Cape May, NJ	3,904

Source: Derived from local average home prices and Places Rated Partnership survey of tax assessors.

illustrates the wide variation in property taxes around the country.

Property taxes can vary locally, too, and be madly confusing to owners. In California, two homes on the same street with identical sales prices and physical characteristics can have substantially different, yet legally impeccable, tax bills if one of them was sold before the approval of Proposition 13 and the other after. In Texas, a home's value can be assessed at different levels at different times of the year by different assessors. In northern Michigan, homeowners pay a lower "winter" bill and a higher "summer" bill whether or not they are year-round residents.

WHAT DIFFERENCE DOES AGE MAKE?

Scuff over the sawdust and around the empty nail kegs, the stacked sheetrock, and the crated fiberglass shower stall in a newly framed ranch in a suburban housing development, and you might wonder why the builder is asking a bundle for something he's putting up so quickly.

They don't build them the way they used to. Porches that shade a house from its "morning side" to its "afternoon side" are rarely found. A porch is now merely a recessed space at the home's entrance. The 10-foot interior ceiling common before World War II has been replaced by the 8-foot standard. The kind of formal stairway with well-turned balusters and waxed rails that Andy Hardy used to slide down is no longer necessary —most new homes are erected on a single level. Milled red oak fascias and moldings have become too expensive for common use; walls are envelopes of three-eighths gypsum board fastened to studs rather than the old "mud jobs" of plaster on lath; and solid six-panel interior doors have lost out to hollow-core flush doors of hemlock veneer.

On the other hand, the seasonal threat of damp and flooded cellars arises less often, simply because there aren't many cellars being excavated. Polyvinyl chloride and copper have replaced galvanized iron for water pipes; cast-iron radiators no longer interfere with furniture arrangement; knob-and-tube wiring has surrendered to safer electrical circuitry; and pressure-treated wood has eliminated termite and dry-rot risks along the sills.

CONSTRUCTION RATES AND PERMIT VALUES

New homes are nearly always built with a construction permit and nearly every construction permit results in a new home. Among retirement places, the rate that new homes are added to the existing housing stock in a five-year period varies considerably. Some areas are lagging. Others are bricklayer and carpenter paradises.

The average value of local construction permits—a figure that includes everything from materials, labor, design work, interest and taxes, profit, and miscellaneous overhead—approaches or exceeds the price of an existing home. The value of the house lot is another issue.

Based on Federal Housing Authority data, the cost of the land on which a home is built represents 22 percent of its price. Like home prices, this varies depending on where the home is located. In Hawaii, the true, freehold cost of the site is more than half the sales price; in California, it's 40 percent; in Kansas, it's 13 percent.

HISTORIC NEIGHBORHOODS

The "filtering theory" of housing states that houses pass down from their high-income original owners to middle-income buyers and finally to lower-income owners. Put another way, richer households tend to live in newer homes and poorer households occupy older homes.

Sounds obvious, no?

However, when the real estate sections from *Yankee* magazine, *Old House Journal*, the New Bern (NC) *Sun Journal*, the Beaufort (SC) *Gazette*, the *Arizona Republic*, the Charleston (SC) *Post & Courier*, to the *New York Times Magazine* list antique Capes, Georgian country mansions, and in-town Victorians built in the last century for hundreds of thousands of dollars, you're looking at an exception to the theory.

Nowhere is this more apparent than in areas with century-old resort histories like Prescott, the Southern Berkshires, St. Augustine, and Santa Rosa–Sonoma.

HOME ENERGY REQUIREMENTS

If you don't count the loan initiation fees and closing costs that new homeowners pay to float their mortgages, then fuel and electricity for the home were among the fastest-rising items on the Consumer Price Index since 1967. What was once a minor and predictable expense, amounting to less than 1 percent of a household's budget 25 years ago, may now equal the cost of medical care or clothing.

Air-Conditioning Needs

Place	Hours over 80°F
Key West–Key Largo–Marathon, FL	3,360
Lake Havasu City, AZ	3,213
Riviera–Bullhead City, AZ	3,213
Yuma, AZ	3,185
Palm Springs–Coachella Valley, CA	2,988
Rockport–Aransas Pass, TX	2,845
Phoenix–Mesa–Scottsdale, AZ	2,819
Mission–McAllen–Alamo, TX	2,653
Las Vegas, NV	2,427
Pompano Beach, FL	2,407

Source: Derived from American Society of Heating, Refrigeration, and Air-Conditioning Engineers, *Standards;* and Department of Defense, *Engineering Weather Data.*

Three factors account for the $1,796 difference between the annual average residential utility bills in Port Angeles, WA, and Yuma, AZ: local climate, the form of energy used to keep interiors comfortable, and the energy's source.

Counting Hours

Texans say their Gulf Coast is one long stretch where air conditioning, like food and water, is a basic necessity without which people go mad and die. Here, a meteorologist measuring humidity with a psychrometer whenever the temperature climbs over 80°F will count nearly 2,500 hours every year when the instrument's bulb stays wet from moist air. New Delhi records similar numbers, and so does Kinshasa, capital of Zaire. These 2,500-odd hours are the equivalent of more than 200 days per year having uncomfortable, sweaty, 12-hour periods of high humidity.

In Las Vegas, Phoenix, and Tucson, the days are much drier, but the number of hours when the temperature is more than 80°F is even greater than the number found on the Texas Gulf Coast. These hours were first counted by Defense Department building engineers in the late 1940s and updated in 1978 for a worldwide inventory of military installations.

Not only are these hours useful for gauging how hot a given place is over time, they also signal how much an evaporative cooler in the desert or a refrigerated air conditioner elsewhere may be humming.

Counting Days

In 1915, Eugene P. Milener, an engineer with the Gas Company of Baltimore, made a discovery for which he received little recognition outside his industry. The amount of natural gas needed to keep houses warm can be accurately predicted for every degree that the outdoor temperature falls below 65°F. Natural gas utilities still use this measurement, called a "heating-degree day," to estimate consumption patterns among their customers.

Heating-degree days are the number of degrees the daily average temperature drops below 65. Heating your home isn't usually necessary when the temperature outdoors is more than 65, but furnaces are fired up when

Heating Needs

Place	Heating-Degree Days
Eagle River, WI	9,643
McCall–Cascade–Payette Valley, ID	8,772
Ketchum–Sun Valley, ID	8,729
Pagosa Springs, CO	8,548
Woodstock, VT	8,387
Kalispell–Flathead Valley, MT	8,378
Houghton Lake, MI	8,218
Lake Winnipesaukee, NH	7,956
Oscoda–Tawas–Huron Shore, MI	7,912
Northern Door Peninsula, WI	7,901

Source: National Oceanic and Atmospheric Administration, *Climatography of the United States,* Series 20.

Atomic Retirement Places

Nuclear-generated power costs more to consumers. In addition, tall, steaming, concrete nuclear power plant cooling towers can be an unnerving sight to some. But these landmarks aren't uncommon and are in or near attractive retirement places.

Place	Nuclear Power Plant
Camden, ME	Maine Yankee
Charlevoix–Boyne City– East Jordan, MI	Big Rock Point
Clemson–Pendleton District, SC	Oconee 1, 2 & 3
Crossville, TN	Watts Bar 1 & 2
East End Long Island, NY	Fitzpatrick
Fredericksburg–Spotsylvania, VA	North Anna 1 & 2
Inverness, FL	Turkey Point 3 & 4
Laguna Beach–Dana Point, CA	San Onofre 2 & 3
Lake Granbury, TX	Comanche Peak 1 & 2
Phoenix–Mesa–Scottsdale, AZ	Palo Verde 1, 2 & 3
San Diego, CA	San Onofre 2 & 3
San Luis Obispo, CA	Diablo Canyon 1 & 2
Southport–Brunswick Islands, NC	Brunswick 1 & 2
Toms River–Barnegat Bay, NJ	Oyster Creek
Vero Beach–Sebastian, FL	St. Lucie 1 & 2
Virginia Beach, VA	Surry 1 & 2
York Beaches, ME	Seabrook

Source: Nuclear Energy Institute, 1994.

---

the outdoors gets colder. Thus, a heating-degree day indicates the number of degrees of heating required to keep a house at 65. If, for example, the temperature on a winter day is 35, that day has 30 heating-degree days, meaning that 30°F of heating are needed.

The average for annual heating-degree days (total heating-degree days over the year) in the United States is 4,579, ranging from none in Hawaii at sea level to nearly 20,000 in Alaska's Brooks Range. The number of annual heating-degree days in a given year tells you how cold it gets and also how often you'll need to run a home's heating system to keep the indoors comfortable.

A Home Energy Geography

Can you recall the Korean War years when the rumbling of coal trucks along their delivery routes was a familiar urban street sound? Three-dollar-a-ton black anthracite was the dominant home heating fuel everywhere east of the Mississippi except for Florida and New England. The blue flame of piped-in natural gas, the dominant heating fuel today, was just starting to burn in new refrigerators, stoves, clothes dryers, and in new home furnaces. And electric power companies were just beginning to offer rate incentives to buyers of total electric homes.

Coal is almost gone from the home-energy scene in spite of heavy marketing of airtight coal stoves as auxiliary heat. The major options, from most expensive to least in cost per million British thermal units (BTU), are electricity, piped-in natural gas, and fuel oil or kerosene. And in rural areas, there's bottled gas and wood.

Electricity. In 1950, the only place where the homes were all-electric was the small desert town of Las Vegas, seat of Nevada's Clark County. The power there was the cheapest in the country because it was generated by falling water at the new Boulder Canyon hydroelectric project some 25 miles southeast.

Power is still cheap in Las Vegas, relative to nuclear-generated or fossil-fuel–generated power that residential customers pay for elsewhere in the country. So is the power that heats and lights homes in the Puget Sound area, the Oregon Cascades, and the Kentucky and Tennessee lakes region, places that also get their power from major hydroelectric projects.

In the future, consumers may not be stuck paying high utility bills sent out by local electric-power monopolies. Las Cruces, NM, recently voted to drop El Paso Electric for a lower-cost supplier, and California is considering allowing ratepayers to choose their own electric company by 2002.

Although most houses are heated with natural gas, electricity is the dominant choice in new homes. The reason: it costs much less to wire a new house for electric resistance heat than to install a gas or oil furnace with piping and sheet-metal hot-air conduits. All-electric homes predominate in 94 places.

Bottled Gas. Bottled or liquefied petroleum (LP) gas comes from oil and is sold in compressed or liquid form. It requires outdoor storage tanks that look like beached, one-man submarines. Unlike piped-in natural gas and electricity, it offers the advantage of an on-hand supply in case of interrupted service.

In rural spots, particularly in the Ozarks and in the north Georgia mountains, it is the fuel of choice for heat and even for running air conditioners and refrigerators. Mobile homes from New England to the Desert Southwest, too, are also heated by bottled gas.

Natural Gas. In 56 retirement places, the major source for heating a house is a byproduct of oil drilling that for many years flamed at the wellhead for lack of a market. Natural gas, a fossil fuel, is inexpensive heat for most householders, mainly because the government regulated its interstate price. Even after deregulation, its price continues to drop relative to inflation.

Natural gas hasn't ever been cheap to residential customers at the ends of the continental transmission lines that start in Louisiana and Texas gas fields, however. Transportation costs explain why natural gas isn't preferred in New England or Mid-Atlantic Metro Belt retirement places, where oil is the least expensive of fuels, or in the Pacific Northwest, where hydro-generated electricity costs the least.

Oil and Kerosene. Though their prices have tumbled recently because of worldwide overproduction, #2 heating oil and kerosene were the only items on the Consumer Price Index to sextuple in cost between 1967 and 1990. High cost is one reason that the number of homes heated with oil has dropped since the 1970s. You won't find the price varying greatly by location, but you will find those distillates of imported crude to be the most common heating fuel in 17 places, mainly in New England, the Mid-Atlantic Metro Belt, and in western North Carolina.

Wood. Anyone who feeds a wood stove has heard the homely proverb about this fuel: it warms you twice, first when you cut and stack it, and second when you watch it burn. From Rocky Mountain piñon to hickory and ash from Ozark forests, it is burned in 3 million homes. Among retirement places, many of the homes in western Montana and in California's Mother Lode country are heated with wood because it is cheap and available right outside a householder's door.

The cost of a cord of good, seasoned hardwood varies all over the map. You can buy half a cord for $300 in Manhattan, or, with a little sweat and permission, you can gather fallen timber in local state forests *gratis*.

Keeping It Running

Utility bills for home heating and cooling, lighting, and running appliances cost $1,580 out on East End Long Island, NY, but only $663 in Coeur d'Alene, ID. Why the difference?

The high number of annual heating-degree days in both places is a sign of long winters, certainly. But in East End Long Island, the cost of home-delivered #2 oil plus the electricity bills mailed out by the Long Island Lighting Company are among the country's highest. As for Coeur d'Alene, homes there are total-electric and get their bills from the Washington Water Power Company, the distributor of cheaper hydro-generated power.

If your only concern is dodging both winter heating and summer air-conditioning bills, head for Maui. Unfortunately, you'll be writing big monthly checks to Maui Electric, Ltd. There are few heated homes here, and air conditioning isn't necessary, but the cost of electricity to keep your water hot, food cool, lamps lit, and appliances running is about as high as it gets anywhere because power is generated by imported oil.

 **GRADING:** Housing

How affordable are homes? A wide gap between prices and the ability of local households to buy may portend high rents, a lower rate of appreciation, and a difficult time at resale.

Is housing more affordable on the Oregon coast than in the southern Appalachians or New England? When it comes to paying property taxes, would you be better off choosing the Ozark corner of Arkansas over Colorado's western slope? Might a move to Florida in February haunt you in August when you realize how much air conditioning costs?

To help answer some of these questions, *Retirement Places Rated* grades each place on housing affordability, using three figures:

1. *Mortgage payments.* Annual mortgage payments are based on an 8.5 percent, 30-year mortgage on the local average sales price of a home, after making a one-tenth down payment.

2. *Property taxes.* Annual property taxes are estimates for a single-family home of average market value using local effective tax rates.

3. *Household income.* Average household income figures come from the Place Profiles in the "Money Matters" chapter. Annual mortgage payments and property taxes, expressed as a percent of average household income, is then scaled against a standard where half the typical 25 percent mortgage lending requirement gets a perfect 100 and three times the 25 percent lending requirement gets a 0.

GRADING EXAMPLE

A growing city near the Colorado-Utah border illustrates the grading method for housing.

Grand Junction, CO (grade: 92)

In the midst of the 1980s energy bust, property was so cheap on Colorado's western slope that Californians who'd just sold their home couldn't find anything in Grand Junction priced high enough to shelter their capital gains. Today there is a housing shortage, so rapidly have homes appreciated here and surrounding Mesa County.

The typical $83,000 construction cost for a new home without lot surpasses the sales price of a resale home with lot. Two areas where prices top $150,000 are Redlands subdivision and the neighborhood near the Tiara Rado golf course fairways.

For all that, housing is more affordable here than elsewhere. Annual mortgage payments and taxes of $7,889 aren't a big strain on a local household's income of $44,700. This produces a grade of 92.

 RANKINGS: Housing

Housing affordability is graded using three criteria: (1) *mortgage payments*, (2) *property taxes*, and (3) *average household income.* Mortgage payments and property taxes are added together and expressed as a percent of local household income. This percent figure is then graded against a standard where half the typical 25 percent mortgage lending requirement gets 100 and three times the 25 percent lending requirement gets a 0.

Grades are rounded two decimal places. Locations with tie grades get the same rank and are listed alphabetically.

Retirement Places from First to Last

Rank	Grade	Rank	Grade	Rank	Grade
1. Lake Martin, AL	99.26	31. Madison, MS	91.47	57. Lake Conroe, TX	88.73
2. Guntersville, AL	98.13	32. Clemson–Pendleton		58. Kerrville, TX	88.68
3. Thomasville, GA	97.66	District, SC	91.31	59. Ocala, FL	88.59
4. Kentucky Lake, KY	96.96	33. Fredericksburg, TX	91.26	60. Leesburg–Lady Lake, FL	88.58
5. Chewelah, WA	96.21	34. Fairhope–Gulf Shores, AL	91.23		
		35. Panama City, FL	91.12	61. St. Jay–Northeast	
6. Mission–McAllen–Alamo,				Kingdom, VT	88.51
TX	95.83	36. New Braunfels, TX	91.09	62. Coeur d'Alene, ID	88.38
7. Branson, MO	95.77	37. Petoskey–Harbor Springs,		63. Williamsburg, VA	88.29
8. Beaver Lake, AR	95.61	MI	91.07	64. Sarasota, FL	88.24
9. Aiken, SC	95.57	38. Gainesville, FL	91.03	65. Newport–Lincoln City, OR	88.19
10. Fayetteville, AR	95.43	39. Smith Mountain Lake, VA	90.88		
		39. Yuma, AZ	90.88	66. Lake Buchanan–Lake LBJ,	
11. Norfork Lake, AR	95.19			TX	87.89
12. Silver City, NM	95.07	41. Traverse City, MI	90.78	67. Bend, OR	87.70
13. Oscoda–Tawas–Huron		42. St. Petersburg–Clearwater,		68. Fort Collins–Loveland, CO	87.31
Shore, MI	94.96	FL	90.77	69. Conway, SC	87.19
14. Hot Springs, AR	94.62	43. State College, PA	90.63	70. Las Cruces, NM	87.04
15. Lake Livingston, TX	93.87	44. Lake Granbury, TX	90.51		
		45. Alpine–Big Bend, TX	90.37	71. Bradenton, FL	86.89
16. Charlevoix–Boyne				72. Daytona Beach, FL	86.88
City–East Jordan, MI	93.78	46. Lake of the Cherokees, OK	90.29	73. Blairsville, GA	86.80
17. Houghton Lake, MI	93.77	47. Florence, OR	90.16	74. New Port Richey, FL	86.76
18. Sebring–Avon Park, FL	93.59	48. Asheville, NC	90.09	75. Melbourne, FL	86.75
19. Kissimmee–St. Cloud, FL	93.48	49. Savannah, GA	90.06		
20. Alamogordo, NM	93.41	50. Bay St. Louis–Pass		76. Ruidoso, NM	86.65
		Christian, MS	89.97	77. Oakhurst–Coarsegold, CA	86.60
21. Delta–Cedaredge, CO	93.33			78. Pompano Beach, FL	86.56
22. Table Rock Lake, MO	93.24	51. Western St. Tammany		79. Pahrump Valley, NV	86.46
23. Maryville, TN	93.16	Parish, LA	89.88	80. Phoenix–Mesa–Scottsdale,	
24. Crossville, TN	92.84	52. Kalispell–Flathead Valley,		AZ	86.43
25. Tryon, NC	92.81	MT	89.63		
		53. Oxford, MS	89.56	81. Sandpoint–Priest River, ID	86.42
26. Montrose, CO	92.54	54. Hamilton–Bitterroot Valley,		82. Bar Harbor, ME	86.20
27. Wenatchee, WA	92.51	MT	89.25	83. Northern Neck, VA	86.19
28. San Antonio, TX	91.83	55. Albuquerque, NM	89.17	84. Medford–Ashland, OR	85.88
29. Grand Junction, CO	91.76			85. Edenton, NC	85.57
30. Lakeland–Winter Haven, FL	91.75	56. Colorado Springs, CO	88.75		

Rank	Grade		Rank	Grade		Rank	Grade
86. Las Vegas, NV	85.55		118. Grants Pass, OR	82.12		152. Santa Fe, NM	74.24
87. Rehoboth Bay–Indian River			119. Woodstock, VT	81.91		153. Boone–Blowing Rock, NC	74.19
Bay, DE	85.48		120. Reno–Sparks, NV			154. St. George–Zion, UT	73.90
88. Vero Beach–Sebastian, FL	85.46			81.81		155. Whidbey Island, WA	73.78
89. Lake of the Ozarks, MO	85.43		121. Charlottesville, VA	81.28			
90. St. Augustine, FL	85.32		122. Northern Door Peninsula,			156. York Beaches, ME	73.42
			WI	81.14		157. Sedona, AZ	71.82
91. Durango, CO	85.14		123. Camden, ME	80.82		158. Southern Berkshire County,	
92. Southern Pines–Pinehurst,			124. Wickenburg, AZ	80.76		MA	71.76
NC	85.07		125. Wimberly–San Marcos, TX	80.50		159. Amherst–Northampton, MA	71.66
93. New Bern, NC	85.00					160. Payson, AZ	71.60
94. McCall–Cascade–Payette			126. Fredericksburg–				
Valley, ID	84.70		Spotsylvania, VA	80.25		161. Placerville–Shingle Springs,	
95. Hendersonville–East Flat			127. Port Angeles–Seqium, WA	80.17		CA	71.00
Rock, NC	84.67		128. Virginia Beach, VA	79.74		162. Annapolis, MD	69.77
			129. Burlington, VT	79.73		163. Amador County, CA	69.44
96. Cedar Creek Lake, TX	84.61		130. Bellingham, WA	79.51		164. Ketchum–Sun Valley, ID	68.98
97. Winchester, VA	84.57					165. Litchfield Hills, CT	68.64
98. Polson–Mission Valley, MT	84.54		131. Hanover, NH	79.49			
99. Inverness, FL	84.41		132. Pike County, PA	78.91		166. Cape Cod, MA	66.15
100. Boca Raton–Delray Beach,			133. Lake Winnipesaukee, NH	78.85		167. Hilton Head Island, SC	66.08
FL	84.24		134. Charleston Sea Islands, SC	78.59		168. Dare Outer Banks, NC	65.57
			135. Taos, NM	78.26		169. Sonora–Groveland–Twain	
101. Eagle River, WI	84.22					Harte, CA	65.39
102. Beaufort, SC	84.08		136. Myrtle Beach–North Myrtle			170. San Juan Islands, WA	64.85
102. Rockport–Aransas Pass,			Beach, SC	78.09			
TX	84.08		137. Naples, FL	77.98		171. East End Long Island, NY	63.67
104. Carson City–Carson Valley,			138. Southport–Brunswick			172. Maui, HI	61.45
NV	83.77		Islands, NC	77.87		173. Riviera–Bullhead City, AZ	60.22
105. Brooksville–Spring Hill, FL	83.61		139. Clayton, GA	77.80		174. Kauai, HI	59.60
			140. Cottonwood–Verde Valley,			175. Santa Rosa–Sonoma, CA	59.53
106. Tucson, AZ	83.52		AZ	77.53			
107. Brevard, NC	83.42					176. St. Simons–Jekyll Islands,	
108. Austin, TX	83.17		141. Prescott–Prescott Valley,			GA	59.40
109. Redding, CA	83.04		AZ	77.35		177. Grass Valley–Nevada City,	
110. Lower Cape May, NJ	82.96		142. Chapel Hill, NC	77.31		CA	59.27
			143. Hiawassee, GA	77.24		178. San Diego, CA	57.16
111. Ocean City, MD	82.94		144. Easton–St.			179. Key West–Key	
112. Athens, GA	82.78		Michaels–Oxford, MD	76.76		Largo–Marathon, FL	54.58
113. Kingman, AZ	82.77		145. Pagosa Springs, CO	76.70		180. Santa Barbara, CA	53.09
114. Port Charlotte–Punta							
Gorda, FL	82.71		146. Port Townsend, WA	76.34		181. Laguna Beach–Dana Point,	
115. Fort Myers–Cape Coral, FL	82.70		147. Lake Havasu City, AZ	76.20		CA	46.42
			148. Toms River–Barnegat Bay,			182. San Luis Obispo, CA	42.79
116. Charles Town–Harpers			NJ	76.12		183. Carmel–Pebble Beach, CA	39.43
Ferry–Shepherdstown, WV	82.69		149. Brookings–Gold Beach, OR	75.90			
117. Hesperia–Apple			150. Paradise–Magalia, CA	75.54			
Valley–Victorville, CA	82.18						
			151. Palm Springs–Coachella				
			Valley, CA	75.00			

PLACE PROFILES: Housing

On the following pages are capsule descriptions of housing features in each place. Data under the first category, **Home Prices**, show (1) the average asking price for an existing home, and (2) the lowest asking price for an existing or new home in the top 10 percent of the market. Next to the heading, **Taxes**, is the estimated annual property tax on the average-priced home.

Figures for heating-degree days, under **Energy Requirements**, are the normal number of annual degrees

of heating needed to keep a home at 65°F when the temperature outdoors is below that mark. Figures for air-conditioning hours represent the normal number of annual hours when the temperature outside is over 80°F.

Annual costs for space and water heating, cooling, lighting, and appliances are to the right of **Utilities**. Underneath is the prevailing heating fuel—natural gas, oil, bottled gas, or wood. After the comma is the most common alternate. "All electric" indicates the homes are heated by electricity. Utility figures do not include costs for water or sewage.

Underneath the **New Construction** heading are (1) the rate at which new, single homes have been added to the local stock over the last five years, and (2) the average value of construction permits taken out for new single homes, exclusive of land.

The **Historic Neighborhoods** section contains the names of historic districts on the National Register of Historic Places that are primarily residential.

Figures under the last heading, **Alternative Housing**, indicate the percent share that condominiums, mobile homes, and apartments have in the local housing mix. Apartments are defined as units in buildings with five or more rental units.

Information comes from these sources: American Gas Association, *Gas Facts* (residential gas bills), 1994; American Society of Heating, Refrigeration, and Air Conditioning Engineers, *Standards*, no date; National Association of Realtors, *Existing Home Sales* (regional price inflation), 1990–1994; Places Rated Partnership survey of state revenue departments and local tax assessors (assessed valuation and typical residential prop-

erty tax rates), 1994; Places Rated Partnership survey of real estate boards (local price inflation); U.S. Department of Commerce, Bureau of the Census, unpublished 1990 census data for housing (alternative housing mix and utility sources), and *Housing Permits and Construction Contracts* (single-family home building rates and estimates for construction costs), monthly, 1990–1994, and National Oceanic and Atmospheric Administration, unpublished Series 20 climate data (normal heating-degree days); U.S. Department of Defense, *Engineering Weather Data* (air-conditioning hours), no date; U.S. Department of Energy, *Electric Sales and Revenue* (residential electric bills), 1994; U.S. Department of Housing and Urban Development, Federal Housing Administration, *Property Characteristics, 1 Family Homes*, 1994; U.S. Department of the Interior, National Register of Historic Places, unpublished historic district housing counts, 1994; and U.S. Department of Labor, Bureau of Labor Statistics, *Consumer Price Index* (residential electricity and natural gas cost inflation), monthly, 1992–1994.

A check mark (✓) highlights a place as one of the 18 best for realistic home values.

✓ Aiken, SC
Home Prices
  Average: $84,000
  Upper tenth: $146,000
Taxes: $961
Energy Requirements
  Heating-degree days: 2,456
  Air-conditioning hours: 1,203
Utilities: $1,336
  Natural Gas, Electric
New Home Construction
  Five-year rate: 11%
  Value: $93,700
Historic Neighborhood
  Aiken Winter Colony
Alternative Housing
  19% trailers, 4% apartments, 1% condos
Grade: 96

Alamogordo, NM
Home Prices
  Average: $72,000
  Upper tenth: $115,000
Taxes: $563
Energy Requirements
  Heating-degree days: 2,908
  Air-conditioning hours: 1,473
Utilities: $1,486
  Natural Gas, Bottled Gas
New Home Construction
  Five-year rate: 3%
  Value: $76,100
Historic Neighborhood
  Tularosa Townsite District
Alternative Housing
  26% trailers, 3% apartments, 1% condos
Grade: 93

Albuquerque, NM
Home Prices
  Average: $110,500
  Upper tenth: $172,000
Taxes: $865

Energy Requirements
  Heating-degree days: 4,425
  Air-conditioning hours: 1,118
Utilities: $1,518
  Natural Gas, Electric
New Home Construction
  Five-year rate: 8%
  Value: $95,300
Historic Neighborhoods
  Eighth Street–Forrester District
  Fourth Ward District
  Huning Highlands
  Los Griegos
  Los Poblanos
  Silver Hill
  Spruce Park
Alternative Housing
  17% apartments, 7% trailers, 2% condos
Grade: 89

Alpine–Big Bend, TX
Home Prices
  Average: $61,500
  Upper tenth: $116,000
Taxes: $1,355
Energy Requirements
  Heating-degree days: 2,559
  Air-conditioning hours: 1,104
Utilities: $1,431
  Natural Gas, Bottled Gas
New Home Construction
  Five-year rate: 1%
  Value: $44,600
Alternative Housing
  23% trailers, 7% apartments
Grade: 90

Amador County, CA
Home Prices
  Average: $153,000
  Upper tenth: $230,000
Taxes: $1,545

Energy Requirements
   Heating-degree days: 2,911
   Air-conditioning hours: 979
Utilities: $1,285
   Wood, Electric
New Home Construction
   Five-year rate: 13%
   Value: $102,700
Alternative Housing
   11% trailers, 3% apartments
Grade: 69

Amherst–Northampton, MA
Home Prices
   Average: $158,500
   Upper tenth: $218,000
Taxes: $2,690
Energy Requirements
   Heating-degree days: 6,404
   Air-conditioning hours: 435
Utilities: $1,419
   Oil, Electric
New Home Construction
   Five-year rate: 6%
   Value: $107,600
Historic Neighborhoods
   Cushman Village
   Dickinson
   East Village
   Fort Hill
   North Amherst Center
   Prospect–Gaylord District
Alternative Housing
   15% apartments, 5% condos, 2% trailers
Grade: 72

Annapolis, MD
Home Prices
   Average: $227,000
   Upper tenth: $356,000
Taxes: $2,906
Energy Requirements
   Heating-degree days: 4,382
   Air-conditioning hours: 742
Utilities: $1,008
   All Electric
New Home Construction
   Five-year rate: 10%
   Value: $93,000
Historic Neighborhood
   Colonial Annapolis
Alternative Housing
   11% apartments, 9% condos, 2% trailers
Grade: 70

Asheville, NC
Home Prices
   Average: $90,000
   Upper tenth: $174,000
Taxes: $1,427
Energy Requirements
   Heating-degree days: 4,308
   Air-conditioning hours: 536
Utilities: $1,480
   Oil, Electric
New Home Construction
   Five-year rate: 8%
   Value: $95,400
Historic Neighborhoods
   Biltmore Village Cottages
   Chestnut Hill District
   Grove Park District
   Charlotte Street Cottages
   Montford Area
Alternative Housing
   16% trailers, 8% apartments, 3% condos
Grade: 90

Athens, GA
Home Prices
   Average: $101,000
   Upper tenth: $174,000
Taxes: $1,584
Energy Requirements
   Heating-degree days: 2,893
   Air-conditioning hours: 1,122
Utilities: $1,549
   Natural Gas, Electric
New Home Construction
   Five-year rate: 8%
   Value: $79,900
Historic Neighborhoods
   Bloomfield Street
   Boulevard District
   Cobbham District
   Dearing Street
   Milledge Avenue
   Milledge Circle
   Oglethorpe Avenue
   Reese Street
   West Hancock Avenue
   Woodlawn District
Alternative Housing
   22% apartments, 7% trailers, 5% condos
Grade: 83

Austin, TX
Home Prices
   Average: $114,500
   Upper tenth: $204,000
Taxes: $2,634
Energy Requirements
   Heating-degree days: 1,688
   Air-conditioning hours: 2,041
Utilities: $1,534
   Natural Gas, Electric
New Home Construction
   Five-year rate: 11%
   Value: $113,300
Historic Neighborhoods
   Bremond Block
   Clarksville
   Hyde Park
   Rainey Street
   Shadow Lawn
   Sixth Street
   Swedish Hill
   Willow-Spence Streets
Alternative Housing
   25% apartments, 5% condos, 3% trailers
Grade: 83

Bar Harbor, ME
Home Prices
   Average: $117,500
   Upper tenth: $218,000
Taxes: $1,451
Energy Requirements
   Heating-degree days: 7,604
   Air-conditioning hours: 170
Utilities: $1,511
   Oil, Wood
New Home Construction
   Five-year rate: 5%
   Value: $74,900
Historic Neighborhoods
   Blue Hill District
   Castine District
   Castine Off-the-Neck
   Somesville District
   West Street
Alternative Housing
   9% trailers, 3% apartments
Grade: 86

Bay St. Louis–Pass Christian, MS
Home Prices
Average: $78,000
Upper tenth: $118,000
Taxes: $1,129
Energy Requirements
Heating-degree days: 1,507
Air-conditioning hours: 2,096
Utilities: $1,280
All Electric
New Home Construction
Five-year rate: 6%
Value: $66,600
Historic Neighborhoods
Beach Boulevard
Main Street
Sycamore Street
Pass Christian Scenic Drive
Alternative Housing
11% apartments, 6% trailers, 2% condos
Grade: 90

Beaufort, SC
Home Prices
Average: $112,000
Upper tenth: $174,000
Taxes: $1,218
Energy Requirements
Heating-degree days: 1,842
Air-conditioning hours: 1,378
Utilities: $1,098
All Electric
New Home Construction
Five-year rate: 14%
Value: $96,200
Historic Neighborhood
Beaufort District
Alternative Housing
10% trailers, 5% apartments, 2% condos
Grade: 84

✓ **Beaver Lake, AR**
Home Prices
Average: $68,000
Upper tenth: $116,000
Taxes: $499
Energy Requirements
Heating-degree days: 3,840
Air-conditioning hours: 966
Utilities: $1,452
Natural Gas, Wood
New Home Construction
Five-year rate: 3%
Value: $58,900
Historic Neighborhood
Eureka Springs District
Alternative Housing
15% trailers, 2% apartments, 1% condos
Grade: 96

Bellingham, WA
Home Prices
Average: $126,500
Upper tenth: $458,000
Taxes: $1,655
Energy Requirements
Heating-degree days: 5,609
Air-conditioning hours: 45
Utilities: $446
All Electric
New Home Construction
Five-year rate: 12%
Value: $94,400
Historic Neighborhood
Eldridge Avenue

Alternative Housing
12% apartments, 12% trailers, 3% condos
Grade: 80

Bend, OR
Home Prices
Average: $104,000
Upper tenth: $230,000
Taxes: $1,154
Energy Requirements
Heating-degree days: 6,926
Air-conditioning hours: 111
Utilities: $1,026
Wood, Electric
New Home Construction
Five-year rate: 21%
Value: $104,400
Alternative Housing
21% trailers, 5% apartments, 1% condos
Grade: 88

Blairsville, GA
Home Prices
Average: $79,500
Upper tenth: $145,000
Taxes: $626
Energy Requirements
Heating-degree days: 4,476
Air-conditioning hours: 599
Utilities: $932
All Electric
New Home Construction
Five-year rate: 17%
Value: $37,100
Alternative Housing
18% trailers, 2% apartments, 1% condos
Grade: 87

Boca Raton–Delray Beach, FL
Home Prices
Average: $174,500
Upper tenth: $292,000
Taxes: $1,424
Energy Requirements
Heating-degree days: 262
Air-conditioning hours: 2,407
Utilities: $1,515
All Electric
New Home Construction
Five-year rate: 11%
Value: $109,900
Alternative Housing
15% condos, 10% apartments, 1% trailers
Grade: 84

Boone–Blowing Rock, NC
Home Prices
Average: $100,500
Upper tenth: $174,000
Taxes: $1,055
Energy Requirements
Heating-degree days: 6,003
Air-conditioning hours: 199
Utilities: $1,480
Oil, Electric
New Home Construction
Five-year rate: 11%
Value: $86,100
Alternative Housing
10% apartments, 9% trailers, 4% condos
Grade: 74

Bradenton, FL
Home Prices
Average: $111,000
Upper tenth: $203,000

Taxes: $906
Energy Requirements
Heating-degree days: 678
Air-conditioning hours: 2,133
Utilities: $1,427
All Electric
New Home Construction
Five-year rate: 11%
Value: $53,300
Historic Neighborhoods
Braden Castle Park
Palmetto District
Alternative Housing
23% trailers, 16% condos, 8% apartments
Grade: 87

✓ **Branson, MO**
Home Prices
Average: $74,000
Upper tenth: $115,000
Taxes: $560
Energy Requirements
Heating-degree days: 4,527
Air-conditioning hours: 975
Utilities: $966
All Electric
New Home Construction
Five-year rate: 3%
Value: $65,900
Alternative Housing
27% trailers, 4% apartments, 2% condos
Grade: 96

Brevard, NC
Home Prices
Average: $99,000
Upper tenth: $175,000
Taxes: $1,236
Energy Requirements
Heating-degree days: 4,059
Air-conditioning hours: 644
Utilities: $993
All Electric
New Home Construction
Five-year rate: 9%
Value: $117,800
Alternative Housing
16% trailers, 4% condos, 2% apartments
Grade: 83

Brookings–Gold Beach, OR
Home Prices
Average: $117,000
Upper tenth: $229,000
Taxes: $1,197
Energy Requirements
Heating-degree days: 4,099
Air-conditioning hours: 12
Utilities: $486
All Electric
New Home Construction
Five-year rate: 12%
Value: $101,400
Alternative Housing
33% trailers, 3% apartments, 2% condos
Grade: 76

Brooksville–Spring Hill, FL
Home Prices
Average: $90,000
Upper tenth: $146,000
Taxes: $734
Energy Requirements
Heating-degree days: 767
Air-conditioning hours: 2,078
Utilities: $1,409
All Electric

New Home Construction
Five-year rate: 16%
Value: $58,500
Alternative Housing
25% trailers, 2% condos, 2% apartments
Grade: 84

Burlington, VT
Home Prices
Average: $146,000
Upper tenth: $218,000
Taxes: $2,672
Energy Requirements
Heating-degree days: 7,771
Air-conditioning hours: 263
Utilities: $1,459
Oil, Natural Gas
New Home Construction
Five-year rate: 7%
Value: $97,000
Historic Neighborhoods
Battery Street
Lakeside Development
Main Street–College Street
Pearl Street
Shelburne Village
South Union Street
South Willard Street
University Green
Wells-Richardson District
Alternative Housing
11% apartments, 9% condos, 6% trailers
Grade: 80

Camden, ME
Home Prices
Average: $126,500
Upper tenth: $270,000
Taxes: $1,760
Energy Requirements
Heating-degree days: 7,297
Air-conditioning hours: 181
Utilities: $1,511
Oil, Wood
New Home Construction
Five-year rate: 5%
Value: $79,700
Historic Neighborhoods
Chestnut Street
High Street
Alternative Housing
9% apartments, 7% trailers, 1% condos
Grade: 81

Cape Cod, MA
Home Prices
Average: $210,000
Upper tenth: $327,000
Taxes: $3,843
Energy Requirements
Heating-degree days: 6,058
Air-conditioning hours: 142
Utilities: $1,363
Oil, Natural Gas
New Home Construction
Five-year rate: 6%
Value: $105,100
Historic Neighborhoods
Barnstable-
Centerville
Cotuit
Craigville
Hyannis Road
Hyannis Port
Mill Way
Old King's Highway
Pleasant–School Street

Santuit
Wianno
Harwich District
Provincetown District
Wellfleet Center
Yarmouth Northside
Alternative Housing
6% condos, 3% apartments, 1% trailers
Grade: 66

Carmel–Monterey–Pebble Beach, CA
Home Prices
Average: $359,000
Upper tenth: $652,000
Taxes: $3,644
Energy Requirements
Heating-degree days: 3,125
Air-conditioning hours: 46
Utilities: $1,305
Natural Gas, Electric
New Home Construction
Five-year rate: 5%
Value: $139,500
Alternative Housing
16% apartments, 6% condos, 2% trailers
Grade: 39

Carson City–Carson Valley, NV
Home Prices
Average: $157,000
Upper tenth: $229,000
Taxes: $1,501
Energy Requirements
Heating-degree days: 5,691
Air-conditioning hours: 644
Utilities: $1,184
Natural Gas, Electric
New Home Construction
Five-year rate: 19%
Value: $111,000
Alternative Housing
14% trailers, 12% apartments, 6% condos
Grade: 84

Cedar Creek Lake, TX
Home Prices
Average: $74,000
Upper tenth: $145,000
Taxes: $1,727
Energy Requirements
Heating-degree days: 2,105
Air-conditioning hours: 1,908
Utilities: $1,353
All Electric
New Home Construction
Five-year rate: 1%
Value: $77,100
Alternative Housing
33% trailers, 2% apartments
Grade: 85

Chapel Hill, NC
Home Prices
Average: $147,500
Upper tenth: $290,000
Taxes: $2,337
Energy Requirements
Heating-degree days: 3,802
Air-conditioning hours: 1,018
Utilities: $1,119
All Electric
New Home Construction
Five-year rate: 13%
Value: $116,700
Historic Neighborhoods
Chapel Hill District

Gimghoul Neighborhood
Rocky Ridge Farm
Alternative Housing
21% apartments, 12% trailers, 8% condos
Grade: 77

Charles Town–Harpers Ferry–Shepherdstown, WV
Home Prices
Average: $111,500
Upper tenth: $203,000
Taxes: $842
Energy Requirements
Heating-degree days: 5,192
Air-conditioning hours: 684
Utilities: $1,093
All Electric
New Home Construction
Five-year rate: 14%
Value: $85,400
Historic Neighborhoods
Harpers Ferry District
Shepherdstown District
Alternative Housing
14% trailers, 7% apartments
Grade: 83

Charleston Sea Islands, SC
Home Prices
Average: $114,500
Upper tenth: $204,000
Taxes: $1,370
Energy Requirements
Heating-degree days: 1,866
Air-conditioning hours: 1,252
Utilities: $1,061
All Electric
New Home Construction
Five-year rate: 10%
Value: $104,000
Historic Neighborhoods
Charleston Peninsula District
McClellanville District
Mount Pleasant District
Rockville District
Secessionville
Alternative Housing
15% apartments, 9% trailers, 7% condos
Grade: 79

✓ Charlevoix–Boyne City–East Jordan, MI
Home Prices
Average: $76,500
Upper tenth: $115,000
Taxes: $1,734
Energy Requirements
Heating-degree days: 7,700
Air-conditioning hours: 261
Utilities: $1,684
Natural Gas, Wood
New Home Construction
Five-year rate: 9%
Value: $71,500
Alternative Housing
9% trailers, 4% condos, 4% apartments
Grade: 94

Charlottesville, VA
Home Prices
Average: $146,500
Upper tenth: $290,000
Taxes: $1,626
Energy Requirements
Heating-degree days: 4,224
Air-conditioning hours: 964
Utilities: $1,593
Natural Gas, Electric

New Home Construction
Five-year rate: 9%
Value: $107,300
Historic Neighborhoods
Ridge Street
Scottsville District
Southwest Mountains District
Wertland Street
Alternative Housing
18% apartments, 4% condos, 4% trailers
Grade: 81

✓ **Chewelah, WA**
Home Prices
Average: $66,500
Upper tenth: $90,000
Taxes: $665
Energy Requirements
Heating-degree days: 7,192
Air-conditioning hours: 228
Utilities: $1,011
Wood, Electric
New Home Construction
Five-year rate: 8%
Value: $80,700
Alternative Housing
25% trailers, 3% apartments
Grade: 96

Clayton, GA
Home Prices
Average: $101,000
Upper tenth: $204,000
Taxes: $879
Energy Requirements
Heating-degree days: 3,806
Air-conditioning hours: 695
Utilities: $1,049
Bottled Gas, Wood
New Home Construction
Five-year rate: 14%
Value: $65,300
Alternative Housing
17% trailers, 1% condos, 1% apartments
Grade: 78

Clemson–Pendleton District, SC
Home Prices
Average: $86,500
Upper tenth: $149,000
Taxes: $796
Energy Requirements
Heating-degree days: 3,367
Air-conditioning hours: 1,180
Utilities: $1,039
All Electric
New Home Construction
Five-year rate: 9%
Value: $82,500
Historic Neighborhoods
Newry District
Seneca District
Pendleton District
Alternative Housing
13% trailers, 4% apartments, 1% condos
Grade: 91

Coeur d'Alene, ID
Home Prices
Average: $87,500
Upper tenth: $143,000
Taxes: $1,830
Energy Requirements
Heating-degree days: 6,239
Air-conditioning hours: 380
Utilities: $663
All Electric

New Home Construction
Five-year rate: 19%
Value: $93,500
Historic Neighborhood
Sherman Park Addition
Alternative Housing
16% trailers, 6% apartments, 2% condos
Grade: 88

Colorado Springs, CO
Home Prices
Average: $108,000
Upper tenth: $172,000
Taxes: $968
Energy Requirements
Heating-degree days: 6,415
Air-conditioning hours: 496
Utilities: $1,144
Natural Gas, Electric
New Home Construction
Five-year rate: 10%
Value: $87,900
Historic Neighborhoods
Boulder Crescent Place
Manitou Springs District
North End
North Weber Street
Alternative Housing
16% apartments, 5% condos, 5% trailers
Grade: 89

Conway, SC
Home Prices
Average: $81,500
Upper tenth: $118,000
Taxes: $836
Energy Requirements
Heating-degree days: 2,482
Air-conditioning hours: 1,572
Utilities: $1,156
All Electric
New Home Construction
Five-year rate: 12%
Value: $77,200
Alternative Housing
5% apartments, 4% trailers, 2% condos
Grade: 87

Cottonwood–Verde Valley, AZ
Home Prices
Average: $94,000
Upper tenth: $112,000
Taxes: $1,147
Energy Requirements
Heating-degree days: 3,579
Air-conditioning hours: 1,101
Utilities: $1,542
Natural Gas, Electric
New Home Construction
Five-year rate: 18%
Value: $73,600
Alternative Housing
15% trailers, 4% apartments
Grade: 78

Crossville, TN
Home Prices
Average: $70,500
Upper tenth: $145,000
Taxes: $465
Energy Requirements
Heating-degree days: 4,521
Air-conditioning hours: 726
Utilities: $717
All Electric

New Home Construction
Five-year rate: 2%
Value: $69,500
Historic Neighborhood
Cumberland Homesteads
Alternative Housing
16% trailers, 5% condos, 2% apartments
Grade: 93

Dare Outer Banks, NC
Home Prices
Average: $153,500
Upper tenth: $290,000
Taxes: $1,136
Energy Requirements
Heating-degree days: 2,804
Air-conditioning hours: 832
Utilities: $1,056
All Electric
New Home Construction
Five-year rate: 12%
Value: $95,300
Historic Neighborhood
Nags Head Beach Cottages
Alternative Housing
11% trailers, 7% condos, 1% apartments
Grade: 66

Daytona Beach, FL
Home Prices
Average: $95,500
Upper tenth: $146,000
Taxes: $779
Energy Requirements
Heating-degree days: 909
Air-conditioning hours: 1,553
Utilities: $1,240
All Electric
New Home Construction
Five-year rate: 10%
Value: $84,300
Historic Neighborhoods
El Pino Parque
Lake Helen District
New Home Smyrna Beach District
South Beach Street
West DeLand District
Alternative Housing
12% trailers, 9% apartments, 9% condos
Grade: 87

Delta–Cedaredge, CO
Home Prices
Average: $64,000
Upper tenth: $113,000
Taxes: $558
Energy Requirements
Heating-degree days: 5,927
Air-conditioning hours: 557
Utilities: $1,123
Natural Gas, Wood
New Home Construction
Five-year rate: 2%
Value: $55,100
Alternative Housing
17% trailers, 1% apartments
Grade: 93

Durango, CO
Home Prices
Average: $112,000
Upper tenth: $172,000
Taxes: $764
Energy Requirements
Heating-degree days: 6,911
Air-conditioning hours: 210

Utilities: $1,096
Natural Gas, Wood
New Home Construction
Five-year rate: 15%
Value: $82,100
Historic Neighborhood
East Third Avenue
Alternative Housing
18% trailers, 6% apartments, 3% condos
Grade: 85

Eagle River, WI
Home Prices
Average: $79,000
Upper tenth: $143,000
Taxes: $2,570
Energy Requirements
Heating-degree days: 9,643
Air-conditioning hours: 173
Utilities: $1,586
Bottled Gas, Wood
New Home Construction
Five-year rate: 8%
Value: $63,000
Alternative Housing
7% trailers, 1% apartments, 1% condos
Grade: 84

East End Long Island, NY
Home Prices
Average: $277,000
Upper tenth: $545,000
Taxes: $5,125
Energy Requirements
Heating-degree days: 5,685
Air-conditioning hours: 174
Utilities: $1,580
Oil, Natural Gas
New Home Construction
Five-year rate: 4%
Value: $87,200
Historic Neighborhoods
East Hampton-
  Briar Patch Road
  Buell's Lane
  Egypt Lane
  Jones Road Area
  North Main Street
  Pantigo Road
  Village District
Greenport Village
Miller Place District
Sag Harbor Village
Saint James District
Southampton-
  Beach Road
  North Main Street
  Village District
  Wickapogue Road
Shelter Island Heights
Village of Branch
Alternative Housing
5% apartments, 2% condos, 2% trailers
Grade: 64

Easton–St. Michaels–Oxford, MD
Home Prices
Average: $206,000
Upper tenth: $584,000
Taxes: $1,533
Energy Requirements
Heating-degree days: 4,139
Air-conditioning hours: 742
Utilities: $1,008
All Electric

New Home Construction
Five-year rate: 9%
Value: $101,200
Historic Neighborhood
Easton District
Alternative Housing
6% apartments, 5% trailers, 2% condos
Grade: 77

Edenton, NC
Home Prices
Average: $90,000
Upper tenth: $174,000
Taxes: $1,008
Energy Requirements
Heating-degree days: 2,918
Air-conditioning hours: 1,100
Utilities: $1,146
All Electric
New Home Construction
Five-year rate: 5%
Value: $76,200
Historic Neighborhood
Edenton District
Alternative Housing
22% trailers, 2% apartments
Grade: 86

Fairhope-Gulf Shores, AL
Home Prices
Average: $90,500
Upper tenth: $146,000
Taxes: $403
Energy Requirements
Heating-degree days: 1,819
Air-conditioning hours: 1,833
Utilities: $1,148
All Electric
New Home Construction
Five-year rate: 17%
Value: $77,800
Historic Neighborhoods
Fairhope Bayfront District
Montrose District
Point Clear District
Fairhope White Avenue
Alternative Housing
18% trailers, 13% condos, 3% apartments
Grade: 91

✓ Fayetteville, AR
Home Prices
Average: $75,000
Upper tenth: $117,000
Taxes: $710
Energy Requirements
Heating-degree days: 4,141
Air-conditioning hours: 966
Utilities: $1,498
Natural Gas, Electric
New Home Construction
Five-year rate: 11%
Value: $74,700
Historic Neighborhoods
Mount Nord District
Shiloh District
Washington-Willow District
Alternative Housing
12% apartments, 10% trailers, 1% condos
Grade: 95

Florence, OR
Home Prices
Average: $90,500
Upper tenth: $146,000
Taxes: $950

Energy Requirements
Heating-degree days: 4,744
Air-conditioning hours: 2
Utilities: $484
All Electric
New Home Construction
Five-year rate: 6%
Value: $102,600
Alternative Housing
17% trailers, 12% apartments
Grade: 90

Fort Collins-Loveland, CO
Home Prices
Average: $109,000
Upper tenth: $172,000
Taxes: $1,212
Energy Requirements
Heating-degree days: 6,368
Air-conditioning hours: 399
Utilities: $1,110
Natural Gas, Electric
New Home Construction
Five-year rate: 14%
Value: $89,300
Historic Neighborhood
Laurel School District
Alternative Housing
13% apartments, 7% trailers, 5% condos
Grade: 87

Fort Myers-Cape Coral, FL
Home Prices
Average: $128,000
Upper tenth: $233,000
Taxes: $1,044
Energy Requirements
Heating-degree days: 418
Air-conditioning hours: 1,890
Utilities: $1,349
All Electric
New Home Construction
Five-year rate: 14%
Value: $88,000
Alternative Housing
19% condos, 17% trailers, 8% apartments
Grade: 83

Fredericksburg, TX
Home Prices
Average: $87,000
Upper tenth: $173,000
Taxes: $1,541
Energy Requirements
Heating-degree days: 2,012
Air-conditioning hours: 1,729
Utilities: $1,507
Natural Gas, Electric
New Home Construction
Five-year rate: 3%
Value: $79,200
Historic Neighborhood
Fredericksburg District
Alternative Housing
14% trailers, 1% apartments
Grade: 91

Fredericksburg-Spotsylvania, VA
Home Prices
Average: $137,000
Upper tenth: $204,000
Taxes: $1,534
Energy Requirements
Heating-degree days: 4,554
Air-conditioning hours: 938
Utilities: $1,027
All Electric

New Home Construction
Five-year rate: 19%
Value: $125,700
Historic Neighborhood
Fredericksburg District
Alternative Housing
11% apartments, 8% trailers, 1% condos
Grade: 80

Gainesville, FL
Home Prices
Average: $88,500
Upper tenth: $146,000
Taxes: $722
Energy Requirements
Heating-degree days: 1,267
Air-conditioning hours: 1,504
Utilities: $1,225
All Electric
New Home Construction
Five-year rate: 10%
Value: $75,800
Historic Neighborhoods
High Springs District
Melrose District
Micanopy District
Newberry District
Northeast Gainesville District
Pleasant Street
Southeast Gainesville District
Alternative Housing
20% apartments, 13% trailers, 6% condos
Grade: 91

Grand Junction, CO
Home Prices
Average: $81,500
Upper tenth: $143,000
Taxes: $852
Energy Requirements
Heating-degree days: 5,548
Air-conditioning hours: 975
Utilities: $1,220
Natural Gas, Electric
New Home Construction
Five-year rate: 9%
Value: $83,000
Historic Neighborhood
North Seventh Street
Alternative Housing
11% trailers, 9% apartments, 3% condos
Grade: 92

Grants Pass, OR
Home Prices
Average: $99,500
Upper tenth: $172,000
Taxes: $1,043
Energy Requirements
Heating-degree days: 4,219
Air-conditioning hours: 700
Utilities: $631
All Electric
New Home Construction
Five-year rate: 9%
Value: $85,700
Alternative Housing
23% trailers, 3% apartments
Grade: 82

Grass Valley–Nevada City, CA
Home Prices
Average: $202,500
Upper tenth: $343,000
Taxes: $2,059

Energy Requirements
Heating-degree days: 4,770
Air-conditioning hours: 474
Utilities: $1,104
Wood, Bottled Gas
New Home Construction
Five-year rate: 11%
Value: $98,900
Alternative Housing
9% trailers, 4% apartments, 1% condos
Grade: 59

✓ Guntersville, AL
Home Prices
Average: $66,500
Upper tenth: $116,000
Taxes: $286
Energy Requirements
Heating-degree days: 3,034
Air-conditioning hours: 1,288
Utilities: $997
All Electric
New Home Construction
Five-year rate: 4%
Value: $72,000
Alternative Housing
16% trailers, 4% apartments
Grade: 98

Hamilton–Bitterroot Valley, MT
Home Prices
Average: $75,000
Upper tenth: $115,000
Taxes: $1,097
Energy Requirements
Heating-degree days: 7,553
Air-conditioning hours: 177
Utilities: $950
Wood, Natural Gas
New Home Construction
Five-year rate: 2%
Value: $72,600
Historic Neighborhood
Hamilton Southside
Alternative Housing
18% trailers, 2% apartments
Grade: 89

Hanover, NH
Home Prices
Average: $137,500
Upper tenth: $218,000
Taxes: $2,813
Energy Requirements
Heating-degree days: 7,573
Air-conditioning hours: 312
Utilities: $1,543
Oil, Wood
New Home Construction
Five-year rate: 4%
Value: $91,600
Historic Neighborhoods
Canaan Street
Haverhill Corner
Hebron Village
Lyme Common
Orford Street
Alternative Housing
11% condos, 9% trailers, 8% apartments
Grade: 79

Hendersonville–East Flat Rock, NC
Home Prices
Average: $105,000
Upper tenth: $175,000
Taxes: $1,533

Energy Requirements
Heating-degree days: 4,203
Air-conditioning hours: 682
Utilities: $1,006
All Electric
New Home Construction
Five-year rate: 10%
Value: $99,900
Historic Neighborhoods
Flat Rock District
Seventh Avenue Depot District
Alternative Housing
19% trailers, 3% condos, 3% apartments
Grade: 85

Hesperia–Apple Valley–Victorville, CA
Home Prices
Average: $143,000
Upper tenth: $205,000
Taxes: $1,549
Energy Requirements
Heating-degree days: 3,127
Air-conditioning hours: 1,495
Utilities: $1,988
Natural Gas, Electric
New Home Construction
Five-year rate: 7%
Value: $112,100
Alternative Housing
11% apartments, 9% trailers, 2% condos
Grade: 82

Hiawassee, GA
Home Prices
Average: $99,500
Upper tenth: $203,000
Taxes: $681
Energy Requirements
Heating-degree days: 4,476
Air-conditioning hours: 599
Utilities: $932
All Electric
New Home Construction
Five-year rate: 16%
Value: $71,400
Alternative Housing
28% trailers, 1% condos
Grade: 77

Hilton Head Island, SC
Home Prices
Average: $256,000
Upper tenth: $345,000
Taxes: $2,395
Energy Requirements
Heating-degree days: 1,851
Air-conditioning hours: 1,378
Utilities: $1,098
All Electric
New Home Construction
Five-year rate: 14%
Value: $199,700
Alternative Housing
9% condos, 6% trailers, 5% apartments
Grade: 66

✓ Hot Springs, AR
Home Prices
Average: $75,500
Upper tenth: $145,000
Taxes: $586
Energy Requirements
Heating-degree days: 3,181
Air-conditioning hours: 1,643
Utilities: $1,445
Natural Gas, Electric

New Home Construction
Five-year rate: 1%
Value: $99,100
Alternative Housing
13% trailers, 6% apartments, 5% condos
Grade: 95

✓ Houghton Lake, MI
Home Prices
Average: $60,000
Upper tenth: $114,000
Taxes: $1,230
Energy Requirements
Heating-degree days: 8,218
Air-conditioning hours: 213
Utilities: $1,743
Natural Gas, Bottled Gas
New Home Construction
Five-year rate: 8%
Value: $48,700
Alternative Housing
12% trailers, 1% apartments
Grade: 94

Inverness, FL
Home Prices
Average: $88,500
Upper tenth: $146,000
Taxes: $722
Energy Requirements
Heating-degree days: 1,025
Air-conditioning hours: 2,086
Utilities: $1,412
All Electric
New Home Construction
Five-year rate: 16%
Value: $41,500
Alternative Housing
31% trailers, 3% condos, 1% apartments
Grade: 84

Kalispell–Flathead Valley, MT
Home Prices
Average: $84,500
Upper tenth: $143,000
Taxes: $1,472
Energy Requirements
Heating-degree days: 8,378
Air-conditioning hours: 205
Utilities: $1,071
Natural Gas, Wood
New Home Construction
Five-year rate: 6%
Value: $89,600
Alternative Housing
16% trailers, 5% apartments, 2% condos
Grade: 90

Kauai, HI
Home Prices
Average: $235,500
Upper tenth: $455,000
Taxes: $2,089
Energy Requirements
Heating-degree days: 0
Air-conditioning hours: 1,091
Utilities: $1,576
All Electric
New Home Construction
Five-year rate: 16%
Value: $124,300
Alternative Housing
5% condos, 4% apartments
Grade: 60

✓Kentucky Lake, KY
Home Prices
Average: $65,500
Upper tenth: $116,000
Taxes: $722
Energy Requirements
Heating-degree days: 3,932
Air-conditioning hours: 1,270
Utilities: $845
All Electric
New Home Construction
Five-year rate: 2%
Value: $81,300
Alternative Housing
18% trailers, 3% apartments
Grade: 97

Kerrville, TX
Home Prices
Average: $94,500
Upper tenth: $174,000
Taxes: $2,176
Energy Requirements
Heating-degree days: 2,218
Air-conditioning hours: 1,813
Utilities: $1,323
All Electric
New Home Construction
Five-year rate: 3%
Value: $90,300
Alternative Housing
18% trailers, 6% apartments, 1% condos
Grade: 89

Ketchum–Sun Valley, ID
Home Prices
Average: $215,500
Upper tenth: $572,000
Taxes: $2,024
Energy Requirements
Heating-degree days: 8,729
Air-conditioning hours: 183
Utilities: $522
All Electric
New Home Construction
Five-year rate: 19%
Value: $208,500
Historic Neighborhood
Bellevue District
Alternative Housing
29% condos, 8% trailers, 5% apartments
Grade: 69

Key West–Key Largo–Marathon, FL
Home Prices
Average: $215,000
Upper tenth: $462,000
Taxes: $1,754
Energy Requirements
Heating-degree days: 100
Air-conditioning hours: 3,360
Utilities: $1,821
All Electric
New Home Construction
Five-year rate: 9%
Value: $78,100
Historic Neighborhoods
Key West District
Pigeon Key
Alternative Housing
22% trailers, 10% condos, 6% apartments
Grade: 55

Kingman, AZ
Home Prices
Average: $76,500
Upper tenth: $112,000

Taxes: $933
Energy Requirements
Heating-degree days: 3,212
Air-conditioning hours: 1,587
Utilities: $1,903
Natural Gas, Electric
New Home Construction
Five-year rate: 28%
Value: $59,100
Alternative Housing
8% trailers, 4% apartments
Grade: 83

Kissimmee–St. Cloud, FL
Home Prices
Average: $97,500
Upper tenth: $146,000
Taxes: $796
Energy Requirements
Heating-degree days: 603
Air-conditioning hours: 2,186
Utilities: $1,444
All Electric
New Home Construction
Five-year rate: 27%
Value: $80,600
Historic Neighborhood
Kissimmee District
Alternative Housing
20% trailers, 9% apartments, 5% condos
Grade: 93

Laguna Beach–Dana Point, CA
Home Prices
Average: $386,000
Upper tenth: $633,000
Taxes: $4,099
Energy Requirements
Heating-degree days: 2,157
Air-conditioning hours: 400
Utilities: $1,299
Natural Gas, Electric
New Home Construction
Five-year rate: 3%
Value: $166,900
Historic Neighborhood
Crystal Cove District
Alternative Housing
19% apartments, 10% condos, 1% trailers
Grade: 46

Lake Buchanan–Lake LBJ, TX
Home Prices
Average: $92,500
Upper tenth: $174,000
Taxes: $2,128
Energy Requirements
Heating-degree days: 2,342
Air-conditioning hours: 1,736
Utilities: $1,298
All Electric
New Home Construction
Five-year rate: 3%
Value: $83,600
Alternative Housing
17% trailers, 3% condos, 1% apartments
Grade: 88

Lake Conroe, TX
Home Prices
Average: $96,500
Upper tenth: $144,000
Taxes: $2,456
Energy Requirements
Heating-degree days: 1,774
Air-conditioning hours: 2,018

Utilities: $1,389
All Electric
New Home Construction
Five-year rate: 13%
Value: $104,700
Alternative Housing
17% trailers, 9% apartments, 3% condos
Grade: 89

Lake Granbury, TX
Home Prices
Average: $98,000
Upper tenth: $174,000
Taxes: $1,989
Energy Requirements
Heating-degree days: 2,625
Air-conditioning hours: 1,866
Utilities: $1,340
All Electric
New Home Construction
Five-year rate: 1%
Value: $121,300
Alternative Housing
35% trailers, 2% condos, 1% apartments
Grade: 91

Lake Havasu City, AZ
Home Prices
Average: $110,000
Upper tenth: $142,000
Taxes: $1,342
Energy Requirements
Heating-degree days: 1,213
Air-conditioning hours: 3,213
Utilities: $1,936
Electric
New Home Construction
Five-year rate: 28%
Value: $82,300
Alternative Housing
6% condos, 4% apartments, 1% trailers
Grade: 76

✓ Lake Livingston, TX
Home Prices
Average: $57,500
Upper tenth: $116,000
Taxes: $1,323
Energy Requirements
Heating-degree days: 2,096
Air-conditioning hours: 1,834
Utilities: $1,329
All Electric
New Home Construction
Five-year rate: n.a.
Value: $51,800
Alternative Housing
29% trailers, 1% condos
Grade: 94

✓ Lake Martin, AL
Home Prices
Average: $63,000
Upper tenth: $116,000
Taxes: $265
Energy Requirements
Heating-degree days: 2,910
Air-conditioning hours: 1,380
Utilities: $1,022
Natural Gas, Electric
New Home Construction
Five-year rate: 3%
Value: $66,900
Alternative Housing
16% trailers, 2% apartments
Grade: 99

Lake of the Cherokees, OK
Home Prices
Average: $67,000
Upper tenth: $146,000
Taxes: $528
Energy Requirements
Heating-degree days: 3,691
Air-conditioning hours: 1,313
Utilities: $991
Wood, Bottled Gas
New Home Construction
Five-year rate: 2%
Value: $64,100
Alternative Housing
28% trailers, 1% condos, 1% apartments
Grade: 90

Lake of the Ozarks, MO
Home Prices
Average: $100,000
Upper tenth: $173,000
Taxes: $591
Energy Requirements
Heating-degree days: 4,317
Air-conditioning hours: 913
Utilities: $948
All Electric
New Home Construction
Five-year rate: 1%
Value: $88,500
Alternative Housing
14% condos, 13% trailers, 1% apartments
Grade: 85

Lake Winnipesaukee, NH
Home Prices
Average: $150,000
Upper tenth: $218,000
Taxes: $3,661
Energy Requirements
Heating-degree days: 7,956
Air-conditioning hours: 224
Utilities: $1,543
Oil, Wood
New Home Construction
Five-year rate: 4%
Value: $113,800
Historic Neighborhoods
Centre Harbor Village
Monument Square
Sanbornton Square
Center Sandwich
Sandwich Lower Corner
Alternative Housing
8% trailers, 6% condos, 3% apartments
Grade: 79

Lakeland–Winter Haven, FL
Home Prices
Average: $83,500
Upper tenth: $145,000
Taxes: $681
Energy Requirements
Heating-degree days: 588
Air-conditioning hours: 1,778
Utilities: $1,313
All Electric
New Home Construction
Five-year rate: 10%
Value: $63,700
Historic Neighborhoods
Beacon Hill–Alta Vista
East Lake Morton District
Mountain Lake Estates
Northeast Bartow District
South Bartow District
South Lake Morton

Alternative Housing
27% trailers, 5% apartments, 3% condos
Grade: 92

Las Cruces, NM
Home Prices
Average: $87,500
Upper tenth: $144,000
Taxes: $685
Energy Requirements
Heating-degree days: 3,155
Air-conditioning hours: 1,157
Utilities: $1,391
Natural Gas, Bottled Gas
New Home Construction
Five-year rate: 11%
Value: $80,000
Historic Neighborhoods
Alameda-Depot District
Mesquite Street
Alternative Housing
25% trailers, 9% apartments, 1% condos
Grade: 87

Las Vegas, NV
Home Prices
Average: $126,500
Upper tenth: $200,000
Taxes: $1,349
Energy Requirements
Heating-degree days: 2,407
Air-conditioning hours: 2,427
Utilities: $1,246
All Electric
New Home Construction
Five-year rate: 30%
Value: $67,600
Historic Neighborhoods
Boulder City
Las Vegas High School Area
Alternative Housing
24% apartments, 10% trailers, 8% condos
Grade: 86

Leesburg–Lady Lake, FL
Home Prices
Average: $93,500
Upper tenth: $174,000
Taxes: $763
Energy Requirements
Heating-degree days: 831
Air-conditioning hours: 2,079
Utilities: $1,410
All Electric
New Home Construction
Five-year rate: 21%
Value: $65,100
Alternative Housing
36% trailers, 4% apartments, 2% condos
Grade: 89

Litchfield Hills, CT
Home Prices
Average: $241,500
Upper tenth: $334,000
Taxes: $3,187
Energy Requirements
Heating-degree days: 6,636
Air-conditioning hours: 295
Utilities: $1,556
Oil, Electric
New Home Construction
Five-year rate: 6%
Value: $106,400
Historic Neighborhoods
Bethlehem Green
Canaan Village

Colebrook Center
Falls Village
Flanders District
Goshen District
Lime Rock District
Litchfield Center
Milton Center
New Home Milford Center
Norfolk District
Sharon District
Sharon Valley
West Goshen
Winsted Green
Alternative Housing
7% apartments, 2% condos
Grade: 69

Lower Cape May, NJ
Home Prices
Average: $137,500
Upper tenth: $272,000
Taxes: $3,520
Energy Requirements
Heating-degree days: 4,693
Air-conditioning hours: 508
Utilities: $1,355
All Electric
New Home Construction
Five-year rate: 3%
Value: $90,400
Alternative Housing
3% trailers, 2% apartments, 2% condos
Grade: 83

Madison, MS
Home Prices
Average: $88,500
Upper tenth: $174,000
Taxes: $917
Energy Requirements
Heating-degree days: 2,467
Air-conditioning hours: 1,576
Utilities: $1,362
Natural Gas, Electric
New Home Construction
Five-year rate: 22%
Value: $81,900
Alternative Housing
17% apartments, 8% trailers, 2% condos
Grade: 91

Maryville, TN
Home Prices
Average: $78,500
Upper tenth: $145,000
Taxes: $887
Energy Requirements
Heating-degree days: 3,937
Air-conditioning hours: 1,053
Utilities: $894
All Electric
New Home Construction
Five-year rate: 3%
Value: $85,000
Historic Neighborhoods
Indiana Avenue Homes
Louisville District
Alternative Housing
12% trailers, 6% apartments, 1% condos
Grade: 93

Maui, HI
Home Prices
Average: $263,500
Upper tenth: $456,000
Taxes: $1,252

Energy Requirements
Heating-degree days: 0
Air-conditioning hours: 1,414
Utilities: $1,725
All Electric
New Home Construction
Five-year rate: 12%
Value: $112,800
Alternative Housing
24% condos, 8% apartments
Grade: 61

McCall–Cascade–Payette Valley, ID
Home Prices
Average: $105,500
Upper tenth: $172,000
Taxes: $1,547
Energy Requirements
Heating-degree days: 8,772
Air-conditioning hours: 78
Utilities: $1,299
Wood, Electric
New Home Construction
Five-year rate: 13%
Value: $95,300
Alternative Housing
15% trailers, 3% condos, 1% apartments
Grade: 85

Medford–Ashland, OR
Home Prices
Average: $102,000
Upper tenth: $171,000
Taxes: $1,216
Energy Requirements
Heating-degree days: 4,611
Air-conditioning hours: 673
Utilities: $625
All Electric
New Home Construction
Five-year rate: 11%
Value: $99,600
Historic Neighborhoods
Hanley District
Hillcrest Orchard District
South Oakdale District
Alternative Housing
17% trailers, 7% apartments, 1% condos
Grade: 86

Melbourne, FL
Home Prices
Average: $115,000
Upper tenth: $177,000
Taxes: $938
Energy Requirements
Heating-degree days: 644
Air-conditioning hours: 2,094
Utilities: $1,414
All Electric
New Home Construction
Five-year rate: 13%
Value: $92,200
Alternative Housing
12% apartments, 9% condos, 4% trailers
Grade: 87

✓ Mission–McAllen–Alamo, TX
Home Prices
Average: $52,500
Upper tenth: $115,000
Taxes: $1,208
Energy Requirements
Heating-degree days: 693
Air-conditioning hours: 2,653
Utilities: $1,592
All Electric

New Home Construction
Five-year rate: 19%
Value: $25,900
Alternative Housing
19% trailers, 7% apartments, 2% condos
Grade: 96

Montrose, CO
Home Prices
Average: $75,500
Upper tenth: $114,000
Taxes: $671
Energy Requirements
Heating-degree days: 6,383
Air-conditioning hours: 467
Utilities: $1,132
Natural Gas, Wood
New Home Construction
Five-year rate: 10%
Value: $54,300
Alternative Housing
23% trailers, 5% apartments, 1% condos
Grade: 93

Myrtle Beach–North Myrtle Beach, SC
Home Prices
Average: $128,500
Upper tenth: $203,000
Taxes: $1,187
Energy Requirements
Heating-degree days: 2,320
Air-conditioning hours: 1,160
Utilities: $1,033
All Electric
New Home Construction
Five-year rate: 12%
Value: $99,600
Alternative Housing
10% condos, 7% trailers, 5% apartments
Grade: 78

Naples, FL
Home Prices
Average: $202,000
Upper tenth: $464,000
Taxes: $1,648
Energy Requirements
Heating-degree days: 326
Air-conditioning hours: 2,316
Utilities: $1,486
All Electric
New Home Construction
Five-year rate: 15%
Value: $109,800
Alternative Housing
37% condos, 11% trailers, 8% apartments
Grade: 78

New Bern, NC
Home Prices
Average: $93,000
Upper tenth: $174,000
Taxes: $1,048
Energy Requirements
Heating-degree days: 2,742
Air-conditioning hours: 1,434
Utilities: $1,259
All Electric
New Home Construction
Five-year rate: 9%
Value: $97,100
Historic Neighborhoods
Ghent District
New Home Bern District
Riverside District

Alternative Housing
17% trailers, 6% apartments, 2% condos
Grade: 85

New Braunfels, TX
Home Prices
Average: $102,000
Upper tenth: $175,000
Taxes: $2,232
Energy Requirements
Heating-degree days: 1,790
Air-conditioning hours: 2,107
Utilities: $1,417
All Electric
New Home Construction
Five-year rate: 11%
Value: $81,400
Historic Neighborhood
Gruene District
Alternative Housing
15% trailers, 5% apartments, 2% condos
Grade: 91

New Port Richey, FL
Home Prices
Average: $80,000
Upper tenth: $120,000
Taxes: $653
Energy Requirements
Heating-degree days: 732
Air-conditioning hours: 2,168
Utilities: $1,438
All Electric
New Home Construction
Five-year rate: 9%
Value: $67,700
Alternative Housing
10% condos, 4% apartments, 3% trailers
Grade: 87

Newport–Lincoln City, OR
Home Prices
Average: $94,000
Upper tenth: $171,000
Taxes: $1,167
Energy Requirements
Heating-degree days: 5,286
Air-conditioning hours: 16
Utilities: $487
All Electric
New Home Construction
Five-year rate: 10%
Value: $91,300
Alternative Housing
20% trailers, 5% apartments, 2% condos
Grade: 88

✓ Norfork Lake, AR
Home Prices
Average: $66,500
Upper tenth: $115,000
Taxes: $584
Energy Requirements
Heating-degree days: 4,103
Air-conditioning hours: 1,276
Utilities: $1,231
All Electric
New Home Construction
Five-year rate: 4%
Value: $67,500
Alternative Housing
17% trailers, 3% apartments, 1% condos
Grade: 95

Northern Door Peninsula, WI
Home Prices
Average: $107,000
Upper tenth: $177,000
Taxes: $3,389
Energy Requirements
Heating-degree days: 7,901
Air-conditioning hours: 286
Utilities: $1,472
Natural Gas, Oil
New Home Construction
Five-year rate: 7%
Value: $74,100
Alternative Housing
4% condos, 4% trailers, 2% apartments
Grade: 81

Northern Neck, VA
Home Prices
Average: $145,000
Upper tenth: $349,000
Taxes: $1,044
Energy Requirements
Heating-degree days: 3,975
Air-conditioning hours: 1,042
Utilities: $1,060
All Electric
New Home Construction
Five-year rate: 10%
Value: $105,900
Historic Neighborhoods
Heathsville District
Reedville District
Lancaster Court House District
Alternative Housing
11% trailers, 1% apartments, 1% condos
Grade: 86

Oakhurst–Coarsegold, CA
Home Prices
Average: $112,500
Upper tenth: $200,000
Taxes: $1,202
Energy Requirements
Heating-degree days: 3,762
Air-conditioning hours: 843
Utilities: $1,794
Natural Gas, Electric
New Home Construction
Five-year rate: 16%
Value: $68,900
Alternative Housing
10% trailers, 6% apartments, 1% condos
Grade: 87

Ocala, FL
Home Prices
Average: $83,500
Upper tenth: $145,000
Taxes: $681
Energy Requirements
Heating-degree days: 930
Air-conditioning hours: 2,076
Utilities: $1,409
All Electric
New Home Construction
Five-year rate: 16%
Value: $42,300
Historic Neighborhoods
Dunnellon Boomtown
McIntosh District
Ocala District
Tuscawilla Park District
Alternative Housing
31% trailers, 4% apartments, 3% condos
Grade: 89

Ocean City, MD
Home Prices
Average: $123,000
Upper tenth: $232,000
Taxes: $1,771
Energy Requirements
Heating-degree days: 4,380
Air-conditioning hours: 772
Utilities: $1,018
All Electric
New Home Construction
Five-year rate: 13%
Value: $93,800
Alternative Housing
34% condos, 10% trailers, 3% apartments
Grade: 83

✓Oscoda–Tawas–Huron Shore, MI
Home Prices
Average: $60,500
Upper tenth: $114,000
Taxes: $1,161
Energy Requirements
Heating-degree days: 7,912
Air-conditioning hours: 227
Utilities: $1,704
Natural Gas, Bottled Gas
New Home Construction
Five-year rate: 5%
Value: $50,700
Historic Neighborhood
Alabaster District
Alternative Housing
8% trailers, 3% apartments, 1% condos
Grade: 95

Oxford, MS
Home Prices
Average: $68,000
Upper tenth: $117,000
Taxes: $939
Energy Requirements
Heating-degree days: 3,482
Air-conditioning hours: 1,629
Utilities: $1,144
All Electric
New Home Construction
Five-year rate: 6%
Value: $46,100
Alternative Housing
18% trailers, 11% apartments
Grade: 90

Pagosa Springs, CO
Home Prices
Average: $100,000
Upper tenth: $172,000
Taxes: $973
Energy Requirements
Heating-degree days: 8,548
Air-conditioning hours: 43
Utilities: $1,058
Wood, Bottled Gas
New Home Construction
Five-year rate: 12%
Value: $108,400
Alternative Housing
15% trailers, 10% condos, 3% apartments
Grade: 77

Pahrump Valley, NV
Home Prices
Average: $97,000
Upper tenth: $149,000
Taxes: $1,056

Energy Requirements
Heating-degree days: 3,299
Air-conditioning hours: 2,152
Utilities: $1,173
Electric
New Home Construction
Five-year rate: n.a.
Value: $67,600
Alternative Housing
20% trailers, 5% condos, 2% apartments
Grade: 86

Palm Springs–Coachella Valley, CA
Home Prices
Average: $176,500
Upper tenth: $288,000
Taxes: $1,913
Energy Requirements
Heating-degree days: 985
Air-conditioning hours: 2,988
Utilities: $2,132
Electric
New Home Construction
Five-year rate: 11%
Value: $120,100
Alternative Housing
10% apartments, 10% condos, 4% trailers
Grade: 75

Panama City, FL
Home Prices
Average: $85,000
Upper tenth: $145,000
Taxes: $694
Energy Requirements
Heating-degree days: 1,681
Air-conditioning hours: 1,908
Utilities: $1,355
All Electric
New Home Construction
Five-year rate: 11%
Value: $57,600
Alternative Housing
17% trailers, 10% condos, 6% apartments
Grade: 91

Paradise–Magalia, CA
Home Prices
Average: $129,000
Upper tenth: $173,000
Taxes: $1,364
Energy Requirements
Heating-degree days: 3,214
Air-conditioning hours: 1,086
Utilities: $1,811
Natural Gas, Electric
New Home Construction
Five-year rate: 8%
Value: $102,800
Alternative Housing
10% apartments, 4% trailers, 2% condos
Grade: 76

Payson, AZ
Home Prices
Average: $106,500
Upper tenth: $142,000
Taxes: $1,299
Energy Requirements
Heating-degree days: 4,296
Air-conditioning hours: 722
Utilities: $1,763
Natural Gas, Wood
New Home Construction
Five-year rate: 6%
Value: $78,100

Alternative Housing
4% trailers, 1% apartments, 1% condos
Grade: 72

Petoskey–Harbor Springs, MI
Home Prices
Average: $93,000
Upper tenth: $173,000
Taxes: $2,530
Energy Requirements
Heating-degree days: 7,573
Air-conditioning hours: 229
Utilities: $1,656
Natural Gas, Wood
New Home Construction
Five-year rate: 7%
Value: $90,000
Historic Neighborhood
Bay View District
Alternative Housing
10% trailers, 5% apartments, 4% condos
Grade: 91

Phoenix–Mesa–Scottsdale, AZ
Home Prices
Average: $117,500
Upper tenth: $200,000
Taxes: $1,434
Energy Requirements
Heating-degree days: 1,350
Air-conditioning hours: 2,819
Utilities: $2,089
All Electric
New Home Construction
Five-year rate: 13%
Value: $105,300
Historic Neighborhoods
Blount Addition
Chelsea Place
Coronado Neighborhood
Encanto-Palmcroft District
Glendale Townsite–Catlin Court
Kenilworth District
Oakland District
Phoenix Homesteads
Portland Street
Roosevelt District
Story District
Victoria Place
Willo District
Woodland District
Alternative Housing
17% apartments, 9% condos, 9% trailers
Grade: 86

Pike County, PA
Home Prices
Average: $144,000
Upper tenth: $218,000
Taxes: $3,001
Energy Requirements
Heating-degree days: 6,167
Air-conditioning hours: 475
Utilities: $1,191
All Electric
New Home Construction
Five-year rate: 12%
Value: $91,500
Alternative Housing
15% trailers
Grade: 79

Placerville–Shingle Springs, CA
Home Prices
Average: $201,500
Upper tenth: $342,000
Taxes: $2,075

Energy Requirements
Heating-degree days: 3,930
Air-conditioning hours: 749
Utilities: $1,249
Wood, Electric
New Home Construction
Five-year rate: 11%
Value: $128,800
Alternative Housing
8% trailers, 5% apartments, 2% condos
Grade: 71

Polson–Mission Valley, MT
Home Prices
Average: $87,000
Upper tenth: $171,000
Taxes: $1,331
Energy Requirements
Heating-degree days: 7,181
Air-conditioning hours: 243
Utilities: $933
All Electric
New Home Construction
Five-year rate: 1%
Value: $64,300
Alternative Housing
18% trailers, 3% apartments
Grade: 85

Pompano Beach, FL
Home Prices
Average: $138,000
Upper tenth: $203,000
Taxes: $1,126
Energy Requirements
Heating-degree days: 262
Air-conditioning hours: 2,407
Utilities: $1,515
All Electric
New Home Construction
Five-year rate: 12%
Value: $107,500
Alternative Housing
16% apartments, 11% condos, 2% trailers
Grade: 87

Port Angeles–Seqium, WA
Home Prices
Average: $119,500
Upper tenth: $172,000
Taxes: $1,530
Energy Requirements
Heating-degree days: 5,695
Air-conditioning hours: 22
Utilities: $442
All Electric
New Home Construction
Five-year rate: 11%
Value: $84,000
Alternative Housing
6% apartments, 2% trailers, 1% condos
Grade: 80

Port Charlotte–Punta Gorda, FL
Home Prices
Average: $109,500
Upper tenth: $203,000
Taxes: $894
Energy Requirements
Heating-degree days: 477
Air-conditioning hours: 2,322
Utilities: $1,488
All Electric
New Home Construction
Five-year rate: 12%
Value: $80,300

Historic Neighborhood
  Punta Gorda District
Alternative Housing
  16% trailers, 12% condos, 4% apartments
Grade: 83

Port Townsend, WA
Home Prices
  Average: $127,500
  Upper tenth: $229,000
Taxes: $1,652
Energy Requirements
  Heating-degree days: 5,041
  Air-conditioning hours: 34
Utilities: $444
  All Electric
New Home Construction
  Five-year rate: 22%
  Value: $63,500
Historic Neighborhoods
  Fort Worden District
  Irondale District
  Port Townsend
Alternative Housing
  20% trailers, 4% apartments, 2% condos
Grade: 76

Prescott–Prescott Valley, AZ
Home Prices
  Average: $115,500
  Upper tenth: $200,000
Taxes: $1,409
Energy Requirements
  Heating-degree days: 4,995
  Air-conditioning hours: 526
Utilities: $1,820
  Natural Gas, Electric
New Home Construction
  Five-year rate: 18%
  Value: $118,100
Historic Neighborhoods
  East Prescott
  Lynx Creek District
  Pine Crest
  West Prescott
Alternative Housing
  13% trailers, 7% condos, 4% apartments
Grade: 77

Redding, CA
Home Prices
  Average: $119,000
  Upper tenth: $200,000
Taxes: $1,274
Energy Requirements
  Heating-degree days: 2,855
  Air-conditioning hours: 1,463
Utilities: $1,924
  Natural Gas, Wood
New Home Construction
  Five-year rate: 13%
  Value: $99,100
Alternative Housing
  19% trailers, 8% apartments, 1% condos
Grade: 83

Rehoboth Bay–Indian River Bay, DE
Home Prices
  Average: $116,500
  Upper tenth: $204,000
Taxes: $1,505
Energy Requirements
  Heating-degree days: 4,341
  Air-conditioning hours: 477
Utilities: $1,326
  Oil, Electric

New Home Construction
  Five-year rate: 11%
  Value: $76,800
Historic Neighborhoods
  Bridgeville
  Laurel
  Lewes
  Milton
  Richards
  South Milford
Alternative Housing
  28% trailers, 5% condos, 2% apartments
Grade: 85

Reno–Sparks, NV
Home Prices
  Average: $156,500
  Upper tenth: $285,000
Taxes: $1,786
Energy Requirements
  Heating-degree days: 5,674
  Air-conditioning hours: 704
Utilities: $1,198
  Natural Gas, Electric
New Home Construction
  Five-year rate: 15%
  Value: $104,800
Alternative Housing
  21% apartments, 11% trailers, 9% condos
Grade: 82

Riviera–Bullhead City, AZ
Home Prices
  Average: $138,000
  Upper tenth: $200,000
Taxes: $1,684
Energy Requirements
  Heating-degree days: 1,309
  Air-conditioning hours: 3,213
Utilities: $1,936
  Electric
New Home Construction
  Five-year rate: 28%
  Value: $80,800
Alternative Housing
  20% trailers, 4% apartments, 3% condos
Grade: 60

Rockport–Aransas Pass, TX
Home Prices
  Average: $85,000
  Upper tenth: $174,000
Taxes: $1,955
Energy Requirements
  Heating-degree days: 1,066
  Air-conditioning hours: 2,845
Utilities: $1,650
  All Electric
New Home Construction
  Five-year rate: 2%
  Value: $72,200
Alternative Housing
  24% trailers, 4% condos, 3% apartments
Grade: 84

Ruidoso, NM
Home Prices
  Average: $94,500
  Upper tenth: $172,000
Taxes: $740
Energy Requirements
  Heating-degree days: 4,105
  Air-conditioning hours: 830
Utilities: $1,372
  Natural Gas, Bottled Gas

New Home Construction
Five-year rate: 4%
Value: $113,600
Historic Neighborhoods
Lincoln District
White Oaks
Alternative Housing
20% trailers, 4% condos, 1% apartments
Grade: 87

St. Augustine, FL
Home Prices
Average: $130,500
Upper tenth: $289,000
Taxes: $1,065
Energy Requirements
Heating-degree days: 1,040
Air-conditioning hours: 1,492
Utilities: $1,221
All Electric
New Home Construction
Five-year rate: 18%
Value: $135,400
Historic Neighborhoods
Abbott Tract
Lincolnville
Model Land Company
St. Augustine Town Plan
Alternative Housing
15% condos, 15% trailers, 7% apartments
Grade: 85

St. George–Zion, UT
Home Prices
Average: $104,500
Upper tenth: $172,000
Taxes: $2,761
Energy Requirements
Heating-degree days: 3,215
Air-conditioning hours: 766
Utilities: $911
All Electric
New Home Construction
Five-year rate: 35%
Value: $79,700
Alternative Housing
16% trailers, 15% condos, 7% apartments
Grade: 74

St. Jay–Northeast Kingdom, VT
Home Prices
Average: $85,500
Upper tenth: $136,000
Taxes: $1,590
Energy Requirements
Heating-degree days: 7,835
Air-conditioning hours: 278
Utilities: $1,459
Oil, Wood
New Home Construction
Five-year rate: 6%
Value: $69,600
Historic Neighborhoods
Maple Street–Clarks Avenue
St. Johnsbury District
St. Johnsbury Main Street
Alternative Housing
11% trailers, 6% apartments, 2% condos
Grade: 89

St. Petersburg–Clearwater, FL
Home Prices
Average: $109,000
Upper tenth: $203,000
Taxes: $889

Energy Requirements
Heating-degree days: 603
Air-conditioning hours: 1,881
Utilities: $1,346
All Electric
New Home Construction
Five-year rate: 5%
Value: $120,300
Historic Neighborhoods
Harbor Oaks District
Pass-a-Grille District
Tarpon Springs District
Alternative Housing
18% condos, 13% apartments, 12% trailers
Grade: 91

St. Simons–Jekyll Islands, GA
Home Prices
Average: $211,500
Upper tenth: $355,000
Taxes: $2,453
Energy Requirements
Heating-degree days: 1,604
Air-conditioning hours: 1,365
Utilities: $1,178
All Electric
New Home Construction
Five-year rate: 8%
Value: $98,100
Alternative Housing
14% condos, 9% apartments, 2% trailers
Grade: 59

San Antonio, TX
Home Prices
Average: $80,500
Upper tenth: $145,000
Taxes: $1,852
Energy Requirements
Heating-degree days: 1,644
Air-conditioning hours: 2,189
Utilities: $1,571
Natural Gas, Electric
New Home Construction
Five-year rate: 4%
Value: $73,100
Historic Neighborhoods
King William District
La Villita
Mission Parkway
Source of the River District
South Alamo Street
South Mary's Street
Alternative Housing
18% apartments, 3% condos, 3% trailers
Grade: 92

San Diego, CA
Home Prices
Average: $255,000
Upper tenth: $457,000
Taxes: $2,723
Energy Requirements
Heating-degree days: 1,256
Air-conditioning hours: 110
Utilities: $1,001
Natural Gas, Electric
New Home Construction
Five-year rate: 4%
Value: $174,500
Alternative Housing
23% apartments, 12% condos, 5% trailers
Grade: 57

San Juan Islands, WA
Home Prices
    Average: $237,500
    Upper tenth: $458,000
Taxes: $1,898
Energy Requirements
    Heating-degree days: 5,341
    Air-conditioning hours: 28
Utilities: $1,218
    Wood, Electric
New Home Construction
    Five-year rate: 25%
    Value: $91,800
Alternative Housing
    11% trailers, 3% apartments, 1% condos
Grade: 65

San Luis Obispo, CA
Home Prices
    Average: $272,500
    Upper tenth: $457,000
Taxes: $3,008
Energy Requirements
    Heating-degree days: 2,498
    Air-conditioning hours: 420
Utilities: $1,369
    Natural Gas, Electric
New Home Construction
    Five-year rate: 6%
    Value: $134,900
Alternative Housing
    12% trailers, 9% apartments, 4% condos
Grade: 43

Sandpoint–Priest River, ID
Home Prices
    Average: $85,000
    Upper tenth: $144,000
Taxes: $1,453
Energy Requirements
    Heating-degree days: 7,694
    Air-conditioning hours: 143
Utilities: $1,299
    Wood, Electric
New Home Construction
    Five-year rate: 10%
    Value: $71,700
Alternative Housing
    17% trailers, 4% condos, 2% apartments
Grade: 86

Santa Barbara, CA
Home Prices
    Average: $320,500
    Upper tenth: $576,000
Taxes: $3,269
Energy Requirements
    Heating-degree days: 2,438
    Air-conditioning hours: 59
Utilities: $1,188
    Natural Gas, Electric
New Home Construction
    Five-year rate: 3%
    Value: $170,600
Historic Neighborhood
    Santa Barbara Presidio
Alternative Housing
    17% apartments, 7% condos, 6% trailers
Grade: 53

Santa Fe, NM
Home Prices
    Average: $164,000
    Upper tenth: $287,000
Taxes: $1,283

Energy Requirements
    Heating-degree days: 5,777
    Air-conditioning hours: 250
Utilities: $1,335
    Natural Gas, Electric
New Home Construction
    Five-year rate: 6%
    Value: $127,300
Historic Neighborhoods
    Barrio de Analco
    Camino del Monte Sol
    Don Gaspar District
    Seton Village
Alternative Housing
    16% trailers, 9% apartments, 4% condos
Grade: 74

Santa Rosa–Sonoma, CA
Home Prices
    Average: $260,000
    Upper tenth: $575,000
Taxes: $2,717
Energy Requirements
    Heating-degree days: 2,883
    Air-conditioning hours: 770
Utilities: $1,603
    Natural Gas, Electric
New Home Construction
    Five-year rate: 8%
    Value: $121,300
Historic Neighborhoods
    Bodega Bay District
    Sonoma Plaza District
Alternative Housing
    10% apartments, 7% trailers, 5% condos
Grade: 60

Sarasota, FL
Home Prices
    Average: $136,500
    Upper tenth: $233,000
Taxes: $1,114
Energy Requirements
    Heating-degree days: 581
    Air-conditioning hours: 2,207
Utilities: $1,451
    All Electric
New Home Construction
    Five-year rate: 10%
    Value: $105,200
Historic Neighborhoods
    Burns Court
    Venice Edgewood District
    Rigby's La Plaza
    Venice Venezia Park
Alternative Housing
    22% condos, 14% trailers, 7% apartments
Grade: 88

Savannah, GA
Home Prices
    Average: $94,000
    Upper tenth: $174,000
Taxes: $1,951
Energy Requirements
    Heating-degree days: 1,847
    Air-conditioning hours: 1,308
Utilities: $1,357
    Natural Gas, Electric
New Home Construction
    Five-year rate: 7%
    Value: $82,800
Historic Neighborhoods
    Ardsley Park–Chatham Crescent
    Fort Screven
    Isle of Hope
    Savannah District

Alternative Housing
12% apartments, 6% trailers, 3% condos
Grade: 90

✓ Sebring–Avon Park, FL
Home Prices
Average: $76,500
Upper tenth: $117,000
Taxes: $624
Energy Requirements
Heating-degree days: 657
Air-conditioning hours: 2,219
Utilities: $1,455
All Electric
New Home Construction
Five-year rate: 11%
Value: $56,400
Alternative Housing
27% trailers, 3% apartments, 3% condos
Grade: 94

Sedona, AZ
Home Prices
Average: $203,500
Upper tenth: $284,000
Taxes: $2,483
Energy Requirements
Heating-degree days: 3,388
Air-conditioning hours: 1,313
Utilities: $1,505
Natural Gas, Wood
New Home Construction
Five-year rate: 9%
Value: $117,900
Alternative Housing
8% apartments, 5% condos, 2% trailers
Grade: 72

✓ Silver City, NM
Home Prices
Average: $66,500
Upper tenth: $114,000
Taxes: $520
Energy Requirements
Heating-degree days: 4,528
Air-conditioning hours: 853
Utilities: $1,428
Natural Gas, Bottled Gas
New Home Construction
Five-year rate: n.a.
Value: $69,500
Historic Neighborhoods
Chihuahua Hill
Pinos Altos
San Lorenzo District
Silver City Homes
Alternative Housing
25% trailers, 3% apartments
Grade: 95

Smith Mountain Lake, VA
Home Prices
Average: $98,000
Upper tenth: $174,000
Taxes: $637
Energy Requirements
Heating-degree days: 4,177
Air-conditioning hours: 850
Utilities: $999
All Electric
New Home Construction
Five-year rate: 14%
Value: $92,400
Historic Neighborhoods
Bedford District

Alternative Housing
19% trailers, 2% condos, 1% apartments
Grade: 91

Sonora–Groveland–Twain Harte, CA
Home Prices
Average: $158,500
Upper tenth: $284,000
Taxes: $1,604
Energy Requirements
Heating-degree days: 3,637
Air-conditioning hours: 873
Utilities: $1,271
Wood, Bottled Gas
New Home Construction
Five-year rate: 9%
Value: $69,100
Historic Neighborhood
Columbia District
Alternative Housing
16% trailers, 3% apartments
Grade: 65

Southern Berkshire County, MA
Home Prices
Average: $173,500
Upper tenth: $218,000
Taxes: $2,325
Energy Requirements
Heating-degree days: 7,445
Air-conditioning hours: 204
Utilities: $1,363
Oil, Natural Gas
New Home Construction
Five-year rate: 4%
Value: $115,600
Historic Neighborhoods
Mill River District
North Egremont District
Sheffield Center
Sheffield Plain
South Egremont Village
Alternative Housing
9% apartments, 3% condos, 2% trailers
Grade: 72

Southern Pines–Pinehurst, NC
Home Prices
Average: $118,500
Upper tenth: $233,000
Taxes: $1,339
Energy Requirements
Heating-degree days: 3,321
Air-conditioning hours: 1,205
Utilities: $1,182
All Electric
New Home Construction
Five-year rate: 12%
Value: $101,900
Historic Neighborhoods
Aberdeen District
Pinehurst District
Southern Pines District
Alternative Housing
17% trailers, 5% condos, 3% apartments
Grade: 85

Southport–Brunswick Islands, NC
Home Prices
Average: $97,000
Upper tenth: $174,000
Taxes: $1,261
Energy Requirements
Heating-degree days: 2,751
Air-conditioning hours: 1,149
Utilities: $1,163
All Electric

New Home Construction
Five-year rate: 13%
Value: $77,600
Historic Neighborhood
Southport District
Alternative Housing
36% trailers, 4% condos, 1% apartments
Grade: 78

State College, PA
Home Prices
Average: $92,500
Upper tenth: $163,000
Taxes: $1,080
Energy Requirements
Heating-degree days: 6,364
Air-conditioning hours: 390
Utilities: $1,479
Oil, Electric
New Home Construction
Five-year rate: 8%
Value: $94,800
Historic Neighborhoods
Bellefonte District
Boalsburg District
Lemont District
Alternative Housing
21% apartments, 9% trailers, 4% condos
Grade: 91

Table Rock Lake, MO
Home Prices
Average: $75,500
Upper tenth: $114,000
Taxes: $571
Energy Requirements
Heating-degree days: 4,745
Air-conditioning hours: 951
Utilities: $1,255
Bottled Gas, Electric
New Home Construction
Five-year rate: 2%
Value: $65,100
Alternative Housing
23% trailers, 1% apartments, 1% condos
Grade: 93

Taos, NM
Home Prices
Average: $100,000
Upper tenth: $200,000
Taxes: $783
Energy Requirements
Heating-degree days: 7,128
Air-conditioning hours: 178
Utilities: $1,458
Natural Gas, Wood
New Home Construction
Five-year rate: 4%
Value: $62,500
Historic Neighborhoods
Fechin District
Hennings District
La Loma Plaza
Ranchos de Taos Plaza
Taos Downtown
Alternative Housing
17% trailers, 3% condos, 2% apartments
Grade: 78

✓ Thomasville, GA
Home Prices
Average: $67,000
Upper tenth: $117,000
Taxes: $777

Energy Requirements
Heating-degree days: 1,602
Air-conditioning hours: 1,627
Utilities: $1,262
All Electric
New Home Construction
Five-year rate: 5%
Value: $73,900
Historic Neighborhoods
Dawson Street
East End
Gordon Avenue
Paradise Park
Tockwotton–Love Place
Alternative Housing
19% trailers, 5% apartments, 1% condos
Grade: 98

Toms River–Barnegat Bay, NJ
Home Prices
Average: $154,000
Upper tenth: $270,000
Taxes: $3,402
Energy Requirements
Heating-degree days: 5,294
Air-conditioning hours: 586
Utilities: $2,067
Natural Gas, Electric
New Home Construction
Five-year rate: 5%
Value: $73,100
Historic Neighborhood
Beach Haven District
Alternative Housing
10% condos, 4% apartments, 3% trailers
Grade: 76

Traverse City, MI
Home Prices
Average: $92,500
Upper tenth: $172,000
Taxes: $1,599
Energy Requirements
Heating-degree days: 7,749
Air-conditioning hours: 305
Utilities: $1,705
Natural Gas, Oil
New Home Construction
Five-year rate: 8%
Value: $81,500
Historic Neighborhoods
Boardman Neighborhood
Central Neighborhood
Alternative Housing
11% trailers, 7% apartments, 3% condos
Grade: 91

Tryon, NC
Home Prices
Average: $98,500
Upper tenth: $175,000
Taxes: $978
Energy Requirements
Heating-degree days: 3,181
Air-conditioning hours: 682
Utilities: $1,006
All Electric
New Home Construction
Five-year rate: 9%
Value: $73,400
Alternative Housing
15% trailers, 2% apartments, 2% condos
Grade: 93

Tucson, AZ
Home Prices
Average: $105,500
Upper tenth: $172,000
Taxes: $1,287
Energy Requirements
Heating-degree days: 1,678
Air-conditioning hours: 2,297
Utilities: $1,892
Natural Gas, Electric
New Home Construction
Five-year rate: 10%
Value: $103,000
Historic Neighborhoods
Armory Park District
Colonia Solana
El Encanto Estates
El Presidio
Iron Horse Expansion
Speedway-Drachman District
West University District
Alternative Housing
18% apartments, 13% trailers, 5% condos
Grade: 84

Vero Beach–Sebastian, FL
Home Prices
Average: $143,000
Upper tenth: $291,000
Taxes: $1,167
Energy Requirements
Heating-degree days: 548
Air-conditioning hours: 2,276
Utilities: $1,473
All Electric
New Home Construction
Five-year rate: 14%
Value: $119,400
Alternative Housing
20% condos, 15% trailers, 6% apartments
Grade: 85

Virginia Beach, VA
Home Prices
Average: $139,500
Upper tenth: $232,000
Taxes: $1,590
Energy Requirements
Heating-degree days: 3,495
Air-conditioning hours: 930
Utilities: $1,025
All Electric
New Home Construction
Five-year rate: 7%
Value: $84,100
Alternative Housing
14% apartments, 8% condos, 2% trailers
Grade: 80

Wenatchee, WA
Home Prices
Average: $97,000
Upper tenth: $171,000
Taxes: $970
Energy Requirements
Heating-degree days: 6,006
Air-conditioning hours: 628
Utilities: $556
All Electric
New Home Construction
Five-year rate: 10%
Value: $94,300
Alternative Housing
12% trailers, 8% apartments, 3% condos
Grade: 93

Western St. Tammany Parish, LA
Home Prices
Average: $116,000
Upper tenth: $175,000
Taxes: $467
Energy Requirements
Heating-degree days: 1,711
Air-conditioning hours: 1,774
Utilities: $1,272
All Electric
New Home Construction
Five-year rate: 15%
Value: $85,300
Historic Neighborhoods
Abita Springs District
Covington St. John Division
Alternative Housing
9% trailers, 4% apartments, 3% condos
Grade: 90

Whidbey Island, WA
Home Prices
Average: $144,500
Upper tenth: $229,000
Taxes: $1,647
Energy Requirements
Heating-degree days: 5,509
Air-conditioning hours: 53
Utilities: $447
All Electric
New Home Construction
Five-year rate: 14%
Value: $86,700
Historic Neighborhood
Central Whidbey Island District
Alternative Housing
13% trailers, 7% apartments, 2% condos
Grade: 74

Wickenburg, AZ
Home Prices
Average: $110,000
Upper tenth: $174,000
Taxes: $1,342
Energy Requirements
Heating-degree days: 2,144
Air-conditioning hours: 2,065
Utilities: $1,781
All Electric
New Home Construction
Five-year rate: 13%
Value: $63,500
Alternative Housing
17% apartments, 6% condos, 3% trailers
Grade: 81

Williamsburg, VA
Home Prices
Average: $111,500
Upper tenth: $292,000
Taxes: $836
Energy Requirements
Heating-degree days: 3,723
Air-conditioning hours: 905
Utilities: $1,017
All Electric
New Home Construction
Five-year rate: 18%
Value: $134,700
Historic Neighborhood
Colonial Williamsburg
Alternative Housing
8% apartments, 8% trailers, 7% condos
Grade: 88

Wimberly–San Marcos, TX
Home Prices
  Average: $102,500
  Upper tenth: $174,000
Taxes: $2,358
Energy Requirements
  Heating-degree days: 1,790
  Air-conditioning hours: 2,107
Utilities: $1,417
  All Electric
New Home Construction
  Five-year rate: 1%
  Value: $62,200
Historic Neighborhood
  Belvin Street District
Alternative Housing
  15% apartments, 14% trailers, 2% condos
Grade: 80

Winchester, VA
Home Prices
  Average: $121,500
  Upper tenth: $203,000
Taxes: $668
Energy Requirements
  Heating-degree days: 5,269
  Air-conditioning hours: 686
Utilities: $948
  All Electric
New Home Construction
  Five-year rate: 12%
  Value: $73,100
Historic Neighborhood
  Winchester District
Alternative Housing
  8% trailers, 2% apartments, 1% condos
Grade: 85

Woodstock, VT
Home Prices
  Average: $126,000
  Upper tenth: $217,000
Taxes: $1,499
Energy Requirements
  Heating-degree days: 8,387
  Air-conditioning hours: 169
Utilities: $1,459
  Oil, Wood
New Home Construction
  Five-year rate: 4%
  Value: $93,100

Historic Neighborhoods
  South Woodstock Village
  Windsor Village
  Woodstock Village
Alternative Housing
  8% trailers, 6% condos, 5% apartments
Grade: 82

York Beaches, ME
Home Prices
  Average: $145,500
  Upper tenth: $218,000
Taxes: $1,877
Energy Requirements
  Heating-degree days: 7,378
  Air-conditioning hours: 206
Utilities: $1,391
  Oil, Electric
New Home Construction
  Five-year rate: 7%
  Value: $79,900
Historic Neighborhoods
  Cape Arundel Summer Colony
  Kennebunk District
  Kennebunkport District
  Kittery Isles of Shoals
  Limerick Upper Village
  Lower Alewive
  West Lebanon District
  York Cliffs
  York District
Alternative Housing
  7% trailers, 6% apartments, 3% condos
Grade: 73

Yuma, AZ
Home Prices
  Average: $82,000
  Upper tenth: $143,000
Taxes: $1,000
Energy Requirements
  Heating-degree days: 927
  Air-conditioning hours: 3,185
Utilities: $2,238
  All Electric
New Home Construction
  Five-year rate: 12%
  Value: $65,500
Historic Neighborhoods
  Brinley Avenue
  Century Heights
Alternative Housing
  38% trailers, 8% apartments, 4% condos
Grade: 91

 ET CETERA: Housing

PROPERTY TAXES

Although the dollar amount of a home's property tax bill seems to inch upward with each reassessment, there is some comfort in knowing that the *rate* homes are being taxed is actually going down.

Over the years while the prices of existing homes were rising, the average effective property tax rate (the tax bill expressed as a percent of a home's fair market value) dropped from 2 percent to less than 1.15 percent nationwide. Experts expect the downward trend to continue.

Nowhere in the United States can you own a home and escape property taxes without specific income and age qualifications. But homeowners in certain states like Louisiana, where the statewide average property tax rate is 0.4 percent, shoulder less of a burden than do homeowners in other states such as Wisconsin, which has an average effective tax rate of 3.1, or nearly 8 times that of Louisiana.

Homestead Exemptions

When you shop for favorable property taxes around the country, be a little circumspect when you hear of states that give retired people additional property tax relief. Are any of these perks, by themselves, worth the move? Read on.

Homestead exemptions are specific dollar amounts deducted from a home's assessed value. The assessed value minus the exemption equals the amount of taxable value for computing property tax. Homeowners in Florida get a $25,000 exemption, for example, while Hawaiians get a $40,000 exemption if their home is their principal residence. A related break is the *homestead credit*, an amount subtracted from the property tax rather than from the assessed value. Ten states also allow additional exemptions or credits to older homeowners without income qualifications.

Do exemptions translate into much hard cash? Except in Alaska—where you can virtually forget property taxes once you turn 65—not really. Based on statewide average property tax rates, you'll save $204 in Hawaii ($255 if you're over 70), $54 in Illinois, $160 in Kentucky, $144 in South Carolina, and $138 in West Virginia.

Property tax exemptions can be an extra benefit in retirement, but if you're planning a move you'd do well to put other considerations such as energy cost and house prices first.

A SINGLE-HOUSE MISCELLANY

Each year, the Federal Housing Authority (FHA) reports on the characteristics of nearly 1 million single-family homes whose mortgages it insures. Here's a geography of nine of these features.

Lot Size. Imagine a house lot with 85 feet of frontage and 100 feet of depth. The 8,500 square feet it encloses is the average lot size for a resale house in the United States. Resale houses sitting on lots over half an acre (21,780 square feet) are more frequently found in Alabama, Connecticut, Georgia, Maine, New Hampshire, North Carolina, South Carolina, and Wisconsin than in the other states.

Construction and Exterior. In frame construction, the wood frame supports the floors and roof; in masonry construction, the exterior masonry wall serves as the support. Except in interior Texas, masonry construction using local stone has virtually disappeared in new houses. Concrete-block masonry construction, however, is a common technique in Arizona and Florida, where either spray-paint or stucco is used on the exterior. Everywhere else, the majority of new houses are of frame construction.

Homestead Exemptions

Fifteen states grant homestead exemptions to everyone, usually expressed as a dollar amount taken off a home's assessed value (AV).

State	Maximum Value of Exemption
Alabama	$4,000 AV on state tax, $2,000 AV on county tax
California	$7,000 "Full Cash Value"
Florida	$25,000 AV
Georgia	$2,000 AV
Hawaii	$40,000 AV
Idaho	$50,000 AV or 50 percent AV, whichever is least
Illinois	$3,500 AV ($4,500 in Cook County)
Indiana	Credit of 4 percent property tax liability
Iowa	$4,850 "Actual Value"
Louisiana	$7,500 AV
Massachusetts	20 percent of average AV (local option)
Mississippi	$5,850 AV
New Mexico	$2,000 AV
Oklahoma	$1,000 AV
Texas	$5,000 AV on school tax
Wisconsin	$9,150 "Full Value" on school tax

Ten states grant exemptions to older homeowners without any income qualification. These may be in addition to exemptions granted everyone.

State	Maximum Value of Exemption
Alaska	$150,000 AV at age 65
Hawaii	$60,000 AV at age 55; $80,000 AV at age 61; $100,000 AV at age 66; $120,000 AV at age 70
Illinois	$5,500 AV at age 65
Kentucky	$21,800 AV at age 65
Mississippi	$6,000 AV at age 65
New Jersey	$250 homestead credit at age 65
South Carolina	$20,000 "Fair Market Value" at age 65
Texas	$15,000 AV on school tax at age 65
Utah	$475 homestead credit at age 65
West Virginia	$20,000 AV at age 65

Source: ACIR, Significant Features of Fiscal Federalism, 1994.

Aluminum siding is the preferred exterior in Maryland and Ohio; cedar shingles or clapboards are the choice in Georgia, Maine, Massachusetts, New Hampshire, and Washington. Exteriors of brick or stucco are preferred in California, Louisiana, Nevada, Oklahoma, South Carolina, and Texas.

Stories. The word *story* originally referred to tiers of stained-glass or painted windows that described a special event. The common definition today is "the space between the floor and the ceiling, roof, or the floor above, in the case of a multi- story home." It has nothing to do with the height of a house; a house that appears from the outside to be two stories may actually be a single story with a cathedral ceiling. Two thirds of existing houses in this country have only one story. However, in Arizona, California, Florida, Louisiana, Mississippi, New Mexico, Oklahoma, and

Texas, single-story houses constitute more than 90 percent of resale homes. Multistory resale homes predominate in the District of Columbia, Maine, Maryland, Massachusetts, New Jersey, New York, and Pennsylvania.

Basements. The basement is an area of full-story height under the first floor not intended for year-round living. Only 15 percent of new houses have basements; they've become too expensive to excavate. In eight states, however, two out of three resale houses have a full basement, reflecting a pattern of locating the furnace below grade and a preference for extra living space. These states are Connecticut, Iowa, Maine, Massachusetts, Minnesota, Missouri, New Hampshire, and Wisconsin.

Most resale houses have no basements at all. More than two-thirds of the houses in Arizona, Florida, Louisiana, Mississippi, New Mexico, and Texas simply rest on a concrete slab poured on the ground. In Alabama, Arkansas, North Carolina, Oregon, South Carolina, and Tennessee, a majority of existing houses have a crawl space, defined as an unfinished accessible space below the first floor that is usually less than full-story height.

Bathrooms. Bathrooms are either full (a tub or shower stall, a sink, and a toilet) or half (just a sink and toilet). Just one of five resale homes have both a full bathroom and a half bathroom. In Hawaii, Mississippi, New Hampshire, New Mexico, North Carolina, and South Carolina, however, more than one-third of resale homes have both full and half bathrooms.

Garages and Carports. Garages, as everyone knows, are completely enclosed shelters for automobiles; carports are roofed shelters that aren't completely enclosed. Six out of 10 houses, new and old, have garages; one in 10 has only a carport. Only in Arizona, Hawaii, Louisiana, and Mississippi is this pattern reversed.

Fireplaces. Flueless, imitation fireplaces, like dinettes and rumpus rooms, are memories of the 1950s. Nearly half of new American homes now have a working fireplace and chimney. Resale homes with a fireplace can be found most frequently in the northern timber states of Idaho, Minnesota, Montana, Oregon, and Washington, and also in North Carolina and Pennsylvania.

Swimming Pools. You won't find new houses built on speculation with in-ground swimming pools anywhere. Builders have learned that few buyers shop for shelter *and* a swimming pool at the same time. Among resale homes, less than 2 percent have them. You're most likely to find them in Arizona, California, Nevada, and surprisingly, Maine and New York.

Enclosed Porches. A porch is a covered addition or recessed space at the entrance of a home. These Main Street lookouts have disappeared from new home markets. You'll find enclosed porches on 8 percent of resale homes in this country. In Connecticut, Iowa, Maine,

Massachusetts, New Jersey, and New York, more than 20 percent of these homes have them.

Resale Houses and New Houses

If a single, detached house is your preference, consider the pluses and minuses of resale houses versus new houses.

In most markets, resale homes are less expensive than equivalent new homes and are available in broader price ranges, with more architectural styles and locations in town. Resale homes usually have had their minor defects, often unforeseen when the home was new, corrected by the seller.

But the age of the structure may signal problems. Repairs to the roof, floor coverings, appliances, and mechanical systems, which have depreciated over the years, may be necessary during the first two years you own the house. More important, as a neighborhood matures, some homes are maintained better than others and price disparities develop, which can affect your own home's value.

New houses in new, homogeneous neighborhoods portend more rapid appreciation in value over equivalent resale houses. You can have a new house covered by an extended homeowner warranty to protect you from major structural defects. If timing permits, you also can customize the house with options and extras and have the opportunity to select colors, appliance brands, and technological features such as heating and air-conditioning systems. But the drawback to new homes in many communities is their 10 to 20 percent price premium over equivalent resale homes.

Buying a new home is more complicated, too, since many more decisions have to be made about finish details and landscaping, all of which may mean frequent site visits to confer with the builder.

Duplexes

If you're a first-time investor considering a home for rental income, a duplex (a house divided into apartments for two households) often is a better buy than a single house because of a better relation between price and income. A duplex might be bought for eight to 10 times its annual rental income, where a single house might cost 13 to 15 times what it could bring in rent.

You might consider buying a duplex, renting one of the apartments, and occupying the other yourself. This is particularly attractive in college towns. From Charlottesville, VA, to Athens, GA, to Austin, TX, college towns have more rental properties and renters than other places. Aside from the income and depreciation you would have from the rental unit, if you live alone, congenial tenants—perhaps a graduate student and family—can watch the house should you want to do some traveling. You can also trade lower rent for maintenance help.

A MOBILE-HOME MISCELLANY

According to the Census Bureau, the average age of a mobile-home owner is climbing past middle age, and persons over 60 now comprise 35 percent of the market. Mobile homes made up one-third of all new housing purchased in the United States last year. Living in one makes sense if you are on a limited budget. It also presents two major problems: (1) this type of housing depreciates in value nearly everywhere, and (2) owners are subject to sometimes arbitrary eviction from mobile-home parks.

Are Mobile Homes Investments?

Whether real estate salespeople tout houses, condos, or mobile homes, they've all learned the five factors that influence prices: quality of original construction, the neighborhood's turnover rate, supply and demand for housing, current upkeep, and location.

With these factors at work in the housing market, mobile homes, like automobiles, tend to go down in value as they get older. According to the American Institute of Real Estate Appraisers, the typical mobile home in a typical park depreciates 10 percent the first year and between 5 and 6 percent each year thereafter.

This isn't the case in all parts of the country. In seven states, all but two of them in the West, mobile homes appreciated at a modest annual rate. These states are Alaska, Arizona, California, Florida, New Jersey, Oregon, and Washington. In the central states, values kept pace with new home costs. In the eastern third of the country, however, mobile homes declined in value from the moment they were first winched onto a permanent pad.

Do mobile homes make good investments? *Yes*, if you want to live in Florida, New Jersey, Arizona, or the Pacific Coast states but can't afford to buy a house or a condo in the competitive real estate markets there. While the appreciation in mobile homes lags behind that of conventional houses, you still have some chance to make money when you sell.

Perhaps, if you have your sights set on a destination in the Rocky Mountain states, the Ozarks, northern Michigan, or Texas but can't afford conventional housing. Search carefully for a well-managed park near popular resorts or natural outdoor endowments.

No, if you're headed for the southeastern states, Pennsylvania, New York, or New England and have enough money to buy conventional housing. Mobile homes here have a history of depreciating while prices for existing site-built homes have gone up.

Tenant Rights for Mobile-Home Owners

Except in New Mexico, the Uniform Residential Landlord and Tenant Act doesn't protect mobile-home owners who rent space in a mobile-home park. In most states, a park owner can evict you for any reason. The park owner rarely gives leases and can demand sharp rent increases and a variety of costly fees once you've spent money moving your mobile home to the park. You may be forced to sell at a loss if the park owner tells you to get out and no other park has space for your home.

Twelve states have passed "just cause" laws to protect mobile-home owners from being arbitrarily evicted from parks, according to a survey by the American Mobilehome Association. Just causes for eviction include nonpayment of rent, being tried and convicted of a crime, violation of reasonable park rules, or conversion of park land to other uses. The states are:

Arizona	Oregon
California	New Jersey
Colorado	New Mexico
Florida	New York
Illinois	Utah
Nevada	Washington

A CONDO MISCELLANY

Condominiums are pushed to younger, first-time home buyers and older persons drawn to maintenance-free living at a lower cost, often in adults-only developments.

Ten Negatives

The complaints reported by the Urban Land Institute 30 years ago in an extensive survey of condominium residents are still being raised today. Among them are:

- noisy children and undesirable neighbors
- pets
- parking problems
- poor association management
- ticky-tacky construction
- dishonest salespeople
- renters in other units
- thin party walls
- long rows of identically designed houses
- unneeded and overpromoted recreation facilities

If you are thinking of condominium living, these complaints are a guide to judging condominium developments. Ask questions of the association and the broker. What are the restrictions on pets? Children? How are they enforced? Does each unit have an assigned parking space? Are there rules in the association's bylaws limiting the number of rental units? What is the average tenure of the unit owners? Of the renters? Are any units set aside for time shares? Is their number restricted?

As a retired person, you are one of the two major targets of condominium marketing. The other is the young person or family buying their first home. Both groups want lower costs, freedom from house and yard maintenance in a ready-made environment, social life, and recreation facilities, all with the tax advantages of ownership. There isn't any reason the two groups can't live together harmoniously in the same development. In well-managed condominiums they do. But in other developments, the mix can prove unhappy.

Legal Protection for Condo Buyers

Twelve states recognize that consumers have little protection when they buy a condominium and have passed laws modeled after the Uniform Condominium Act (1980) drawn up by the National Conference of Commissioners on Uniform State Laws. They are:

Maine	North Carolina
Minnesota	Pennsylvania
Missouri	Rhode Island
Nebraska	Texas
New Hampshire	Virginia
New Mexico	Washington

The act covers owners' associations, developers' activities, eminent domain, separate titles and taxation, and safeguards for condominium buyers. Among its provisions are:

- The developer must provide you with a Public Offering Statement, accurately and fully disclosing a schedule for completion of all construction, the total number of condominium units, the bylaws of the owners' association, copies of any contracts or leases that you must sign, a current balance sheet and projected one-year budget for the owners' association, and a statement of the monthly common assessments you'll have to pay.
- After signing a purchase agreement, you still have 15 days to cool off, after which you can either cancel the agreement without penalty or accept conveyance of the property.
- If you buy a condominium without first being given the Public Offering Statement, you are entitled to receive from the developer an amount equal to 10 percent of the sales price of the unit you bought.
- The developer and real estate agent must guarantee that the unit you are buying is free from defective materials, is built according to sound engineering and construction standards, and conforms to local codes.

CAVEAT EMPTOR: SUBDIVISION LOTS

Every year real estate developers ring up billions of dollars in interstate land sales. During the 1970s, one of the results of this lucrative business was to leave 1 million Americans with real estate they didn't want and couldn't sell. Many of these buyers who found themselves holding title to swampland or desert were older adults looking for a spot to put up a vacation home or permanent residence.

Buying out-of-state land is always risky, especially if you don't visit the property. Even if you do see the homesite before buying, it may be very difficult to be sure the developer will actually follow through on promised amenities. The slick promotional brochure will describe golf courses, landscaped parks, swimming pools, clubhouses, and marinas, but any promise not clearly outlined in the sales contract isn't enforceable. What you consider to be a sound investment may turn out to be no more of a sure thing than your prospects at the $2 window at the track.

A Land Buyer's Rights

Federal legislation amended in 1984 to protect the land buyer applies to brokers and developers who subdivide land into 100 or more lots and sell or advertise them in more than one state. Some of the provisions are:

- The buyer has seven calendar days to back out of any sales agreement. A legal or legitimate reason isn't necessary for cancellation.
- A buyer who fails to receive a property report before signing a purchase agreement may cancel the agreement up to two years from the time of signing.
- A buyer who doesn't receive a warranty deed within 180 days of signing a purchase agreement may, in most cases, cancel the agreement.
- Buyers who legally revoke their contracts are entitled to a refund.
- For a period up to three years after signing the purchase contract, the buyer may sue the seller if the developer:
  Sells property without giving the property report to the buyer before contract signing.
  Sells any property when the property report contains any false facts or omits a material fact.
  Distributes promotional material inconsistent with material in the property report.

A RENTER'S MISCELLANY

The kind of apartment building you choose to live in makes a difference in your monthly costs. In larger cities and in college towns where apartments are a big part of the housing mix, rents for a typical four-room, 850-square-foot unit are higher in high-rise elevator buildings (U.S. average: $650) than in walkups or elevator buildings of three stories or fewer (U.S. average: $540), according to the current Institute of Real Estate Management survey. The least expensive kind of building is the garden apartment, defined as a group of low-rise apartment buildings on a large landscaped lot under one manager. The national monthly rental for this kind of building is $485.

You'll find tenant turnover rates, defined as newly occupied apartments as a percentage of all the apartments in the building during the previous year, also vary by the kind of building. High-rise elevator buildings have the lowest turnover (U.S. average: 39 percent), whereas the turnover rate in walk-ups and elevator buildings of three or fewer stories is half again that rate (U.S. average: 57 percent). The kind of apartment building with the most transient population is the garden apartment, in which 63 percent of the tenants moved in within the previous 12 months.

Search out NORCs

While over 1 million people live in planned retirement developments, even more live in Naturally Occurring Retirement Communities.

NORCs, as they are called by architects and planners, are usually apartment neighborhoods that attract older people by word-of-mouth because of their safety and convenience, and because landlords keep the properties in tip-top shape. NORCs are age-integrated since the original tenants were younger and, over time, came to be outnumbered by older tenants.

NORCs aren't considered retirement communities by their own residents or landlords. For their part, NORC landlords wish to encourage the trend: tenants are long-term and stable, dependable in paying rent, and generally cause less wear and tear on the property. Vacated apartments do not remain unrented nearly as long in NORCs as they do in other complexes. Attractive housing for older people is attractive to younger people as well, though the reverse isn't necessarily true.

The Rule of 156

When fine old apartment buildings were being converted to condominiums during the 1970s, one way of determining a fair price for tenants who had first option to buy was to multiply their last month's rent by 156. Buying an apartment that rented for $600 a month, for example, would cost $93,600.

It can work in reverse. To estimate rent for a house or a condominium, divide its market value by 156. Using this rule plus the prices of houses given in the Place Profiles, it isn't difficult to figure roughly what it would cost you to rent a house in a given area, assuming that the landlord has realistic expectations for the rate of return on property.

In Maui, the rent would be about $1,700; in Cape Cod, $1,350; in Hot Springs, Arkansas, $485. The rule of 156 may seem unfair to landlords, since there is only an 8 percent return from which maintenance and taxes must be paid. Bear in mind, however, that landlords rarely buy houses for the rental income they may bring;

rather, they buy them for their market appreciation and rent them during the interim to cover expenses.

Renters' Legal Rights

Twenty states have passed landlord-tenant laws based on the Uniform Residential Landlord and Tenant Act (1972), a model law drawn by the National Conference of Commissioners on Uniform State Laws. These states are:

Alaska	Montana
Arizona	Nebraska
Connecticut	New Mexico
Florida	Oklahoma
Hawaii	Oregon
Iowa	Rhode Island
Kansas	South Carolina
Kentucky	Tennessee
Michigan	Virginia
Mississippi	Washington

The landlord-tenant act defines rights and obligations of both parties to a lease on an apartment house, and it also specifies the way disputes can be resolved. Among its provisions are:

- If your dispute with a landlord leads you to complain to the local housing board, join a tenants' group, or bring suit against the landlord, your landlord may not retaliate by cutting services, raising your rent, or evicting you.
- If the landlord doesn't make needed repairs, and the cost of the repairs isn't more than $100 or half the rent, whichever is greater, you may make repairs and deduct the expense from your monthly rent.
- After you vacate the apartment or house, any money you've deposited as security must be returned. If there are any deductions from the deposit for damages or other reasons, these deductions must be itemized.
- If the landlord doesn't live up to the terms of the lease, you may recover damages in small claims court.

YOUR $125,000 DECISION

Prior to 1987, capital gains were taxed up to a maximum of 20 percent. Capital gains are now treated as ordinary income. Your home is a capital asset; if you sell it at a profit, your capital gains are taxable in the year you sell. A loss on the sale, however, isn't deductible.

There are two exceptions to this rule that can help you put off the payment of taxes or eliminate them altogether: the "rollover" available to sellers of any age and the one-time exclusion, which can be taken advantage of only by sellers 55 and over.

The Rollover. If you sell your house at a profit, the tax on the profit may be postponed if, within two years from the date you sell, you buy another house and pay as much or more than the sale price of your old house. This time limit works forward and backward: you can buy the new house as long as 24 months before or 24 months after you sell your old house. If you anticipate retiring, this rule allows you to buy a vacation home up to two years before you sell your principal residence and claim the rollover when you move into the vacation home for full-time living.

If the price of your new home is less than the sale price of your old one, part of the profit will be taxable during the year. The profit will also be taxable during the year in which you sold in the event that you don't buy a new principal residence but instead rent an apartment or house.

The rollover can be used over and over again until the day you sell your home and don't buy another. When that happens, the taxes are due on all the accumulated profits realized in all your principal residences sold over prior years. That is an ideal time to claim the one-time exclusion.

The Exclusion. If either you or your spouse are 55 by the day you sell your home at a profit, and you've owned and used the home as your principal residence for at least three of the five years ending on the day the property is sold, you can elect to exclude up to $125,000 of profit from tax altogether ($62,500 for married persons filing separately).

The exclusion can be claimed only once, so don't use it to shelter a paltry gain if you anticipate an even larger gain later on. Also, if you sell your house and buy another, you can postpone all or part of your gain anyway. If you take the exemption and later wish you hadn't, you can revoke your decision within three years after filing your return for the year the sale occurred or within two years of the time the tax for that year was paid, whichever is later.

Remember, too, that once the exclusion is claimed by a married couple, it cannot be claimed again by either spouse. Divorced or widowed persons who jointly used the exemption with their previous spouses are branded for life in the eyes of the IRS.

HOME-EQUITY CONVERSION: LIVING ON THE HOUSE

If you're over 65 and own a home, you're likely to possess an asset that has appreciated dramatically over the years. Economists put the total value of homes owned by people over 65 in the United States at more than $1 trillion.

Home-equity conversion, or reverse-equity plans, are designed to help older house-rich and cash-poor homeowners unlock the value of their home and convert it into additional retirement income without being forced to move. Unlike common home-equity loans available to most homeowners, you don't have to show sufficient monthly income for a commercial bank's

---

Mortgage Taxes

When a home is sold, most states collect a tax from the seller to cover the cost of recording the deed changes. In nine states, a tax on the mortgage is collected from the buyer. While most of these states grant exemptions, taking out a $100,000 mortgage can mean paying a tax ranging from $1,000 in New York ($2,000 in New York City) to $100 in Oklahoma.

Alabama	0.15%
California	0.11
Florida	0.35
Kansas	0.26
Minnesota	0.23
New York	1.00
Oklahoma	0.10
Tennessee	0.115
Virginia	0.15

Source: ACIR, *Significant Features of Fiscal Federalism*, 1994.

---

approval. Some plans involve actual transfer of title to the property; others do not. Some provide income for only a specified period; others provide income for life.

Deciding which plan is best takes careful thought; interested homeowners should seek the advice of an attorney for help in weighing the benefits and liabilities of specific plans. The following are three major variations:

A **Reverse Appreciation Mortgage** (RAM) is a loan paid out in monthly installments to the homeowner by a lender, thereby creating a debt (hence the word mortgage) that increases each month. The house must be free of mortgage or lien, since the amount of the loan is determined by the price the home would fetch if the property were put up for sale. The loan comes due at the end of the term or when the owner dies or decides to sell the property. The RAM is repaid out of money from the sale of the house or from other resources.

A **sale-leaseback** lets you stay in your home for the rest of your life as long as you're physically able. You sell your house to an investor who leases the property back to you at a fixed rent for as long as you can or want to live in the house. You receive a down payment and a monthly mortgage payment from the investor, who is responsible for taxes, maintenance, and insurance on the property. The investor takes full possession of the property when you choose to move out of the house or in the event of your death.

Deferred payment loans are home-improvement loans offered most often by city governments or neighborhood housing service agencies. They are

Property Tax Deferrals

Older persons can legally postpone payment of all or part of their property taxes. In property tax deferral programs, the state pays the tax for the owner and puts a lien on the property, secured by its sale value. Generally, below market interest is charged each year on the amount postponed. The tax-deferral loan comes due when the home is sold, given away, or when the owner dies, in which case the heirs or estate must pay what's due.

To be eligible, you usually have to be over 65, though in some cases the minimum age is lower or there is none. Most of the programs also have a limit on how much income you can earn, ranging from $14,000 to $32,000. Some programs have no income limit. Deferral programs function statewide in:

State	Contact
California	State Controller's Office
Illinois	County Treasurer's Office
Maine	State Department of Revenue
Oregon	County Assessor's Office
Washington	County Assessor's Office
Wisconsin	State Department of Revenue

Local-option programs are also available in nine other states: Colorado, Connecticut, Florida, Georgia, Massachusetts, New Hampshire, Texas, Utah, and Virginia.

generally open to all ages and charge low or no interest. The loan comes due when the owner dies or sells the property. In either case, the deferred loan is then paid out of cash from the sale of the house or at the estate settlement.

NUCLEAR HOT SPOTS

Would you mind living near a nuclear power plant? Given the record of the industry after 1,000 reactor years of commercial operation in this country, even proponents of nuclear power would admit that fears about a catastrophic meltdown or low-level environmental contamination are legitimate.

Because of a lower demand for electricity, construction and regulatory delays, skyrocketing costs, and concerns about reactor safety after the Three Mile Island and Chernobyl incidents, the growth of nuclear power has slowed considerably. Utility planners are simply unwilling to take the risk of investing billions in a 12- to 14-year process of building a nuclear plant and then face the possibility of not being allowed to operate it. As a result, plans for 76 power plants have been canceled over the past decade, and not one nuclear plant has been ordered since 1978.

Alabama: 7,377 megawatts total capacity. *Houston County*: Farley #1 (1977), Farley #2 (1981). *Jackson County*: Bellefonte #2 (indefinite), Belle-

fonte #1 (indefinite). *Morgan County*: Browns Ferry #1 (1974), Browns Ferry #2 (1975), Browns Ferry #3 (1977).

Arizona: 3,810 megawatts total capacity. *Maricopa County*: Palo Verde #1 (1986), Palo Verde #2 (1986), Palo Verde #3 (1988).

Arkansas: 1,694 megawatts total capacity. *Pope County*: Arkansas Nuclear #1 (1974), Arkansas Nuclear #2 (1980).

California: 5,694 megawatts total capacity. *San Diego County*: San Onofre #2 (1983), San Onofre #3 (1984). *San Luis Obispo County*: Diablo Canyon #1 (1985), Diablo Canyon #2 (1986).

Connecticut: 3,262 megawatts total capacity. *Middlesex County*: Haddam Neck (1968). *New London County*: Millstone #1 (1970), Millstone #2 (1975), Millstone #3 (1986).

Florida: 3,846 megawatts total capacity. *Citrus County*: Crystal River #3 (1977). *Dade County*: Turkey Point #3 (1972), Turkey Point #4 (1973). *St. Lucie County*: St. Lucie #1 (1976), St. Lucie #2 (1983).

Georgia: 3,758 megawatts total capacity. *Appling County*: Edwin I. Hatch #1 (1975), Edwin I. Hatch #2 (1979). *Burke County*: Vogtle #1 (1987), Vogtle #2 (1989).

Illinois: 12,815 megawatts total capacity. *Byron County*: Byron #1 (1985), Byron #2 (1987). *De Witt County*: Clinton (1987). *Grundy County*: Dresden #2 (1970), Dresden #3 (1971). *La Salle County*: La Salle #1 (1984), La Salle #2 (1984). *Lake County*: Zion #1 (1973), Zion #2 (1974). *Rock Island County*: Quad Cities #1 (1972), Quad Cities #2 (1972). *Will County*: Braidwood #1 (1988), Braidwood #2 (1988).

Iowa: 565 megawatts total capacity. *Linn County*: Duane Arnold (1975).

Kansas: 1,150 megawatts total capacity. *Coffee County*: Wolf Creek (1985).

Louisiana: 2,015 megawatts total capacity. *St. Charles Parish*: Waterford #3 (1985). *West Feliciana Parish*: River Bend (1986).

Maine: 840 megawatts total capacity. *Lincoln County*: Maine Yankee (1972).

Maryland: 1,650 megawatts total capacity. *Calvert County*: Calvert Cliffs #1 (1975), Calvert Cliffs #2 (1977).

Massachusetts: 545 megawatts total capacity. *Plymouth County*: Pilgrim (1972).

Michigan: 4,009 megawatts total capacity. *Berrien County*: Donald Cook #1 (1975), Donald Cook #2 (1978). *Charlevoix County*: Big Rock Point (1965). *Monroe County*: Fermi #2 (1988). *Van Buren County*: Palisades (1971).

Minnesota: 1,605 megawatts total capacity. *Goodhue County*: Prairie Island #1 (1973), Prairie Island #2 (1974). *Wright County*: Monticello (1971).

Nuclear Power Plants in the United States

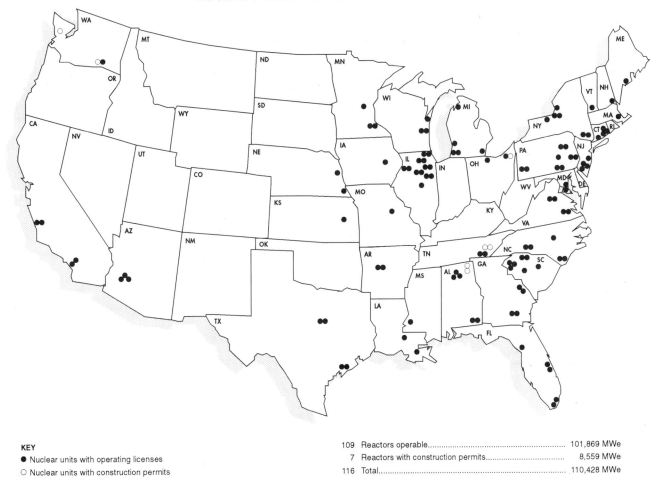

KEY
- ● Nuclear units with operating licenses
- ○ Nuclear units with construction permits

109	Reactors operable..	101,869 MWe
7	Reactors with construction permits..................................	8,559 MWe
116	Total..	110,428 MWe

Mississippi: 1,250 megawatts total capacity. *Claiborne County*: Grand Gulf (1985).

Missouri: 1,150 megawatts total capacity. *Callaway County*: Callaway (1984).

Nebraska: 1,252 megawatts total capacity. *Namaha County*: Cooper (1974). *Washington County*: Fort Calhoun #1 (1973).

New Hampshire: 650 megawatts total capacity. *Rockingham County*: Seabrook (1990).

New Jersey: 3,947 megawatts total capacity. *Ocean County*: Oyster Creek (1969). *Salem County*: Salem #1 (1977), Salem #2 (1981), Hope Creek (1986).

New York: 4,911 megawatts total capacity. *Oswego County*: Nine Mile Point #1 (1969), Nine Mile Point #2 (1988). *Suffolk County*: Fitzpatrick (1975). *Wayne County*: Ginna (1970). *Westchester County*: Indian Point #2 (1973), Indian Point #3 (1976).

North Carolina: 4,698 megawatts total capacity. *Brunswick County*: Brunswick #1 (1977), Brunswick #2 (1975). *Mecklenburg County*: William McGuire #1 (1981), William McGuire #2 (1984). *Wake County*: Shearon Harris (1987).

Ohio: 3,259 megawatts total capacity. *Lake County*: Perry #1 (1987), Perry #2 (indefinite). *Ottawa County*: Davis-Besse (1977).

Pennsylvania: 8,009 megawatts total capacity. *Beaver County*: Beaver Valley #1 (1976), Beaver Valley #2 (1987). *Dauphin County*: Three Mile Island (1974). *Luzerne County*: Susquehanna #1 (1983), Susquehanna #2 (1985). *Montgomery County*: Limerick #1 (1986), Limerick #2 (1990). *York County*: Peach Bottom #2 (1974), Peach Bottom #3 (1974).

South Carolina: 6,435 megawatts total capacity. *Darlington County*: H.B. Robinson #2 (1971). *Fairfield County*: Summer (1984). *Oconee County*: Oconee #1 (1973), Oconee #2 (1973), Oconee #3 (1974). *York County*: Catawba (1986).

Tennessee: 4,650 megawatts total capacity. *Hamilton County*: Sequoyah #1 (1981), Sequoyah #2 (1982). *Rhea County*: Watts Bar #1 (indefinite), Watts Bar #2 (indefinite).

Texas: 4,800 megawatts total capacity. *Matagorda County*: South Texas Project #1 (1988), South Texas Project #2 (1989). *Somervell County*: Comanche Peak #1 (1990), Comanche Peak #2 (1993).

Vermont: 504 megawatts total capacity. *Windham County*: Vermont Yankee (1972).

Virginia: 3,414 megawatts total capacity. *Louisa County*: North Anna #1 (1978), North Anna #2 (1980). *Surry County*: Surry #1 (1972), Surry #2 (1973).

Washington: 1,000 megawatts total capacity. *Benton County*: WPPSS #2 (1984).

Wisconsin: 1,505 megawatts total capacity. *Kewaunee County*: Kewaunee (1974). *Manitowoc County*: Point Beach #1 (1970), Point Beach #2 (1972).

CLIMATE

"The fortunate people of the planet," John Kenneth Galbraith once wrote, "are those who live by the seasons. There is far more difference between a Vermont farm in the summer and that farm in the winter than there is between San Diego and São Paulo. This means that people who live where the seasons are good and strong have no need to travel; they can stay at home and let change come to them. This simple truth will one day be recognized and then we will see a great reverse migration from Florida to Maine and on into Quebec."

That might cause many white-shoed Sun Belt real estate promoters to sit up and say "Huh?" They can relax, however. Demographers forecast the march to the sun will continue well into the next century.

What else is new? Americans say they prefer a mild, sunny climate. When asked where in the country these climates are, they point to the fast-growing lower half of the Pacific Coast, the Desert Southwest, Florida, and 1anywhere along the South Atlantic and Gulf coasts. This area, between 25 and 35 degrees latitude, has been drawing older adults for decades.

But other places north of the Mason-Dixon line and hundreds of miles inland from beaches are drawing older adults. Many of these locations see mild climates, too. Some of their names might surprise you.

What has always been surprising is the variety of global climates found right here at home. Northern maritime, mild Mediterranean, southerly mountain, desert, tropical "paradise," desert highland, rugged northern continental, windward slope, leeward slope, and humid subtropical climates—you name it, you'll meet up with it somewhere in the United States.

Climate can't be bought, built, remodeled, or relocated. A place's climate is there for keeps, and the weather events that make up a place's climate—rain, snow, heat, cold, drought, wind—will have a profound effect on the rest of your life.

FACTORS TO KEEP IN MIND

If you can live anywhere you wish and are open to all the variety this country offers, know that a combination of water, latitude and longitude, elevation, prevailing winds, mountains, and urban development lies behind any area's climate.

Water, particularly an ocean, takes the edge off temperature. It warms up slowly, holds much more heat than land, and cools more slowly. Places on the water tend to be cooler in summer and warmer in winter than others away from water. The hottest it gets in July on the Santa Monica Pier in Los Angeles is 75°F; meanwhile, 15 miles north in the San Fernando Valley, it's 95°F.

Golfers in the suburbs west of Boston store their clubs from Thanksgiving until the onset of Spring. Golfers 45 miles southeast on Cape Cod, with ocean on three sides, can play almost all year 'round.

Places located in the country's heartland see wide swings of temperature. These continental climates tend to be even more rigorous in the higher *latitudes.* The closer to the poles you get, the more exaggerated are the seasonal shifts because polar and very northerly locations undergo the greatest seasonal variation in the amount and intensity of sunlight. In Fairbanks, Alaska, for example, the average day in December is only 4 hours long. In late June, the day lengthens to 18 hours and the sun's heat is intense. Places in the North and Far North, then, experience Siberian winters and sun-baked summers.

Though some medical studies show reduced odds of heart disease and cancer the higher one lives above sea level, a higher *elevation* can have the same negative effect on comfort as a higher latitude. Each 1,000 feet above sea level lowers a thermometer reading by 3.3°F. In New Mexico, for example, there is a difference of just 3°F in annual average temperature between Clayton and Lordsburg, two places with similar elevations. But Clayton is on the edge of the plains, while Lordsburg is 440 miles southwest in high desert. On the other hand, at two weather stations just 15 miles apart, but differing in elevation by 4,700 feet, the average annual temperatures differ by 16°F.

To understand how *prevailing winds* influence climate, consider a pair of places 3,200 miles apart: Bellingham, Washington, and Bar Harbor, Maine. Both sit high in northern latitudes on their respective coasts. Both peek through some of the foggiest mornings in the United States. You'd naturally suppose the two have similar climates. But Bellingham is milder because of the winds that blow from west to east across the continent. The West Coast is a landfall for air that has moved thousands of miles over water; even cities far inland still feel some of the beneficial effects of the Pacific winds. Interior cities in the east feel few consequences of the Atlantic save on those rare occasions when the prevailing wind direction turns. Sad to say, this reversal of wind direction often means a storm.

Mountains deflect and channel winds, rain, and snow. Mountain people aren't relating folk tales when they tell visitors that the weather on one side of a mountain range is radically different from that on the other. In winter, the Great Divide shields Colorado Springs from much of the Arctic air that moves down the continent. In summer, the hidden, windward side of the city's mountain vista is a lush, evergreen parkland at lower elevations; the leeward side where the city sits is a semi-arid steppe descending to dry, shortgrass prairie.

Finally, *urban development* makes heat islands with-in the surrounding countryside. Phoenix–Mesa–Scottsdale now has night temperatures 8°F warmer than they were 50 years ago when the area was a small cowtown and winter resort. Population here has increased 12-fold. Concrete and asphalt stores the sun's radiant energy better than desert sand ever did, and automobile pollution is trapped overhead in a high-pressure cell. In general, wind speed, visibility, sunshine, and heating needs are less in the center of cities than in the nearby country, but temperature, cloudiness, thunderstorm frequency, and air pollution levels are higher.

MAJOR CLIMATE REGIONS

Mountains indeed mark the major climate regions of the United States. The Pacific Coast is quite mild, the northern portion of the Great Interior quite rigorous. The Great Basin lying between the Cascade–Sierra Nevada range to the west and the Rocky Mountains to the east is noted for dryness. Some of the best climates for variety and mildness are found in the southern portion of this area. The southern half of the Appalachian Mountains also offers climates both mild and variable.

Most Americans live in the large climatic zone that includes the Great Plains and Central Lowlands regions. Ironically, this zone also happens to be the least desirable for human comfort. Those who live in its northern part are hit by severe winters and hot, humid summers with springs and autumns that are all too short. In the southern portion, winters are milder and springs and autumns are longer, but the steam-bath summers are uncomfortable.

The climate of the East Coast is similar to that of the Great Interior, but milder and somewhat damper. Right on the coast, winters are milder and summers noticeably cooler. Several retirement places with excellent climates are here, notably New Jersey's Cape May and Ocean counties, Ocean City in Maryland, and Rehoboth Bay–Indian River Bay in southern Delaware.

The high country that includes the Rockies, the Cascades, the Sierra Nevadas, and the northern half of the Appalachians is home to resort areas owing to the cool, crisp, sunny summers with cold nights, and winters that provide plenty of snow for outdoor sports. Several places in the valleys are popular with older adults who prefer a stimulating yet not too mild climate.

Hawaii is the only state situated in the tropical zone, officially defined as any area where temperatures don't drop below 64°F. These islands experience small temperature changes, with summer averaging only 4° to 8°F higher than winter. Moisture-bearing trade winds from over the Pacific provide a system of natural ventilation for the heat associated with these tropical climates.

Climate Regions of the United States

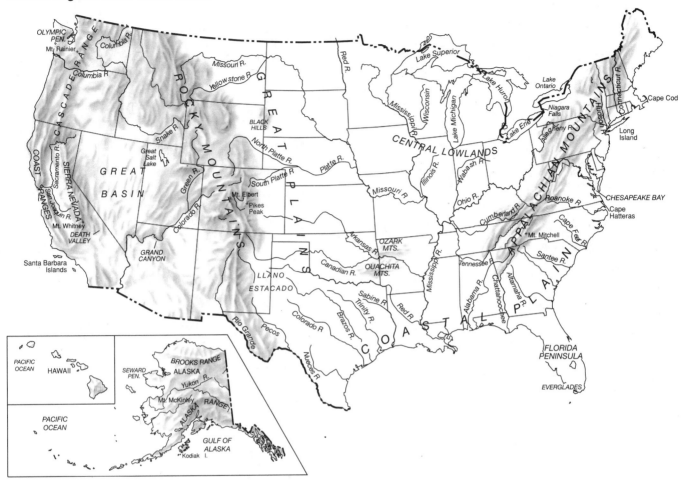

SO, WHAT'S COMFORTABLE?

Mop the sweat from pulling a balky lawnmower's starter cord a dozen times on a July afternoon, hack away at the ice on the car's windshield one morning in January, or look out the window on any wet and gray day and you're forgiven for fantasizing about a place where it's never hot or cold and always bright.

It is a fantasy, indeed. Not only would you likely get bored with an endless sequence of identically dry, sunny days with tepid temperatures, you'd also find that none of the places profiled here have climates that match this pattern 365 days a year.

Temperature

Beware of chamber of commerce blandishments about a place's annual average temperature. San Francisco's is 57°F. So is St. Louis's. But San Francisco enjoys both a diurnal (24-hour) temperature range of 12°F and an annual range (the difference between January's and July's average temperatures) of 12°F. St. Louis has a diurnal range of 17°F and an annual range of 47°F. The temperature swings in these two cities highlight the difference between a marine climate and a continental

climate. San Francisco's climate is somewhat cool and remarkably stable year 'round. St. Louis's is neither.

Among retirement regions, the greatest annual temperature ranges (up to 77°F) are found in the North Woods, the Rocky Mountains, and northern parts of New England. The greatest diurnal temperature swings (up to 40°F) are in high desert parts of the Rio Grande and Desert Southwest regions. The smallest diurnal and annual temperature swings are in Hawaii and along the Pacific Coast.

Humidity

After air temperature, humidity is the major factor in climatic comfort. Anyone who has sweated out a hot, humid summer knows humidity heightens heat. In hot, humid climates, heat is retained in the damp air even after the sunset, resulting in nights that are almost as hot as the days.

Wind Chill

Wind chill is the same thing as heat loss. Anyone who has turned their face away from a stiff winter blow

Cloudy Places

A day is *clear* if clouds form less than 30 percent of the daytime sky, *partly cloudy* if they form 40 to 70 percent of it, and *cloudy* if they form more than 80 percent. Some spots see cloudiness two out of every three of their days.

	Cloudy Days
Brookings–Gold Beach, OR	239
Florence, OR	239
Newport–Lincoln City, OR	239
Bellingham, WA	229
Port Angeles–Seqium, WA	229
Port Townsend, WA	229
San Juan Islands, WA	229
Whidbey Island, WA	227
Polson–Mission Valley, MT	213
Kalispell–Flathead Valley, MT	213
Charlevoix–Boyne City–East Jordan, MI	210
Petoskey–Harbor Springs, MI	210
Traverse City, MI	210
Hamilton–Bitterroot Valley, MT	208
Burlington, VT	206

Source: NOAA, *Local Climatological Data.* Some of the above figures come from the nearest "First Order" station.

Foggy Places

Fog is a cloud that touches the ground. A day of fog is defined as one on which thick fog—less than half a mile visibility—occurred once during the day.

Bellingham, WA	90 days
San Juan Islands, WA	90
Port Townsend, WA	90
Port Angeles–Seqium, WA	90
Asheville, NC	78
Blairsville, GA	78
Boone–Blowing Rock, NC	78
Brevard, NC	78
Clayton, GA	78
Hendersonville–East Flat Rock, NC	78
Hiawassee, GA	78

Source: NOAA, *Local Climatological Data.* Some of the above figures come from the nearest "First Order" station.

Snowy Places

Most locations profiled in these pages see less than six inches of snow, and 50 of these experience not even a trace. Below are 13, however, that get more than six feet in a normal year.

	Average Snowfall
McCall–Cascade–Payette Valley, ID	159 inches
Pagosa Springs, CO	119
Charlevoix–Boyne City–East Jordan, MI	96
Sandpoint–Priest River, ID	91
Petoskey–Harbor Springs, MI	90
Traverse City, MI	90
Woodstock, VT	90
St. Jay–Northeast Kingdom, VT	88
Hanover, NH	78
Bar Harbor, ME	76
Burlington, VT	76
Houghton Lake, MI	76
Durango, CO	75

Source: NOAA, *Climatography of the United States.*

Damp Places

In Florida, cars can be sponged clean using nothing more than the heavy morning dew. Mushrooms on the Pacific Northwest coast get enormous quickly.

	Humidity
Brookings–Gold Beach, OR	75%
Florence, OR	75
Newport–Lincoln City, OR	75
Port Angeles–Seqium, WA	74
Port Townsend, WA	74
Maui, HI	72
Bellingham, WA	70
San Juan Islands, WA	70
Whidbey Island, WA	70
Key West–Key Largo–Marathon, FL	67
Petoskey–Harbor Springs, MI	67
Traverse City, MI	67
Kauai, HI	67

Source: NOAA, *Local Climatological Data.* Figures are annual averages nearest to 12 noon. Some of the above figures come from the nearest "First Order" station.

Dry Places

In some places with low humidities, it's cheaper and more efficient to cool interiors with evaporative air conditioners (swamp coolers) rather than the more expensive refrigerated air conditioners.

	Humidity
Las Vegas, NV	24%
Pahrump Valley, NV	24
St. George–Zion, UT	24
Tucson, AZ	30
Wickenburg, AZ	31
Hesperia–Apple Valley–Victorville, CA	32
Kingman, AZ	32
Lake Havasu City, AZ	32
Palm Springs–Coachella Valley, CA	32
Phoenix–Mesa–Scottsdale, AZ	32
Riviera–Bullhead City, AZ	32
Yuma, AZ	32

Source: NOAA, *Local Climatological Data.* Figures are annual averages nearest to 12 noon. Some of the above figures come from the nearest "First Order" station.

swears to this. When the wind rises over five miles per hour and the thermometer reads 45°F or less, you'll start to feel temperatures on exposed skin colder than still air.

Again You Wonder, "What's Comfortable?"

Is searching for the ideal year-round retirement climate merely an illusion, much like the quest for perfect health, an honest man, or the Holy Grail?

Perhaps it is. Thousands of retired persons living in Florida vacate during the Sunshine State's summers for a cottage on the Jersey Shore, the New England Coast, or a cabin in the southern Appalachians. Thousands of others shun the broiling Desert Southwest summers for Sierra or Rocky Mountain foothills. Still others, absolutely bored by the unvarying paradise-like climate in the Virgin Islands or Hawaii, head back to the mainland in search of four-season weather.

This migration isn't exclusively American. Older

adults from northern Europe who live in Spain, southern Italy, Greece, or North Africa routinely pack up and return to their native country for a summer climate that's milder than the one on the Mediterranean coast.

Having acknowledged this, it is still possible to rate places that approach a climatic ideal by pointing to conditions that detract from maximum comfort. Please read on.

 GRADING: Climate

Mild won't always mean a winterless, perpetually Mediterranean climate; it is simply the absence of great variations or extremes of temperature. As we get older, we tend to be better off in comfortable, stable weather conditions than we are in climates that make large physiological demands and where radical weather changes come on quickly.

Winter Mildness

To grade how mild winters are, two measures are weighted equally: (1) *winter severity*, or the average apparent temperature from November through April, and (2) *winter length*, or the number of days during these months when the temperature falls below freezing.

Winter severity is scaled against a standard where 0°F gets a 0, and 55°F gets 100. Note that apparent temperatures during this period are influenced by wind chill.

Winter length is scaled against a standard where 365 freezing days throughout the year gets a 0, and no freezing days receives a perfect 100.

Summer Mildness

To grade how mild the summers are, two things get the same weight: (1) *summer severity*, or the average apparent temperature from May through October, and (2) *summer length*, or the number of 90°F days that would feel like they were 95°F, if relative humidity were taken into account.

Summer severity is scaled against a standard where 95°F gets a 0, and 55°F gets 100. Note that apparent temperatures during this period are influenced by relative humidity.

Summer length is scaled against a standard where 365 95°F days a year gets 0, and no 95°F days receives a perfect 100.

Hazardousness

Because they are predictable from decades of weather records, snow and thunderstorms are normal, if inconvenient weather events in retirement places. To grade for relative freedom from these hazards, *Retirement Places Rated* weights snow twice as heavily as thunderstorms. The result is scaled against a standard where no snow and no thunderstorms gets 100, and three times the annual average snow and storm days for the retirement places gets a 0.

Seasonal Affect

To grade the weather's psychological influence, the number of cloudy (more than 80 percent cloud cover) and wet (precipitation greater than 0.1 of an inch) days are weighted twice as heavily as the number of fog (visibility less than one-half mile) days.

The result is scaled against a standard where no foggy, wet, or cloudy days gets a perfect 100, and year-round fog, precipitation, and cloudiness gets a 0.

 RANKINGS: Climate

A place's overall grade for climate comes from averaging four broad factors: (1) *winter mildness*, (2) *summer mildness*, (3) *hazardousness*, and (4) *seasonal affect*.

Grades are rounded two decimal places. Locations with tie grades get the same rank and are listed alphabetically.

Retirement Places from First to Last

Rank	Grade
1. Carmel–Monterey–Pebble Beach, CA	94.39
2. Santa Barbara, CA	92.97
3. San Luis Obispo, CA	92.78
4. Laguna Beach–Dana Point, CA	92.75
5. San Diego, CA	91.39
6. Brookings–Gold Beach, OR	89.42
7. Santa Rosa–Sonoma, CA	88.37
8. Florence, OR	88.21
9. Newport–Lincoln City, OR	87.99
10. Kauai, HI	87.21
11. Port Angeles–Seqium, WA	86.50
12. Maui, HI	86.25
13. San Juan Islands, WA	85.99
14. Whidbey Island, WA	85.85
15. Port Townsend, WA	85.75
16. Paradise–Magalia, CA	84.61
17. Bellingham, WA	82.76
18. Placerville–Shingle Springs, CA	81.60
19. Alpine–Big Bend, TX	81.56
20. Dare Outer Banks, NC	81.52
21. Grants Pass, OR	81.39
22. Hesperia–Apple Valley–Victorville, CA	81.37
23. Sonora–Groveland–Twain Harte, CA	81.25
24. Kingman, AZ	80.69
25. Redding, CA	80.43
26. Myrtle Beach, SC	80.42
27. Pahrump Valley, NV	80.19
28. Southport–Brunswick Islands, NC	80.09
29. Amador County, CA	79.65
29. Hilton Head Island, SC	79.65
31. St. Simons–Jekyll Islands, GA	79.60
32. Oakhurst–Coarsegold, CA	79.56
33. Medford–Ashland, OR	79.44
34. Grass Valley–Nevada City, CA	78.98
35. Edenton, NC	78.94
36. Silver City, NM	78.92
37. Beaufort, SC	78.86
38. Las Vegas, NV	78.84
39. Panama City, FL	78.71
40. Rockport–Aransas Pass, TX	78.66
41. Lower Cape May, NJ	78.57
42. Charleston Sea Islands, SC	78.56
43. Virginia Beach, VA	78.50
44. Fredericksburg, TX	78.46
45. Mission–McAllen–Alamo, TX	78.40
46. Palm Springs–Coachella Valley, CA	78.33
47. Lake Buchanan–Lake LBJ, TX	78.31
48. New Bern, NC	78.29
49. Aiken, SC	78.23
50. Tucson, AZ	78.17
51. Riviera–Bullhead City, AZ	78.06
52. Key West–Key Largo–Marathon, FL	77.95

Rank	Grade
52. San Antonio, TX	77.95
54. Austin, TX	77.94
55. Yuma, AZ	77.90
56. Bay St. Louis–Pass Christian, MS	77.86
57. Las Cruces, NM	77.84
58. Lake Havasu City, AZ	77.80
59. Daytona Beach, FL	77.72
60. Athens, GA	77.71
61. Clayton, GA	77.70
62. Savannah, GA	77.68
63. Vero Beach–Sebastian, FL	77.65
64. St. Augustine, FL	77.53
65. Conway, SC	77.46
66. Tryon, NC	77.44
67. Blairsville, GA	77.40
67. Hiawassee, GA	77.40
69. Wickenburg, AZ	77.38
70. New Braunfels, TX	77.37
71. Melbourne, FL	77.31
72. Clemson–Pendleton District, SC	77.18
73. Wimberly–San Marcos, TX	77.16
74. Alamogordo, NM	77.14
75. Cedar Creek Lake, TX	77.11
76. Lake Martin, AL	76.98
76. Ocean City, MD	76.98
78. St. George–Zion, UT	76.97
79. Fairhope–Gulf Shores, AL	76.89
80. Phoenix–Mesa–Scottsdale, AZ	76.82
81. East End Long Island, NY	76.81
82. Ruidoso, NM	76.75
83. Kerrville, TX	76.65
84. Williamsburg, VA	76.54
85. Rehoboth Bay–Indian River Bay, DE	76.47
86. Easton–St. Michaels–Oxford, MD	76.42
86. Smith Mountain Lake, VA	76.42
88. Brevard, NC	76.37
89. Western St. Tammany Parish, LA	76.31
90. Hendersonville–East Flat Rock, NC	76.29
91. Asheville, NC	76.24
92. Prescott–Prescott Valley, AZ	76.20
93. Chapel Hill, NC	76.19
94. Annapolis, MD	76.18
95. New Port Richey, FL	76.16
96. Lake Granbury, TX	76.10
96. Oxford, MS	76.10
98. Maryville, TN	76.00
99. Cape Cod, MA	75.99
100. Gainesville, FL	75.98
100. Sarasota, FL	75.98
102. Brooksville–Spring Hill, FL	75.77
103. Carson City–Carson Valley, NV	75.74
104. Lake Conroe, TX	75.59
105. Cottonwood–Verde Valley, AZ	75.53

Rank	Grade
106. Toms River–Barnegat Bay, NJ	75.52
107. Lake Livingston, TX	75.47
108. St. Petersburg–Clearwater, FL	75.45
109. Bradenton, FL	75.30
110. Southern Pines–Pinehurst, NC	75.26
111. Thomasville, GA	75.24
112. Leesburg–Lady Lake, FL	75.13
112. Madison, MS	75.13
114. Albuquerque, NM	75.12
115. Sedona, AZ	75.11
116. Northern Neck, VA	75.06
117. Pompano Beach, FL	74.95
118. Inverness, FL	74.91
119. Crossville, TN	74.81
120. Guntersville, AL	74.80
121. Payson, AZ	74.79
122. Boca Raton–Delray Beach, FL	74.75
123. Kissimmee–St. Cloud, FL	74.73
123. Reno–Sparks, NV	74.73
125. Hot Springs, AR	74.66
126. Lakeland–Winter Haven, FL	74.42
127. Ocala, FL	74.40
128. Lake of the Cherokees, OK	74.28
129. Charlottesville, VA	74.16
130. Naples, FL	74.03
131. Wenatchee, WA	73.87
132. Beaver Lake, AR	73.80
133. Bend, OR	73.70
134. Santa Fe, NM	73.58
135. Fort Myers–Cape Coral, FL	73.55
136. Kentucky Lake, KY	73.26
136. Winchester, VA	73.26
138. Norfork Lake, AR	73.19
138. Sebring–Avon Park, FL	73.19
140. Port Charlotte–Punta Gorda, FL	73.12
141. Fayetteville, AR	73.09
142. Fredericksburg–Spotsylvania, VA	72.90
143. Table Rock Lake, MO	72.51
144. Branson, MO	72.49
145. Delta–Cedaredge, CO	72.22
146. Charles Town–Harpers Ferry–Shepherdstown, WV	72.07
147. Boone–Blowing Rock, NC	71.69
148. Montrose, CO	71.23
149. Taos, NM	71.01
150. Ketchum–Sun Valley, ID	70.85
151. Lake of the Ozarks, MO	70.83
152. Grand Junction, CO	70.81
153. Hamilton–Bitterroot Valley, MT	70.62
154. Kalispell–Flathead Valley, MT	70.48
155. Polson–Mission Valley, MT	70.30
156. Chewelah, WA	69.91
157. Colorado Springs, CO	69.55
158. State College, PA	69.44

Rank	Grade	Rank	Grade	Rank	Grade
159. Northern Door Peninsula, WI	69.28	168. Oscoda–Tawas–Huron Shore, MI	67.19	177. St. Jay–Northeast Kingdom, VT	61.81
160. Coeur d'Alene, ID	69.22	169. York Beaches, ME	66.53	178. Petoskey–Harbor Springs, MI	61.69
		170. Lake Winnipesaukee, NH	65.95	179. Traverse City, MI	61.34
161. Fort Collins–Loveland, CO	68.94			180. Woodstock, VT	61.18
162. Pike County, PA	68.68	171. Bar Harbor, ME	65.64		
163. Amherst–Northampton, MA	68.59	172. Durango, CO	64.31		
164. Camden, ME	67.79	173. Hanover, NH	63.66	181. Charlevoix–Boyne City–East Jordan, MI	60.69
165. Southern Berkshire County, MA	67.64	174. Burlington, VT	63.48	182. Pagosa Springs, CO	57.09
		175. Sandpoint–Priest River, ID	63.35	183. McCall–Cascade–Payette Valley, ID	51.82
166. Litchfield Hills, CT	67.39				
167. Eagle River, WI	67.23	176. Houghton Lake, MI	63.02		

PLACE PROFILES: Climate

The following pages describe climate at weather stations in 183 places. Temperature and precipitation data come from the National Oceanic and Atmospheric Administration (NOAA) series 20 publications. Data for humidity, wind speed, days with fog and thunderstorms, as well as clear, partly cloudy, and cloudy days are derived from the nearest station reporting in NOAA's *Local Climatological Data*.

The temperature and precipitation data are NOAA's "30-Year Normals" or averages collected over three decades. Every 10 years, the data for the new decade are added into the normal, and the data for the earliest 10 years are dropped to flatten out anomalies and weather extremes. Events such as a freak blizzard in Albuquer-

que or a heat wave that might occur once every 50 years in Coeur d'Alene have little effect on each place's 30-year normals.

The prose summaries describe each place's location and its distinctive climate and landscape features. *Location* details the place's elevation and its latitude north of the equator and longitude west of Greenwich, England. With these coordinates, you can roughly determine whether one place is farther north, south, east, or west from another.

When *landscape* is described, it is usually how the terrain influences a place's climate and what varieties of vegetation grow there naturally. Few people would deny that landscape is an important element on its own; for

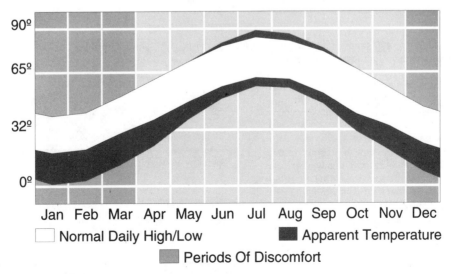

PRECIPITATION

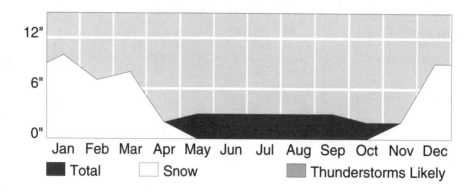

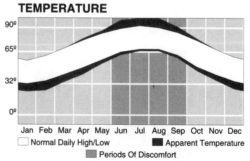

many, it is as important as climate. Some prefer mountains or seacoasts, others rolling hills or flatwoods forests, while still others favor stark desert vistas. Rather than rating landscapes, they are described briefly here and the decision left up to you.

The descriptions for *climate* are capsule summaries of each location's type and general features. To help you visualize the annual temperature and precipitation patterns for each place, look at graphic boxes to the right.

Under the TEMPERATURE box on the previous page, the white band shows the normal high and low air temperatures as they rise and fall over the year. The dark band underneath shows the apparent temperature, which is air temperature influenced by winter wind chill and summer humidity.

Under the PRECIPITATION box above is the amount of rain and snow for each month of the year. The white lumps that occur in many places during winter months indicate snow. Rainfall is shown by the dark wave. A vertical band shows thunderstorms in the months they occur most frequently.

Rounding out each place's climate picture are annual summaries for relative humidity observed nearest to noon, wind speed, snowfalls and rainfalls, clear, partly cloudy, and cloudy days, storm days, very hot and very cold days, and precipitation days (days on which there is at least 0.1 inch of precipitation).

A check mark (✓) preceding a place's name highlights it as one of the top 18 places for climate mildness.

Aiken, SC

Location: 33.33 N, 81.43 W, at 490 feet, on the western border of the state across the Savannah River from Augusta, GA.

Landscape: Generally flat, with gentle slopes and local relief of less than 100 feet. Near the fall line that divides the upcountry Piedmont Plateau and the Coastal Plain low country. To the west are low-rise sandhills. The trees are a mixed forest of southern yellow pine, oak, and hickory.

Climate: Warm and mild, with occasional hot spells. In the winter, measurable snow is a rarity and remains on the ground only a short time. While frosts are typical in late spring or early fall, in 100 years of weather records a temperature of zero or colder has never been reached.

Winter mildness: 92   **Hazard free:** 79
Summer mildness: 66   **Seasonal affect:** 74

TEMPERATURE

ANNUAL
Humidity: 56%
Wind Speed: 6.9 mph
DAYS
0º or below: 0
32º or below: 46
90º or above: 65
Clear: 113
Partly Cloudy: 107
Cloudy: 145

PRECIPITATION

ANNUAL
Precipitation: 51.0"
Snow: 1.8"
DAYS
Precipitation: 72
Thunderstorm: 42
Fog: 33

Grade: 78

Alamogordo, NM

Location: 32.54 N, 105.57 W, at 4,303 feet, in the south-central part of the state, 55 miles north of El Paso, TX.

Landscape: Near the west base of the Sacramento Mountains and east of the Tularosa Basin. Typical desert in appearance. The native vegetation includes thorny shrubs of mesquite and creosote bush. Juniper and pinyon pine start in higher elevations to the east.

Climate: Desert character with long, hot, usually dry summers. Precipitation at this time of year is in heavy thunderstorms. Winters are moderate but subject to occasional frost. Rains are widespread and usually gentle. Winter daily high and low temperature changes can be dramatic.

Winter mildness: 84	**Hazard free:** 80
Summer mildness: 63	**Seasonal affect:** 89

Grade: 77

TEMPERATURE

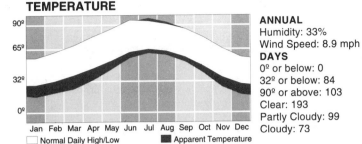

Normal Daily High/Low ■ Apparent Temperature ▨ Periods Of Discomfort

ANNUAL
Humidity: 33%
Wind Speed: 8.9 mph
DAYS
0º or below: 0
32º or below: 84
90º or above: 103
Clear: 193
Partly Cloudy: 99
Cloudy: 73

PRECIPITATION

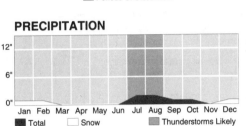

■ Total □ Snow ▨ Thunderstorms Likely

ANNUAL
Precipitation: 12.7"
Snow: 4.3"
DAYS
Precipitation: 27
Thunderstorm: 36
Fog: 2

Albuquerque, NM

Location: 35.05 N, 106.39 W, at 4,943 feet, 55 miles SW of Santa Fe, the state capital.

Landscape: On the upper Rio Grande River opposite a pass between the Sandia and Manzano mountains to the east. It is encircled by sections of the Cibola National Forest. Common vegetation includes sagebrush or shadscale, and a mixture of short grasses. There may be willows and sedges along streams in the area.

Climate: Arid continental. The low humidity and cool nights make the summer heat much less oppressive. There are no muggy days. Winters are moderate and clear, but with freezing nights. Half the moisture falls between July and September in the form of brief but severe thunderstorms. These storms have a moderating effect on the heat and do not greatly interfere with outdoor activities. Long drizzles do not occur.

Winter mildness: 72	**Hazard free:** 72
Summer mildness: 73	**Seasonal affect:** 87

Grade: 75

TEMPERATURE

Normal Daily High/Low ■ Apparent Temperature ▨ Periods Of Discomfort

ANNUAL
Humidity: 34%
Wind Speed: 9.1 mph
DAYS
0º or below: 1
32º or below: 119
90º or above: 63
Clear: 168
Partly Cloudy: 110
Cloudy: 87

PRECIPITATION

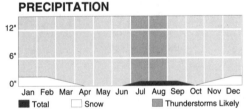

■ Total □ Snow ▨ Thunderstorms Likely

ANNUAL
Precipitation: 8.9"
Snow: 10.2"
DAYS
Precipitation: 28
Thunderstorm: 41
Fog: 5

Alpine–Big Bend, TX

Location: 30.21 N, 103.39 W, at 4,480 feet, in west Texas, 190 miles SE of El Paso.

Landscape: In a high valley flanked by the Davis Mountains to the north and the Glass Mountains to the east. Canyons and extensive rangeland contrast with the high mountains. In the valleys and on the lower slopes are many varieties of cactus and after a good rain, wildflowers are abundant.

Climate: Chihuahuan Desert moderated by altitude. Summers are long and, but for occasional thunderstorms, generally dry. Winters are brief and mild, though subject to occasional morning frosts.

Winter mildness: 89	**Hazard free:** 81
Summer mildness: 71	**Seasonal affect:** 89

Grade: 82

TEMPERATURE

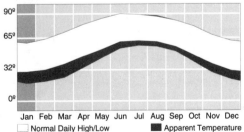

Normal Daily High/Low ■ Apparent Temperature ▨ Periods Of Discomfort

ANNUAL
Humidity: 33%
Wind Speed: 8.9 mph
DAYS
0º or below: 0
32º or below: 60
90º or above: 67
Clear: 193
Partly Cloudy: 99
Cloudy: 73

PRECIPITATION

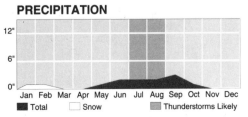

■ Total □ Snow ▨ Thunderstorms Likely

ANNUAL
Precipitation: 16.9"
Snow: 2.5"
DAYS
Precipitation: 28
Thunderstorm: 36
Fog: 2

Amador County, CA

Location: The weather station is Jackson, 38.21 N, 120.46 W, at 1,975 feet, 40 miles SE of Sacramento, the state capital.

Landscape: In the higher grassy hills of the western slope of the Sierra Nevada Mountains with steep gradients from mountain to valley. Canyons cut the forested slope, giving dramatic relief. Snow-fed rivers, lakes, and reservoirs promote wildflowers and low-growing shrubs. Digger pine and blue oak are found at higher elevations.

Climate: Sierran forest climate in the transition zone between the dry western desert and the wetter Pacific coast. Mountain temperature changes can vary greatly both daily and seasonally. Prevailing west winds influence conditions jointly with elevation. The summers are long, hot, and generally dry. Most of the annual precipitation falls as rain rather than snow.

Winter mildness: 85	**Hazard free:** 80
Summer mildness: 73	**Seasonal affect:** 82

Grade: 80

TEMPERATURE

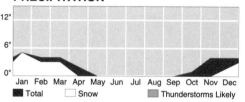

ANNUAL
Humidity: 58%
Wind Speed: 7.8 mph
DAYS
0º or below: 0
32º or below: 77
90º or above: 59
Clear: 189
Partly Cloudy: 75
Cloudy: 101

PRECIPITATION

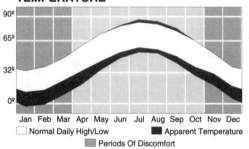

ANNUAL
Precipitation: 29.9"
Snow: 14.1"
DAYS
Precipitation: 49
Thunderstorm: 14
Fog: 34

Amherst–Northampton, MA

Location: 42.22 N, 72.31 W, at 320 feet, in the western part of the state, 70 miles west of Boston and 50 miles north of Hartford, CT.

Landscape: In the center of the long Connecticut Valley, with the Berkshire Hills of the Appalachians visible to the west. Curved ridges are covered by typical Appalachian oak forest mixed with beech, birch, walnut, maple, elm, and sweet chestnut. Willow, ash, or elm are found in poorly drained coves. Quabbin Reservoir lies to the east.

Climate: Hot continental, with typical New England seasonal temperature extremes. Summers are generally mild and free of thunderstorms, but with occasional hot, muggy days. Winters are long with a snow cover that is deep and lasting.

Winter mildness: 60	**Hazard free:** 44
Summer mildness: 88	**Seasonal affect:** 71

Grade: 69

TEMPERATURE

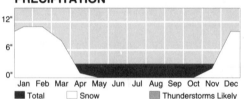

ANNUAL
Humidity: 56%
Wind Speed: 8.5 mph
DAYS
0º or below: 11
32º or below: 151
90º or above: 10
Clear: 80
Partly Cloudy: 108
Cloudy: 177

PRECIPITATION

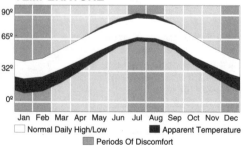

ANNUAL
Precipitation: 42.5"
Snow: 44.8"
DAYS
Precipitation: 75
Thunderstorm: 33
Fog: 28

Annapolis, MD

Location: 38.58 N, 76.29 W, at 41 feet, on the Severn River near its mouth on the western shore of the Chesapeake Bay, 27 miles SE of Baltimore.

Landscape: The wide Severn River drains low, long rolling suburban hills into the upper bay. Native vegetation is typical southeastern mixed forest with broadleaf deciduous and needleleaf evergreen trees.

Climate: Subtropical with a definite marine influence. Summers are hot and humid though often lifted somewhat by a bay breeze. Winters are chilly and rainy. Snow is minimal and doesn't last long.

Winter mildness: 77	**Hazard free:** 74
Summer mildness: 77	**Seasonal affect:** 74

Grade: 76

TEMPERATURE

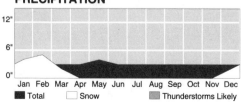

ANNUAL
Humidity: 53%
Wind Speed: 9.2 mph
DAYS
0º or below: 0
32º or below: 85
90º or above: 27
Clear: 106
Partly Cloudy: 108
Cloudy: 151

PRECIPITATION

ANNUAL
Precipitation: 41.8"
Snow: 14.4"
DAYS
Precipitation: 73
Thunderstorm: 27
Fog: 25

Asheville, NC

Location: 35.36 N, 82.33 W, at 2,134 feet, on the French Broad River in western North Carolina.

Landscape: The entire valley is called the Asheville Plateau and is flanked on the east and west by mountain ranges. Thirty miles south, the Blue Ridge Mountains form an escarpment with 2,700 feet average elevation. Peaks nearby include Mount Mitchell (6,684 feet), 20 miles northeast, and Big Pisgah (5,721 feet), 16 miles southwest. Forests are dominated by tall, broadleaf trees such as oak, hickory, walnut, maple, and basswood. There are lower layers of small trees and shrubs; dogwood, blueberry, and haw.

Climate: Temperate but invigorating. Considerable variation in temperature occurs from day to day throughout the year. The valley has a pronounced effect on wind direction, which is mostly from the northwest. Destructive weather events are rare.

Winter mildness: 76   **Hazard free:** 66
Summer mildness: 84   **Seasonal affect:** 71

Grade: 76

TEMPERATURE

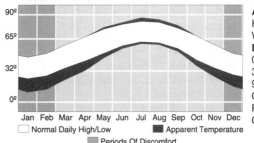

ANNUAL
Humidity: 58%
Wind Speed: 7.6 mph
DAYS
0º or below: 1
32º or below: 101
90º or above: 9
Clear: 102
Partly Cloudy: 113
Cloudy: 150

PRECIPITATION

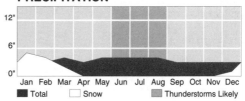

ANNUAL
Precipitation: 47.6"
Snow: 14.3"
DAYS
Precipitation: 75
Thunderstorm: 45
Fog: 77

Athens, GA

Location: 33.57 N, 83.22 W, at 662 feet, in the Piedmont Plateau of northeast Georgia, 60 miles east of Atlanta.

Landscape: Local elevations range between 600 and 800 feet in rolling to hilly terrain. Streams drain to the Savannah River. The countryside is agricultural. The forests are dominated by stands of southern yellow pine, with some mixed hardwood.

Climate: The Atlantic Ocean 200 miles to the southeast, the Gulf of Mexico 275 miles to the south, and the southern Appalachian Mountains to the north and northwest, all exert some influence on the city's climate. Summers are warm and humid, but prolonged periods of extreme heat are noticeably absent. Precipitation is evenly distributed throughout the year. Cold spells are short lived and are broken up by periods of warm southerly airflow.

Winter mildness: 88   **Hazard free:** 75
Summer mildness: 70   **Seasonal affect:** 74

Grade: 78

TEMPERATURE

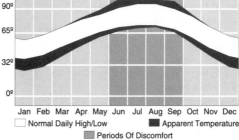

ANNUAL
Humidity: 55%
Wind Speed: 7.4 mph
DAYS
0º or below: 0
32º or below: 52
90º or above: 51
Clear: 113
Partly Cloudy: 105
Cloudy: 147

PRECIPITATION

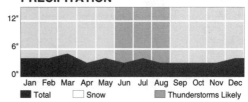

ANNUAL
Precipitation: 49.7"
Snow: 2.2"
DAYS
Precipitation: 70
Thunderstorm: 51
Fog: 38

Austin, TX

Location: 30.16 N, 97.44 W, at 501 feet, on the Balcones Escarpment which separates the Texas hill country from the blackland prairies of East Texas.

Landscape: Elevations within the city limits vary from 400 to 900 feet above sea level spreading over a sequence of low hills and wide terraces. Native trees include cedar, oak, walnut, mesquite, and pecan. The Highland Lakes have been formed by a series of dams on the Colorado River which curves through the city.

Climate: Prairie. Although summers are hot, night temperatures usually drop into the 70s. Winters are mild, with below-freezing temperatures on fewer than 25 days. Prevailing winds are southerly, though strong northers may bring cold spells which rarely last more than a few days. Precipitation is well distributed. Summer brings some heavy thunderstorms. Winter rains are slow and steady.

Winter mildness: 99   **Hazard free:** 81
Summer mildness: 55   **Seasonal affect:** 79

Grade: 78

TEMPERATURE

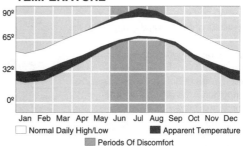

ANNUAL
Humidity: 56%
Wind Speed: 9.2 mph
DAYS
0º or below: 0
32º or below: 21
90º or above: 107
Clear: 116
Partly Cloudy: 114
Cloudy: 135

PRECIPITATION

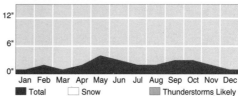

ANNUAL
Precipitation: 31.9"
Snow: 0.8"
DAYS
Precipitation: 47
Thunderstorm: 40
Fog: 22

Bar Harbor, ME

Location: 44.23 N, 68.12 W, at 20 feet, on the heavily glaciated Maine coast, 35 miles east of Augusta, the state capital.

Landscape: On the northeast shore of Mount Desert Island where glacial features are characteristic in the many lakes, islands, and rocky coastline. Elevations range from sea level to 1,530-foot Mt. Cadiliac providing a dramatic combination of mountains, sheer cliff, and ocean. Tortuous mountain trails crisscross Mount Desert. Native vegetation includes a mix of northern hardwoods and spruce.

Climate: Warm continental climate produces winters that are moderately long and can be severe if the predominate weather is coming from the Carolina Coast. The Atlantic Ocean moderates the cold winds from the Canadian Arctic regions. Summer weather is mild but changeable as it is affected by the tropical storms that sweep up the Atlantic coast.

Winter mildness: 56   **Hazard free:** 24
Summer mildness: 94   **Seasonal affect:** 71

Grade: 66

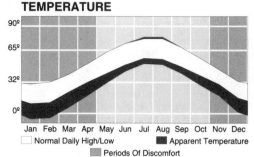

TEMPERATURE
Normal Daily High/Low — Apparent Temperature — Periods Of Discomfort

ANNUAL
Humidity: 58%
Wind Speed: 8.8 mph
DAYS
0º or below: 16
32º or below: 158
90º or above: 4
Clear: 102
Partly Cloudy: 98
Cloudy: 165

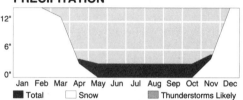

PRECIPITATION
Total — Snow — Thunderstorms Likely

ANNUAL
Precipitation: 45.8"
Snow: 74.7"
DAYS
Precipitation: 76
Thunderstorm: 17
Fog: 48

Bay St. Louis–Pass Christian, MS

Location: 30.18 N, 89.19 W, at 28 feet, along the thickly settled stretch of Gulf of Mexico coast. New Orleans is 60 miles west.

Landscape: Flat, consisting of low-lying delta floodplains sloping down to sand beaches and shallow harbors and bays. Gulf Islands National Seashore lies offshore in the Mississippi Sound. Native trees are temperate rainforest evergreen, oak, laurel, and magnolia. There are large areas of loblolly and slash pine in the sandy upland areas. Tree ferns, small palms, and shrubs make up the lower growth.

Climate: Subtropical. The Gulf waters modify local climate, an effect not felt farther inland. Summers are hot and humid, though temperatures of 90°F or higher occur only half as often here as they do in Hattiesburg, 60 miles north. Rainfall is plentiful and is heaviest in July, with totals in March and September following close behind.

Winter mildness: 100   **Hazard free:** 66
Summer mildness: 63   **Seasonal affect:** 75

Grade: 78

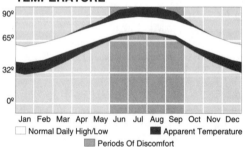

TEMPERATURE
Normal Daily High/Low — Apparent Temperature — Periods Of Discomfort

ANNUAL
Humidity: 63%
Wind Speed: 9.0 mph
DAYS
0º or below: 0
32º or below: 15
90º or above: 55
Clear: 103
Partly Cloudy: 115
Cloudy: 147

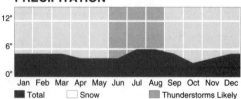

PRECIPITATION
Total — Snow — Thunderstorms Likely

ANNUAL
Precipitation: 61.8"
Snow: 0.7"
DAYS
Precipitation: 73
Thunderstorm: 74
Fog: 27

Beaufort, SC

Location: 32.26 N, 80.40 W, at 11 feet, on Port Royal, one of the Sea Islands, 45 miles south of Charleston and 35 miles north of Savannah, GA.

Landscape: The land is low and flat with elevations averaging under 25 feet. Port Royal is one of dozens of islands at the southern tip of the state of various shapes and sizes, with fresh and saltwater streams, inlets, rivers, and sounds. Most have many swampy areas. Beech, sweet gum, magnolia, pine, and oak are common trees.

Climate: Subtropical, on the edge of the climate enjoyed by Florida and the Caribbean Islands. The surrounding water produces mild winters, hot summers with regular thunderstorms, and seasonal temperatures that shift slowly. The inland Appalachian Mountains block most cold air from the northern interior.

Winter mildness: 97   **Hazard free:** 75
Summer mildness: 65   **Seasonal affect:** 74

Grade: 79

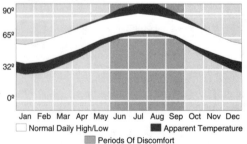

TEMPERATURE
Normal Daily High/Low — Apparent Temperature — Periods Of Discomfort

ANNUAL
Humidity: 60%
Wind Speed: 8.6 mph
DAYS
0º or below: 0
32º or below: 28
90º or above: 56
Clear: 103
Partly Cloudy: 109
Cloudy: 153

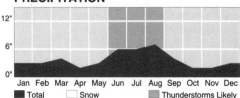

PRECIPITATION
Total — Snow — Thunderstorms Likely

ANNUAL
Precipitation: 51.4"
Snow: 0.3"
DAYS
Precipitation: 71
Thunderstorm: 55
Fog: 28

Beaver Lake, AR

Location: 36.25 N, 93.51 W, at 1,112 feet, in northwest Arkansas 35 miles NE of Fayetteville.

Landscape: This reservoir is part of the large power- and flood-control project in the White River Basin. The lake's 450-mile shoreline is surrounded by tall bluffs, forests, and meadows. Elevations in this region of the Ozark Plateau vary from 500 feet to 1,400 feet. The countryside is rugged, forested, and scattered with farms. Oak and hickory predominate with lower layers of weakly developed small trees and shrubs of redbud and dogwood.

Climate: Primarily modified continental, with warm, humid summers and mild winters. In any given year, the climate can vary from warm and humid maritime to cold and dry continental, but it is relatively free from climatic extremes.

Winter mildness: 80   **Hazard free:** 63
Summer mildness: 72   **Seasonal affect:** 76

TEMPERATURE

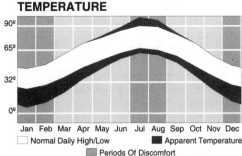

Normal Daily High/Low   Apparent Temperature
Periods Of Discomfort

ANNUAL
Humidity: 57%
Wind Speed: 10.7 mph
DAYS
0º or below: 1
32º or below: 84
90º or above: 51
Clear: 115
Partly Cloudy: 96
Cloudy: 154

PRECIPITATION

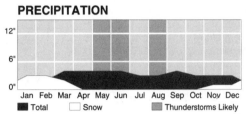

Total   Snow   Thunderstorms Likely

ANNUAL
Precipitation: 44.4"
Snow: 12.3"
DAYS
Precipitation: 60
Thunderstorm: 56
Fog: 20

Grade: 74

✓ Bellingham, WA

Location: 48.45 N, 122.29 W, at 60 feet, on Bellingham Bay at lower Whatcom Falls, 40 miles south of Vancouver, British Columbia.

Landscape: Dominated by the broad, glacier-carved Skagit River Valley with fjords and deep undersea troughs. East of Bellingham are the North Cascade Mountains and Mt. Baker (10,775 feet). The San Juan Islands are in nearby Puget Sound. Native vegetation is predominately needleleaf forest of Douglas fir, red cedar, and spruce.

Climate: Marine. Winter days are mild, but the nights are chilly. Summers are cool with low precipitation. The cooler air temperatures reduce evaporation and produce a very damp, humid climate with heavy cloud cover.

Winter mildness: 79   **Hazard free:** 85
Summer mildness: 97   **Seasonal affect:** 60

TEMPERATURE

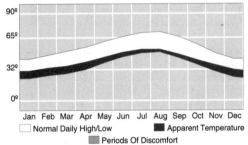

Normal Daily High/Low   Apparent Temperature
Periods Of Discomfort

ANNUAL
Humidity: 70%
Wind Speed: 6.7 mph
DAYS
0º or below: 0
32º or below: 68
90º or above: 0
Clear: 51
Partly Cloudy: 84
Cloudy: 230

PRECIPITATION

Total   Snow   Thunderstorms Likely

ANNUAL
Precipitation: 36.2"
Snow: 13.3"
DAYS
Precipitation: 91
Thunderstorm: 5
Fog: 89

Grade: 83

Bend, OR

Location: 44.03 N, 121.19 W, at 3,629 feet, along the western border of the Harney Basin and the Great Sandy Desert, near the center of the state 130 miles SE of Portland.

Landscape: The Cascades rise immediately west of the city and terrace upwards to crests of 10,000 feet about 10 miles away. The rolling plateau extends south and east from Bend into California, Nevada, and Idaho. The lower elevation is a steppe or shortgrass prairie of grama, needlegrass, and wheatgrass. Forests to the west are Douglas fir, red cedar, and spruce.

Climate: Continental climate of the Great Basin. The mountains moderate the more extreme temperatures of summer. Because the high Cascades block the moisture-laden Pacific winds, rain here is generally light with only one day per year with rainfall of an inch or more. Moderate days and cool nights characterize temperatures here.

Winter mildness: 56   **Hazard free:** 60
Summer mildness: 97   **Seasonal affect:** 75

TEMPERATURE

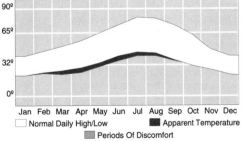

Normal Daily High/Low   Apparent Temperature
Periods Of Discomfort

ANNUAL
Humidity: 59%
Wind Speed: 4.8 mph
DAYS
0º or below: 4
32º or below: 196
90º or above: 13
Clear: 116
Partly Cloudy: 79
Cloudy: 170

PRECIPITATION

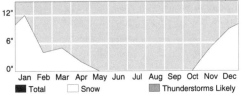

Total   Snow   Thunderstorms Likely

ANNUAL
Precipitation: 11.7"
Snow: 39.0"
DAYS
Precipitation: 31
Thunderstorm: 8
Fog: 49

Grade: 74

Blairsville, GA

Location: 34.52 N, 83.57 W, at 1,926 feet, in the Dahlonega Plateau of the Appalachians, 80 miles north and east of Atlanta, and about 80 miles east along the Tennessee line from Chattanooga.

Landscape: On the Nottley River amid many lakes, streams, and waterfalls in rugged mountain high country. Brasstown Bald (4,784 feet), the highest mountain in Georgia, is a short distance southeast. The nearby Chattahoochee National Forest is a typical eastern deciduous forest with pine, oak, red maple, and black gum trees. Sassafras and shagbark hickory, dogwood, and azalea are early spring bloomers.

Climate: Continental climate strongly influenced by nearby mountains and higher mountains farther north. Summer heat is moderated by the higher elevations. Summers are pleasant, with warm days and cool nights. Winters are cloudy, cold but not severe. Spring is changeable and sometimes stormy. Fall is clear and sunny, with chilly nights.

Winter mildness: 76	**Hazard free:** 74
Summer mildness: 84	**Seasonal affect:** 69
Grade: 77	

TEMPERATURE

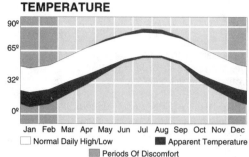

ANNUAL
Humidity: 60%
Wind Speed: 7.6 mph
DAYS
0º or below: 0
32º or below: 93
90º or above: 14
Clear: 102
Partly Cloudy: 113
Cloudy: 150

PRECIPITATION

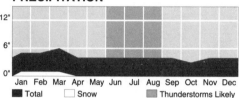

ANNUAL
Precipitation: 57.2"
Snow: 6.0"
DAYS
Precipitation: 95
Thunderstorm: 45
Fog: 77

Boca Raton–Delray Beach, FL

Location: 26.12 N, 80.05 W, at 16 feet, along the densely settled Atlantic coast in the southeastern part of the state, between Palm Beach and Miami.

Landscape: The Boca Raton Inlet and its lakes were once mariners' refuges. The Gulf Stream flows northward two miles offshore, its nearest approach to the Florida coast. Most of the swampland has been drained for development. Outer coastal plain growth at the eastern edge of the Everglades is primarily saw grass and mangrove.

Climate: Because of its southerly location near the ocean, the area has an equable climate. Winters are pleasantly warm. Summers are hot and humid, but are tempered by the ocean breeze. Cumulus clouds often shade the land without completely obscuring the sun. The moist unstable air in this area results in frequent short rain showers from May through October.

Winter mildness: 100	**Hazard free:** 65
Summer mildness: 54	**Seasonal affect:** 75
Grade: 75	

TEMPERATURE

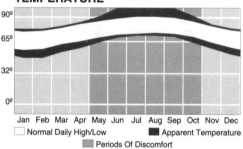

ANNUAL
Humidity: 60%
Wind Speed: 9.6 mph
DAYS
0º or below: 0
32º or below: 0
90º or above: 94
Clear: 75
Partly Cloudy: 158
Cloudy: 132

PRECIPITATION

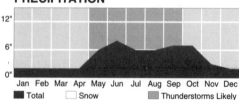

ANNUAL
Precipitation: 59.2"
Snow: 0.0"
DAYS
Precipitation: 80
Thunderstorm: 77
Fog: 28

Boone–Blowing Rock, NC

Location: 36.13 N, 81.40 W, at 3,266 feet, 50 miles NE of Asheville atop the Blue Ridge Mountains in the northwestern corner of the state near the Tennessee line.

Landscape: Rough highland with deep gorges, mountain trails, and rising elevations of the southern Appalachians. There are many streams that cut through the forests. A typical heavy Appalachian oak forest covers the mountains with a mix of pine, oak, maple, beech, hickory, and birch.

Climate: Hot continental moderated by the altitude. Winters are long and cold. The rest of the year is mild and invigorating. Considerable variation in temperature occurs from day to night throughout the year. Precipitation is constant and plentiful with long, snowy winters and rainy seasons in spring and summer. Destructive weather events are rare.

Winter mildness: 69	**Hazard free:** 38
Summer mildness: 93	**Seasonal affect:** 69

Grade: 72

TEMPERATURE

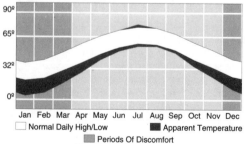

ANNUAL
Humidity: 58%
Wind Speed: 7.6 mph
DAYS
0º or below: 1
32º or below: 113
90º or above: 1
Clear: 102
Partly Cloudy: 113
Cloudy: 150

PRECIPITATION

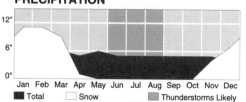

ANNUAL
Precipitation: 65.3"
Snow: 44.9"
DAYS
Precipitation: 96
Thunderstorm: 45
Fog: 77

Bradenton, FL

Location: 27.30 N, 82.34 W, at 19 feet, on the south bank of the Manatee River near its mouth at Tampa Bay midway on Florida's west coast, 50 miles south of Tampa.

Landscape: The southern Gulf Coastal Plains are flat and irregular with less than 300 feet variation in altitude over the gently rolling area. Most of the numerous streams are sluggish. Marshes, swamps, and lakes are numerous. Evergreen oaks, laurel, and magnolia are common but the trees are not tall and the leaf canopy is less dense. There is a well-developed underbrush of ferns, shrubs, and herbaceous plants.

Climate: Subtropical and humid. Winters are mild but inclined to be rainy. Summers are hot with frequent, heavy thunderstorms.

Winter mildness: 100   **Hazard free:** 58
Summer mildness: 58   **Seasonal affect:** 78

TEMPERATURE

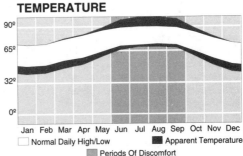

Normal Daily High/Low   Apparent Temperature
Periods Of Discomfort

ANNUAL
Humidity: 55%
Wind Speed: 8.4 mph
DAYS
0º or below: 0
32º or below: 4
90º or above: 85
Clear: 102
Partly Cloudy: 142
Cloudy: 121

PRECIPITATION

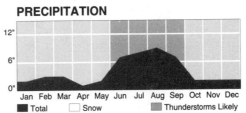

Total   Snow   Thunderstorms Likely

ANNUAL
Precipitation: 53.7"
Snow: 0.0"
DAYS
Precipitation: 71
Thunderstorm: 92
Fog: 22

Grade: 75

Branson, MO

Location: 36.38 N, 93.13 W, at 722 feet, 50 miles south of Springfield near the Arkansas state line.

Landscape: There are several important lakes and rivers in this area of the Ozark Plateau. The rounded mountains rise somewhat steeply from river valleys and impounded lakes. Oak-hickory forests are tall, providing a dense cover in summer, colorful foliage in fall, but are completely bare in winter. Pines are evidence of second-growth forest. Lower layers of shrub and flowering trees are common.

Climate: Hot continental with hot summers and cool winters. Precipitation is adequate throughout the year usually falling as rain. Winters may be cold enough for snow, but the typical precipitation is icy rain during brief, intense cold snaps. Spring arrives early and is pleasant.

Winter mildness: 74   **Hazard free:** 59
Summer mildness: 76   **Seasonal affect:** 75

TEMPERATURE

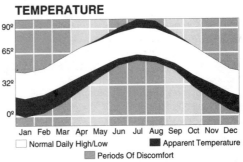

Normal Daily High/Low   Apparent Temperature
Periods Of Discomfort

ANNUAL
Humidity: 57%
Wind Speed: 10.7 mph
DAYS
0º or below: 4
32º or below: 102
90º or above: 43
Clear: 115
Partly Cloudy: 96
Cloudy: 154

PRECIPITATION

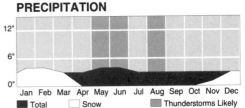

Total   Snow   Thunderstorms Likely

ANNUAL
Precipitation: 42.2"
Snow: 16.1"
DAYS
Precipitation: 61
Thunderstorm: 56
Fog: 20

Grade: 72

Brevard, NC

Location: 35.14 N, 82.44 W, at 2,230 feet, in the mountains near the South Carolina border, 40 miles from Asheville.

Landscape: High rounded slopes of the southern Appalachians, with steep gorges and precipitous cliffs, are found in this area. Nearby are the Appalachian Trail and Blue Ridge Parkway. Also near are the Pisgah and Nantahala National Forests, with oak, beech, walnut, ash, sweet chestnut, and hornbeam. Native laurel blooms in the spring.

Climate: Hot continental moderated by the altitude. This is especially notable in summer with markedly less humidity and cooler nights than cities in similar latitude. Winters are short, but cold and cloudy. Precipitation, mainly mountain rain, is plentiful and well distributed throughout the year.

Winter mildness: 76   **Hazard free:** 70
Summer mildness: 84   **Seasonal affect:** 69

TEMPERATURE

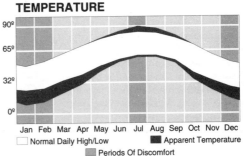

Normal Daily High/Low   Apparent Temperature
Periods Of Discomfort

ANNUAL
Humidity: 58%
Wind Speed: 7.6 mph
DAYS
0º or below: 1
32º or below: 111
90º or above: 9
Clear: 102
Partly Cloudy: 113
Cloudy: 150

PRECIPITATION

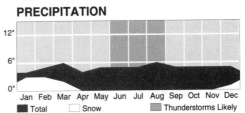

Total   Snow   Thunderstorms Likely

ANNUAL
Precipitation: 67.1"
Snow: 10.9"
DAYS
Precipitation: 91
Thunderstorm: 45
Fog: 77

Grade: 76

✓ Brookings–Gold Beach, OR

Location: 42.03 N, 124.17 W, at 113 feet, on the southern Oregon coast, 270 miles south of Portland.

Landscape: Port cities on the Pacific backed by the Klamath Mountains to the east. Many streams, including the Rogue River, drain the mountain wilderness. An escarpment rises from the rocky beaches. Syskiyou National Forest includes Brewer weeping spruce and Port Orford cedar. Wild azalea, myrtlewood, and a stand of redwood trees are among the native vegetation along the coast.

Climate: Mild marine. Daytime high temperatures can reach 70°F in winter and infrequently top that point in the hottest part of summer. Nights are chilly throughout the year. Precipitation is constant from November through March.

Winter mildness: 94 **Hazard free:** 96
Summer mildness: 96 **Seasonal affect:** 60

Grade: 89

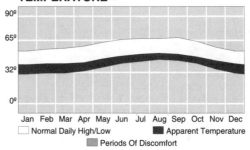

TEMPERATURE

ANNUAL
Humidity: 75%
Wind Speed: 8.6 mph
DAYS
0º or below: 0
32º or below: 8
90º or above: 1
Clear: 49
Partly Cloudy: 76
Cloudy: 240

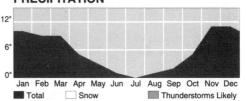

PRECIPITATION

ANNUAL
Precipitation: 72.6"
Snow: 0.3"
DAYS
Precipitation: 101
Thunderstorm: 8
Fog: 41

Brooksville–Spring Hill, FL

Location: 28.33 N, 82.23 W, at 126 feet, in the west central part of the state, 25 miles NE of Tampa.

Landscape: Hilly country unusual for Florida. To the east lies the Green Swamp, composed of lakes, rivers, forests, and sandhills. Nearby Withlacoochee State Forest contains a typical mix of hardwood, longleaf, and slash pine. Aromatic and evergreen bayberry and sweet bay are scattered throughout.

Climate: Subtropical. Warmed by nearby Gulf of Mexico. Winters are sunny, mild, and dry. Summers are hot, humid, and beset by frequent thunderstorms that provide half of the area's annual precipitation.

Winter mildness: 100 **Hazard free:** 63
Summer mildness: 57 **Seasonal affect:** 77

Grade: 76

TEMPERATURE

ANNUAL
Humidity: 54%
Wind Speed: 8.6 mph
DAYS
0º or below: 0
32º or below: 4
90º or above: 93
Clear: 91
Partly Cloudy: 147
Cloudy: 127

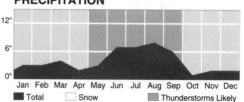

PRECIPITATION

ANNUAL
Precipitation: 53.8"
Snow: 0.0"
DAYS
Precipitation: 71
Thunderstorm: 81
Fog: 26

Burlington, VT

Location: 44.28 N, 73.12 W, at 113 feet, on the eastern shore of Lake Champlain, 75 miles south of Montreal, Quebec.

Landscape: The highest peaks of the Adirondacks in New York state are visible 35 miles to the west across the lake. The foothills of Vermont's Green Mountains begin 10 miles to the east and southeast. Native vegetation includes conifer and deciduous trees. Northern white pine, eastern hemlock, maple, oak, and beech are common.

Climate: The summer, while not long, is pleasant. Fall is cool. Winters are cold, with brief, intense cold snaps formed by high pressure systems moving down from central Canada. Lake Champlain's tempering effect produces temperatures along the lakeshore from 5°F to 10°F warmer than those at the airport 3.5 miles inland. Because of its location in the path of the St. Lawrence Valley storm track, this is one of the cloudiest cities in the United States.

Winter mildness: 54 **Hazard free:** 21
Summer mildness: 92 **Seasonal affect:** 68

Grade: 63

TEMPERATURE

ANNUAL
Humidity: 60%
Wind Speed: 8.9 mph
DAYS
0º or below: 25
32º or below: 156
90º or above: 6
Clear: 57
Partly Cloudy: 101
Cloudy: 207

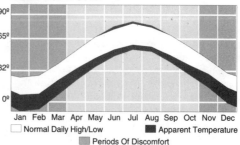

PRECIPITATION

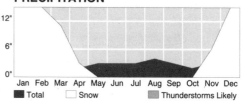

ANNUAL
Precipitation: 34.5"
Snow: 74.6"
DAYS
Precipitation: 75
Thunderstorm: 23
Fog: 15

Camden, ME

Location: 44.12 N, 69.04 W, at 33 feet, on Penobscot Bay in the center of Maine's seacoast, some 70 air miles NE of Portland.

Landscape: Although low-lying, the coastal terrain is very rugged and rocky in most places, allowing for hundreds of bays, islands, peninsulas, and harbors. Immediately to the west are low-rise mountains. Vegetation consists of evergreen coniferous trees, maple, birch, and scrub oak. The area inland is dotted with marshes, ponds, and lakes.

Climate: The Atlantic Ocean has a considerable modifying effect on the local climate, resulting in cool summers and winters that are mild for so northerly a location. Winter snows can be heavy, however. Though fall is generally mild, spring comes late and the weather isn't really warm until late June.

Winter mildness: 56   **Hazard free:** 37
Summer mildness: 93   **Seasonal affect:** 71

TEMPERATURE

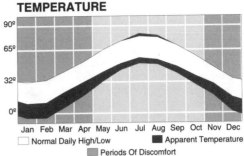

Normal Daily High/Low   Apparent Temperature
Periods Of Discomfort

ANNUAL
Humidity: 59%
Wind Speed: 8.8 mph
DAYS
0º or below: 16
32º or below: 158
90º or above: 4
Clear: 102
Partly Cloudy: 98
Cloudy: 165

PRECIPITATION

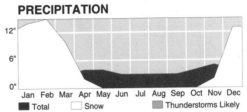

Total   Snow   Thunderstorms Likely

ANNUAL
Precipitation: 47.3"
Snow: 60.2"
DAYS
Precipitation: 76
Thunderstorm: 17
Fog: 48

Grade: 68

Cape Cod, MA

Location: 41.41 N, 69.57 W, at 46 feet, 60 miles SE of Boston on a hooked peninsula jutting out 65 miles into the Atlantic Ocean.

Landscape: Only 120 miles wide and bounded by Cape Cod Bay to the north and west, Buzzards Bay to the west, and Vineyard and Nantucket sounds in the south. The western end of the cape is higher and hillier than the eastern, or "outer cape," which is almost flat and treeless. The sandy soil of glacial origin is arranged in rolling hills and dunes. The northern hook, designated a national seashore, embraces an area of dunes, marshes, lakes, and pinewood.

Climate: Mild maritime. Summer temperatures are usually ideal for outdoor recreation. Both zero- and 90-degree days are very rare. Because the Cape extends into the warm Gulf Stream, its climate is moderate compared with that of the mainland, with warmer winters and cooler summers.

Winter mildness: 67   **Hazard free:** 64
Summer mildness: 93   **Seasonal affect:** 72

TEMPERATURE

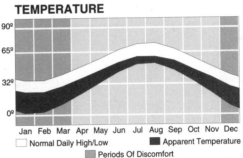

Normal Daily High/Low   Apparent Temperature
Periods Of Discomfort

ANNUAL
Humidity: 57%
Wind Speed: 12.5 mph
DAYS
0º or below: 1
32º or below: 122
90º or above: 1
Clear: 99
Partly Cloudy: 103
Cloudy: 163

PRECIPITATION

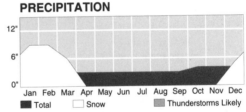

Total   Snow   Thunderstorms Likely

ANNUAL
Precipitation: 45.1"
Snow: 30.2"
DAYS
Precipitation: 77
Thunderstorm: 18
Fog: 23

Grade: 76

✓ Carmel–Monterey–Pebble Beach, CA

Location: 36.33 N, 121.55 W, at 237 feet, on the Carmel River at the southern point of Monterey Bay, 80 miles south of San Francisco.

Landscape: The sea pushes back the land in a great sweeping coastal indentation where sandy and rocky beaches verge on tidepools. Local relief comes mainly from the Diablo and Santa Lucia mountains that rise to the east above the Pacific Ocean in high, grassy bluffs. Cypress and pine groves predominate in the mixed evergreen forest.

Climate: The ocean is the biggest climate factor. Cool temperatures and sea breezes keep the weather mild all year long. Fog and wind are common. Precipitation falls only from October through March.

Winter mildness: 98   **Hazard free:** 98
Summer mildness: 94   **Seasonal affect:** 84

TEMPERATURE

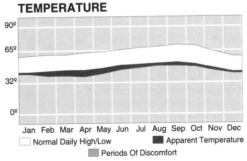

Normal Daily High/Low   Apparent Temperature
Periods Of Discomfort

ANNUAL
Humidity: 61%
Wind Speed: 6.1 mph
DAYS
0º or below: 0
32º or below: 1
90º or above: 2
Clear: 146
Partly Cloudy: 115
Cloudy: 104

PRECIPITATION

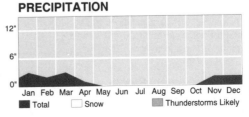

Total   Snow   Thunderstorms Likely

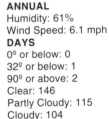

ANNUAL
Precipitation: 18.7"
Snow: 0.1"
DAYS
Precipitation: 35
Thunderstorm: 3
Fog: 18

Grade: 94

Carson City–Carson Valley, NV

Location: 39.10 N, 119.46 W, at 4,665 feet, 30 miles south of Reno and 14 miles east of Lake Tahoe.

Landscape: Near the eastern foothills of the Sierra Nevada Range and on the edge of the Great Basin, a major drainage sink for the Rockies. The rivers here flow into landlocked lakes or simply evaporate in the desert. Sagebrush and saltbrush are common in the high country desert. The Sierran forest is mountain hemlock, red fir, lodgepole pine and western white pine.

Climate: Mediterranean highland characterized by a long, unbroken, dry summer. Winters are cold, but short. West winds prevail and influence the temperature and humidity. Much of the moisture from the Pacific that would fall as rain is blocked by the mountains. At higher elevations winter precipitation will fall as snow.

Winter mildness: 63	**Hazard free:** 70
Summer mildness: 87	**Seasonal affect:** 85

Grade: 76

TEMPERATURE

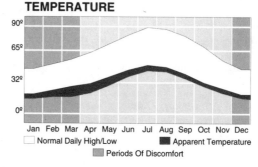

ANNUAL
Humidity: 39%
Wind Speed: 6.6 mph
DAYS
0° or below: 3
32° or below: 169
90° or above: 37
Clear: 159
Partly Cloudy: 93
Cloudy: 113

PRECIPITATION

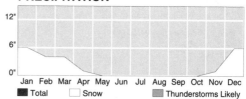

ANNUAL
Precipitation: 10.9"
Snow: 23.9"
DAYS
Precipitation: 23
Thunderstorm: 0
Fog: 7

Cedar Creek Lake, TX

Location: 32.10 N, 96.04 W, at 460 feet, in East Texas about 70 air miles SE of Dallas.

Landscape: The surrounding rolling to hilly terrain drains to the Neches River on the east and the Trinity River on the west. The grass is bluestem prairie. The trees are pine, post oak, blackjack oak, and Texas hickory.

Climate: Prairie, with hot summers. Rainfall is about 39 inches annually, evenly distributed, though July and August are somewhat dry. Winters are mild, with temperatures almost always rising above freezing in the daytime. There are no zero temperatures on record. Spring and fall are the best seasons. This provides a long growing season but there are sufficient changes to make the weather interesting. Flowers bloom as late as December, as early as March.

Winter mildness: 94	**Hazard free:** 77
Summer mildness: 59	**Seasonal affect:** 79

Grade: 77

TEMPERATURE

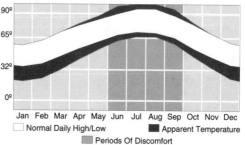

ANNUAL
Humidity: 55%
Wind Speed: 10.8 mph
DAYS
0° or below: 0
32° or below: 40
90° or above: 96
Clear: 137
Partly Cloudy: 97
Cloudy: 131

PRECIPITATION

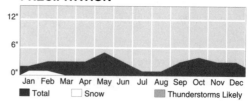

ANNUAL
Precipitation: 39.7"
Snow: 2.8"
DAYS
Precipitation: 56
Thunderstorm: 45
Fog: 11

Chapel Hill, NC

Location: 35.54 N, 79.03 W, at 503 feet, in the transition zone between the Coastal Plain and the Piedmont Plateau, 35 miles west of Raleigh, the state capital.

Landscape: The topography of the Piedmont is rolling, with elevations from 200 feet to 500 feet within a 10-mile radius. Broadleaf deciduous and needleleaf evergreen trees make up the medium-tall forests. Loblolly pine and other southern yellow pine mix with hickory, sweet gum, red maple, and winged elm. Low shrubs of dogwood, viburnum, and blueberry are common.

Climate: Subtropical. Because the western mountains form a partial barrier to cold air masses moving eastward from the nation's interior, there are very few days in the heart of winter when the temperature falls below 20°F. Tropical air is present during much of the summer, bringing warm temperatures and high humidity. In midsummer, afternoon temperatures reach 90°F or higher every fourth day.

Winter mildness: 79	**Hazard free:** 73
Summer mildness: 76	**Seasonal affect:** 74

Grade: 76

TEMPERATURE

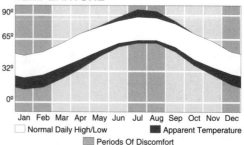

ANNUAL
Humidity: 54%
Wind Speed: 7.8 mph
DAYS
0° or below: 0
32° or below: 91
90° or above: 39
Clear: 112
Partly Cloudy: 105
Cloudy: 148

PRECIPITATION

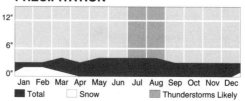

ANNUAL
Precipitation: 46.0"
Snow: 7.9"
DAYS
Precipitation: 74
Thunderstorm: 44
Fog: 34

Charles Town–Harpers Ferry–Shepherdstown, WV

Location: 39.17 N, 77.51 W, at 513 feet, near the meeting point for Virginia, Maryland, and West Virginia, 52 miles NW of Washington, D.C.

Landscape: Rolling farmland and foothills of the Alleghany Mountain Range, west of the Blue Ridge Parkway. Steep hills and mountains rise up in long ridges, curving north to south. The Shenandoah and Potomac rivers offer both whitewater rapids and lazy stretches of calm fishing waters. Appalachian oak forest is dominated by tall, broadleafed trees that provide continuous dense covering in summer but are bare by November. Common trees are oak, beech, birch, hickory, maple, and a shrub undergrowth. Pines are a ready secondary growth.

Climate: Hot continental with warm, humid summers, cool falls, and somewhat cold and snowy winters. Precipitation is evenly distributed throughout the year.

Winter mildness: 69
Summer mildness: 80
Hazard free: 58
Seasonal affect: 74

Grade: 72

TEMPERATURE

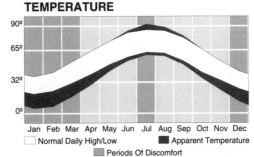

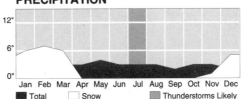

ANNUAL
Humidity: 55%
Wind Speed: 8.1 mph
DAYS
0º or below: 1
32º or below: 119
90º or above: 31
Clear: 102
Partly Cloudy: 112
Cloudy: 151

PRECIPITATION

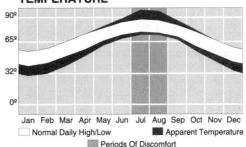

ANNUAL
Precipitation: 37.5"
Snow: 27.2"
DAYS
Precipitation: 71
Thunderstorm: 36
Fog: 23

Charleston Sea Islands, SC

Location: 32.46 N, 79.56 W, at 118 feet, between the Ashley and Cooper rivers, on the state's central coast.

Landscape: Generally level with sandy to sandy-loam soil. Because of the low elevation, a portion of the city and nearby coastal islands are vulnerable to tidal flooding. The coastal marshes and interior swamps are dominated by moss-draped oak, sweet and black gums, and bald cypress. Grasses and cattails grow in the more open marsh areas.

Climate: Temperate subtropical modified considerably by the ocean. Summer is warm and humid, but temperatures over 100°F are infrequent. Nearly half of the annual total rainfall occurs during the summer. From late September to early November, the weather is cool and sunny. Prewinter cold spells begin in November. Winters are mild; temperatures of 32°F or less are very unusual. Spring is warm, windy, and stormy.

Winter mildness: 96
Summer mildness: 66
Hazard free: 74
Seasonal affect: 75

Grade: 79

TEMPERATURE

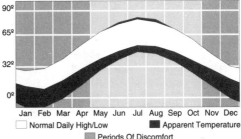

ANNUAL
Humidity: 59%
Wind Speed: 8.6 mph
DAYS
0º or below: 0
32º or below: 36
90º or above: 52
Clear: 103
Partly Cloudy: 109
Cloudy: 153

PRECIPITATION

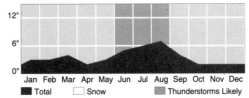

ANNUAL
Precipitation: 48.5"
Snow: 0.7"
DAYS
Precipitation: 66
Thunderstorm: 55
Fog: 28

Charlevoix–Boyne City–East Jordan, MI

Location: 45.19 N, 85.15 W, at 592 feet, on the Lake Michigan coast, 250 miles NW of Lansing, the state capital.

Landscape: Lake Charlevoix is one of the largest in the state. The rivers and inlets along its glaciated shores are low relief and forested. Elevations in the area provide access to both downhill and cross-country skiing. Native vegetation includes maple, oak, and birch hardwoods mixed in the mainly coniferous forest stands of northern white pine.

Climate: Winters in this warm continental region are moderately long and severe. Snow usually stays on the ground through April. Seasonal temperatures can vary considerably. Summers are pleasant because of the tempering effect of Lake Michigan. Spring and summer rains are usual.

Winter mildness: 54
Summer mildness: 93
Hazard free: 3
Seasonal affect: 68

Grade: 61

TEMPERATURE

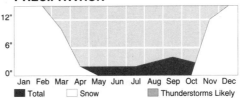

ANNUAL
Humidity: 66%
Wind Speed: 10.7 mph
DAYS
0º or below: 18
32º or below: 169
90º or above: 5
Clear: 66
Partly Cloudy: 88
Cloudy: 211

PRECIPITATION

ANNUAL
Precipitation: 31.6"
Snow: 94.4"
DAYS
Precipitation: 73
Thunderstorm: 23
Fog: 22

Charlottesville, VA

Location: 38.01 N, 78.32 W, at 480 feet, in the center of Virginia's Albemarle County on the Central Piedmont Plateau, 110 miles SW of Washington, D.C.

Landscape: The Blue Ridge Mountains are on the western edge of the county. These and several smaller ranges make relief rolling to quite steep. Elevations range from 300 feet to 800 feet, with some points in the Blue Ridge as high as 3,200 feet. Southeastern mixed forest is medium-tall to tall broad-leaf deciduous oak, hickory, sweet gum, red maple, and winged elm, together with loblolly, and shortleaf pine.

Climate: Modified continental, with mild winters and warm, humid summers. The mountains produce various steering and blocking effects on storms and air masses. Chesapeake Bay further modifies the climate, making it warmer in winter, cooler in summer. Precipitation is well distributed throughout the year.

Winter mildness: 78   **Hazard free:** 60
Summer mildness: 78   **Seasonal affect:** 74

Grade: 74

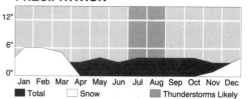

TEMPERATURE

ANNUAL
Humidity: 54%
Wind Speed: 7.7 mph
DAYS
0° or below: 0
32° or below: 87
90° or above: 31
Clear: 112
Partly Cloudy: 107
Cloudy: 146

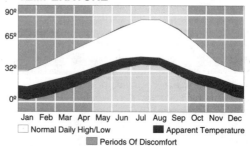

PRECIPITATION

ANNUAL
Precipitation: 47.3"
Snow: 23.3"
DAYS
Precipitation: 72
Thunderstorm: 40
Fog: 38

Chewelah, WA

Location: 48.16 N, 117.43 W, at 1,671 feet, in the northeastern part of the state 50 miles midway between Canada and Spokane.

Landscape: In meadowlands on the floor of the Colville River Valley. The town is surrounded by mountainous benchland. The nearby Selkirk Range and Huckleberry Mountains are forested by a variety of evergreens including cedar, larch, fir, and pine.

Climate: Warm continental. The seasonal temperature shifts are moderated because of the mountain protection from wind and severe storms. Summer days are warm with little humidity. There are well-defined seasons that include much winter snow.

Winter mildness: 56   **Hazard free:** 53
Summer mildness: 92   **Seasonal affect:** 70

Grade: 70

TEMPERATURE

ANNUAL
Humidity: 58%
Wind Speed: 8.9 mph
DAYS
0° or below: 9
32° or below: 178
90° or above: 27
Clear: 85
Partly Cloudy: 87
Cloudy: 193

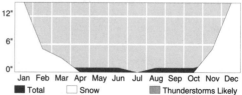

PRECIPITATION

ANNUAL
Precipitation: 21.2"
Snow: 46.8"
DAYS
Precipitation: 57
Thunderstorm: 10
Fog: 47

Clayton, GA

Location: 34.52 N, 83.24 W, at 1,925 feet, in the Mountain and Intermountain Plateau province of northeast Georgia some 90 miles NE of Atlanta.

Landscape: Hilly to mountainous, with elevations averaging 1,500 feet. To the north, some of the mountains rise above 3,000 feet. Chattahoochee National Forest is a typical mixed deciduous forest of the eastern mountain states with oak, beech, birch, walnut, maple, ash, hornbeam. Pines readily develop as second growth where there has been logging or fire.

Climate: Nearby mountains, and higher mountains farther north, have a marked influence. Summer heat is tempered by the higher elevations. Generally, places halfway up the mountain slopes remain warmer during winter nights than do places on the valley floor. Summers are quite pleasant, with warm days and cool nights. Winters are cold but not severe. Spring is changeable and sometimes stormy. Fall is clear and sunny, with chilly nights.

Winter mildness: 79   **Hazard free:** 74
Summer mildness: 82   **Seasonal affect:** 69
Grade: 78

TEMPERATURE

ANNUAL
Humidity: 60%
Wind Speed: 7.6 mph
DAYS
0° or below: 0
32° or below: 93
90° or above: 14
Clear: 102
Partly Cloudy: 113
Cloudy: 150

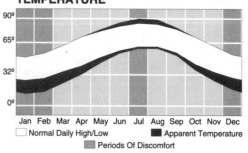

PRECIPITATION

ANNUAL
Precipitation: 57.2"
Snow: 6.0"
DAYS
Precipitation: 95
Thunderstorm: 45
Fog: 77

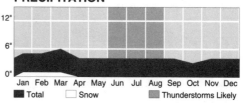

Clemson–Pendleton District, SC

Location: 34.41 N, 82.57 W, at 950 feet in the extreme northwestern part of the state, 25 miles SW of Greenville.

Landscape: The high parts of the Blue Ridge foothills yield a broken outline. Here is a curving valley with typical Up-Country forests of beech, sweet gum, magnolia, pine, and oak. Rhododendrons, azaleas, and kalmias bloom in spring.

Climate: In the transition between hot continental and sub-tropical. Winters are brief, with negligible snowfalls. Summers are longer than in more northerly locations, and less humid and stormy than others in the low country 150 miles southeast of here. Precipitation is distributed throughout the year with a maximum in early spring.

Winter mildness: 84　　**Hazard free:** 77
Summer mildness: 72　　**Seasonal affect:** 74

Grade: 77

TEMPERATURE

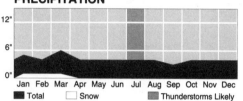

Normal Daily High/Low　　Apparent Temperature
Periods Of Discomfort

ANNUAL
Humidity: 55%
Wind Speed: 6.9 mph
DAYS
0° or below: 0
32° or below: 70
90° or above: 49
Clear: 122
Partly Cloudy: 100
Cloudy: 143

PRECIPITATION

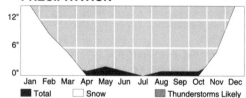

Total　　Snow　　Thunderstorms Likely

ANNUAL
Precipitation: 54.4"
Snow: 4.4"
DAYS
Precipitation: 81
Thunderstorm: 42
Fog: 33

Coeur d'Alene, ID

Location: 47.40 N, 116.46 W, at 2,152 feet, on Coeur d'Alene Lake in the state's northwest panhandle, 30 miles east of Spokane, WA.

Landscape: The Coeur d'Alene Mountains are a division of the Bitterroot Range of the Northern Rocky Mountains. They shelter the city with a rough triangle of forested hills or low mountains for about 60 miles along the Montana border from Pend Oreille Lake to the St. Joe River. The Coeur d'Alene National Forest spreads across most of the range. To the north and northwest lies Rathdrum Prairie. Within a 10-mile radius of the city, several mountain peaks rise over 4,000 feet. Mixed coniferous-deciduous forest predominates here.

Climate: Can be generally described as temperate, with clear, dry summers and rainy, snowy winters. Though seasonal variation is large, it is less wide-ranging than in most other locations this far north.

Winter mildness: 65　　**Hazard free:** 40
Summer mildness: 89　　**Seasonal affect:** 69

Grade: 69

TEMPERATURE

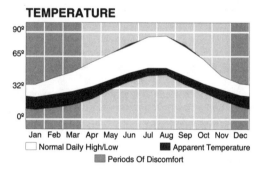

Normal Daily High/Low　　Apparent Temperature
Periods Of Discomfort

ANNUAL
Humidity: 59%
Wind Speed: 8.9 mph
DAYS
0° or below: 3
32° or below: 139
90° or above: 27
Clear: 85
Partly Cloudy: 87
Cloudy: 193

PRECIPITATION

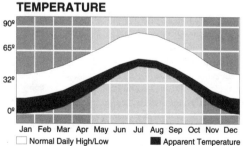

Total　　Snow　　Thunderstorms Likely

ANNUAL
Precipitation: 26.0"
Snow: 59.9"
DAYS
Precipitation: 66
Thunderstorm: 10
Fog: 47

Colorado Springs, CO

Location: 38.50 N, 104.49 W, at 6,008 feet, on the eastern slope of Colorado's Rocky Mountains, 75 miles south of Denver.

Landscape: Relatively flat and semiarid. Immediately to the west, the mountains rise abruptly to heights ranging from 10,000 feet to 14,000 feet. To the east lies the gently undulating prairie land of eastern Colorado with typical prairie short grasses and woody shrubs. The land slopes upward to the north, reaching an average height of 8,000 feet within 20 miles at the top of Palmer Lake Divide. High plains prairie meet the foothills of the Rockies where there are stands of mixed spruce-fir forests.

Climate: The wide range of outlying elevations helps to give Colorado Springs the pleasant plains-and-mountain mixture that has established it as a resort. Precipitation is generally light, with 80 percent of it falling as rain from April to October.

Winter mildness: 60　　**Hazard free:** 36
Summer mildness: 89　　**Seasonal affect:** 83

Grade: 70

TEMPERATURE

Normal Daily High/Low　　Apparent Temperature
Periods Of Discomfort

ANNUAL
Humidity: 38%
Wind Speed: 10.1 mph
DAYS
0° or below: 7
32° or below: 161
90° or above: 17
Clear: 127
Partly Cloudy: 119
Cloudy: 119

PRECIPITATION

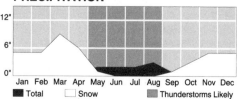

Total　　Snow　　Thunderstorms Likely

ANNUAL
Precipitation: 16.2"
Snow: 41.7"
DAYS
Precipitation: 30
Thunderstorm: 56
Fog: 21

Conway, SC

Location: 33.50 N, 79.03 W, at 25 feet, on the coastal plain inland, 20 miles NW of Myrtle Beach.

Landscape: On the relatively flat coastal plain. Surrounded by low-country swamplands drained by the tea-colored water of the Waccamaw River. The hinterland is agricultural with second-growth tall forests of longleaf, loblolly, and slash pines. Live oaks, azaleas, and other bright flowering shrubs are also native.

Climate: Subtropical. Winter is extremely mild and without snow. The Blue Ridge Mountains inland block the cold air from the interior. Summer is warm and humid, with frequent heavy thunderstorms. The nearby Atlantic has a pronounced modifying effect on temperatures. Some tropical storms reach inland every few years.

Winter mildness: 91
Summer mildness: 66
Hazard free: 77
Seasonal affect: 74

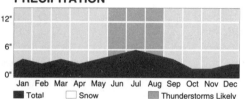

TEMPERATURE

ANNUAL
Humidity: 56%
Wind Speed: 8.8 mph
DAYS
0° or below: 0
32° or below: 51
90° or above: 65
Clear: 111
Partly Cloudy: 103
Cloudy: 151

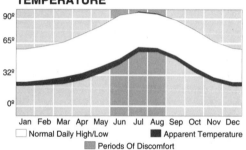

PRECIPITATION

ANNUAL
Precipitation: 50.8"
Snow: 1.5"
DAYS
Precipitation: 77
Thunderstorm: 47
Fog: 24

Grade: 77

Cottonwood-Verde Valley, AZ

Location: 34.44 N, 112.00 W, at 3,314 feet, 50 miles north of Phoenix.

Landscape: The Verde River runs through this high valley near the western edge of the Mongollon Rim. Nearby, are many high peaks, canyons, and mesas. Cottonwood trees line the river. Pondorosa pine and other conifers are in the high country and sagebrush and native grasses cover the valley floor. The shrubs must tolerate alkaline conditions, as soils are poorly drained.

Climate: Mountain steppe. There are strong daily and seasonal temperature changes. The usual winter flow of air is from the Pacific Ocean. This brings frequent, heavy snows. Cold air masses from Canada sometimes bring temperatures well below zero higher up in the mountains. Moisture-bearing winds from the southeast Gulf region bring brief summer rains from July through September.

Winter mildness: 72
Summer mildness: 77
Hazard free: 68
Seasonal affect: 88

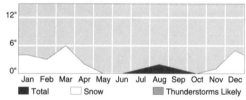

TEMPERATURE

ANNUAL
Humidity: 33%
Wind Speed: 6.3 mph
DAYS
0° or below: 0
32° or below: 150
90° or above: 32
Clear: 211
Partly Cloudy: 84
Cloudy: 70

PRECIPITATION

ANNUAL
Precipitation: 15.8"
Snow: 22.9"
DAYS
Precipitation: 39
Thunderstorm: 23
Fog: 11

Grade: 76

Crossville, TN

Location: 35.57 N, 85.50 W, at 1,863 feet, on the Cumberland Plateau near the center of the state, 62 miles west of Knoxville.

Landscape: High, rolling foothills of the Appalachian Mountains are on the eastern horizon. This is a timberland plateau of eastern deciduous forest. Common trees are hickory, oak, beech, birch, walnut, and maple. These tall broadleafed trees provide a dense foliage during summer and completely shed their leaves in winter. Low shrubs develop in spring.

Climate: Hot continental climate characterized by long, mild summers and cool winters. Daily and seasonal temperature changes are not dramatic. Precipitation, almost all of it rain, is well distributed throughout the year with slight increases in the summer.

Winter mildness: 77
Summer mildness: 81
Hazard free: 62
Seasonal affect: 72

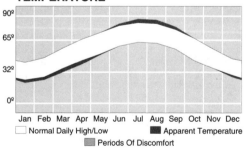

TEMPERATURE

ANNUAL
Humidity: 61%
Wind Speed: 4.4 mph
DAYS
0° or below: 1
32° or below: 88
90° or above: 32
Clear: 111
Partly Cloudy: 96
Cloudy: 158

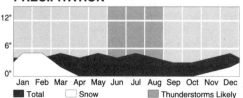

PRECIPITATION

ANNUAL
Precipitation: 55.5"
Snow: 16.4"
DAYS
Precipitation: 84
Thunderstorm: 51
Fog: 33

Grade: 75

Dare Outer Banks, NC

Location: 35.54 N, 75.40 W, at 5 feet, on the state's northwest coast, 60 miles south of Virginia Beach, VA.

Landscape: Principally barrier islands consisting of white-sand beaches, dunes, wetlands, and hardwood forest. There are extensive coastal marshes and interior swamps, dominated by gums and cypress. Cape Hatteras National Seashore, extending 75 miles along the coast, protects over 30,000 acres.

Climate: Subtropical, with humid, hot summers and winters that are mild. January and February nights can be freezing, due to the effect of wind chill. Rain falls throughout the year. Summer brings heavy thunderstorms. Occasional tropical storms from the Atlantic may strike this coastal location.

Winter mildness: 92 **Hazard free:** 79
Summer mildness: 76 **Seasonal affect:** 74

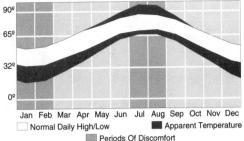

TEMPERATURE

ANNUAL
Humidity: 65%
Wind Speed: 11.1 mph
DAYS
0º or below: 0
32º or below: 32
90º or above: 5
Clear: 108
Partly Cloudy: 101
Cloudy: 156

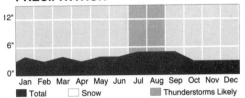

PRECIPITATION

ANNUAL
Precipitation: 52.1"
Snow: 2.1"
DAYS
Precipitation: 73
Thunderstorm: 42
Fog: 15

Grade: 82

Daytona Beach, FL

Location: 29.12 N, 81.01 W, at 10 feet, on the Halifax River and Intracoastal Waterway along the state's Atlantic coast.

Landscape: On a tidewater lagoon. The surrounding land is flat with sandy soil. There is no rise above 35 feet. Coastal plain vegetation in this area is cabbage palm and sea grape. The climax forest is mixed evergreen, oak, and magnolia.

Climate: Nearness to the ocean results in a climate tempered by both onshore and offshore breezes. Summer is hot and humid, but a sea breeze usually starts at midday and common afternoon thundershowers lower temperatures to more comfortable levels. Winters can have cold airflows from the north, but usually are mild because of the city's ocean setting and southerly latitude.

Winter mildness: 100 **Hazard free:** 65
Summer mildness: 63 **Seasonal affect:** 75

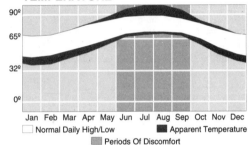

TEMPERATURE

ANNUAL
Humidity: 60%
Wind Speed: 8.7 mph
DAYS
0º or below: 0
32º or below: 6
90º or above: 56
Clear: 98
Partly Cloudy: 133
Cloudy: 134

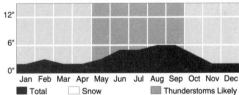

PRECIPITATION

ANNUAL
Precipitation: 47.9"
Snow: 0.0"
DAYS
Precipitation: 78
Thunderstorm: 77
Fog: 28

Grade: 78

Delta–Cedaredge, CO

Location: 38.44 N, 108.04 W, at 4,953 feet, in the western part of the state, 45 miles SE of Grand Junction.

Landscape: Within the sage desert and shortgrass prairie of the Colorado Plateau. Ranchland and orchards mark the gently rolling lowland. Lakes and streams here are fed from mountain snows; the Gunnison and Uncompahgre Rivers flow through steep canyons. Sagebrush and cactus are found in the canyons. Pine, spruce, and aspen forests cover the subalpine areas.

Climate: Desert-steppe brings varied seasonal and daily temperature changes. Summers are dry and comfortable due to the high altitude. Winters are cold with moderate snow cover in the elevations through May. Humidity is low, and precipitation is scant but for brief mountain thunderstorms.

Winter mildness: 65 **Hazard free:** 61
Summer mildness: 80 **Seasonal affect:** 83

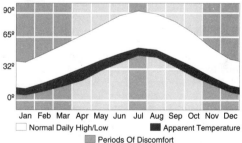

TEMPERATURE

ANNUAL
Humidity: 41%
Wind Speed: 8.1 mph
DAYS
0º or below: 6
32º or below: 132
90º or above: 65
Clear: 137
Partly Cloudy: 106
Cloudy: 122

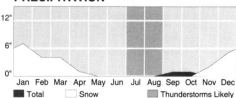

PRECIPITATION

ANNUAL
Precipitation: 8.9"
Snow: 23.9"
DAYS
Precipitation: 34
Thunderstorm: 35
Fog: 8

Grade: 72

Durango, CO

Location: 37.16 N, 107.52 W, at 6,523 feet in the state's southwestern corner, 250 air miles SW of Denver.
Landscape: High in the Animas River valley surrounded by red bluffs. The sharply uplifted peaks of the San Juan Mountains provide dramatic relief. The San Juan National Forest is typical of the pine and aspen subalpine growth with steppe shrubs and grasses.
Climate: Semiarid continental causes definite seasonal temperature variations. Warm, dry summers blend into short, crisp falls. Winters are long and extremely snowy. Daily temperature changes are notable throughout the year as the nights chill considerably from daytime highs.

Winter mildness: 52   **Hazard free:** 17
Summer mildness: 92   **Seasonal affect:** 81

Grade: 64

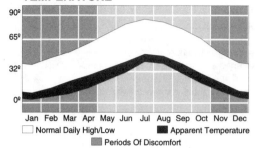

TEMPERATURE

☐ Normal Daily High/Low   ■ Apparent Temperature
▨ Periods Of Discomfort

ANNUAL
Humidity: 40%
Wind Speed: 8.1 mph
DAYS
0º or below: 11
32º or below: 211
90º or above: 18
Clear: 137
Partly Cloudy: 106
Cloudy: 122

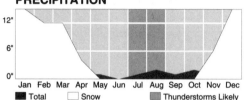

PRECIPITATION

■ Total   ☐ Snow   ▨ Thunderstorms Likely

ANNUAL
Precipitation: 19.3"
Snow: 72.5"
DAYS
Precipitation: 44
Thunderstorm: 35
Fog: 8

Eagle River, WI

Location: 45.55 N, 89.14 W, at 1,647 feet, near the western end of Michigan's Upper Peninsula.
Landscape: Generally level. The entire area was once part of a great, dense white pine forest but is now covered with second growth. Within a 20-mile radius of the town are more than 200 lakes.
Climate: Continental, and largely determined by the movement and interaction of large air masses. Weather changes can be expected every few days in winter and spring. Winters are long and cold. This should be considered a rigorous climate with an average of 27 days when the temperature drops below zero. Summers are warm and pleasant, with cool nights. Spring and fall are short, with rapid transition from winter to summer and vice versa.

Winter mildness: 47   **Hazard free:** 43
Summer mildness: 97   **Seasonal affect:** 72

Grade: 67

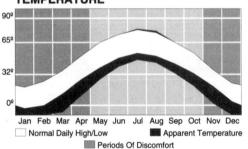

TEMPERATURE

☐ Normal Daily High/Low   ■ Apparent Temperature
▨ Periods Of Discomfort

ANNUAL
Humidity: 63%
Wind Speed: 10.0 mph
DAYS
0º or below: 27
32º or below: 162
90º or above: 7
Clear: 86
Partly Cloudy: 102
Cloudy: 177

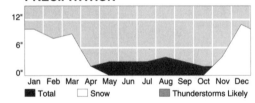

PRECIPITATION

■ Total   ☐ Snow   ▨ Thunderstorms Likely

ANNUAL
Precipitation: 31.0"
Snow: 45.0"
DAYS
Precipitation: 63
Thunderstorm: 33
Fog: 24

East End Long Island, NY

Location: 40.58 N, 72.11 W, at 55 feet, at the extreme tip of Long Island, 120 miles east of New York City.
Landscape: The eastern end of Long Island, where the Atlantic Ocean meets Long Island Sound, is divided into two narrow peninsulas by four bays. The surrounding land is suburban and agricultural. Small trees and shrubs make up the undergrowth. Common specimen trees are oak, beech, birch, hickory, tulip tree, and sweet chestnut.
Climate: Hot continental, with fewer seasonal and daily temperature fluctuations especially where tempered by the effects of the surrounding salt water. Precipitation is distributed throughout the year. Summers have hot and humid stretches, but are generally warm and dry. Winters can be cold with icy rain. Snowfall is light and lasts but a little while.

Winter mildness: 71   **Hazard free:** 69
Summer mildness: 88   **Seasonal affect:** 74

Grade: 77

TEMPERATURE

☐ Normal Daily High/Low   ■ Apparent Temperature
▨ Periods Of Discomfort

ANNUAL
Humidity: 59%
Wind Speed: 9.0 mph
DAYS
0º or below: 1
32º or below: 99
90º or above: 6
Clear: 99
Partly Cloudy: 117
Cloudy: 149

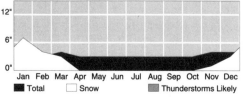

PRECIPITATION

■ Total   ☐ Snow   ▨ Thunderstorms Likely

ANNUAL
Precipitation: 45.7"
Snow: 19.9"
DAYS
Precipitation: 71
Thunderstorm: 27
Fog: 38

Easton-St. Michaels-Oxford, MD

Location: 38.46 N, 76.04 W, at 38 feet, in the tidewater region along the eastern shore of Chesapeake Bay, near the head of Tred Avon River, 150 miles NE of Little Rock, the state capital.
Landscape: There is precious little relief in the long, low hills cut by streams and inlets from the Bay. Inland, the land is developed agricultural. The native vegetation is typical southeastern mixed forest with broadleaf deciduous and needleleaf evergreen trees. In the towns are holly and magnolias.
Climate: Subtropical with a definite marine influence. Summers are hot and humid though often lifted somewhat by a bay breeze. Some winters can be freezing and snowy, but normally are chilly and rainy. Snow is minimal and short-lasting.

Winter mildness: 78   **Hazard free:** 74
Summer mildness: 77   **Seasonal affect:** 74

Grade: 76

TEMPERATURE

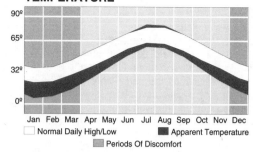

Normal Daily High/Low   Apparent Temperature
Periods Of Discomfort

ANNUAL
Humidity: 59%
Wind Speed: 9.0 mph
DAYS
0° or below: 1
32° or below: 99
90° or above: 6
Clear: 99
Partly Cloudy: 117
Cloudy: 149

PRECIPITATION

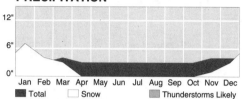

Total   Snow   Thunderstorms Likely

ANNUAL
Precipitation: 45.7"
Snow: 19.9"
DAYS
Precipitation: 71
Thunderstorm: 27
Fog: 38

Edenton, NC

Location: 36.03 N, 76.36 W, at 5 feet, on Albemarle Sound in northeast coastal area, 65 miles SSW of Virginia Beach, VA.
Landscape: At the mouth of the Chowan River on Albemarle Sound west of Kitty Hawk and the Barrier Islands. The woods are evergreens, oak, bald cypress, laurel, and magnolia mixed with loblolly and slash pine. The native undergrowth consists of fern, small palms, shrubs and herbaceous plants.
Climate: Subtropical, with humid, hot, coastal plain summers. Winters are mild, but with some freezing nights. Snow is negligible but rain falls throughout the year. Spring and summer can bring heavy thunderstorms, and occasional tropical storms from the Atlantic may reach this location.

Winter mildness: 88   **Hazard free:** 76
Summer mildness: 73   **Seasonal affect:** 74

Grade: 79

TEMPERATURE

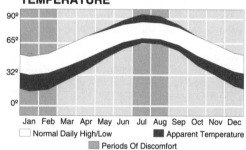

Normal Daily High/Low   Apparent Temperature
Periods Of Discomfort

ANNUAL
Humidity: 58%
Wind Speed: 11.1 mph
DAYS
0° or below: 0
32° or below: 52
90° or above: 31
Clear: 106
Partly Cloudy: 106
Cloudy: 153

PRECIPITATION

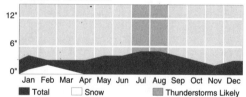

Total   Snow   Thunderstorms Likely

ANNUAL
Precipitation: 48.5"
Snow: 5.5"
DAYS
Precipitation: 73
Thunderstorm: 42
Fog: 20

Fairhope-Gulf Shores, AL

Location: 30.31 N, 87.54 W, at 122 feet, 35 miles south of Mobile on the Gulf of Mexico near the entrance to Mobile Bay.
Landscape: Gulf coastal plain where ecologies range from sea level sandy beaches and saltmarshes to typical southern pine forests. Local relief ranges from sea level to less than 250 feet inland.
Climate: Subtropical. Although destructive hurricanes are extremely infrequent, this seems due more to chance than to location. The area is subject to hurricanes from the West Indies and the Gulf of Mexico. The normal annual rainfall amount here is one of the highest in the continental United States. It is evenly distributed throughout the year, with a slight maximum at the height of the summer thunderstorm season. The growing season averages 274 days, enough for citrus fruits to be grown in the area.

Winter mildness: 98   **Hazard free:** 67
Summer mildness: 63   **Seasonal affect:** 73

Grade: 77

TEMPERATURE

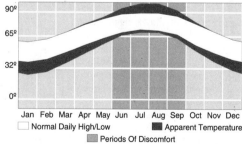

Normal Daily High/Low   Apparent Temperature
Periods Of Discomfort

ANNUAL
Humidity: 56%
Wind Speed: 9.0 mph
DAYS
0° or below: 0
32° or below: 21
90° or above: 74
Clear: 103
Partly Cloudy: 115
Cloudy: 147

PRECIPITATION

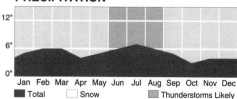

Total   Snow   Thunderstorms Likely

ANNUAL
Precipitation: 65.1"
Snow: 0.3"
DAYS
Precipitation: 80
Thunderstorm: 73
Fog: 40

Fayetteville, AR

Location: 36.03 N, 94.09 W, at 1,334 feet, in northwestern Arkansas, 50 miles north of Fort Smith.

Landscape: Situated on the White River in the Boston Mountains. Elevations near here reach over 2,000 feet in the highest parts of the Ozark Plateau. This is rugged, wooded mountain country. Broadleaf deciduous oak and hickory predominate, with lower layers of weakly developed small trees and shrubs, especially redbud and dogwood.

Climate: Modified continental, with hot, humid summers and briefer winters than other locations at this latitude. Winter to winter can vary from warm and humid maritime to cold and dry continental, but are relatively free from climatic extremes. Snowfalls are minimal, but precipitation in January and February can be icy rain.

Winter mildness: 76   **Hazard free:** 64
Summer mildness: 74   **Seasonal affect:** 75

Grade: 73

TEMPERATURE

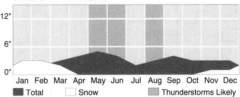

ANNUAL
Humidity: 57%
Wind Speed: 10.7 mph
DAYS
0º or below: 2
32º or below: 102
90º or above: 47
Clear: 115
Partly Cloudy: 96
Cloudy: 154

PRECIPITATION

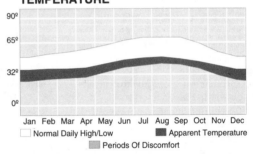

ANNUAL
Precipitation: 44.0"
Snow: 11.7"
DAYS
Precipitation: 62
Thunderstorm: 56
Fog: 20

✓ Florence, OR

Location: 43.59 N, 124.06 W, at 23 feet, at the mouth of the Siuslaw River near the center of Oregon's Pacific coast, 60 miles west of Eugene.

Landscape: Minimal elevation from extensive sand dunes and beach. Low growth of sea grass, rhododendrons, and evergreen shrub lead to a taller forest of cedar, hemlock, and Douglas fir in the foothills of the Coast Range.

Climate: Mild marine with heavy rainfall especially in winter and spring. Humidity is always high, but daily maximum temperatures are comfortable throughout the year. Winters may produce ocean storms and occasional light snow. Falls are clear, lengthy, and pleasant.

Winter mildness: 91   **Hazard free:** 93
Summer mildness: 97   **Seasonal affect:** 60

Grade: 88

TEMPERATURE

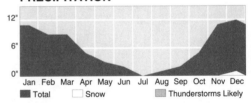

ANNUAL
Humidity: 75%
Wind Speed: 8.6 mph
DAYS
0º or below: 0
32º or below: 8
90º or above: 1
Clear: 49
Partly Cloudy: 76
Cloudy: 240

PRECIPITATION

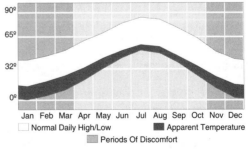

ANNUAL
Precipitation: 76.5"
Snow: 3.0"
DAYS
Precipitation: 101
Thunderstorm: 8
Fog: 41

Fort Collins–Loveland, CO

Location: 40.35 N, 105.05 W, at 5,003 feet, on the Cache la Poudre River in the eastern foothills of the Rockies' Front Range, 55 miles north of Denver.

Landscape: Lies close to some of the most spectacular mountain terrain in the country. Steep cliffs, high waterfalls, and forested mountain slopes cut by swift rivers are all found to the west. Within 30 miles to the east, the landscape settles into grassland prairies of the Great Plains.

Climate: Near the center of the continent, Fort Collins and Loveland are removed from any major source of airborne moisture and are further shielded from rainfall by the high Rockies to the west. In wintertime, cold air masses from Canada may bring snow and sub-freezing temperatures at night. In summer, hot air from the desert southwest brings daytime temperatures of 90°F. However, felt heat is low because of dryness.

Winter mildness: 59   **Hazard free:** 36
Summer mildness: 88   **Seasonal affect:** 83

Grade: 69

TEMPERATURE

ANNUAL
Humidity: 39%
Wind Speed: 8.7 mph
DAYS
0º or below: 11
32º or below: 167
90º or above: 22
Clear: 115
Partly Cloudy: 130
Cloudy: 120

PRECIPITATION

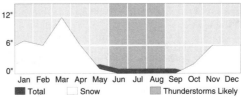

ANNUAL
Precipitation: 15.1"
Snow: 47.3"
DAYS
Precipitation: 33
Thunderstorm: 41
Fog: 9

Fort Myers–Cape Coral, FL

Location: 26.38 N, 81.52 W, at 10 feet, on the broad Caloosahatchee River in southwestern Florida, 120 miles SSE of Tampa.

Landscape: This area is the western terminus of the Okeechobee Waterway, linking the Atlantic Ocean and the Gulf of Mexico, about 15 miles away. The land is level and low. The climax growth of the coastal plain in this area north of the Everglades is evergreen-oak and magnolia. Spanish moss trails from Evangeline oak and bald cypress. Tree ferns, small palms, and shrubs make up the lower layer.

Climate: Subtropical. Summer and winter temperature extremes are checked by the influence of the Gulf. Mild winters have many bright, warm days. Nights are moderately cool. Rainfall averages more than 50 inches annually, with two-thirds of this total coming daily between June and September. Most rain falls as late afternoon or early evening thunderstorms, bringing relief from the heat.

Winter mildness: 100 **Hazard free:** 58
Summer mildness: 51 **Seasonal affect:** 80
Grade: 74

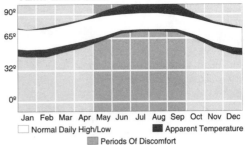

TEMPERATURE

ANNUAL
Humidity: 55%
Wind Speed: 8.1 mph
DAYS
0º or below: 0
32º or below: 0
90º or above: 113
Clear: 99
Partly Cloudy: 167
Cloudy: 99

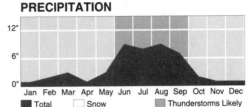

PRECIPITATION

ANNUAL
Precipitation: 53.4"
Snow: 0.0"
DAYS
Precipitation: 72
Thunderstorm: 92
Fog: 20

Fredericksburg, TX

Location: 30.16 N, 98.52 W, at 1,702 feet, on the Pedernales River, 80 miles west of Austin, the state capital.

Landscape: In a high, green valley, in the transition from rich Blacklands to Edwards Plateau foothills. The town is encircled by hills with granite and limestone outcroppings. Native vegetation includes cedar, juniper, oak, and prairie grasses.

Climate: Prairie. Summer days are hot but nights are pleasantly cool. Winters are mild with few, brief cold spells. Rainfall is distributed fairly evenly throughout the year. Humidity is generally a comfortable 55 percent.

Winter mildness: 95 **Hazard free:** 80
Summer mildness: 60 **Seasonal affect:** 79

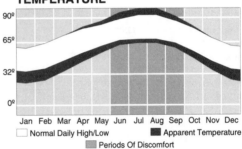

TEMPERATURE

ANNUAL
Humidity: 56%
Wind Speed: 9.2 mph
DAYS
0º or below: 0
32º or below: 39
90º or above: 97
Clear: 116
Partly Cloudy: 114
Cloudy: 135

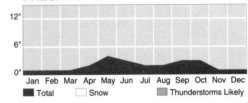

PRECIPITATION

ANNUAL
Precipitation: 30.0"
Snow: 1.1"
DAYS
Precipitation: 43
Thunderstorm: 40
Fog: 22

Grade: 78

Fredericksburg–Spotsylvania, VA

Location: 38.18 N, 77.27 W, at 60 feet, 42 miles south of Washington, D.C., and 40 miles north of Richmond.

Landscape: Rolling hill country at the head of navigation of the Rappahannock River in northeastern Virginia. The woods are a southeastern mixed forest of medium-tall to tall broadleaf deciduous oak, hickory, sweet gum, red maple, and winged elm, together with loblolly, and shortleaf pine. The undergrowth is dogwood, viburnum, blueberry, youpon, and numerous woody vines.

Climate: Modified continental, with cool winters and warm, humid summers. The Blue Ridge Mountains to the west produce various steering and blocking effects on storms and air masses. Chesapeake Bay further modifies the climate, making it warmer in winter and cooler in summer. Precipitation is well distributed throughout the year.

Winter mildness: 73 **Hazard free:** 66
Summer mildness: 75 **Seasonal affect:** 75

Grade: 73

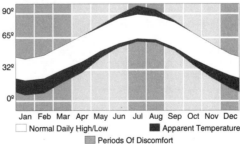

TEMPERATURE

ANNUAL
Humidity: 58%
Wind Speed: 8.1 mph
DAYS
0º or below: 1
32º or below: 112
90º or above: 49
Clear: 112
Partly Cloudy: 107
Cloudy: 146

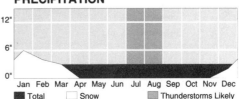

PRECIPITATION

ANNUAL
Precipitation: 40.7"
Snow: 16.9"
DAYS
Precipitation: 72
Thunderstorm: 40
Fog: 23

Gainesville, FL

Location: 29.39 N, 82.19 W, at 147 feet, in north central Florida, 66 miles SW of Jacksonville.

Landscape: Flat-to-rolling ranch and farm country, with some geological relief in limestone sinkholes and caverns. Native trees are longleaf and slash pines. Gallberry, saw palmetto, and fetterbush make up the undergrowth. Plants normally found in ravines of the Appalachian Mountains are at home here.

Climate: Subtropical in character, with a small annual range of temperature change. Humid, hot summer afternoons are cooled by frequent, heavy thunderstorms. Winters are mild, with warm days and cool nights.

Winter mildness: 100   **Hazard free:** 64
Summer mildness: 58   **Seasonal affect:** 76

TEMPERATURE

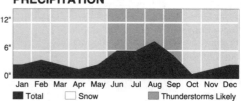

ANNUAL
Humidity: 59%
Wind Speed: 6.4 mph
DAYS
0º or below: 0
32º or below: 21
90º or above: 98
Clear: 91
Partly Cloudy: 147
Cloudy: 127

PRECIPITATION

ANNUAL
Precipitation: 51.8"
Snow: 0.1"
DAYS
Precipitation: 70
Thunderstorm: 80
Fog: 41

Grade: 76

Grand Junction, CO

Location: 39.04 N, 108.33 W, at 4,597 feet, in the Grand Valley of western Colorado, at the confluence of the Colorado and Gunnison rivers, 20 miles east of the Utah border.

Landscape: Nearby is the lake-studded Grand Mesa, the Colorado National Monument, and Grand Mesa and Uncompahgre National forests. Sagebrush and cactus are found in the canyons; pine, spruce, and aspen forests cover the subalpine areas.

Climate: The interior location, coupled with the ring of high mountains, results in low rainfall. Winter snows are frequent, light, and do not remain long. In the summer, relative humidity is very low, making the region as dry as parts of Arizona. Sunny days predominate in all seasons. The city's climate is marked by wide seasonal temperature changes; thanks to the protection of the surrounding mountains, sudden and severe weather changes are infrequent.

Winter mildness: 66   **Hazard free:** 61
Summer mildness: 75   **Seasonal affect:** 83

Grade: 71

TEMPERATURE

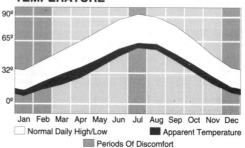

ANNUAL
Humidity: 41%
Wind Speed: 8.1 mph
DAYS
0º or below: 6
32º or below: 132
90º or above: 65
Clear: 137
Partly Cloudy: 106
Cloudy: 122

PRECIPITATION

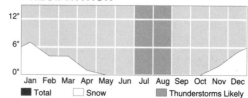

ANNUAL
Precipitation: 8.6"
Snow: 23.9"
DAYS
Precipitation: 34
Thunderstorm: 35
Fog: 8

Grants Pass, OR

Location: 42.26 N, 123.19 W, at 948 feet, on the Rogue River, in southwestern Oregon, 120 miles south of Eugene.

Landscape: In the midst of rugged terrain in the foothills of the Siskiyous. The Rogue River is swift whitewater here. Southwest is 'The Redwood Highway' and the Illinois Valley. The common trees in the dense Pacific conifer forest are Douglas fir, western red cedar, western hemlock, silver fir, and Sitka spruce.

Climate: Generally mild highland. The moderate temperatures of the Pacific are altered somewhat by the Coast Range. Nights are always cool, as are the days but for a brief period between July and August. Winter is the rainy season. Summers are dry.

Winter mildness: 82   **Hazard free:** 91
Summer mildness: 81   **Seasonal affect:** 72

Grade: 81

TEMPERATURE

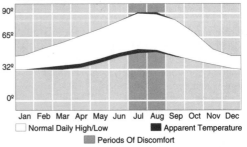

ANNUAL
Humidity: 59%
Wind Speed: 4.8 mph
DAYS
0º or below: 0
32º or below: 68
90º or above: 53
Clear: 116
Partly Cloudy: 79
Cloudy: 170

PRECIPITATION

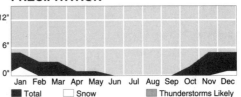

ANNUAL
Precipitation: 31.0"
Snow: 5.3"
DAYS
Precipitation: 62
Thunderstorm: 8
Fog: 49

Grass Valley–Nevada City, CA

Location: 39.15 N, 121.01 W, at 2,519 feet, on the western slope of the Sierra Nevadas, 60 miles NE of Sacramento.

Landscape: In a long, steeply sloping mountainous region. The Sacramento Valley to the west softens the terrain somewhat. The transition zone between grassland and Sierran forest is found here. Conifers and shrubs cover the slopes. At higher elevations, digger pine and blue oak form open stands. In the montane zone at 4,000 to 6,000 feet the most important trees are western yellow pine, Douglas fir, sugar pine, white fir, and incense cedar.

Climate: Mediterranean, characterized by winter rainfall and dry summers. The higher elevation of the Sierra foothills tempers the summer heat. Winters are milder here than at other locations on the eastern slope of the Sierras. There are frequent freezing temperatures at night, and an occasional blizzard.

Winter mildness: 74   **Hazard free:** 77
Summer mildness: 84   **Seasonal affect:** 81

Grade: 79

TEMPERATURE

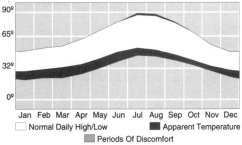

□ Normal Daily High/Low   ■ Apparent Temperature
■ Periods Of Discomfort

ANNUAL
Humidity: 58%
Wind Speed: 7.9 mph
DAYS
0º or below: 0
32º or below: 117
90º or above: 39
Clear: 189
Partly Cloudy: 75
Cloudy: 101

PRECIPITATION

■ Total   □ Snow   ▨ Thunderstorms Likely

ANNUAL
Precipitation: 56.0"
Snow: 16.7"
DAYS
Precipitation: 59
Thunderstorm: 14
Fog: 34

Guntersville, AL

Location: 34.21 N, 86.17 W, at 592 feet, on Guntersville Lake in northeast Alabama, at the southernmost point of the Tennessee River.

Landscape: Created by impoundment, the 30-mile long, island-dotted lake is at the base of the Appalachian Mountain range. The highlands are covered from shore to higher elevations with typical southeastern deciduous broadleaf forest with mixed southern yellow pine. There are high bluffs, caves, and mountain springs in the rolling foothill country.

Climate: Subtropical with hot, humid summers and short, mild winters. Precipitation is distributed throughout the year with a maximum in spring. Thunderstorms are common in summer. There may be snow but it is usually a light dusting and melts quickly.

Winter mildness: 83   **Hazard free:** 72
Summer mildness: 69   **Seasonal affect:** 73

Grade: 75

TEMPERATURE

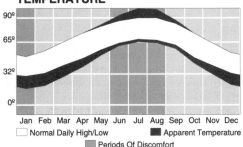

□ Normal Daily High/Low   ■ Apparent Temperature
■ Periods Of Discomfort

ANNUAL
Humidity: 57%
Wind Speed: 8.2 mph
DAYS
0º or below: 0
32º or below: 85
90º or above: 61
Clear: 102
Partly Cloudy: 101
Cloudy: 162

PRECIPITATION

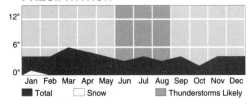

■ Total   □ Snow   ▨ Thunderstorms Likely

ANNUAL
Precipitation: 53.2"
Snow: 2.3"
DAYS
Precipitation: 79
Thunderstorm: 57
Fog: 19

Hamilton–Bitterroot Valley, MT

Location: 46.14 N, 114.09 W, at 3,572 feet on the Bitterroot River in extreme western Montana, 45 miles south of Missoula.

Landscape: There are strong contrasts between rolling sub-alpine woodland, open parkland of the high valley, lakes and high glaciated peaks of the Bitterroot Mountains. Semiarid steppe conditions are good for the short grasses of the prairie. Scattered shrubs and low trees give way to evergreen forests. Ponderosa pine, pinyon-juniper and Douglas fir are frequent associates.

Climate:: Semiarid steppe, with most precipitation falling as snow in winter from October through May. Snow is especially heavy in the higher altitudes. Winters are cold and long. Summers hot, dry, clear and all too brief.

Winter mildness: 56   **Hazard free:** 49
Summer mildness: 95   **Seasonal affect:** 72

Grade: 71

TEMPERATURE

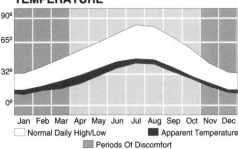

□ Normal Daily High/Low   ■ Apparent Temperature
■ Periods Of Discomfort

ANNUAL
Humidity: 61%
Wind Speed: 6.2 mph
DAYS
0º or below: 10
32º or below: 170
90º or above: 17
Clear: 74
Partly Cloudy: 82
Cloudy: 209

PRECIPITATION

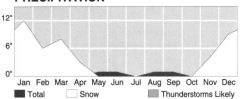

■ Total   □ Snow   ▨ Thunderstorms Likely

ANNUAL
Precipitation: 13.3"
Snow: 43.3"
DAYS
Precipitation: 37
Thunderstorm: 23
Fog: 26

Hanover, NH

Location: 43.42 N, 72.17 W, at 531 feet, on the Connecticut River in western New Hampshire, 135 miles NW of Boston.

Landscape: The Green Mountains of Vermont lie west, the White Mountains northeast of this upper Connecticut River Valley location. Low hills flank the river. The surrounding forest is mixed conifer and deciduous, with northern white pine, eastern hemlock, maple, oak, and beech.

Climate: Northerly latitude assures the variety and vigor of a true New England climate. The summer, while not long, is pleasant. Fall is cool and clear and runs through October. Winters are cold, with brief, intense cold snaps formed by high pressure systems moving down from central Canada and Hudson Bay. Snows are deep and long-lasting. Spring is called *breakup,* or *mud season.*

Winter mildness: 54   **Hazard free:** 21
Summer mildness: 91   **Seasonal affect:** 71

Grade: 64

TEMPERATURE

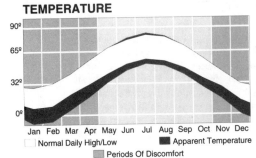

Normal Daily High/Low — Apparent Temperature — Periods Of Discomfort

ANNUAL
Humidity: 56%
Wind Speed: 8.5 mph
DAYS
0° or below: 23
32° or below: 167
90° or above: 7
Clear: 90
Partly Cloudy: 110
Cloudy: 165

PRECIPITATION

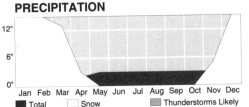

Total — Snow — Thunderstorms Likely

ANNUAL
Precipitation: 37.4"
Snow: 76.8"
DAYS
Precipitation: 75
Thunderstorm: 19
Fog: 49

Hendersonville–East Flat Rock, NC

Location: 35.19 N, 82.27 W, at 2,146 feet, just above the South Carolina border in the southwestern part of the state, 20 miles south of Asheville.

Landscape: The relief is mostly broken, mountainous, and rugged, with some very steep slopes and high waterfalls. There is a large intermountain valley, with rolling to strongly rolling mountain meadows. The Appalachian oak forest includes beech, birch, hickory, walnut, maple, elm, ash, sweet chestnut, and lower layers of small trees and shrubs.

Climate: Warm continental, with considerable differences in temperature between winter and summer. It is mild and pleasant from late spring to late fall, and summer nights are always cool even following hot afternoons. Winters are short, with light snowfalls.

Winter mildness: 75   **Hazard free:** 69
Summer mildness: 84   **Seasonal affect:** 70

Grade: 76

TEMPERATURE

Normal Daily High/Low — Apparent Temperature — Periods Of Discomfort

ANNUAL
Humidity: 58%
Wind Speed: 7.6 mph
DAYS
0° or below: 0
32° or below: 109
90° or above: 11
Clear: 102
Partly Cloudy: 113
Cloudy: 150

PRECIPITATION

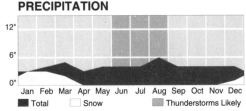

Total — Snow — Thunderstorms Likely

ANNUAL
Precipitation: 56.1"
Snow: 11.0"
DAYS
Precipitation: 82
Thunderstorm: 45
Fog: 77

Hesperia–Apple Valley–Victorville, CA

Location: 34.32 N, 117.17 W, at 2,715 feet, in the Victor Valley, 78 miles NE of Los Angeles.

Landscape: On the southwestern edge of the Mohave Desert and north of the San Bernardino Mountains and National Forest. This is dramatic country where mountain peaks thousands of feet high look down on valleys that lie below sea level. Sierran forest of coniferous and shrub at lower elevations; digger pine and blue oak in open or woodland stands.

Climate: Arid wilderness. Effects of desert and alpine terrain show in the hot, dry summers. Nights are invariably much cooler than the days. Most of the annual precipitation falls in the winter as rain on the lower slopes, in great amounts of snow in the higher mountains, and just a trace on the valley floor.

Winter mildness: 84   **Hazard free:** 95
Summer mildness: 66   **Seasonal affect:** 93

Grade: 81

TEMPERATURE

Normal Daily High/Low — Apparent Temperature — Periods Of Discomfort

ANNUAL
Humidity: 32%
Wind Speed: 7.8 mph
DAYS
0° or below: 0
32° or below: 79
90° or above: 104
Clear: 241
Partly Cloudy: 75
Cloudy: 49

PRECIPITATION

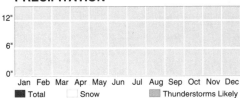

Total — Snow — Thunderstorms Likely

ANNUAL
Precipitation: 5.5"
Snow: 1.2"
DAYS
Precipitation: 12
Thunderstorm: 7
Fog: 1

Hiawassee, GA

Location: 34.57 N, 83.45 W, at 1,980 feet, in the Mountain and Intermountain Plateau province of northeast Georgia some 90 miles NE of Atlanta.

Landscape: Hilly to mountainous, with elevations averaging 1,500 feet. To the north, some of the mountains rise above 3,000 feet. Chattahoochee National Forest is a typical eastern mountain deciduous collection of oak, beech, birch, walnut, maple, ash, and hornbeam. Pines readily develop as second growth where there has been logging or fire.

Climate: Nearby mountains, and higher mountain ranges farther north, have a marked influence. Summer heat is tempered by the higher elevations. The contrast of valley and hill exposures results in wide variations in winter low temperatures. Summers are long, generally clear, and pleasant, with warm days and cool nights. Winters are cold but short. Spring is changeable and sometimes stormy. Fall is clear and sunny, with chilly nights.

Winter mildness: 76	**Hazard free:** 74
Summer mildness: 84	**Seasonal affect:** 69
Grade: 77	

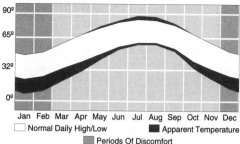

TEMPERATURE

Normal Daily High/Low — Apparent Temperature — Periods Of Discomfort

ANNUAL
Humidity: 60%
Wind Speed: 7.6 mph
DAYS
0º or below: 0
32º or below: 93
90º or above: 14
Clear: 102
Partly Cloudy: 113
Cloudy: 150

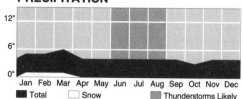

PRECIPITATION

Total — Snow — Thunderstorms Likely

ANNUAL
Precipitation: 57.2"
Snow: 6.0"
DAYS
Precipitation: 95
Thunderstorm: 45
Fog: 77

Hilton Head Island, SC

Location: 32.13 N, 80.45 W, at 8 feet, on Hilton Head Island, one of the Sea Islands, 45 miles south of Charleston and 35 miles north of Savannah, GA.

Landscape: The land is low and flat with elevations mostly under 25 feet. There are dozens of islands of various shapes and sizes, and on them are fresh and saltwater streams, inlets, rivers, and sounds. The interior forest are medium to tall stands of mixed loblolly and shortleaf pines, plus oak, hickory, red maple, and winged elm.

Climate: Subtropical, just on the edge of the climate enjoyed by Florida and the Caribbean Islands. The surrounding water produces mild winters, hot and humid summers, and temperatures that shift slowly. The inland Appalachian Mountains block much cold air from the northern interior, and the Gulf Stream moderates the climate considerably.

Winter mildness: 97	**Hazard free:** 79
Summer mildness: 66	**Seasonal affect:** 74

Grade: 80

TEMPERATURE

Normal Daily High/Low — Apparent Temperature — Periods Of Discomfort

ANNUAL
Humidity: 59%
Wind Speed: 8.6 mph
DAYS
0º or below: 0
32º or below: 28
90º or above: 56
Clear: 103
Partly Cloudy: 109
Cloudy: 153

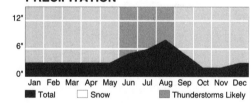

PRECIPITATION

Total — Snow — Thunderstorms Likely

ANNUAL
Precipitation: 51.4"
Snow: 0.3"
DAYS
Precipitation: 71
Thunderstorm: 47
Fog: 28

Hot Springs, AR

Location: 34.30 N, 93.03 W, at 579 feet, on the Ouachita River 36 miles SW of Little Rock, the state capital.

Landscape: At the eastern edge of the Ouachita Mountains and the Ouachita National Forest of central Arkansas. There are 47 thermal springs here. In the protected forests, mixed broadleaf deciduous trees such as oak, maple, sweet gum, and hickory thrive. Needleleaf evergreens and lower layers of weakly developed small trees and shrubs such as redbud and dogwood are common.

Climate: The irregular topography, with elevations varying from 400 feet to 1,000 feet, has considerable effect on the microclimate of the area, particularly on temperature extremes, ground fog, and precipitation. Winter is short, wet, with temperatures falling below freezing half the nights. Summers are hot, humid, and long. Spring and fall are changeable and pleasant.

Winter mildness: 87	**Hazard free:** 70
Summer mildness: 65	**Seasonal affect:** 75

Grade: 75

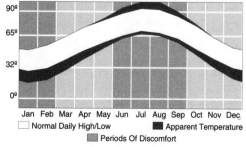

TEMPERATURE

Normal Daily High/Low — Apparent Temperature — Periods Of Discomfort

ANNUAL
Humidity: 57%
Wind Speed: 7.8 mph
DAYS
0º or below: 0
32º or below: 56
90º or above: 78
Clear: 118
Partly Cloudy: 100
Cloudy: 147

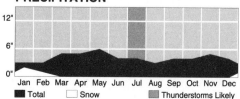

PRECIPITATION

Total — Snow — Thunderstorms Likely

ANNUAL
Precipitation: 56.5"
Snow: 4.7"
DAYS
Precipitation: 72
Thunderstorm: 56
Fog: 16

Houghton Lake, MI

Location: 44.19 N, 84.46 W, at 1,138 feet, in Michigan's central plateau. The largest inland lake in the state, it is 180 miles NW of Detroit.

Landscape: The land around the lake is level to rolling, gradually dropping off toward the east and, more rapidly, to the south. In the north are hills and ridges 100 to 300 feet higher. The region has thick woods and abundant streams and lakes. In the transitional forest there is mixed conifer, mostly northern white pine, and a few deciduous species.

Climate: The daily and seasonal temperature range is greater here than along Michigan's shorelines where the modifying effects of the Great Lakes can be felt. Rainfall is heaviest in the summer, with 60 percent of it falling between April and September. Winters here are cold and snowy, though not as snowy as those in locations to the north and west. Cloudiness is greatest in late fall and winter.

Winter mildness: 51
Summer mildness: 95
Hazard free: 18
Seasonal affect: 69

Grade: 63

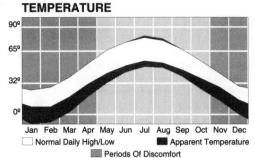

TEMPERATURE

ANNUAL
Humidity: 63%
Wind Speed: 8.9 mph
DAYS
0° or below: 24
32° or below: 172
90° or above: 3
Clear: 65
Partly Cloudy: 99
Cloudy: 201

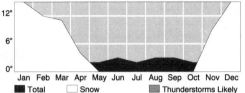

PRECIPITATION

ANNUAL
Precipitation: 28.3"
Snow: 74.0"
DAYS
Precipitation: 71
Thunderstorm: 31
Fog: 29

Inverness, FL

Location: 28.50 N, 82.20 W, at 38 feet in Florida's west central lakes country, 55 miles north of Tampa.

Landscape: The Green Swamp, the source of five rivers and 70 percent of the state's water, lies east of here. Composed of lakes, rivers, forests, and sandhills. Withlacoochee State Forest encloses a typical mix of hardwood, longleaf, and slash pine. Aromatic and evergreen bayberry and sweet bay are scattered throughout.

Climate: Subtropical, with a small annual range of temperature. Humid, hot summers are somewhat cooled by regular, heavy afternoon thunderstorms. Winters are extremely mild.

Winter mildness: 100
Summer mildness: 55
Hazard free: 63
Seasonal affect: 76

Grade: 75

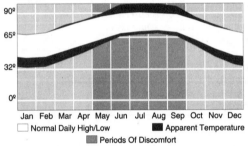

TEMPERATURE

ANNUAL
Humidity: 54%
Wind Speed: 8.6 mph
DAYS
0° or below: 0
32° or below: 8
90° or above: 109
Clear: 91
Partly Cloudy: 147
Cloudy: 127

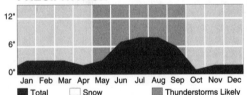

PRECIPITATION

ANNUAL
Precipitation: 53.4"
Snow: 0.0"
DAYS
Precipitation: 76
Thunderstorm: 81
Fog: 26

Kalispell–Flathead Valley, MT

Location: 48.11 N, 114.18 W, at 2,946 feet, in the Flathead valley at the western gateway to Glacier National Park, about 70 air miles north of Missoula.

Landscape: The Continental Divide is 40 miles east of here. The nearby mountains rise 4,500 feet above the valley floor. In addition to Flathead Lake, the valley contains four smaller lakes and numerous streams and sloughs. Conditions are good for the short prairie grasses. Scattered shrubs and low trees give way to evergreen forests. Ponderosa pine, pinyon-juniper, and Douglas fir are frequent associates.

Climate: The high mountains to the east block cold air from Alberta in the wintertime, and assure frequent and beneficial rains by cooling the moist ocean air arriving from the west. There is more precipitation on the eastern side of the valley than the western. Winter is cold and snowy. Summers are pleasant and dry.

Winter mildness: 54
Summer mildness: 98
Hazard free: 50
Seasonal affect: 71

Grade: 70

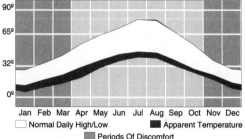

TEMPERATURE

ANNUAL
Humidity: 61%
Wind Speed: 6.6 mph
DAYS
0° or below: 10
32° or below: 170
90° or above: 17
Clear: 71
Partly Cloudy: 80
Cloudy: 214

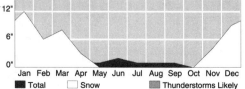

PRECIPITATION

ANNUAL
Precipitation: 16.5"
Snow: 43.3"
DAYS
Precipitation: 37
Thunderstorm: 22
Fog: 32

✓ Kauai, HI

Location: The weather station is Lihue, 21.59 N, 159.22 W, at 207 feet, on the settled east coast of the volcanic island, 95 air miles NW of Honolulu.

Landscape: The northernmost of the major Hawaiian Islands, it is also the most verdant and known as the Garden Isle. Consisting mainly of Mt. Waialeale and marginal lowlands dissected by fertile valleys and deep fissures. Strands of native plants include varieties of fern and palm, and shrub, forest, bog, and moss lichen.

Climate: Mild marine tropical, characterized by a two-season year. Temperature conditions are mild and uniform everywhere but high elevations. There are marked geographic differences in rainfall. Mt. Waialeale is the wettest spot on earth, with an annual rainfall exceeding 40 feet. The exceptionally steep rainfall gradient ensures a much drier leeward coast. Easterly trade winds dominate. This is associated with brisk sea breezes in the afternoon.

Winter mildness: 100   **Hazard free:** 98
Summer mildness: 71   **Seasonal affect:** 88
Grade: 89

TEMPERATURE

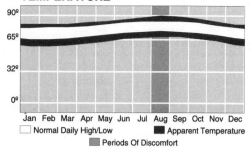

□ Normal Daily High/Low   ■ Apparent Temperature
▨ Periods Of Discomfort

ANNUAL
Humidity: 66%
Wind Speed: 12.8 mph
DAYS
0º or below: 0
32º or below: 0
90º or above: 17
Clear: 131
Partly Cloudy: 143
Cloudy: 91

PRECIPITATION

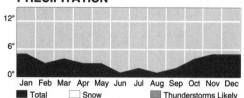

■ Total   □ Snow   ▨ Thunderstorms Likely

ANNUAL
Precipitation: 43.0"
Snow: 0.0"
DAYS
Precipitation: 19
Thunderstorm: 4
Fog: 0

Kentucky Lake, KY

Location: The weather station is Murray, 36.36 N, 88.19 W, at 480 feet, in the western part of the state, 100 miles NW of Nashville, TN.

Landscape: Kentucky Lake is one of the world's largest man-made lakes, formed more than 40 years ago by damming the Tennessee River. Relief is minimal. The surrounding country is gently rolling and heavily forested with oak, hickory, walnut, maple, elm, ash, and sweet chestnut with lower layers of small trees and shrubs.

Climate: Hot continental, with moderately cold winters and warm, humid summers. Precipitation is ample and well distributed throughout the year. Most days, even those in winter, are suitable for outdoor activity. Spring and fall are the most comfortable seasons. Fall, the sunniest season, is remarkably free from storms or cold.

Winter mildness: 79   **Hazard free:** 63
Summer mildness: 72   **Seasonal affect:** 74

Grade: 73

TEMPERATURE

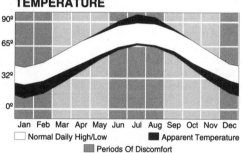

□ Normal Daily High/Low   ■ Apparent Temperature
▨ Periods Of Discomfort

ANNUAL
Humidity: 58%
Wind Speed: 7.8 mph
DAYS
0º or below: 1
32º or below: 84
90º or above: 51
Clear: 109
Partly Cloudy: 99
Cloudy: 157

PRECIPITATION

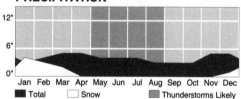

■ Total   □ Snow   ▨ Thunderstorms Likely

ANNUAL
Precipitation: 53.6"
Snow: 10.8"
DAYS
Precipitation: 74
Thunderstorm: 59
Fog: 19

Kerrville, TX

Location: 30.03 N, 99.08 W, at 1,645 feet, at the edge of the Edwards Plateau, 75 miles west of Austin, the state capital.

Landscape: Kerr County lies across the hills, valleys, and uplands of the rolling Hill Country of southwest Texas. There are breaks into the deep valleys of the Guadalupe River and its tributaries. The area is covered with cedars and live oaks.

Climate: Prairie continental in character, with wide swings of temperature both daily and seasonally, especially in the winter. Winter precipitation is mostly slow, steady, light rain. Summer months are drier and hot. Falls are pleasant but can be stormy due both to "northers" and Gulf storms moving north.

Winter mildness: 92   **Hazard free:** 81
Summer mildness: 58   **Seasonal affect:** 79

TEMPERATURE

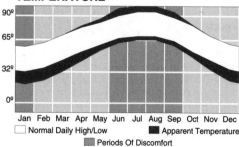

□ Normal Daily High/Low   ■ Apparent Temperature
▨ Periods Of Discomfort

ANNUAL
Humidity: 56%
Wind Speed: 9.2 mph
DAYS
0º or below: 0
32º or below: 53
90º or above: 107
Clear: 116
Partly Cloudy: 114
Cloudy: 135

PRECIPITATION

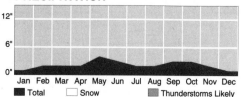

■ Total   □ Snow   ▨ Thunderstorms Likely

ANNUAL
Precipitation: 34.2"
Snow: 0.8"
DAYS
Precipitation: 49
Thunderstorm: 40
Fog: 22

Grade: 77

Ketchum-Sun Valley, ID

Location: 43.41 N, 114.21 W, at 5,821 feet, at the edge of Idaho's Sawtooth recreation area, 100 miles east of Boise.

Landscape: Sits high among even higher, rugged mountains. There are several flat or nearly flat glaciated valleys, some of which are several miles wide. The native vegetation is a mixed coniferous forest comprised of Douglas fir, Engelmann spruce and cedar-hemlock.

Climate: Semiarid steppe. Summers are crisp, clear, and dry. Winters are long and cold. Annual precipitation comes almost entirely as light and dry snow, and accumulates to some depth. The prevailing winds are westerlies. Seasonal and daily temperature changes are extreme, but would be even more so if not moderated by the mountains.

Winter mildness: 49   **Hazard free:** 62
Summer mildness: 97   **Seasonal affect:** 72

Grade: 71

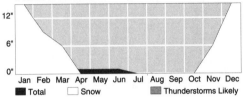

TEMPERATURE

Normal Daily High/Low — Apparent Temperature — Periods Of Discomfort

ANNUAL
Humidity: 59%
Wind Speed: 8.8 mph
DAYS
0° or below: 10
32° or below: 185
90° or above: 12
Clear: 120
Partly Cloudy: 90
Cloudy: 155

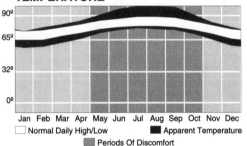

PRECIPITATION

Total — Snow — Thunderstorms Likely

ANNUAL
Precipitation: 15.9"
Snow: 60.2"
DAYS
Precipitation: 80
Thunderstorm: 14
Fog: 47

Key West-Key Largo-Marathon, FL

Location: 24.33 N, 81.47 W, at 7 feet, at the end of the long island chain swinging in a southwesterly arc from the tip of the Florida peninsula, 160 miles south of Miami.

Landscape: Key West sits on a sand and coral island 3 1/2 miles long and 1 mile wide. The average elevation along the entire island chain is just 8 feet. The waters surrounding these islands are shallow, and there is little wave action because outlying reefs break the surf. Much of the shoreline is filled mangrove swamp.

Climate: Because of the Gulf Stream, the Florida Keys have a notably mild, tropical-maritime climate in which the average winter temperatures are only about 14 degrees lower than in summer. Summers are hot, humid, and stormy, although prevailing easterly tradewinds and sea breezes make the heat tolerable.

Winter mildness: 100   **Hazard free:** 71
Summer mildness: 59   **Seasonal affect:** 79

Grade: 78

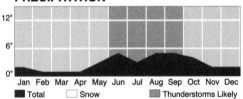

TEMPERATURE

Normal Daily High/Low — Apparent Temperature — Periods Of Discomfort

ANNUAL
Humidity: 67%
Wind Speed: 11.2 mph
DAYS
0° or below: 0
32° or below: 0
90° or above: 46
Clear: 103
Partly Cloudy: 156
Cloudy: 106

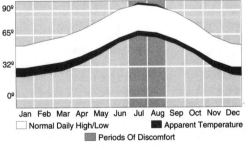

PRECIPITATION

Total — Snow — Thunderstorms Likely

ANNUAL
Precipitation: 39.6"
Snow: 0.0"
DAYS
Precipitation: 84
Thunderstorm: 64
Fog: 1

Kingman, AZ

Location: 35.11 N, 114.03 W, at 3,334 feet, in the dry Peacock Mountains in northwestern Arizona, 90 miles SE .of Las Vegas, NV.

Landscape: Sits some 2,000 feet above the Colorado River Valley in high plateau country. Lakes Mead, Mohave, and Havasu are principal sources of water and recreation. Ground cover is primarily sagebrush and native grasses. In the upper elevations are sparse conifer stands.

Climate: Arid steppe, with strong daily and seasonal temperature changes. Winters are clear, long, and extremely mild with some flow of air from as far as the Pacific Ocean. There is a hot, sunbaked stretch from July through September. Except for brief periods in spring and summer, there is no measurable precipitation.

Winter mildness: 86   **Hazard free:** 95
Summer mildness: 63   **Seasonal affect:** 92

Grade: 81

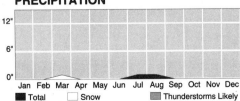

TEMPERATURE

Normal Daily High/Low — Apparent Temperature — Periods Of Discomfort

ANNUAL
Humidity: 32%
Wind Speed: 7.8 mph
DAYS
0° or below: 0
32° or below: 61
90° or above: 101
Clear: 241
Partly Cloudy: 75
Cloudy: 49

PRECIPITATION

Total — Snow — Thunderstorms Likely

ANNUAL
Precipitation: 9.8'
Snow: 2.4"
DAYS
Precipitation: 23
Thunderstorm: 7
Fog: 1

Kissimmee–St. Cloud, FL

Location: 28.17 N, 81.24 W, at 19 feet at the head of Lake Tohopekaliga in central Florida, 30 miles SW of Orlando.
Landscape: Situated amid clear lakes in gently rolling hill country. Flood-plain grasses and pine flatwoods mix with live oak hammocks. Forests are a typical mix of hardwood, longleaf, and slash pine. Aromatic and evergreen bayberry and sweet bay are scattered throughout.
Climate: Subtropical, with a small annual range of temperature change. Warmed by both the Gulf of Mexico and the Atlantic. Winters are sunny, mild, and dry. Summers are hot, humid, and beset by frequent thunderstorms that provide half of the area's annual precipitation.

Winter mildness: 100   **Hazard free:** 63
Summer mildness: 54   **Seasonal affect:** 77

TEMPERATURE

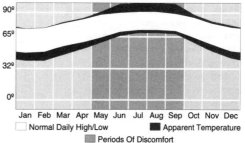
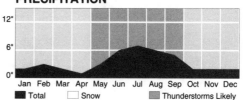

ANNUAL
Humidity: 54%
Wind Speed: 8.6 mph
DAYS
0° or below: 0
32° or below: 3
90° or above: 108
Clear: 91
Partly Cloudy: 147
Cloudy: 127

PRECIPITATION

ANNUAL
Precipitation: 46.1"
Snow: 0.0"
DAYS
Precipitation: 73
Thunderstorm: 81
Fog: 26

Grade: 75

✓ Laguna Beach–Dana Point, CA

Location: 33.32 N, 117.47 W, at 44 feet, on the Pacific Ocean 40 miles south of Los Angeles.
Landscape: Steep hills rise from two lagoons at the head of Laguna canyon. Trees and shrubs must withstand severe summer drought and evaporation. Following a wet winter, hard-leaved evergreens such as pinyon and cypress are more abundant.
Climate: Ocean breezes keep the weather mild throughout the year. Morning fog and low clouds are common in cooler seasons. There is not much precipitation, and what rain there is falls mostly in winter.

Winter mildness: 100   **Hazard free:** 98
Summer mildness: 87   **Seasonal affect:** 84

TEMPERATURE

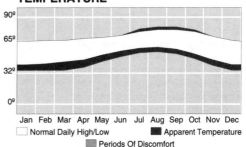
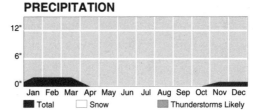

ANNUAL
Humidity: 61%
Wind Speed: 7.5 mph
DAYS
0° or below: 0
32° or below: 3
90° or above: 2
Clear: 146
Partly Cloudy: 115
Cloudy: 104

PRECIPITATION

ANNUAL
Precipitation: 12.2"
Snow: 0.0"
DAYS
Precipitation: 21
Thunderstorm: 3
Fog: 38

Grade: 93

Lake Buchanan–Lake LBJ, TX

Location: 30.45 N, 98.25 W, at 1,270 feet, on the Colorado River at the northern end of the Highland Lakes region, 50 miles NW of Austin, the state capital.
Landscape: In the cedar and oak Hill Country of central Texas. Granite cliffs, limestone bluffs, and caverns are prominent geologic features. Cypress trees grow on the river banks and bluebonnet and other wildflowers bloom with sufficient rainfall.
Climate: Prairie. Summer days are hot, but nights are pleasantly cool. Winters are mild with few, brief cold spells. Rainfall is distributed fairly evenly throughout the year. Humidity is generally a comfortable 55 percent.

Winter mildness: 96   **Hazard free:** 81
Summer mildness: 59   **Seasonal affect:** 80

TEMPERATURE

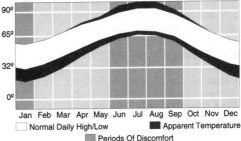
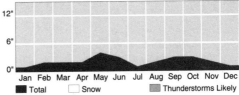

ANNUAL
Humidity: 56%
Wind Speed: 9.2 mph
DAYS
0° or below: 0
32° or below: 21
90° or above: 107
Clear: 116
Partly Cloudy: 114
Cloudy: 135

PRECIPITATION

ANNUAL
Precipitation: 31.2"
Snow: 0.8"
DAYS
Precipitation: 40
Thunderstorm: 40
Fog: 22

Grade: 78

Lake Conroe, TX

Location: 30.21 N, 95.33 W, at 201 feet, in the Texas Gulf Plain, 40 miles north of downtown Houston.
Landscape: On a flood plain at the southern edge of the Big Thicket area with rolling hills and many small lakes. The area is rapidly becoming suburbanized with some loss to the surrounding piney woods and dense deciduous forests.
Climate: Subtropical. Summer days are hot and humid but the nights are pleasantly cool. Winters are mild with few, brief cold spells. Rainfall is distributed evenly throughout the year, but arrives in major storms.

Winter mildness: 98   **Hazard free:** 72
Summer mildness: 56   **Seasonal affect:** 74

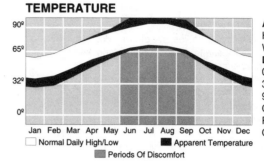

TEMPERATURE

☐ Normal Daily High/Low   ■ Apparent Temperature
■ Periods Of Discomfort

ANNUAL
Humidity: 59%
Wind Speed: 7.9 mph
DAYS
0º or below: 0
32º or below: 28
90º or above: 108
Clear: 94
Partly Cloudy: 114
Cloudy: 157

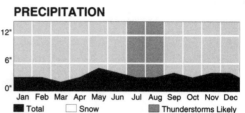

PRECIPITATION

■ Total   ☐ Snow   ■ Thunderstorms Likely

ANNUAL
Precipitation: 47.3"
Snow: 0.3"
DAYS
Precipitation: 64
Thunderstorm: 61
Fog: 31

Grade: 76

Lake Granbury, TX

Location: 32.26 N, 97.47 W, at 722 feet, on the Brazos River, 40 miles SW of Ft. Worth.
Landscape: In the Grand Prairie region with distant mesa and butte vistas. The native vegetation includes post oak, black-jack oak, Texas hickory, and bluestem parkland grasses.
Climate: Prairie. Summer days are hot but nights are pleasantly cool. Winters are mild with few, brief cold spells. Rainfall is distributed fairly evenly throughout the year. Humidity is generally less than 60 percent.

Winter mildness: 91   **Hazard free:** 77
Summer mildness: 59   **Seasonal affect:** 79

TEMPERATURE

☐ Normal Daily High/Low   ■ Apparent Temperature
■ Periods Of Discomfort

ANNUAL
Humidity: 59%
Wind Speed: 7.9 mph
DAYS
0º or below: 0
32º or below: 40
90º or above: 96
Clear: 137
Partly Cloudy: 97
Cloudy: 131

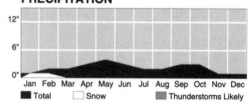

PRECIPITATION

■ Total   ☐ Snow   ■ Thunderstorms Likely

ANNUAL
Precipitation: 32.5"
Snow: 2.8"
DAYS
Precipitation: 47
Thunderstorm: 45
Fog: 31

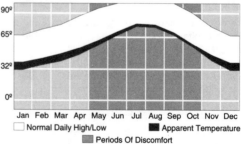

Grade: 76

Lake Havasu City, AZ

Location: 34.29 N, 114.19 W, at 602 feet, in extreme western Arizona, above Parker Dam on the Colorado River, 100 miles SE of Las Vegas, NV.
Landscape: On the Colorado River, west of the Mohave Mountains. The center is the 45-mile-long Lake Havasu, with redwall limestone canyon, steep slopes, and gorges. This is the edge of the Sonoran Desert where growth is low shrub and saguaro. Creosote bush, geraniums, and sedums are common especially after a wet winter.
Climate: Desert, with strong daily and seasonal temperature changes. Winters are clear, long, and extremely mild with some flow of air from as far as the Pacific Ocean. There is a long, hot, sunbaked stretch from May through October. Except for a handful of days in spring and summer, there is no measurable precipitation.

Winter mildness: 100   **Hazard free:** 97
Summer mildness: 38   **Seasonal affect:** 93

TEMPERATURE

☐ Normal Daily High/Low   ■ Apparent Temperature
■ Periods Of Discomfort

ANNUAL
Humidity: 32%
Wind Speed: 7.8 mph
DAYS
0º or below: 0
32º or below: 14
90º or above: 178
Clear: 241
Partly Cloudy: 75
Cloudy: 49

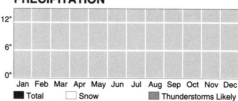

PRECIPITATION

■ Total   ☐ Snow   ■ Thunderstorms Likely

ANNUAL
Precipitation: 4.5"
Snow: 0.0"
DAYS
Precipitation: 11
Thunderstorm: 7
Fog: 1

Grade: 78

Lake Livingston, TX

Location: 30.37 N, 95.01 W, at 131 feet, in the Trinity River valley 75 miles NE of Houston.

Landscape: On the southern edge of Big Thicket area with rolling hills and many small lakes. Native vegetation includes post and blackjack oak, and Texas hickory stands mixed with piney woods.

Climate: Prairie. Summer days are hot but nights are pleasantly cool. Winters are mild with a few, brief cold spells overnight. Rainfall is distributed fairly evenly throughout the year. Humidity is generally a comfortable 60 percent or less.

Winter mildness: 94   **Hazard free:** 72
Summer mildness: 59   **Seasonal affect:** 75

Grade: 75

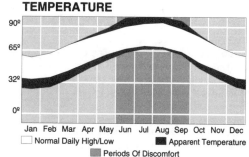

TEMPERATURE

ANNUAL
Humidity: 59%
Wind Speed: 7.9 mph
DAYS
0º or below: 0
32º or below: 41
90º or above: 99
Clear: 94
Partly Cloudy: 114
Cloudy: 157

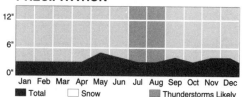

PRECIPITATION

ANNUAL
Precipitation: 48.7"
Snow: 0.8"
DAYS
Precipitation: 65
Thunderstorm: 61
Fog: 11

Lake Martin, AL

Location: 32.56 N, 85.57 W, at 707 feet, 40 miles NE of Montgomery, the state capital.

Landscape: Created on the Tallapoosa River by Alabama Power Company decades ago. The lake has some 700 miles of irregular shoreline. In the sandhills further north, the land slopes gently. Streams are numerous. Forests are mixed deciduous and needleleaf evergreen. Varieties include predominately southern yellow pine and small stands of oak, black gum, and red maple.

Climate: Hot continental. From June through September, humidity and temperature conditions show little daily change. In summer, precipitation is from local heat thundershowers in the afternoon. Rain is abundant and includes all types and intensities from December through March. Hard winter freezes are infrequent; snow is rare enough to be a curiosity.

Winter mildness: 90   **Hazard free:** 73
Summer mildness: 67   **Seasonal affect:** 74

Grade: 77

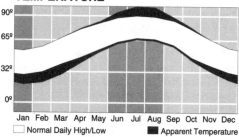

TEMPERATURE

ANNUAL
Humidity: 55%
Wind Speed: 6.7 mph
DAYS
0º or below: 0
32º or below: 40
90º or above: 75
Clear: 109
Partly Cloudy: 105
Cloudy: 151

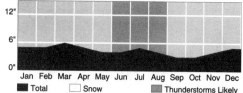

PRECIPITATION

ANNUAL
Precipitation: 57.9"
Snow: 0.3"
DAYS
Precipitation: 74
Thunderstorm: 58
Fog: 21

Lake of the Cherokees, OK

Location: 36.33 N, 94.45 W, at 739 feet, near the western slope of the Ozark Mountains, 75 miles NE of Tulsa.

Landscape: The forested hills drop to the 1,300-mile shore of Grand Lake, a major impoundment on the Neosho River. Foothills give way to low-relief plain and rivers. Forest and prairie grow side by side: deciduous oak-hickory forests with elm, sycamore, bur oak, redbud, and buckeye stand next to vast stretches of bluestem grasses.

Climate: Prairie, with hot summers and winters that are moderate with occasional hard freezes. Annual precipitation is moderate and usually falls as rain. Humidity is mild.

Winter mildness: 81   **Hazard free:** 69
Summer mildness: 68   **Seasonal affect:** 78

Grade: 74

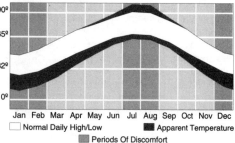

TEMPERATURE

ANNUAL
Humidity: 55%
Wind Speed: 10.3 mph
DAYS
0º or below: 1
32º or below: 78
90º or above: 73
Clear: 127
Partly Cloudy: 102
Cloudy: 136

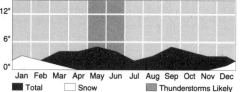

PRECIPITATION

ANNUAL
Precipitation: 46.4"
Snow: 8.8"
DAYS
Precipitation: 61
Thunderstorm: 50
Fog: 10

Lake of the Ozarks, MO

Location: 38.00 N, 92.44 W, at 1,043 feet, on the Osage River, 44 miles SW of Jefferson City, the state capital.
Landscape: There are 1,150 miles of irregular shoreline on the lake, formed when the Osage River was dammed in the rolling, open country of south-central Missouri. The slopes are wooded with oak, maple, sweet gum, and hickory, mixed with secondary-growth spruce and pine.
Climate: Hot continental with hot, humid summers and cold winters. Apparent temperatures, especially those caused by cold and wind, are pronounced throughout the year. Snow is neither deep nor long-lasting.

Winter mildness: 75   **Hazard free:** 57
Summer mildness: 72   **Seasonal affect:** 75

Grade: 71

TEMPERATURE
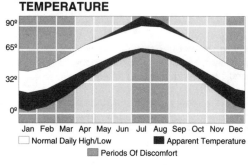

ANNUAL
Humidity: 59%
Wind Speed: 10.7 mph
DAYS
0º or below: 3
32º or below: 104
90º or above: 58
Clear: 115
Partly Cloudy: 96
Cloudy: 154

PRECIPITATION
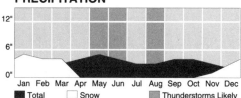

ANNUAL
Precipitation: 43.5"
Snow: 18.4"
DAYS
Precipitation: 66
Thunderstorm: 56
Fog: 20

Lake Winnipesaukee, NH

Location: 43.36 N, 71.19 W, at 504 feet, in central New Hampshire near the southern edge of the White Mountains, 30 miles NE of Concord, the state capital.
Landscape: From the island-dotted glacier lake to the ski resorts around North Conway, the terrain rises dramatically from elevations of about 2,000 feet to more than 6,000 feet in the Presidential Range. The area is generally rugged, scenic, and heavily forested. Interspersed between ranges and peaks are broad valleys. The mixed conifer and deciduous forest is transitional. Northern white pine, eastern hemlock, maple, oak, and beech are common.
Climate: Rigorous continental, with mild, clear summer days and cool nights. Falls are pleasant and famous throughout the region for bright foliage colors. Winters are long, snowy, and sometimes subfreezing for periods of several days to a week. Springs are changeable.

Winter mildness: 52   **Hazard free:** 34
Summer mildness: 93   **Seasonal affect:** 71

Grade: 66

TEMPERATURE

ANNUAL
Humidity: 54%
Wind Speed: 6.7 mph
DAYS
0º or below: 14
32º or below: 170
90º or above: 11
Clear: 90
Partly Cloudy: 110
Cloudy: 165

PRECIPITATION

ANNUAL
Precipitation: 40.5"
Snow: 62.8"
DAYS
Precipitation: 75
Thunderstorm: 19
Fog: 49

Lakeland–Winter Haven, FL

Location: 28.02 N, 81.57 W, at 211 feet, in central Florida, 42 miles east of Tampa.
Landscape: In the rolling lake-ridge section, 50 miles from the Gulf of Mexico and 70 miles from the Atlantic Ocean. Here one can find the highest elevation in the Florida peninsula. Flood-plain prairies and pine flatwoods mix with live oak hammocks. Forests are typical mix of hardwood, longleaf, and slash pine. Aromatic and evergreen bayberry and sweet bay are scattered throughout.
Climate: Subtropical. The proximity of the Gulf of Mexico and the Atlantic Ocean bring pleasant winters. Days are bright and warm, nights are cool, and rainfall is light to moderate. Occasionally, major cold waves overspread the area, bringing temperatures down below freezing. The high temperature and humidity during the long summers are moderated by afternoon thundershowers.

Winter mildness: 100   **Hazard free:** 63
Summer mildness: 53   **Seasonal affect:** 77

Grade: 74

TEMPERATURE
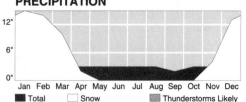

ANNUAL
Humidity: 54%
Wind Speed: 8.6 mph
DAYS
0º or below: 0
32º or below: 3
90º or above: 108
Clear: 91
Partly Cloudy: 147
Cloudy: 127

PRECIPITATION
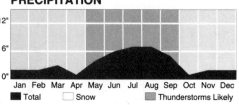

ANNUAL
Precipitation: 47.5"
Snow: 0.0"
DAYS
Precipitation: 73
Thunderstorm: 81
Fog: 26

Las Cruces, NM

Location: 32.18 N, 106.46 W, at 3,883 feet, near the southern edge of the state, 40 miles NW of El Paso, TX.

Landscape: The wide, level Rio Grande valley runs northwest to southeast through here. Rolling desert borders the southwest and west. About 12 miles east the Organ Mountains, with peaks above 8,500 feet, form a rugged backdrop. The northwest portion of the valley narrows to low hills and buttes. The vegetation is dry-desert with negligible groundcover. Only plants adapted to the highly alkaline conditions survive. These include thorn scrub, savanna, or steppe grassland, prickly pear, and saguaro cactus. In this higher altitude there are belts of oak and juniper woodland.

Climate: Desert continental, characterized by low rainfall, hot summers with cool nights, and mild and sunny winters. The rainfall is light, almost all of it falling during the summer growing months in brief showers. Drizzles are unknown.

Winter mildness: 85
Summer mildness: 64
Hazard free: 79
Seasonal affect: 90

Grade: 78

TEMPERATURE

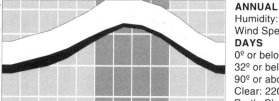

ANNUAL
Humidity: 33%
Wind Speed: 8.9 mph
DAYS
0º or below: 0
32º or below: 65
90º or above: 105
Clear: 193
Partly Cloudy: 99
Cloudy: 73

PRECIPITATION

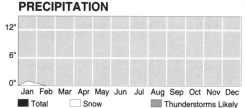

ANNUAL
Precipitation: 9.4"
Snow: 5.3"
DAYS
Precipitation: 22
Thunderstorm: 36
Fog: 2

Las Vegas, NV

Location: 36.10 N, 115.08 W, at 2,028 feet, just west of the Colorado River valley. Los Angeles is 300 miles SW.

Landscape: Near the center of a broad desert valley surrounded by mountains from 2,000 to 10,000 feet higher than the valley's floor. These mountains act as effective barriers to moisture-laden storms moving in from the Pacific Ocean. The thick-branched Joshua tree grows among creosote bushes and jumbled boulders in the Mohave Desert region.

Climate: Summers are typical of a desert climate. Humidity is low with maximum temperatures in the 100-degree levels. Nearby mountains contribute to relatively cool nights. Spring and fall are ideal, rarely interrupted by adverse weather conditions. Winters, too, are mild, with daytime averages of 60°F, clear skies, and warm sunshine. There are very few overcast or rainy days.

Winter mildness: 94
Summer mildness: 51
Hazard free: 93
Seasonal affect: 91

Grade: 79

TEMPERATURE

ANNUAL
Humidity: 23%
Wind Speed: 9.3 mph
DAYS
0º or below: 0
32º or below: 33
90º or above: 132
Clear: 220
Partly Cloudy: 79
Cloudy: 66

PRECIPITATION

ANNUAL
Precipitation: 4.1"
Snow: 1.2"
DAYS
Precipitation: 13
Thunderstorm: 13
Fog: 0

Leesburg–Lady Lake, FL

Location: 28.48 N, 81.52 W, at 80 feet, in Florida's central lakes region 40 miles NW of Orlando.

Landscape: Composed of lakes, rivers, forests, and sandhills. Withlacoochee State Forest is typical mix of hardwood, longleaf, and slash pine. Aromatic and evergreen bayberry and sweet bay are scattered throughout.

Climate: Subtropical, with a small range of annual temperature change. Humid, hot summers are cooled by frequent afternoon thunderstorms. Winters are extremely mild, with warm days and cool nights.

Winter mildness: 100
Summer mildness: 55
Hazard free: 63
Seasonal affect: 77

Grade: 75

TEMPERATURE

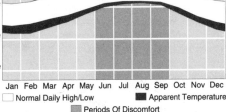

ANNUAL
Humidity: 54%
Wind Speed: 8.6 mph
DAYS
0º or below: 0
32º or below: 4
90º or above: 106
Clear: 91
Partly Cloudy: 147
Cloudy: 127

PRECIPITATION

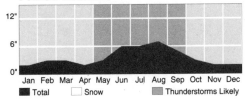

ANNUAL
Precipitation: 48.8"
Snow: 0.0"
DAYS
Precipitation: 73
Thunderstorm: 81
Fog: 26

Litchfield Hills, CT

Location: 41.48 N, 73.07 W, at 593 feet, in the state's northwest corner, 25 miles west of Hartford, the state capital.
Landscape: In the midst of low Berkshire Mountain foothills with many forest-rimmed lakes next to open fields and meadows. The woods are eastern hardwood forest dominated by tall, broadleaf trees that provide dense cover in summer, brilliant color in fall, and are bare in winter. Common are maple, oak, beech, birch, walnut, ash, and sweet chestnut.
Climate: Hot continental with large temperature variations from season to season. Winters receive Canadian air, which sweeps down the Hudson Valley to the west. December through February is cold with long-lasting snow. Spring is short. Summers are clear, warm, and ideal. Falls extend through mid-November. Precipitation is moderate and evenly distributed throughout the year.

Winter mildness: 62   **Hazard free:** 34
Summer mildness: 88   **Seasonal affect:** 71

Grade: 67

TEMPERATURE

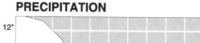

ANNUAL
Humidity: 56%
Wind Speed: 8.5 mph
DAYS
0º or below: 6
32º or below: 135
90º or above: 19
Clear: 80
Partly Cloudy: 108
Cloudy: 177

PRECIPITATION

ANNUAL
Precipitation: 49.3"
Snow: 62.2"
DAYS
Precipitation: 78
Thunderstorm: 20
Fog: 28

Lower Cape May, NJ

Location: 38.56 N, 74.54 W, at 10 feet, 50 miles south of Atlantic City, at the southern tip of the state where the Intracoastal Waterway swings into Delaware Bay.
Landscape: Surrounding flat terrain is composed of tidal marshes and beach sand. The dunes provide vantage points for observing bird migrations along the Atlantic flyway. The Wildwood resorts are on a barrier island to the northeast. The interior woods are evergreen and laurel.
Climate: Continental, but the moderating influence of the Atlantic Ocean is apparent throughout the year. Summers are relatively cooler, winters warmer than those of other places at the same latitude. During the warm season, sea breezes in the late morning and afternoon prevent excessive heat. Fall is long, lasting until almost mid-November. Warming is somewhat delayed in the spring.

Winter mildness: 78   **Hazard free:** 77
Summer mildness: 83   **Seasonal affect:** 73

Grade: 79

TEMPERATURE

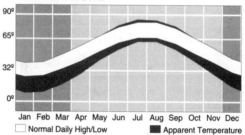

ANNUAL
Humidity: 57%
Wind Speed: 10.1 mph
DAYS
0º or below: 0
32º or below: 72
90º or above: 8
Clear: 94
Partly Cloudy: 110
Cloudy: 161

PRECIPITATION

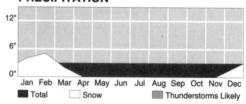

ANNUAL
Precipitation: 40.5"
Snow: 15.1"
DAYS
Precipitation: 64
Thunderstorm: 20
Fog: 44

Madison, MS

Location: 32.27 N, 90.07 W, at 335 feet on Ross Barnett Reservoir, 17 miles north of Jackson, the state capital.
Landscape: Damming the Pearl River created the 43-mile-long lake. Rolling hills of the central coastal plain are predominant but there are no topographical features that influence the weather. The woods are mixed broadleafed deciduous and southern yellow pine.
Climate: Subtropical. In summer, southerly winds and accompanying Gulf air predominate, resulting in a warm, humid maritime climate with afternoon thundershowers. Winters are mild and somewhat cloudy, with a short stretch of freezing nights.

Winter mildness: 91   **Hazard free:** 69
Summer mildness: 62   **Seasonal affect:** 75

Grade: 75

TEMPERATURE

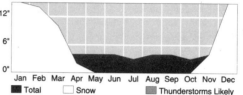

ANNUAL
Humidity: 58%
Wind Speed: 7.4 mph
DAYS
0º or below: 0
32º or below: 50
90º or above: 83
Clear: 113
Partly Cloudy: 103
Cloudy: 149

PRECIPITATION

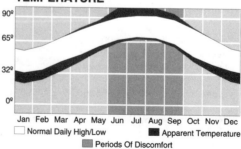
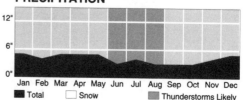

ANNUAL
Precipitation: 55.4"
Snow: 1.4"
DAYS
Precipitation: 69
Thunderstorm: 66
Fog: 22

Maryville, TN

Location: 35.45 N, 83.58 W, at 945 feet, in the foothills of the Great Smoky Mountains of eastern Tennessee, 16 miles south of Knoxville.

Landscape: To the east are the highest peaks in eastern North America. Well drained by lakes and rivers, including the Little Tennessee River. There is a large stand of virgin red spruce in the Great Smoky Mountains National Park. Common trees are hickory, oak, beech, birch, walnut, and maple. These tall, broadleafed trees provide a dense foliage during summer and completely shed their leaves in winter.

Climate: Hot continental, characterized by hot, humid summers and cool, cloudy, wet winters. Daily and seasonal temperature changes are not abrupt. In summer nights, there is a pleasant moderating effect where a steady wind, a draw caused by the many streams and waterfalls, pulls the cool air down from the mountains to the lowlands.

Winter mildness: 81 **Hazard free:** 68
Summer mildness: 77 **Seasonal affect:** 72

Grade: 76

TEMPERATURE

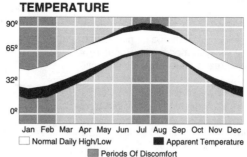

ANNUAL
Humidity: 60%
Wind Speed: 7.0 mph
DAYS
0º or below: 1
32º or below: 74
90º or above: 28
Clear: 97
Partly Cloudy: 106
Cloudy: 162

PRECIPITATION

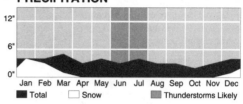

ANNUAL
Precipitation: 47.1"
Snow: 10.9"
DAYS
Precipitation: 83
Thunderstorm: 47
Fog: 31

✓ Maui, HI

Location: The weather station is Lahaina, 20.52 N, 156.41 W, at 20 feet, on Auau Channel on the island's west coast, 125 air miles from Honolulu.

Landscape: With an area of 728 square miles, Maui is the 2nd largest of the Hawaiian chain. It was created by two volcanoes, which make up east and west peninsulas connected by a valleylike isthmus seven miles wide. The peaks of west Maui rise to almost 6,000 feet, and those southeast to over 10,000 feet. Native plants include varieties of fern and palm, and shrub, forest, bog, and moss lichen.

Climate: Mild marine tropical. Daily and seasonal air temperature changes are small. Summer days can be hot, owing to high humidity. There is marked variation in rainfall depending on the season and place. Leeward coastal areas are drier than the lower mountains of western Maui. Winds are persistently from the northeast.

Winter mildness: 100 **Hazard free:** 96
Summer mildness: 69 **Seasonal affect:** 84

Grade: 86

TEMPERATURE

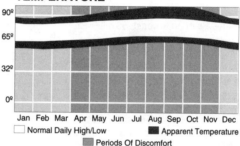

ANNUAL
Humidity: 72%
Wind Speed: 12.2 mph
DAYS
0º or below: 0
32º or below: 0
90º or above: 17
Clear: 54
Partly Cloudy: 182
Cloudy: 129

PRECIPITATION

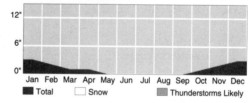

ANNUAL
Precipitation: 16.5"
Snow: 0.0"
DAYS
Precipitation: 19
Thunderstorm: 8
Fog: 0

McCall–Cascade–Payette Valley, ID

Location: 44.54 N, 116.06 W, at 5,031 feet in the Payette River valley, 95 miles north of Boise, the state capital.

Landscape: In the Salmon River Mountains, along the Salmon and Snake rivers. There are high mountain peaks and broad river-drained valleys. Mixed coniferous-deciduous forest predominates comprised of Douglas fir, Engelmann spruce, and cedar-hemlock.

Climate: Highland continental, characterized by wide daily and seasonal temperature changes. Winters are severe, with heavy snowfall. Summer days are warm to hot and usually dry because westerly air masses draw the dry climate of the Pacific coast.

Winter mildness: 45 **Hazard free:** −48
Summer mildness: 100 **Seasonal affect:** 68

Grade: 52

TEMPERATURE

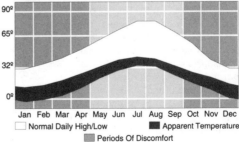

ANNUAL
Humidity: 59%
Wind Speed: 8.9 mph
DAYS
0º or below: 18
32º or below: 224
90º or above: 4
Clear: 85
Partly Cloudy: 87
Cloudy: 193

PRECIPITATION

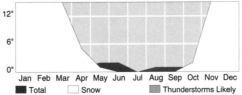

ANNUAL
Precipitation: 27.6"
Snow: 158.4"
DAYS
Precipitation: 73
Thunderstorm: 10
Fog: 47

Medford–Ashland, OR

Location: 42.19 N, 122.52 W, at 1,374 feet, in extreme southwest Oregon, 25 miles north of the California border.
Landscape: In a mountain valley formed by the Rogue River and one of its tributaries, Bear Creek. Most of the valley ranges in elevation from 1,300 to 1,400 feet above sea level. Principal trees of the dense Pacific conifer forest are Douglas fir, western red cedar, western hemlock, silver fir, and Sitka-spruce.
Climate: Moderate continental, with marked seasonal characteristics. Late fall, winter, and early spring are cloudy, damp, and cool. The remainder of the year is warm, dry, and sunny. The rain shadow afforded by the Siskiyous and the Coast Range results in relatively light rainfall. Snowfalls are very light and seldom remain on the ground more than 24 hours. Winters are mild, with the temperatures just dipping below freezing during December and January nights.

Winter mildness: 78   **Hazard free:** 87
Summer mildness: 80   **Seasonal affect:** 73

Grade: 79

TEMPERATURE

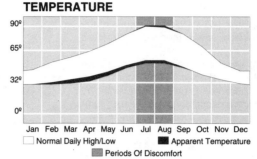

ANNUAL
Humidity: 59%
Wind Speed: 4.8 mph
DAYS
0º or below: 0
32º or below: 86
90º or above: 54
Clear: 116
Partly Cloudy: 79
Cloudy: 170

PRECIPITATION

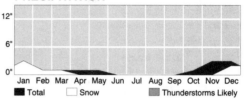

ANNUAL
Precipitation: 18.9"
Snow: 8.9"
DAYS
Precipitation: 49
Thunderstorm: 8
Fog: 49

Melbourne, FL

Location: 28.04 N, 80.36 W, at 21 feet, on the Intracoastal Waterway in the center of Florida's Atlantic coast, 58 miles SE of Orlando.
Landscape: Flat, Florida coastal topography, with miles of hard, sandy beach. Inland, the land rises slightly to 30 feet. Native vegetation includes sea-oat grass, seagrape and cabbage palm.
Climate: Subtropical. Nearness to the Atlantic results in a climate tempered by land and sea breezes. Temperatures in summer may top 90°F during the late morning or early afternoon, but they are cut short by a midday sea breeze and afternoon convective thundershowers, which lower temperatures to comfortable levels. Winters can have cold airflows from the north, but usually are mild because of the city's ocean setting and southerly latitude.

Winter mildness: 100   **Hazard free:** 65
Summer mildness: 61   **Seasonal affect:** 77

Grade: 77

TEMPERATURE

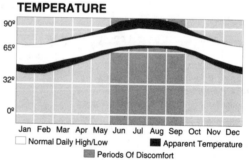

ANNUAL
Humidity: 60%
Wind Speed: 8.4 mph
DAYS
0º or below: 0
32º or below: 2
90º or above: 65
Clear: 98
Partly Cloudy: 133
Cloudy: 134

PRECIPITATION

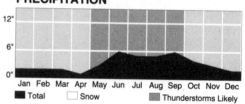

ANNUAL
Precipitation: 45.5"
Snow: 0.0"
DAYS
Precipitation: 65
Thunderstorm: 77
Fog: 28

Mission–McAllen–Alamo, TX

Location: 26.12 N, 98.13 W, at 124 feet, on the border with Mexico in the lower Rio Grande valley of south Texas. The river empties into the Gulf of Mexico 75 miles east of here.
Landscape: Flat topography with little relief. Date palms, bougainvillea, and winter poinsettias color the valley towns, but the native upland sage and chaparral has lost out to intensive development, agricultural and urban.
Climate: Subtropical, influenced by the Gulf of Mexico. Winters are clear, with warm days and cool nights. Summers are long, hot, and humid. The Sierra Madre Oriental Mountains in Mexico block dry air from the Chihuahuan Desert, but both effect the climate of this river plain.

Winter mildness: 100   **Hazard free:** 88
Summer mildness: 51   **Seasonal affect:** 80

Grade: 78

TEMPERATURE

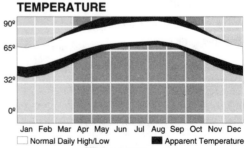

ANNUAL
Humidity: 60%
Wind Speed: 11.5 mph
DAYS
0º or below: 0
32º or below: 7
90º or above: 104
Clear: 97
Partly Cloudy: 132
Cloudy: 136

PRECIPITATION

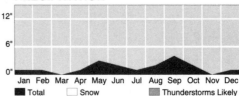

ANNUAL
Precipitation: 22.8"
Snow: 0.0"
DAYS
Precipitation: 34
Thunderstorm: 26
Fog: 27

Montrose, CO

Location: 38.28 N, 107.52 W, at 5,801 feet, in the Uncompahgre River valley, 50 miles SE of Grand Junction.

Landscape: Within the sage desert and shortgrass prairie of the Colorado Plateau. The western vista is the Uncompahgre Plateau, rising over 9,000 feet. Ranchland and orchards mark the gently rolling lowland. Lakes and streams here are fed from mountain snows; the Uncompahgre River flows through steep canyons. Pine, spruce, and aspen forests cover the subalpine areas; sagebrush and cactus are found in the canyons.

Climate: Desert-steppe brings varied seasonal and daily temperature changes. Summers are dry and comfortable due to the high altitude. Winters are cold with moderate snow cover in the elevations through May. Humidity is low, and precipitation is scant but for brief mountain thunderstorms.

Winter mildness: 59 **Hazard free:** 56
Summer mildness: 86 **Seasonal affect:** 83

Grade: 71

TEMPERATURE

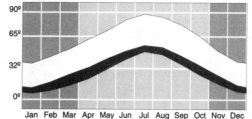

ANNUAL
Humidity: 40%
Wind Speed: 8.1 mph
DAYS
0º or below: 7
32º or below: 168
90º or above: 34
Clear: 137
Partly Cloudy: 106
Cloudy: 122

PRECIPITATION

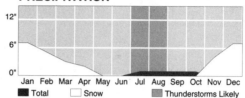

ANNUAL
Precipitation: 9.7"
Snow: 30.2"
DAYS
Precipitation: 27
Thunderstorm: 35
Fog: 8

Myrtle Beach, SC

Location: 33.41 N, 78.53 W, at 30 feet, 100 miles NE of Charleston, in the center of the Atlantic coast.

Landscape: The area known as the Grand Strand is flat, has a populated area only a few blocks wide, and extends 43 miles up and down the shore. Elevations are no greater than 50 feet above sea level. There are many more trees and wooded areas than usually found in a beach area. The beaches themselves are white sand. Inland is low and swampy, with stands of southern yellow pine mixed with hickory, sweet gum, and other deciduous trees. The grasses are bluestem, panicums, and longleaf uniola in the coastal marshes.

Climate: Subtropical. Mild winters and warm summers are the rule. The ocean has a pronounced modifying effect on temperatures. The Blue Ridge Mountains inland block the cold air from the interior. Some tropical storms reach the area every few years.

Winter mildness: 93 **Hazard free:** 77
Summer mildness: 73 **Seasonal affect:** 74

Grade: 80

TEMPERATURE

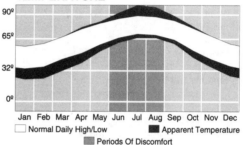

ANNUAL
Humidity: 56%
Wind Speed: 8.8 mph
DAYS
0º or below: 0
32º or below: 42
90º or above: 20
Clear: 111
Partly Cloudy: 103
Cloudy: 151

PRECIPITATION

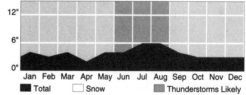

ANNUAL
Precipitation: 52.6"
Snow: 1.7"
DAYS
Precipitation: 74
Thunderstorm: 47
Fog: 24

Naples, FL

Location: 26.08 N, 81.47 W, at 9 feet, on Florida's southern Gulf of Mexico coast, 25 miles south of Ft. Myers.

Landscape: Flat topography. The area lies on a seven-mile mainland beach. Nearby are mangrove islands. To the east is the Big Cypress Swamp and beyond, the Everglades. Native vegetation includes cypress, evergreen oaks, laurel, small palms, and tropical shrubs.

Climate: Subtropical. Summer and winter temperature extremes are checked by the influence of the Gulf. Summer heat is exacerbated by humidity. Winters have many bright, warm days and moderately cool nights. Rainfall averages more than 50 inches annually, with two-thirds coming daily between June and September. Most rain falls as late afternoon or early evening thunderstorms, bringing welcome relief from the heat.

Winter mildness: 100 **Hazard free:** 58
Summer mildness: 54 **Seasonal affect:** 78

Grade: 74

TEMPERATURE

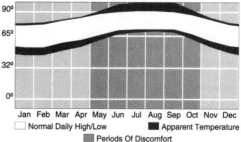

ANNUAL
Humidity: 55%
Wind Speed: 8.4 mph
DAYS
0º or below: 0
32º or below: 0
90º or above: 101
Clear: 102
Partly Cloudy: 142
Cloudy: 121

PRECIPITATION

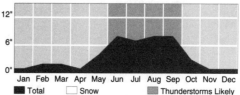

ANNUAL
Precipitation: 51.1"
Snow: 0.0"
DAYS
Precipitation: 72
Thunderstorm: 92
Fog: 20

New Bern, NC

Location: 35.06 N, 77.02 W, at 15 feet, at the mouth of the Neuse River, which empties into Pamlico Sound off North Carolina's Atlantic coast. The area is 100 miles SE of Raleigh, the state capital.

Landscape: In this central tidewater savanna there are bluffs, marshes, lakes, and rivers. The confluence of the Neuse River and the Trent make this level land somewhat swampy. The woods are an oak-hickory forest with short trees, small and leathery leaves, and a canopy that is less dense. In town are live oak, laurel, holly, and magnolia with an underbrush of shrubs and herbaceous plants.

Climate: Subtropical, with humid, hot summers and winters that are mild. Rain falls throughout the year. Spring and summer can bring heavy thunderstorms. Occasional storms from the Atlantic may strike this coastal location.

Winter mildness: 89	**Hazard free:** 75
Summer mildness: 71	**Seasonal affect:** 74

Grade: 78

TEMPERATURE

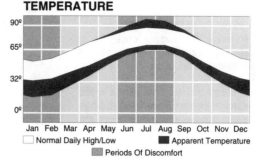

Jan Feb Mar Apr May Jun Jul Aug Sep Oct Nov Dec
☐ Normal Daily High/Low   ■ Apparent Temperature
☐ Periods Of Discomfort

ANNUAL
Humidity: 56%
Wind Speed: 11.1 mph
DAYS
0º or below: 0
32º or below: 53
90º or above: 39
Clear: 106
Partly Cloudy: 106
Cloudy: 153

PRECIPITATION

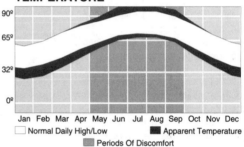

Jan Feb Mar Apr May Jun Jul Aug Sep Oct Nov Dec
■ Total   ☐ Snow   ■ Thunderstorms Likely

ANNUAL
Precipitation: 54.2"
Snow: 3.2"
DAYS
Precipitation: 77
Thunderstorm: 48
Fog: 20

New Braunfels, TX

Location: 29.42 N, 98.07 W, at 623 feet, on the Balcones Escarpment in south-central Texas, 30 miles NE of San Antonio.

Landscape: Arid grassland with shrubs and low trees, and low hills. The deep, winding Comal River flows into the Guadalupe. Nearby Landa Park, Natural Bridge Caverns, and Canyon Lake mark the region. Caladium grow along the riverbanks. As the land rises to the Edwards Plateau, oak and juniper mix with mesquite and buffalo grass.

Climate: Prairie, with warm days and cool nights in winter, and a long, hot summer. Though miles from the Gulf, the area is influenced by moist, marine air. Most of the annual precipitation falls as rain in May and in September.

Winter mildness: 98	**Hazard free:** 83
Summer mildness: 54	**Seasonal affect:** 79

Grade: 77

TEMPERATURE

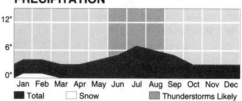

Jan Feb Mar Apr May Jun Jul Aug Sep Oct Nov Dec
☐ Normal Daily High/Low   ■ Apparent Temperature
☐ Periods Of Discomfort

ANNUAL
Humidity: 55%
Wind Speed: 9.3 mph
DAYS
0º or below: 0
32º or below: 28
90º or above: 122
Clear: 107
Partly Cloudy: 118
Cloudy: 140

PRECIPITATION

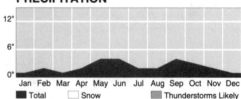

Jan Feb Mar Apr May Jun Jul Aug Sep Oct Nov Dec
■ Total   ☐ Snow   ■ Thunderstorms Likely

ANNUAL
Precipitation: 34.3"
Snow: 0.5"
DAYS
Precipitation: 46
Thunderstorm: 36
Fog: 21

New Port Richey, FL

Location: 28.14 N, 82.43 W, at 30 feet, on Florida's central Gulf coast, 30 miles north of Tampa.

Landscape: Inland is hilly country unusual to Florida. With-lacoochee State Forest is typical mix of hardwood, longleaf, and slash pine. Aromatic and evergreen bayberry and sweet bay are scattered throughout.

Climate: Subtropical, with temperatures modified throughout the year by the waters of the Gulf. Afternoon thunderstorms are frequent during summer, resulting in drastic temperature drops. Snowfall is negligible, and freezing temperatures, even at night, are rare.

Winter mildness: 100	**Hazard free:** 62
Summer mildness: 59	**Seasonal affect:** 78

Grade: 76

TEMPERATURE

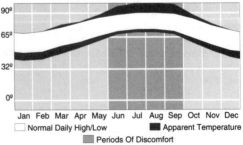

Jan Feb Mar Apr May Jun Jul Aug Sep Oct Nov Dec
☐ Normal Daily High/Low   ■ Apparent Temperature
☐ Periods Of Discomfort

PRECIPITATION

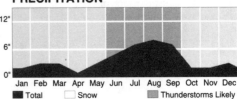

Jan Feb Mar Apr May Jun Jul Aug Sep Oct Nov Dec
■ Total   ☐ Snow   ■ Thunderstorms Likely

ANNUAL
Humidity: 57%
Wind Speed: 8.4 mph
DAYS
0º or below: 0
32º or below: 4
90º or above: 76
Clear: 102
Partly Cloudy: 142
Cloudy: 121

ANNUAL
Precipitation: 51.0"
Snow: 0.0"
DAYS
Precipitation: 70
Thunderstorm: 85
Fog: 22

✓ Newport–Lincoln City, OR

Location: 44.38 N, 124.03 W, at 177 feet, directly on Oregon's Pacific Coast, 55 miles west of Salem, the state capital.

Landscape: Parts of the cities sit at the water's edge, more is built on level bench land about 150 feet above sea level. Just to the east, the foothills of the Coast Range begin a steep ascent to ridges that are 2,000 to 3,000 feet high. The principal trees of the dense Pacific conifer forests nearby are Douglas fir, western red cedar, western hemlock, silver fir, and Sitka-spruce.

Climate: Marine climate typical of Oregon's coastal area. Temperature extremes are almost nonexistent. Warm, moist air from the Pacific make summers mild and pleasant. In the winter, the air releases moisture over the cold landmass, resulting in a constant cloud cover and rain from November through March. Most of the annual precipitation falls during these months.

Winter mildness: 88 **Hazard free:** 95
Summer mildness: 100 **Seasonal affect:** 58

Grade: 88

TEMPERATURE

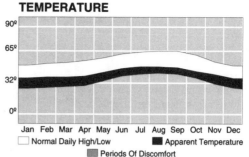

□ Normal Daily High/Low ■ Apparent Temperature
▨ Periods Of Discomfort

ANNUAL
Humidity: 75%
Wind Speed: 8.6 mph
DAYS
0º or below: 0
32º or below: 30
90º or above: 0
Clear: 49
Partly Cloudy: 76
Cloudy: 240

PRECIPITATION

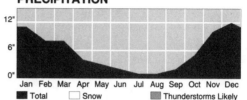

■ Total □ Snow ▨ Thunderstorms Likely

ANNUAL
Precipitation: 71.9"
Snow: 2.0"
DAYS
Precipitation: 126
Thunderstorm: 7
Fog: 41

Norfork Lake, AR

Location: 36.20 N, 92.23 W, at 756 feet, near the center of the Arkansas-Missouri border 100 air miles north of Little Rock, the state capital.

Landscape: Though in the center of the Ozark Mountains, gently rolling hills surround Lake Norfork, formed by damming the White River. The thick woods are broadleaf deciduous forests of oak, hickory, maple, sweet gum, and walnut.

Climate: Hot continental, with warm summers and winters with mild days and freezing nights. In a given year, the climate can vary from warm and humid maritime to cold and dry continental, but it is relatively free from climatic extremes.

Winter mildness: 78 **Hazard free:** 65
Summer mildness: 72 **Seasonal affect:** 75

Grade: 73

TEMPERATURE

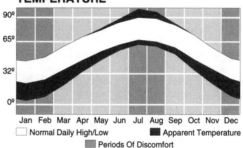

□ Normal Daily High/Low ■ Apparent Temperature
▨ Periods Of Discomfort

ANNUAL
Humidity: 57%
Wind Speed: 10.7 mph
DAYS
0º or below: 1
32º or below: 90
90º or above: 56
Clear: 115
Partly Cloudy: 96
Cloudy: 154

PRECIPITATION

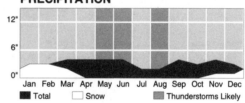

■ Total □ Snow ▨ Thunderstorms Likely

ANNUAL
Precipitation: 44.2"
Snow: 10.9"
DAYS
Precipitation: 63
Thunderstorm: 55
Fog: 20

Northern Door Peninsula, WI

Location: The weather station is Sturgeon Bay, 44.51 N, 87.23 W, at 660 feet, on Wisconsin's Door Peninsula between Green Bay and Lake Michigan. The site is 180 miles NW of Madison, the state capital.

Landscape: Characterized by rolling woodlands, limestone bluffs, and 250 miles of rocky shoreline. Glacier effects predominate. The woods contain northern hardwoods of maple, oak, beech, and birch, mixed with pine, eastern hemlock, and eastern red cedar.

Climate: Continental, and largely influenced by Lakes Michigan and Superior. Winters are moderately long and severe. Snow falls early and lasts late. Summers are mild, with cool evenings and nights. A distinct, four-season climate, with springs and autumns that are all too short.

Winter mildness: 54 **Hazard free:** 49
Summer mildness: 93 **Seasonal affect:** 72

Grade: 69

TEMPERATURE

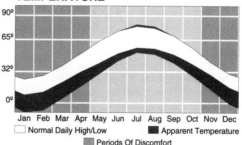

□ Normal Daily High/Low ■ Apparent Temperature
▨ Periods Of Discomfort

ANNUAL
Humidity: 63%
Wind Speed: 10.0 mph
DAYS
0º or below: 19
32º or below: 159
90º or above: 3
Clear: 86
Partly Cloudy: 102
Cloudy: 177

PRECIPITATION

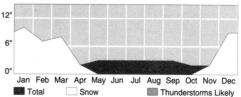

■ Total □ Snow ▨ Thunderstorms Likely

ANNUAL
Precipitation: 31.5"
Snow: 39.1"
DAYS
Precipitation: 63
Thunderstorm: 33
Fog: 24

Northern Neck, VA

Location: 37.46 N, 76.28 W, at 98 feet, on a peninsula between Virginia's Rappahannock and Potomac rivers that extends into Chesapeake Bay. Richmond, the state capital, is 40 miles SE.

Landscape: Tidewater country of low hills, streams, and marsh. The woods inland are a typical southeastern mixed forest with tall oak, hickory, sweet gum, red maple, and winged elm. At least half of the stands are filled with second-growth loblolly and shortleaf pine. Coastal marshes and interior swamps are dominated by gums and cypress. An undergrowth of dogwood, viburnum, blueberry, youpon, and numerous woody vines is prevalent.

Climate: Mild winters and hot, humid summers. Spring and autumn are especially pleasant. Precipitation is evenly distributed throughout the year, mostly as rain. Thunderstorms are likely in midsummer.

Winter mildness: 79   **Hazard free:** 68
Summer mildness: 75   **Seasonal affect:** 75

Grade: 75

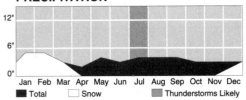

TEMPERATURE

Jan Feb Mar Apr May Jun Jul Aug Sep Oct Nov Dec
☐ Normal Daily High/Low   ■ Apparent Temperature
▨ Periods Of Discomfort

ANNUAL
Humidity: 58%
Wind Speed: 10.7 mph
DAYS
0º or below: 0
32º or below: 88
90º or above: 39
Clear: 106
Partly Cloudy: 106
Cloudy: 153

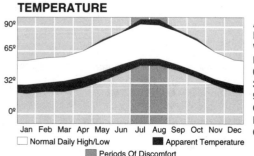

PRECIPITATION

Jan Feb Mar Apr May Jun Jul Aug Sep Oct Nov Dec
■ Total   ☐ Snow   ▨ Thunderstorms Likely

ANNUAL
Precipitation: 42.7"
Snow: 16.7"
DAYS
Precipitation: 70
Thunderstorm: 36
Fog: 20

Oakhurst–Coarsegold, CA

Location: 37.19 N, 119.39 W, at 2,289 feet, in California's southern mines country 150 miles east of San Francisco.

Landscape: In these high foothills is a jumble of ravines, buttes, and wooded peaks, watered by streams from the Sierra Nevada Mountains. Yosemite National Park is immediately north with waterfalls, acres of forest, and glacier-carved valleys. Rivers drain into the broad San Joaquin Valley to the west. The lower hills are covered by close-growing cypress and pinyon. In the higher elevations is a combination of digger pine and blue oak.

Climate: Sierran forest climate in the transition zone between the dry west coast desert and the wet west coast farther north. Prevailing west winds influence conditions jointly with elevation. Therefore the summers are long and generally dry.

Winter mildness: 82   **Hazard free:** 80
Summer mildness: 76   **Seasonal affect:** 82

Grade: 80

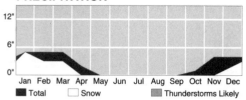

TEMPERATURE

Jan Feb Mar Apr May Jun Jul Aug Sep Oct Nov Dec
☐ Normal Daily High/Low   ■ Apparent Temperature
▨ Periods Of Discomfort

ANNUAL
Humidity: 58%
Wind Speed: 7.9 mph
DAYS
0º or below: 0
32º or below: 77
90º or above: 59
Clear: 189
Partly Cloudy: 75
Cloudy: 101

PRECIPITATION

Jan Feb Mar Apr May Jun Jul Aug Sep Oct Nov Dec
■ Total   ☐ Snow   ▨ Thunderstorms Likely

ANNUAL
Precipitation: 32.7"
Snow: 14.1"
DAYS
Precipitation: 49
Thunderstorm: 14
Fog: 34

Ocala, FL

Location: 29.11 N, 82.08 W, at 99 feet, in north central Florida, 25 miles south of Gainesville and 90 miles west of Daytona Beach and the Atlantic Ocean.

Landscape: This is low, ridge country with deposits of pure limestone, just west of Ocala National Forest. Artesian springs and outlets form the Silver River. Stands of sand pine, longleaf, slash, and other yellow southern pine mix with hardwoods of the Eastern deciduous forest.

Climate: Subtropical, with a small annual range of temperature changes. Precipitation is light, except from May through September. Summers are hotter and more humid than coastal locations, but are cooled by afternoon thunderstorms. Winters are mild, with warm days and cool nights.

Winter mildness: 100   **Hazard free:** 63
Summer mildness: 53   **Seasonal affect:** 76

Grade: 74

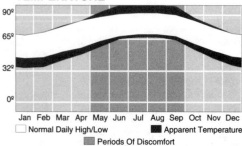

TEMPERATURE

Jan Feb Mar Apr May Jun Jul Aug Sep Oct Nov Dec
☐ Normal Daily High/Low   ■ Apparent Temperature
▨ Periods Of Discomfort

ANNUAL
Humidity: 54%
Wind Speed: 8.6 mph
DAYS
0º or below: 0
32º or below: 12
90º or above: 120
Clear: 91
Partly Cloudy: 147
Cloudy: 127

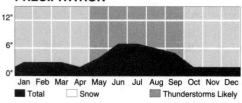

PRECIPITATION

Jan Feb Mar Apr May Jun Jul Aug Sep Oct Nov Dec
■ Total   ☐ Snow   ▨ Thunderstorms Likely

ANNUAL
Precipitation: 51.6"
Snow: 0.0"
DAYS
Precipitation: 77
Thunderstorm: 81
Fog: 26

Ocean City, MD

Location: 38.20 N, 75.05 W, at 8 feet, on the Atlantic coast of southeastern Maryland 100 miles SE of Washington, D.C.
Landscape: A 10-mile barrier beach that forms a chain of bays along the Atlantic shore. Assateague Island National Seashore is a narrow barrier island and a southern extension of Ocean City's barrier beach. The coastal marsh and interior swamps are dominated by gums and cypress with an understory of grasses and sedges.
Climate: Subtropical, characterized by milder winters than locations farther north, thanks to the Atlantic. Summers are somewhat hot and humid. Precipitation is evenly distributed throughout the year as rain though there may be summer drought. Frost occurs nearly every winter but snow is infrequent.

Winter mildness: 78   **Hazard free:** 76
Summer mildness: 79   **Seasonal affect:** 72

TEMPERATURE

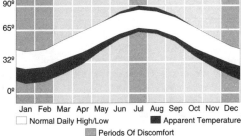

Normal Daily High/Low   ■ Apparent Temperature
■ Periods Of Discomfort

ANNUAL
Humidity: 56%
Wind Speed: 9.1 mph
DAYS
0º or below: 0
32º or below: 83
90º or above: 25
Clear: 96
Partly Cloudy: 104
Cloudy: 165

PRECIPITATION

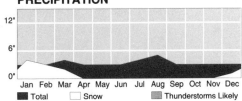

■ Total   □ Snow   ■ Thunderstorms Likely

ANNUAL
Precipitation: 45.3"
Snow: 11.9"
DAYS
Precipitation: 73
Thunderstorm: 28
Fog: 34

Grade: 77

Oscoda–Tawas–Huron Shore, MI

Location: 44.25 N, 83.20 W, at 387 feet, in northern Michigan on Lake Huron, 120 miles NE of Lansing, the state capital.
Landscape: At the mouth of the Au Sable River with the Huron National Forest lying inland. This is a more rugged coast on an upland plateau where relief is minimal. The forest is pine and hemlock.
Climate: The daily and seasonal temperature range is modified by Lake Huron. Rainfall is heaviest in the summer. Winters here are cold and snowy, though not as snowy as locations to the north and west. Summer is mild, with cool nights. Cloudiness is greatest in late fall and winter.

Winter mildness: 53   **Hazard free:** 38
Summer mildness: 94   **Seasonal affect:** 71

TEMPERATURE

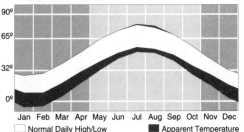

Normal Daily High/Low   ■ Apparent Temperature
■ Periods Of Discomfort

ANNUAL
Humidity: 60%
Wind Speed: 8.1 mph
DAYS
0º or below: 17
32º or below: 166
90º or above: 4
Clear: 67
Partly Cloudy: 105
Cloudy: 193

PRECIPITATION

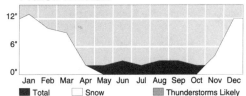

■ Total   □ Snow   ■ Thunderstorms Likely

ANNUAL
Precipitation: 30.0"
Snow: 52.0"
DAYS
Precipitation: 63
Thunderstorm: 32
Fog: 27

Grade: 67

Oxford, MS

Location: 34.22 N, 89.31 W, at 416 feet, in north-central Mississippi, 75 miles SE of Memphis.
Landscape: Rolling hill country near the Sardis Reservoir and two other lakes. The surrounding Holly Springs National Forest protects a typical southeastern mixed forest of medium-tall to tall broadleaf deciduous and needleleaf evergreen trees.
Climate: Hot continental to subtropical. Though not in the path of storms coming up from the Gulf or down from Canada, the area is influenced by both. Winter, wet with frequent drizzle and infrequent light snowfall, has mild days and cold nights. Summer is hot and humid. Spring and autumn are pleasant and long-lasting.

Winter mildness: 85   **Hazard free:** 73
Summer mildness: 69   **Seasonal affect:** 75

TEMPERATURE

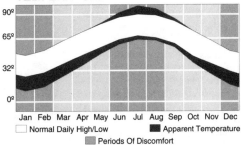

Normal Daily High/Low   ■ Apparent Temperature
■ Periods Of Discomfort

ANNUAL
Humidity: 56%
Wind Speed: 8.9 mph
DAYS
0º or below: 0
32º or below: 57
90º or above: 67
Clear: 119
Partly Cloudy: 96
Cloudy: 150

PRECIPITATION

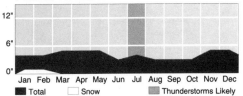

■ Total   □ Snow   ■ Thunderstorms Likely

ANNUAL
Precipitation: 55.7"
Snow: 3.3"
DAYS
Precipitation: 72
Thunderstorm: 53
Fog: 10

Grade: 76

Pagosa Springs, CO

Location: 37.16 N, 107.00 W, at 7,105 feet, on the San Juan River in southwestern Colorado, 230 air miles from Denver.

Landscape: On a high mountain plateau. Peaks of the San Juan Mountains are a distant vista to the north and east. The geothermal springs, canyons, mesas, and mountains provide dramatic relief. Pine, spruce, and aspen forests cover the subalpine areas.

Climate: Semiarid steppe. High altitude brings just two seasons: an eight-month winter and a sunny, four-month summer. Temperature variations are great both daily and annually. Snowfall in this region is legendary.

Winter mildness: 42   **Hazard free:** −23
Summer mildness: 100   **Seasonal affect:** 81

Grade: 57

TEMPERATURE

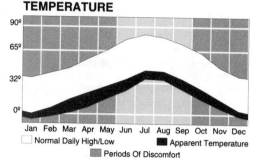

Normal Daily High/Low   Apparent Temperature
Periods Of Discomfort

ANNUAL
Humidity: 40%
Wind Speed: 8.1 mph
DAYS
0º or below: 36
32º or below: 243
90º or above: 2
Clear: 115
Partly Cloudy: 130
Cloudy: 120

PRECIPITATION

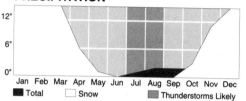

Total   Snow   Thunderstorms Likely

ANNUAL
Precipitation: 19.9"
Snow: 116.4"
DAYS
Precipitation: 47
Thunderstorm: 34
Fog: 8

Pahrump Valley, NV

Location: 36.10 N, 115.08 W, at 2,028 feet, just west of the Colorado River valley. Los Angeles is 300 miles SW and Las Vegas is 35 miles east.

Landscape: In a desert valley with mountains from 2,000 to 10,000 feet on the horizon. These mountains act as effective barriers to moisture-laden storms moving in from the Pacific Ocean. In the environs, thick-branched Joshua trees grow among creosote bushes and jumbled boulders.

Climate: Summers are typical of a desert climate. Humidity is low with maximum temperatures topping 100 degrees. Nearby mountains contribute to relatively cool nights. Spring and fall are ideal, rarely interrupted by adverse weather conditions. Winters, too, are mild, with daytime averages of 60°F, clear skies, and warm sunshine. There are very few overcast or rainy days.

Winter mildness: 89   **Hazard free:** 93
Summer mildness: 59   **Seasonal affect:** 91

Grade: 80

TEMPERATURE

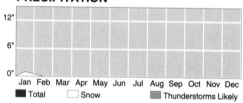

Normal Daily High/Low   Apparent Temperature
Periods Of Discomfort

ANNUAL
Humidity: 23%
Wind Speed: 9.3 mph
DAYS
0º or below: 0
32º or below: 33
90º or above: 132
Clear: 220
Partly Cloudy: 79
Cloudy: 66

PRECIPITATION

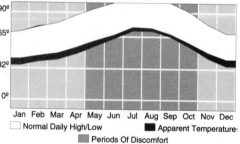

Total   Snow   Thunderstorms Likely

ANNUAL
Precipitation: 4.8"
Snow: 1.2"
DAYS
Precipitation: 13
Thunderstorm: 13
Fog: 0

Palm Springs–Coachella Valley, CA

Location: 33.49 N, 116.32 W, at 466 feet, in California's desert country, 100 miles east of Los Angeles.

Landscape: In the Coachella Valley at the foot of Mt. San Jacinto, where the San Gorgonio Pass funnels Pacific warmed air that sometimes includes Los Angeles smog. This is the edge of the Sonoran Desert, known sometimes as the upper Colorado Desert. Joshua Tree National Monument is immediately northeast. Desert cactus, palm, and broadleaf evergreen scrub pine are typical growth.

Climate: Arid desert surrounding rapid urbanization. Summers are dry and hot, with afternoon temperatures topping 100°F. Nights are cooler. Most of the annual precipitation, such as it is, falls in the winter as brief rain.

Winter mildness: 100   **Hazard free:** 97
Summer mildness: 40   **Seasonal affect:** 94

Grade: 78

TEMPERATURE

Normal Daily High/Low   Apparent Temperature
Periods Of Discomfort

ANNUAL
Humidity: 32%
Wind Speed: 7.8 mph
DAYS
0º or below: 0
32º or below: 7
90º or above: 180
Clear: 241
Partly Cloudy: 75
Cloudy: 49

PRECIPITATION

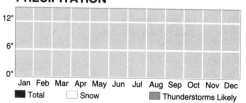

Total   Snow   Thunderstorms Likely

ANNUAL
Precipitation: 5.3"
Snow: 0.1"
DAYS
Precipitation: 9
Thunderstorm: 7
Fog: 1

Panama City, FL

Location: 30.09 N, 85.39 W, at 33 feet, on the Gulf of Mexico in Florida's northwestern panhandle. Tallahassee, the state capital, is 120 miles east.

Landscape: Sandy coastal region of shallow bays, white beaches, and dunes. Elevations range from a few feet above sea level to more than 100 feet. The interior swamp includes evergreen oaks and members of the laurel and magnolia families. The longleaf, loblolly, and slash pines represent second-growth forest.

Climate: Subtropical. The Florida panhandle is cooler in summer than the central part of the state, and still pleasant in winter. The Yucatan Current runs near here bringing its moderating influence.

Winter mildness: 100 **Hazard free:** 69
Summer mildness: 65 **Seasonal affect:** 74

Grade: 79

TEMPERATURE

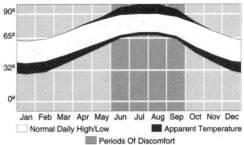

ANNUAL
Humidity: 60%
Wind Speed: 8.4 mph
DAYS
0º or below: 0
32º or below: 17
90º or above: 57
Clear: 108
Partly Cloudy: 121
Cloudy: 136

PRECIPITATION

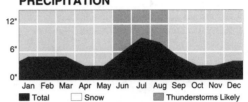

ANNUAL
Precipitation: 65.1"
Snow: 0.2"
DAYS
Precipitation: 82
Thunderstorm: 69
Fog: 34

✓ Paradise–Magalia, CA

Location: 39.44 N, 121.38 W, at 1,708 feet, on Paradise Ridge in California Sierra Nevada foothills, 92 miles north of Sacramento, the state capital.

Landscape: Steep slopes climb to high mountains. Stream-cut canyons drain to the Sacramento River. Tall digger pine and blue oak dominate the forest. Lower rounded hills are grass covered. Open meadows and woodlands alternate.

Climate: Distinctly four seasons. Temperature is moderated by the altitude. Winter is the rainy season and summer is long and dry.

Winter mildness: 93 **Hazard free:** 98
Summer mildness: 71 **Seasonal affect:** 83

Grade: 85

TEMPERATURE

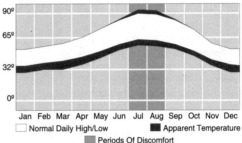

ANNUAL
Humidity: 58%
Wind Speed: 7.8 mph
DAYS
0º or below: 0
32º or below: 17
90º or above: 74
Clear: 177
Partly Cloudy: 77
Cloudy: 111

PRECIPITATION

ANNUAL
Precipitation: 52.7"
Snow: 0.4"
DAYS
Precipitation: 39
Thunderstorm: 4
Fog: 8

Payson, AZ

Location: 34.14 N, 111.19 W, at 4,887 feet, in the Tonto Basin near Arizona's Mogollon Rim. Phoenix is 65 miles SE.

Landscape: Surrounded by the Tonto National Forest. The Mazatzal Mountains of central Arizona and higher peaks of the White Mountains are nearby. In the higher ridges the cover is Ponderosa, juniper, and pinyon pine. Lower, sagebrush, and native grasses grow in the dry, alkaline soil.

Climate: Semiarid mountain steppe. There are strong daily and seasonal temperature changes. The usual winter flow of air is from the Pacific Ocean. This brings snow. Cold air masses from Canada sometimes drive temperatures well below freezing in the high plateau and mountainous regions. Moisture-bearing winds from the southeast Gulf region bring summer rain from July through September.

Winter mildness: 70 **Hazard free:** 67
Summer mildness: 77 **Seasonal affect:** 88

Grade: 75

TEMPERATURE

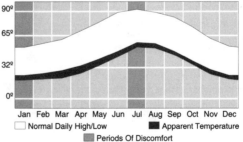

ANNUAL
Humidity: 33%
Wind Speed: 6.3 mph
DAYS
0º or below: 0
32º or below: 144
90º or above: 64
Clear: 211
Partly Cloudy: 84
Cloudy: 70

PRECIPITATION

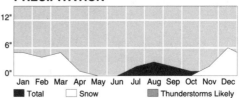

ANNUAL
Precipitation: 22.1"
Snow: 24.4"
DAYS
Precipitation: 40
Thunderstorm: 23
Fog: 1

Petoskey–Harbor Springs, MI

Location: 45.22 N, 84.57 W, at 786 feet, on the south shore of Little Traverse Bay on Lake Michigan, some 30 miles south of the Mackinac Straits separating Michigan's upper and lower peninsulas.

Landscape: Generally level or gently undulating, with sandy and gravelly soils. The region abounds with lakes. Local beaches and gravel pits yield colorful fossilized stones. Elevations in the area provide access to both downhill and cross-country skiing. The forest is pine and hemlock.

Climate: Though rigorous because of its interior and northerly location, the climate is modified by the presence of two Great Lakes. Consequently, summertime temperatures average at least five degrees cooler than locations in the southern part of the state. However, winters are quite severe, with cold spells that may last for a week and snowfall that averages almost 90 inches.

Winter mildness: 54   **Hazard free:** 8
Summer mildness: 93   **Seasonal affect:** 68

Grade: 62

TEMPERATURE
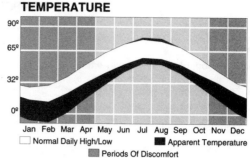

ANNUAL
Humidity: 67%
Wind Speed: 10.7 mph
DAYS
0º or below: 18
32º or below: 169
90º or above: 5
Clear: 66
Partly Cloudy: 88
Cloudy: 211

PRECIPITATION
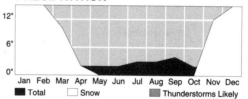

ANNUAL
Precipitation: 31.4"
Snow: 88.4"
DAYS
Precipitation: 73
Thunderstorm: 23
Fog: 22

Phoenix–Mesa–Scottsdale, AZ

Location: 33.27 N, 112.04 W, at 1,082 feet, in the center of the Salt River Valley, on a broad, oval, nearly flat plain.

Landscape: To the south, west, and north are nearby mountain ranges. The famous Superstition Mountains, which rise to an elevation of 5,000 feet, are 35 miles east. The Sonoran Desert can bloom with saguaro, cholla, and cereus, but creosote bush is most common. The paloverde tree can put out small leaves in rainy seasons, but usually depends on its green or blue-green bark for survival.

Climate: Typical desert, with low annual rainfall and low humidity. Daytime temperatures are hot throughout the summer. Winters are mild, but nighttime temperatures can drop below freezing December through February. Most days are clear and sunny and the valley floor is generally free of wind except during the thunderstorm season in July and August.

Winter mildness: 100   **Hazard free:** 89
Summer mildness: 41   **Seasonal affect:** 90

Grade: 77

TEMPERATURE
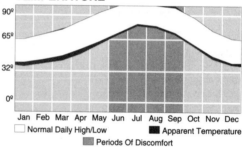

ANNUAL
Humidity: 31%
Wind Speed: 6.3 mph
DAYS
0º or below: 0
32º or below: 8
90º or above: 169
Clear: 211
Partly Cloudy: 84
Cloudy: 70

PRECIPITATION
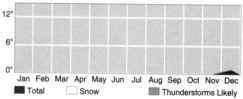

ANNUAL
Precipitation: 7.7"
Snow: 0.0"
DAYS
Precipitation: 19
Thunderstorm: 23
Fog: 1

Pike County, PA

Location: 41.19 N, 74.48 W, at 1,185 feet, across the Delaware River from New York state. New York City is 80 miles SE.

Landscape: The Delaware River drains this highland region between the Catskills and the Pocono Mountains. These are long, flat-topped or rounded ridges that rise to 4,000 feet. Many streams and glacial lakes lie among the wooded hills. White pine, eastern hemlock, and red spruce mix with deciduous trees like red maple, sassafras, oak, beech, and birch. Mountain laurel, dogwood, dwarf sumac, and fern fill out the lower growth layers.

Climate: Hot continental with summers moderated by altitude. Winter is cold and cloudy. Precipitation is evenly distributed throughout the year with snow likely to fall in December and last until spring. Severe weather disturbances are unlikely.

Winter mildness: 62   **Hazard free:** 45
Summer mildness: 86   **Seasonal affect:** 71

Grade: 69

TEMPERATURE
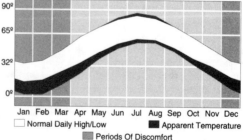

ANNUAL
Humidity: 56%
Wind Speed: 7.6 mph
DAYS
0º or below: 6
32º or below: 145
90º or above: 16
Clear: 68
Partly Cloudy: 113
Cloudy: 184

PRECIPITATION
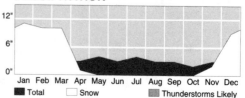

ANNUAL
Precipitation: 43.2"
Snow: 45.1"
DAYS
Precipitation: 76
Thunderstorm: 31
Fog: 18

✓ Placerville–Shingle Springs, CA

Location: 38.43 N, 120.48 W, at 1,866 feet, in California's northern mines country. Sacramento, the state capital, is 40 miles west.

Landscape: Rounded, grass-covered foothills of Sierra Nevada mountains rise from the Sacramento Valley to high, craggy peaks to the east. In the rolling valleys are sandy-bottom stream beds lined with sycamore, willow, and cottonwood. Tall digger pine and blue oak dominate the higher forest.

Climate: Mediterranean, characterized by winter rainfall. Summers are hot, though tempered by the higher elevation of the Sierra foothills. Winter days are mild, with occasional freezing nights.

Winter mildness: 82 **Hazard free:** 90
Summer mildness: 77 **Seasonal affect:** 82

TEMPERATURE

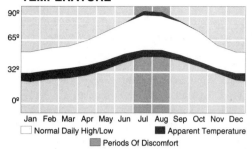

☐ Normal Daily High/Low ■ Apparent Temperature
▨ Periods Of Discomfort

ANNUAL
Humidity: 58%
Wind Speed: 7.9 mph
DAYS
0º or below: 0
32º or below: 77
90º or above: 59
Clear: 189
Partly Cloudy: 75
Cloudy: 101

PRECIPITATION

■ Total ☐ Snow ▨ Thunderstorms Likely

ANNUAL
Precipitation: 36.7"
Snow: 3.8"
DAYS
Precipitation: 49
Thunderstorm: 14
Fog: 34

Grade: 82

Polson–Mission Valley, MT

Location: 47.41 N, 114.09 W, at 2,931 feet, on the southern end of Flathead Lake 60 miles north of Missoula.

Landscape: The Mission range of the Rocky Mountains lies east, and the Coeur d'Alene Mountains lie southwest of this valley plateau. Streams and lakes of many sizes are in the area. The short prairie grasses, scattered shrubs and low trees give way to the forests of evergreen. Ponderosa pine, pinyon-juniper, and Douglas fir are frequent associates.

Climate: Semiarid steppe, with most precipitation falling as winter snow, especially in the higher altitudes. Winters can be cold and long. Summers are warm, dry and too brief.

Winter mildness: 57 **Hazard free:** 50
Summer mildness: 93 **Seasonal affect:** 71

TEMPERATURE

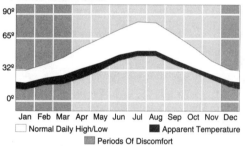

☐ Normal Daily High/Low ■ Apparent Temperature
▨ Periods Of Discomfort

ANNUAL
Humidity: 61%
Wind Speed: 6.6 mph
DAYS
0º or below: 10
32º or below: 170
90º or above: 17
Clear: 71
Partly Cloudy: 80
Cloudy: 214

PRECIPITATION

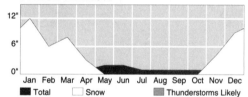

■ Total ☐ Snow ▨ Thunderstorms Likely

ANNUAL
Precipitation: 16.7"
Snow: 43.3"
DAYS
Precipitation: 37
Thunderstorm: 22
Fog: 32

Grade: 70

Pompano Beach, FL

Location: 26.14 N, 80.07 W, at 17 feet along the densely settled Atlantic coast in the southeastern part of the state, between Palm Beach and Miami.

Landscape: Ocean beach along Florida's Gold Coast, near the eastern edge of the Everglades. Formerly a mangrove swamp, now completely drained and urbanized. Inland on the coastal plain, bald cypress and palmetto shrubs dominate the swamps and evergreen oak and laurel grow on drier areas.

Climate: Subtropical, in a southerly location near the ocean and warmed by the Gulf Stream. Winters are pleasantly warm. Summer daytime temperatures are high, but tempered by the ocean breeze. Cumulus clouds gather which shade the land without completely obscuring the sun. The moist, unstable air in this area results in frequent showers, usually of short duration.

Winter mildness: 100 **Hazard free:** 65
Summer mildness: 54 **Seasonal affect:** 76

TEMPERATURE

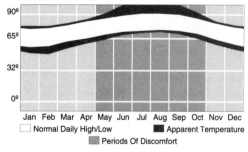

☐ Normal Daily High/Low ■ Apparent Temperature
▨ Periods Of Discomfort

ANNUAL
Humidity: 60%
Wind Speed: 8.4 mph
DAYS
0º or below: 0
32º or below: 0
90º or above: 94
Clear: 98
Partly Cloudy: 133
Cloudy: 134

PRECIPITATION

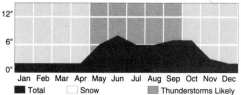

■ Total ☐ Snow ▨ Thunderstorms Likely

ANNUAL
Precipitation: 59.2"
Snow: 0.0"
DAYS
Precipitation: 80
Thunderstorm: 77
Fog: 7

Grade: 75

✓ Port Angeles–Seqium, WA

Location: 48.07 N, 123.25 W, at 32 feet, on Washington's Olympic Peninsula. Victoria, capital of British Columbia, is 20 miles by ferry across Juan de Fuca Strait.

Landscape: A variety of terrain from the rocky coastline to peaks rising nearly 8,000 feet in the Olympic Mountains immediately to the south. Rivers and lakes drain the forested peninsula. Pacific needleleaf forests grow densely and have some of the world's largest trees. Douglas fir, western red cedar, and Sitka-spruce are dominant. A shrub undergrowth is present in the forests.

Climate: Generally mild throughout the year because of the modifying influence of the Pacific Ocean. Annual rainfall is moderate-heavy with maximum precipitation in winter due to the maritime polar air masses. There are traces of snow. Summer tends to be foggy.

Winter mildness: 83   **Hazard free:** 92
Summer mildness: 99   **Seasonal affect:** 63

Grade: 86

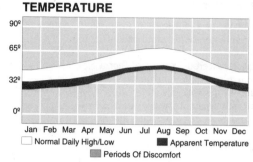

TEMPERATURE

ANNUAL
Humidity: 73%
Wind Speed: 6.7 mph
DAYS
0º or below: 0
32º or below: 41
90º or above: 0
Clear: 51
Partly Cloudy: 84
Cloudy: 230

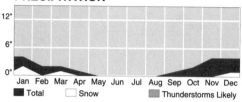

PRECIPITATION

ANNUAL
Precipitation: 25.0"
Snow: 6.1"
DAYS
Precipitation: 64
Thunderstorm: 5
Fog: 89

Port Charlotte–Punta Gorda, FL

Location: 26.58 N, 82.05 W, at 11 feet, at the northern end of Charlotte Harbor on the Gulf of Mexico, 44 miles south of Sarasota.

Landscape: Flat, level terrain crossed by rivers and streams. The woods are temperate evergreen, laurel, and magnolia. The lower level of growth includes tree ferns, small palms, and shrubs.

Climate: Subtropical. Summer and winter temperature extremes are checked by the influence of the Gulf. Mild winters have many bright, warm days. Nights are moderately cool. Rainfall averages nearly 50 inches annually, with two-thirds of this total coming daily between June and September. Most rain falls as late afternoon or early evening thunderstorms, bringing welcome relief from the heat.

Winter mildness: 100   **Hazard free:** 58
Summer mildness: 51   **Seasonal affect:** 78

Grade: 73

TEMPERATURE

ANNUAL
Humidity: 55%
Wind Speed: 8.4 mph
DAYS
0º or below: 0
32º or below: 1
90º or above: 120
Clear: 102
Partly Cloudy: 142
Cloudy: 121

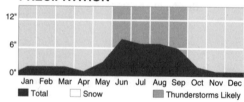

PRECIPITATION

ANNUAL
Precipitation: 48.3"
Snow: 0.0"
DAYS
Precipitation: 71
Thunderstorm: 92
Fog: 20

✓ Port Townsend, WA

Location: 48.07 N, 122.45 W, at 16 feet, on Washington's Olympic Peninsula, at the eastern end of the Strait of Juan de Fuca where Admiralty Inlet leads into Puget Sound. Seattle is 45 miles south.

Landscape: In the midst of a variety of terrain, from the rocky, glaciated coastline, to peaks rising nearly 8,000 feet in the Olympic Mountains to the west. Rivers and lakes drain the forested peninsula. Pacific needleleaf forests grow densely and have some of the world's largest trees. Douglas fir, western red cedar, and Sitka-spruce are dominant. A shrub undergrowth is present in the forests.

Climate: Predominantly marine, with cool summers, mild winters, moist air, and small daily temperature variation. Summers are cool and dry. Like most other places in this region, the area is often foggy and cloudy.

Winter mildness: 85   **Hazard free:** 92
Summer mildness: 96   **Seasonal affect:** 60

Grade: 86

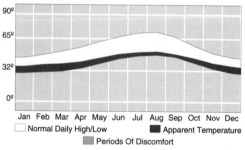

TEMPERATURE

ANNUAL
Humidity: 73%
Wind Speed: 6.7 mph
DAYS
0º or below: 0
32º or below: 41
90º or above: 0
Clear: 51
Partly Cloudy: 84
Cloudy: 230

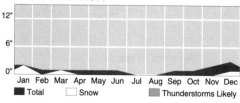

PRECIPITATION

ANNUAL
Precipitation: 21.0"
Snow: 6.1"
DAYS
Precipitation: 91
Thunderstorm: 5
Fog: 89

Prescott–Prescott Valley, AZ

Location: 34.32 N, 112.28 W, at 5,368 feet, in Arizona's mountainous west-central section, 75 miles north of Phoenix.
Landscape: In a mile-high basin among pine-dotted mountains rich in minerals. In the higher ridges of the Prescott National Forest the growth is Ponderosa, juniper, and pinyon pine. Sagebrush and native grasses dominate the dry, alkaline soil at lower elevations.
Climate: Semiarid mountain steppe, with strong daily and seasonal temperature changes. The usual winter flow of air is from the Pacific Ocean, bringing frequent snow. Cold air masses from Canada sometimes drive temperatures below freezing in the high plateau and mountainous regions. Moisture-bearing winds from the southeast Gulf region bring summer rain from July through September.

Winter mildness: 67   **Hazard free:** 68
Summer mildness: 84   **Seasonal affect:** 88

Grade: 76

TEMPERATURE

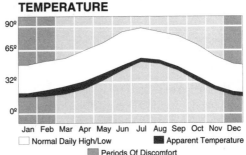

☐ Normal Daily High/Low   ■ Apparent Temperature
■ Periods Of Discomfort

ANNUAL
Humidity: 33%
Wind Speed: 6.3 mph
DAYS
0º or below: 0
32º or below: 150
90º or above: 32
Clear: 211
Partly Cloudy: 84
Cloudy: 70

PRECIPITATION

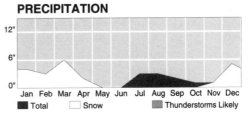

■ Total   ☐ Snow   ■ Thunderstorms Likely

ANNUAL
Precipitation: 19.6"
Snow: 22.9"
DAYS
Precipitation: 39
Thunderstorm: 23
Fog: 11

Redding, CA

Location: 40.35 N, 122.23 W, at 557 feet, in the Sacramento Valley some 150 miles north of Sacramento and 100 miles south of the Oregon border.
Landscape: Mountains surround the city on three sides, forming a huge horseshoe. The Coast Range is 30 miles west, the Sierra Nevada system 40 miles east, and the Cascade Range about 50 miles north-northeast. The western part of the valley floor is mostly rolling hills with scrub oak trees. The Sacramento River flows in a north-south direction through the eastern portion of the valley.
Climate: Precipitation is confined mostly to rain during the winter and spring months. Snowfall is infrequent and light. June through September are hot months and temperatures can exceed 100°F. Temperatures almost always drop into comfortable ranges at night. The summer and fall are nearly cloudless.

Winter mildness: 90   **Hazard free:** 91
Summer mildness: 64   **Seasonal affect:** 83

Grade: 80

TEMPERATURE

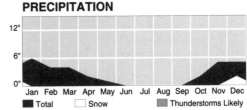

☐ Normal Daily High/Low   ■ Apparent Temperature
■ Periods Of Discomfort

ANNUAL
Humidity: 42%
Wind Speed: 7.2 mph
DAYS
0º or below: 0
32º or below: 44
90º or above: 100
Clear: 177
Partly Cloudy: 77
Cloudy: 111

PRECIPITATION

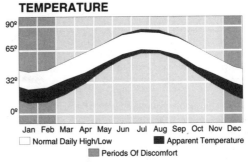

■ Total   ☐ Snow   ■ Thunderstorms Likely

ANNUAL
Precipitation: 33.3"
Snow: 4.2"
DAYS
Precipitation: 36
Thunderstorm: 10
Fog: 13

Rehoboth Bay–Indian River Bay, DE

Location: 38.43 N, 75.04 W, at 16 feet, on Delaware Bay and the Atlantic coast, 100 miles east of Washington, D.C.
Landscape: Very nearly a flat topography. A long barrier beach separates the Bays from the Atlantic Ocean. Coastal sand dunes and beaches are a sharp contrast with stands of pine. Streams flow from inland lakes to coastal marshlands before emptying into the bays.
Climate: Along the northern edge of the subtropical zone. Seasonal and daily temperature variations are moderate. Winters can be cold with snow that is scant and usually doesn't last long. Summers can be hot and humid but are tempered by onshore breezes.

Winter mildness: 77   **Hazard free:** 73
Summer mildness: 80   **Seasonal affect:** 72

Grade: 76

TEMPERATURE

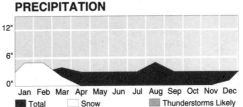

☐ Normal Daily High/Low   ■ Apparent Temperature
■ Periods Of Discomfort

ANNUAL
Humidity: 54%
Wind Speed: 9.1 mph
DAYS
0º or below: 0
32º or below: 91
90º or above: 18
Clear: 96
Partly Cloudy: 104
Cloudy: 165

PRECIPITATION

■ Total   ☐ Snow   ■ Thunderstorms Likely

ANNUAL
Precipitation: 44.3"
Snow: 14.9"
DAYS
Precipitation: 71
Thunderstorm: 30
Fog: 34

Reno–Sparks, NV

Location: 39.31 N, 119.48 W, at 4,498 feet, near the northern shore of Lake Tahoe, in a semiarid plateau lying in the lee of the Sierra Nevadas.

Landscape: At the west edge of Truckee Meadows, on the edge of the Great Basin, a major drainage for the Rockies. The Sierras rise to elevations of 9,000 to 10,000 feet. Hills to the east reach 6,000 to 7,000 feet. The Truckee River, flowing from the Sierra Nevada east through Reno, drains into Pyramid Lake to the northeast. Sagebrush and saltbrush are common in the high country desert east of here.

Climate: Desert. Sunshine is abundant throughout the year. Temperatures are mild, but the daily range may exceed 45 degrees. Afternoon temperatures are moderate, and only ten days a year fail to reach a level above freezing. Humidity is very low during the summer months and moderately low during winter.

Winter mildness: 62   **Hazard free:** 72
Summer mildness: 84   **Seasonal affect:** 85

Grade: 75

TEMPERATURE

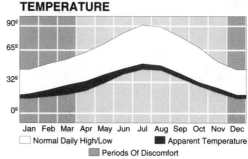

☐ Normal Daily High/Low   ■ Apparent Temperature
■ Periods Of Discomfort

ANNUAL
Humidity: 39%
Wind Speed: 6.6 mph
DAYS
0º or below: 2
32º or below: 174
90º or above: 52
Clear: 159
Partly Cloudy: 93
Cloudy: 113

PRECIPITATION

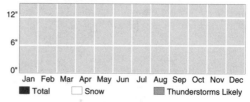

■ Total   ☐ Snow   ■ Thunderstorms Likely

ANNUAL
Precipitation: 7.5"
Snow: 22.7"
DAYS
Precipitation: 23
Thunderstorm: 14
Fog: 7

Riviera–Bullhead City, AZ

Location: 35.09 N, 114.34 W, at 540 feet in extreme western Arizona, on the Colorado River, 78 miles SE of Las Vegas, NV.

Landscape: Deep gorges line the banks of the Colorado, which roars down from impounded Lake Mead past the Black Mountains to the east and the Great Salt Lake Desert west in Nevada. Sagebrush, shadscale, fourwing saltbrush, and spiny hopsage are all tolerant of the poorly drained alkaline soils.

Climate: Desert, with strong daily and seasonal temperature changes. Winters are clear, long, and extremely mild with some flow of air from as far as the Pacific Ocean. There is a long, hot, sunbaked stretch from May through October. Except for a handful of days in spring and summer, there is no measurable precipitation.

Winter mildness: 100   **Hazard free:** 97
Summer mildness: 39   **Seasonal affect:** 94

Grade: 78

TEMPERATURE

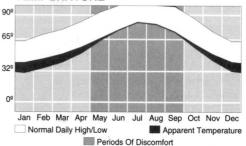

☐ Normal Daily High/Low   ■ Apparent Temperature
■ Periods Of Discomfort

ANNUAL
Humidity: 32%
Wind Speed: 7.6 mph
DAYS
0º or below: 0
32º or below: 6
90º or above: 164
Clear: 241
Partly Cloudy: 75
Cloudy: 49

PRECIPITATION

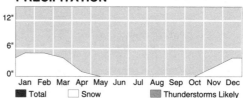

■ Total   ☐ Snow   ■ Thunderstorms Likely

ANNUAL
Precipitation: 4.7"
Snow: 0.0"
DAYS
Precipitation: 10
Thunderstorm: 7
Fog: 1

Rockport–Aransas Pass, TX

Location: 28.01 N, 97.03 W, at 6 feet, 30 miles NE of Corpus Christi on the Gulf of Mexico.

Landscape: Aransas County is a flat coastal plain, with many bays and inlets. Elevations range from sea level to 50 feet. The sandy loam and coastal clay soils are dotted with mesquite and live oak.

Climate: Humid subtropical. The heat is moderated by the prevailing southeasterly winds off the Gulf producing a climate that is predominantly maritime. Summers are warm and humid. Winters are pleasantly mild, with freezing temperatures occurring only at night, and only about 10 times per year. Spring and fall are the most pleasant months, with moderate temperatures and changeable weather.

Winter mildness: 100   **Hazard free:** 87
Summer mildness: 53   **Seasonal affect:** 78

Grade: 79

TEMPERATURE

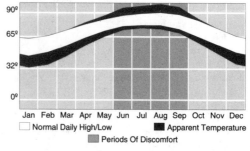

☐ Normal Daily High/Low   ■ Apparent Temperature
■ Periods Of Discomfort

ANNUAL
Humidity: 62%
Wind Speed: 12.0 mph
DAYS
0º or below: 0
32º or below: 7
90º or above: 104
Clear: 103
Partly Cloudy: 121
Cloudy: 141

PRECIPITATION

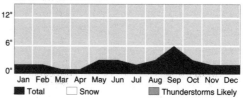

■ Total   ☐ Snow   ■ Thunderstorms Likely

ANNUAL
Precipitation: 35.1"
Snow: 0.1"
DAYS
Precipitation: 44
Thunderstorm: 28
Fog: 29

Ruidoso, NM

Location: 33.20 N, 105.41 W, at 6,641 feet, in south-central New Mexico, 115 miles north of El Paso, TX.

Landscape: In the Sacramento Mountains with the Tularosa Valley to the west. Thorny desert shrubs of mesquite and creosote bush thrive in lower elevations; juniper and pinyon in higher elevations to the east.

Climate: Highland, with cold winters, and short hot summers. Daily and seasonal temperature changes are pronounced. There is snow, but most precipitation falls as light rain and is evenly distributed throughout the year.

Winter mildness: 73   **Hazard free:** 75
Summer mildness: 76   **Seasonal affect:** 88

Grade: 77

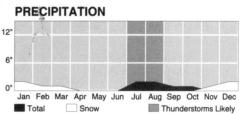

TEMPERATURE

□ Normal Daily High/Low   ■ Apparent Temperature
■ Periods Of Discomfort

ANNUAL
Humidity: 33%
Wind Speed: 8.9 mph
DAYS
0º or below: 1
32º or below: 129
90º or above: 58
Clear: 193
Partly Cloudy: 99
Cloudy: 73

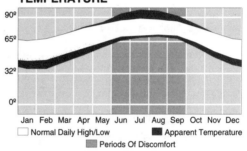

PRECIPITATION

■ Total   □ Snow   ■ Thunderstorms Likely

ANNUAL
Precipitation: 12.8"
Snow: 9.1"
DAYS
Precipitation: 31
Thunderstorm: 36
Fog: 5

St. Augustine, FL

Location: 29.51 N, 81.16 W, at 5 feet, on the Atlantic coast in northeastern Florida, 40 miles south of Jacksonville.

Landscape: On a peninsula with the Matanzas and North rivers on the east and south and the San Sebastian on the west. These rivers and saltwater lagoons lie between the city and Anastasia Island and the Atlantic Ocean beyond, serving as a port of entry on the Atlantic Intracoastal Waterway. There are Coquina quarries. The surrounding terrain is level. The pines begin to yield to palms. Broadleafed deciduous trees do not make up much of the forest.

Climate: Subtropical. The atmosphere is heavily humid. Average daily sunshine ranges from five-and-one-half hours in December to nine hours in May. The greatest amount of rain, mostly in the form of local thundershowers, falls during the late summer months.

Winter mildness: 100   **Hazard free:** 71
Summer mildness: 60   **Seasonal affect:** 75

Grade: 78

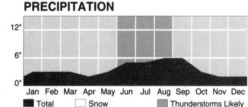

TEMPERATURE

□ Normal Daily High/Low   ■ Apparent Temperature
■ Periods Of Discomfort

ANNUAL
Humidity: 55%
Wind Speed: 8.0 mph
DAYS
0º or below: 0
32º or below: 15
90º or above: 82
Clear: 96
Partly Cloudy: 127
Cloudy: 142

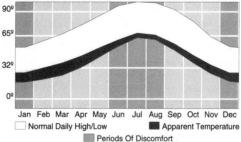

PRECIPITATION

■ Total   □ Snow   ■ Thunderstorms Likely

ANNUAL
Precipitation: 48.8"
Snow: 0.0"
DAYS
Precipitation: 70
Thunderstorm: 65
Fog: 38

St. George–Zion, UT

Location: 37.06 N, 113.34 W, at 2,880 feet, in the broad Virgin River Valley of southwestern Utah, 122 miles NE of Las Vegas, NV.

Landscape: Fifteen miles north, the Pine Valley Mountains rise to over 10,000 feet. The same distance west are the Beaver Dam Mountains, rising to 7,000 feet. To the east and south is high plateau land. Canyon walls of sandstone in hues of red, gray, yellow, brown, and volcanic cinder cone rock formations provide relief. On the edge of the Mojave Desert, vegetation is sparse. Cacti and thorny shrubs are most prevalent, as are creosote bush and chamiso.

Climate: Semiarid desert-steppe. The most striking features are bright sunshine, small annual precipitation, dryness and purity of air, and large daily variations in temperature. Summers are characterized, by hot, dry weather and low humidity. Winters are short and mild, with the Rocky Mountains blocking cold air masses from the north and east.

Winter mildness: 82   **Hazard free:** 91
Summer mildness: 58   **Seasonal affect:** 91
Grade: 77

TEMPERATURE

□ Normal Daily High/Low   ■ Apparent Temperature
■ Periods Of Discomfort

ANNUAL
Humidity: 23%
Wind Speed: 9.3 mph
DAYS
0º or below: 0
32º or below: 89
90º or above: 125
Clear: 220
Partly Cloudy: 79
Cloudy: 66

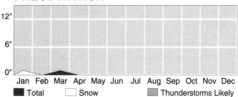

PRECIPITATION

■ Total   □ Snow   ■ Thunderstorms Likely

ANNUAL
Precipitation: 8.2"
Snow: 3.0"
DAYS
Precipitation: 20
Thunderstorm: 13
Fog: 0

St. Jay–Northeast Kingdom, VT

Location: 44.25 N, 72.01 W, at 588 feet, in Vermont's upper Connecticut River valley 33 miles east of Montpelier, the state capital.

Landscape: The Green Mountains form the western boundary, the Connecticut River the eastern. This area is comprised of low rugged hills, lowlands dotted with glacial lakes, ponds, bogs, and swamps. The woods are a transitional forest of mixed conifer and deciduous trees. Northern white pine, eastern hemlock, maple, oak, and beech are common.

Climate: Northerly latitude assures the variety and vigor of a true New England climate. The summer, while not long, is pleasant. Fall is cool, extending through October. Winters are cold and snowy, with brief, intense cold snaps formed by high-pressure systems moving down from central Canada and Hudson Bay.

Winter mildness: 52
Summer mildness: 92

Hazard free: 12
Seasonal affect: 72

Grade: 62

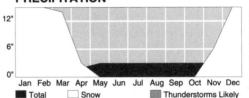

TEMPERATURE

ANNUAL
Humidity: 56%
Wind Speed: 8.5 mph
DAYS
0º or below: 28
32º or below: 173
90º or above: 9
Clear: 90
Partly Cloudy: 110
Cloudy: 165

PRECIPITATION

ANNUAL
Precipitation: 37.2"
Snow: 86.0"
DAYS
Precipitation: 81
Thunderstorm: 19
Fog: 15

St. Petersburg–Clearwater, FL

Location: 27.46 N, 82.40 W, at 44 feet, on Florida's central Gulf coast near the tip of Pinellas Peninsula, adjacent to Tampa Bay.

Landscape: This is flat country connected on the east and south by bridges to Tampa and the mainland. A string of sand-reef island resorts lie to the west. Outer coastal plain forest of evergreen, southern yellow pine, and laurel.

Climate: Temperature throughout the year is modified by the waters of the Gulf of Mexico and surrounding bays. Thunderstorms are frequent during late summer afternoons. The resulting temperature drop feels good. Snowfall is negligible, and freezing temperatures are rare.

Winter mildness: 100
Summer mildness: 57

Hazard free: 62
Seasonal affect: 78

Grade: 75

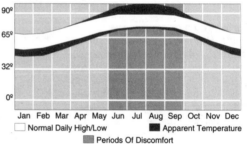

TEMPERATURE

ANNUAL
Humidity: 57%
Wind Speed: 8.4 mph
DAYS
0º or below: 0
32º or below: 0
90º or above: 78
Clear: 102
Partly Cloudy: 142
Cloudy: 121

PRECIPITATION

ANNUAL
Precipitation: 48.6"
Snow: 0.0"
DAYS
Precipitation: 69
Thunderstorm: 85
Fog: 22

St. Simons–Jekyll Islands, GA

Location: 31.13 N, 81.21 W, at 10 feet, on the Intracoastal Waterway 65 miles south of Savannah, GA, and 54 miles north of Jacksonville, FL.

Landscape: Flat, with no elevation higher than 20 feet. Shell beaches blend into the surrounding marshlands. The outer coastal plain, reached by a causeway, is a temperate rainforest that includes Evangeline oak, long-leaf pine, laurel, Bayonet palmettos, holly, and magnolia. Flowers bloom through the winter and climbing vines are prevalent.

Climate: The area enjoys mild and relatively short winters due to the moderating effect of coastal waters. Summers are warm and humid, but very high temperatures are rare. Heat waves are usually interrupted by thundershowers. Even in the summer the nights are usually pleasant. Most of the annual rain falls in the summer and early autumn.

Winter mildness: 100
Summer mildness: 66

Hazard free: 70
Seasonal affect: 75

Grade: 80

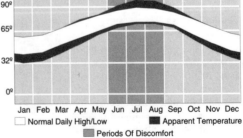

TEMPERATURE

ANNUAL
Humidity: 53%
Wind Speed: 8.0 mph
DAYS
0º or below: 0
32º or below: 16
90º or above: 42
Clear: 96
Partly Cloudy: 127
Cloudy: 142

PRECIPITATION

ANNUAL
Precipitation: 49.6"
Snow: 0.1"
DAYS
Precipitation: 68
Thunderstorm: 65
Fog: 38

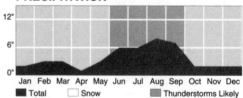
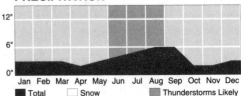

San Antonio, TX

Location: 29.25 N, 98.29 W, at 675 feet, in the south-central Texas blacklands, 150 miles north of Mexico.

Landscape: Rolling country between the Edwards Plateau and the Gulf Coastal Plain. The headwaters of the San Antonio River, which winds through the downtown area, is here on the Balcones Escarpment. Soils are blackland clay and silty loam. Vegetation consists of grasses and live oak trees, along with mesquite and cacti.

Climate: Prairie. Two-season, with mild weather during normal winter months and a long, hot summer. Though 140 miles from the Gulf of Mexico, the city feels the influence of its hot, moist air. Thunderstorms and rains have occurred in every month of the year. They are most common during the summer, with most rain falling in May and September. The winds during the winter are from the north, and from the south in the summer.

Winter mildness: 99   **Hazard free:** 83

Summer mildness: 54   **Seasonal affect:** 79

Grade: 78

TEMPERATURE

☐ Normal Daily High/Low   ■ Apparent Temperature
■ Periods Of Discomfort

ANNUAL
Humidity: 55%
Wind Speed: 9.3 mph
DAYS
0º or below: 0
32º or below: 23
90º or above: 112
Clear: 107
Partly Cloudy: 118
Cloudy: 140

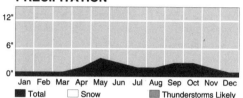

PRECIPITATION

■ Total   ☐ Snow   ■ Thunderstorms Likely

ANNUAL
Precipitation: 31.0"
Snow: 0.7"
DAYS
Precipitation: 46
Thunderstorm: 36
Fog: 21

✓ San Diego, CA

Location: 32.43 N, 117.09 W, at 13 feet, just above the Mexican border on San Diego Bay and the Pacific.

Landscape: Backed by coastal foothills and mountains to the east. Relief is further provided by cliffs that rise from the bay. Stream valleys are narrow where they drain the hills. Evergreens with thick, hard leaves like eucalyptus are prevalent. California live oak, tan oak, and California laurel are also common. Chaparral is a low-growing shrub.

Climate: Typically marine, sometimes called Mediterranean. There are no freezing days and few 90-degree days each year. Dry, mild summers and springs that are cooler, with some rain are the only seasons. Storms are practically unknown. Sunshine is abundant though there is considerable fog along the coast, and many low clouds in early morning and evening during the summer.

Winter mildness: 100   **Hazard free:** 99

Summer mildness: 82   **Seasonal affect:** 85

Grade: 91

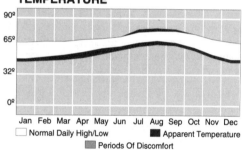

TEMPERATURE

☐ Normal Daily High/Low   ■ Apparent Temperature
■ Periods Of Discomfort

ANNUAL
Humidity: 61%
Wind Speed: 6.9 mph
DAYS
0º or below: 0
32º or below: 0
90º or above: 4
Clear: 147
Partly Cloudy: 116
Cloudy: 102

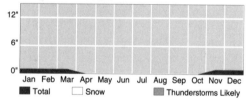

PRECIPITATION

■ Total   ☐ Snow   ■ Thunderstorms Likely

ANNUAL
Precipitation: 9.9"
Snow: 0.0"
DAYS
Precipitation: 19
Thunderstorm: 2
Fog: 24

✓ San Juan Islands, WA

Location: Friday Harbor is 48.32 N, 123.00 W, at 91 feet, in the midst of an archipelago of 172 islands that make up San Juan County in northwestern Washington, 20 miles offshore from Bellingham.

Landscape: A submerged mountain chain in upper Puget Sound where the straits of Juan de Fuca and Georgia meet at the Canadian border. Mt. Constitution, at 2,409 feet, is the highest point on the islands. Many are low, flat or flat-topped hills, with wooded forests of Sitka-spruce and western hemlock. Madrona, with a red-skinned trunk, is scattered throughout the coniferous forests at these low levels.

Climate: Marine, with mild summers, cool winters, moist air, and small daily temperature variation. Summers are dry. Like most other places in this region, the area is often foggy and cloudy.

Winter mildness: 84   **Hazard free:** 92

Summer mildness: 97   **Seasonal affect:** 62

Grade: 86

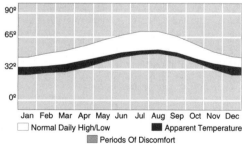

TEMPERATURE

☐ Normal Daily High/Low   ■ Apparent Temperature
■ Periods Of Discomfort

ANNUAL
Humidity: 70%
Wind Speed: 6.7 mph
DAYS
0º or below: 0
32º or below: 39
90º or above: 0
Clear: 51
Partly Cloudy: 84
Cloudy: 230

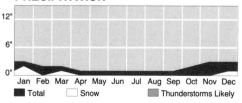

PRECIPITATION

■ Total   ☐ Snow   ■ Thunderstorms Likely

ANNUAL
Precipitation: 26.2"
Snow: 6.2"
DAYS
Precipitation: 73
Thunderstorm: 5
Fog: 89

✓ San Luis Obispo, CA

Location: 35.17 N, 120.39 W, at 234 feet, in the foothills of the Santa Lucia Mountains, 75 miles NW of Santa Barbara.
Landscape: Wooded San Luis Obispo Creek has stretches of fast-falling water. The Santa Lucia Mountains rise to cliff-top, ocean views. Cypress, and pine groves predominate in the mixed evergreen forest.
Climate: Mediterranean with generally two seasons. The ocean is the biggest climate influence. Cool temperatures and sea breezes keep the weather mild most of the year. Fog and wind are common; rain falls mainly during the winter months.

Winter mildness: 99   **Hazard free:** 98
Summer mildness: 88   **Seasonal affect:** 85

TEMPERATURE

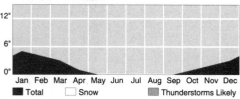

ANNUAL
Humidity: 61%
Wind Speed: 6.1 mph
DAYS
0º or below: 0
32º or below: 3
90º or above: 12
Clear: 146
Partly Cloudy: 115
Cloudy: 104

PRECIPITATION

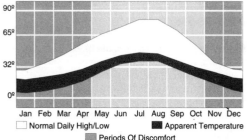

ANNUAL
Precipitation: 23.5"
Snow: 0.0"
DAYS
Precipitation: 28
Thunderstorm: 3
Fog: 18

Grade: 93

Sandpoint–Priest River, ID

Location: 48.16 N, 116.33 W, at 2,086 feet, in the Idaho panhandle, 50 miles south of the Canadian border
Landscape: Pend Oreille Lake, near the outflow of the Pend Oreille River, is one of many area lakes and streams. The Kaniksu National Forest is mixed coniferous and deciduous. Douglas fir, hemlock, and cedar predominate in this high valley surrounded by mountain ranges.
Climate: Can be generally described as rigorous, with dry summers and snowy winters. Though seasonal variation is large, it is less so than most other locations this far north. Fall is pleasant but all too short.

Winter mildness: 53   **Hazard free:** 13
Summer mildness: 96   **Seasonal affect:** 68

TEMPERATURE

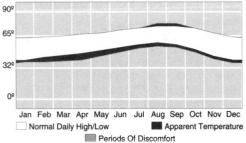

ANNUAL
Humidity: 59%
Wind Speed: 8.9 mph
DAYS
0º or below: 7
32º or below: 187
90º or above: 15
Clear: 85
Partly Cloudy: 87
Cloudy: 193

PRECIPITATION

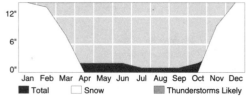

ANNUAL
Precipitation: 31.4"
Snow: 89.3"
DAYS
Precipitation: 80
Thunderstorm: 10
Fog: 47

Grade: 63

✓ Santa Barbara, CA

Location: 34.25 N, 119.42 W, at 100 feet, in the Santa Maria Valley, 150 miles NW of Los Angeles.
Landscape: The valley is flat and fertile, opening onto the Pacific Ocean at the base of the Santa Ynez Mountains. It is bounded by the foothills of the San Rafael Mountains, the Solomon Hills, and the Casmalia Hills. Cypress and pine groves predominate in the mixed evergreen forest.
Climate: Mediterranean, including a rainy season typical of the California coast in winter. During the rest of the year, particularly from June to October, there is little or no precipitation. Clear, sunshiny afternoons prevail on most days. At night and in the morning, however, the California stratus and fog appear.

Winter mildness: 98   **Hazard free:** 99
Summer mildness: 89   **Seasonal affect:** 85

TEMPERATURE

ANNUAL
Humidity: 60%
Wind Speed: 6.1 mph
DAYS
0º or below: 0
32º or below: 10
90º or above: 4
Clear: 146
Partly Cloudy: 115
Cloudy: 104

PRECIPITATION

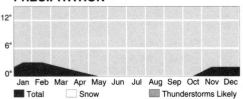

ANNUAL
Precipitation: 16.3"
Snow: 0.0"
DAYS
Precipitation: 21
Thunderstorm: 2
Fog: 18

Grade: 93

Santa Fe, NM

Location: 35.40 N, 105.56 W, at 6,947 feet, in the north-central part of the state, 60 miles from Albuquerque.

Landscape: In the northern Rio Grande Valley on the Santa Fe River in the rolling foothills of the rugged Sangre de Cristo Mountains. Westward the terrain slopes to the Rio Grande River some 20 miles away. The high mountains protect the city from much of winter's cold. Engelmann spruce and subalpine fir cover the higher slopes; ponderosa pine is on the lower, drier, more exposed slopes.

Climate: Highland steppe, with winters that are crisp, clear, and sunny, with considerable daytime warming. Summers are warm, pleasant, dry, and invigorating. Long cloudy periods are unknown.

Winter mildness: 62	**Hazard free:** 50
Summer mildness: 91	**Seasonal affect:** 87

Grade: 74

TEMPERATURE

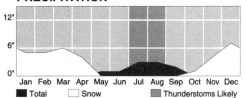

ANNUAL
Humidity: 34%
Wind Speed: 9.1 mph
DAYS
0º or below: 4
32º or below: 169
90º or above: 8
Clear: 168
Partly Cloudy: 110
Cloudy: 87

PRECIPITATION

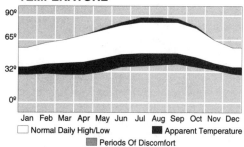

ANNUAL
Precipitation: 17.0"
Snow: 33.7"
DAYS
Precipitation: 33
Thunderstorm: 41
Fog: 5

✓ Santa Rosa–Sonoma, CA

Location: 38.26 N, 122.42 W, at 177 feet, in the Russian River Valley, 50 miles north of San Francisco.

Landscape: This valley runs parallel to the Pacific Coast with only low hills, 300 feet to 500 feet, between it and the ocean 25 miles southwest. Higher hills rise 10 miles to the east leading into the foothills of the Coast Ranges. Principal trees of the conifer forest are Douglas fir, western red cedar, western hemlock, and Sitka-spruce.

Climate: The nearness of the ocean and the surrounding topography join with the prevailing westerly circulation to produce a predominantly southerly air flow year 'round. However, the area is sufficiently far inland to assure it a varied climate. Summers are warm, winters cool, and there is a daily temperature shift. There is less fog and drizzle here than other points south.

Winter mildness: 92	**Hazard free:** 99
Summer mildness: 82	**Seasonal affect:** 83

Grade: 88

TEMPERATURE

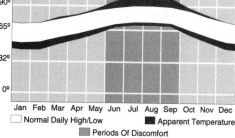

ANNUAL
Humidity: 65%
Wind Speed: 10.6 mph
DAYS
0º or below: 0
32º or below: 37
90º or above: 34
Clear: 160
Partly Cloudy: 100
Cloudy: 105

PRECIPITATION

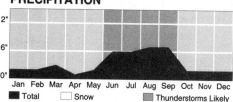

ANNUAL
Precipitation: 30.3"
Snow: 0.0"
DAYS
Precipitation: 46
Thunderstorm: 2
Fog: 14

Sarasota, FL

Location: 27.20 N, 82.32 W, at 27 feet, sheltered from the Gulf of Mexico behind Longboat Key on Sarasota Bay. St. Petersburg is 20 miles north.

Landscape: The southern Gulf Coastal Plains are flat and irregular. There is less than 200 feet variation in altitude over the gently rolling areas. Most of the numerous streams are sluggish; and marshes, swamps, and lakes are numerous. Evergreen oaks, laurel, and magnolia are common. Trees are not tall and the leaf canopy is less dense. There is a well-developed underbrush of ferns, shrubs, and herbaceous plants.

Climate: Subtropical. Temperature throughout the year is modified by the waters of the Gulf of Mexico and surrounding bays. Thunderstorms are frequent during late-summer afternoons, rapidly cooling the hot, humid days. Winters are mild. Snow and freezing temperatures are rare.

Winter mildness: 100	**Hazard free:** 62
Summer mildness: 58	**Seasonal affect:** 78

Grade: 76

TEMPERATURE

ANNUAL
Humidity: 55%
Wind Speed: 8.4 mph
DAYS
0º or below: 0
32º or below: 0
90º or above: 78
Clear: 102
Partly Cloudy: 142
Cloudy: 121

PRECIPITATION

ANNUAL
Precipitation: 47.2"
Snow: 0.0"
DAYS
Precipitation: 71
Thunderstorm: 85
Fog: 22

Savannah, GA

Location: 32.05 N, 81.06 W, at 42 feet, on Georgia's north coastal border at the mouth of the Savannah River and Atlantic Ocean.

Landscape: Surrounded by flat land, low and marshy to the north and east, rising to several feet above sea level to the west and south. About half the land to the west and south is clear of trees and the other half is woods, much of which lie in swamp. The outer coastal plain is a temperate rainforest that includes live oak, loblolly pine, laurel, and magnolia.

Climate: Subtropical. Summer temperatures are moderated by thundershowers almost every afternoon. Sunshine is adequate in all seasons; seldom are there more than two or three days in succession without it. The long growing season is accompanied by abundant rain.

Winter mildness: 97   **Hazard free:** 72
Summer mildness: 63   **Seasonal affect:** 74

Grade: 78

TEMPERATURE

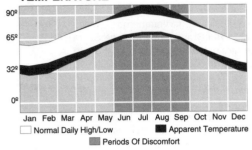

ANNUAL
Humidity: 53%
Wind Speed: 7.9 mph
DAYS
0º or below: 0
32º or below: 31
90º or above: 69
Clear: 104
Partly Cloudy: 110
Cloudy: 151

PRECIPITATION

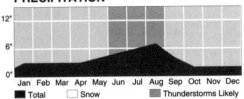

ANNUAL
Precipitation: 49.2"
Snow: 0.4"
DAYS
Precipitation: 68
Thunderstorm: 61
Fog: 39

Sebring–Avon Park, FL

Location: 27.29 N, 81.26 W, at 131 feet, circling Lake Jackson in south-central Florida, 90 miles south of Orlando, and east of St. Petersburg on the Gulf, and west of Fort Pierce on the Atlantic coast.

Landscape: Highland lakes region with sandy ridges giving relief to low, level muckland and flatland. Hardwood hammock and cabbage palms are dense in the rainforest of Highlands Hammock State Park.

Climate: Subtropical, with a surplus of moisture. As in other Florida locations, the humid, hot summer is cooled by afternoon thunderstorms. Winters are mild. Annual range of temperature changes is small.

Winter mildness: 100   **Hazard free:** 63
Summer mildness: 50   **Seasonal affect:** 76

Grade: 73

TEMPERATURE

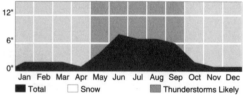

ANNUAL
Humidity: 54%
Wind Speed: 8.6 mph
DAYS
0º or below: 0
32º or below: 4
90º or above: 137
Clear: 91
Partly Cloudy: 147
Cloudy: 127

PRECIPITATION

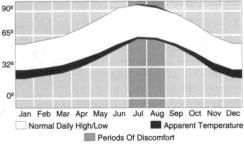

ANNUAL
Precipitation: 49.6"
Snow: 0.0"
DAYS
Precipitation: 76
Thunderstorm: 81
Fog: 26

Sedona, AZ

Location: 34.52 N, 111.45 W, at 4,280 feet, in Oak Creek Canyon 90 miles north of Phoenix and 17 miles south of Flagstaff.

Landscape: Overlooks red-hued rocks and buttes of the canyon whose steep walls rise 1,200 feet. The forest is Ponderosa pine, Douglas fir, and at higher elevations, subalpine fir and Engelmann spruce.

Climate: Semiarid mountain steppe. There are strong daily and seasonal temperature changes. The usual winter flow of air is from the Pacific Ocean. This brings frequent snows. Cold air from Canada sometimes drives temperatures below freezing here. Moisture-bearing winds from the southeast Gulf region bring brief summer rains from July through September.

Winter mildness: 73   **Hazard free:** 68
Summer mildness: 75   **Seasonal affect:** 88

Grade: 75

TEMPERATURE

ANNUAL
Humidity: 33%
Wind Speed: 6.8 mph
DAYS
0º or below: 0
32º or below: 150
90º or above: 32
Clear: 211
Partly Cloudy: 84
Cloudy: 70

PRECIPITATION

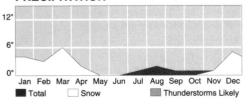

ANNUAL
Precipitation: 18.7"
Snow: 22.9"
DAYS
Precipitation: 39
Thunderstorm: 23
Fog: 11

Silver City, NM

Location: 32.46 N, 108.16 W, at 5,851 feet, in southwestern New Mexico, 170 miles east of Tucson, Arizona.

Landscape: East of the Continental Divide in the foothills of the Pinos Altos Range at the edge of the Gila National Forest. Here there are wild ranges, high cliffs, and remote canyons. The Chihuahuan desert vegetation includes creosote, ceniza, and ocotillo shrubs. Juniper and pinyons are common on rocky outcrops. Ponderosa pine, Douglas fir, white fir, and spruce occur in the high forests.

Climate: Desert continental. The rainfall is light and falls in brief showers through late summer and fall. Drizzles are unknown. Summers are hot, but the nights are cool. Winters tend to be mild and sunny, with freezing nights.

Winter mildness: 72	**Hazard free:** 83
Summer mildness: 79	**Seasonal affect:** 90

Grade: 79

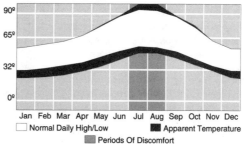

TEMPERATURE

Normal Daily High/Low — Apparent Temperature — Periods Of Discomfort

ANNUAL
Humidity: 58%
Wind Speed: 7.9 mph
DAYS
0º or below: 0
32º or below: 64
90º or above: 83
Clear: 189
Partly Cloudy: 75
Cloudy: 101

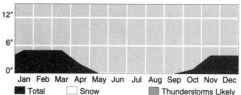

PRECIPITATION

Total — Snow — Thunderstorms Likely

ANNUAL
Precipitation: 31.6"
Snow: 0.9"
DAYS
Precipitation: 43
Thunderstorm: 14
Fog: 34

Smith Mountain Lake, VA

Location: 37.02 N, 79.32 W, at 795 feet, in foothills on the eastern slope of the Blue Ridge Mountains of southwest Virginia. Roanoke is 20 miles NW.

Landscape: This 22,000-acre lake has 500 miles of irregular shoreline. The woods are a typical southeastern mixed forest of medium-tall to tall oak, hickory, sweet gum, red maple, and winged elm, together with loblolly and shortleaf pine. The undergrowth is dogwood, viburnum, blueberry, youpon, and numerous woody vines.

Climate: Hot continental, with four distinct seasons. Winters are short, summers somewhat hot and humid. Spring and autumn are ideal. Precipitation is evenly distributed throughout the year, mostly as rain. In mid-summer, mountain thunderstorms are likely.

Winter mildness: 78	**Hazard free:** 69
Summer mildness: 80	**Seasonal affect:** 74

Grade: 76

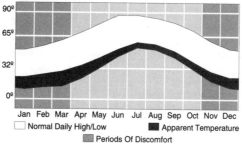

TEMPERATURE

Normal Daily High/Low — Apparent Temperature — Periods Of Discomfort

ANNUAL
Humidity: 33%
Wind Speed: 8.9 mph
DAYS
0º or below: 1
32º or below: 129
90º or above: 58
Clear: 193
Partly Cloudy: 99
Cloudy: 73

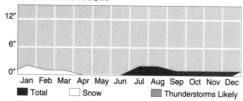

PRECIPITATION

Total — Snow — Thunderstorms Likely

ANNUAL
Precipitation: 15.4"
Snow: 6.6"
DAYS
Precipitation: 22
Thunderstorm: 23
Fog: 2

Sonora-Groveland-Twain Harte, CA

Location: The weather station is Sonora, 37.59 N, 120.23 W, at 1,854 feet. Sacramento is 93 miles NW.

Landscape: In the foothills of the Sierra Nevada Mountains at the edge of the Stanislaus National Forest. Five rivers drain the region. Chaparral of the low elevations gives way to digger pine and several oak species in the higher mountains.

Climate: Sierran forest climate in the transition zone between the dry west-coast desert and the wet west coast farther north. Prevailing west winds influence conditions jointly with elevation. Therefore the summers are long and generally dry. Most of the precipitation falls as rain rather than snow.

Winter mildness: 84	**Hazard free:** 93
Summer mildness: 72	**Seasonal affect:** 82

Grade: 81

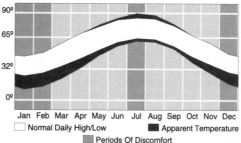

TEMPERATURE

Normal Daily High/Low — Apparent Temperature — Periods Of Discomfort

ANNUAL
Humidity: 54%
Wind Speed: 8.1 mph
DAYS
0º or below: 0
32º or below: 89
90º or above: 28
Clear: 102
Partly Cloudy: 112
Cloudy: 151

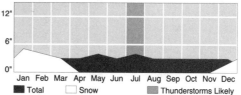

PRECIPITATION

Total — Snow — Thunderstorms Likely

ANNUAL
Precipitation: 42.9"
Snow: 16.0"
DAYS
Precipitation: 74
Thunderstorm: 36
Fog: 23

Southern Berkshire County, MA

Location: The weather station is Great Barrington, 42.11 N, 73.21 W, at 721 feet, in the extreme southwestern corner of the state near the New York and Connecticut state lines.

Landscape: The Berkshire Valley is enclosed by the Berkshire Plateau in the east and the Taconic Mountains in the west. Rolling, open meadows are watered by the headwaters of the Housatonic River. A typical northern deciduous forest covers the uplands with maple, birch, beech, oak, and a scattering of pine. The low growth is shrub, herb, and fern.

Climate: Hot continental, with large temperature variations from season to season. Winters receive Canadian air sweeping down the Hudson Valley to the west. December through February is cold with long-lasting snow. Spring is short. Summers are clear, warm, and ideal. Falls extend through mid-November. Precipitation is moderate and evenly distributed throughout the year.

Winter mildness: 59   **Hazard free:** 34
Summer mildness: 91   **Seasonal affect:** 71

Grade: 68

TEMPERATURE

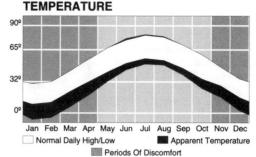

Normal Daily High/Low   Apparent Temperature
Periods Of Discomfort

ANNUAL
Humidity: 56%
Wind Speed: 8.5 mph
DAYS
0º or below: 6
32º or below: 135
90º or above: 19
Clear: 80
Partly Cloudy: 108
Cloudy: 177

PRECIPITATION

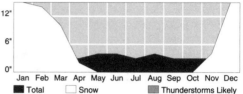

Total   Snow   Thunderstorms Likely

ANNUAL
Precipitation: 44.8"
Snow: 62.2"
DAYS
Precipitation: 75
Thunderstorm: 20
Fog: 28

Southern Pines–Pinehurst, NC

Location: 35.10 N, 79.23 W, at 512 feet, 75 miles south of Chapel Hill in the southern heartland of the state.

Landscape: In gently rolling sandhill country between the foothills of the Uwharrie Mountains and the coastal plains. The woods are a hardwood swamp forest with broadleaf deciduous and needleleaf evergreens.

Climate: Mild winters and hot humid summers are the rule. Precipitation is evenly distributed throughout the year, but peaks slightly in midsummer or early spring thunderstorms. Occasionally there will be summer droughts. Frost occurs nearly every winter but snow is infrequent.

Winter mildness: 78   **Hazard free:** 75
Summer mildness: 73   **Seasonal affect:** 74

Grade: 75

TEMPERATURE

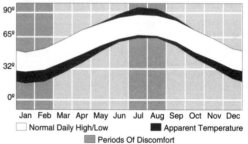

Normal Daily High/Low   Apparent Temperature
Periods Of Discomfort

ANNUAL
Humidity: 54%
Wind Speed: 7.8 mph
DAYS
0º or below: 0
32º or below: 111
90º or above: 43
Clear: 112
Partly Cloudy: 105
Cloudy: 148

PRECIPITATION

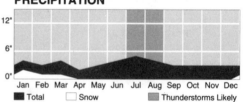

Total   Snow   Thunderstorms Likely

ANNUAL
Precipitation: 46.8"
Snow: 5.7"
DAYS
Precipitation: 74
Thunderstorm: 44
Fog: 34

Southport–Brunswick Islands, NC

Location: 33.55 N, 78.01 W, at 34 feet, on the Atlantic Ocean in North Carolina's extreme southeastern corner, 25 miles south of Wilmington.

Landscape: The surrounding terrain, typical of the state's Coastal Plain, is low-lying. The average elevation is less than 40 feet and level. There are many rivers, creeks, and lakes nearby. Considerable swampy growth surrounds the many water sites. Large tracts of southern mixed forest alternate with cultivated fields.

Climate: A strong maritime influence. Summers are warm and humid, but excessive heat is rare. During the colder part of the year, polar air reaches the coastal areas causing sharp temperature drops. Rainfall is ample and well distributed, with most occurring in summer in the form of thundershowers. In winter, rain may fall steadily for several days. Snowfall is slight.

Winter mildness: 90   **Hazard free:** 77
Summer mildness: 74   **Seasonal affect:** 74

Grade: 80

TEMPERATURE

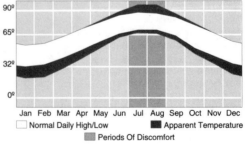

Normal Daily High/Low   Apparent Temperature
Periods Of Discomfort

ANNUAL
Humidity: 56%
Wind Speed: 8.8 mph
DAYS
0º or below: 0
32º or below: 42
90º or above: 20
Clear: 111
Partly Cloudy: 103
Cloudy: 151

PRECIPITATION

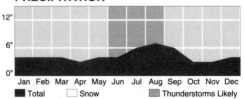

Total   Snow   Thunderstorms Likely

ANNUAL
Precipitation: 57.0"
Snow: 1.7"
DAYS
Precipitation: 74
Thunderstorm: 47
Fog: 24

State College, PA

Location: 40.47 N, 77.51 W, at 1,157 feet, in Centre County, the geographic center of Pennsylvania.

Landscape: Elevations vary from 977 feet to 2,400 feet. There are rolling meadows of the Nittany Valley and foothills of the Allegheny Plateau that rises to the west. Forests of pine, hemlock, and hardwoods of beech, maple, oak, ash, and cherry were once more common before the clear-cut harvests. The surrounding higher elevations are now covered with second-growth forests.

Climate: Hot continental. The weather is moderated by the surrounding mountain elevations and protected by its eastern slope location. This translates to drier, somewhat less humid seasons. Winters are cold and snowy, with thick cloud cover. Summer and fall are the most pleasant seasons of the year.

Winter mildness: 63   **Hazard free:** 41
Summer mildness: 88   **Seasonal affect:** 72

Grade: 69

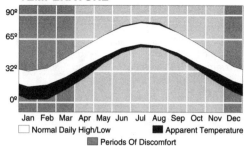

TEMPERATURE

ANNUAL
Humidity: 54%
Wind Speed: 7.6 mph
DAYS
0º or below: 5
32º or below: 131
90º or above: 8
Clear: 86
Partly Cloudy: 109
Cloudy: 170

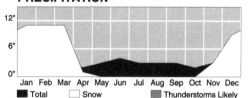

PRECIPITATION

ANNUAL
Precipitation: 37.5"
Snow: 48.0"
DAYS
Precipitation: 76
Thunderstorm: 31
Fog: 18

Table Rock Lake, MO

Location: 36.40 N, 93.52 W, at 1,324 feet, just above the Arkansas state line, 50 miles south of Springfield.

Landscape: One of several lakes on the Ozark Plateau formed by river impoundment. The rounded mountains rise somewhat steeply from river valleys and the lakeshore. Oak-hickory forests are tall, providing a dense cover in summer, colorful foliage in fall, but are bare in winter. Pines are evident of second-growth forest. Lower layers of shrub, dogwood, and redbud are common.

Climate: Hot continental, with hot summers and cold winters. Precipitation is adequate throughout the year, usually falling as rain. Winters may be cold enough for snow, but more usual is an icy rain during brief, intense cold snaps. Spring arrives early and is pleasant.

Winter mildness: 74   **Hazard free:** 59
Summer mildness: 77   **Seasonal affect:** 75

Grade: 73

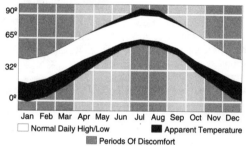

TEMPERATURE

ANNUAL
Humidity: 57%
Wind Speed: 10.7 mph
DAYS
0º or below: 4
32º or below: 102
90º or above: 43
Clear: 115
Partly Cloudy: 96
Cloudy: 154

PRECIPITATION

ANNUAL
Precipitation: 44.4"
Snow: 16.1"
DAYS
Precipitation: 62
Thunderstorm: 56
Fog: 20

Taos, NM

Location: 36.24 N, 105.34 W, at 6,983 feet, 55 miles north of Sante Fe.

Landscape: On a branch of the Rio Grande in the Sangre de Cristo Mountains, near Wheeler Peak, highest point in New Mexico. The relief includes deep gorges, mountainous skylines, and wide valleys. Typical steppe vegetation consists of numerous short grasses, scattered shrubs, and low trees. Engelmann spruce and subalpine fir cover the intermediate slopes, and ponderosa pine is on the lower, drier, more exposed slopes.

Climate: Steppe and semiarid continental. Precipitation is evenly distributed throughout the year, falling as rain in summer storms and snow in the cold winters. Summers are clear, mild, and ideal.

Winter mildness: 56   **Hazard free:** 41
Summer mildness: 93   **Seasonal affect:** 87

Grade: 71

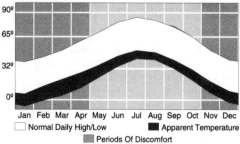

TEMPERATURE

ANNUAL
Humidity: 34%
Wind Speed: 9.1 mph
DAYS
0º or below: 6
32º or below: 172
90º or above: 7
Clear: 168
Partly Cloudy: 110
Cloudy: 87

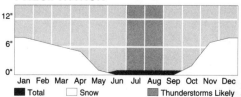

PRECIPITATION

ANNUAL
Precipitation: 12.4"
Snow: 45.7"
DAYS
Precipitation: 34
Thunderstorm: 41
Fog: 5

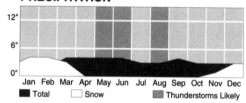

Thomasville, GA

Location: 30.50 N, 83.58 W, at 250 feet, in the extreme southern part of the state, 35 miles NE of Tallahassee, FL.
Landscape: At the western edge of the coastal plain in low, gently sloping pinelands near the Ochlockonee River. Stands of temperate rainforest of evergreen and laurel occur. Noted for profusion of moss-covered oaks and roses, azaleas, camellias, and other ornamental shrubs.
Climate: Subtropical with no freezing winters. Summers are hot and humid. The annual temperature range is small to moderate. Rainfall is abundant and well distributed throughout the year.

Winter mildness: 98	**Hazard free:** 63
Summer mildness: 59	**Seasonal affect:** 75

TEMPERATURE

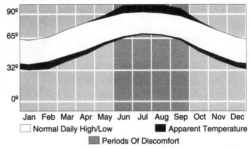

ANNUAL
Humidity: 54%
Wind Speed: 6.3 mph
DAYS
0º or below: 0
32º or below: 34
90º or above: 94
Clear: 101
Partly Cloudy: 129
Cloudy: 135

PRECIPITATION

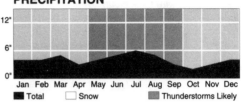

ANNUAL
Precipitation: 52.1"
Snow: 0.4"
DAYS
Precipitation: 71
Thunderstorm: 82
Fog: 50

Grade: 75

Toms River–Barnegat Bay, NJ

Location: 39.57 N, 74.12 W, at 40 feet, in the center of New Jersey's Atlantic coast, 95 miles south of New York City.
Landscape: Surrounding flat terrain is composed of tidal marshes and beach sand. The dunes provide vantage points for observing bird migrations along the Atlantic flyway. Inland is a forest of mixed evergreens.
Climate: Hot continental, with the moderating influence of the Atlantic apparent throughout the year. Summers are relatively cooler, winters warmer than those of other places at the same latitude. During the warm season, sea breezes in the late morning and afternoon prevent excessive heat, and on occasion, may lower the temperature 15 degrees within a half hour. Fall is long, lasting until almost mid-November. On the other hand, warming is somewhat delayed in the spring. Precipitation is moderate and well distributed throughout the year.

Winter mildness: 70	**Hazard free:** 73
Summer mildness: 84	**Seasonal affect:** 72

TEMPERATURE

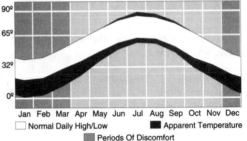

ANNUAL
Humidity: 58%
Wind Speed: 10.1 mph
DAYS
0º or below: 2
32º or below: 110
90º or above: 17
Clear: 94
Partly Cloudy: 110
Cloudy: 161

PRECIPITATION

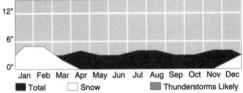

ANNUAL
Precipitation: 47.1"
Snow: 15.7"
DAYS
Precipitation: 74
Thunderstorm: 27
Fog: 44

Grade: 76

Traverse City, MI

Location: 44.45 N, 85.37 W, at 599 feet, on Grand Traverse Bay in northwestern Michigan.
Landscape: The tip of the 20-mile-long Old Mission Peninsula, jutting into the bay from the city, is exactly midway between the Equator and the North Pole. The terrain is generally level or gently undulating, with sandy and gravelly soils. The region abounds with lakes ideal for fishing and summer recreation. The forest is pine and hemlock. Maple, oak, and birch are occasional deciduous trees.
Climate: Though rigorous because of its interior and northerly location, the climate is modified by the presence of Great Lakes on either side of the Michigan peninsula. Consequently, summertime temperatures average at least 5 degrees cooler than locations in the southern part of the state. However, winters are quite severe, with cold spells that may last for a week and snowfall that averages almost 90 inches.

Winter mildness: 53	**Hazard free:** 9
Summer mildness: 93	**Seasonal affect:** 68

TEMPERATURE

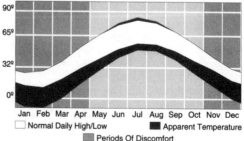

ANNUAL
Humidity: 67%
Wind Speed: 10.7 mph
DAYS
0º or below: 18
32º or below: 169
90º or above: 5
Clear: 66
Partly Cloudy: 88
Cloudy: 211

PRECIPITATION

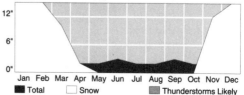

ANNUAL
Precipitation: 29.8"
Snow: 88.4"
DAYS
Precipitation: 73
Thunderstorm: 22
Fog: 22

Grade: 61

Tryon, NC

Location: 35.12 N, 82.14 W, at 1,085 feet, just above the South Carolina border 25 miles south of Asheville.

Landscape: Central mountain region with the Blue Ridge away to the north over Hogbark Mountain. Sassafras Mountain, at 1,085 feet, lies west. Nearby are waterfalls and valleys of rolling farmland, together with lakes and ski areas. The surrounding Appalachian oak forest also includes tulip tree, sweet chestnut, birch, hickory, walnut, and maple. In spring, a low layer of herbs quickly develops but is reduced after the trees reach full foliage and shade the ground.

Climate: Hot continental, with a strong annual temperature cycle of cool winters and warm summers. Precipitation, usually rain, is adequate in all months. Spring comes earlier in this thermal belt than just a few miles north or south.

Winter mildness: 85   **Hazard free:** 73
Summer mildness: 74   **Seasonal affect:** 73

Grade: 77

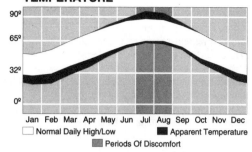

TEMPERATURE

ANNUAL
Humidity: 55%
Wind Speed: 6.9 mph
DAYS
0º or below: 0
32º or below: 70
90º or above: 41
Clear: 122
Partly Cloudy: 100
Cloudy: 143

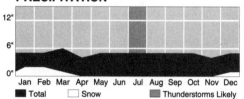

PRECIPITATION

ANNUAL
Precipitation: 65.3"
Snow: 8.2"
DAYS
Precipitation: 83
Thunderstorm: 42
Fog: 33

Tucson, AZ

Location: 32.13 N, 110.55 W, at 2,437 feet, on the Santa Cruz River, 120 miles SE of Phoenix and 60 miles above the Mexican border.

Landscape: At the foot of the Catalina Mountains in a broad, flat to gently rolling valley floor rimmed by mountains. To the northeast, the Coronado National Forest is typical of pine, spruce, fir forests of the higher elevations.

Climate: Desert. A sunny, dry climate and a unique desert-mountain location. There is a long, hot season beginning in April that ends in October. High temperatures are modified by low humidity. Tucson lies in the zone receiving more sunshine than any other in the United States. Clear skies or very thin, high clouds permit intense surface heating during the day and active radiational cooling at night. Summer is the rainy season with active thunderstorms.

Winter mildness: 99   **Hazard free:** 80
Summer mildness: 51   **Seasonal affect:** 89

Grade: 78

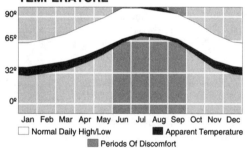

TEMPERATURE

ANNUAL
Humidity: 30%
Wind Speed: 8.3 mph
DAYS
0º or below: 0
32º or below: 18
90º or above: 141
Clear: 195
Partly Cloudy: 90
Cloudy: 80

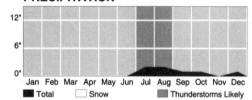

PRECIPITATION

ANNUAL
Precipitation: 12.0"
Snow: 1.1"
DAYS
Precipitation: 18
Thunderstorm: 41
Fog: 2

Vero Beach–Sebastian, FL

Location: 27.38 N, 80.24 W, at 17 feet, on Florida's east coast, 50 miles north of Palm Beach.

Landscape: On the coastal plain northeast of Lake Okeechobee in the midst of miles of dunes and barrier beach broken by the Indian River. Native vegetation includes sea-oat grass, seagrape and cabbage palm.

Climate: Subtropical. Nearness to the Atlantic results in a climate tempered by land and sea breezes. Apparent temperatures in summer may top 90°F during the late morning or early afternoon, but they are cut short by a midday sea breeze and afternoon convective thundershowers. Winters can have cold airflows from the north, but usually are mild because of the area's ocean setting and southerly latitude.

Winter mildness: 100   **Hazard free:** 68
Summer mildness: 61   **Seasonal affect:** 76

Grade: 78

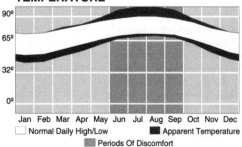

TEMPERATURE

ANNUAL
Humidity: 59%
Wind Speed: 8.4 mph
DAYS
0º or below: 0
32º or below: 2
90º or above: 65
Clear: 98
Partly Cloudy: 133
Cloudy: 134

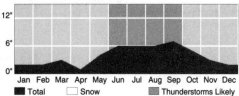

PRECIPITATION

ANNUAL
Precipitation: 51.2"
Snow: 0.2"
DAYS
Precipitation: 77
Thunderstorm: 69
Fog: 15

Virginia Beach, VA

Location: 36.51 N, 75.58 W, at 16 feet, at the entrance to Chesapeake Bay, 90 miles SE of Richmond, the state capital.
Landscape: Low, level land that extends south to the North Carolina border. Back Bay is a brackish lagoon and a national wildlife refuge, paralleling the ocean in the south of the city. Southeastern mixed forest has medium-tall to tall oak, hickory, sweet gum, red maple, and winged elm. At least half of the stands are filled with loblolly and shortleaf pine. The extensive coastal marshes and interior swamps are dominated by gums and cypress.
Climate: Subtropical. In a favorable geographic position north of the track of hurricanes and tropical storms and south of high-latitude storm systems. Winters are mild. Springs and falls are especially pleasant. Summers, though, are warm, humid, and long. A temperature of zero has never been recorded here, although there is occasional snow.

Winter mildness: 85	**Hazard free:** 77
Summer mildness: 75	**Seasonal affect:** 74

Grade: 78

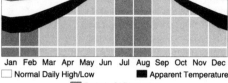

TEMPERATURE

Normal Daily High/Low Apparent Temperature Periods Of Discomfort

ANNUAL
Humidity: 58%
Wind Speed: 10.7 mph
DAYS
0º or below: 0
32º or below: 54
90º or above: 32
Clear: 106
Partly Cloudy: 106
Cloudy: 153

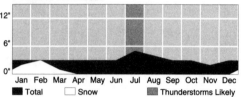

PRECIPITATION

Total Snow Thunderstorms Likely

ANNUAL
Precipitation: 44.6"
Snow: 7.7"
DAYS
Precipitation: 74
Thunderstorm: 36
Fog: 20

Wenatchee, WA

Location: 47.25 N, 120.18 W, at 645 feet, in central Washington, 85 miles SE of Seattle.
Landscape: At the juncture of the Wenatchee and Columbia rivers. The rounded, shrubbed Wenatchee Mountains lie to the southwest and the Columbia Plain stretches east in juniper grasslands. The uplands are moderately dissected, hilly, and steep. The tablelands are loess-covered and fertile.
Climate: Steppe-grassland. Generally shielded from the wet Pacific-driven weather by the Cascade Range. Summers are warm and nearly rainless. Winters are cool, foggy, and rainy. Snow is plentiful in the higher mountains.

Winter mildness: 67	**Hazard free:** 68
Summer mildness: 84	**Seasonal affect:** 73

Grade: 74

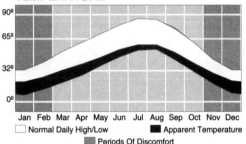

TEMPERATURE

Normal Daily High/Low Apparent Temperature Periods Of Discomfort

ANNUAL
Humidity: 58%
Wind Speed: 8.9 mph
DAYS
0º or below: 1
32º or below: 118
90º or above: 33
Clear: 85
Partly Cloudy: 87
Cloudy: 193

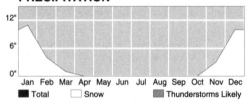

PRECIPITATION

Total Snow Thunderstorms Likely

ANNUAL
Precipitation: 8.3"
Snow: 30.7"
DAYS
Precipitation: 26
Thunderstorm: 10
Fog: 48

Western St. Tammany Parish, LA

Location: 30.28 N, 90.06 W, at 30 feet, on the north shore of Lake Pontchartrain. A 24-mile causeway across the lake connects the parish with New Orleans.
Landscape: On a low, level area of alluvial plain in the Lower Mississippi Valley. Swamp- and marshlands support cypress, small palms, tree ferns, shrubs, and herbaceous plants. Evergreen-oak and magnolia forests are the natural climax vegetation.
Climate: Subtropical. Best described as humid. Lake Pontchartrain and the nearby Gulf of Mexico modify the temperature and decrease its range. Heavy and frequent rains are typical. There are daily afternoon thunderstorms from mid-June through September. From December to March, precipitation is likely to be steady rain of two or three days duration. During the winter and spring, cold rain forms fogs.

Winter mildness: 98	**Hazard free:** 69
Summer mildness: 60	**Seasonal affect:** 74

Grade: 76

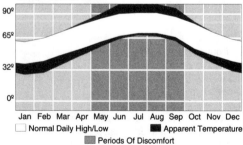

TEMPERATURE

Normal Daily High/Low Apparent Temperature Periods Of Discomfort

ANNUAL
Humidity: 62%
Wind Speed: 8.2 mph
DAYS
0º or below: 0
32º or below: 32
90º or above: 91
Clear: 102
Partly Cloudy: 118
Cloudy: 145

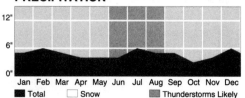

PRECIPITATION

Total Snow Thunderstorms Likely

ANNUAL
Precipitation: 62.7"
Snow: 0.5"
DAYS
Precipitation: 76
Thunderstorm: 68
Fog: 27

✓ Whidbey Island, WA

Location: Station is Coupeville, 48.08 N, 122.35 W, at 50 feet, on the Saratoga Passage in Puget Sound Basin, 40 miles above Seattle.

Landscape: At 40 miles long, it is one of the largest offshore islands in the continental United States. The coast has rocky banks indented by coves and inlets. Inland are gently rolling hills with patches of Douglas fir, red cedar, and spruce.

Climate: Marine, characterized by moderate temperatures, a pronounced though not sharply defined rainy season, and considerable cloudiness, particularly during the winter. Occasionally, severe winter storms come in from the north. Summers are warm and pleasant; winters are mild and rainy.

Winter mildness: 82   **Hazard free:** 90
Summer mildness: 97   **Seasonal affect:** 66

Grade: 86

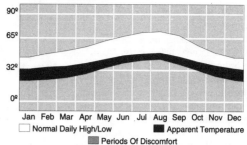

TEMPERATURE

ANNUAL
Humidity: 70%
Wind Speed: 9.0 mph
DAYS
0º or below: 0
32º or below: 52
90º or above: 3
Clear: 56
Partly Cloudy: 80
Cloudy: 229

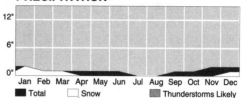

PRECIPITATION

ANNUAL
Precipitation: 21.1"
Snow: 6.6"
DAYS
Precipitation: 62
Thunderstorm: 7
Fog: 43

Wickenburg, AZ

Location: 33.58 N, 112.43 W, at 2,903 feet, in west-central Arizona, 30 miles NW of Phoenix.

Landscape: In the Harcuvar Mountains on the Hassayampa River at the northern edge of the Sonoran Desert. Native vegetation includes mixed grasses, chaparral brush, and oak-juniper woodlands.

Climate: Semiarid mountain steppe. There are strong daily and seasonal temperature changes. The usual winter flow of air is from the Pacific, though cold air from Canada sometimes drives temperatures below freezing in the high plateau and mountainous regions. Summer is dry with daytime temperatures topping 100°F.

Winter mildness: 91   **Hazard free:** 89
Summer mildness: 52   **Seasonal affect:** 90

Grade: 77

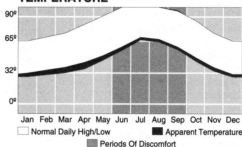

TEMPERATURE

ANNUAL
Humidity: 31%
Wind Speed: 6.3 mph
DAYS
0º or below: 0
32º or below: 63
90º or above: 152
Clear: 211
Partly Cloudy: 84
Cloudy: 70

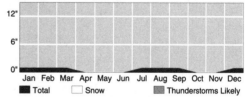

PRECIPITATION

ANNUAL
Precipitation: 12.2"
Snow: 0.2"
DAYS
Precipitation: 20
Thunderstorm: 23
Fog: 1

Williamsburg, VA

Location: 37.16 N, 76.42 W, at 86 feet, on a tidewater peninsula between the James and York rivers, 40 miles midway between Richmond and Norfolk.

Landscape: Elevated slightly on a ridge, the country is low and level to gently rolling field. The southeastern mixed forest has medium-tall to tall oak, hickory, sweet gum, red maple, and winged elm. At least half of the stands are filled with loblolly and shortleaf pine. The extensive coastal marshes and interior swamps are dominated by gums and cypress.

Climate: Hot continental. Winter is mild, while spring and fall are ideal. Summers, though, are warm, humid, and long. Precipitation is evenly distributed as rain, though there is occasional snow. The area lies north of the hurricane and tropical storm track and south of high-latitude storm systems.

Winter mildness: 80   **Hazard free:** 75
Summer mildness: 75   **Seasonal affect:** 74

Grade: 77

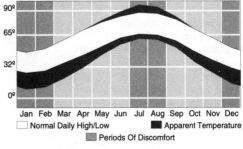

TEMPERATURE

ANNUAL
Humidity: 58%
Wind Speed: 10.7 mph
DAYS
0º or below: 0
32º or below: 85
90º or above: 37
Clear: 106
Partly Cloudy: 106
Cloudy: 153

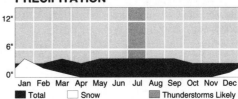

PRECIPITATION

ANNUAL
Precipitation: 47.1"
Snow: 9.7"
DAYS
Precipitation: 75
Thunderstorm: 36
Fog: 20

Wimberly–San Marcos, TX

Location: 29.59 N, 98.03 W, at 840 feet, 35 miles midway between Austin and San Antonio.

Landscape: The San Marcos River rises from springs here. Caves and lakes dot the nearby central hill country. Along the water courses are cypress and juniper-oak stands.

Climate: Prairie. Although summers are hot, night temperatures usually drop into the 70s. Winters are mild. Prevailing winds are southerly, though strong northers may bring cold spells, which rarely last more than a few days. Precipitation is well distributed, but heaviest in late spring with a secondary rainfall peak in September. Summer brings some heavy thunderstorms. Winter rains are slow and steady.

Winter mildness: 98   **Hazard free:** 81
Summer mildness: 54   **Seasonal affect:** 79

Grade: 77

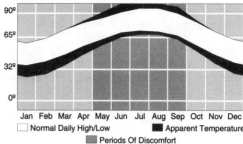

TEMPERATURE

Normal Daily High/Low — Apparent Temperature — Periods Of Discomfort

ANNUAL
Humidity: 56%
Wind Speed: 9.2 mph
DAYS
0° or below: 0
32° or below: 28
90° or above: 122
Clear: 116
Partly Cloudy: 114
Cloudy: 135

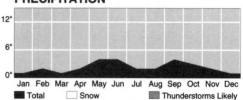

PRECIPITATION

Total — Snow — Thunderstorms Likely

ANNUAL
Precipitation: 34.3"
Snow: 0.5"
DAYS
Precipitation: 46
Thunderstorm: 40
Fog: 22

Winchester, VA

Location: 39.11 N, 78.09 W, at 720 feet, near the northern entrance of the Shenandoah Valley. Washington, D.C., is 80 miles SE.

Landscape: Low, rolling country between the Appalachian and Blue Ridge Mountains. The mixed forest has medium tall to tall oak, hickory, sweet gum, red maple, winged elm, and loblolly and southern yellow pine.

Climate: Hot continental, modified only slightly by the mountains to the west. Winters are wet and cold. Summers are warm but less humid than lower elevations. Precipitation is evenly distributed throughout the year, mostly as rain. In mid-summer, thunderstorms are likely.

Winter mildness: 71   **Hazard free:** 59
Summer mildness: 82   **Seasonal affect:** 75

Grade: 73

TEMPERATURE

Normal Daily High/Low — Apparent Temperature — Periods Of Discomfort

ANNUAL
Humidity: 55%
Wind Speed: 8.1 mph
DAYS
0° or below: 0
32° or below: 106
90° or above: 25
Clear: 102
Partly Cloudy: 112
Cloudy: 151

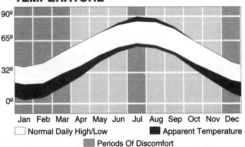

PRECIPITATION

Total — Snow — Thunderstorms Likely

ANNUAL
Precipitation: 37.9"
Snow: 26.6"
DAYS
Precipitation: 70
Thunderstorm: 36
Fog: 23

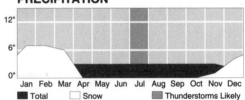

Woodstock, VT

Location: 43.37 N, 72.31 W, at 705 feet, just west of the Connecticut River and New Hampshire line, and 60 miles south of Montpelier, the state capital.

Landscape: In the upper Connecticut River Valley with the Green Mountains rising to the west. Rivers cut through steep gorges giving high relief to the winding valleys. The forests are transitional woods of mixed conifer and deciduous trees. Northern white pine, eastern hemlock, maple, oak, and beech are common.

Climate: Northerly latitude assures the variety and vigor of a true New England climate. The summer, while not long, is clear and warm. Fall is cool, extending through October. Winters are cold, with brief, intense cold snaps formed by high pressure systems moving down from central Canada and Hudson Bay. Snows are deep and long-lasting. Spring is called *breakup* or *mud season*.

Winter mildness: 48   **Hazard free:** 10
Summer mildness: 95   **Seasonal affect:** 71

Grade: 61

TEMPERATURE

Normal Daily High/Low — Apparent Temperature — Periods Of Discomfort

ANNUAL
Humidity: 56%
Wind Speed: 8.5 mph
DAYS
0° or below: 35
32° or below: 186
90° or above: 6
Clear: 90
Partly Cloudy: 110
Cloudy: 165

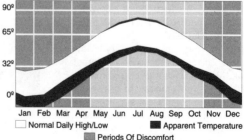

PRECIPITATION

Total — Snow — Thunderstorms Likely

ANNUAL
Precipitation: 40.1"
Snow: 89.3"
DAYS
Precipitation: 78
Thunderstorm: 19
Fog: 49

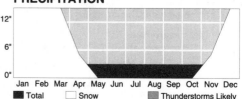

York Beaches, ME

Location: 43.23 N, 70.32 W, at 51 feet, on Maine's southern Atlantic coast, 35 miles south of Portland.

Landscape: Low hills drained by marsh and stream rise at the mouth of the York River on the Atlantic Ocean. The shore is marked by natural harbors, inlets, and sandy beaches. Native vegetation is mixed evergreen of pine and spruce with some maple and oak. The low-lying areas support typical marsh grasses and cattails.

Climate: Hot continental. Moderated somewhat by the ocean, winters can be cold, damp, and snowy. Summer days are clear and warm; the nights pleasantly cool.

Winter mildness: 57 **Hazard free:** 29
Summer mildness: 93 **Seasonal affect:** 71

Grade: 67

TEMPERATURE

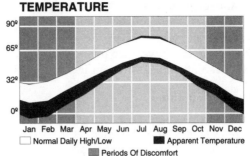

Normal Daily High/Low — Apparent Temperature — Periods Of Discomfort

ANNUAL
Humidity: 59%
Wind Speed: 8.8 mph
DAYS
0º or below: 14
32º or below: 157
90º or above: 6
Clear: 102
Partly Cloudy: 98
Cloudy: 165

PRECIPITATION

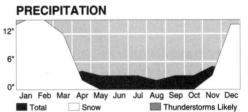

Total — Snow — Thunderstorms Likely

ANNUAL
Precipitation: 44.3"
Snow: 68.7"
DAYS
Precipitation: 76
Thunderstorm: 18
Fog: 48

Yuma, AZ

Location: 32.43 N, 114.37 W, at 137 feet, in the extreme southwest corner of Arizona, near the California and Mexican borders.

Landscape: The land is typical desert steppe, with dry, sandy, and dusty soil. There is scant vegetation. Sagebrush and prairie shortgrass are common. Craggy buttes and mountains take their characteristic texture from wind erosion rather than water erosion. Surrounding mountain ranges are the dominant geologic feature. They include the Trigo, Chocolate, Castle Dome, Mohawk, and Gila ranges.

Climate: Definite desert. Home heating is necessary during the nights from late October to mid-April. It is very dry, with many places in the world receiving more rain in a year than has fallen in Yuma in the past 90 years. Yuma is officially the sunniest place in America.

Winter mildness: 100 **Hazard free:** 97
Summer mildness: 39 **Seasonal affect:** 93

Grade: 78

TEMPERATURE

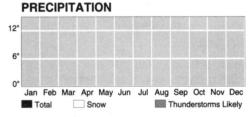

Normal Daily High/Low — Apparent Temperature — Periods Of Discomfort

ANNUAL
Humidity: 32%
Wind Speed: 7.8 mph
DAYS
0º or below: 0
32º or below: 2
90º or above: 174
Clear: 241
Partly Cloudy: 75
Cloudy: 49

PRECIPITATION

Total — Snow — Thunderstorms Likely

ANNUAL
Precipitation: 3.2"
Snow: 0.0"
DAYS
Precipitation: 12
Thunderstorm: 7
Fog: 1

ET CETERA: Climate

CLIMATE AND HEALTH

There is no proven link between longevity and climate. True, the three places on the globe with the highest portion of centenarians—the Caucasus Mountains, the mountains of Bolivia, and northwestern India—are in southerly latitudes at high elevations. But in America where records have been kept for generations, a similar situation does not exist. In fact, most of the longest average life spans are recorded in three states with severe winters—Minnesota, North Dakota, and Iowa.

People with certain chronic diseases are much more comfortable in some climates than in others. Asthmatics do best in warm, dry places that have a minimum of airborne allergens and no molds. People with rheumatism or arthritis find comfort in warm, moist southerly climates where the weather is constant and the atmospheric pressure swings least. Those suffering from tuberculosis or emphysema seem to do best in the lower elevations of mountains with lots of clear air and sunshine.

A brief classic in bioclimatology is H. E. Landsberg's

Weather and Health (see "Relocation Resources" at the end of this book). Landsberg details the relationships between climate and the aggravation of various physical afflictions. Drawing on this and other sources, *Retirement Places Rated* describes some basic weather phenomena and suggests how they can affect the way you feel.

Weather Stages: Beware of 3 and 4

The weather changes that cause the body to react have been studied by meteorologists and classified into six basic stages that make up the clear-stormy-clear cycle repeated all over the planet. The stages in the cycle are linked to some of the joys and tragedies of existence.

Stage 1. Cool, high-pressure air, with few clouds and moderate winds, followed by . . .
Stage 2. Perfectly clear, dry air, high pressure, and little wind, leading to . . .
Stage 3. Considerable warming, steady or slightly falling pressure, and some high clouds, until . . .
Stage 4. The warm, moist air gets into the lower layers; pressure falls, clouds thicken, precipitation is common, and the wind picks up speed; then . . .
Stage 5. An abrupt change takes place; showery precipitation is accompanied by cold, gusty winds, rapidly rising pressure, and falling humidity as the moisture in the air is released.
Stage 6. Gradually, the pressure rises still further and the clouds diminish; temperatures reach low levels and the humidity continues to drop, leading back to . . .
Stage 1. Cool, high-pressure air . . .

Of course, these phases aren't equally long, either in any given sequence or in the course of a year. During winter, all six stages may follow one another within three days while in the summer two weeks may pass before the cycle is completed.

The beautiful weather stages 1 and 2 stimulate the body very little. They make no demands that can't be met by adequate clothing and shelter. In contrast, weather stages 4 and 5 are often violent. They stir us up mentally and physically.

There is no question weather stages affect the body. Hospital birth and death records prove it. In pregnancy, in far more cases than statistical accident permits, labor begins on days that are in weather stage 3. Heart attacks peak in weather stages 3 and 4 and drop in stages 1 and 6. Bleeding ulcers and migraines peak in stage 4.

Weather influences mood and conduct. There is a strong link between weather stage 3 and suicide, behavior problems in schoolchildren, and street riots. A study in Poland showed that accident rates in factory workers doubled during cyclonic weather conditions (stages 3 and 4: periods of falling pressure, rising temperatures and humidity signaling the onset of stormy weather) and returned to normal low levels in fair weather. Animals are affected, too. Dogcatchers are busiest during stages 3, 4, and 5 because dogs become restless, stray from their homes, and wander through the streets.

More on Comfort

As the six weather stages suggest, everyday comfort is influenced by three basic climatic factors: humidity, temperature, and barometric pressure.

Humidity. The amount of moisture in the air is closely related to air temperature in determining the comfort level of the atmosphere. Much of the discomfort and nervous tension experienced at the approach of stormy weather (weather stage 4) is the product of rising temperatures and humidity.

High levels of atmospheric moisture, such as those felt most of the time in the Pacific Northwest and along the Gulf Coast and South Atlantic Coast, aren't usually the cause of direct discomfort except in persons suffering from certain types of arthritis or rheumatism. But even in these cases, the mild temperatures found in these locations usually don't do much to offset discomfort. In fact, the stability of the barometric pressure in these areas makes them ideal for people with muscle and joint pain.

But damp air combined with low temperatures can be uncomfortable. Most people who live through damp winters, especially in places with high winds, complain that the cold, wet wind goes right through them. Moreover, the harmful effect of cold, damp air on pulmonary diseases has long been known. With this in mind, it's smart to think carefully about moving to New England coastal locations—Cape Cod and the Maine coast, for example—where these conditions are winter trademarks.

Perhaps the most noticeable drawback to very moist air is the variety of organisms it supports. Bacteria and the spores of fungi and molds thrive in moist air but are almost absent in dry air. If the air is moist and also warm, the problem is multiplied. People susceptible to bacterial skin infections, fungal infections such as athlete's foot, or mold allergies should consider places with high humidities carefully.

On the other end of the spectrum, very dry air produces perceptible effects immediately and can cause discomfort within a day. When the relative humidity falls below 50 percent, most persons experience dry nasal passages and perhaps a dry, tickling throat. In the Desert Southwest, where the humidity can drop to 20 percent or less in some locations, many people experience nosebleeds, flaking skin, and constant sore throats.

Temperature. Many bioclimatologists maintain that the body is most comfortable and productive at "65–65," meaning an air temperature of 65 degrees with 65 percent humidity. High relative humidity intensifies the felt effect of high temperatures (see the table "Temperature, Humidity, and Apparent Temperature") because it impairs the evaporative cooling effect of sweating.

At apparent temperatures as low as 80 to 90°F, a person may begin to suffer symptoms of heat stress. The degree of heat stress experienced will vary depending on

Temperature, Humidity, and Apparent Temperature

Apparent Temperature

	0	5	10	15	20	25	30	35	40	45	50	55	60	65	70	75	80	85	90	95	100
110	99	102	105	108	112	117	123	130	137	143	150										
105	95	97	100	102	105	109	113	118	123	129	135	142	149								
100	91	93	95	97	99	101	104	107	110	115	120	126	132	138	144						
95	87	88	90	91	93	94	96	98	101	104	107	110	114	119	124	130	136				
90	83	84	85	86	87	88	90	91	93	95	96	98	100	102	106	109	113	117	122		
85	78	79	80	81	82	83	84	85	86	87	88	89	90	91	93	95	97	99	102	105	108
80	73	74	75	76	77	77	78	79	79	80	81	82	83	85	86	86	87	88	89	91	
75	69	69	70	71	72	72	73	73	74	74	75	75	76	76	77	77	78	78	79	79	80
70	64	64	65	65	66	66	67	67	68	68	69	69	70	70	70	70	71	71	71	71	72

Relative Humidity (%)

Locate the air temperature at the left and the relative humidity along the bottom. The intersection of the horizontal row of figures opposite the temperature with the vertical row of figures above the relative humidity is the apparent temperature. For example, an air temperature of 85 degrees feels like 89 degrees at 55 percent relative humidity; but when the humidity is 90 percent, 85 degrees feels like 102.

age, health, and body characteristics. Infants, young children, and older adults are most likely to be affected by high temperature/humidity combinations.

The map "Apparent Temperatures (July)" shows how felt temperatures vary across the country. The places in America where the highest temperatures are constantly recorded are mainly in the desert areas of the Great Basin (the southern half of the plateau between the Sierra Nevada to the west and the Rocky Mountains to the east), the Great Interior Valley of California, and parts of the High Plains regions of New Mexico, Oklahoma, and Texas. These areas are generally dry, so the effects of the high temperatures on the body are not particularly noticeable or damaging. This is especially true of locations west of eastern New Mexico.

States along the Gulf Coast and the South Atlantic Coast have temperatures that are less spectacularly high but humidity that can be oppressive. Most people would

Apparent Temperatures (July)

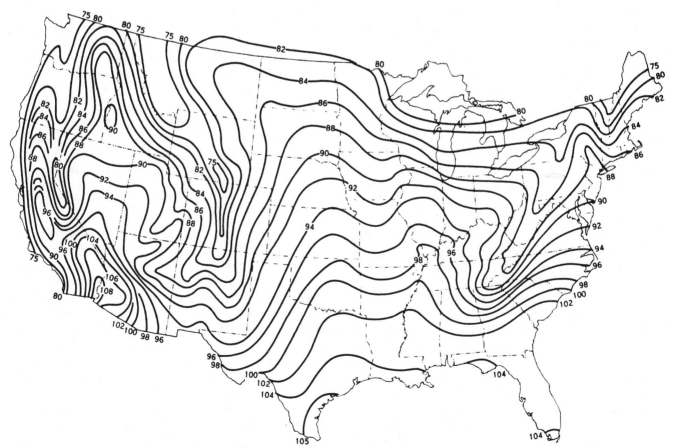

Source: National Oceanic and Atmospheric Administration, National Climatic Center, Asheville, North Carolina.

find a 90-degree day in Fairhope–Gulf Shores or Daytona Beach far more uncomfortable than they would a day of the same temperature in Las Vegas or Yuma.

What about cold temperatures? Throughout the 1960s and 1970s, most older adults shunned cold weather in favor of the hot and sunny beach climates of the Sun Belt. Now, many are discovering the benefits of seasonal change and some cold weather, particularly around the holiday season. *Retirement Places Rated* includes many retirement places that have cold weather. Some of these—most notably in Michigan, Wisconsin, and Montana—have winters that can be rigorous and are not for the faint of heart.

Cold weather can have an adverse effect on persons with heart or circulatory ailments. These diseases follow a seasonal pattern, with a peak of deaths occurring in January and February. The cooling of the extremities places greater stress on the heart as it tries to maintain a safe body temperature. Breathing very cold air can tax the heart-lung system, and some persons who have hardening of the coronary arteries may get chest pains when outdoors in a cold wind.

Cold weather can also increase blood pressure with adverse consequences for those with circulatory problems. Although polar weather inhibits the survival of respiratory germs, these microbes thrive in a damp, cloudy, cool climate and contribute to a high incidence of influenza, bronchitis, and colds.

As the body gets older, its circulatory system loses effectiveness. Add to this another natural consequence of aging—the decreased rate of metabolism that keeps the body warm—and you have partially explained older adults' needs for higher household temperatures. The expense of heating costs in a cool climate, therefore, may offset the appeal of seasonal changes and winter weather.

But despite the dangers of heat or cold extremes, sudden wide shifts of temperature in either direction constitute a threat to health. When the weather—and especially the temperature—changes suddenly and dramatically, the rates of cardiac arrest, respiratory distress, stroke, and other medical emergencies skyrocket.

Sudden atmospheric cooling can bring on attacks of asthma, bronchitis, and stroke. Heart attacks and associated symptoms are more frequent following these periods. Often these are produced by changing air masses during autumn, particularly by the passage of a cold frontal system following a dropping barometer.

A sudden rise in the temperature may precipitate its own assortment of medical emergencies, among them heat stroke, heart attack, and stroke. Because the body recuperates during the night, the nighttime maximum air temperature is far more significant than the daytime maximum during a heat wave. A hot night prevents the body from reestablishing its thermal equilibrium and tends to lessen the amount of sleep a person gets, increasing fatigue. Hospital employees call these sudden temperature shifts, which cause so much discomfort and harm, "ambulance weather."

Barometric pressure. Though most people may be unaware of the source of their discomfort, barometric pressure and its wide and rapid fluctuations are powerful influences on performance, comfort, and health. Pressure changes are felt more keenly by older adults, whose bodies are generally more sensitive to change.

Recalling weather stage 4, the rapid fall of pressure that signals the arrival of storms and advancing cold fronts can trigger episodes of asthma, heart disease, stroke, and pain in the joints. People with rheumatism or arthritis may suffer unduly if they live in places where pressure changes are continual and rapid. The map "Pressure Changes from Day to Day (February)" shows the regions with greatest and least pressure changes during an average day in February, when joint pain and other discomforts reach their peak.

As the map shows, the northern and eastern sections of the country experience the biggest swings, averaging a barometric change of .20 inch to .25 inch from one day to the next. In summer, when pressure changes are relatively small, the average change in these regions is approximately .10 inch. States in the southern latitudes, particularly Florida and southern California, show the least change, only about .10 inch in February and less than .05 inch in summer. Of course, these figures are averages, and along the Gulf and Atlantic coasts, large and rapid pressure changes are occasionally caused by hurricanes.

The map offers another reason why so many older adults choose Florida and the Gulf Coast. Additionally, due to the stabilizing and modifying effects that large bodies of water have on temperature and pressure, weather conditions by seacoasts are steadier than those of most inland, desert, or mountain locations.

Although the climates found in Florida and the other Gulf states are not as pleasant year 'round as they are hyped, subtropical climates—hot, humid, monotonous, and even wearying as they are to some—are just about perfect for people with severe rheumatoid joint pain or those who cannot tolerate sudden changes in the weather.

Questing for Relief

People with heart conditions should definitely avoid extreme heat and cold, rapid temperature variations, and wide and sudden pressure swings. This can rule out most interior regions as well as northerly ones, even those on coastal locations.

Places that have warm, mild, and steady weather are recommended. Mountains and high altitudes should be avoided on two counts: less oxygen and strain caused by steep grades. Best bets are southerly coastal locations where sea-level, oxygen-rich air and stable pressures and temperatures predominate most of the year.

Look along the coast of the Mid-Atlantic Metro Belt southward all the way around the Florida peninsula and westward along the Gulf. Also look along the southern third of the Pacific coastline.

Emphysema brings a completely different set of

Pressure Changes from Day to Day (February)

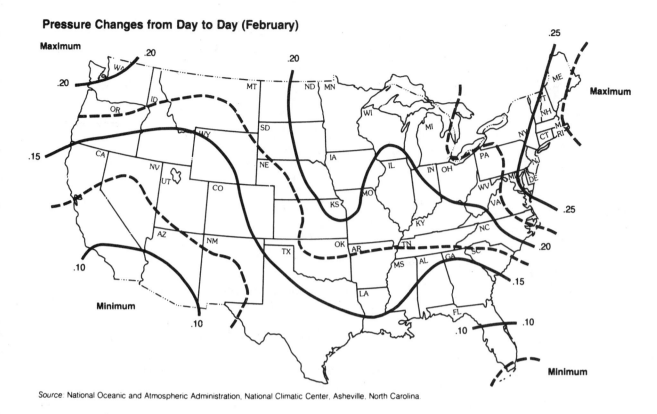

Source: National Oceanic and Atmospheric Administration, National Climatic Center, Asheville, North Carolina.

problems and solutions. In general, excessive dampness combined with cool or cold weather is harmful. This eliminates the Pacific Northwest, New England, and the North Woods. Southerly coastal locations are better, but the air is perhaps still too damp. Seek out warm, sunny, dry climates such as those found in Arizona, New Mexico, Utah, Nevada, and the interior valleys of California. Remember to avoid high elevations.

Asthma is a complex disorder not completely understood. While it is believed to be an autoimmune disorder similar to allergies, it may be precipitated or worsened by different things in different individuals. Your wisest course is to consult medical specialists first to determine the specific cause of your attacks. Asthmatics seem to do best in the pollen-free, dry, warm air found in the Desert Southwest. Because the air on the desert floor can be dusty, seeking a moderate altitude there may be beneficial.

Tuberculosis, recently considered a waning disease, is on the rise. It generally strikes people who have weakened resistance to infection, making older adults more susceptible than the rest of the population. Treatment is multifaceted, but an area that is mild, dry, sunny, and has clear air helps a great deal.

Mountain locations have always been popular and can provide relief if the altitude isn't excessive. Because dampness isn't recommended, the dry, sunny places in the southern Rockies are preferable to locations in the Southern Highlands. Ocean breezes are thought to be beneficial, too, and may be better for people who cannot tolerate the more rugged climate of the interior mountains. Hawaii or the southern California Coast would be ideal.

For people with rheumatic pains, and discomfort in amputated limbs or in old scar tissue, the warm and steady climates of the subtropics are perfect. Here the surrounding water keeps temperatures and pressures from shifting quickly, and the prevailing warmth is soothing. It would be hard to miss with any seafront location from Myrtle Beach, South Carolina, south to the Florida Keys, around and up the west coast of the Florida peninsula, westward along the Gulf and down all the way to the mouth of the Rio Grande.

Life at the Top

Many mountain resorts got their start as 19th-century health retreats. Back then, "night air" and "bad air" were seen as causes for chronic respiratory diseases. The antidote prescribed was "pine air" and a high altitude.

While most mountain air is clear and relatively free from pollutants, it also contains less oxygen. A rapid change to a high altitude is risky for people with heart diseases and arteriosclerosis. If you suffer from asthma, emphysema, or anemia, you should consult local physicians before moving to any place more than 2,000 feet above sea level. Even if all indications point to a positive reaction, it would be wise to take up residence for at least several months before making a permanent move.

For those who can tolerate the high country, the advantages of such locations are well known. Because atmospheric temperature decreases with increasing elevation (about 3.3°F per 1,000 feet), places at high elevations in southerly locales (such as Santa Fe or Asheville enjoy the long summers and mild winters typical of the South, and also the cool summers, crisp autumns, and absence of mugginess usually associated with more northerly areas.

Since altitude puts a certain amount of stress on the body's circulatory system and lungs, becoming acclimated to high places leads to good health. A higher altitude accelerates respiration and increases the lung capacity, strengthens the heart, increases the metabolic rate, and boosts the number and proportion of red blood cells.

In the United States, the highest town with a post office is Climax, Colorado. At 11,350 feet, Climax is beyond the comfort range of many older adults. Up here, a 3-minute egg takes 7 minutes to boil, corn on the cob needs to be on the fire 45 minutes, and homebrewed beer matures in half the expected time. Yet many of the 4,000 residents love it. The incidence of infection is amazingly low, and insects are practically unknown. In the East, the highest town of any size is Highlands, North Carolina, in the Great Smoky Mountains. Though less than half as high as Climax, Highlands and the neighboring towns offer the cool, clear air and invigorating climate that have long drawn people to the mountains.

NATURAL HAZARDS

Perhaps no natural sight was more dramatic on live television than the 1980 eruption of Mount St. Helens. A blast equal to 10 million tons of TNT blew off the topmost 1,300 feet of the mountain. Fortunately, volcanoes usually give warning. Even more fortunately, the places where volcanic activity is a hazard are few.

Other violent natural events are more common and, though less cataclysmic than a full-blown volcanic eruption, can cause great damage and threaten lives. Many of these natural hazards follow definite geographic patterns, and some places are at greater risk than others.

The Sun Belt Is Also a Storm Belt

Most severe storms occur in the southern half of the nation. For this reason, you might say the Sun Belt is also a storm belt.

Thunderstorms and Lightning. Thunderstorms are common and don't usually cause death. But lightning kills 200 Americans a year. The most common natural danger, at any given moment there are about 2,000 thunderstorms in progress around the globe. In the time it takes you to read this paragraph, lightning will have struck 700 times.

Florida, the Sunshine State, is actually the country's stormiest state, with three times as much thunder and lightning as any other. California, Oregon, and Washington are the three most storm-free states. In a typical year, coastal California locations average between two and five thunderstorm episodes. Most American locations average between 35 and 50. Florida's west coast averages 90.

The Place Profiles earlier in this chapter tell how many thunderstorm days each place can expect in an average year. The southeastern quadrant of our country generally receives more rain and thunderstorms than the rest, although the thunderstorms of the Great Plains are awesome spectacles.

Tornadoes. While they are not nearly as large or long-lived as hurricanes and release much less force, tornadoes have more killing power concentrated in a small area than any other storm. For absolute ferocity and wind speed, a tornado has no rival.

The hallmark of this vicious inland storm is the huge funnel cloud that sweeps and bounces along the ground, destroying buildings, sweeping up cars, trains, livestock, and trees, and sucking them up hundreds of feet into the whirling vortex. Wind speeds close to 300 miles per hour have been recorded.

Although no one can tell for certain just where particular tornadoes might touch down, their season, origin, and direction of travel are fairly predictable. Tornado season reaches its peak in late spring and early summer. After forming in the intense heat and rising air of the plains, these storms proceed toward the northeast at speeds averaging 25 to 40 miles per hour. Most tornadoes do not last long or travel far. Half of all tornadoes reported travel less than 5 miles on the ground; a rare few have been tracked for more than 200 miles.

Nearly one-third of all tornadoes ever reported in the United States have occurred within the boundaries of Kansas, Oklahoma, and Texas. In fact, an area 150 miles on either side of a line drawn from Abilene, Texas, to Omaha, Nebraska, is called Tornado Alley. Among retirement spots, the lake locations in Oklahoma, any location in Texas or Arkansas, and even spots in Kentucky and Tennessee have a high potential for tornado damage and danger.

Hurricanes. On the North Carolina coast from the Brunswick Islands up to the Outer Banks, blue hurricane evacuation markers along the back routes direct travelers to inland safety.

Giant tropical cyclonic storms that start at sea, hurricanes are unmatched for sheer power over a very large area. They last for days, measure hundreds of miles across, and release tremendous energy in the form of high winds, torrential rains, lightning, and tidal surges. They usually occur in late summer and fall, and strike the Gulf states and southern segments of the Atlantic Coast, though they will also strike locations farther north. Like thunderstorms, hurricanes are much less frequent and less severe on the Pacific Coast.

Hurricanes usually originate in the tropical waters of the Atlantic Ocean. They occur toward summer's end because it takes that long for the water temperature and evaporation rate to rise sufficiently to begin the cyclonic, counterclockwise rotation of a wind system around a low-pressure system. When the winds are less than 39 miles per hour, the cyclone becomes a tropical depression. When winds speed up to between 39 and 74 miles per hour, the depression becomes a tropical storm. When the winds top 74 miles per hour, the storm becomes a hurricane.

Often the greatest danger and destruction from hurricanes aren't winds but tidal surges that sweep ashore with seas 15 feet or more higher than normal high tides. Although Florida and the southern coasts are most vulnerable to hurricanes, low-lying locations as far north as Cape Cod and the Maine coast aren't immune.

Earthquake Risks

California and the Pacific Northwest may be relatively free of the thunderstorms, tornadoes, and hurricanes that buffet other parts of the country. But these states are in the area of the country most prone to earthquake damage. A glance at the map "Earthquake Hazard Zones," which predicts not only the probability of earthquakes but also their severity, confirms this.

All retirement places in California, Nevada, and Utah have the potential for substantial earthquake damage. Locations in Oregon are relatively safe, but the Puget Sound area of Washington has experienced two major shocks in the past 35 years. Portions of Montana and Idaho also are very vulnerable to earthquakes.

Other pockets of earthquake risk might surprise you. Albuquerque is situated in a danger area, and so is Silver City. The resorts on the South Carolina and Georgia coasts sit in the middle of a quake-sensitive zone that was the site of the 1886 Charleston quake, the strongest ever measured east of the Mississippi. The entire New England region shares a danger roughly comparable to this area. Boston has suffered a severe quake and remains prone today. A series of quakes occurred in southeastern Missouri in 1811–12, changing the course of the Mississippi River and creating a major lake. There is still some risk in this area, which includes the retirement places in western Kentucky and Tennessee and part of the Ozarks.

Can Anyone Win?

After studying the maps, you may come to the dismal conclusion that you cannot win: where one natural disaster area stops, another begins. Some areas, like the coasts of South Carolina and Georgia, appear to possess a triple-whammy combination of earthquake, tornado, and hurricane hazards.

Studying the map more closely, you might begin to detect retirement areas that seem safer than others. One such area is the Pacific Northwest, with the exception of the significant earthquake risk around Puget Sound. Parts of Arizona, Utah, and New Mexico, too, are relatively free from disaster risk. The southern Appalachians, despite a moderate earthquake risk, do not experience many storms due to the protection of the mountains. But some parts of that region are flood-prone. And moderate earthquake risk seems almost unavoidable anywhere but the frigid North Central Plains or the steamy, tornado-ridden flatlands of Texas and the Gulf states.

So, as with most things in life, when it comes to avoiding natural disasters, you can only pay your money and take your chances.

HAY FEVER SUFFERERS, TAKE NOTE

It does not come from hay nor does it cause a fever, but that's little consolation to the 18 million Americans afflicted. Hay fever is an allergic reaction of the eyes, nose, or throat to certain airborne particles. These particles may be any of pollen from seed-bearing trees, grasses, and weeds, or spores from certain molds. The term originated in Britain when people assumed its feverlike symptoms had something to do with the fall haying.

Most persons might think that once they're into adulthood, they already know whether they have hay

Tornado and Hurricane Risk Areas

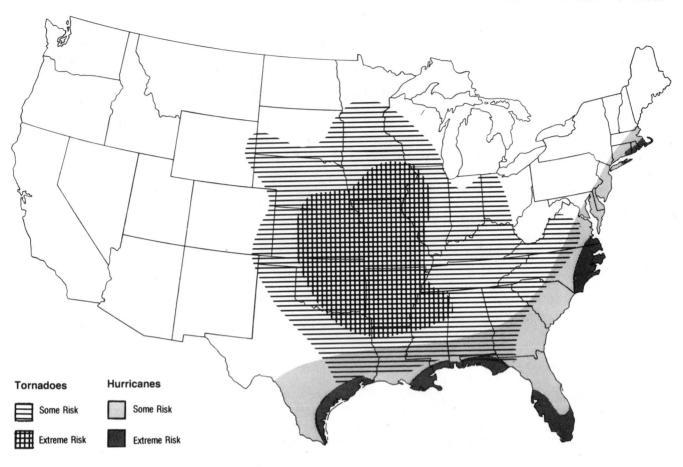

Tornadoes

⊟ Some Risk

▦ Extreme Risk

Hurricanes

☐ Some Risk

■ Extreme Risk

Earthquake Hazard Zones

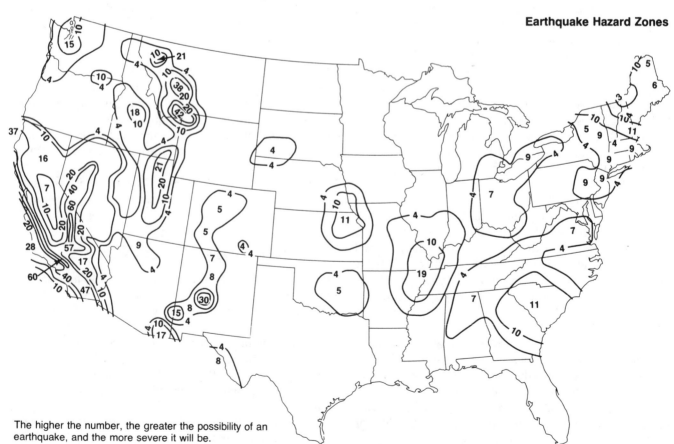

The higher the number, the greater the possibility of an earthquake, and the more severe it will be.

Source: U.S. Geological Survey Open-File Report 76-416, 1976.

fever. But if you move, would you suddenly develop a baffling runny nose and minor sore throat? Allergy problems aren't always alleviated by relocation, and sometimes a new allergen, absent where you used to live, can turn up to cause you problems.

In the Arctic, because of low temperature, poor soil, and small and primitive vegetation, nobody suffers from it. In the tropics and subtropics, because the plants are generally flowered and produce pollen so heavy it cannot become airborne, few complain of it.

Live in a temperate region and you'll find irritating pollen. The best market for over-the-counter antihistamines in America is the heartland where grasses and trees without flowers predominate. Farming disrupts the soil here, encouraging the growth of weeds (especially the most devilish of them all, ragweed). It extends from the Rockies to the Appalachian chain, and from the Canadian border down to the mid-South.

Alas, nowhere in this country except Alaska and the southern half of Florida will you escape entirely. It's simply a question of degree. Some places, once havens for asthmatics and hay-fever sufferers, aren't any longer. Examples include many of the fast-growing areas of the Desert Southwest. In the 1950s, Tucson was virtually free of ragweed pollen. Its desert location prevented the growth of weeds, grasses, and trees that cause hay fever. As more and more people moved into the area, more trees were planted and lawns seeded. The result? A pollen index that's still good but not nearly as good as it used to be.

PERSONAL SAFETY

In Chapel Hill, the cops are worried about gun thefts in town and in nearby Carboro. Several sporting goods shops have been hit, and in many home burglaries the take includes a rifle or handgun. Everyone notes the irony: houses are broken into for the guns homeowners bought to protect themselves from a rash of break-ins. The rising spiral means more guns on the street.

In Barnstable District Court on Cape Cod one spring day, two dozen persons are arraigned for offenses that wouldn't open the eyes of a *Miami Herald* police reporter: possession of marijuana and conspiracy to violate controlled substance laws, operating under the influence and speeding, breaking and entering with intent to commit a felony, giving a false name to a police officer, and assault and battery.

In a coffee shop up in Wisconsin's Door County peninsula, the talk one winter morning concerns a condo break-in. Missing are a shopping bag of Pampers and a baby's crib. Left behind are a state-of-the-art stereo system, Waterford crystal, the silver, and a closet full of high-fashion ski-wear. Maybe we should all start locking our doors, the locals in the coffee shop agree.

Chapel Hill does have a crime problem, Door County has none, and Cape Cod hasn't much of one until the summer tourists come. Indeed, the odds of your being a crime victim in three out of four of the 183 places profiled in *Retirement Places Rated* are below the national average.

Check the police log printed in the newspapers of some places and you'll wonder whether anything interesting goes on there at all. A drunk-and-disorderly, a car break-in, a bar fight, all are just occasional items hidden among the traffic accidents, animal complaints, and fishing violations.

Some places seem so safe you couldn't pay someone to assault you. Others, by comparison, are just plain dangerous. If you decide to settle in Door County, the odds of your meeting up with violent crime in a year are 1 in 6,579. Should you settle in Key West, the chances rise to 1 in 72. One could say that life in the Florida Keys is almost a hundred times more dangerous than it is on the Lake Michigan shore in northern Wisconsin.

But raw odds distort the local crime picture. In spite of the popular idea that older persons are the preferred targets of crooks, you are more likely to have your pocket picked or your purse snatched than you are of being victimized by all other crimes. So why the need for a chapter on personal safety if your retirement years are statistically safer than all the years preceding?

The simple answer is that you are a different kind of crime victim whenever you have to trim back shrubbery along your home's foundation to limit a thief's potential

---

Crime Trends

Is personal safety improving for some places and getting worse in others? The answer to both parts of the question is yes.

Getting Safer

Beaver Lake, AR
Carmel–Pebble Beach, CA
Key West–Key Largo–Marathon, FL
Redding, CA
Yuma, AZ

Getting More Dangerous

Aiken, SC
Amherst–Northampton, MA
Beaufort, SC
Branson, MO
Chapel Hill, NC
Charleston Sea Islands, SC
Fort Myers–Cape Coral, FL
Guntersville, AL
Hilton Head Island, SC
Maryville, TN
Panama City, FL
Port Charlotte–Punta Gorda, FL
Rehoboth Bay–Indian River Bay, DE
Savannah, GA
Sebring–Avon Park, FL
Silver City, NM
Southern Pines–Pinehurst, NC
Southport–Brunswick Islands, NC
Winchester, VA

The five places that are becoming safer saw a steady drop in both violent and property crimes reported to police over the latest five years for which data are available. Nineteen other places experienced a rise in both categories of crime over the same period.

---

hiding places, or have to get rid of the mailbox and install a mail slot in your front door, or have to check your car's door locks when driving down a darkened avenue, or have to keep feeling for your wallet at street festivals, or have to use only empty elevators, or have to stay indoors evenings more than you really care to. In some places such tactics are advised, in others they are merely prudent, and in still others they may not be necessary at all.

CRIME RISK: SEVERAL CONNECTIONS

Why some places are safer than others is a topic guaranteed to get politicians, police, and citizens into arguments. For all the debate, experts recognize several factors.

Climate has a striking connection with lawbreaking. Police respond to more disturbance calls on the day after summer temperatures are highest than on any other days of the year. The numbers of burglaries, vandalisms, and rapes increase with ambient temperatures up to 85 degrees Fahrenheit. Indeed, in the Sun Belt and in the Frost Belt, cops and criminals are busiest throughout July and August when all crimes except robbery are the likeliest to happen. Since people spend more time outdoors during these months, they are more exposed. Homes, too, are more unprotected during this time of year because they are left with open windows and unlocked doors. Robbery is the cold-weather exception. It is highest in December when shoppers and retail stores doing brisk holiday business make tempting targets.

Time of day and the *photoperiod*, or length of the day, are two other factors. After sundown is the time most cars are stolen, most persons and businesses are robbed, most persons are assaulted, and most thefts are committed. Burglaries, purse-snatchings and pocket-pickings, on the other hand, happen more often during daylight hours. Some police dispatchers contend that the number of daylight minutes is a predictor of the kind of 911 calls they handle.

Population size is closely tied to crime rates. Safer places—Fredericksburg in the Texas Hill Country and Norfork Lake in northern Arkansas, for instance—are rural. More dangerous places are urban. There are exceptions, certainly. Key West's crime rate resembles San Antonio's.

Even local *traffic* plays a role. The ease with which a criminal can drive off down the street, escape onto an arterial road, and disappear among commuters on the Interstate is an encouragement. One reason places on islands and peninsulas have lower crime rates is that few crooks are dumb enough to commit robberies if their escape is over a long bridge or causeway.

Age and *sex* figure into the equation. Some 40 million persons in this country have arrest records for misdeeds other than traffic violations. The proportion of suspects who are male is much higher than their proportion in the general population. Half the persons picked up by police for violent and property crimes are under 20 years of age and four-fifths are male. None of this should be taken to mean that persons hold up convenience stores, boost Chevrolet Camaros, or duke it out in disco parking lots because they are young and male, but these characteristics are associated with other factors in crime.

The *economy* also plays a role. In most places, each time the unemployment rate goes up the police make more arrests. But joblessness and loss of income won't automatically make a place unsafe. Many of the safer places in this book are poorer than average and suffer job losses during business slumps. More affluent areas, given similar sets of circumstances, aren't nearly as safe as they seem: rich offenders are arrested less often than poor ones, especially on suspicion. Once arrested, they are convicted with less frequency. This is especially true in juvenile cases involving thefts and break-ins.

Transience affects crime rates. A warning sign for crooks is a stable neighborhood where people know one another and look out for one another's safety and property no matter how many police cruise the area. High neighborhood turnover leading to more strangers living next to each other leads to higher crime rates. Resort areas that draw transients—Las Vegas, Daytona Beach, or Myrtle Beach, for instance—have serious crime problems. When visitors are added to the year-round residents, the higher population betters the odds that victim and crook will meet.

Police strength, too, is linked to the local crime rate. In Manhattan, there are 1,300 police officers per square mile; in most rural counties there are between 1 and 3 sworn uniformed officers for every 1,000 residents. In the sparsely settled Montana Rockies and parts of the desert well east of Los Angeles, however, state police need an average 30 minutes or more to respond to calls.

It's natural to think personal safety in a place rises or falls in proportion to the size of the local police force, but it just isn't so. Police enforce traffic codes, investigate accidents, find lost children, and calm down fighting spouses. They battle crime, too, but most of what they do is after the fact. They respond to complaints; they interview victims and fill out reports; they follow up on tips; and they collar suspects and bring them to book. A large number of police per capita, however, is usually an indication of a high-crime area rather than an area where crime is being foiled.

Other factors related to criminal activity include the practices of local prosecutors, judges, juries, and parole boards; the attitudes of the community toward crime; and the willingness of ordinary citizens to report crime.

TRACKING CRIME

Every year some 16,000 police departments send figures of the number of crimes reported in their cities and towns to the FBI in Washington. Because of their seriousness, frequency, and likelihood of being reported, eight crimes make up the FBI's Crime Index. Four are classified as violent and four are property crimes.

Violent Crime

Murder is the most reported of all crimes and has the highest rate of charges being laid. Incidence is at an all-time high in the United States. Half of all victims knew their killers, perhaps even sat across from them at the breakfast table the morning of the crime. Victims and killers are becoming less connected, however, because of random violence. Based on the number of unsolved killings each year and an increase in slayings involving strangers, the FBI estimates at least 25 serial killers are on the loose.

Rape, too, frequently involves acquainted victims and aggressors. It is the most underreported of crimes and also has the highest proportion of "unfounded" complaints. Rape victims are always female by current crime reporting standards.

Robbery is the violent crime that most often involves more than one criminal, and is the one violent crime committed less out of anger than as a way of making a

---

Crime Compared with Other Events in Life

The rates for some violent crimes are higher than those of other harmful life events. For example, the risk of being a victim of violent crime is higher than the risk of being affected by divorce, death from cancer, or injury or death from a fire. Anyone over 15 years old runs a greater risk of being a violent crime victim, with or without injury, than being hurt in a traffic accident. Still, a person is much more likely to die from natural causes than from being a victim of crime.

Event	Annual Rate per 1,000 Adults
Accidental injury, all circumstances	290.000
Accidental injury at home	105.000
Personal Theft	**82.000**
Accidental injury at work	68.000
Accidental injury in an automobile	23.000
Divorce	23.000
Death, all causes	11.000
Aggravated Assault	**9.000**
Death of a spouse	9.000
Robbery	**7.000**
Heart disease death	4.000
Cancer death	2.000
Accidental death, all circumstances	0.500
Pneumonia/influenza death	0.300
Automobile accidental death	0.200
Suicide	0.200
Injury from fire	0.100
Murder	**0.100**
Death from fire	0.003

Source: Bureau of Justice Statistics, *Report to the Nation on Crime and Justice.* 1988.

---

living. It differs from common theft because it involves force or threat, thereby placing the victim in fear.

Assault is simply an attempt, successful or not, to injure another person. Its rate is highest in August and lowest in February, higher in the West than in other parts of the country, and higher in areas with resort or military economies.

Property Crime

Most *burglaries*, jailed pros say, are planned for hours and pulled off in minutes. The typical target is the home or apartment. Nearly half of the incidents involve walking in rather than breaking in. The typical time is between 9:00 and 11:00 A.M. or between 1:00 and 3:00 P.M. when you're least likely to be inside.

Theft, after drunk driving, is the most common crime in North America. Walking off with an unattended garden hose is one example; shoplifting a Russian sable coat is another. In almost all of the cases, the victim never sees the offender.

Auto theft, it's been said, is a victimless crime because you get over your loss with a check from the insurance company. The typical incident, peaking in the summer during school recess, involves an unlocked car in a shopping mall parking lot. Around Phoenix and in

Safer vs. More Dangerous Places

A look at the crime rates in the Place Profiles later in this chapter makes one thing stand out. Whether crimes of violence (which account for just 10 percent of lawbreaking) or property crime, larger Sun Belt areas suffer more from criminal activity than smaller, more rural places.

Property Crime

Dangerous Places	Rate
Key West–Key Largo–Marathon, FL	10,284
San Antonio, TX	10,278
Austin, TX	9,756
Albuquerque, NM	8,913
Oxford, MS	8,655

Safest Places	Rate
Hiawassee, GA	655
Norfork Lake, AR	1,088
Blairsville, GA	1,324
Northern Neck, VA	1,371
Southern Berkshire County, MA	1,454

Note: The property crime rate is the sum of rates for burglary, theft, and auto theft. The U.S. average is 5,045.

Violent Crime

Dangerous Places	Rate
Pompano Beach, FL	1,709
Key West–Key Largo–Marathon, FL	1,381
Albuquerque, NM	1,334
St. Simons–Jekyll Islands, GA	1,310
Gainesville, FL	1,236

Safest Places	Rate
Northern Door Peninsula, WI	24
Hiawassee, GA	35
Table Rock Lake, MO	67
Hamilton–Bitterroot Valley, MT	71
Bar Harbor, ME	78

Note: The violent crime rate is the sum of rates for murder, rape, robbery, and aggravated assault. The U.S. average is 714.

---

larger cities along Interstate 10 in the California desert, stealing cars is an underground art.

Because victims often believe it futile to file complaints, many crimes aren't reported. This affects the accuracy of the Crime Index. Even if a complaint is filed, the investigating officer's definition of the crime may affect the numbers. A snatched purse, for instance, is either a robbery or a larceny depending on the jurisdiction. Likewise, a slap in the face is either an aggravated or simple assault depending on motive.

Moreover, some police departments have either padded the figures to oust a judge considered soft on crime or to persuade the city council to increase the department's budget, or they fudged the number of crimes to create an image of effective law enforcement.

In some rural areas, too, car thefts and parking-lot fights growing out of teenage highjinks aren't added to the statistics. Sheriffs punish the offenders informally with a night in jail, restitution, and some community service.

It's important to distinguish between the *incidence* of crime and the crime *rate*. Incidence is simply how many crimes are reported in a given place. The more people living in a place, the greater the crime incidence.

Police throughout San Diego County log 24,000 violent crimes a year. In Bernalillo County, New Mexico (greater Albuquerque), their counterparts investigate nearly 6,000. Is San Diego more dangerous than Albuquerque? Hardly. San Diego's violent crime rate per 100,000 residents is 855; Albuquerque's is 1,334. While San Diego is safer than Albuquerque, both have violent crime rates higher than the national average—714.

 GRADING: Personal Safety

The one crime cops file the most reports on is theft: a stolen bike, a necklace missing from a jewelry retailer's display case, hubcaps disappearing from a used-car lot. Yet these heists are counted as heavily as murders to determine crime rates. When it comes to comparing places, this method doesn't show relative danger.

A more realistic way to grade for personal safety is simple: For each place, Places Rated averages the rates for violent and property crimes for the latest five-year period, but since property crimes are much less serious than crimes against people, they get one-tenth the weight of violent crimes. Each place starts with a base score of zero and points are added according to these indicators:

1. *Violent crime rate*. The rates for murder, robbery, and aggravated assault are added together.
2. *Property crime rate*. The rates for burglary, theft, and auto theft are totaled, and the result is divided by 10.

The sum of a place's violent crime rate and one-tenth its property crime rate is then scaled against a standard

Florida's Defense

In 1931, while researching his famous piece "The Worst American State," H. L. Mencken found the best source for data on causes of death was the life insurance industry and that, when it came to murder, Florida had the highest rate.

After six decades, not much is different. Most retirement places in Florida rank near the bottom in personal safety. Of all the states, Florida has the highest rates for violent crime and for property crime. The state is the setting for Edna Buchanan's, Carl Hiassen's, Elmore Leonard's, and John D. MacDonald's best-selling crime fiction, and its largest city, Miami, the focus of world attention after several lurid murders of foreign tourists.

This isn't entirely fair. Local crime rates are figured per 100,000 residents. But the state draws millions of four-season visitors. A truer way to measure crime rates, notes Florida's Department of Law Enforcement, would be to add a place's average daily number of tourists to its number of year-round residents, then determine the rate. The results would produce dramatically lower crime rates and improve the Sunshine State's national image.

where no crime gets a perfect 100 and rates five times the national average get a 0.

GRADING EXAMPLES

A New England college town, a Texas college town, a spa in the Arkansas Ouachitas, and a popular Florida resort show the scoring method for personal safety.

Amherst–Northampton, Massachusetts (grade: 91)

Higher crime rates go along with young populations. Amherst–Northampton is an exception to the rule. One of every four people here is a student at the Five Colleges—Amherst, Hampshire, Mount Holyoke, Smith, and the University of Massachusetts. Yet the Amherst–Northampton area sees crime rates far below the national average. Unfortunately, crime rates that fell throughout the 1980s are on the rise in the 1990s.

Among the 3,500 crimes reported to the police in a typical year, nearly one-third involve theft. Adding Amherst–Northampton's violent crime rate (173) to one-tenth its property crime rate (221) produces a total score of 394 and a grade of 91.

Alpine–Big Bend, TX (grade: 84)

This small place in low, dry, green mountains three hours southeast of El Paso has, in Sul Ross State University, a higher portion of college students in its population than Amherst–Northampton. The area sees few robberies and burglaries. Escape only leads into empty ranching country and the law out here have aircraft.

Alpine has had several sensational murders, however. Recently prisoners in the county lockup were moved to more secure facilities in a neighboring county seat to cut down on drug smuggling. For all that, the area's violent crime rate (454) and one-tenth the property crime rate (334) gives the area a better-than-average grade of 84.

Hot Springs, AR (grade: 81)

If Sun Belt resorts are saddled with high crime rates, this one is an exception. Adding its violent crime rate (410) to one-tenth its property crime rate (517) results in a total score of 927, a middlingly safe record good for a grade of 81.

It wasn't always this way. Up until 1967, when Governor Winthrop Rockefeller ordered state troopers to break up the craps tables, bulldoze the slot machines into a gravel pit, and close down the brothels, Hot Springs had a hundred-year, wide-open tradition for lawlessness.

Today, the locals will tell you that one-third of the annual crime occurs during the spring racing season at Oaklawn Park, and that the only other thing that distinguishes this retirement place in the eyes of the law is the phenomenal number of speeding tickets handed out on I-30 and on US 270 by the Arkansas Highway Patrol's Troop K.

Pompano Beach, Florida (grade: 50)

If there are a million visitors in Florida on a typical day, a hundred thousand of them are probably having fun on a Broward County beach. Given New England's weather, undergraduates from Amherst–Northampton's Five Colleges no doubt join the student migration here each spring break.

That's just the problem, according to Florida's Division of Tourism. Resorts here see too much carousing by young outsiders, plus scams by professional crooks from the Frost Belt and not a little violence carried out by persons just passing through. Because statistics don't take into account the number of visitors when per capita crime rates are figured, resorts seem more dangerous places to live in than they actually are.

Certainly Pompano Beach has less crime than neighboring Miami to the south and West Palm Beach–Boca Raton–Delray Beach immediately north. Lumping year-round residents and seasonal visitors together when calculating the crime rate might brighten the picture. Even so, the violent crime rate (1,709) and one-tenth the property crime rate (791) here are far above the national average producing a score of 2,500 and a grade of 50.

RANKINGS: Personal Safety

In ranking 183 places for personal safety, *Retirement Places Rated* uses two critera: (1) the **violent crime rate**, and (2) the **property crime rate** divided by 10. The total is then graded against a standard where five times the national average gets a 0 and no crime gets 100.

Grades are rounded two decimal places. Locations with tie grades get the same rank and are listed alphabetically.

Retirement Places from First to Last

Rank	Grade	Rank	Grade	Rank	Grade
1. Hiawassee, GA	98.35	43. Pike County, PA	91.40	81. Williamsburg, VA	88.10
2. Blairsville, GA	96.34	44. Guntersville, AL	91.38	82. Bend, OR	88.09
3. Norfork Lake, AR	96.01	45. Montrose, CO	91.28	83. Maryville, TN	88.03
4. Hamilton–Bitterroot Valley, MT	95.95			84. Lake Martin, AL	87.93
5. Northern Door Peninsula, WI		46. St. George–Zion, UT	91.24	85. Western St. Tammany	
	95.65	47. Brookings–Gold Beach, OR	91.14	Parish, LA	87.87
6. Smith Mountain Lake, VA	95.64	48. Hendersonville–East Flat		86. Grand Junction, CO	87.80
7. Southern Berkshire County, MA	95.31	Rock, NC	90.97	87. Bay St. Louis–Pass	
8. Fredericksburg, TX	95.29	49. Inverness, FL	90.93	Christian, MS	87.40
9. Northern Neck, VA	94.82	50. Sonora–Groveland–Twain		88. Alamogordo, NM	87.39
10. Whidbey Island, WA	94.49	Harte, CA	90.89	89. Charlottesville, VA	87.30
				90. Virginia Beach, VA	87.29
11. Bar Harbor, ME	94.47	51. St. Jay–Northeast Kingdom, VT	90.84		
12. Clayton, GA	94.30	52. Oscoda–Tawas–Huron		91. Kalispell–Flathead Valley, MT	87.28
13. Table Rock Lake, MO	94.17	Shore, MI	90.70	92. Laguna Beach–Dana Point, CA	87.26
14. Kentucky Lake, KY	94.16	53. Lake Winnipesaukee, NH	90.57	93. Bellingham, WA	87.13
15. Lake of the Ozarks, MO	94.06	54. Fairhope–Gulf Shores, AL	90.39	94. Alpine–Big Bend, TX	87.06
		54. Fredericksburg–Spotsylvania, VA	90.39	95. New Port Richey, FL	87.00
16. Tryon, NC	94.01				
17. Lake of the Cherokees, OK	93.66	56. Toms River–Barnegat Bay, NJ	90.35	96. Durango, CO	86.97
18. Brevard, NC	93.58	57. Port Townsend, WA	90.28	97. Edenton, NC	86.96
19. Polson–Mission Valley, MT	93.33	58. Traverse City, MI	90.27	98. Asheville, NC	86.92
20. Hanover, NH	93.29	59. Port Angeles–Seqium, WA	90.00	99. Sandpoint–Priest River, ID	86.71
		60. Grass Valley–Nevada City, CA	89.93	100. Burlington, VT	86.65
21. Charles Town–Harpers Ferry–Shepherdstown, WV	93.22				
22. Camden, ME	93.17	61. Payson, AZ	89.69	100. Lake Havasu City, AZ	86.65
23. Southport–Brunswick Islands, NC	93.13	62. Grants Pass, OR	89.66	102. Cedar Creek Lake, TX	86.43
24. Litchfield Hills, CT	93.12	63. Madison, MS	89.45	103. Annapolis, MD	86.40
25. Amador County, CA	92.97	63. Beaver Lake, AR	89.45	103. Coeur d'Alene, ID	86.40
		65. Clemson–Pendleton District, SC	89.44	105. Medford–Ashland, OR	86.34
25. Amherst–Northampton, MA	92.97				
27. Wimberly–San Marcos, TX	92.94	66. Lake Livingston, TX	89.38	106. Ketchum–Sun Valley, ID	86.10
28. Charlevoix–Boyne City–East Jordan, MI	92.93	67. Carmel–Monterey–Pebble Beach, CA	89.32	107. Santa Rosa–Sonoma, CA	85.96
29. San Juan Islands, WA	92.89	68. Wickenburg, AZ	89.27	108. Taos, NM	85.87
30. Woodstock, VT	92.85	69. Fayetteville, AR	89.11	109. Easton–St. Michaels–Oxford, MD	85.54
		70. Kauai, HI	89.08	110. Newport–Lincoln City, OR	85.46
31. Boone–Blowing Rock, NC	92.79				
32. Chewelah, WA	92.54	71. Southern Pines–Pinehurst, NC	88.91	111. Carson City–Carson Valley, NV	85.37
33. York Beaches, ME	92.51	72. Petoskey–Harbor Springs, MI	88.83	112. Florence, OR	84.83
34. State College, PA	92.49	73. Fort Collins–Loveland, CO	88.63	113. Hot Springs, AR	84.78
35. Lake Buchanan–Lake LBJ, TX	92.26	74. East End Long Island, NY	88.54	114. Wenatchee, WA	84.75
		75. Kerrville, TX	88.52	115. Lake Conroe, TX	84.72
36. Lake Granbury, TX	92.23	76. Prescott–Prescott Valley, AZ	88.51		
37. Cottonwood–Verde Valley, AZ	92.18	77. San Luis Obispo, CA	88.50	116. Paradise–Magalia, CA	84.70
38. Eagle River, WI	92.09	78. Winchester, VA	88.47	117. Santa Barbara, CA	84.53
39. Delta–Cedaredge, CO	92.07	79. Pagosa Springs, CO	88.41	118. McCall–Cascade–Payette Valley, ID	84.50
40. Sedona, AZ	92.00	80. Placerville–Shingle Springs, CA	88.21	119. Colorado Springs, CO	83.76
				120. Maui, HI	83.43
41. Crossville, TN	91.98				
42. Port Charlotte–Punta Gorda, FL	91.77			121. Santa Fe, NM	83.14
				122. Redding, CA	83.10
				123. Ruidoso, NM	83.05

Rank	Grade	Rank	Grade	Rank	Grade
124. Chapel Hill, NC	83.00	144. Oakhurst–Coarsegold, CA	80.12	166. Austin, TX	74.84
125. Riviera–Bullhead City, AZ	82.95	145. Thomasville, GA	79.99	167. Beaufort, SC	74.65
				168. Hesperia–Apple Valley–Victorville, CA	74.45
126. Dare Outer Banks, NC	82.65	146. Sarasota, FL	79.68	169. Phoenix–Mesa–Scottsdale, AZ	74.25
127. Houghton Lake, MI	82.59	147. Conway, SC	78.96	170. Ocean City, MD	74.23
128. Pahrump Valley, NV	82.58	148. Athens, GA	78.85		
129. Las Cruces, NM	82.49	148. Oxford, MS	78.85		
130. Vero Beach–Sebastian, FL	82.09	150. Reno–Sparks, NV	78.82	171. San Antonio, TX	73.33
		151. Panama City, FL	78.24	172. Ocala, FL	72.62
131. Rehoboth Bay–Indian River Bay, DE	82.03	152. Naples, FL	78.03	173. Kissimmee–St. Cloud, FL	71.83
132. New Braunfels, TX	81.91	153. Melbourne, FL	77.95	174. St. Petersburg–Clearwater, FL	71.29
133. Kingman, AZ	81.87	154. Las Vegas, NV	77.59	175. Bradenton, FL	70.69
134. New Bern, NC	81.75	155. St. Augustine, FL	77.52		
135. Mission–McAllen–Alamo, TX	81.67			176. Palm Springs–Coachella Valley, CA	70.67
		156. Hilton Head Island, SC	77.27	177. Charleston Sea Islands, SC	70.10
136. Branson, MO	81.63	157. Silver City, NM	77.15	178. Lakeland–Winter Haven, FL	69.16
137. Leesburg–Lady Lake, FL	81.59	158. Rockport–Aransas Pass, TX	76.98	179. St. Simons–Jekyll Islands, GA	66.67
138. Aiken, SC	81.30	159. Daytona Beach, FL	76.87	180. Gainesville, FL	65.53
139. Brooksville–Spring Hill, FL	81.08	160. Savannah, GA	75.90		
140. Cape Cod, MA	81.05	161. San Diego, CA	75.77	181. Albuquerque, NM	63.47
		162. Boca Raton–Delray Beach, FL	75.72	182. Key West–Key Largo–Marathon, FL	60.45
141. Sebring–Avon Park, FL	80.85	163. Yuma, AZ	75.71	183. Pompano Beach, FL	58.97
142. Lower Cape May, NJ	80.60	164. Myrtle Beach, SC	75.61		
143. Fort Myers–Cape Coral, FL	80.23	165. Tucson, AZ	74.90		

PLACE PROFILES: Personal Safety

The following Place Profiles show each place's average annual rates for seven crimes: murder, rape, robbery, aggravated assault, burglary, theft, and motor-vehicle theft for the latest five years for which data are available.

The rates for these crimes are grouped into **Violent** and **Property** categories and a total rate for these categories is given. To the right of the totals are symbols indicating their trends over five years. Nineteen places have two arrows pointing up (▲), meaning the rates rose in both categories. Just 6 have two arrows pointing down (▼), meaning the rates dropped in both catego-

ries. Another 39 have dashes (–) after their violent and property totals, meaning these rates are unchanged. The remaining places typically show rises in property crime and unchanged or falling violent crime.

All figures are derived from the FBI's unpublished "Crime by County" annual reports for the latest five years for which data are available.

A check mark (✓) preceding a place's name highlights it as one of the top 18 places for personal safety.

Place	Violent Crime Rates						Property Crime Rates					Grade
	Murder	Rape	Robbery	Assault	Total	Trend	Burglary	Theft	Auto Theft	Total	Trend	
United States	**9.2**	**38.6**	**255.1**	**411.1**	**714**	–	**1,241**	**3,160**	**644**	**5,045**	–	**80**
Aiken, SC	12.5	51.1	112.3	529.6	706	▲	1,452	2,520	363	4,336	▲	81
Alamogordo, NM	5.1	9.0	35.4	280.1	330	–	1,111	3,105	171	4,387	▼	87
Albuquerque, NM	11.3	59.0	295.8	968.1	1,334	▲	2,552	5,718	644	8,913	▼	63
Alpine–Big Bend, TX	12.2	21.2	17.2	403.8	454	–	986	2,252	101	3,339	▼	87
Amador County, CA	1.3	8.1	9.8	159.3	179	–	745	1,631	119	2,495	▼	93
Amherst–Northampton, MA	1.9	14.0	18.0	173.3	207	▲	526	1,433	250	2,209	▲	93
Annapolis, MD	3.6	27.9	123.1	239.0	394	–	973	2,911	465	4,349	▲	86
Asheville, NC	6.3	29.5	106.3	195.5	338	–	1,433	2,841	323	4,596	▲	87
Athens, GA	8.0	55.6	220.3	341.0	625	–	2,003	4,161	473	6,637	▲	79
Austin, TX	8.2	58.4	235.0	255.7	557	–	2,317	6,754	685	9,756	▼	75
✓ **Bar Harbor, ME**	1.3	18.3	3.9	54.2	78	–	682	1,823	90	2,595	–	94
Bay St. Louis–Pass Christian, MS	8.6	117.5	72.5	177.8	376	–	1,793	1,826	292	3,911	–	87

Place	Violent Crime Rates						Property Crime Rates					Grade
	Murder	Rape	Robbery	Assault	Total	Trend	Burglary	Theft	Auto Theft	Total	Trend	
United States	**9.2**	**38.6**	**255.1**	**411.1**	**714**	**–**	**1,241**	**3,160**	**644**	**5,045**	**–**	**80**
Beaufort, SC	7.9	64.4	116.4	708.3	897	▲	1,823	4,371	280	6,473	▲	75
Beaver Lake, AR	4.3	24.8	14.9	305.3	349	▼	1,039	1,719	178	2,936	▼	89
Bellingham, WA	3.2	61.6	38.1	163.9	267	–	1,021	3,880	272	5,173	–	87
Bend, OR	3.5	40.7	34.3	120.5	199	–	1,120	3,822	322	5,264	▲	88
✓ Blairsville, GA	5.3	13.8	3.5	67.9	90	–	677	572	76	1,324	▲	96
Boca Raton–Delray Beach, FL	6.7	40.1	183.2	565.4	795	–	1,982	4,225	631	6,839	▼	76
Boone–Blowing Rock, NC	3.3	11.6	10.3	118.5	144	–	780	2,082	96	2,958	▼	93
Bradenton, FL	6.0	54.8	255.0	771.2	1,087	▲	2,262	4,216	508	6,986	–	71
Branson, MO	9.4	43.8	47.3	393.7	494	▲	1,242	4,861	143	6,246	▲	82
✓ Brevard, NC	3.8	31.3	10.9	152.7	199	–	627	1,206	90	1,923	▼	94
Brookings–Gold Beach, OR	3.0	26.0	10.4	114.8	154	–	1,015	2,662	178	3,854	▼	91
Brooksville–Spring Hill, FL	2.9	29.1	59.6	599.8	691	–	1,296	3,137	183	4,616	▼	81
Burlington, VT	2.7	42.9	31.9	74.9	152	–	1,383	4,958	270	6,611	▼	87
Camden, ME	3.9	9.6	10.7	79.7	104	–	622	2,390	108	3,121	▲	93
Cape Cod, MA	2.2	30.8	40.5	576.1	650	▲	1,629	3,119	300	5,048	▼	81
Carmel–Monterey–Pebble Beach, CA	6.6	34.6	62.1	244.0	347	▼	945	1,923	162	3,031	▼	89
Carson City–Carson Valley, NV	0.8	36.5	64.2	389.0	491	▲	838	2,937	233	4,008	–	85
Cedar Creek Lake, TX	6.6	14.0	28.8	409.9	459	▲	1,589	1,954	133	3,676	▼	86
Chapel Hill, NC	8.0	36.1	87.2	305.6	437	▲	1,746	3,987	255	5,987	▲	83
Charles Town–Harpers Ferry–Shepherdstown, WV	3.4	14.1	39.0	106.6	163	–	802	1,522	176	2,500	–	93
Charleston Sea Islands, SC	10.6	64.8	249.0	802.8	1,127	▲	1,680	4,654	611	6,944	▲	70
Charlevoix–Boyne City–East Jordan, MI	0.0	43.7	11.2	139.4	194	–	443	1,806	116	2,365	–	93
Charlottesville, VA	5.7	33.9	85.7	205.7	331	–	753	3,464	212	4,429	▼	87
Chewelah, WA	2.6	24.9	5.0	64.6	97	–	837	2,628	112	3,576	▼	93
✓ Clayton, GA	7.1	8.8	16.6	115.2	148	–	1,109	719	166	1,994	–	94
Clemson–Pendleton District, SC	6.2	24.8	29.0	280.4	340	–	823	2,069	139	3,032	–	89
Coeur d'Alene, ID	3.4	42.6	25.5	281.5	353	–	1,102	3,482	172	4,756	▲	86
Colorado Springs, CO	4.6	58.1	94.7	252.9	410	–	1,297	4,117	379	5,794	▼	84
Conway, SC	11.8	48.7	102.1	558.9	721	–	1,587	3,613	404	5,604	▼	79
Cottonwood–Verde Valley, AZ	8.8	22.4	14.3	207.1	253	–	743	1,350	147	2,240	▼	92
Crossville, TN	0.0	10.7	58.3	96.7	166	–	750	1,876	601	3,227	–	92
Dare Outer Banks, NC	7.8	29.4	26.5	269.1	333	–	2,278	4,740	226	7,244	▲	83
Daytona Beach, FL	7.9	56.4	225.8	535.9	826	–	1,865	3,568	397	5,831	▼	77
Delta–Cedaredge, CO	3.6	9.2	9.2	238.9	261	–	621	1,508	91	2,221	▲	92
Durango, CO	3.2	25.3	22.4	270.1	321	–	804	3,780	142	4,726	–	87
Eagle River, WI	6.7	13.4	7.9	126.9	155	–	1,158	1,839	275	3,272	▼	92
East End Long Island, NY	3.0	10.6	118.1	154.3	286	–	966	2,563	592	4,121	▲	89
Easton–St. Michaels–Oxford, MD	5.4	32.9	85.8	439.5	564	–	773	2,238	161	3,172	–	86
Edenton, NC	9.2	21.7	73.7	350.7	455	▼	1,030	2,256	108	3,394	▲	87
Fairhope–Gulf Shores, AL	4.2	18.2	37.8	226.2	287	–	849	2,002	139	2,990	–	90
Fayetteville, AR	5.9	28.5	29.8	144.0	208	–	1,063	3,172	315	4,550	–	89
Florence, OR	3.0	47.8	104.9	183.9	340	–	1,292	4,241	312	5,846	▲	85
Fort Collins–Loveland, CO	2.2	40.9	17.0	221.6	282	–	735	3,225	148	4,108	▼	89
Fort Myers–Cape Coral, FL	7.8	36.9	283.0	329.1	657	▲	1,654	3,122	701	5,477	▲	80

Place	Violent Crime Rates						Property Crime Rates					Grade
	Murder	Rape	Robbery	Assault	Total	Trend	Burglary	Theft	Auto Theft	Total	Trend	
United States	**9.2**	**38.6**	**255.1**	**411.1**	**714**	**–**	**1,241**	**3,160**	**644**	**5,045**	**–**	**80**
✓ Fredericksburg, TX	2.4	8.1	5.9	77.0	93	–	584	1,266	85	1,936	▼	95
Fredericksburg–Spotsylvania, VA	4.3	13.0	59.6	122.1	199	–	511	3,077	278	3,866	▼	90
Gainesville, FL	8.6	68.7	282.2	876.7	1,236	–	2,657	5,491	493	8,641	▲	66
Grand Junction, CO	5.7	22.8	34.3	205.0	268	–	920	3,608	228	4,756	▲	88
Grants Pass, OR	6.6	39.7	50.7	57.1	154	–	1,104	3,389	265	4,757	–	90
Grass Valley–Nevada City, CA	1.8	20.2	19.3	277.0	318	–	801	1,966	185	2,952	▲	90
Guntersville, AL	6.1	16.6	28.3	215.9	267	▲	696	1,694	193	2,583	▲	91
✓ Hamilton–Bitterroot Valley, MT	1.7	5.0	3.3	60.9	71	–	222	1,446	92	1,759	–	96
Hanover, NH	2.0	17.2	5.3	72.2	97	–	605	2,417	97	3,119	▲	93
Hendersonville–East Flat Rock, NC	7.4	23.9	40.7	194.2	266	–	1,005	1,615	221	2,841	▲	91
Hesperia–Apple Valley–Victorville, CA	12.1	44.5	277.6	637.8	972	–	1,825	3,062	961	5,849	–	74
✓ Hiawassee, GA	0.0	3.2	0.0	31.7	35	–	410	216	30	655	▲	98
Hilton Head Island, SC	7.3	63.5	90.8	641.0	803	▲	1,733	3,825	262	5,820	▲	77
Hot Springs, AR	9.3	42.9	138.7	219.0	410	–	1,525	3,341	307	5,173	▲	85
Houghton Lake, MI	3.1	82.5	24.5	252.5	363	–	2,749	3,769	464	6,983	▼	83
Inverness, FL	5.0	11.0	30.7	228.3	275	–	1,019	1,614	140	2,773	▼	91
Kalispell–Flathead Valley, MT	2.0	37.7	18.0	121.7	179	–	812	4,819	326	5,957	▲	87
Kauai, HI	3.2	34.9	26.0	117.5	182	–	1,219	3,364	251	4,834	▼	89
✓ Kentucky Lake, KY	1.7	11.5	10.8	150.1	174	–	527	1,211	79	1,818	▲	94
Kerrville, TX	6.5	32.0	23.4	293.1	355	–	1,083	2,204	159	3,446	▲	89
Ketchum–Sun Valley, ID	4.4	23.3	5.9	347.7	381	–	1,096	3,327	234	4,657	▲	86
Key West–Key Largo–Marathon, FL	6.9	60.6	301.6	1,012.0	1,381	▼	2,866	6,747	671	10,284	▼	60
Kingman, AZ	9.1	14.9	47.1	416.1	487	▼	1,987	3,801	383	6,171	▼	82
Kissimmee–St. Cloud, FL	5.6	53.8	185.1	648.2	893	▲	2,861	4,943	431	8,235	▼	72
Laguna Beach–Dana Point, CA	4.3	20.6	95.9	260.5	381	–	1,026	2,431	490	3,947	–	87
Lake Buchanan–Lake LBJ, TX	4.0	21.3	10.7	168.2	204	–	897	1,690	85	2,672	–	92
Lake Conroe, TX	9.0	30.1	71.2	357.9	468	–	1,429	2,775	421	4,626	▼	85
Lake Granbury, TX	3.4	7.5	12.8	158.8	182	–	958	1,812	139	2,909	–	92
Lake Havasu City, AZ	6.8	15.5	26.1	336.6	385	▼	1,470	2,466	346	4,282	–	87
Lake Livingston, TX	7.8	16.4	33.9	253.8	312	–	1,398	1,769	183	3,350	–	89
Lake Martin, AL	11.8	20.2	37.4	452.2	522	–	646	1,419	74	2,139	▼	88
✓ Lake of the Cherokees, OK	5.6	14.1	9.2	126.8	156	–	804	1,309	193	2,306	–	94
✓ Lake of the Ozarks, MO	2.2	4.4	10.1	143.3	160	–	961	988	69	2,018	▲	94
Lake Winnipesaukee, NH	2.9	48.1	17.4	102.0	170	–	1,008	2,875	160	4,043	–	91
Lakeland–Winter Haven, FL	9.7	39.7	281.3	711.1	1,041	–	2,461	5,149	771	8,381	▼	69
Las Cruces, NM	6.3	50.8	81.1	327.4	466	▲	1,840	3,772	400	6,012	▼	82
Las Vegas, NV	12.3	63.0	387.6	283.2	746	–	1,581	3,752	856	6,190	–	78
Leesburg–Lady Lake, FL	5.7	45.6	89.4	553.9	695	–	1,625	2,335	310	4,269	▼	82
Litchfield Hills, CT	2.3	23.9	20.6	90.6	138	–	639	1,925	249	2,814	▲	93
Lower Cape May, NJ	4.8	64.5	121.1	296.6	487	–	1,730	4,986	235	6,951	▲	81
Madison, MS	5.0	38.2	61.4	174.9	280	–	862	2,585	183	3,630	▼	89
Maryville, TN	1.8	44.2	54.3	223.1	323	▲	873	2,789	394	4,056	▲	88
Maui, HI	3.2	33.5	54.0	208.0	299	–	1,788	4,973	346	7,107	▼	83

Place	Violent Crime Rates						Property Crime Rates					Grade
	Murder	Rape	Robbery	Assault	Total	Trend	Burglary	Theft	Auto Theft	Total	Trend	
United States	**9.2**	**38.6**	**255.1**	**411.1**	**714**	**–**	**1,241**	**3,160**	**644**	**5,045**	**–**	**80**
McCall–Cascade–Payette Valley, ID	3.1	65.7	3.1	422.8	495	–	1,521	2,666	311	4,497	▲	85
Medford–Ashland, OR	3.1	46.5	46.9	266.8	363	–	932	3,514	241	4,687	–	86
Melbourne, FL	4.7	34.9	153.9	525.0	718	–	1,664	4,222	362	6,249	–	78
Mission–McAllen–Alamo, TX	6.8	22.6	66.6	386.9	483	–	1,857	3,832	647	6,336	▲	82
Montrose, CO	0.8	5.7	15.5	139.5	162	–	614	2,945	137	3,696	–	91
Myrtle Beach, SC	10.6	52.9	156.8	464.1	684	–	2,332	5,204	479	8,015	▼	76
Naples, FL	8.3	78.2	153.0	544.5	784	–	1,764	3,431	353	5,548	▼	78
New Bern, NC	6.8	30.4	141.8	445.0	624	–	1,559	3,075	244	4,878	▲	82
New Braunfels, TX	5.0	8.1	55.4	563.4	632	▲	1,421	2,994	290	4,705	–	82
New Port Richey, FL	4.5	23.7	57.2	294.2	380	–	1,171	2,705	249	4,125	▼	87
Newport–Lincoln City, OR	4.6	39.2	40.8	267.9	353	–	1,386	3,662	284	5,332	▼	85
✓ Norfork Lake, AR	3.2	8.9	3.8	118.1	134	–	103	921	65	1,088	–	96
✓ Northern Door Peninsula, WI	1.6	5.4	2.3	15.2	24	–	508	1,808	88	2,404	▲	96
✓ Northern Neck, VA	2.8	15.8	5.5	154.5	179	–	509	801	61	1,371	▼	95
Oakhurst–Coarsegold, CA	12.7	46.5	138.5	584.7	782	▼	1,640	2,231	416	4,288	▲	80
Ocala, FL	10.1	56.2	270.2	724.6	1,061	▲	1,999	3,711	362	6,073	▼	73
Ocean City, MD	7.9	57.6	73.4	652.6	792	▲	1,767	5,686	333	7,785	▼	74
Oscoda–Tawas–Huron Shore, MI	2.6	57.0	5.3	197.5	262	–	1,023	1,912	109	3,044	▲	91
Oxford, MS	2.0	47.2	66.5	307.5	423	–	1,781	6,666	208	8,655	▼	79
Pagosa Springs, CO	4.0	26.0	18.3	360.9	409	▲	681	2,180	106	2,967	▼	88
Pahrump Valley, NV	10.0	25.0	135.0	500.0	670	–	700	2,835	380	3,915	–	83
Palm Springs–Coachella Valley, CA	10.9	38.6	254.4	797.6	1,101	–	2,155	3,610	1,096	6,861	▼	71
Panama City, FL	7.9	59.5	91.8	547.1	706	▲	1,492	4,391	313	6,196	▲	78
Paradise–Magalia, CA	6.1	41.6	59.4	340.4	448	–	1,426	3,025	393	4,844	▼	85
Payson, AZ	3.0	28.4	17.7	264.7	314	–	678	2,318	147	3,142	▲	90
Petoskey–Harbor Springs, MI	2.4	88.6	12.7	136.7	240	–	804	3,454	143	4,401	▲	89
Phoenix–Mesa–Scottsdale, AZ	8.7	42.2	211.7	505.5	768	–	1,921	5,021	1,066	8,009	▼	74
Pike County, PA	0.7	23.6	16.8	142.0	183	–	1,919	1,342	151	3,412	▼	91
Placerville–Shingle Springs, CA	6.0	28.8	53.1	259.8	348	–	1,399	2,051	259	3,708	▼	88
Polson–Mission Valley, MT	1.5	23.5	9.5	81.1	116	–	592	1,968	350	2,909	▼	93
Pompano Beach, FL	16.2	54.8	526.9	1,111.0	1,709	–	2,280	4,670	954	7,905	▼	59
Port Angeles–Seqium, WA	1.7	47.8	20.5	118.6	189	–	854	3,172	181	4,206	▼	90
Port Charlotte–Punta Gorda, FL	4.5	14.7	49.8	133.6	203	▲	901	1,894	195	2,991	▲	92
Port Townsend, WA	4.0	40.1	9.9	146.8	201	–	968	2,762	182	3,912	▲	90
Prescott–Prescott Valley, AZ	7.6	22.1	22.2	319.3	371	–	726	2,398	167	3,291	▼	89
Redding, CA	5.3	55.8	75.4	420.7	557	▼	1,389	2,962	374	4,725	▼	83
Rehoboth Bay–Indian River Bay, DE	5.0	101.1	72.4	510.8	689	▲	1,104	2,795	155	4,054	▲	82
Reno–Sparks, NV	6.8	93.5	208.7	371.8	681	▼	1,302	4,396	400	6,098	–	79
Riviera–Bullhead City, AZ	11.9	9.8	60.9	405.9	488	–	2,040	2,972	490	5,502	▼	83
Rockport–Aransas Pass, TX	3.3	50.2	28.0	640.2	722	▲	2,191	4,260	356	6,807	▼	77
Ruidoso, NM	9.7	45.0	29.0	417.8	502	▲	2,111	2,935	267	5,313	▼	83

Place	Violent Crime Rates						Property Crime Rates					Grade
	Murder	Rape	Robbery	Assault	Total	Trend	Burglary	Theft	Auto Theft	Total	Trend	
United States	9.2	38.6	255.1	411.1	714	–	1,241	3,160	644	5,045	–	80
St. Augustine, FL	8.2	31.3	143.5	590.6	774	▲	1,460	4,218	285	5,963	–	78
St. George–Zion, UT	3.6	35.3	12.5	90.7	142	–	587	3,124	203	3,914	▲	91
St. Jay–Northeast Kingdom, VT	0.0	25.0	4.9	136.3	166	–	887	2,831	203	3,921	–	91
St. Petersburg–Clearwater, FL	6.5	47.3	324.1	713.1	1,091	–	1,687	4,412	484	6,584	▼	71
St. Simons–Jekyll Islands, GA	14.6	86.2	273.2	936.1	1,310	–	1,952	4,754	498	7,205	▼	67
San Antonio, TX	17.2	53.3	275.7	250.7	597	▲	2,455	6,489	1,334	10,278	▼	73
San Diego, CA	9.3	35.6	276.4	533.9	855	▲	1,396	3,302	1,510	6,208	▼	76
San Juan Islands, WA	0.0	15.5	2.0	72.8	90	–	816	2,444	169	3,429	▲	93
San Luis Obispo, CA	2.7	37.7	43.2	278.5	362	–	833	2,369	181	3,383	▼	89
Sandpoint–Priest River, ID	6.9	25.6	14.2	361.5	408	–	1,147	2,675	190	4,013	▲	87
Santa Barbara, CA	4.1	39.3	94.9	355.1	493	–	1,153	3,083	255	4,491	▼	85
Santa Fe, NM	8.1	23.4	87.4	369.4	488	–	1,196	3,631	565	5,392	–	83
Santa Rosa–Sonoma, CA	4.0	41.5	76.9	300.5	423	–	1,159	2,843	321	4,323	▼	86
Sarasota, FL	5.4	33.2	160.7	403.1	603	–	1,790	4,256	306	6,352	–	80
Savannah, GA	16.8	58.7	377.0	299.2	752	▲	1,811	4,763	589	7,163	▲	76
Sebring–Avon Park, FL	6.8	31.2	115.2	505.3	659	▲	1,745	2,950	387	5,083	▲	81
Sedona, AZ	4.0	27.6	11.8	222.2	266	–	720	1,409	87	2,216	▲	92
Silver City, NM	6.7	29.8	23.4	854.0	914	▲	1,257	3,320	208	4,785	▲	77
✓ Smith Mountain Lake, VA	3.4	6.0	15.0	72.4	97	–	414	1,172	103	1,688	–	96
Sonora–Groveland–Twain Harte, CA	4.1	17.0	13.6	196.0	231	–	983	2,091	169	3,244	▲	91
✓ Southern Berkshire County, MA	1.4	7.1	3.5	128.6	141	–	502	859	93	1,454	▲	95
Southern Pines–Pinehurst, NC	9.6	17.7	60.0	253.3	341	▲	1,086	2,076	189	3,351	▲	89
Southport–Brunswick Islands, NC	9.2	7.5	24.7	124.9	166	▲	1,049	1,359	113	2,522	▲	93
State College, PA	0.7	31.7	13.4	92.2	138	–	587	2,520	91	3,198	▼	92
✓ Table Rock Lake, MO	0.0	0.0	0.0	66.7	67	–	994	1,861	28	2,883	–	94
Taos, NM	2.8	18.2	27.6	427.0	476	–	1,080	2,618	155	3,852	–	86
Thomasville, GA	10.4	29.4	218.2	459.4	717	–	1,422	3,313	285	5,020	▼	80
Toms River–Barnegat Bay, NJ	1.6	20.9	44.4	148.8	216	–	798	2,708	216	3,721	▼	90
Traverse City, MI	1.3	98.0	16.6	137.8	254	–	657	2,627	107	3,392	▼	90
✓ Tryon, NC	5.5	7.0	5.5	168.1	186	–	874	795	120	1,789	▼	94
Tucson, AZ	8.0	59.7	153.6	476.8	698	–	1,533	6,223	556	8,312	▼	75
Vero Beach–Sebastian, FL	4.4	52.1	117.9	403.0	577	–	1,577	3,176	386	5,139	▲	82
Virginia Beach, VA	5.8	34.8	113.1	85.7	240	–	1,011	4,046	292	5,349	–	87
Wenatchee, WA	6.6	70.1	53.0	163.5	293	–	1,382	4,687	290	6,360	–	85
Western St. Tammany Parish, LA	5.8	38.9	48.4	277.6	371	–	1,196	2,278	212	3,687	▼	88
✓ Whidbey Island, WA	2.4	19.9	9.6	73.4	105	–	422	1,764	120	2,305	▼	94
Wickenburg, AZ	8.7	21.3	68.0	188.8	287	–	979	2,253	440	3,673	▼	89
Williamsburg, VA	7.6	36.7	75.7	210.3	330	–	510	3,273	165	3,948	–	88
Wimberly–San Marcos, TX	4.9	22.1	12.5	185.5	225	–	917	1,036	97	2,050	–	93
Winchester, VA	3.9	28.2	49.2	213.8	295	▲	660	3,232	183	4,075	▲	88
Woodstock, VT	0.5	15.4	7.5	96.2	120	–	790	2,249	124	3,162	▼	93
York Beaches, ME	1.9	21.3	18.3	71.2	113	–	791	2,489	154	3,434	–	93
Yuma, AZ	6.4	35.3	84.1	616.7	743	▼	1,393	5,462	518	7,373	▼	76

ET CETERA: Personal Safety

ARE YOU MORE VULNERABLE THAN OTHERS?

Most older adults' dread of crime is out of proportion to the odds of becoming a victim. But the impact of a burglary, robbery, or a fraud are certainly real. It is hard enough for anyone to return to a ransacked home or bounce back after being robbed on the street or defrauded of savings. Why shouldn't older adults living on fixed incomes be more fearful when the impact of these crimes is deeper and longer lasting?

Besides common sense defenses that include staying away from dark streets, locking your doors and windows, not talking to strangers, and being alert and accompanied when going out, here are a few more defenses drawn from various sources, including the Dade County (Miami) Department of Public Safety and the U.S. Department of Justice.

Burglary Defenses

For most homes, minimum security (defined by police as foiling entry into a home through any door or window except by destructive force) is enough to stop all but the dumbest or most dogged burglars. It's usually *after* they've been burglarized, experts note, that people learn additional ways to make their homes secure.

If your home is going to be hit, the chances are greater that it will happen during the day while you are out (even if you're gardening in the backyard) than at night when you're asleep, and that the burglar will be an unemployed young person who lives in or knows the neighborhood, and that the job will be done on the spur of the moment because the home looks empty and easy to enter.

From the viewpoint of the crook, the job's quick rewards also entail the risk of doing time in jail. He may turn back at any of three points:

1. Casing the house. If doors and windows are in plain sight and the sounds are unmistakable that someone is inside, most intruders will turn down the risk and search instead for an easier target.

Tactics for Defense:
- Trim or remove shrubbery near doors and windows to limit an intruder's potential hiding places.
- Leave your air conditioner's fan on when you are away; most burglaries occur in August, and a silent air conditioner is the crook's tip to an empty house.
- If you leave the house during the day, walk out to the sidewalk and turn and wave at the front door.
- Tune in a radio or a television to a talk program, turn on a porch light and yard light and one or two interior lights (the bathroom is one of the best rooms in which to leave a light on) if you are going out for the evening.

2. Entering the house. Even if the front door is unlocked, an intruder commits a crime once he is inside the house—whether or not anything is stolen. If doors and windows are locked and it looks as if it will take time and energy to break in, he will often go elsewhere.

3. Prowling the house. A burglar inside a target house is a very dangerous person to confront; however, he might still be discouraged if he could not quickly find loot or if he thought the police were on their way.

Tactics for Defense:
- Maintain a secure closet (not a safe) with an outward-opening door for storing furs, cameras, guns, silverware, and jewelry; on the door, install a one-inch deadbolt lock. Place an annunciator alarm on the inside. If the door is paneled or of hollow-core construction, strengthen it with 3/4-inch plywood or galvanized sheet steel backing.
- Install a telephone extension in your bedroom and add a rim lock with a 1-inch deadbolt to the interior side of the bedroom door (ideally, a "thumb turn" with no exterior key); then if you hear an intruder, you can retreat to the bedroom, lock the door, and call the police.

In addition, you should avoid:

- Displaying guns on interior walls that can be seen from the street. Guns are big drawing cards for burglars.
- Hiding door keys in the mailbox, under the doormat, atop the door casing, in a flowerpot, or any secret place seasoned burglars search first.
- Keeping a safe in your house. If an intruder finds a safe, he will assume you have something of great value and may come back later and force you to open it.
- Leaving window fans and air conditioners in unlocked windows when you are away from home.
- Entering your home or calling out if you find a window or door forced when you return home. Go to a neighbor and call the police. Wait there until the police come.
- Attaching tags on your key ring that identify you, your car, or your address.

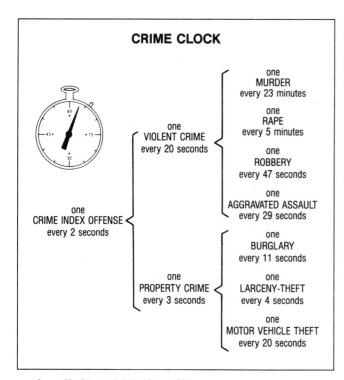

CRIME CLOCK

one
CRIME INDEX OFFENSE
every 2 seconds

one
VIOLENT CRIME
every 20 seconds

one
MURDER
every 23 minutes

one
RAPE
every 5 minutes

one
ROBBERY
every 47 seconds

one
AGGRAVATED ASSAULT
every 29 seconds

one
PROPERTY CRIME
every 3 seconds

one
BURGLARY
every 11 seconds

one
LARCENY-THEFT
every 4 seconds

one
MOTOR VEHICLE THEFT
every 20 seconds

Source: FBI, *Crime in the United States*, 1993.

Figures are for 1993.

Personal Larceny Defenses

Personal larceny with contact, a police blotter term for purse-snatching and pocket-picking, is the only crime that strikes older adults more frequently than the rest of the population. It is a common way a street crook gets cash in a hurry. The target is the person who looks the easiest to attack, has the most money or valuables to lose, and appears the least likely to give chase.

Purses. If you can do without a purse, do without it. Instead, tuck money and credit cards in an inside pocket. If you must carry a purse, carry it under your arm with its opening facing down; if you're attacked, let the purse's contents fall to the ground, then sit down on the sidewalk before you are knocked down.

Wallets. Never carry a wallet in your back pocket; even an amateur can lift it and escape before you realize what's happening. Carry it in the front pocket of your trousers; pin this pocket closed above the wallet with a safety pin, or wrap a large rubber band around the wallet so that it can't be withdrawn smoothly and can't fall through if your pocket is cut by a razor blade.

In addition, you should avoid:

- Letting strangers stop you for conversation.
- Approaching cars parked on the street with motors running.
- Flashing your jewelry or cash. This is a signal to street thugs, especially if you seem neither strong nor quick. They may follow you to a more convenient spot for a holdup.
- Walking close to building entrances or shrubbery.

- Getting separated from your purse or wallet in a crowded rest room or other public place, or leaving your purse or wallet unattended in a shopping cart, or on a counter.
- Mingling with adolescents leaving school or groups of adolescents anywhere.
- Using shortcuts, alleys, or dark ways, and walking through sparsely traveled areas or near thick trees and shrubs.

SECURE HOUSING DEVELOPMENTS

If you are considering life in a development—whether a high-rise apartment or condominium, trailer park, townhouse complex, housing tract, or enclosed dwelling with adjoining courtyards and interior patios—check for these basic security factors.

Opportunity for surveillance. The ease with which residents and police patrols can watch what is going on is determined by the design of the building complex. The ability to survey and question strangers depends on how each residence is designed and its relationship to neighboring dwellings. The nearness of elevator doors to apartment entrances, the number of apartments opening onto each landing, the location and nearness of parking lots and open spaces, the layout of streets and walkways, the evenness and intensity of exterior and interior lighting—all of these factors affect ease of surveillance.

All entryways and walkways should be clearly visible to residents and police at any time of day or night. This means the landscaping surrounding them should be low and free from obstacles and heavy foliage. Walkways should be evenly illuminated at night with lamps that are not so bright as to cause light "tunnels."

Clustered housing units where residents know their neighbors encourage watchfulness. In large buildings, if only a few apartments open onto a common landing or hallway, the same sort of neighborly concern is promoted.

Differentiation of space and territory. The most dangerous places within large buildings are interior public areas with no definite territorial boundaries. Areas seemingly belonging to no one are, in effect, open to everyone. When places are definitely marked off, an intruder will be more obvious, and owners and neighbors will be alerted to potential danger more quickly.

Access control. Obviously, the quality of locks, doors, door frames, and windows affects the ease with which your residence can be entered. Yet many builders give little attention to these details. Still less attention may be given to entrances, a surprising fact when you consider that the design and layout of entrances are crucial elements in security, since they define territory and boundaries to residents, visitors, and intruders.

Entrances and exits to a complex should be limited in number, and entrance routes should pass near activity

Neighborhood Crime Watches

It is not uncommon to see a crime in progress without recognizing it as such. Here are some situations that might be observed in any neighborhood. These are situations a trained police officer would investigate if he or she were making the observation.

Situations Involving Vehicles

Situations	Possible Significance
Moving vehicles, especially if moving slowly without lights, following an aimless or repetitive course	Casing for a place to rob or burglarize; drug pusher, sex offender, or vandal
Parked, occupied vehicle, especially at an unusual hour	Lookout for burglary in progress (sometimes two people masquerading as lovers)
Vehicle parked in neighbor's drive being loaded with valuables, even if the vehicle looks legitimate, i.e., moving van or commercial van	Burglary or larceny in progress
Abandoned vehicle with or without license plate	Stolen or abandoned after being used in a crime
Persons loitering around parked cars	Burglary of vehicle contents, theft of accessories, vandalism
Persons detaching accessories and mechanical parts	Theft or vandalism
Apparent business transactions from a vehicle near school, park, or quiet residential neighborhood	Drug sales
Persons being forced into vehicle	Kidnapping, rape, robbery
Objects thrown from a moving vehicle	Disposal of contraband

Situations Involving Property

Situations	Possible Significance
Property in homes, garages, or storage areas, especially if several items of the same kind such as TVs and bicycles	Storage of stolen property

Situations Involving Property

Situations	Possible Significance
Property in vehicles, especially meaningful at night or if property is household goods, appliances, unmounted tape decks, stereo equipment	Stolen property, burglary in progress
Property being removed from a house or building; meaningful if residents are at work, on vacation, or are known to be absent	Burglary or larceny in progress
Open doors, broken doors or windows, or other signs of a forced entry	Burglary in progress or the scene of a recent burglary

Situations Involving Persons

Situations	Possible Significance
Door-to-door solicitors—especially significant if one goes to the back of the house and one stays in front. Can be men or women, clean-cut and well dressed	Casing for burglary, burglary in progress, soliciting violation
Waiting in front of a house	Lookout for burglary in progress
Forced entry or entry through window	Burglary, vandalism, theft
Persons short-cutting through yards	Fleeing the scene of a crime
Persons running, especially if carrying items of value	Fleeing the scene of a crime
Person carrying property, especially if property isn't boxed or wrapped	Offender leaving the scene of a burglary, robbery, or larceny
High volume of human traffic in and out of residence	Drug sales, vice activities, "fence" operation

areas so that those who come and go can be observed by many people. An increasingly popular type of retirement community designed for metropolitan areas high in crime (like many found in Florida, for example) consists of an enclosed complex of either condominium townhouses or cluster homes surrounded by a wall or secure fence and connected by courtyards and terraces. The entrance in these developments is usually a single gate guarded by a watchman who probably has closed-circuit television and elaborate communications systems.

Siting and clustering. The placement of buildings on the grounds and their relationship to one another affect the ease of access. In complexes where the design allows anyone to wander at will between dwellings or through courtyards, the opportunity for crime increases. When residences are clustered so that entrances face each other and access is limited, strangers are less likely to wander through and are more apt to be questioned if they do. The practice of clustering units together, then, limits access naturally and unobtrusively, while it provides a setting for the casual social contacts between neighbors that promote security.

Despite the obvious feeling of security that walls, fences, guard posts, and television scanners provide for retired persons in a community setting, too heavy a concentration of these precautions should be a warning flag to the potential resident. Security measures piled on top of one another, like excessive numbers of police with attack dogs, are an indicator of unacceptably high crime in the area. If you sense an inordinate preoccupation with security, it's wise to ask about crime or simply eliminate the community from your list altogether.

TYPICAL FRAUDS

P. T. Barnum is credited with the wise but cynical comment that there is "a sucker born every minute and two [con men] to take advantage of him." He spoke from bitter experience; twice in his lifetime he was the victim of swindlers.

Why do people continue to fall for con games? The answer is that the proposals sound too good to pass up and are presented with urgency by persons who appear to be sincere and honest. The favorite targets of these crooks are older adults who are likely to have liquid assets in their savings accounts.

It's hard to believe that people can still be taken in by the "pigeon drop," a thousand-year-old scam in which the "mark" is expected to ante up some of his or her own money in order to be cut in on an imaginary find of a small fortune. A similar game involves persuading a victim to help bank examiners and the FBI catch an embezzler by withdrawing some of his or her funds and turning them over to the supposed law-enforcement officer.

Both of these scams have been exposed time after time, yet victims continue to be bilked out of millions of dollars every year. Consumer and business frauds, too, net billions for their perpetrators. Here are some common examples.

Building Inspector and Contractor Scams

Code violation frauds are perpetrated by crooks working in tandem. One poses as a building inspector who "discovers" serious violations and the need for immediate repairs, for example, to a homeowner's furnace. Shortly afterward the accomplice arrives, pretending to be a repairman who can perform the needed work at low cost. Typically, little or nothing is done to the furnace, but the victim gets a bill for several hundred dollars.

Home improvement swindles are played by con men who usually show up late in the day offering to perform some service such as installing insulation at half price. They claim they have just finished a job in the neighborhood and have material left over, which accounts for the good deal they can pass on to you. You have to make up your mind on the spot and shell out the money immediately. The job probably never gets finished, and the materials used are worth even less than the bargain price you paid.

Work-at-Home Schemes

Work-at-home schemes are targeted toward older adults who respond to newspaper and magazine advertisements such as the following examples noted in a recent U.S. House of Representatives hearing on mail fraud.

IDEAS, INVENTIONS, new products needed by innovative manufacturers. Marketing assistance available to individuals, tinkerers, universities, companies. Call free: 1-800-528-6050. Arizona residents: 1-800-352-0458, extension 831.

EARN $200 weekly, part-time, taking short phone messages at home. Call 1-615-779-3235, extension 267.

Assemble electronic devices in your home during spare time. $300.00 to $600.00/week possible. Experience, knowledge, not necessary. No investment. Write for free information. Electronic Development Lab, Drawer 1560-L, Pinellas Park, FL 33565.

The ads promise extra income each month, all yours for addressing envelopes, making wreaths or plaques in your living room, knitting baby bootees, assembling fishing tackle in your basement, growing earthworms, watching television, or raising house plants at home. U.S. Postal Service investigators, who have been looking into these scams for years, say that they haven't encountered one legitimate work-at-home offer that requires payment from the person who responds to the ad.

That's the key to work-at-home scams. A fee is required in order for the person to get in on the opportunity. The promotor claims that the money is for a start-up kit or for other expenses. The promise is that the promoter will buy back the finished product or that he will arrange for it to be purchased by others in the marketplace. Unfortunately, the promoter seldom if ever buys back the products, and the consumer is not only robbed of his or her initial cash outlay but is also stuck with a large quantity of products for which there is no market.

Commodities Sales

Commodities swindles have become one of the biggest consumer frauds in years. Government investigators estimate these schemes are defrauding the public of as much as $1 billion a year.

The term commodities refers to a wide range of investments, from metals and gems to wholesale food products and foreign currencies. Although most investment firms are reputable, there is a growing number of firms that illegally sell or exchange investments to the unwary. Because commodities issues are complex, even highly educated persons are taken in. Indeed, convicted swindlers have testified in recent congressional hearings that the preferred customer is a retired physician, engineer, college professor, or military officer. Moreover, according to these crooks, the best telephone area codes in the country to call are the Midwest and Far West because, they allege, people there are less cynical.

Commodities investments are perfect vehicles for swindlers, since the payment of profits to investors can often be deferred for six months to a year, leaving plenty of time for the operators to skip town before the investors suspect a scam. Moreover, since commodities are by nature very complicated and risky investments, many investors are never sure whether they've been had or not.

There are two basic ways to invest in commodities. The first is to pay the full price and take immediate possession of the items. The second is to buy on margin, which involves putting up a percentage of the total purchase price with the balance being due on a future date.

A commodities scheme typically involves a boiler room full of telephones in which 10 to 100 salespeople make calls to persons who responded to newspaper advertising. The salespersons are paid by commission, and high-pressure sales are the name of the game. In many cases, a sale is consummated on the telephone. If the person called doesn't agree to purchase anything in the initial call, he or she will be inundated with literature and harassed until a sale is made. The salesperson usually requires the deposit to be wired from the investor's bank, leaving no time for second thoughts.

SERVICES

"Here comes the Gray Peril," local planners in attractive rural spots whispered to one another in the early 1980s. "They will bid up real estate, string out the visiting nurses, slow down traffic, tap into Meals on Wheels, and vote down school bond issues, all without contributing a nickel to the economy."

How times change. Today, places are courting retired persons as ardently as they chase fickle tourists and light industry. Alamagordo, NM, offers to pay half your moving costs. Hot Springs, AR, calls out the volunteer Blue Coats to show you around and even buy you lunch. Mississippi cancels taxes on Social Security and all public and private pensions and ponders free license plates.

Not for nothing. A retired household moving in from outside can have the same impact as three new light industrial jobs, some planners figure. Local economies get better when they float on a cushion of Social Security, pensions, and asset income. Talk to a trust officer in a bank in downtown Grand Junction, CO, and Eagle River, WI, and he or she will bend your ear about how they wouldn't be in business if not for the millions they oversee for older depositors.

Some rural spots owe their growth to older adults who moved there *because* the area was short on services —and short on taxes, too. To the confusion of officials,

after bouncing over dirt roads and smelling landfill effluvia the newcomers soon show up at county offices demanding better services and offer higher property taxes in return.

But the myth lingers in many rural areas that foot-loose older adults want big-city benefits without paying for them. Let's look at five: continuing education, office-based physicians, public libraries, public transportation, and short-term general hospitals.

CONTINUING EDUCATION

When we look back over our lives, we find that the autobiographies we wanted to write are different from the ones that finally get written. There is one thread embedded in the stories: the quick passage through school in youth to a long period of raising a family and working throughout the middle years, ending up in retirement that's all too short. "Is that all there is?" sang Peggy Lee.

School, then a job, then retirement—the *linear life* some call it—doesn't fit people's lengthening life spans anymore. Retirement, frankly, is a period of boredom and anxiety for some who miss the world of work. For others, it would be an empty time indeed if there weren't opportunities for learning new things.

Read the smarmy feature articles in newspapers 10 years ago about the grandmother who started her masters in social work or the retired USMC Major-General who got an A in Art History and you'd think older students were interlopers in the classroom.

They aren't. Gray-haired students cruise the stadium parking lot at the University of Arkansas for an open slot, push a tray down the cafeteria line at the Viking Union at Western Washington University, and scold you for smoking on the steps at the University of Vermont's library.

The average age of students is rising, particularly at public colleges. To fill classrooms, colleges and universities cut tuition fees or waive them for retired people who want to earn a degree, finish one, or just study for no other reason than fulfillment.

Of the 183 places featured in this book, 126 have at least one college. *Two-year* colleges include junior colleges, community colleges, and technical institutes that offer at least one year of college-level courses leading to an associate degree or are creditable toward a bachelor's degree. *Four-year* colleges offer undergraduate courses leading to a bachelor of arts or bachelor of science degree.

HEALTH CARE

For many of us, health care tips the balance in decisions about whether to stay in familiar territory or move to a distant place. In later life, sitting in a doctor's waiting room comes more frequently. Short hospital stays are a likelihood. With each passing year, the bills for physician fees and prescriptions get bigger and bigger.

Retirement Places Rated doesn't judge the quality of health care; it simply looks at the place's supply. While larger places have an edge, this doesn't mean quality health care in a small Ozark clinic is a contradiction. Nor does it necessarily mean that you're better off in a university medical center in San Antonio. The quality of medical care people get depends on their ability to pay for it, the luck of the draw, professional competence, and human error.

Physicians and Their Specialties

Not every M.D. is listed in the Yellow Pages. Some are hospital administrators, medical school professors, journalists, lawyers, or researchers for pharmaceutical companies. Others work for the federal government's Public Health Service, Veteran's Administration, or Department of Defense service branches. Still others are in residency training or are full-time members of hospital staffs. When it comes to doctors, what really counts is the number who have offices and see patients.

Where doctors end up practicing is determined by sentiment, their perceptions of local quality of life, or both. But mainly it's economics. The beginning physician has invested three to seven years in graduate

> **Paging Dr. Finder**
>
> Learning whether cardiologists, urologists, psychiatrists, or other specialists practice in a distant area needn't be a telephonic drudge. Call the local hospital's public relations office for a free copy of their Physician Locator or M.D. Directory. Hospitals in competitive markets know they will more likely have you as a customer when you're ill if they can introduce you early on to an M.D. that uses their facilities.
>
> These "Dr. Finders" aren't mere telephone contact sheets. Often they are photo galleries of physicians with capsule resumes on their education from college through medical school to residency, their specialties, and their board certifications. You can also learn if they take walk-in patients, accept Medicare assignments, and whether another doctor will cover for them on their day off. Some of these guides even detail their civic clubs and what they like to do on weekends.

medical education and frequently has to start out with a monstrous loan to repay.

Some begin work on a hospital staff, develop a practice, get loose from the hospital, and open an office. Others are recruited into partnerships or group practices through advertisements such as these from the *Journal of the American Medical Association.*

NORTH CAROLINA: EXPANDING GROUP RECRUITING TWO EXPERIENCED Emergency Physicians. Double coverage and flexible schedule. Excellent total compensation package includes paid vacation. CME time and occurrence malpractice. 22,000 census. Waterfront community. Community hospital closest to Outer Banks and ocean. Send C.V. to Box 1945, c/o JAMA.

CARDIOLOGIST—BC/BE WANTED TO JOIN A WELL-ESTABLISHED SOLO, Board Certified, noninvasive Cardiologist in a nice Oregon coastal community. Facility available for Echo-Doppler, Holter, Stress test, Cardiac Nuclear Studies, Temporary and Permanent Pacemaker, Swan Ganz, HIS bundle. Excellent salary and benefits. Early partnership. Send C.V. to Box 6199, c/o JAMA.

By whatever means they launch themselves professionally, the major concern of new M.D.s who wish to specialize is a place's covered (i.e., insured) census (i.e., population size).

Depending on how they spend their professional hours, the American Medical Association (AMA) classifies office-based physicians into four groups. Unless they specialize in pediatrics, obstetrics, or child psychiatry, experts predict their typical patients will be in their 60s by the year 2000.

Hospital Services

The American Hospital Association (AHA) classifies hospital services into 85 categories.

Adult day-care program

Alcohol/drug abuse or dependency inpatient unit

Alcohol/drug abuse or dependency outpatient services

Alzheimer's diagnostic/assessment services

Angioplasty

Arthritis treatment center

Birthing room/LDRP room

Blood bank

Burn-care unit

Cardiac catheterization laboratory

Cardiac intensive-care unit

Cardiac rehabilitation program

Chaplaincy/Pastoral care services

Chronic obstructive pulmonary disease services

Community health promotion

Comprehensive geriatric assessment

CT scanner

Diagnostic radioisotope facility

Emergency department

Emergency department social work services

Emergency response (geriatric)

Ethics committee

Extracorporeal shock wave lithotripter

Fitness center

General inpatient care for AIDS/ARC

Genetic counseling/screening services

Geriatric acute-care unit

Geriatric clinics

Health sciences library

Hemodialysis

Histopathology laboratory

HIV/AIDS unit

Home health services

Hospice

Magnetic resonance imaging

Mammography diagnostic

Mammography screening

Medical surgical or other intensive-care unit

Megavoltage radiation therapy

Neonatal intensive-care unit

Noninvasive cardiac assessment services

Obstetrics unit

Occupational health services

Occupational therapy services

Oncology services

Open-heart surgery

Organ/tissue transplant

Organized outpatient services

Organized social work services

Orthopedic surgery

Outpatient social work services

Outpatient surgery services

Patient education

Patient representative services

Pediatric acute inpatient unit

Physical therapy services

Psychiatric child/adolescent services

Psychiatric consultation/liaison services

Psychiatric education services

Psychiatric emergency services

Psychiatric geriatric services

Psychiatric inpatient services

Psychiatric outpatient services

Psychiatric partial hospitalization program

Radioactive implants

Recreational therapy services

Rehabilitation inpatient unit

Rehabilitation outpatient services

Reproductive health services

Respiratory therapy services

Respite care

Senior membership program

Single photon emission computerized tomography (SPECT)

Skilled nursing or other long-term-care facility

Specialized outpatient program for AIDS/ARC

Speech therapy services

Sports medicine clinic/services

Therapeutic radioisotope facility

Trauma center (certified)

Ultrasound

Volunteer services department

Women's health center/services

Worksite health promotion

X-ray radiation therapy

Source: American Hospital Association, *Guide to the Health Care Field*, 1994.

General/family practitioners use all accepted methods of medical care. They treat diseases and injuries, provide preventive care, do routine checkups, prescribe drugs, and do some surgery. They also refer patients to medical specialists.

Medical specialists focus on specific medical disciplines such as cardiology, allergy, gastroenterology, or dermatology. They are the largest of the AMA groups because, frankly, specializing is where the money is. They are likely to give attention to surgical and nonsurgical approaches to treatment. If it is decided that surgery is the method of treatment, they refer patients to surgeons.

Surgical specialists, the best-paid of the AMA's groups, operate on a regular basis several times a week. The letters F.A.C.S. (Fellow of the American College of Surgeons) after a surgeon's name indicate that he or she has passed an evaluation of surgical training and skills as well as ethical fitness.

Other specialists concentrate on disciplines as familiar as psychiatry and neurology, or as exotic as diagnostic radiology, aerospace medicine, and forensic pathology.

Short-Term General Hospitals

The word health can also mean its opposite, illness. A hospital is not really a health-care institution; its business is to take care of sick people. The truly healthy need little medical care except for an occasional shot or checkup; the unhealthy need a lot more.

Just as not all M.D.s see patients, not all hospitals handle typical illnesses and emergencies. Many of the 6,480 U.S. hospitals exclusively treat chronic diseases or alcohol and drug addiction, or they may be burn centers, psychiatric hospitals, or rehabilitation hospitals. *Retirement Places Rated* counts only general hospitals where most patients stay less than 30 days. Nearly all are certified for Medicare participation and most are accredited for acute care by the Joint Commission on Accreditation of Health Care Organizations (JCAHO).

Though most operate as nonprofits, general hospitals are actually businesses that can't afford to go deeply into the red. They offer common services such as an emergency department, respiratory therapy, intensive care, ultrasound, blood bank, a histopathology laboratory, and outpatient surgery. Some stake out market niches with an additional menu—a sports medicine clinic, for example, or a women's health center, an open-heart surgery unit, a certified trauma center, or an X-ray radiation therapy unit.

Two of every three hospitals are *nonteaching*. That is, they are staffed almost entirely by "attending physicians" who have an outside practice, are paid by the patient, and have admitting privileges at the hospital.

Teaching hospitals grant admitting privileges to attending physicians, but they also employ full-time "house staff," taking in first-year and advanced residents and a teaching faculty. The attending physician heads a team of house staff members to make important

---

AMA Physician Categories

The American Medical Association (AMA) classifies a physician as a family practitioner, general practitioner, medical specialist, surgeon, or other specialist by 35 specialties in which the physician reports spending the largest number of his or her professional hours.

General/Family Practitioners
General Practice
Family Practice

Medical Specialists
Allergy
Cardiovascular Diseases
Dermatology
Gastroenterology
Internal Medicine
Pediatrics
Pediatric Allergy
Pediatric Cardiology
Pulmonary Diseases

Surgical Specialists
General Surgery
Neurological Surgery
Obstetrics and Gynecology
Ophthalmology
Orthopedic Surgery
Otolaryngology
Plastic Surgery
Colon and Rectal Surgery
Thoracic Surgery
Urology

Other Specialists
Aerospace Medicine
Anesthesiology
Child Psychiatry
Diagnostic Radiology
Forensic Pathology
Neurology
Occupational Medicine
Psychiatry
Pathology
Physical Medicine and Rehabilitation
General Preventive Medicine
Public Health
Radiology
Therapeutic Radiology

---

decisions about a patient's care. The patient pays the attending physician; the hospital pays the house staff.

If an area appeals to you, but it hasn't a hospital, don't be discouraged. There are usually good facilities a short drive away. Residents of Ocean City on Maryland's Eastern Shore may have to drive to Baltimore for specialized care, but Dorchester General Hospital up the shore in Cambridge or Peninsula General Hospital in Salisbury are more than adequate for routine care.

PUBLIC LIBRARIES

Enter the Craven County library in the heart of New Bern, NC, plop down in an armchair among the local

Using the Library: Reading Quotients

How many books sit on a library's shelves tells half the story of local reading. How often people check them out—the library's circulation—is the other half.

When circulation is added to the number of books and the sum is divided by the population served, the result is the reading quotient, a rough indicator of reading habits. The U.S. average is 8.0. In several places, it's more than twice that number.

Place	Reading Quotient
McCall–Cascade–Payette Valley, ID	40.7
East End Long Island, NY	36.4
Taos, NM	28.7
Chewelah, WA	25.7
San Juan Islands, WA	23.4
Ruidoso, NM	21.2
Bar Harbor, ME	20.7
Camden, ME	19.4
Southern Berkshire County, MA	19.4
Wickenburg, AZ	17.9
Chapel Hill, NC	17.6
Williamsburg, VA	17.1
Northern Door Peninsula, WI	16.8
Lake Winnepesaukee, NH	16.2

Source: Derived from National Center for Education Statistics, unpublished Federal-State Cooperative System library data.

histories, bestsellers, out-of-town newspapers, and data terminals, and you'll get so comfortable in the quiet you'll want to hang out there all day long.

Until its door is padlocked after a municipal budget cut, one service taken for granted is the local public library. There are more than 8,500 systems in this country. From all that, you might expect libraries to be the most plentiful of public services.

They are. Though you'll find current fiction and nonfiction on the shelves everywhere, you won't always locate issues of *Morningstar*, *InfoWorld*, or *American Demographics*.

Libraries and library resources are concentrated in larger places. Albuquerque's 1.7 million books are shelved in the main building on NW Copper Avenue and in 13 neighborhood branches; San Diego's 77 libraries house 4 million books. But the size of the collection tells only half the story. Measured by the number of books per person, the supply is greater in smaller places, especially college towns and towns in New England where the public library is well into its second century of operation.

PUBLIC TRANSPORTATION

In Hot Springs, AR, a small fleet of Orion and Vintage Trolley buses run by IT, the Intracity Transit, helps townspeople and tourists alike dodge congestion. In Las Vegas, new diesel Flyer buses operated by CAT, the Citizens Area Transit, roar 24 hours a day over routes serving the casinos south of downtown and part of the day over other routes that reach the suburban-desert frontier. In both places, transit is a municipal budget-buster. In spite of rising fares and a portion of the local sales tax, they would operate at a loss if it weren't for federal grant money.

If it's a toss-up between Cape Cod and Cape May in your mind, in which place can you do without a car? Probably neither one, unless you find a leisure-living development with its own vans or a neighborhood with a nearby bus stop. Transit routes are mapped so that a limited number of buses can serve the greatest number of persons who don't own an automobile and need a reliable, cheap way to get to work or into town for shopping.

However, in places where the tab for parking in a downtown garage costs $10, where rush-hour traffic approaches grid-lock, where distances are long and time always seems short, the options for public transportation in some places really count.

GRADING: Services

That services are in greater supply in bigger places than in smaller ones is simple common sense. This doesn't mean your need for a cardiologist or an allergist, a public library that gets *Value Line* and the *Wall Street Journal*, a convenient public transit alternative to driving a car, and a schedule of college courses can be met only in places the scale of Phoenix or San Diego.

Admittedly, grading places by their services can't be done to everyone's satisfaction. Services constitute a laundry list of everything from trash pickup and street

repair, to emergency medical teams and firefighters, to gypsy moth spraying and sewage treatment.

If you agree that hospital services, physicians who treat patients, public transit, public libraries, and the chance to take a college course or finish a degree is as good a set of services as any other, then you won't always be disappointed by smaller places, particularly college towns with a medical school.

In spotlighting these services, *Retirement Places Rated* doesn't judge the quality of local hospitals, the credentials of local physicians, the breadth of local college course offerings, or the local bus fleet's current state of repair. This guide simply indicates the presence of selected services that most persons agree enhance retirement living.

A place's final grade is the average of grades it receives in the following five areas.

Office-based Physicians

Among every 100,000 people in the United States, 22 are M.D.s in general/family practice, another 50 are medical specialists, and 41 are surgeons.

Each place's own figures for their three physician groups are scaled against a standard where one and a half times the national average gets a perfect 100 and none gets a 0.

Public Libraries

The 643 million books in America's public libraries works out to 2.64 per person. The $734 million these libraries spend on books each year works out to $2.84 per person.

Each place's books per person and dollars per person figures are scaled against a standard where one and a half times the national average gets a perfect 100 and no libraries gets a 0. Places that are part of larger library systems are graded by the figures for the library system's legal service area.

Continuing Education

Grading here is based on the percent of a place's population enrolled in colleges and universities. Because two-year institutions cost less and are more likely to grant fee waivers to older adults, they are weighted one and a half times that of private four-year colleges. Because public four-year colleges have the same cost advantages plus a greater variety of courses listed in

their catalogs as two-year institutions, they are weighted two and a half times that of private four-year colleges.

The resulting weighted percent figure is then scaled against a standard where twice the national average gets a perfect 100 and no local colleges and universities gets a 0. Enrollment figures are the sum of full-time and part-time students. Institutions offering only graduate-level courses aren't counted.

Public Transportation

Based on Federal Transit Administration figures for the average distance (35,485 miles) a bus travels over its route in revenue service per year, the fleet mileage in each retirement place is divided by the population and then scaled against a standard where no public transit gets a 0, and 6 or more miles per capita gets 100.

For example, the 132 CAT buses in Las Vegas log a total of 4,684,020 miles in scheduled service annually. This works out to 5.09 miles for each person, good for a grade of 90. Only *fixed route* systems that pick up passengers at regular stops on a published schedule are counted. Except for the San Diego Trolley, fixed route public transit and "the bus" are synonymous in 80 retirement places.

Short-term General Hospital Services

Grading here is based on the count of American Hospital Association (AHA) defined services available in local hospitals. This figure is then scaled against a standard where all 85 AHA services gets a perfect 100 and no services a 0.

For example, the 55 unduplicated services available within Traverse City's two hospitals—the Munson Medical Center and Traverse City Community Hospital—is good for a grade of 91. As you may expect, all AHA-defined services are available among Phoenix's, San Antonio's, and San Diego's many hospitals, earning each of those large areas a grade of 100.

 RANKINGS: Services

Five criteria make up the score for a retirement place's supply of selected services: (1) *continuing education*, (2) *office-based physicians*, (3) *public libraries*, (4) *public transporation*, and (5) *short-term general hospital services*.

Grades are rounded two decimal places. Locations that are tied get the same rank and are listed alphabetically.

Retirement Places from First to Last

Rank	Grade	Rank	Grade	Rank	Grade
1. Gainesville, FL	98.76	6. Austin, TX	93.95	11. Camden, ME	91.85
2. Chapel Hill, NC	97.04	6. Williamsburg, VA	93.95	12. State College, PA	90.74
3. Albuquerque, NM	95.03	8. Athens, GA	93.35	13. Charlottesville, VA	90.63
4. Hanover, NH	94.77	9. Reno–Sparks, NV	92.75	14. San Diego, CA	90.44
5. Burlington, VT	94.71	10. Tucson, AZ	92.28	15. Santa Barbara, CA	89.76

Rank	Grade
16. Traverse City, MI	89.62
17. Bellingham, WA	89.15
18. San Antonio, TX	88.90
19. Charleston Sea Islands, SC	88.86
20. Port Angeles–Seqium, WA	88.77
21. Savannah, GA	88.26
22. Phoenix–Mesa–Scottsdale, AZ	87.56
23. Fayetteville, AR	87.32
24. Paradise–Magalia, CA	87.16
25. Southern Berkshire County, MA	87.08
26. Medford–Ashland, OR	86.61
27. Myrtle Beach–North Myrtle Beach, SC	85.94
28. Durango, CO	85.85
29. Kentucky Lake, KY	85.67
30. Las Vegas, NV	85.64
31. St. Petersburg–Clearwater, FL	85.43
32. Amherst–Northampton, MA	85.25
33. Boone–Blowing Rock, NC	84.82
34. Fort Collins–Loveland, CO	84.46
35. San Luis Obispo, CA	83.57
36. Colorado Springs, CO	83.53
37. Melbourne, FL	83.20
38. Cape Cod, MA	82.82
39. Coeur d'Alene, ID	82.74
40. Hot Springs, AR	82.14
41. Pompano Beach, FL	81.99
42. Bar Harbor, ME	81.80
43. Palm Sprins–Coachella Valley, CA	81.53
44. Asheville, NC	81.05
45. Conway, SC	81.02
46. Las Cruces, NM	81.00
47. Santa Rosa–Sonoma, CA	80.86
48. Daytona Beach, FL	79.76
49. Annapolis, MD	79.75
50. Boca Raton–Delray Beach, FL	79.18
51. Hilton Head Island, SC	78.95
52. Lakeland–Winter Haven, FL	76.34
53. Fort Myers–Cape Coral, FL	76.22
54. New Bern, NC	76.16
55. Toms River–Barnegat Bay, NJ	75.43
56. Redding, CA	75.37
57. Charles Town–Harpers Ferry–Shepherdstown, WV	75.19
58. Beaufort, SC	75.00
59. Litchfield Hills, CT	74.60
60. Mission–McAllen–Alamo, TX	74.54
61. Ketchum–Sun Valley, ID	74.50
62. Hesperia–Apple Valley–Victorville, CA	74.36
63. Bradenton, FL	73.75
64. Woodstock, VT	73.66
65. Key West–Key Largo–Marathon, FL	73.43
66. Sedona, AZ	72.64
67. Port Townsend, WA	72.53
68. Carmel–Monterey–Pebble Beach, CA	72.01

Rank	Grade
69. Sonora–Groveland–Twain Harte, CA	71.92
70. Clemson–Pendleton District, SC	71.16
71. Grand Junction, CO	71.01
72. East End Long Island, NY	70.73
73. York Beaches, ME	70.56
74. Petoskey–Harbor Springs, MI	70.49
75. Santa Fe, NM	70.11
76. Southern Pines–Pinehurst, NC	69.73
77. Bay St. Louis–Pass Christian, MS	69.58
78. Oxford, MS	69.50
79. Silver City, NM	69.10
80. Alpine–Big Bend, TX	69.01
81. Lower Cape May, NJ	68.53
82. Cottonwood–Verde Valley, AZ	68.30
82. Prescott–Prescott Valley, AZ	68.30
84. Amador County, CA	68.01
85. Fredericksburg–Spotsylvania, VA	67.89
86. Sarasota, FL	67.77
87. Placerville–Shingle Springs, CA	67.60
88. Virginia Beach, VA	67.51
89. St. Jay–Northeast Kingdom, VT	67.49
90. Wenatchee, WA	67.39
91. Winchester, VA	67.34
92. Carson City–Carson Valley, NV	66.85
93. Kalispell–Flathead Valley, MT	66.75
94. Wimberly–San Marcos, TX	66.65
95. Bend, OR	66.48
96. St. Simons–Jekyll Islands, GA	66.30
97. Rehoboth Bay–Indian River Bay, DE	65.68
98. St. George–Zion, UT	65.37
99. Lake Winnipesaukee, NH	65.21
100. Kauai, HI	64.56
100. New Port Richey, FL	64.56
102. Hendersonville–East Flat Rock, NC	64.15
103. Panama City, FL	63.94
104. Kerrville, TX	63.90
105. Polson–Mission Valley, MT	63.76
106. Alamogordo, NM	63.62
107. Thomasville, GA	63.48
108. Maui, HI	62.72
109. Laguna Beach–Dana Point, CA	62.44
110. Yuma, AZ	62.20
111. Aiken, SC	61.85
112. Grass Valley–Nevada City, CA	61.84
113. Brevard, NC	61.47
114. Fairhope–Gulf Shores, AL	61.44
115. Ocala, FL	60.92
116. St. Augustine, FL	60.65
117. Branson, MO	60.48

Rank	Grade
118. Grants Pass, OR	60.30
119. Lake Martin, AL	60.17
120. Sebring–Avon Park, FL	59.52
121. Kingman, AZ	59.32
121. Lake Havasu City, AZ	59.32
121. Riviera–Bullhead City, AZ	59.32
124. Hiawassee, GA	58.67
125. Leesburg–Lady Lake, FL	58.20
126. Maryville, TN	58.19
127. Cedar Creek Lake, TX	57.63
128. Smith Mountain Lake, VA	56.32
129. Western St. Tammany Parish, LA	54.98
130. Easton–St. Michaels–Oxford, MD	54.97
131. Guntersville, AL	54.55
132. Southport–Brunswick Islands, NC	54.33
133. Kissimmee–St. Cloud, FL	54.27
134. Ruidoso, NM	54.11
134. Vero Beach–Sebastian, FL	54.11
136. Ocean City, MD	54.04
137. Madison, MS	53.85
138. Chewelah, WA	53.35
139. Florence, OR	53.23
140. Northern Door Peninsula, WI	53.22
141. Edenton, NC	52.62
142. Newport–Lincoln City, OR	52.27
143. Naples, FL	52.00
144. Wickenburg, AZ	51.93
145. Port Charlotte–Punta Gorda, FL	51.33
146. Whidbey Island, WA	51.31
147. Eagle River, WI	51.17
148. Northern Neck, VA	50.99
149. Payson, AZ	50.70
150. Montrose, CO	50.68
151. McCall–Cascade–Payette Valley, ID	50.64
152. Norfork Lake, AR	50.43
153. Delta–Cedaredge, CO	49.99
154. Lake of the Ozarks, MO	49.95
155. Taos, NM	49.91
156. Charlevoix–Boyne City–East Jordan, MI	49.26
157. Pahrump Valley, NV	48.98
158. Tryon, NC	48.94
159. Fredericksburg, TX	48.74
159. Houghton Lake, MI	48.74
161. Beaver Lake, AR	48.67
162. Hamilton–Bitterroot Valley, MT	48.66
163. Oscoda–Tawas–Huron Shore, MI	48.56
164. Inverness, FL	48.37
165. Lake Buchanan–Lake LBJ, TX	47.68
166. Clayton, GA	47.51
167. New Braunfels, TX	47.25
168. Sandpoint–Priest River, ID	46.96
169. Lake Conroe, TX	46.93
170. Brookings–Gold Beach, OR	46.84

Rank	Grade	Rank	Grade	Rank	Grade
171. Brooksville–Spring Hill, FL	46.55	176. Lake Granbury, TX	41.21	181. Rockport–Aransas Pass,	
172. Blairsville, GA	46.34	177. San Juan Islands, WA	39.79	TX	29.90
173. Oakhurst–Coarsegold, CA	45.64	178. Lake Livingston, TX	39.62	182. Pike County, PA	29.68
174. Crossville, TN	45.24	179. Pagosa Springs, CO	35.11	183. Table Rock Lake, MO	29.19
175. Lake of the Cherokees, OK	43.10	180. Dare Outer Banks, NC	32.32		

PLACE PROFILES: Services

The following pages show college-level continuing education, office-based physicians, public library, public transportation, and short-term general hospital services in each of the 183 places.

Under the heading **Continuing Education** are (1) the names of community or two-year colleges and their enrollments, and (2) the names and enrollments of local institutions granting at least a bachelor's degree. A • next to the college's name indicates it is publicly controlled.

Office-based Physicians, the second heading, details how many M.D.s practice in the county according to the American Medical Association's basic classifications of general/family practice, surgery, and medical specialties.

Under **Public Libraries** is the number of libraries in the library system serving the retirement place, including all central city, suburban, and rural branches, with total figures on the size of their book holdings and systemwide reading quotients.

Public Transportation names the local transit agency that regularly operates over a fixed route, picking up passengers at regular stops on a published schedule. The number of vehicles in the agency's fleet is also given.

Short-term General Hospital Services names local hospitals accredited by the Joint Commission on Accreditation of Health Care Organizations (JCAHO) and certified for Medicare participation by the U.S. Department of Health and Human Services.

A • next to the hospital name indicates it is an AMA-approved teaching hospital. Veterans (VA) hospitals and military hospitals are also named. Because VA hospitals aren't part of the Medicare system, and because only military veterans may be patients, they aren't counted when determining a place's grade.

The sources for the information are the American Hospital Association, *Guide to the Health Care Field* (hospital accreditation and services), 1994; American Library Association, *American Library Directory* (public library locations), 1994, and *Output Measures for Public Libraries* (public library quality standards), 1987; American Medical Association, *Physician Characteristics and Distribution* (office-based physician classifications and number by county), 1994; Community Transportation Association of America, *Directory of UMTA-Funded Rural and Specialized Transit Systems* (rural fixed-route transit systems and fleet sizes), 1994; Places Rated Partnership survey of state library association annual reports, 1994; U.S. Department of Defense, Veterans Administration, *Annual Report* (VA hospital locations), 1994; U.S. Department of Education, National Center for Education Statistics, *Directory of Postsecondary Institutions* (college and university types and enrollments), 1994; and *Public Libraries in the United States* (public library collections and budgets), 1994; U.S. Department of Health and Human Services, Bureau of Health-Care Professions, *Area Resource File* (hospital services by county), 1993; and U.S. Department of Transportation, Federal Transit Administration, *Section 15 Report* (urban fixed-route transit systems and fleet sizes), 1994.

A check mark (✓) preceding a place's name highlights it as one of the top 18 for services.

Aiken, SC
Continuing Education (71)
  Two-year
   • Aiken Technical College: 1,903
  Four-year
   • University of South Carolina: 2,966
Office-based Physicians (78)
  General/Family Practitioners: 16
  Medical Specialists: 31
  Surgical Specialists: 31
Public Libraries (75)
  Part of Aiken-Bamberg-Edgefield Library System
   14 branches; 192,146 books
   $1.20 p/c book funds, 4.1 reading quotient
Short-term General Hospital Services (85)
  Aiken Regional Medical Centers
Grade: 62

Alamogordo, NM
Continuing Education (66)
  Two-year
   • New Mexico State University: 1,759
Office-based Physicians (80)
  General/Family Practitioners: 11
  Medical Specialists: 7
  Surgical Specialists: 9
Public Libraries (93)
  Alamogordo Public Library
   1 branch; 111,103 books
   $1.90 p/c book funds, 9.6 reading quotient
Short-term General Hospital Services (79)
  Gerald Champion Memorial
  Holloman Air Force Hospital
Grade: 64

✓ Albuquerque, NM
Continuing Education (84)
Two-year
- Albuquerque Technical-Vocational Institute: 9,741

Four-year
- University of New Mexico: 23,955

Office-based Physicians (98)
General/Family Practitioners: 148
Medical Specialists: 373
Surgical Specialists: 297

Public Libraries (94)
Albuquerque–Bernalillo County Library
14 branches; 1,771,836 books
$2.40 p/c book funds, 9.6 reading quotient

Public Transportation (100)
Albuquerque Sun Tran, 108 buses

Short-term General Hospital Services (99)
Kirtland Air Force Hospital
- Lovelace Medical Center
- Presbyterian Hospital
Presbyterian Kaseman
Presbyterian Northside
St. Joseph Medical Center
St. Joseph Northeast Heights
St. Joseph West Mesa Hospital
- University Hospital
VA Medical Center

Grade: 95

Alpine–Big Bend, TX
Continuing Education (100)
Four-year
- Sul Ross State University: 2,290

Office-based Physicians (79)
General/Family Practitioners: 3

Public Libraries (97)
Alpine Public Library
2 branches; 53,422 books
$0.90 p/c book funds, 12.2 reading quotient

Short-term General Hospital Services (68)
Big Bend Regional Medical Center

Grade: 69

Amador County, CA
Office-based Physicians (88)
General/Family Practitioners: 16
Medical Specialists: 7
Surgical Specialists: 4

Public Libraries (89)
Amador County Library
6 branches; 110,847 books
$1.00 p/c book funds, 8.0 reading quotient

Public Transportation (100)
Amador Rapid Transit, 9 buses

Short-term General Hospital Services (63)
Sutter Amador Hospital

Grade: 68

Amherst–Northampton, MA
Continuing Education (100)
Four-year
Amherst College: 1,602
Hampshire College: 1,316
Mount Holyoke College: 1,988
Smith College: 3,058
- University of Massachusetts: 26,032

Office-based Physicians (94)
General/Family Practitioners: 50
Medical Specialists: 86
Surgical Specialists: 43

Public Libraries (98)
23 independent libraries; 741,342 books
$2.80 p/c book funds, 12.1 reading quotient

Public Transportation (50)
Pioneer Valley Transit Authority, 9 buses

Short-term General Hospital Services (85)
Cooley Dickinson Hospital
Mary Lane Hospital
Northampton VA Medical Center

Grade: 85

Annapolis, MD
Continuing Education (81)
Two-year
Anne Arundel Community College: 12,152

Four-year
St. Johns College: 460

Office-based Physicians (86)
General/Family Practitioners: 77
Medical Specialists: 176
Surgical Specialists: 155

Public Libraries (94)
Part of Annapolis and Anne Arundel Public Library
14 branches; 1,099,122 books
$3.60 p/c book funds, 14.0 reading quotient

Public Transportation (51)
Annapolis Public Transit, 12 buses

Short-term General Hospital Services (86)
Anne Arundel Medical Center
- Crownsville Hospital Center
Kimbrough Army Community Hospital

Grade: 80

Asheville, NC
Continuing Education (73)
Two-year
- Asheville Buncombe Community College: 3,467

Four-year
Montreat-Anderson College: 387
- University of North Carolina: 3,271
Warren Wilson College: 573

Office-based Physicians (99)
General/Family Practitioners: 69
Medical Specialists: 127
Surgical Specialists: 107

Public Libraries (82)
Asheville-Buncombe Library System
9 branches; 146,980 books
$2.60 p/c book funds, 6.6 reading quotient

Public Transportation (57)
Asheville City Coach, 15 buses

Short-term General Hospital Services (93)
- Memorial Mission
St. Joseph's
VA Medical Center

Grade: 81

✓ Athens, GA
Continuing Education (100)
Four-year
- University of Georgia: 28,395

Office-based Physicians (97)
General/Family Practitioners: 21
Medical Specialists: 42
Surgical Specialists: 66

Public Libraries (82)
Athens Regional Library System
9 branches; 237,590 books
$1.80 p/c book funds, 6.4 reading quotient

Public Transportation (100)
Athens Transit System, 16 buses

Short-term General Hospital Services (88)
Athens Regional Medical Center
St. Mary's Hospital

Grade: 93

✓ Austin, TX
Continuing Education (95)
Two-year
- Austin Community College: 24,251

Four-year
Concordia Lutheran College: 680
Huston-Tillotson College: 714
St. Edward's University: 3,086
• University of Texas: 49,617
Office-based Physicians (95)
General/Family Practitioners: 184
Medical Specialists: 333
Surgical Specialists: 323
Public Libraries (85)
Austin Public Library
22 branches; 1,031,060 books
$1.80 p/c book funds, 8.1 reading quotient
Public Transportation (100)
Capital Metro, 139 buses
Short-term General Hospital Services (95)
• Brackenridge Hospital
St. David's Hospital
Seton Medical Center
South Austin Medical Center
Grade: 94

Bar Harbor, ME
Continuing Education (32)
Four-year
College of the Atlantic: 227
Office-based Physicians (95)
General/Family Practitioners: 21
Medical Specialists: 19
Surgical Specialists: 18
Public Libraries (100)
19 independent libraries; 284,179 books
$4.60 p/c book funds, 20.7 reading quotient
Public Transportation (97)
Downeast Transportation, 8 buses
Short-term General Hospital Services (85)
Blue Hill Memorial
Maine Coast Memorial
Mount Desert Island Hospital
Grade: 82

Bay St. Louis–Pass Christian, MS
Office-based Physicians (89)
General/Family Practitioners: 41
Medical Specialists: 65
Surgical Specialists: 87
Public Libraries (81)
Hancock County Library System
Harrison County Library System
13 branches; 382,715 books
$1.32 p/c book funds, 5.4 reading quotient
Public Transportation (85)
Coast RTA, 8 buses
Short-term General Hospital Services (93)
Biloxi Regional Medical Center
Biloxi VA Medical Center
Garden Park Community Hospital
Gulf Coast Medical Center
Hancock Medical Center
Keesler Air Force Medical Center
Memorial Hospital at Gulfport
Grade: 70

Beaufort, SC
Continuing Education (68)
Two-year
• Technical College of the Lowcountry: 1,210
• University of South Carolina: 896
Office-based Physicians (92)
General/Family Practitioners: 20
Medical Specialists: 32
Surgical Specialists: 53
Public Libraries (82)
Part of Beaufort County Library
4 branches; 113,022 books
$2.00 p/c book funds, 3.9 reading quotient

Public Transportation (50)
Lowcountry RTA, 3 buses
Short-term General Hospital Services (84)
Beaufort Memorial Hospital
Naval Hospital
Grade: 75

Beaver Lake, AR
Office-based Physicians (91)
General/Family Practitioners: 12
Medical Specialists: 2
Surgical Specialists: 2
Public Libraries (82)
Part of North Arkansas Regional Library
10 branches; 138,678 books
$1.70 p/c book funds, 6.7 reading quotient
Short-term General Hospital Services (71)
Carroll General Hospital
Eureka Springs Hospital
Grade: 49

✓**Bellingham, WA**
Continuing Education (89)
Two-year
• Whatcom Community College: 2,702
Four-year
• Western Washington University: 9,732
Office-based Physicians (94)
General/Family Practitioners: 52
Medical Specialists: 53
Surgical Specialists: 60
Public Libraries (96)
Bellingham Public Library
Whatcom County Rural Library District
13 branches; 416,572 books
$3.80 p/c book funds, 15.2 reading quotient
Public Transportation (82)
Whatcom Transit, 18 buses
Short-term General Hospital Services (85)
St. Joseph Hospital
Grade: 89

Bend, OR
Continuing Education (66)
Two-year
• Central Oregon Community College: 3,036
Office-based Physicians (95)
General/Family Practitioners: 27
Medical Specialists: 33
Surgical Specialists: 52
Public Libraries (83)
Deschutes County Library
4 branches; 130,977 books
$1.90 p/c book funds, 9.6 reading quotient
Short-term General Hospital Services (88)
Central Oregon District Hospital
• St. Charles Medical Center
Grade: 66

Blairsville, GA
Office-based Physicians (89)
General/Family Practitioners: 6
Medical Specialists: 2
Surgical Specialists: 2
Public Libraries (80)
Part of Mountain Regional Library System
4 branches; 74,414 books
$0.80 p/c book funds, 7.5 reading quotient
Short-term General Hospital Services (63)
Union General Hospital
Grade: 46

Boca Raton–Delray Beach, FL
Continuing Education (69)
Two-year
• Palm Beach Community College: 21,191

Four-year
   College of Boca Raton: 1,164
   • Florida Atlantic University: 11,459
   Palm Beach Atlantic College: 1,426
Office-based Physicians (94)
   General/Family Practitioners: 168
   Medical Specialists: 671
   Surgical Specialists: 549
Public Libraries (88)
   4 Independent Library Systems
   14 branches; 786,875 books
   $3.52 p/c book funds, 6.5 reading quotient
Public Transportation (50)
   COTRAN, 20 buses
Short-term General Hospital Services (95)
   Bethesda Memorial Hospital
   Boca Raton Community Hospital
   Delray Community Hospital
   Palm Beach Regional Hospital
   West Boca Medical Center
Grade: 79

Boone–Blowing Rock, NC
Continuing Education (100)
   Four-year
   • Appalachian State University: 11,931
Office-based Physicians (95)
   General/Family Practitioners: 13
   Medical Specialists: 16
   Surgical Specialists: 23
Public Libraries (79)
   Part of Appalachian Regional Library
   6 branches; 157,318 books
   $1.50 p/c book funds, 6.4 reading quotient
Public Transportation (66)
   Appalcart, 4 buses
Short-term General Hospital Services (85)
   Blowing Rock Hospital
   Watauga County Hospital
Grade: 85

Bradenton, FL
Continuing Education (64)
   Two-year
   • Manatee Community College: 7,874
Office-based Physicians (88)
   General/Family Practitioners: 51
   Medical Specialists: 91
   Surgical Specialists: 90
Public Libraries (77)
   Manatee County Public Library
   4 branches; 209,280 books
   $1.70 p/c book funds, 6.3 reading quotient
Public Transportation (50)
   Manatee County Transit, 9 buses
Short-term General Hospital Services (90)
   L. W. Blake Hospital
   Manatee Memorial Hospital
Grade: 74

Branson, MO
Continuing Education (77)
   Four-year
   College of the Ozarks: 1,512
Office-based Physicians (78)
   General/Family Practitioners: 7
   Medical Specialists: 2
   Surgical Specialists: 4
Public Libraries (67)
   2 independent libraries; 20,999 books
   $1.00 p/c book funds, 1.0 reading quotient
Short-term General Hospital Services (80)
   Skaggs Community Hospital
Grade: 60

Brevard, NC
Continuing Education (63)
   Two-year
   Brevard College: 779
Office-based Physicians (91)
   General/Family Practitioners: 9
   Medical Specialists: 6
   Surgical Specialists: 9
Public Libraries (91)
   Transylvania County Library
   1 branch; 58,991 books
   $3.00 p/c book funds, 11.5 reading quotient
Short-term General Hospital Services (62)
   Transylvania Community Hospital
Grade: 61

Brookings–Gold Beach, OR
Office-based Physicians (86)
   General/Family Practitioners: 8
   Medical Specialists: 4
   Surgical Specialists: 1
Public Libraries (95)
   5 independent libraries; 85,356 books
   $2.30 p/c book funds, 13.2 reading quotient
Short-term General Hospital Services (53)
   Curry General Hospital
Grade: 47

Brooksville–Spring Hill, FL
Office-based Physicians (80)
   General/Family Practitioners: 24
   Medical Specialists: 36
   Surgical Specialists: 25
Public Libraries (73)
   Hernando County Public Library System
   5 branches; 106,985 books
   $1.20 p/c book funds, 5.5 reading quotient
Short-term General Hospital Services (79)
   Brooksville Regional Hospital
   Oak Hill Hospital
   Spring Hill Regional Hospital
Grade: 47

✓**Burlington, VT**
Continuing Education (95)
   Two-year
   Champlain College: 1,916
   Four-year
   Burlington College: 173
   St. Michael's College: 2,577
   Trinity College: 1,118
   • University of Vermont: 11,076
Office-based Physicians (100)
   General/Family Practitioners: 48
   Medical Specialists: 133
   Surgical Specialists: 102
Public Libraries (90)
   23 independent libraries; 362,801 books
   $2.07 p/c book funds, 9.1 reading quotient
Public Transportation (97)
   Chittenden County Transit, 24 buses
Short-term General Hospital Services (92)
   Fanny Allen Hospital
   Medical Center Hospital of Vermont
Grade: 95

✓**Camden, ME**
Continuing Education (84)
   Four-year
   Colby College: 1,767
   Thomas College: 1,026
Office-based Physicians (95)
   General/Family Practitioners: 10
   Medical Specialists: 24
   Surgical Specialists: 17

Public Libraries (100)
12 independent libraries; 187,073 books
$3.50 p/c book funds, 19.4 reading quotient
Public Transportation (100)
Coastal Transit, 10 buses
Short-term General Hospital Services (80)
Penobscot Bay Medical Center
Grade: 92

Cape Cod, MA
Continuing Education (59)
Two-year
• Cape Cod Community College: 4,496
Office-based Physicians (92)
General/Family Practitioners: 45
Medical Specialists: 98
Surgical Specialists: 79
Public Libraries (77)
32 independent libraries; 740,360 books
$1.20 p/c book funds, 4.7 reading quotient
Public Transportation (100)
Cape Cod RTA, 43 buses
Short-term General Hospital Services (86)
• Cape Cod Hospital
Falmouth Hospital
Grade: 83

Carmel–Monterey–Pebble Beach, CA
Continuing Education (86)
Two-year
• Hartnell College: 6,762
• Monterey Peninsula College: 6,505
Office-based Physicians (88)
General/Family Practitioners: 82
Medical Specialists: 128
Surgical Specialists: 134
Public Libraries (92)
Part of 4 Independent Library Systems
21 branches; 770,050 books
$2.43 p/c book funds, 9.8 reading quotient
Short-term General Hospital Services (94)
Community Hospital of the Monterey Peninsula
Grade: 72

Carson City–Carson Valley, NV
Continuing Education (80)
Two-year
• Western Nevada Community College: 5,320
Office-based Physicians (88)
General/Family Practitioners: 18
Medical Specialists: 21
Surgical Specialists: 24
Public Libraries (85)
Carson City Library
Douglas County Library
3 branches; 171,370 books
$1.40 p/c book funds, 8.4 reading quotient
Short-term General Hospital Services (82)
Carson Tahoe Hospital
Grade: 67

Cedar Creek Lake, TX
Continuing Education (80)
Two-year
• Trinity Valley Community College: 4,275
Office-based Physicians (79)
General/Family Practitioners: 15
Medical Specialists: 4
Surgical Specialists: 8
Public Libraries (70)
Clint Murchison Memorial Library
4 branches; 82,600 books
$0.30 p/c book funds, 3.8 reading quotient
Short-term General Hospital Services (60)
East Texas Medical Center–Athens
Grade: 58

✓**Chapel Hill, NC**
Continuing Education (100)
Four-year
• University of North Carolina: 23,878
Office-based Physicians (100)
General/Family Practitioners: 61
Medical Specialists: 164
Surgical Specialists: 100
Public Libraries (91)
Chapel Hill Public Library
1 branch; 98,851 books
$2.70 p/c book funds, 17.6 reading quotient
Public Transportation (100)
Durham–Chapel Hill Transit, 27 buses
Short-term General Hospital Services (94)
• University of North Carolina Hospitals
Grade: 97

Charles Town–Harpers Ferry–Shepherdstown, WV
Continuing Education (93)
Four-year
• Shepherd College: 3,694
Office-based Physicians (79)
General/Family Practitioners: 7
Medical Specialists: 7
Surgical Specialists: 6
Public Libraries (82)
4 independent libraries; 100,301 books
$0.50 p/c book funds, 7.3 reading quotient
Public Transportation (56)
Eastern Panhandle Transit Authority, 3 buses
Short-term General Hospital Services (66)
Jefferson Memorial Hospital
Grade: 75

Charleston Sea Islands, SC
Continuing Education (80)
Two-year
Johnson and Wales University: 567
• Trident Technical College: 6,939
Four-year
Charleston Southern University: 2,158
• College of Charleston: 7,726
Office-based Physicians (100)
General/Family Practitioners: 88
Medical Specialists: 279
Surgical Specialists: 270
Public Libraries (91)
Charleston County Library
15 branches; 659,488 books
$2.90 p/c book funds, 6.3 reading quotient
Public Transportation (76)
South Carolina Electric & Gas, 34 buses
Short-term General Hospital Services (98)
Baker Hospital
Bon Secours–St. Francis Hospital
• Charleston Memorial Hospital
• MUSC Medical Center
Naval Hospital
• Roper Hospital
Trident Regional Medical Center
VA Medical Center
Grade: 89

Charlevoix–Boyne City–East Jordan, MI
Office-based Physicians (83)
General/Family Practitioners: 6
Medical Specialists: 5
Surgical Specialists: 3
Public Libraries (95)
6 independent libraries; 78,468 books
$3.00 p/c book funds, 8.0 reading quotient
Short-term General Hospital Services (68)
Charlevoix Area Hospital
Grade: 49

✓Charlottesville, VA
Continuing Education (100)
Two-year
- Piedmont Virginia Community College: 4,203

Four-year
- University of Virginia: 21,110

Office-based Physicians (100)
General/Family Practitioners: 39
Medical Specialists: 204
Surgical Specialists: 151
Public Libraries (89)
Part of Jefferson-Madison Regional Library
8 branches; 335,135 books
$2.50 p/c book funds, 11.1 reading quotient
Public Transportation (67)
Charlottesville Transit, 11 buses
Short-term General Hospital Services (98)
Martha Jefferson Hospital
- University of Virginia Medical Center

Grade: 91

Chewelah, WA
Office-based Physicians (90)
General/Family Practitioners: 17
Medical Specialists: 3
Surgical Specialists: 3
Public Libraries (100)
Part of 3 Independent Library Systems
3 branches; 47,453 books
$9.02 p/c book funds, 25.7 reading quotient
Short-term General Hospital Services (77)
St. Joseph's Hospital
Grade: 53

Clayton, GA
Office-based Physicians (93)
General/Family Practitioners: 6
Medical Specialists: 3
Surgical Specialists: 3
Public Libraries (81)
Part of Northeast Georgia Regional Library
6 branches; 161,129 books
$1.10 p/c book funds, 7.7 reading quotient
Short-term General Hospital Services (63)
Rabun County Memorial Hospital
Ridgecrest Hospital
Grade: 48

Clemson–Pendleton District, SC
Continuing Education (100)
Two-year
- Tri-County Technical College: 2,935

Four-year
Central Wesleyan College: 934
- Clemson University: 15,714

Office-based Physicians (88)
General/Family Practitioners: 100
Medical Specialists: 63
Surgical Specialists: 85
Public Libraries (79)
Oconee County Library System
Part of Pickens County Library System
9 branches; 208,229 books
$1.52 p/c book funds, 4.9 reading quotient
Short-term General Hospital Services (89)
Oconee Memorial Hospital
Grade: 71

Coeur d'Alene, ID
Continuing Education (67)
Two-year
- North Idaho College: 2,820

Office-based Physicians (94)
General/Family Practitioners: 36
Medical Specialists: 20
Surgical Specialists: 28

Public Libraries (79)
Coeur d'Alene Public Library
Kootenai County District Library
8 branches; 150,087 books
$0.70 p/c book funds, 9.6 reading quotient
Public Transportation (87)
North Idaho Express, 11 buses
Short-term General Hospital Services (87)
Kootenai Medical Center
Grade: 83

Colorado Springs, CO
Continuing Education (72)
Two-year
Nazarene Bible College: 424
- Pikes Peak Community College: 7,791

Four-year
Colorado College: 1,955
- University of Colorado: 6,650

Office-based Physicians (88)
General/Family Practitioners: 76
Medical Specialists: 153
Surgical Specialists: 174
Public Libraries (96)
Pikes Peak Library District
14 branches; 912,656 books
$4.40 p/c book funds, 9.7 reading quotient
Public Transportation (64)
Colorado Springs Transit, 39 buses
Short-term General Hospital Services (97)
Air Force Academy Hospital
Memorial Hospital
- Penrose–St. Francis Healthcare System

Grade: 84

Conway, SC
Continuing Education (98)
Two-year
- Horry-Georgetown Technical College: 1,984

Four-year
- University of Coastal Carolina: 4,080

Office-based Physicians (87)
General/Family Practitioners: 37
Medical Specialists: 37
Surgical Specialists: 60
Public Libraries (72)
Part of Horry County Memorial Library
6 branches; 159,952 books
$0.89 p/c book funds, 3.7 reading quotient
Public Transportation (67)
Coastal Rapid Public Transit, 4 buses
Short-term General Hospital Services (82)
Conway Hospital
Grade: 81

Cottonwood–Verde Valley, AZ
Continuing Education (73)
Two-year
- Yavapai College: 6,003

Four-year
Prescott College: 593
Office-based Physicians (86)
General/Family Practitioners: 34
Medical Specialists: 30
Surgical Specialists: 35
Public Libraries (92)
Part of Yavapai County Library District
18 branches; 294,385 books
$2.70 p/c book funds, 10.2 reading quotient
Short-term General Hospital Services (91)
Marcus J. Lawrence Medical Center
Grade: 68

Crossville, TN
Office-based Physicians (89)
General/Family Practitioners: 9

Medical Specialists: 8
Surgical Specialists: 17
Public Libraries (61)
Art Circle Public Library
1 branch; 14,524 books
$0.50 p/c book funds, 6.1 reading quotient
Short-term General Hospital Services (77)
Cumberland Medical Center
Grade: 45

Dare Outer Banks, NC
Office-based Physicians (78)
General/Family Practitioners: 8
Medical Specialists: 2
Public Libraries (84)
Part of East Albemarle Regional Library
5 branches; 151,933 books
$1.60 p/c book funds, 7.0 reading quotient
Grade: 32

Daytona Beach, FL
Continuing Education (81)
Two-year
• Daytona Beach Community College: 10,250
Four-year
Bethune Cookman College: 2,145
Embry-Riddle Aeronautical University: 11,215
Stetson University: 3,092
Office-based Physicians (87)
General/Family Practitioners: 79
Medical Specialists: 120
Surgical Specialists: 144
Public Libraries (75)
Volusia County Public Library
15 branches; 756,128 books
$1.10 p/c book funds, 7.3 reading quotient
Public Transportation (60)
VOTRAN, 34 buses
Short-term General Hospital Services (96)
Bert Fish Medical Center
Daytona Medical Center
Fish Memorial Hospital at Deland
• Halifax Medical Center
Memorial Hospital–Ormond Beach
Peninsula Medical Center
West Volusia Memorial Hospital
Grade: 80

Delta–Cedaredge, CO
Office-based Physicians (86)
General/Family Practitioners: 8
Medical Specialists: 4
Surgical Specialists: 2
Public Libraries (90)
5 independent libraries; 70,528 books
$1.70 p/c book funds, 12.1 reading quotient
Short-term General Hospital Services (73)
Delta County Memorial Hospital
Grade: 50

Durango, CO
Continuing Education (96)
Four-year
• Fort Lewis College: 3,939
Office-based Physicians (100)
General/Family Practitioners: 17
Medical Specialists: 10
Surgical Specialists: 24
Public Libraries (88)
3 independent libraries; 93,483 books
$2.20 p/c book funds, 8.9 reading quotient
Public Transportation (62)
The Durango Lift, 3 buses
Short-term General Hospital Services (84)
Mercy Medical Center
Grade: 86

Eagle River, WI
Office-based Physicians (88)
General/Family Practitioners: 9
Medical Specialists: 2
Surgical Specialists: 1
Public Libraries (100)
9 independent libraries; 94,836 books
$3.90 p/c book funds, 15.2 reading quotient
Short-term General Hospital Services (68)
Eagle River Memorial Hospital
Northwoods Hospital
Grade: 51

East End Long Island, NY
Continuing Education (63)
Four-year
Long Island University Southampton College: 1,257
Office-based Physicians (92)
General/Family Practitioners: 236
Medical Specialists: 817
Surgical Specialists: 546
Public Libraries (100)
11 independent libraries; 372,437 books
$13.92 p/c book funds, 36.4 reading quotient
Short-term General Hospital Services (99)
Eastern Long Island Hospital
Southampton Hospital
• Southside Hospital
Grade: 71

Easton–St. Michaels–Oxford, MD
Office-based Physicians (100)
General/Family Practitioners: 10
Medical Specialists: 27
Surgical Specialists: 30
Public Libraries (90)
Talbot County Free Library
2 branches; 101,958 books
$1.20 p/c book funds, 9.8 reading quotient
Short-term General Hospital Services (85)
Memorial Hospital
Grade: 55

Edenton, NC
Office-based Physicians (96)
General/Family Practitioners: 6
Medical Specialists: 3
Surgical Specialists: 7
Public Libraries (90)
Part of Pettigrew Regional Library
4 branches; 120,881 books
$2.00 p/c book funds, 7.9 reading quotient
Short-term General Hospital Services (78)
Chowan Hospital
Grade: 53

Fairhope–Gulf Shores, AL
Continuing Education (62)
Two-year
• Faulkner State Junior College: 3,109
Office-based Physicians (85)
General/Family Practitioners: 28
Medical Specialists: 25
Surgical Specialists: 29
Public Libraries (82)
10 independent libraries; 178,013 books
$1.60 p/c book funds, 6.3 reading quotient
Short-term General Hospital Services (78)
Mercy Medical
North Baldwin Hospital
South Baldwin Hospital
Thomas Hospital
Grade: 61

Fayetteville, AR
Continuing Education (97)
Four-year
• University of Arkansas: 14,433
Office-based Physicians (96)
General/Family Practitioners: 45
Medical Specialists: 46
Surgical Specialists: 59
Public Libraries (83)
Part of Ozarks Regional Library
14 branches; 288,626 books
$2.00 p/c book funds, 6.8 reading quotient
Public Transportation (69)
Ozark Transit, 12 buses
Short-term General Hospital Services (92)
Fayetteville City Hospital
Springdale Memorial Hospital
VA Medical Center
• Washington Regional Medical Center
Grade: 87

Florence, OR
Office-based Physicians (95)
General/Family Practitioners: 106
Medical Specialists: 125
Surgical Specialists: 131
Public Libraries (98)
Siuslaw Public Library District
1 branch; 50,257 books
$4.40 p/c book funds, 15.4 reading quotient
Short-term General Hospital Services (73)
Cottage Grove Hospital
McKenzie-Willamette Hospital
Peace Harbor Hospital
Sacred Heart General Hospital
Grade: 53

Fort Collins–Loveland, CO
Continuing Education (98)
Four-year
• Colorado State University: 26,837
Office-based Physicians (94)
General/Family Practitioners: 87
Medical Specialists: 56
Surgical Specialists: 80
Public Libraries (87)
5 independent libraries; 362,632 books
$2.30 p/c book funds, 11.0 reading quotient
Public Transportation (50)
TRANSFORT, 12 buses
Short-term General Hospital Services (94)
• Estes Park Medical Center
McKee Medical Center
• Poudre Valley Hospital
Grade: 84

Fort Myers–Cape Coral, FL
Continuing Education (57)
Two-year
• Edison Community College: 8,695
Office-based Physicians (88)
General/Family Practitioners: 63
Medical Specialists: 160
Surgical Specialists: 163
Public Libraries (95)
Lee County Library System
13 branches; 603,015 books
$4.90 p/c book funds, 8.3 reading quotient
Public Transportation (50)
Lee County Transit, 25 buses
Short-term General Hospital Services (91)
Cape Coral Hospital
East Pointe Hospital
Gulf Coast Hospital
Lee Memorial Hospital
Southwest Florida Regional Medical Center
Grade: 76

Fredericksburg, TX
Office-based Physicians (100)
General/Family Practitioners: 12
Medical Specialists: 5
Surgical Specialists: 10
Public Libraries (80)
Pioneer Memorial Library
1 branch; 38,933 books
$0.80 p/c book funds, 7.7 reading quotient
Short-term General Hospital Services (63)
Hill Country Memorial Hospital
Grade: 49

Fredericksburg–Spotsylvania, VA
Continuing Education (76)
Four-year
• Mary Washington College: 3,744
Office-based Physicians (90)
General/Family Practitioners: 15
Medical Specialists: 42
Surgical Specialists: 45
Public Libraries (88)
Part of Central Rappahannock Regional Library
6 branches; 207,539 books
$3.10 p/c book funds, 9.4 reading quotient
Short-term General Hospital Services (85)
Mary Washington Hospital
Grade: 68

✓ Gainesville, FL
Continuing Education (100)
Two-year
• Santa Fe Community College: 10,140
Four-year
• University of Florida: 34,098
Office-based Physicians (100)
General/Family Practitioners: 70
Medical Specialists: 193
Surgical Specialists: 168
Public Libraries (98)
Alachua County Library District
8 branches; 451,052 books
$5.30 p/c book funds, 9.9 reading quotient
Public Transportation (97)
Gainesville RTS, 32 buses
Short-term General Hospital Services (99)
• Alachua General Hospital
North Florida Regional Medical Center
• Shands Hospital at the University of Florida
VA Medical Center
Grade: 99

Grand Junction, CO
Continuing Education (79)
Four-year
• Mesa State College: 4,613
Office-based Physicians (94)
General/Family Practitioners: 38
Medical Specialists: 34
Surgical Specialists: 39
Public Libraries (87)
Mesa Public Library District
6 branches; 200,000 books
$2.20 p/c book funds, 8.7 reading quotient
Short-term General Hospital Services (95)
Community Hospital
Family Health West
• St. Mary's Hospital and Medical Center
VA Medical Center
Grade: 71

Grants Pass, OR
Continuing Education (66)
Two-year
• Rogue Community College: 2,312

Office-based Physicians (90)
General/Family Practitioners: 20
Medical Specialists: 19
Surgical Specialists: 22
Public Libraries (76)
Josephine County Library System
2 branches; 138,330 books
$0.20 p/c book funds, 6.9 reading quotient
Short-term General Hospital Services (69)
Josephine Memorial Hospital
Southern Oregon Medical Center
Grade: 60

Grass Valley–Nevada City, CA
Office-based Physicians (92)
General/Family Practitioners: 34
Medical Specialists: 30
Surgical Specialists: 37
Public Libraries (72)
Nevada County Library System
4 branches; 91,544 books
$0.90 p/c book funds, 4.7 reading quotient
Public Transportation (64)
Nevada County TC, 9 buses
Short-term General Hospital Services (81)
Sierra Nevada Memorial Hospital
Tahoe Forest Hospital District
Grade: 62

Guntersville, AL
Continuing Education (38)
Two-year
• Snead State Junior College: 603
Office-based Physicians (83)
General/Family Practitioners: 24
Medical Specialists: 8
Surgical Specialists: 10
Public Libraries (86)
6 independent libraries; 173,249 books
$1.60 p/c book funds, 7.3 reading quotient
Short-term General Hospital Services (66)
Boaz-Albertville Medical Center
Guntersville-Arab Medical Center
Grade: 55

Hamilton–Bitterroot Valley, MT
Office-based Physicians (86)
General/Family Practitioners: 10
Medical Specialists: 3
Surgical Specialists: 4
Public Libraries (80)
3 independent libraries; 55,993 books
$0.60 p/c book funds, 5.4 reading quotient
Short-term General Hospital Services (78)
Marcus Daly Memorial Hospital
Grade: 49

✓ **Hanover, NH**
Continuing Education (94)
Four-year
Dartmouth College: 4,862
• Plymouth State College: 4,365
Office-based Physicians (100)
General/Family Practitioners: 27
Medical Specialists: 93
Surgical Specialists: 62
Public Libraries (92)
41 independent libraries; 554,794 books
$1.80 p/c book funds, 8.2 reading quotient
Public Transportation (92)
Advance Transit, 12 buses
Short-term General Hospital Services (96)
Alice Peck Day Memorial Hospital
Cottage Hospital
Littleton Regional Hospital
• Mary Hitchcock Memorial Hospital
Speare Memorial Hospital
Grade: 95

Hendersonville–East Flat Rock, NC
Continuing Education (56)
Two-year
• Blue Ridge Community College: 1,449
Office-based Physicians (93)
General/Family Practitioners: 20
Medical Specialists: 27
Surgical Specialists: 35
Public Libraries (89)
Henderson County Public Library
5 branches; 142,793 books
$2.70 p/c book funds, 10.2 reading quotient
Short-term General Hospital Services (84)
Pardee Memorial Hospital
Park Ridge Hospital
Grade: 64

Hesperia–Apple Valley–Victorville, CA
Continuing Education (60)
Two-year
• Victor Valley College: 4,858
Office-based Physicians (87)
General/Family Practitioners: 308
Medical Specialists: 569
Surgical Specialists: 486
Public Libraries (78)
Part of San Bernardino County Library System
28 branches; 1,058,911 books
$1.65 p/c book funds, 4.2 reading quotient
Public Transportation (50)
Victor Valley Transit Authority, 18 buses
Short-term General Hospital Services (98)
St. Mary Desert Valley Hospital
Victor Valley Community Hospital
Grade: 74

Hiawassee, GA
Continuing Education (78)
Two-year
Young Harris College: 435
Office-based Physicians (86)
General/Family Practitioners: 3
Medical Specialists: 1
Public Libraries (80)
Part of Mountain Regional Library System
4 branches; 74,414 books
$0.80 p/c book funds, 7.5 reading quotient
Short-term General Hospital Services (50)
Hospital Authority of Towns County
Grade: 59

Hilton Head Island, SC
Continuing Education (77)
Two-year
• Technical College of the Lowcountry: 1,210
• University of South Carolina, Beaufort: 896
Office-based Physicians (92)
General/Family Practitioners: 20
Medical Specialists: 32
Surgical Specialists: 53
Public Libraries (82)
Part of Beaufort County Library System
4 branches; 113,022 books
$2.00 p/c book funds, 3.9 reading quotient
Public Transportation (61)
Lowcountry RTA, 3 buses
Short-term General Hospital Services (84)
Hilton Head Hospital
Grade: 79

Hot Springs, AR
Continuing Education (59)
Two-year
• Garland County Community College: 1,744
Office-based Physicians (94)
General/Family Practitioners: 21

Medical Specialists: 38
Surgical Specialists: 34
Public Libraries (77)
Part of Tri Lakes Regional Library
4 branches; 143,626 books
$1.10 p/c book funds, 4.4 reading quotient
Public Transportation (95)
Hot Springs Intra-City Transit, 12 buses
Short-term General Hospital Services (87)
AMI National Park Medical Center
St. Joseph's Regional Health Center
Grade: 82

Houghton Lake, MI
Continuing Education (77)
Two-year
• Kirtland Community College: 1,271
Office-based Physicians (75)
General/Family Practitioners: 5
Medical Specialists: 1
Surgical Specialists: 1
Public Libraries (92)
3 independent libraries; 81,882 books
$2.20 p/c book funds, 6.7 reading quotient
Grade: 49

Inverness, FL
Office-based Physicians (82)
General/Family Practitioners: 15
Medical Specialists: 36
Surgical Specialists: 28
Public Libraries (84)
Citrus County Library System
7 branches; 125,930 books
$2.40 p/c book funds, 6.5 reading quotient
Short-term General Hospital Services (76)
Citrus Memorial Hospital
Seven Rivers Community Hospital
Grade: 48

Kalispell–Flathead Valley, MT
Continuing Education (62)
Two-year
• Flathead Valley Community College: 1,824
Office-based Physicians (97)
General/Family Practitioners: 31
Medical Specialists: 30
Surgical Specialists: 26
Public Libraries (86)
Flathead County Library
5 branches; 164,213 books
$1.20 p/c book funds, 10.8 reading quotient
Short-term General Hospital Services (89)
Kalispell Regional Hospital
North Valley Hospital
Grade: 67

Kauai, HI
Continuing Education (56)
Two-year
• Kauai Community College: 1,231
Office-based Physicians (91)
General/Family Practitioners: 20
Medical Specialists: 22
Surgical Specialists: 20
Public Libraries (96)
Part of Hawaii State Library System
5 local branches; 158,778 books
$3.89 p/c book funds, 8.8 reading quotient
Short-term General Hospital Services (80)
Kauai Veterans Memorial Hospital
Wilcox Memorial Hospital
Grade: 65

Kentucky Lake, KY
Continuing Education (99)
Four-year
• Murray State University: 8,079
Office-based Physicians (83)
General/Family Practitioners: 13
Medical Specialists: 9
Surgical Specialists: 17
Public Libraries (85)
Calloway County Public Library
Marshall County Public Library
4 branches; 160,159 books
$1.13 p/c book funds, 9.6 reading quotient
Public Transportation (77)
Murray-Calloway County Transit Authority, 7 buses
Short-term General Hospital Services (84)
Marshall County Hospital
Murray Calloway County Hospital
Grade: 86

Kerrville, TX
Continuing Education (53)
Four-year
Schreiner College: 592
Office-based Physicians (91)
General/Family Practitioners: 9
Medical Specialists: 16
Surgical Specialists: 19
Public Libraries (88)
Butt-Holdsworth Memorial Library
1 branch; 80,745 books
$2.30 p/c book funds, 8.1 reading quotient
Short-term General Hospital Services (87)
Sid Peterson Memorial Hospital
Starlite Village Hospital
VA Medical Center
Grade: 64

Ketchum–Sun Valley, ID
Office-based Physicians (100)
General/Family Practitioners: 9
Medical Specialists: 7
Surgical Specialists: 13
Public Libraries (97)
3 independent libraries; 23,244 books
$3.30 p/c book funds, 10.5 reading quotient
Public Transportation (100)
Ketchum–Sun Valley Transit, 3 buses
Short-term General Hospital Services (75)
Wood River Medical Center
Grade: 75

Key West–Key Largo–Marathon, FL
Continuing Education (64)
Two-year
• Florida Keys Community College: 2,734
Office-based Physicians (84)
General/Family Practitioners: 15
Medical Specialists: 23
Surgical Specialists: 28
Public Libraries (81)
Monroe County Public Library System
4 branches; 150,303 books
$1.30 p/c book funds, 5.6 reading quotient
Public Transportation (71)
Key West Port and Transit Authority, 9 buses
Short-term General Hospital Services (67)
Fishermen's Hospital
Lower Florida Keys Health Systems
Mariners Hospital
Grade: 73

Kingman, AZ
Continuing Education (67)
Two-year
• Mohave Community College: 4,967

Office-based Physicians (79)
General/Family Practitioners: 23
Medical Specialists: 22
Surgical Specialists: 29
Public Libraries (69)
Part of Mohave County Library District
9 branches; 81,771 books
$0.90 p/c book funds, 3.7 reading quotient
Short-term General Hospital Services (81)
Kingman Regional Medical Center
Grade: 59

Kissimmee–St. Cloud, FL
Continuing Education (18)
Four-year
Florida Bible College: 180
Florida Christian College: 124
Office-based Physicians (79)
General/Family Practitioners: 19
Medical Specialists: 31
Surgical Specialists: 31
Public Libraries (95)
Osceola County Library System
8 branches; 220,000 books
$4.50 p/c book funds, 6.5 reading quotient
Short-term General Hospital Services (79)
Florida Hospital Kissimmee
Osceola Regional Hospital
St. Cloud Hospital
Grade: 54

Laguna Beach–Dana Point, CA
Continuing Education (25)
Four-year
Art Institute of Southern California: 127
Office-based Physicians (97)
General/Family Practitioners: 792
Medical Specialists: 1,575
Surgical Specialists: 1,313
Public Libraries (91)
Part of Orange County Public Library System
27 branches; 2,023,612 books
$3.71 p/c book funds, 7.0 reading quotient
Short-term General Hospital Services (99)
Mission Hospital Regional Medical Center
Saddleback Memorial Medical Center
Grade: 62

Lake Buchanan–Lake LBJ, TX
Office-based Physicians (84)
General/Family Practitioners: 12
Medical Specialists: 2
Surgical Specialists: 6
Public Libraries (91)
Burnet County Library System
Llano County Library System
7 branches; 118,741 books
$1.76 p/c book funds, 12.6 reading quotient
Short-term General Hospital Services (63)
Highland Lakes Medical Center
Llano Memorial Hospital
Grade: 48

Lake Conroe, TX
Office-based Physicians (73)
General/Family Practitioners: 26
Medical Specialists: 27
Surgical Specialists: 35
Public Libraries (75)
Part of Montgomery County Library System
7 branches; 177,007 books
$1.40 p/c book funds, 3.9 reading quotient
Short-term General Hospital Services (86)
Doctors Hospital
• Medical Center Hospital
Memorial Hospital–The Woodlands
Grade: 47

Lake Granbury, TX
Office-based Physicians (70)
General/Family Practitioners: 4
Medical Specialists: 2
Surgical Specialists: 5
Public Libraries (71)
Hood County Library
1 branch; 31,575 books
$0.80 p/c book funds, 3.6 reading quotient
Short-term General Hospital Services (65)
Hood General Hospital
Grade: 41

Lake Havasu City, AZ
Continuing Education (67)
Two-year
• Mohave Community College: 4,967
Office-based Physicians (79)
General/Family Practitioners: 23
Medical Specialists: 22
Surgical Specialists: 29
Public Libraries (69)
Part of Mohave County Library District
9 branches; 81,771 books
$0.90 p/c book funds, 3.7 reading quotient
Short-term General Hospital Services (81)
Havasu Samaritan Regional Hospital
Kingman Regional Medical Center
Grade: 59

Lake Livingston, TX
Office-based Physicians (66)
General/Family Practitioners: 10
Medical Specialists: 1
Surgical Specialists: 2
Public Libraries (82)
8 independent libraries; 106,990 books
$0.91 p/c book funds, 6.3 reading quotient
Short-term General Hospital Services (50)
Polk County Memorial Hospital
Trinity Memorial Hospital
Grade: 40

Lake Martin, AL
Continuing Education (74)
Two-year
• Central Alabama Community College: 2,097
Office-based Physicians (84)
General/Family Practitioners: 10
Medical Specialists: 8
Surgical Specialists: 8
Public Libraries (74)
4 independent libraries; 173,916 books
$0.70 p/c book funds, 2.5 reading quotient
Short-term General Hospital Services (69)
Lakeshore Community Hospital
Russell Hospital
Grade: 60

Lake of the Cherokees, OK
Office-based Physicians (81)
General/Family Practitioners: 8
Medical Specialists: 3
Surgical Specialists: 4
Public Libraries (78)
Part of Eastern Oklahoma District Library
13 branches; 222,816 books
$1.60 p/c book funds, 4.9 reading quotient
Short-term General Hospital Services (57)
Grove General Hospital
Grade: 43

Lake of the Ozarks, MO
Office-based Physicians (80)
General/Family Practitioners: 8
Surgical Specialists: 6

Public Libraries (90)
Camden County Library District
6 branches; 66,331 books
$2.50 p/c book funds, 9.5 reading quotient
Short-term General Hospital Services (80)
Lake of the Ozarks General Hospital
Grade: 50

Lake Winnipesaukee, NH
Continuing Education (47)
Two-year
• New Hampshire Technical College: 1,068
Office-based Physicians (94)
General/Family Practitioners: 27
Medical Specialists: 34
Surgical Specialists: 40
Public Libraries (100)
29 independent libraries; 475,514 books
$3.73 p/c book funds, 16.2 reading quotient
Short-term General Hospital Services (85)
Huggins Hospital
Lakes Region General Hospital
Memorial Hospital
Grade: 65

Lakeland–Winter Haven, FL
Continuing Education (63)
Two-year
• Polk Community College: 6,712
Four-year
Florida Southern College: 2,691
Southeastern College Assemblies of God: 1,130
Warner Southern College: 423
Webber College: 250
Office-based Physicians (87)
General/Family Practitioners: 67
Medical Specialists: 157
Surgical Specialists: 154
Public Libraries (89)
7 independent libraries; 409,914 books
$2.20 p/c book funds, 8.1 reading quotient
Public Transportation (50)
Citrus CONNECT, 14 buses
Short-term General Hospital Services (92)
Bartow Memorial Hospital
Lake Wales Medical Centers
Lakeland Regional Medical Center
Midflorida Health Center
Polk General Hospital
Winter Haven Hospital
Grade: 76

Las Cruces, NM
Continuing Education (96)
Two-year
• New Mexico State University, Dona Ana: 3,290
Four-year
• New Mexico State University: 14,812
Office-based Physicians (87)
General/Family Practitioners: 37
Medical Specialists: 40
Surgical Specialists: 42
Public Libraries (90)
3 independent libraries; 177,950 books
$2.40 p/c book funds, 7.6 reading quotient
Public Transportation (50)
ROADRUNNER, 8 buses
Short-term General Hospital Services (82)
Memorial Medical Center
Grade: 81

Las Vegas, NV
Continuing Education (70)
Two-year
• Clark County Community College: 12,955
Four-year
• University of Nevada: 17,938

Office-based Physicians (85)
General/Family Practitioners: 134
Medical Specialists: 319
Surgical Specialists: 290
Public Libraries (86)
Las Vegas–Clark County District Library
28 branches; 1,190,380 books
$2.70 p/c book funds, 6.4 reading quotient
Public Transportation (90)
Las Vegas Transit, 32 buses
Short-term General Hospital Services (97)
Boulder City Hospital
Desert Springs Hospital
Lake Mead Hospital Medical Center
Nellis Air Force Hospital
St. Rose Dominican Hospital
Sunrise Hospital and Medical Center
• University Medical Center
Valley Hospital Medical Center
• Womens Hospital
Grade: 86

Leesburg–Lady Lake, FL
Continuing Education (45)
Two-year
• Lake-Sumter Community College: 2,192
Office-based Physicians (85)
General/Family Practitioners: 37
Medical Specialists: 51
Surgical Specialists: 56
Public Libraries (77)
7 independent libraries; 273,963 books
$1.20 p/c book funds, 5.2 reading quotient
Short-term General Hospital Services (84)
Florida Hospital
Leesburg Regional Medical Center
South Lake Memorial Hospital
Grade: 58

Litchfield Hills, CT
Continuing Education (47)
Two-year
• Northwestern Connecticut Community College: 2,204
Office-based Physicians (88)
General/Family Practitioners: 27
Medical Specialists: 89
Surgical Specialists: 55
Public Libraries (100)
29 independent libraries; 812,117 books
$3.20 p/c book funds, 12.1 reading quotient
Public Transportation (50)
Northwestern Connecticut Transit District, 7 buses
Short-term General Hospital Services (89)
Charlotte Hungerford Hospital
New Milford Hospital
Sharon Hospital
Winsted Memorial Hospital
Grade: 75

Lower Cape May, NJ
Office-based Physicians (80)
General/Family Practitioners: 16
Medical Specialists: 23
Surgical Specialists: 17
Public Libraries (100)
4 independent libraries; 438,961 books
$5.30 p/c book funds, 11.1 reading quotient
Public Transportation (90)
Fare-Free Transportation, 9 buses
Short-term General Hospital Services (73)
Burdette Tomlin Memorial Hospital
Grade: 69

Madison, MS
Continuing Education (56)
Four-year
Tougaloo College: 956

Office-based Physicians (86)
General/Family Practitioners: 17
Medical Specialists: 23
Surgical Specialists: 4
Public Libraries (80)
Madison County–Canton Public Library
4 branches; 87,450 books
$1.40 p/c book funds, 4.5 reading quotient
Short-term General Hospital Services (47)
Madison General Hospital
Grade: 54

Maryville, TN
Continuing Education (45)
Four-year
Maryville College: 841
Office-based Physicians (86)
General/Family Practitioners: 18
Medical Specialists: 33
Surgical Specialists: 28
Public Libraries (75)
Blount County Public Library
1 branch; 61,365 books
$1.20 p/c book funds, 6.4 reading quotient
Short-term General Hospital Services (85)
Blount Memorial Hospital
Grade: 58

Maui, HI
Continuing Education (52)
Two-year
• Maui Community College: 1,995
Office-based Physicians (91)
General/Family Practitioners: 32
Medical Specialists: 44
Surgical Specialists: 53
Public Libraries (96)
Part of Hawaii State Library System
8 local branches; 315,184 books
$3.89 p/c book funds, 8.8 reading quotient
Short-term General Hospital Services (75)
Lanai Community Hospital
Maui Memorial Hospital
Molokai General Hospital
Grade: 63

McCall–Cascade–Payette Valley, ID
Office-based Physicians (95)
General/Family Practitioners: 4
Medical Specialists: 2
Surgical Specialists: 2
Public Libraries (100)
2 independent libraries; 40,035 books
$4.20 p/c book funds, 40.7 reading quotient
Short-term General Hospital Services (59)
McCall Memorial Hospital
Valley County Hospital
Grade: 51

Medford–Ashland, OR
Continuing Education (72)
Four-year
• Southern Oregon State College: 5,196
Office-based Physicians (95)
General/Family Practitioners: 48
Medical Specialists: 77
Surgical Specialists: 80
Public Libraries (91)
Jackson County Library System
15 branches; 344,110 books
$2.90 p/c book funds, 9.5 reading quotient
Public Transportation (83)
Rogue Valley Transportation District, 20 buses
Short-term General Hospital Services (92)
Ashland Community Hospital
Providence Hospital
Rogue Valley Medical Center
Grade: 87

Melbourne, FL
Continuing Education (89)
Two-year
• Brevard Community College: 19,248
Four-year
Florida Institute of Technology: 6,199
Office-based Physicians (88)
General/Family Practitioners: 85
Medical Specialists: 167
Surgical Specialists: 148
Public Libraries (96)
Brevard County Library System
15 branches; 1,726,565 books
$2.40 p/c book funds, 10.9 reading quotient
Public Transportation (50)
Space Coast Area Transit, 11 buses
Short-term General Hospital Services (94)
Cape Canaveral Hospital
Holmes Regional Medical Center
Parrish Medical Center
Patrick Air Force Hospital
Wuesthoff Hospital
Grade: 83

Mission–McAllen–Alamo, TX
Continuing Education (69)
Four-year
• University of Texas–Pan American: 12,337
Office-based Physicians (79)
General/Family Practitioners: 83
Medical Specialists: 70
Surgical Specialists: 81
Public Libraries (75)
8 independent libraries; 481,177 books
$1.10 p/c book funds, 4.4 reading quotient
Public Transportation (60)
Valley Transit, 38 buses
Short-term General Hospital Services (90)
Edinburg Hospital
Knapp Medical Center
• McAllen Medical Center
Mission Hospital
Rio Grande Regional Hospital
Grade: 75

Montrose, CO
Office-based Physicians (83)
General/Family Practitioners: 3
Medical Specialists: 5
Surgical Specialists: 11
Public Libraries (85)
Montrose Library District
6 branches; 62,348 books
$1.40 p/c book funds, 7.1 reading quotient
Short-term General Hospital Services (85)
Montrose Memorial Hospital
Grade: 51

Myrtle Beach–North Myrtle Beach, SC
Continuing Education (88)
Two-year
• Horry-Georgetown Technical College: 1,984
Four-year
• University of South Carolina, Coastal: 4,080
Office-based Physicians (87)
General/Family Practitioners: 37
Medical Specialists: 37
Surgical Specialists: 60
Public Libraries (78)
Part of Horry County Memorial Library System
7 branches; 224,439 books
$1.30 p/c book funds, 4.6 reading quotient
Public Transportation (96)
Coastal Rapid Public Transit, 12 buses
Short-term General Hospital Services (82)
Grand Strand General Hospital
Grade: 86

Naples, FL
Office-based Physicians (91)
General/Family Practitioners: 40
Medical Specialists: 77
Surgical Specialists: 84
Public Libraries (86)
Collier County Public Library
6 branches; 246,421 books
$2.60 p/c book funds, 7.6 reading quotient
Short-term General Hospital Services (84)
Naples Community Hospital
Grade: 52

New Bern, NC
Continuing Education (61)
Two-year
• Craven Community College: 2,193
Office-based Physicians (88)
General/Family Practitioners: 11
Medical Specialists: 31
Surgical Specialists: 40
Public Libraries (71)
Part of Craven–Pamlico–Carteret Regional Library
8 branches; 202,029 books
$0.50 p/c book funds, 5.1 reading quotient
Public Transportation (73)
Craven County Department of Transportation, 9 buses
Short-term General Hospital Services (87)
Cherry Point Naval Hospital
Craven Regional Medical Authority
Grade: 76

New Braunfels, TX
Office-based Physicians (87)
General/Family Practitioners: 21
Medical Specialists: 8
Surgical Specialists: 12
Public Libraries (77)
3 independent libraries; 79,935 books
$1.00 p/c book funds, 5.7 reading quotient
Short-term General Hospital Services (73)
McKenna Memorial Hospital
Grade: 47

New Port Richey, FL
Continuing Education (75)
Two-year
• Pasco Hernando Community College: 5,795
Four-year
St. Leo College: 6,071
Trinity College of Florida: 159
Office-based Physicians (82)
General/Family Practitioners: 55
Medical Specialists: 115
Surgical Specialists: 76
Public Libraries (86)
Pasco County Library System
9 branches; 388,243 books
$2.80 p/c book funds, 7.4 reading quotient
Short-term General Hospital Services (80)
Bayonet Point–Hudson Medical Center
Dade City Hospital
East Pasco Medical Center
New Port Richey Hospital
North Bay Medical Center
Grade: 65

Newport–Lincoln City, OR
Office-based Physicians (86)
General/Family Practitioners: 11
Medical Specialists: 11
Surgical Specialists: 7
Public Libraries (95)
6 independent libraries; 124,900 books
$3.00 p/c book funds, 12.4 reading quotient

Short-term General Hospital Services (81)
North Lincoln Hospital
Pacific Communities Hospital
Grade: 52

Norfork Lake, AR
Office-based Physicians (94)
General/Family Practitioners: 11
Medical Specialists: 12
Surgical Specialists: 17
Public Libraries (80)
Baxter County Library
3 branches; 55,514 books
$1.30 p/c book funds, 7.7 reading quotient
Short-term General Hospital Services (78)
Baxter County Regional Hospital
Grade: 50

Northern Door Peninsula, WI
Office-based Physicians (86)
General/Family Practitioners: 7
Medical Specialists: 4
Surgical Specialists: 9
Public Libraries (100)
Part of Door County Library
8 branches; 153,471 books
$3.60 p/c book funds, 16.8 reading quotient
Short-term General Hospital Services (80)
Door County Memorial Hospital
Grade: 53

Northern Neck, VA
Office-based Physicians (100)
General/Family Practitioners: 15
Medical Specialists: 8
Surgical Specialists: 10
Public Libraries (83)
2 independent libraries; 34,592 books
$1.97 p/c book funds, 5.8 reading quotient
Short-term General Hospital Services (72)
Rappahannock General Hospital
Grade: 51

Oakhurst–Coarsegold, CA
Office-based Physicians (76)
General/Family Practitioners: 13
Medical Specialists: 17
Surgical Specialists: 18
Public Libraries (79)
Madera County Library
5 branches; 145,436 books
$1.30 p/c book funds, 4.7 reading quotient
Short-term General Hospital Services (73)
Chowchilla District Memorial Hospital
Madera Community Hospital
Grade: 46

Ocala, FL
Continuing Education (63)
Two-year
• Central Florida Community College: 6,246
Office-based Physicians (84)
General/Family Practitioners: 36
Medical Specialists: 59
Surgical Specialists: 62
Public Libraries (73)
Part of Central Florida Regional Library
11 branches; 180,000 books
$1.40 p/c book funds, 3.6 reading quotient
Short-term General Hospital Services (85)
Marion Community Hospital
Munroe Regional Medical Center
Grade: 61

Ocean City, MD
Office-based Physicians (71)
General/Family Practitioners: 7

Medical Specialists: 4
Surgical Specialists: 1
Public Libraries (99)
Worcester County Library
4 branches; 160,783 books
$3.70 p/c book funds, 12.4 reading quotient
Public Transportation (100)
Ocean City Bus System, 7 buses
Grade: 54

Oscoda–Tawas–Huron Shore, MI
Office-based Physicians (83)
General/Family Practitioners: 8
Medical Specialists: 3
Surgical Specialists: 7
Public Libraries (86)
Part of Iosco-Arenac District Library
9 branches; 99,675 books
$1.80 p/c book funds, 6.0 reading quotient
Short-term General Hospital Services (74)
Tawas St. Joseph Hospital
Grade: 49

Oxford, MS
Continuing Education (100)
Four-year
• University of Mississippi: 11,288
Office-based Physicians (93)
General/Family Practitioners: 10
Medical Specialists: 10
Surgical Specialists: 18
Public Libraries (82)
Part of First Regional Library
12 branches; 313,979 books
$1.20 p/c book funds, 6.1 reading quotient
Short-term General Hospital Services (73)
Baptist Memorial Hospital–North Mississippi
Grade: 70

Pagosa Springs, CO
Office-based Physicians (78)
General/Family Practitioners: 2
Public Libraries (98)
Upper San Juan–Sisson Library
1 branch; 20,600 books
$3.50 p/c book funds, 13.4 reading quotient
Grade: 35

Pahrump Valley, NV
Office-based Physicians (70)
General/Family Practitioners: 4
Medical Specialists: 1
Surgical Specialists: 1
Public Libraries (78)
Doris Shirky Community Library
1 branch; 16,900 books
$0.85 p/c book funds, 7.8 reading quotient
Grade: 49

Palm Springs–Coachella Valley, CA
Continuing Education (62)
Two-year
• College of the Desert: 7,231
Office-based Physicians (84)
General/Family Practitioners: 229
Medical Specialists: 396
Surgical Specialists: 362
Public Libraries (80)
Part of 3 Independent Library Systems
31 branches; 1,462,325 books
$1.56 p/c book funds, 5.7 reading quotient
Public Transportation (90)
SUNBUS, 37 buses
Short-term General Hospital Services (91)
Canyon Springs Hospital
Desert Hospital

• Eisenhower Memorial Hospital
John F. Kennedy Memorial Hospital
San Gorgonio Memorial Hosptial
Grade: 82

Panama City, FL
Continuing Education (71)
Two-year
• Gulf Coast Community College: 5,966
Office-based Physicians (86)
General/Family Practitioners: 20
Medical Specialists: 44
Surgical Specialists: 51
Public Libraries (71)
Part of Northwest Regional Library System
8 branches; 149,483 books
$1.00 p/c book funds, 3.3 reading quotient
Short-term General Hospital Services (91)
Bay Medical Center
Gulf Coast Hospital
Tyndall Air Force Base Hospital
Grade: 64

Paradise–Magalia, CA
Continuing Education (94)
Two-year
• Butte College: 7,928
Four-year
• California State University, Chico: 14,979
Office-based Physicians (94)
General/Family Practitioners: 63
Medical Specialists: 77
Surgical Specialists: 91
Public Libraries (74)
Butte County Library
6 branches; 255,635 books
$0.90 p/c book funds, 4.0 reading quotient
Public Transportation (82)
Butte County Transit, 5 buses
Short-term General Hospital Services (91)
Biggs-Gridley Memorial Hospital
Chico Community Hospital
Feather River Hospital
N.T. Enloe Memorial Hospital
Oroville Hospital
Grade: 87

Payson, AZ
Office-based Physicians (83)
General/Family Practitioners: 11
Medical Specialists: 7
Surgical Specialists: 9
Public Libraries (96)
Gila County Library District
8 branches; 158,303 books
$2.70 p/c book funds, 8.4 reading quotient
Short-term General Hospital Services (75)
Cobre Valley Community Hospital
Payson Regional Medical Center
Grade: 51

Petoskey–Harbor Springs, MI
Continuing Education (79)
Two-year
• North Central Michigan College: 1,932
Office-based Physicians (100)
General/Family Practitioners: 6
Medical Specialists: 41
Surgical Specialists: 34
Public Libraries (93)
6 independent libraries; 83,199 books
$2.50 p/c book funds, 8.8 reading quotient
Short-term General Hospital Services (80)
Northern Michigan Hospital
Grade: 70

Phoenix–Mesa–Scottsdale, AZ
Continuing Education (79)
Two-year
- Gateway Community College: 6,821
- Glendale Community College: 18,512
- Mesa Community College: 19,818
- Paradise Valley Community College: 5,557
- Phoenix Community College: 12,837
- Rio Salado Community College: 10,480
- Scottsdale Community College: 9,612
- South Mountain Community College: 3,288

Four-year
- Arizona State University: 42,952
  Grand Canyon University: 1,813
  Ottawa University: 1,577
  Western International University: 1,247

Office-based Physicians (91)
General/Family Practitioners: 506
Medical Specialists: 1,043
Surgical Specialists: 979

Public Libraries (90)
14 Independent Library Systems
40 branches; 4,191,620 books
$3.10 p/c book funds, 9.1 reading quotient

Public Transportation (78)
Phoenix Transit System, 274 buses

Short-term General Hospital Services (100)
Arrowhead Community Hospital and Medical Center
Boswell Memorial Hospital
Chandler Regional Hospital
Community Hospital Medical Center
Desert Samaritan Medical Center
- Good Samaritan Regional Medical Center
Hayden Veterans Medical Center
Lincoln Hospital and Health Center
Luke Air Force Hospital
- Maricopa Medical Center
Maryvale Samaritan Medical Center
Mesa General Hospital Medical Center
Mesa Lutheran Hospital
- Phoenix Baptist Hospital and Medical Center
Phoenix General Hospital and Medical Center
Phoenix Memorial Hospital
- St. Joseph's Hospital and Medical Center
St. Luke's Medical Center
- Scottsdale Memorial Hospital
- Scottsdale Memorial Hospital–North
Tempe St. Luke's Hospital
Thunderbird Samaritan Medical Center
Valley Lutheran Hospital
Vencor Hospital–Phoenix
Webb Memorial Hospital
Grade: 88

Pike County, PA
Office-based Physicians (71)
General/Family Practitioners: 5
Medical Specialists: 3
Surgical Specialists: 2

Public Libraries (77)
Pike County Public Library
6 branches; 46,390 books
$1.10 p/c book funds, 4.2 reading quotient
Grade: 30

Placerville–Shingle Springs, CA
Continuing Education (38)
Two-year
- Lake Tahoe Community College: 1,083

Office-based Physicians (88)
General/Family Practitioners: 43
Medical Specialists: 30
Surgical Specialists: 40

Public Libraries (81)
El Dorado County Library
5 branches; 183,763 books
$1.80 p/c book funds, 5.3 reading quotient

Public Transportation (50)
El Dorado Transit, 7 buses

Short-term General Hospital Services (82)
Barton Memorial Hospital
Marshall Hospital
Grade: 68

Polson–Mission Valley, MT
Continuing Education (64)
Two-year
Salish Kootenai Community College: 684

Office-based Physicians (96)
General/Family Practitioners: 17
Medical Specialists: 2

Public Libraries (90)
5 independent libraries; 74,975 books
$1.30 p/c book funds, 8.1 reading quotient

Short-term General Hospital Services (69)
St. Joseph Hospital
St. Luke Community Hospital
Grade: 64

Pompano Beach, FL
Continuing Education (75)
Two-year
- Broward Community College: 23,547

Four-year
Nova University: 9,320

Office-based Physicians (93)
General/Family Practitioners: 221
Medical Specialists: 889
Surgical Specialists: 659

Public Libraries (89)
Part of Broward County Division of Libraries
32 branches; 1,936,342 books
$3.30 p/c book funds, 6.6 reading quotient

Public Transportation (57)
Broward County Transit, 52 buses

Short-term General Hospital Services (96)
- Cleveland Clinic Hospital
- Coral Springs Medical Center
- Hollywood Medical Center
- Memorial Hospital
- North Broward Medical Center
- Plantation General Hospital
- Universal Medical Center
- University Hospital
Grade: 82

Port Angeles–Seqium, WA
Continuing Education (71)
Two-year
- Peninsula College: 2,715

Office-based Physicians (97)
General/Family Practitioners: 34
Medical Specialists: 18
Surgical Specialists: 24

Public Libraries (91)
North Olympic Library System
4 branches; 178,065 books
$2.30 p/c book funds, 12.6 reading quotient

Public Transportation (100)
Clallam Transit System, 12 buses

Short-term General Hospital Services (85)
Forks Community Hospital
Olympic Memorial Hospital
Grade: 89

Port Charlotte–Punta Gorda, FL
Office-based Physicians (87)
General/Family Practitioners: 20
Medical Specialists: 58
Surgical Specialists: 50

Public Libraries (79)
Charlotte-Glades Library System
5 branches; 138,877 books
$1.90 p/c book funds, 4.8 reading quotient

Short-term General Hospital Services (90)
Bon Secours–St. Joseph Hospital
Fawcett Memorial Hospital
Medical Center Hospital
Grade: 51

Port Townsend, WA
Office-based Physicians (91)
General/Family Practitioners: 11
Medical Specialists: 3
Surgical Specialists: 5
Public Libraries (98)
Jefferson County Rural Library District
2 branches; 68,693 books
$4.20 p/c book funds, 14.5 reading quotient
Public Transportation (98)
Jefferson Transit Authority, 4 buses
Short-term General Hospital Services (77)
Jefferson General Hospital
Grade: 73

Prescott–Prescott Valley, AZ
Continuing Education (73)
Two-year
• Yavapai College: 6,003
Four-year
Prescott College: 593
Office-based Physicians (86)
General/Family Practitioners: 34
Medical Specialists: 30
Surgical Specialists: 35
Public Libraries (92)
Part of Yavapai County Library District
18 branches; 294,385 books
$2.70 p/c book funds, 10.2 reading quotient
Short-term General Hospital Services (91)
VA Medical Center
Yavapai Regional Medical Center
Grade: 68

Redding, CA
Continuing Education (74)
Two-year
• Shasta College: 8,454
Four-year
Simpson College: 429
Office-based Physicians (93)
General/Family Practitioners: 57
Medical Specialists: 51
Surgical Specialists: 75
Public Libraries (70)
Shasta County Library
3 branches; 235,554 books
$0.20 p/c book funds, 3.5 reading quotient
Public Transportation (50)
Redding Area Bus, 8 buses
Short-term General Hospital Services (90)
Mayers Memorial Hospital District
• Mercy Medical Center
Redding Medical Center
Grade: 75

Rehoboth Bay–Indian River Bay, DE
Continuing Education (60)
Two-year
• Delaware Technical Community College: 2,989
Office-based Physicians (92)
General/Family Practitioners: 32
Medical Specialists: 44
Surgical Specialists: 50
Public Libraries (90)
14 independent libraries; 315,858 books
$2.20 p/c book funds, 9.3 reading quotient
Short-term General Hospital Services (87)
Beebe Medical Center
Milford Memorial Hospital
Nanticoke Memorial Hospital
Grade: 66

✓**Reno–Sparks, NV**
Continuing Education (86)
Two-year
• Truckee Meadows Community College: 9,741
Four-year
Sierra Nevada College: 313
• University of Nevada: 11,487
Office-based Physicians (95)
General/Family Practitioners: 67
Medical Specialists: 157
Surgical Specialists: 155
Public Libraries (87)
Washoe County Library
8 branches; 497,181 books
$2.40 p/c book funds, 6.2 reading quotient
Public Transportation (100)
CITIFARE, 52 buses
Short-term General Hospital Services (96)
Lougaris VA Medical Center
St. Mary's Regional Medical Center
Sparks Family Hospital
• Washoe Medical Center
Grade: 93

Riviera–Bullhead City, AZ
Continuing Education (67)
Two-year
• Mohave Community College: 4,967
Office-based Physicians (79)
General/Family Practitioners: 23
Medical Specialists: 22
Surgical Specialists: 29
Public Libraries (69)
Part of Mohave County Library District
9 branches; 81,771 books
$0.90 p/c book funds, 3.7 reading quotient
Short-term General Hospital Services (81)
Bullhead Community Hospital
Grade: 59

Rockport–Aransas Pass, TX
Office-based Physicians (67)
General/Family Practitioners: 3
Medical Specialists: 1
Public Libraries (83)
Aransas County Public Library
1 branch; 50,140 books
$0.60 p/c book funds, 7.4 reading quotient
Grade: 30

Ruidoso, NM
Office-based Physicians (98)
General/Family Practitioners: 7
Medical Specialists: 2
Surgical Specialists: 7
Public Libraries (100)
Ruidoso Public Library
1 branch; 34,605 books
$5.80 p/c book funds, 21.2 reading quotient
Short-term General Hospital Services (73)
Lincoln County Medical Center
Grade: 54

St. Augustine, FL
Continuing Education (51)
Four-year
Flagler College: 1,204
Office-based Physicians (90)
General/Family Practitioners: 25
Medical Specialists: 37
Surgical Specialists: 27
Public Libraries (82)
St. Johns County Public Library
4 branches; 90,211 books
$2.40 p/c book funds, 5.6 reading quotient
Short-term General Hospital Services (80)
Flagler Hospital
Grade: 61

St. George–Zion, UT
Continuing Education (67)
Two-year
- Dixie College: 2,528

Office-based Physicians (81)
General/Family Practitioners: 12
Medical Specialists: 8
Surgical Specialists: 20

Public Libraries (90)
Washington County Public Library
4 branches; 144,001 books
$1.90 p/c book funds, 14.7 reading quotient

Short-term General Hospital Services (89)
Dixie Regional Medical Center

Grade: 65

St. Jay–Northeast Kingdom, VT
Continuing Education (79)
Four-year
- Lyndon State College: 1,344

Office-based Physicians (86)
General/Family Practitioners: 4
Medical Specialists: 9
Surgical Specialists: 11

Public Libraries (94)
18 independent libraries; 125,648 books
$1.60 p/c book funds, 9.4 reading quotient

Short-term General Hospital Services (78)
Northeastern Vermont Regional Hospital

Grade: 67

St. Petersburg–Clearwater, FL
Continuing Education (59)
Two-year
- St. Petersburg Junior College: 18,680

Four-year
Clearwater Christian College: 351
Eckerd College: 1,323

Office-based Physicians (93)
General/Family Practitioners: 200
Medical Specialists: 479
Surgical Specialists: 399

Public Libraries (100)
Clearwater Public Library
5 branches; 431,355 books
$3.98 p/c book funds, 13.7 reading quotient

Public Transportation (78)
Pinellas Suncoast Transit, 104 buses

Short-term General Hospital Services (97)
Bay Pines VA Medical Center
- Bayfront Medical Center
Clearwater Community Hospital
Edward White Hospital
Helen Ellis Memorial Hospital
Mease Hospital Countryside
Mease Hospital Dunedin
Medical Center Hospital
Morton F. Plant Hospital
Northside Hospital
Palms of Pasadena Hospital
Pinellas Community Hospital
St. Anthony's Hospital
University General Hospital
Women's Hospital and Medical Center

Grade: 85

St. Simons–Jekyll Islands, GA
Continuing Education (86)
Two-year
- Brunswick College: 1,441

Office-based Physicians (93)
General/Family Practitioners: 13
Medical Specialists: 28
Surgical Specialists: 35

Public Libraries (77)
Part of Glynn County Regional Library
8 branches; 289,456 books
$0.60 p/c book funds, 7.7 reading quotient

Short-term General Hospital Services (76)
Southeast Georgia Regional Medical Center

Grade: 66

✓ San Antonio, TX
Continuing Education (74)
Two-year
- Palo Alto College: 4,086
- St. Philips College: 5,204
- San Antonio College: 20,082

Four-year
Incarnate Word College: 2,556
Our Lady of the Lake University: 2,693
St. Mary's University: 4,045
Trinity University: 2,538
- University of Texas: 15,489

Office-based Physicians (93)
General/Family Practitioners: 299
Medical Specialists: 617
Surgical Specialists: 579

Public Libraries (78)
San Antonio Public Library
21 branches; 1,868,350 books
$1.10 p/c book funds, 4.5 reading quotient

Public Transportation (100)
San Antonio VIA, 486 buses

Short-term General Hospital Services (100)
Audie Murphy Memorial Veterans Hospital
- Baptist Medical Center
- Bexar County Hospital District
Brooke Army Medical Center
Metropolitan Hospital
- Nix Medical Center
Northeast Baptist Hospital
- St. Luke's Lutheran Hospital
- San Antonio Regional Hospital
- Santa Rosa Health Care Corporation
Southeast Baptist Hospital
Southwest General Hospital
- Southwest Texas Methodist Hospital
Village Oaks Medical Center
Wilford Hall Air Force Medical Center

Grade: 89

✓ San Diego, CA
Continuing Education (81)
Two-year
- Cuyamaca College: 3,614
- Grossmont College: 15,357
Kelsey-Jenney College: 594
- Mira Costa College: 7,517
- Palomar College: 16,707
- San Diego City College: 13,737
- San Diego Mesa College: 23,410
- San Diego Miramar College: 5,378
- Southwestern College: 13,010

Four-year
- California State University, San Marcos: 650
Christian Heritage College: 327
Coleman College: 893
National University: 8,836
Point Loma Nazarene College: 2,256
- San Diego State University: 34,155
United States International University: 2,254
- University of California: 17,797
University of San Diego: 6,027

Office-based Physicians (94)
General/Family Practitioners: 662
Medical Specialists: 1,483
Surgical Specialists: 1,228

Public Libraries (82)
8 Independent Library Systems
77 branches; 4,039,169 books
$1.81 p/c book funds, 6.6 reading quotient
Public Transportation (95)
North County Transit District, 120 buses
San Diego Transit, 254 buses
The Trolley, 59 buses
Short-term General Hospital Services (100)
Alvarado Hospital Medical Center
Camp Pendleton Naval Medical Center
Coronado Hospital
Fallbrook Hospital District
• Green Hospital of Scripps Clinic
• Grossmont Hospital
Harbor View Medical Center
• Kaiser Foundation Hospital
• Mercy Hospital and Medical Center
Mission Bay Memorial Hospital
Palomar Medical Center
Paradise Valley Hospital
Pomerado Hospital
Scripps Memorial–Chula Vista
Scripps Memorial–Encinitas
Scripps Memorial–La Jolla
Sharp Cabrillo Hospital
Sharp Chula Vista Medical Center
• Sharp Memorial Hospital
• Tri-City Medical Center
• UC San Diego Medical Center
Vencor Hospital San Diego
VA Medical Center
Villaview Community Hospital
Grade: 90

San Juan Islands, WA
Office-based Physicians (99)
General/Family Practitioners: 6
Medical Specialists: 5
Surgical Specialists: 5
Public Libraries (100)
Orcas Island Library District
3 branches; 52,934 books
San Juan Island Library District
$8.70 p/c book funds, 23.4 reading quotient
Grade: 40

San Luis Obispo, CA
Continuing Education (91)
Two-year
• Cuesta Community College: 7,127
Four-year
• California Polytechnic State University: 15,912
Office-based Physicians (95)
General/Family Practitioners: 81
Medical Specialists: 102
Surgical Specialists: 103
Public Libraries (87)
San Luis Obispo City-County Library
15 branches; 327,722 books
$2.80 p/c book funds, 10.4 reading quotient
Public Transportation (52)
San Luis Obispo RTA, 17 buses
Short-term General Hospital Services (93)
AMI Sierra Vista Regional Medical Center
Arroyo Grande Community Hospital
French Hospital Medical Center
San Luis Obispo General Hospital
Twin Cities Community Hospital
Grade: 84

Sandpoint–Priest River, ID
Office-based Physicians (85)
General/Family Practitioners: 8
Medical Specialists: 6
Surgical Specialists: 6

Public Libraries (85)
3 independent libraries; 51,955 books
$1.90 p/c book funds, 8.1 reading quotient
Short-term General Hospital Services (65)
Bonner General Hospital
Grade: 47

✓ **Santa Barbara, CA**
Continuing Education (90)
Two-year
• Allan Hancock College: 7,975
• Santa Barbara City College: 11,031
Four-year
• University of California: 18,391
Westmont College: 1,268
Office-based Physicians (96)
General/Family Practitioners: 101
Medical Specialists: 232
Surgical Specialists: 202
Public Libraries (85)
Santa Barbara Public Library
15 branches; 591,144 books
$2.20 p/c book funds, 8.3 reading quotient
Public Transportation (86)
Santa Barbara MTD, 51 buses
Short-term General Hospital Services (92)
Goleta Valley Community Hospital
Marian Medical Center
St. Francis Medical Center
• Santa Barbara Cottage Hospital
Santa Ynez Valley Hospital
Valley Community Hospital
Vandenberg Air Force Hospital
Grade: 90

Santa Fe, NM
Continuing Education (70)
Two-year
• Institute of American Indian Arts: 208
• Santa Fe Community College: 2,705
Four-year
College of Santa Fe: 1,052
St. John's College: 469
Office-based Physicians (96)
General/Family Practitioners: 42
Medical Specialists: 47
Surgical Specialists: 54
Public Libraries (96)
6 independent libraries; 242,061 books
$3.00 p/c book funds, 13.3 reading quotient
Short-term General Hospital Services (88)
St. Vincent Hospital
Grade: 70

Santa Rosa–Sonoma, CA
Continuing Education (79)
Two-year
• Santa Rosa Junior College: 20,479
Four-year
• Sonoma State University: 6,129
Office-based Physicians (97)
General/Family Practitioners: 175
Medical Specialists: 212
Surgical Specialists: 203
Public Libraries (85)
Sonoma County Library
12 branches; 641,083 books
$2.20 p/c book funds, 7.8 reading quotient
Public Transportation (50)
Sonoma County Transit, 18 buses
Short-term General Hospital Services (93)
• Community Hospital
Healdsburg General Hospital
Kaiser Foundation Hospital
Palm Drive Hospital
Grade: 81

Sarasota, FL
Continuing Education (18)
Four-year
Ringling School of Art and Design: 508
University of Sarasota: 134
Office-based Physicians (99)
General/Family Practitioners: 74
Medical Specialists: 218
Surgical Specialists: 193
Public Libraries (79)
Sarasota County Public Library System
6 branches; 373,508 books
$1.60 p/c book funds, 7.5 reading quotient
Public Transportation (50)
Sarasota County Transit Authority, 20 buses
Short-term General Hospital Services (93)
Doctors Hospital of Sarasota
Englewood Community Hospital
Sarasota Memorial Hospital
Venice Hospital
Grade: 68

Savannah, GA
Continuing Education (77)
Two-year
Savannah Technical Institute: 2,156
Four-year
• Armstrong State College: 4,170
Savannah College of Art and Design: 1,979
• Savannah State College: 2,319
Office-based Physicians (93)
General/Family Practitioners: 37
Medical Specialists: 114
Surgical Specialists: 129
Public Libraries (80)
Part of Chatham–Effingham–Liberty Regional Library
20 branches; 565,968 books
$1.10 p/c book funds, 5.3 reading quotient
Public Transportation (100)
Chatham Area Transit, 49 buses
Short-term General Hospital Services (92)
Candler Hospital
• Memorial Medical Center
St. Joseph's Hospital
Grade: 88

Sebring–Avon Park, FL
Continuing Education (67)
Two-year
• South Florida Community College: 2,576
Office-based Physicians (90)
General/Family Practitioners: 17
Medical Specialists: 29
Surgical Specialists: 25
Public Libraries (76)
Highlands County Library System
3 branches; 94,655 books
$1.20 p/c book funds, 6.1 reading quotient
Short-term General Hospital Services (65)
Highlands Regional Medical Center
Walker Memorial Hospital
Grade: 60

Sedona, AZ
Continuing Education (97)
Four-year
• Northern Arizona University, Flagstaff: 16,994
Office-based Physicians (88)
General/Family Practitioners: 34
Medical Specialists: 41
Surgical Specialists: 44
Public Libraries: (90)
Part of Coconino Library District
7 branches; 275,022 books
$2.20 p/c book funds, 8.9 reading quotient

Short-term General Hospital Services (87)
Flagstaff Medical Center
Page Hospital
Tuba City Indian Medical Center
Grade: 73

Silver City, NM
Continuing Education (84)
Four-year
• Western New Mexico University: 1,764
Office-based Physicians (89)
General/Family Practitioners: 8
Medical Specialists: 9
Surgical Specialists: 10
Public Libraries (96)
The Public Library
2 branches; 48,519 books
$2.90 p/c book funds, 12.7 reading quotient
Short-term General Hospital Services (77)
Gila Regional Medical Center
Grade: 69

Smith Mountain Lake, VA
Continuing Education (63)
Two-year
• Paul D. Camp Community College: 1,441
Four-year
Ferrum College: 1,208
Office-based Physicians (68)
General/Family Practitioners: 16
Medical Specialists: 3
Surgical Specialists: 4
Public Libraries (82)
2 independent libraries; 83,902 books
$1.30 p/c book funds, 6.4 reading quotient
Short-term General Hospital Services (68)
Bedford County Memorial Hospital
Franklin Memorial Hospital
Grade: 56

Sonora–Groveland–Twain Harte, CA
Continuing Education (67)
Two-year
• Columbia College: 2,012
Office-based Physicians (89)
General/Family Practitioners: 17
Medical Specialists: 16
Surgical Specialists: 18
Public Libraries (68)
Tuolumne County Free Library
12 branches; 88,651 books
$0.30 p/c book funds, 5.3 reading quotient
Public Transportation (50)
Tuolumne County TA, 3 buses
Short-term General Hospital Services (85)
Sonora Community Hospital
Tuolumne General Hospital
Grade: 72

Southern Berkshire County, MA
Continuing Education (48)
Four-year
Simons Rock College: 330
Office-based Physicians (94)
General/Family Practitioners: 23
Medical Specialists: 101
Surgical Specialists: 63
Public Libraries (100)
15 independent libraries; 315,966 books
$5.40 p/c book funds, 19.4 reading quotient
Public Transportation (100)
Berkshire RTA, 7 buses
Short-term General Hospital Services (93)
Fairview Hospital
Grade: 87

Southern Pines–Pinehurst, NC
Continuing Education (66)
Two-year
  • Sandhills Community College: 2,145
Office-based Physicians (93)
General/Family Practitioners: 9
Medical Specialists: 28
Surgical Specialists: 45
Public Libraries (100)
Southern Pines Public Library
  1 branch; 39,353 books
  $5.80 p/c book funds, 13.6 reading quotient
Short-term General Hospital Services (89)
Moore Regional Hospital
Grade: 70

Southport–Brunswick Islands, NC
Continuing Education (45)
Two-year
  • Brunswick Community College: 712
Office-based Physicians (75)
General/Family Practitioners: 10
Medical Specialists: 5
Surgical Specialists: 10
Public Libraries (74)
Brunswick County Library
  3 branches; 61,450 books
  $1.10 p/c book funds, 4.6 reading quotient
Short-term General Hospital Services (77)
Brunswick Hospital
J. Arthur Dosher Memorial Hospital
Grade: 54

✓ State College, PA
Continuing Education (100)
Four-year
  • Pennsylvania State University: 38,864
Office-based Physicians (89)
General/Family Practitioners: 31
Medical Specialists: 47
Surgical Specialists: 41
Public Libraries (81)
  4 independent libraries; 206,483 books
  $1.60 p/c book funds, 7.0 reading quotient
Public Transportation (100)
CENTRE LINE, 24 buses
Short-term General Hospital Services (84)
Centre Community Hospital
Grade: 91

Table Rock Lake, MO
Office-based Physicians (61)
General/Family Practitioners: 3
Public Libraries (85)
Stone County Library
  2 branches; 61,155 books
  $0.80 p/c book funds, 5.8 reading quotient
Grade: 29

Taos, NM
Office-based Physicians (88)
General/Family Practitioners: 8
Medical Specialists: 5
Surgical Specialists: 6
Public Libraries (100)
  2 independent libraries; 48,273 books
  $6.00 p/c book funds, 28.7 reading quotient
Short-term General Hospital Services (62)
Holy Cross Hospital
Grade: 50

Thomasville, GA
Continuing Education (45)
Four-year
  Thomas College: 360
Office-based Physicians (98)
General/Family Practitioners: 11
Medical Specialists: 21
Surgical Specialists: 28
Public Libraries (81)
Thomas County Public Library
  5 branches; 71,080 books
  $1.30 p/c book funds, 5.2 reading quotient
Short-term General Hospital Services (93)
John D. Archbold Memorial Hospital
Grade: 63

Toms River–Barnegat Bay, NJ
Continuing Education (58)
Two-year
  • Ocean County College: 7,424
Four-year
  Georgian Court College: 2,316
Office-based Physicians (84)
General/Family Practitioners: 35
Medical Specialists: 200
Surgical Specialists: 149
Public Libraries (91)
Ocean County Library
  19 branches; 784,128 books
  $3.40 p/c book funds, 9.6 reading quotient
Public Transportation (50)
Ocean County DOT, 10 buses
Short-term General Hospital Services (93)
Community Medical Center
Kimball Medical Center
Medical Center of Ocean County
Southern Ocean County Hospital
Grade: 75

✓ Traverse City, MI
Continuing Education (76)
Two-year
  • Northwestern Michigan College: 4,391
Office-based Physicians (96)
General/Family Practitioners: 14
Medical Specialists: 52
Surgical Specialists: 49
Public Libraries (85)
  6 independent libraries; 116,639 books
  $2.40 p/c book funds, 7.9 reading quotient
Public Transportation (100)
BATA Bus, 20 buses
Short-term General Hospital Services (91)
Munson Medical Center
Traverse City Community Hospital
Grade: 90

Tryon, NC
Office-based Physicians (90)
General/Family Practitioners: 6
Medical Specialists: 2
Surgical Specialists: 4
Public Libraries (85)
Polk County Public Library
  1 branch; 34,841 books
  $1.50 p/c book funds, 8.2 reading quotient
Short-term General Hospital Services (69)
St. Luke's Hospital
Grade: 49

✓ Tucson, AZ
Continuing Education (87)
Two-year
  • Pima Community College: 26,766
Four-year
  • University of Arizona: 35,735
Office-based Physicians (93)
General/Family Practitioners: 132
Medical Specialists: 462
Surgical Specialists: 374

Public Libraries (82)
Tucson-Pima Library System
18 branches; 1,119,997 books
$1.70 p/c book funds, 9.1 reading quotient
Public Transportation (100)
Tucson SUN TRAN, 152 buses
Short-term General Hospital Services (99)
Carondelet St. Joseph's Hospital
• Carondelet St. Mary's Hospital
Davis Monthan Air Force Hospital
El Dorado Hospital and Medical Center
• Kino Community Hospital
Northwest Hospital
Tucson General Hospital
• Tucson Medical Center
• University Medical Center
VA Medical Center
Grade: 92

Vero Beach–Sebastian, FL
Office-based Physicians (94)
General/Family Practitioners: 22
Medical Specialists: 53
Surgical Specialists: 62
Public Libraries (94)
Indian River County Library
3 branches; 145,430 books
$4.60 p/c book funds, 8.0 reading quotient
Short-term General Hospital Services (83)
Indian River Memorial Hospital
Sebastian River Medical Center
Grade: 54

Virginia Beach, VA
Continuing Education (14)
Four-year
Regent University: 715
Office-based Physicians (89)
General/Family Practitioners: 98
Medical Specialists: 150
Surgical Specialists: 136
Public Libraries (93)
Virginia Beach Public Library
9 branches; 724,968 books
$4.00 p/c book funds, 10.6 reading quotient
Public Transportation (60)
Tidewater Regional Transit, 35 buses
Short-term General Hospital Services (82)
Sentara Bayside Hospital
• Virginia Beach General Hospital
Grade: 68

Wenatchee, WA
Continuing Education (71)
Two-year
• Wenatchee Valley College: 2,493
Office-based Physicians (100)
General/Family Practitioners: 27
Medical Specialists: 32
Surgical Specialists: 39
Public Libraries (93)
Part of North Central Regional Library
25 branches; 425,362 books
$3.30 p/c book funds, 10.3 reading quotient
Short-term General Hospital Services (73)
Central Washington Hospital
Lake Chelan Community Hospital
Grade: 67

Western St. Tammany Parish, LA
Office-based Physicians (90)
General/Family Practitioners: 29
Medical Specialists: 70
Surgical Specialists: 66

Public Libraries (93)
Part of St. Tammany Parish Library
10 branches; 338,555 books
$3.70 p/c book funds, 9.3 reading quotient
Short-term General Hospital Services (91)
Highland Park Medical Center
Northshore Regional Medical Center
St. Tammany Parish Hospital
Slidell Memorial Hospital and Medical Center
Grade: 55

Whidbey Island, WA
Office-based Physicians (81)
General/Family Practitioners: 16
Medical Specialists: 5
Surgical Specialists: 14
Public Libraries (92)
Part of Sno-Isle Regional Library
21 branches; 971,931 books
$3.70 p/c book funds, 11.0 reading quotient
Short-term General Hospital Services (84)
Oak Harbor Naval Hospital
Whidbey General Hospital
Grade: 51

Wickenburg, AZ
Office-based Physicians (91)
General/Family Practitioners: 506
Medical Specialists: 1,043
Surgical Specialists: 979
Public Libraries (97)
Wickenburg Public Library
1 branch; 27,000 books
$1.08 p/c book funds, 17.9 reading quotient
Short-term General Hospital Services (72)
Wickenburg Community Hospital
Grade: 52

✓ **Williamsburg, VA**
Continuing Education (100)
Four-year
• College of William and Mary: 7,672
Office-based Physicians (100)
General/Family Practitioners: 19
Medical Specialists: 35
Surgical Specialists: 28
Public Libraries (97)
Williamsburg Regional Library
1 branch; 128,671 books
$4.50 p/c book funds, 17.1 reading quotient
Public Transportation (95)
James City County Transit System, 8 buses
Short-term General Hospital Services (78)
Williamsburg Community Hospital
Grade: 94

Wimberly–San Marcos, TX
Continuing Education (100)
Four-year
• Southwest Texas State University: 20,940
Office-based Physicians (80)
General/Family Practitioners: 12
Medical Specialists: 14
Surgical Specialists: 15
Public Libraries (83)
5 independent libraries; 125,521 books
$1.50 p/c book funds, 6.0 reading quotient
Short-term General Hospital Services (71)
Central Texas Medical Center
Grade: 67

Winchester, VA
Continuing Education (74)
Two-year
• Lord Fairfax Community College: 2,599
Four-year
Shenandoah University: 1,158

Office-based Physicians (96)
General/Family Practitioners: 11
Medical Specialists: 51
Surgical Specialists: 53
Public Libraries (80)
The Handley Library
2 branches; 93,984 books
$1.80 p/c book funds, 4.7 reading quotient
Short-term General Hospital Services (87)
Winchester Medical Center
Grade: 67

Woodstock, VT
Office-based Physicians (88)
General/Family Practitioners: 8
Medical Specialists: 33
Surgical Specialists: 15
Public Libraries (91)
31 independent libraries; 290,869 books
$1.60 p/c book funds, 8.2 reading quotient
Public Transportation (100)
Advance Transit, 12 buses
Short-term General Hospital Services (89)
Mt. Ascutney Hospital and Health Center
Springfield Hospital
White River VA Medical Center
Grade: 74

York Beaches, ME
Continuing Education (41)
Four-year
University of New England: 1,259

Office-based Physicians (84)
General/Family Practitioners: 35
Medical Specialists: 43
Surgical Specialists: 41
Public Libraries (92)
25 independent libraries; 566,669 books
$1.80 p/c book funds, 9.1 reading quotient
Public Transportation (50)
Biddeford–Saco–Old Orchard Beach Transit, 9 buses
Short-term General Hospital Services (85)
Goodall Hospital
Southern Maine Medical Center
York Hospital
Grade: 71

Yuma, AZ
Continuing Education (67)
Two-year
• Arizona Western College: 4,913
Office-based Physicians (80)
General/Family Practitioners: 17
Medical Specialists: 28
Surgical Specialists: 32
Public Libraries (85)
Yuma County Library District
5 branches; 200,969 books
$2.10 p/c book funds, 7.8 reading quotient
Short-term General Hospital Services (79)
Yuma Regional Medical Center
Grade: 62

ET CETERA: Services

FINDING THE RIGHT DOCTOR

Chances are good that you'll have to choose a new physician at some point; even if you don't move after retirement, your doctor might. Finding a replacement for the person in whom you've put so much trust isn't always easy.

Give some thought to the kind of doctor you are most comfortable with. Do you want to place complete faith in your physician? Or do you have questions about your treatment? Do you like a cooperative arrangement, in which you and your doctor work as a team? It's very important to most people that they have a doctor who will listen to their complaints, worries, and concerns, rather than one who may make patients feel that they're questioning the doctor's authority.

If you're planning to move, you might ask your present doctor if he or she knows anything about the doctors in the area where you are going. Or you can get names from the nearest hospital at the new location, from friends you make, from medical societies, and from new neighbors.

When you have decided whom you want to contact, call that doctor's office, saying that you are a prospective patient, and ask to speak to the doctor briefly. You may have to agree to call back, but making a connection with a professional voice is an important step. If you can't arrange this, if the doctor is too busy, you probably

ought to go to the next name on your list. You need a physician who is readily accessible.

When you do make contact, tell the doctor enough about yourself so that he or she has a good idea of who you are and what your problems may be. If the doctor sounds right to you, you could ask about fees, house calls (yes, they are again being made when necessary), and emergencies. Or you may wish to save some of these questions for a personal visit. It is important to establish through the initial phone call or visit that you and the doctor will be at ease with each other.

Evaluate the doctor's attitude. If he or she doesn't want to bother with you now, you will probably get that don't-bother-me treatment sooner or later when dealing with specific problems. Make sure that

- You can openly discuss your feelings and personal concerns about sexual and emotional problems.
- The doctor isn't vague, impatient, or unwilling to answer all your questions about the causes and treatment of your physical problems.
- The doctor takes a thorough history on you and asks about past physical and emotional problems, family medical history, medication you

are taking, and other matters affecting your health.

- The doctor doesn't always attribute your problems to getting older, and that he or she doesn't automatically prescribe drugs rather than deal with real causes of your medical problems.
- The doctor has an associate to whom you can turn should your doctor retire or die.

Talk with the doctor about the transfer of your medical records. Some doctors like to have them, especially if there is any specific medical problem or chronic condition. Other doctors prefer not to see them, and to develop new records.

Even if you feel fine, arrange to have a physical or at least a quick checkup. This is more for the doctor's benefit than for yours, but it will help you, too. Should an emergency occur, the doctor will have basic information about you and some knowledge of your needs, and you will avoid the stress of trying to work with a doctor who has to learn about you in an emergency.

FINDING THE RIGHT LAWYER

When you move from one state to another, you enter a new legal environment. Even if your will is legal in your new state (and it may not be), it might not do the best possible job. When you resettle, see a lawyer in your new area to make certain your will is one your state will recognize. Some states, for example, require that the executor of a will be a resident of the state where the deceased lived. For a legal checkup, you might have to contact a family lawyer.

Lawyering is a competitive field. In the past, lawyer and clients usually found each other in the Rotary Club, at a church supper, or on the golf course. Since 1977, when the Supreme Court struck down laws barring the legal profession from advertising, many lawyers have gotten quite adept at promoting themselves. Just look up "Lawyers" in a telephone book's Yellow Pages, and you'll be surprised by the techniques many firms borrow from consumer goods advertising. Specialists for 24-hour divorces, personal bankruptcy, workers' compensation, and personal injury claims abound. Somewhere hidden among the listings is a professional who can advise you. How do you find him or her?

- *Satisfied clients.* If a friend or neighbor has used a lawyer's services, ask what sort of matter the lawyer handled. Some lawyers, especially in large cities, specialize in a certain branch of law and aren't interested in taking on cases outside their specialty. They aren't family lawyers.
- *Lawyers referral service.* Most state bar associations have a referral service with a toll-free telephone number. Typically, the name you are given is an attorney who practices where you

live, specializes in your legal problem, and is next up in the association's database to be referred. You can have a first interview with him or her for a stated—and very modest—fee. In that interview, you can find out whether you'll need further legal services and, if so, you can decide whether you want to continue with the lawyer to whom you were referred. You will be under no obligation to do so if you do not want to.

- *Local bar association.* If the referral service lists no lawyer in your area, try the local bar association. If you don't find it in the telephone book, inquire for the president's name at the county courthouse. You can then ask him or her for the name of a good lawyer. Be sure to make it clear that you are asking, in their capacity as president of the local association, for the name of a reliable attorney who can perform the kind of service you are seeking.

Don't Put Off Your Will

It's human nature to avoid thinking about the need for a will. Seven out of every 10 people die without one, and eight of 10 who do have a will fail to keep it up to date. If you don't have a will when you die, the state where you live in your retirement years will write one for you according to its own statutes, and the assets you may have worked hard to accumulate will be distributed according to its laws.

Don't put off making a will because of imagined costs. A lawyer can tell you the basic fee in advance; it's usually $100 to $250 for a simple document. And it may save your heirs thousands. Once you have a will, make a note to yourself in your calendar to review it every year. Births, marriages, deaths, hard feelings, the patching up of hard feelings, plus changes in your finances, in your health, or in federal or state laws—any of these may affect your will. Regular, periodic review helps ensure that you won't forget to make needed adjustments.

If death and taxes are inevitable—as the old saying goes—so are taxes after death. But it isn't all bad. No estate smaller than $600,000 is subject to federal tax. State tax exemptions vary greatly and often change, another reason for keeping the document up to date.

Where should you keep your will? Put it in a safe place, but don't hide it behind a painting or under a rug. If you conceal it too well, a court may rule that you don't have one! Your lawyer should have a signed copy, and the original should be in a logical place, such as a safety-deposit box or your desk. Be sure your spouse, a close relative, or a friend knows where both the copies and the original are.

DRIVER LICENSING

When you settle in a new state, you have to surrender your out-of-state driver's license and get a new one. The time to get this done ranges from immediately in 12 states, up to 30 days in 14 states, up to 90 days in 9 other states, and 120 days in Wyoming. New Hampshire and Vermont allow you as much time as your former state gives newcomers. Hawaii lets you keep your license until it expires.

Required Tests

For a new resident with a valid driver's license from a former state, the requirement for getting a license from the new state varies. All states now require vision testing. In Connecticut and New Hampshire, all other tests aside from vision may be waived. Washington requires you to get behind the wheel with a license examiner for a road test; in 29 other states, a road test may be waived or required at the discretion of the examiner.

Problem Drivers

Forty-two states belong to the National Driver License Compact, an agreement among states to share information on drivers who accumulate tickets in one jurisdiction and try to escape control in another. If your license has been revoked, you won't get a new one simply by moving to another state. Every license application is checked with the National Driver Register, a federal data file of persons whose license to drive has been revoked.

DRIVING DANGER SIGNALS

Researching the records of insurance companies and state police agencies, Dr. Leon Pastalan of the University of Michigan found that older drivers receive a high number of tickets for the following five different traffic violations:

- Rear-end collisions
- Dangerously slow driving
- Failure to yield the right-of-way
- Driving the wrong way on one-way streets
- Illegal turns

Even though people age at different rates, normal changes that affect eyesight, muscle reflexes, and hearing are the reasons older adults are ticketed for these moving violations more often than the rest of the population. Simply recognizing your limitations will help you become a better driver.

Eyesight. Ninety percent of all sensory input needed to drive a car comes through the eyes. As vision becomes less sharp, the typical rectangular black-and-white road signs get harder to read. Night driving is especially risky, because the older we get, the more illumination we need. For example, an 80-year-old needs three times the light that a 20-year-old needs to read. Other problems include loss of depth perception (a major cause of rear-end collisions) and limited peripheral vision (dangerous when making turns at intersections).

Driver Age Discrimination?

Once you start feeling your age, will insurance companies and state highway safety committees consider you dangerous when you get behind the wheel of your automobile?

On the face of it, older drivers have a better accident record than younger drivers. People over 60 represent one in eight persons in this country yet are involved in only one in 15 of the automobile accidents. But the National Safety Council notes that people over 60 drive much less than younger people and actually have a poorer accident record in terms of the miles they drive.

The American Medical Association and the American Association of Motor Vehicle Administrators have recommended that, while no one's license should be placed in jeopardy just because the driver is older, states should reexamine older drivers more frequently than younger drivers. Fourteen states and Washington, D.C., now require special examinations* based solely on age.

California	Reexamination waived for "clean record" drivers under 70.
Colorado	Reexamination waived for "clean record" drivers under 70.
Hawaii	License renewal every two years for drivers over 65.
Illinois	Complete reexamination every four years for age 69 to 80; every two years for drivers age 81 to 86; every year 87 and older.
Indiana	Complete reexamination every three years for drivers over 75.
Iowa	License renewal every two years for drivers over 70.
Louisiana	Physical reexamination every four years for drivers over 60.
Maine	Vision reexamination at age 40, age 52, and 65 and over.
New Hampshire	Complete reexamination for drivers over 75.
New Mexico	License renewal every year for drivers over 75.
Oregon	Vision reexamination at age 50 and over.
Pennsylvania	Physical examination on a random basis for drivers over 45.
Rhode Island	License renewal every two years for drivers over 70.
Utah	Reexamination waived for "clean record" drivers under 70.
Washington, D.C.	Vision and reaction examination for drivers over 70; complete reexamination at age 75 and over.

Source: U.S. Federal Highway Administration, *Driver License Administration Requirements and Fees.*

* California, Delaware, Georgia, Nevada, New Jersey, Oregon, and Pennsylvania also require doctors to report conditions that impair driving ability.

Getting a Driver's License After Moving

	Time Limit	Rules of the Road	Signs and Signals	Vision	Road Test	NDR Compact
Alabama	30 days	•	•	•		•
Alaska	90 days	•	•	•		•
Arizona	immediately	•	•	•	○	•
Arkansas	30 days	•	•	•		•
California	10 days	•	•	•		•
Colorado	30 days	•	•	•	○	•
Connecticut	60 days	○	○	•	○	
Delaware	60 days		•	•	○	•
District of Columbia	30 days	•		•	○	•
Florida	30 days	○	○	•	○	•
Georgia	30 days	•	•	•		•
Hawaii	*	•	•	•	○	•
Idaho	90 days	•	•	•		•
Illinois	90 days	•	•	•		•
Indiana	60 days	•	•	•		•
Iowa	immediately	•	•	•		•
Kansas	90 days	•	•	•		•
Kentucky	immediately	•	•	•		
Louisiana	90 days			•	○	•
Maine	30 days	•		•	○	•
Maryland	30 days	○	○	•	○	•
Massachusetts	immediately	•		•		
Michigan	immediately	•	•	•		
Minnesota	60 days	•	•	•	○	•
Mississippi	60 days	•	•	•	○	•
Missouri	immediately	•	•	•	○	•
Montana	90 days	○	○	•	○	•
Nebraska	30 days	•	•	•	○	•
Nevada	45 days	•	•	•	○	•
New Hampshire	60 days	○		•	○	•
New Jersey	60 days	•		•	○	•
New Mexico	30 days	•		•		•
New York	30 days	•	•	•		•
North Carolina	30 days	•	•	•	○	
North Dakota	60 days	•	•	•	○	•
Ohio	30 days	•	•	•	○	•
Oklahoma	immediately	•	•	•	○	•
Oregon	immediately	•	•	•	○	•
Pennsylvania	60 days	•	•	•	○	
Rhode Island	30 days	•	•	•		•
South Carolina	90 days			•	○	•
South Dakota	90 days	•	•	•	○	•
Tennessee	30 days	○	○	•	○	•
Texas	30 days	•	•	•	○	
Utah	60 days	•	•	•		•
Vermont	6 months	○	○	•	○	•
Virginia	30 days	•	•	•		•
Washington	30 days	•	•	•	•	•
West Virginia	immediately	•	•	•		•
Wisconsin	immediately	•	•	•	○	
Wyoming	120 days	•	•	•	○	•

Source: U.S. Federal Highway Administration, *Driver License Administration Requirements and Fees.*

*In Hawaii, a driver's license from any state is valid until its expiration if the driver is over 18.

•Required

○May be required or waived at the discretion of the examiner.

You can adjust to these dangers by not driving at night, having regular eye checkups, wearing gray or green-tinted sunglasses on days with high sun glare, and replacing your car's standard rearview mirror with a wide-angle one to aid peripheral vision.

Muscle reflexes. Many people slow down as they get

older. Strength may dwindle, neck and shoulder joints may stiffen, and you may tire sooner. Most important to driving, your reflex reactions may slow. All of these symptoms can affect how safely you enter a busy freeway, change lanes to pass a plodding 18-wheel truck, or avoid a rear-end fender bender.

Ask your physician if any of the medication you're taking might decrease your alertness and ability to drive defensively. On long road trips, take along a companion to share the driving and break the day's distance into short stretches to reduce fatigue. Don't get caught on freeways and major arterial streets during morning and evening rush hours.

Hearing. One in every five persons over 55 and one of every three persons over 65 has impaired hearing. It is a gradual condition and can go unnoticed for a long time. When you can't hear an ambulance siren, a ticket for failing to yield the right-of-way to an emergency vehicle is the likely consequence.

You can be aware of hearing loss by having periodic checkups. When you drive, open a window, turn off the radio, keep the air-conditioner fan on low speed, and cut unnecessary conversation.

COLLEGE TUITION BREAKS

Forty states waive or reduce tuition in their public colleges for persons who've reached a specific age. It's the law in 28 of the states; in the other 11, it's a policy adopted by the state's Board of Regents or its Board of Higher Education. It is common practice for individual

College Tuition Waivers for Older Adults

	Law	Policy	Minimum Age	All State-Funded Institutions
Alabama		•	60	
Alaska		•	60	•
Arkansas	•		60	•
California		•	60	
Connecticut	•		62	•
Delaware	•		60	•
District of Columbia		•	60	•
Florida	•		60	•
Georgia	•		62	•
Hawaii	•		60	•
Idaho		•	60	•
Illinois	•		65	•
Indiana	•		60	•
Kansas		•	60	•
Kentucky	•		65	•
Louisiana	•		60	•
Maine		•	65	•
Maryland	•		60	•
Massachusetts	•		60	•
Michigan	•		60	
Minnesota	•		62	•
Montana	•		62	•
Nevada		•	62	•
New Hampshire		•	65	•
New Jersey	•		65	•
New Mexico	•		65	•
New York	•		60	•
North Carolina	•		65	•
North Dakota		•	65	•
Ohio	•		60	•
Oklahoma		•	65	•
Oregon		•	65	•
Rhode Island	•		60	•
South Carolina	•		60	•
South Dakota		•	65	•
Tennessee	•		65	•
Texas	•		65	•
Utah	•		62	•
Virginia	•		60	•
Washington	•		60	•
Wisconsin	•		62	•

Source: Senate Special Committee on Aging, *Lifelong Learning for an Aging Society,* 1992; Places Rated Partnership survey.

Establishing Residency for Tuition Benefits

Legal residency is not only important for tax purposes, it's a necessary step to qualify for in-state tuition fees or tuition waivers at local public colleges.

Of the states that offer some form of tuition reduction or waiver, most require proof of at least one year of residency. Here are several steps to take to satisfy that requirement:

- Ask the local county clerk for a certificate of domicile.
- Get a driver's license, and register your car in the new state.
- If you don't drive, ask the driver's license authority for a nondriver identification card. All states now issue them; some are similar to the driver's license format. Delaware, Illinois, and Minnesota will issue an ID card to all persons, not just nondrivers.
- File your final state income tax in your former state; file state and federal income taxes in the new state.
- At first opportunity, register and vote in an election in your new state.

colleges and universities in all of the 50 states to establish their own tuition reduction policies.

The limitations on this benefit vary. All states grant it on a space-available basis, which simply means that older students who want to take advantage of the tuition break are admitted to courses only after tuition-paying students have enrolled. Eight states grant the benefit only for auditing courses, that is, enrolling for no credit. Four states—Illinois, Maryland, Indiana, and Virginia—look at the student's income to determine eligibility.

ALABAMA

There is no legislation or state policy to waive or reduce tuition for older adults in state-funded colleges and universities. Tuition and general student fees are waived for courses in all state-funded two-year colleges.

ALASKA

State policy waives tuition for residents 60 years or older at state-funded universities on a space-available basis.

ARIZONA

There is no legislation or state policy within the university or community college system to waive or reduce tuition for older adults.

ARKANSAS

Tuition and general student fees are waived for credit courses on a space-available basis for older adults at any state institutions of higher learning.

CALIFORNIA

Tuition and general student fees may be waived only at participating campuses of the California State University system for credit courses on a space-available basis.

COLORADO

There is no legislation or state policy to waive or reduce tuition for older adults.

CONNECTICUT

State law waives tuition at all state-funded two-year colleges; unless student is admitted to degree-granting programs at state universities, tuition waived only on a space-available basis.

DELAWARE

State law waives application, course, registration, and other fees for credit courses on a space-available basis. Students must be formal degree candidates.

DISTRICT OF COLUMBIA

Tuition waived in courses taken for credit or audited at all University of the District of Columbia campuses.

FLORIDA

Tuition fees are waived for courses taken by residents over 60 who attend classes for credit at state universities on a space-available basis. No academic credit is given under the waiver.

GEORGIA

Tuition fees are waived only for credit courses on a space-available basis. Dental, medical, veterinary, and law school courses are excluded.

HAWAII

Tuition and general student fees are waived at the University of Hawaii campuses for regularly scheduled credit courses on a space-available basis.

IDAHO

State policy reduces registration fee to $20 plus $5 fee per credit hour is charged for courses on a space-available basis.

ILLINOIS

Older persons who have been accepted in regularly scheduled credit courses, and whose income is less than $14,000, are eligible for tuition waivers on a space-available basis.

INDIANA

With certain limitations, 50 percent of the tuition fee is waived for older adults who are not working full time and who have a high school degree.

IOWA

There is no legislation or state policy within the university or community college system to waive or reduce tuition for older adults.

KANSAS

Tuition and general student fees at state-funded universities are waived only for auditing courses on a space-available basis.

KENTUCKY

Tuition and general student fees are waived at any state-funded institution of higher learning, for residents only, for regularly scheduled credit courses on a space-available basis.

LOUISIANA

Tuition and other registration fees are waived for courses on a space-available basis, provided that sufficient funds are appropriated by the legislature to reimburse colleges and universities affected.

MAINE

Tuition and fees are waived for undergraduate courses on a space-available basis.

MARYLAND

Tuition fees are waived for two-year college courses on a space-available basis, and up to three university or four-year college courses per term on a space available basis for students whose income is derived from retirement benefits and who aren't employed full time.

MASSACHUSETTS

Tuition fees are waived for courses if the college or university is not overenrolled.

MICHIGAN

Community colleges may waive tuition for older students meeting admission requirements.

MINNESOTA

Except for an administration fee of $6 a credit hour, collected only when a course is taken for credit, tuition and activity fees are waived to attend courses for credit, to audit any course offered for credit, or to enroll in any noncredit adult vocational education courses on a space-available basis.

MISSISSIPPI

There is no legislation or state policy within the university or community college system to waive or reduce tuition for older adults.

MISSOURI

There is no legislation or state policy within the university or community college system to waive or reduce tuition for older adults.

MONTANA

Tuition may be waived at the discretion of the regents of the Montana university system.

NEBRASKA

There is no legislation or state policy within the university or community college system to waive or reduce tuition for older adults.

NEVADA

Registration fees are waived only for regularly scheduled courses which may be audited or taken for credit. Consent of the instructor may be required.

NEW HAMPSHIRE

State policy waives tuition fees on a space-available basis.

NEW JERSEY

Tuition fees may be waived for courses on a space-available basis at each public institution of higher education.

NEW MEXICO

Tuition may be reduced to $5 per credit hour up to a maximum of six credit hours per semester for older residents on a space-available basis.

NEW YORK

Tuition fees may be waived only for auditing courses on a space-available basis at institutions of the state university system.

NORTH CAROLINA

Tuition fees are waived for auditing courses or for taking courses for credit on a space-available basis.

NORTH DAKOTA

Tuition fees are waived only for auditing courses on a space-available basis.

OHIO

Tuition and matriculation fees are waived only for auditing courses on a space-available basis.

OKLAHOMA

Tuition fees are waived only for auditing courses on a space-available basis.

OREGON

Tuition fees are waived for auditing courses on a space-available basis.

PENNSYLVANIA

There is no legislation or state policy within the university or community college system to waive or reduce tuition for older adults.

RHODE ISLAND

Tuition and general student fees are waived for credit courses on a space-available basis at the discretion of the institution.

SOUTH CAROLINA

Tuition fees are waived for courses, for credit or audit, at any state-supported institution on a space-available basis.

SOUTH DAKOTA

Tuition fees are reduced to 50 percent of resident tuition.

TENNESSEE

Tuition and registration fees are waived for auditing or taking for credit courses on a space-available basis. The board of regents may charge a service fee not to exceed $50/quarter or $75/semester. The waiver does not apply at medical, dental. or pharmacy schools.

TEXAS

Tuition fees may be waived for auditing courses on a space-available basis by the governing board of any state-supported institution.

UTAH

Tuition fees (but not quarterly registration fees) are waived for courses on a space-available basis.

VERMONT

There is no legislation or state policy within the university or community college system to waive or reduce tuition for older adults.

VIRGINIA

Tuition and registration fees are waived on a space-available basis, if the student has a federal taxable income not exceeding $10,000. Registration is limited to no more than three courses in any one term, quarter, or semester if the person is not enrolled for academic credit.

WASHINGTON

Depending on the institution, and for no more than two courses per term, tuition and general student fees may be waived for courses taken for credit and waived entirely for courses taken for audit. There may be a nominal fee of $5 charged per term for auditing.

WEST VIRGINIA

There is no legislation or state policy within the university or community college system to waive or reduce tuition for older adults.

WISCONSIN

Tuition fees are waived for auditing courses within the state university system.

WYOMING

There is no legislation or state policy within the university or community college system to waive or reduce tuition for older adults.

WORKING

Since the late 1980s, states from Washington to South Carolina have taken to the idea that enticing older outsiders to their cities and towns was a cleaner economic move than chasing light industrial employers. The impact of a new, affluent couple moving in could be the same as three new jobs at good pay, they estimated.

For all that, diesel logging trucks are still a common sight on coastal U.S. 17 from Virginia Beach to Savannah, on route 12 in Vermont, and on U.S. 93 in western Montana. On Colorado's western slope, Montrose still has a huge candy factory and awaits the opening of an experimental airplane plant. In the Arkansas Ozarks, the radio still broadcasts help-wanted ads for workers at local chicken-processors.

If places had to rely on older newcomers for their economic futures, they'd starve. Payrolls everywhere are still earned the old-fashioned way—by agriculture, mining, manufacturing, construction, and a lot of retail trade and services. However, which places will gain new jobs over the next five years is important if you're thinking of starting a second career.

OLDER PERSONS DO WORK

Near Beaver Lake, Arkansas, a man and wife, both retired from the U.S. Army Corps of Engineers, breed AKC Schipperke dogs and take in stray animals for later adoption. They advertise their Skips in *Dog World* and buyers come from all over the Mississippi and Ohio valleys. For them, it's a matter of being your own boss and doing something you love rather than working a temporary job at Tyson's Foods, in nearby Springdale, when that employer is especially busy.

In a Chapel Hill haberdashery, a woman stands near the Hathaway and Pendleton shelves in the shirt alcove. The boys from Duke, UNC, and State are her customers, especially during the job-interviewing season. They haven't a clue about what goes into a good shirt or even how to wash it. She likes this retail job much better than the one she had selling linens and bedding at a department store in a mall near Raleigh.

In Eagle River, Wisconsin, a World War II veteran tells how his teenage friend is mystified that the man doesn't quit his $4.25-an-hour commander's job at American Legion Post #431 and get behind the counter at McDonald's out on Highway 17. The teenager promises to pull strings with the day manager to start the older friend at $6.00. For some odd reason, says the man, he can't drum into the kid's head that the commander's job requires organizational and human relations skills, and is far more fun and interesting than fast food, even if it were done for free.

A thousand miles south, a charming woman runs the visitor's drop-in center on Central Avenue in downtown Hot Springs, Arkansas. Amid rackfuls of brochures, booklets, maps, pamphlets, and broadsides, she talks with American and foreign tourists all day long. "Ask me a question and I'll be happy to answer it. And if I don't know the answer," she adds, "I'll be happy to make one up." Her work is voluntary; so are other options at St. Joseph's hospital auxiliary, or helping high school kids with reading problems.

All are retired and each works in his own way—as a volunteer, through self-employment, or at a part-time job. Though working after retirement is by no means a concern of every older adult, it is to many. In the years immediately after retirement, nearly one in four people take a short-schedule, seasonal, or temporary job. Another one in four would do the same thing, according to surveys, but several things stand in the way.

Social Security Rules

If you're going back to work, "Social Security giveth, and Social Security taketh away," notes retirement-expert Bob Menchin. The amount of money you can earn on the job and still collect the benefits coming to you is limited. If you're under 65 and your income exceeds $8,040, your benefits will be reduced by $1 for every $2 you're earning over that amount. If you're between 65 and 70 and earning more than $11,160, your benefits will be cut by $1 for every $3 you're paid over the ceiling. After age 70, these reductions no longer apply.

Keeping your earnings under the exempt amount is understandable. Not only would half or more of your excess earnings be lost through Social Security reductions, but they would be subject to income taxes as well as Social Security withholding. Explaining this to an employer unfortunately makes it seem as if you're limited in motivation.

The Market for Part-Time Jobs

Even though the number of part-time jobs has increased by 21 percent over the past decade, most of these positions are low-skill, low-paid ones with few benefits.

The big reason that there aren't more better-paying and challenging part-time jobs is the high cost to employers. Training and administrative costs, for instance, are the same for full- and part-time workers. A short work week boosts the hourly costs to employers for these expenses. In contrast, jobs that require little training—such as hamburger flipping, counter help, aisle sweeping, or cashiering—won't significantly raise the costs to employers, particularly if the job has no benefit package.

Age Discrimination

In spite of the law protecting anyone between the ages of 40 and 70 from being passed over in hiring or being involuntarily retired solely on the basis of age, this kind

---

Farms, Forests, and Mines

Just outside the built-up areas of most retirement places is an agricultural, forestry, and mining outback. Equipment sales yards on the commercial strips in town offer the clue: John Deere tractors, Ingersoll-Rand pumps, Dresser rock drills. At least one in seven workers in the following areas have a job in these slow-growing or no-growing industries.

Delta–Cedaredge, CO
Fredericksburg, TX
Lake Livingston, TX
Lake of the Cherokees, OK
Newport–Lincoln City, OR
Oakhurst–Coarsegold, CA
Polson–Mission Valley, MT
Silver City, NM
Wenatchee, WA
Yuma, AZ

Source: Woods & Poole Economics, Inc., employment forecasts.

---

of discrimination still happens everywhere in the world of work.

It is also one of the most difficult job-market issues to identify. Few, if any, employers support discriminatory business practices; they are open to lawsuits if they do. Yet a large number of older workers have experienced discrimination. About the only advice career counselors can offer is that fair treatment usually comes from working for a supervisor older than yourself.

JOB FORECASTS IN RETIREMENT PLACES

Economists who follow employment trends have an old joke: If you take each local planner's forecast for job growth in his or her area and add them all together, the total number of jobs forecasted would require that every man, woman, and child hold down one day job and moonlight two others.

Fortunately, forecasters at the national level try to adopt a more balanced perspective. Although no one can predict the future with certainty, predicting where jobs will be plentiful over the next few years isn't a matter of gazing into a crystal ball. Forecasters use reliable indicators.

To start, jobs come to where the people are. In other words, any place that has a concentration of people and is also growing is by definition a jobs Mecca.

Secondly, the hot industries—retail trade, services, and finance, insurance, and real estate (known as FIRE) will stay hot. With variation between places, this is where the real action is expected to occur in the remaining years of the 20th century. And with variation among employers, these industries are precisely the ones where *good* part-time jobs are found.

Military Economies

At least 1 in every 12 workers in the following places gets paid by the Department of Defense. Military cutbacks and base closings throughout the 1990s may hit their economies hard. For good reason several of their representatives are sitting on the Armed Services Committee in Congress.

> Alamogordo, NM
>
> Bay St. Louis–Pass Christian, MS
>
> Beaufort, SC
>
> Charleston Sea Islands, SC
>
> Colorado Springs, CO
>
> Hilton Head Island, SC
>
> New Bern, NC
>
> Oscoda–Tawas–Huron Shore, MI
>
> San Diego, CA
>
> Virginia Beach, VA
>
> Whidbey Island, WA
>
> Yuma, AZ

Source: Woods & Poole Economics, Inc., employment forecasts.

College-Town Competition

For all the lively goings-on in places dominated by the higher education calendar, they aren't ideal places for older adults to track down an interesting part-time or seasonal job. The competition is especially stiff in the following places, where the number of younger persons who look for a part-time job is more than seven times the number of persons in their late 50s and early 60s searching for the same thing.

> Amherst–Northampton, MA
>
> Athens, GA
>
> Austin, TX
>
> Boone–Blowing Rock, NC
>
> Burlington, VT
>
> Chapel Hill, NC
>
> Charlottesville, VA
>
> Clemson–Pendleton District, SC
>
> Fort Collins–Loveland, CO
>
> Gainesville, FL
>
> Las Cruces, NM
>
> Oxford, MS
>
> State College, PA
>
> Virginia Beach, VA

Source: Woods & Poole Economics, Inc., population forecasts.

Unemployment Threat

If you see a good number of light-manufacturing plants with full parking lots and notice lots of hardhat construction workers aboard growling earth-moving machines at new residential and commercial developments, you'll know that in flush times jobs are easy to find here and the pay is just great. You can also assume that, should a recession roll in, this place may be hard hit by unemployment.

One of the few things you'll find economists agreeing on is that places with large numbers of workers in manufacturing and construction are harshly affected during business slumps.

In contrast to boom-and-bust places, there are others where the pace isn't quite as fast, and where large numbers of white-collar workers commute to downtown or suburban jobs with financial, real estate, and insurance firms. Others find their work at colleges and universities, at big medical centers in the area, or at local resorts. The employment mix in these areas is more balanced, with most of the weight going to the white-collar sector.

Finally, there are places at the opposite extreme from industrial places, not because they are thriving, but because manufacturing plays no part in their existence. These have nearly pure white-collar economies characterized by people working almost exclusively in retail trade, services, finance, insurance, and real estate.

Even though in retirement you may have little to worry about regarding being without a full-time job, local unemployment may still affect you in unforeseen ways. By boosting the competition for available work, high unemployment limits your chances of finding a part-time job should you ever want one.

Just as places can be rated for mild climates and their supply of public golf links, so also can they be rated for how vulnerable they are to joblessness during a bad business cycle. The unemployment threat is:

High

- ■ if factory workers and construction workers hold down more than 35 percent . . .
- ■ or if Department of Defense workers and military hold down more than 12 percent . . .
- ■ or if together they hold down more than 40 percent *of all the jobs in the area.*

Moderate

- ☐ if the number of construction workers and factory workers is between 20 and 35 percent . . .
- ☐ or the number of military and other workers for the Defense Department is between 6 and 12 percent . . .
- ☐ or if together they number between 25 and 40 percent *of all employment in the area.*

Low

- □ if factory and construction workers total less than 20 percent . . .
- □ or Department of Defense workers and military are less than 6 percent . . .
- □ or if together they are less than 25 percent *of all the jobs in the area.*

Among *Retirement Places Rated*'s 183 locations, the unemployment threat is high in 11, moderate in 50, and low in 122.

What Are the Odds?

Think of how much competition you'll meet in tracking down a good seasonal or short-schedule job. Are there crowds of voluntary part-time workers pounding the pavement everywhere, or are the odds more favorable in Phoenix and Chapel Hill than in Orlando or Albuquerque?

"Voluntary" part-timers are persons who want only part-time jobs rather than persons who resignedly take a temporary, seasonal, or short-schedule job because there's nothing else available. There are 13 million voluntary part-timers in this country. Most are older adults, 19- to 23-year-old college students, and women ages 38 to 54 easing back into the workplace.

To measure competition, *Retirement Places Rated* compares the population of these two latter groups to persons in their early 60s. In each place, the part-time job competition is:

- ■ **Unfavorable** if the number of college-age persons and women reentering the job market is more than five times the number of persons in their early 60s.
- ⊡ **Average** if the number of college-age persons and women reentering the job market is between three and five times the number of persons in their early 60s.
- □ **Favorable** if the number of college-age persons and women reentering the job market is less than three times the number of persons in their early 60s.

Among *Retirement Places Rated*'s 183 locations, the competition is favorable in 97, average in 73, and unfavorable in 13.

GRADING: Working

If you've taken early retirement from your lifelong career and want to launch a new one or simply land an interesting part-time job, are the prospects rosier in Redding, Reno, or Ruidoso?

To help you answer the question, *Retirement Places Rated* compares two factors in each place: the percentage rate of job growth over the next five years, and the total number of new full-time equivalent jobs forecasted in retail trade, services, and the so-called FIRE industries in each place. (A full-time equivalent job is typically held by one worker; occasionally, two workers share it. Two full-time equivalent jobs roughly translate into three part-time jobs of 25 hours per week.)

The two factors—number of new jobs and rate of growth—are multiplied together to produce a score which is then scaled against a standard where no growth or net job loss equals 0 and job gains at a rate 5 times the national average produces a perfect 100.

RANKINGS: Working

In ranking 183 places for job growth, *Retirement Places Rated* uses two criteria: (1) the number of new jobs forecast between now and the year 2000 in Services, Retail Trade, and the FIRE industries (Finance, Insurance, and Real Estate), and (2) the rate of increase in these new jobs.

Forecasts are for the entire county in which the place is located. Grades are rounded two decimal places. Locations with tie grades, usually within the same county, get the same rank and are listed alphabetically.

Retirement Places from First to Last

Rank	Score	Rank	Score	Rank	Score
1. San Diego, CA	100.00	53. Santa Barbara, CA	69.06	108. Payson, AZ	55.35
2. Phoenix–Mesa–Scottsdale, AZ	99.05	54. Savannah, GA	68.67	109. Hendersonville–East Flat Rock, NC	54.93
2. Wickenburg, AZ	99.05	55. Lakeland–Winter Haven, FL	68.60	110. Amador County, CA	54.79
4. Laguna Beach–Dana Point, CA	98.87	56. Ocala, FL	68.53	111. Ocean City, MD	54.63
5. Las Vegas, NV	95.37	57. Carmel–Monterey–Pebble Beach, CA	67.80	112. Petoskey–Harbor Springs, MI	54.53
6. Boca Raton–Delray Beach, FL	94.33	58. Bend, OR	67.70	113. Charlottesville, VA	54.24
7. Pompano Beach, FL	87.67	59. Sedona, AZ	67.69	114. Port Townsend, WA	54.04
8. Palm Springs–Coachella Valley, CA	87.06	60. San Luis Obispo, CA	67.67	115. Lake Winnipesaukee, NH	53.80
9. Fort Myers–Cape Coral, FL	86.77	61. Gainesville, FL	67.62	116. Charlevoix–Boyne City–East Jordan, MI	53.57
10. Tucson, AZ	86.37	62. Traverse City, MI	67.41	117. Port Angeles–Sequim, WA	52.95
11. St. Petersburg–Clearwater, FL	85.91	63. St. Simons–Jekyll Islands, GA	67.17	118. Bar Harbor, ME	52.88
12. Kissimmee–St. Cloud, FL	84.56	64. Santa Fe, NM	66.82	119. Panama City, FL	52.86
12. New Port Richey, FL	84.56	65. Redding, CA	66.62	120. Southern Pines–Pinehurst, NC	52.79
14. Hesperia–Apple Valley–Victorville, CA	84.41	66. Placerville–Shingle Springs, CA	66.36	121. New Bern, NC	52.50
15. Bradenton, FL	83.23	67. Bellingham, WA	66.08	122. Smith Mountain Lake, VA	52.43
16. Austin, TX	82.56	68. Key West–Key Largo–Marathon, FL	65.66	123. Kalispell–Flathead Valley, MT	52.19
17. Conway, SC	81.69	69. Asheville, NC	65.59	124. Kerrville, TX	52.08
17. Myrtle Beach, SC	81.69	70. Pahrump Valley, NV	65.28	125. Amherst–Northampton, MA	51.92
19. Maui, HI	80.30	70. New Braunfels, TX	65.28	126. Charleston Sea Islands, SC	51.46
20. Kingman, AZ	80.15	72. York Beaches, ME	64.77	127. Crossville, TN	51.32
20. Lake Havasu City, AZ	80.15	73. Coeur d'Alene, ID	64.74	128. Northern Door Peninsula, WI	50.79
20. Riviera–Bullhead City, AZ	80.15	74. Kauai, HI	64.62	129. Grants Pass, OR	50.37
23. Santa Rosa–Sonoma, CA	79.52	75. Chapel Hill, NC	63.80	130. Camden, ME	50.27
24. Sarasota, FL	79.22	76. Paradise–Magalia, CA	63.17	131. Carson City–Carson Valley, NV	49.85
25. Annapolis, MD	78.92	77. Medford–Ashland, OR	62.61	132. Beaver Lake, AR	49.40
26. San Antonio, TX	78.45	78. Burlington, VT	62.51	133. Norfork Lake, AR	49.07
27. Mission–McAllen–Alamo, TX	77.72	79. Florence, OR	62.39	134. Litchfield Hills, CT	48.57
28. Naples, FL	77.18	80. Branson, MO	62.35	135. Southern Berkshire County, MA	48.32
29. Brooksville–Spring Hill, FL	75.87	81. Western St. Tammany Parish, LA	61.57	136. Athens, GA	48.30
30. Lake Conroe, TX	75.25	81. Toms River–Barnegat Bay, NJ	61.57	137. Table Rock Lake, MO	48.19
31. Leesburg–Lady Lake, FL	75.17	83. Virginia Beach, VA	60.49	138. Silver City, NM	48.16
32. Daytona Beach, FL	74.79	84. Fayetteville, AR	60.30	139. Wimberly–San Marcos, TX	47.68
33. Albuquerque, NM	74.24	85. Las Cruces, NM	60.02	140. Oxford, MS	47.61
34. Melbourne, FL	73.66	86. Beaufort, SC	59.68	141. San Juan Islands, WA	46.99
35. East End Long Island, NY	72.89	86. Hilton Head Island, SC	59.68	142. Woodstock, VT	46.61
36. Port Charlotte–Punta Gorda, FL	72.71	88. Cape Cod, MA	59.61	143. Eagle River, WI	46.43
37. Vero Beach–Sebastian, FL	72.47	89. Taos, NM	58.96	144. Montrose, CO	46.03
38. Clemson–Pendleton District, SC	71.87	90. Lower Cape May, NJ	58.93	145. Sandpoint–Priest River, ID	45.44
39. Cottonwood–Verde Valley, AZ	71.68	91. Fredericksburg–Spotsylvania, VA	58.91	146. McCall–Cascade–Payette Valley, ID	44.90
39. Prescott–Prescott Valley, AZ	71.68	92. Hanover, NH	58.12	147. Cedar Creek Lake, TX	44.87
41. Aiken, SC	71.57	93. Yuma, AZ	57.94	148. Brookings–Gold Beach, OR	44.47
42. St. George–Zion, UT	71.48	94. Winchester, VA	57.78	149. Bay St. Louis–Pass Christian, MS	44.37
43. Colorado Springs, CO	70.84	95. State College, PA	57.68	150. Charles Town–Harpers Ferry–Shepherdstown, WV	43.77
43. Southport–Brunswick Islands, NC	70.84	96. Maryville, TN	57.34	151. Hot Springs, AR	43.27
45. Fairhope–Gulf Shores, AL	70.58	97. Sebring–Avon Park, FL	56.86	152. Lake Livingston, TX	43.26
46. Grass Valley–Nevada City, CA	70.15	98. Boone–Blowing Rock, NC	56.51	153. Clayton, GA	42.05
47. St. Augustine, FL	69.85	99. Lake Granbury, TX	56.48	154. Brevard, NC	41.88
48. Fort Collins–Loveland, CO	69.43	100. Lake of the Ozarks, MO	56.38	155. Ketchum–Sun Valley, ID	41.16
49. Reno–Sparks, NV	69.33	101. Madison, MS	56.36	156. Lake Buchanan–Lake LBJ, TX	40.89
50. Rehoboth Bay–Indian River Bay, DE	69.29	102. Grand Junction, CO	56.11	157. Kentucky Lake, KY	40.58
51. Inverness, FL	69.27	102. Oakhurst–Coarsegold, CA	56.11	158. Lake of the Cherokees, OK	39.30
52. Dare Outer Banks, NC	69.08	104. Whidbey Island, WA	55.72	159. Fredericksburg, TX	38.39
		105. Sonora–Groveland–Twain Harte, CA	55.65	160. Blairsville, GA	37.60
		106. Wenatchee, WA	55.55		
		107. Guntersville, AL	55.38		

Rank	Score		Rank	Score		Rank	Score
161. Northern Neck, VA	37.10		171. Ruidoso, NM	25.82		176. Houghton Lake, MI	17.25
162. Newport–Lincoln City, OR	36.28		172. Hamilton–Bitterroot Valley, MT	23.35		177. Thomasville, GA	14.38
163. Pagosa Springs, CO	34.79					178. Edenton, NC	13.40
164. Williamsburg, VA	34.73		173. Oscoda–Tawas–Huron Shore, MI	22.21		179. Alpine–Big Bend, TX	11.78
165. Durango, CO	34.35		174. St. Jay–Northeast Kingdom, VT	21.47		180. Hiawassee, GA	10.06
166. Chewelah, WA	32.71		175. Easton–St. Michaels–Oxford, MD	20.01		181. Rockport–Aransas Pass, TX	10.04
167. Lake Martin, AL	27.09					182. Tryon, NC	9.04
168. Alamogordo, NM	26.97					183. Delta–Cedaredge, CO	0.00
169. Pike County, PA	26.61						
170. Polson–Mission Valley, MT	26.32						

PLACE PROFILES: Working

The following chart shows the number of new jobs forecasted in each place for Services, Retail Trade, and FIRE (Finance, Insurance, and Real Estate), the industries where most older adults find new opportunity and also where the most part-time, seasonal, and short-schedule jobs are found.

The chart also characterizes the local unemployment threat—low (represented by a □), moderate (represented by a ⊡), or high (represented by a ■); and the competition for part-time work—favorable (represented by a □), average (represented by a ⊡), or unfavorable (represented by a ■).

All figures are county totals and are derived from current employment forecasts by Woods & Poole Economics, Inc., of Washington, D.C., and are used here with permission.

A check mark (✓) in front of a place's name highlights it as one of the top 18 places for part-time job opportunities between 1995 and 2000.

Place	Unemployment Threat	Services	Retail	FIRE	Competition	Grade
Aiken, SC	■	1,580	2,640	270	⊡	72
Alamogordo, NM	■	160	100	50	□	27
Albuquerque, NM	□	8,060	3,600	1,460	□	74
Alpine–Big Bend, TX	□	50	20	0	□	12
Amador County, CA	□	570	300	120	■	55
Amherst–Northampton, MA	□	1,250	540	130	□	52
Annapolis, MD	□	8,830	3,650	1,860	⊡	79
Asheville, NC	⊡	2,180	2,850	70	□	66
Athens, GA	□	490	960	150	□	48
✓ Austin, TX	□	14,590	3,180	4,660	⊡	83
Bar Harbor, ME	⊡	620	540	160	□	53
Bay St. Louis–Pass Christian, MS	⊡	690	570	170	□	44
Beaufort, SC	■	560	1,300	380	⊡	60
Beaver Lake, AR	⊡	370	220	30	⊡	49
Bellingham, WA	□	1,870	2,320	170	⊡	66
Bend, OR	⊡	1,670	1,410	490	⊡	68
Blairsville, GA	⊡	120	100	30	⊡	38
✓ Boca Raton–Delray Beach, FL	□	27,540	14,020	5,750	⊡	94
Boone–Blowing Rock, NC	□	580	820	130	⊡	57
✓ Bradenton, FL	□	9,860	2,330	630	⊡	83
Branson, MO	□	1,310	640	80	□	62
Brevard, NC	⊡	310	230	90	□	42
Brookings–Gold Beach, OR	□	230	240	50	□	44
Brooksville–Spring Hill, FL	□	2,430	1,780	270	■	76
Burlington, VT	⊡	2,550	1,100	590	□	63
Camden, ME	⊡	660	350	70	□	50
Cape Cod, MA	□	1,580	1,650	650	□	60
Carmel–Monterey–Pebble Beach, CA	⊡	3,820	1,350	900	⊡	68
Carson City–Carson Valley, NV	□	830	550	300	□	50
Cedar Creek Lake, TX	□	420	260	80	□	45
Chapel Hill, NC	□	940	1,560	660	⊡	64
Charles Town–Harpers Ferry–Shepherdstown, WV	⊡	300	210	80	⊡	44
Charleston Sea Islands, SC	⊡	3,220	640	(210)	□	51
Charlevoix–Boyne City–East Jordan, MI	⊡	270	440	100	□	54
Charlottesville, VA	□	1,830	1,500	260	□	54
Chewelah, WA	⊡	140	70	70	⊡	33
Clayton, GA	⊡	70	200	90	□	42
Clemson–Pendleton District, SC	⊡	2,560	4,130	520	⊡	72

Place	Unemployment Threat	Services	Retail	FIRE	Competition	Grade
Coeur d'Alene, ID	□	1,640	1,020	240	⊡	65
Colorado Springs, CO	■	5,960	2,350	840	□	71
✓ Conway, SC	□	3,530	6,230	1,720	□	82
Cottonwood–Verde Valley, AZ	□	1,670	1,670	830	■	72
Crossville, TN	⊡	410	520	60	□	51
Dare Outer Banks, NC	□	750	1,350	410	⊡	69
Daytona Beach, FL	□	4,700	5,150	1,350	□	75
Delta–Cedaredge, CO	□	10	0	(10)	□	0
Durango, CO	□	270	190	(30)	□	34
Eagle River, WI	□	310	220	70	□	46
East End Long Island, NY	□	12,250	1,050	2,270	□	72
Easton–St. Michaels–Oxford, MD	⊡	40	50	110	□	20
Edenton, NC	⊡	20	80	0	□	13
Fairhope–Gulf Shores, AL	□	1,700	1,760	650	⊡	71
Fayetteville, AR	⊡	1,530	950	340	□	60
Florence, OR	□	3,020	2,090	240	□	62
Fort Collins–Loveland, CO	⊡	3,470	2,180	230	⊡	69
✓ Fort Myers–Cape Coral, FL	□	9,360	6,930	2,860	⊡	87
Fredericksburg, TX	□	170	170	60	□	38
Fredericksburg–Spotsylvania, VA	□	1,630	1,400	280	■	59
Gainesville, FL	□	4,100	1,570	540	□	68
Grand Junction, CO	□	1,200	780	230	□	56
Grants Pass, OR	⊡	460	500	250	□	50
Grass Valley–Nevada City, CA	⊡	1,870	990	650	■	70
Guntersville, AL	■	480	860	160	⊡	55
Hamilton–Bitterroot Valley, MT	□	100	70	20	□	73
Hanover, NH	□	1,790	630	200	□	58
Hendersonville–East Flat Rock, NC	⊡	550	800	190	□	55
✓ Hesperia–Apple Valley–Victorville, CA	□	15,290	8,360	2,750	⊡	84
Hiawassee, GA	⊡	20	20	10	□	10
Hilton Head Island, SC	■	560	1,300	380	⊡	60
Hot Springs, AR	□	540	380	150	□	43
Houghton Lake, MI	□	50	60	0	□	17
Inverness, FL	□	1,390	1,540	620	⊡	69
Kalispell–Flathead Valley, MT	□	840	630	180	⊡	52
Kauai, HI	□	1,690	860	220	⊡	65
Kentucky Lake, KY	⊡	170	320	80	⊡	41
Kerrville, TX	□	550	400	190	⊡	52
Ketchum–Sun Valley, ID	⊡	90	190	110	□	41
Key West–Key Largo–Marathon, FL	□	1,950	1,380	390	⊡	66
Kingman, AZ	□	2,730	2,670	1,140	■	80
✓ Kissimmee–St. Cloud, FL	□	5,030	3,750	960	⊡	85
✓ Laguna Beach–Dana Point, CA	⊡	64,900	8,690	22,810	□	99
Lake Buchanan–Lake LBJ, TX	□	280	100	110	□	41
Lake Conroe, TX	□	3,390	1,760	420	⊡	75
Lake Granbury, TX	□	630	320	130	⊡	56
Lake Havasu City, AZ	□	2,730	2,670	1,140	■	80
Lake Livingston, TX	□	300	210	50	⊡	43
Lake Martin, AL	■	90	140	0	⊡	27
Lake of the Cherokees, OK	□	240	120	60	□	39
Lake of the Ozarks, MO	□	500	720	130	□	56
Lake Winnipesaukee, NH	□	620	1,230	200	□	54
Lakeland–Winter Haven, FL	□	2,690	4,520	570	□	69
Las Cruces, NM	□	1,270	850	300	⊡	60
✓ Las Vegas, NV	□	34,410	10,670	4,180	⊡	95
Leesburg–Lady Lake, FL	□	3,410	2,490	1,020	⊡	75
Litchfield Hills, CT	⊡	1,330	150	290	□	49
Lower Cape May, NJ	□	1,160	1,070	350	□	59
Madison, MS	□	550	760	250	⊡	56
Maryville, TN	⊡	780	1,070	40	⊡	57
Maui, HI	□	5,280	2,710	950	⊡	80
McCall–Cascade–Payette Valley, ID	□	150	180	30	⊡	45
Medford–Ashland, OR	□	1,590	1,870	270	□	63
Melbourne, FL	⊡	6,060	4,130	1,360	□	74
Mission–McAllen–Alamo, TX	□	4,310	5,130	780	⊡	78
Montrose, CO	□	290	280	70	□	46
✓ Myrtle Beach, SC	□	3,530	6,230	1,720	□	82
Naples, FL	□	5,220	2,020	910	⊡	77
New Bern, NC	■	720	810	150	□	53
New Braunfels, TX	□	930	1,560	270	⊡	65
✓ New Port Richey, FL	□	6,110	4,670	1,500	■	85
Newport–Lincoln City, OR	□	120	350	(10)	□	36
Norfork Lake, AR	⊡	640	150	50	⊡	49
Northern Door Peninsula, WI	⊡	560	460	40	□	51

Place	Unemployment Threat	Services	Retail	FIRE	Competition	Grade
Northern Neck, VA	⊡	260	90	50	□	37
Oakhurst–Coarsegold, CA	□	930	520	80	⊡	56
Ocala, FL	□	2,510	1,740	760	□	69
Ocean City, MD	□	560	830	250	□	55
Oscoda–Tawas–Huron Shore, MI	■	50	110	20	□	22
Oxford, MS	□	250	430	50	□	48
Pagosa Springs, CO	□	110	70	10	□	35
Pahrump Valley, NV	□	1,490	210	110	⊡	65
✓ Palm Springs–Coachella Valley, CA	□	15,010	7,540	3,490	⊡	87
Panama City, FL	⊡	1,070	1,210	80	□	53
Paradise–Magalia, CA	□	2,200	1,120	520	⊡	63
Payson, AZ	⊡	380	500	190	⊡	55
Petoskey–Harbor Springs, MI	□	880	310	40	⊡	55
✓ Phoenix–Mesa–Scottsdale, AZ	□	48,280	23,870	15,440	⊡	99
Pike County, PA	□	190	0	50	□	27
Placerville–Shingle Springs, CA	□	1,570	1,210	450	⊡	66
Polson–Mission Valley, MT	□	160	80	10	□	26
✓ Pompano Beach, FL	□	23,530	10,920	3,950	⊡	88
Port Angeles–Seqium, WA	□	760	530	80	⊡	53
Port Charlotte–Punta Gorda, FL	□	1,840	2,420	260	■	73
Port Townsend, WA	□	490	330	70	⊡	54
Prescott–Prescott Valley, AZ	□	1,670	1,670	830	■	72
Redding, CA	□	2,100	1,770	390	⊡	67
Rehoboth Bay–Indian River Bay, DE	⊡	1,590	2,010	1,630	□	69
Reno–Sparks, NV	□	5,030	2,330	750	□	69
Riviera–Bullhead City, AZ	□	2,730	2,670	1,140	■	80
Rockport–Aransas Pass, TX	□	10	10	40	□	10
Ruidoso, NM	□	120	70	20	□	26
St. Augustine, FL	□	1,890	1,520	430	□	70
St. George–Zion, UT	□	1,930	970	310	■	71
St. Jay–Northeast Kingdom, VT	⊡	110	60	20	□	21
✓ St. Petersburg–Clearwater, FL	□	15,340	11,070	3,890	□	86
St. Simons–Jekyll Islands, GA	□	1,670	1,300	380	□	67
San Antonio, TX	□	15,540	5,860	2,420	□	78
✓ San Diego, CA	⊡	55,810	25,090	12,670	□	100
San Juan Islands, WA	□	210	200	120	□	47
San Luis Obispo, CA	□	2,800	800	1,830	⊡	68
Sandpoint–Priest River, ID	⊡	270	230	80	⊡	45
Santa Barbara, CA	□	5,400	1,100	1,230	□	69
Santa Fe, NM	□	1,850	1,740	520	⊡	67
Santa Rosa–Sonoma, CA	□	8,430	3,000	2,530	⊡	80
Sarasota, FL	□	6,910	4,670	1,760	□	79
Savannah, GA	□	3,180	2,880	550	□	69
Sebring–Avon Park, FL	□	690	810	170	□	57
Sedona, AZ	□	1,670	1,670	830	■	68
Silver City, NM	⊡	350	230	30	⊡	48
Smith Mountain Lake, VA	■	180	230	130	□	52
Sonora–Groveland–Twain Harte, CA	□	670	420	310	⊡	56
Southern Berkshire County, MA	⊡	1,400	380	220	□	48
Southern Pines–Pinehurst, NC	⊡	980	350	160	□	53
Southport–Brunswick Islands, NC	□	1,120	1,110	620	⊡	71
State College, PA	□	1,120	1,470	240	□	58
Table Rock Lake, MO	□	420	150	80	□	48
Taos, NM	□	740	490	110	□	59
Thomasville, GA	⊡	50	90	0	□	14
Toms River–Barnegat Bay, NJ	□	2,620	1,360	750	□	62
Traverse City, MI	□	2,330	1,340	260	⊡	67
Tryon, NC	⊡	20	20	20	□	9
✓ Tucson, AZ	□	14,630	8,140	2,230	⊡	86
Vero Beach–Sebastian, FL	□	2,780	1,420	800	⊡	72
Virginia Beach, VA	⊡	2,730	3,610	1,400	□	60
Wenatchee, WA	□	1,000	580	90	□	56
Western St. Tammany Parish, LA	□	1,180	1,530	110	□	62
Whidbey Island, WA	■	930	510	200	⊡	56
✓ Wickenburg, AZ	□	48,280	23,870	15,440	⊡	99
Williamsburg, VA	□	140	570	100	⊡	35
Wimberly–San Marcos, TX	□	220	340	120	⊡	48
Winchester, VA	⊡	950	1,130	20	⊡	58
Woodstock, VT	⊡	860	220	150	□	47
York Beaches, ME	⊡	1,700	1,840	400	□	65
Yuma, AZ	⊡	910	890	250	□	58

ET CETERA: Working

It's dryly said that finding any job means having to listen to No, No, No, No, No . . . and No one more time before finally hearing Yes. Landing a good part-time job isn't any different, except when it means creating one with an employer who isn't looking, or interviewing an employer who is looking but hasn't the slightest idea what to do with an older applicant. In these situations, you may be in for a long series of No's.

SOME UNVOICED EMPLOYER OBJECTIONS

While job discrimination because of age is against the law, you might still be a victim of what labor economists call "statistical" discrimination when an employer assumes several things about all older persons applying for a job:

- You want a job that isn't available.
- You have old-fashioned, conservative values.
- You haven't the same economic incentive to work that younger workers have.
- You don't have the stamina or the flexibility.
- You want more money because you have more experience.
- You'll call in sick more often than younger workers.
- Your fringe coverage—life insurance, health insurance, and pension benefits—will cost more than fringes for younger applicants.
- Your prospects for staying with a job and justifying the employer's investment in on-the-job training are less than those of a younger worker.
- You're preoccupied with the past; a slate upon which nothing more can be written.

All of these objections somehow work themselves into the "overqualified" catch-all; it's the word most frequently used by an employer when turning down older people who've applied for a job.

Anyone who has worked 20, 30, or 40 years is overqualified by standard definition. Why not ask the employer what he or she means by being overqualified? If you'll go to work at the going rate, plus bring experience and maturity to the job, won't that mean that the cost of your productivity will be less than or equal to a younger worker's? If you're already covered by Medicare and Social Security, won't the employer avoid the cost of health insurance and a pension plan if you're hired? If the average tenure of younger workers in certain jobs is less than the shelf life of yogurt, won't you be a better bet for longevity?

PART-TIME JOB SEARCHING

The number of part-time jobs increased 21 percent over the past decade. Most of these jobs are found in retail trade, services, and in finance, insurance, and real estate. Here are some useful strategies for searching out good opportunities.

Focus on Small Businesses and Nonprofit Organizations. Large employers often have policies against part-time employment. Smaller companies are more flexible. Moreover, small businesses compete with larger employers for good workers, not by offering more money, but by offering informal, adaptable working conditions. Finally, many small businesses in the remainder of the 1990s will be started by older castoffs from corporations; in fact, economists expect more job creation in organizations with fewer than 250 employees than in larger firms.

Many of the most interesting jobs are found in the nonprofit sector—libraries, museums, colleges and universities, and human service organizations. Like small businesses, they offer flexibility instead of big money.

Respond to Full-Time Job Openings. If you've identified an employer that can use your skills, buttonhole the boss for a full-time job. If he or she hasn't any, suggest a part-time alternative. If the company has no experience with part-timers, suggest a trial period.

Too often part-timers pass by advertised positions that are full-time. Many 8-hour-a-day jobs can be shared.

Don't Forget the Government. Part-time opportunities are expanding within the federal government, partly because of a 12-year-old law that requires federal agencies to introduce short-schedule positions and prorate compensation and benefits according to the number of hours worked. The good jobs, however, are reserved for persons who've previously worked for Uncle Sam for at least three years.

All state governments have agencies with part-time positions. The key is identifying the agencies and where in the state the positions are (don't assume there are no state government jobs outside of the capital city). A good place to start is the state's aging or adult services office (listed under "Relocation Resources" in the Appendix of this book).

Try Temporary Work. One major reason why agencies that supply temporary workers are hiring older persons is that the work is usually full-time for a limited period. For job-seekers with child-care needs, this isn't the most attractive situation. Agencies specializing in clerical work dominate the Yellow Pages, but firms that

Part-time Employers: A Short Directory

Depending on the product or service they sell, America's millions of private businesses are pigeonholed into more than 20,000 slots by the federal government. Here's a selected list, grouped under the three broadest classes—Retail Trade; Finance, Insurance, and Real Estate; and Services—that (1) are found nearly everywhere, (2) offer part-time and seasonal flexibility, and (3) are businesses where older adults are finding jobs.

RETAIL TRADE

BUILDING MATERIALS AND GARDEN SUPPLIES
Lumber and Other Building Materials
Paint, Glass, and Wallpaper Stores
Hardware Stores
Retail Nurseries and Garden Stores
Mobile Home Dealers

GENERAL MERCHANDISE STORES
Department Stores
Variety Stores

FOOD STORES
Grocery Stores
Meat and Fish Markets
Fruit and Vegetable Markets
Candy, Nut, and Confectionery Stores
Dairy Products Stores
Retail Bakeries

AUTOMOTIVE DEALERS AND SERVICE STATIONS
New and Used Car Dealers
Auto- and Home-Supply Stores
Gasoline Service Stations
Boat Dealers
Recreational Vehicle Dealers
Motorcycle Dealers

APPAREL AND ACCESSORY STORES
Men's & Boys' Clothing Stores
Women's Clothing Stores
Women's Accessory & Specialty Stores
Children's and Infants' Wear Stores
Family Clothing Stores
Shoe Stores

FURNITURE AND HOME FURNISHINGS STORES
Furniture Stores
Household Appliance Stores
Radio, TV, and Electronic Stores

MISCELLANEOUS RETAIL
Drug Stores and Proprietary Stores
Liquor Stores
Used Merchandise Stores
Nonstore Retailers (Mail Order Firms)

FINANCE, INSURANCE, AND REAL ESTATE

DEPOSITORY INSTITUTIONS
Commercial Banks
Savings Institutions
Credit Unions

NONDEPOSITORY INSTITUTIONS
Federally Sponsored Credit Institutions
Personal Credit Institutions
Business Credit Institutions
Mortgage Bankers and Brokers

INSURANCE CARRIERS
Life Insurance
Medical Service and Health Insurance
Fire, Marine, and Casualty Insurance
Surety Insurance
Title Insurance
Pension, Health, and Welfare Funds

REAL ESTATE
Real Estate Operators and Lessors
Real Estate Agents and Managers
Title Abstract Offices
Subdividers and Developers

SERVICES

HOTELS AND OTHER LODGING PLACES
Hotels and Motels
Rooming and Boarding Houses
Camps and Recreational Vehicle Parks
Membership-Basis Organization Hotels

engage part-time engineers, accountants, and health-care professionals are growing.

Volunteer. The "Me" Decade has given way to the "Decency" Decade, if you follow pop sociologists on the talk shows. Today, one of every four Americans over 14 is involved in some kind of volunteer work. The value of all their volunteered time adds up to more than $100 billion a year.

Volunteer positions frequently turn into paid positions. If anything, they provide the setting for polishing up existing job skills and acquiring new skills and experience for seeking paid employment.

Part-time Employers: A Short Directory (continued)

SERVICES (continued)

PERSONAL SERVICES
Laundry, Cleaning, and Garment Services
Photographic Studios, Portrait
Beauty Shops
Barber Shops
Shoe Repair and Shoeshine Parlors
Funeral Service and Crematories

BUSINESS SERVICES
Advertising
Credit Reporting and Collection
Mailing, Reproduction, Stenographic
Services to Buildings
Miscellaneous Equipment Rental and Leasing
Personnel Supply Services
Computer and Data Processing Services

AUTO REPAIR, SERVICES, AND PARKING
Automotive Rentals
Automobile Parking
Automotive Repair Shops

MISCELLANEOUS REPAIR SERVICES
Electrical Repair Shops
Watch, Clock, and Jewelry Repair
Reupholstery and Furniture Repair

MOTION PICTURES
Motion Picture Production and Services
Motion Picture Distribution and Services
Motion Picture Theaters
Video Tape Rental

AMUSEMENT AND RECREATION SERVICES
Dance Studios, Schools, and Halls
Producers, Orchestras, Entertainers
Bowling Centers
Commercial Sports
Miscellaneous Amusement, Recreation Services

HEALTH SERVICES
Offices and Clinics of Medical Doctors
Offices and Clinics of Dentists
Offices of Osteopathic Physicians
Office of Other Health Practitioners
Nursing and Personal Care Facilities
Hospitals
Medical and Dental Laboratories
Home Health Care Services

LEGAL SERVICES
Legal Services

EDUCATIONAL SERVICES
Elementary and Secondary Schools
Colleges and Universities
Libraries
Vocational Schools

SOCIAL SERVICES
Individual and Family Services
Job Training and Related Services
Child Day Care Services
Residential Care

MUSEUMS, BOTANICAL, ZOOLOGICAL GARDENS
Museums and Art Galleries
Botanical and Zoological Gardens

MEMBERSHIP ORGANIZATIONS
Business Associations
Professional Organizations
Labor Organizations
Civic and Social Associations
Political Organizations
Religious Organizations

ENGINEERING AND MANAGEMENT SERVICES
Engineering and Architectural Services
Accounting, Auditing, and Bookkeeping
Research and Testing Services
Management and Public Relations

LEISURE LIVING

Like mild and dry climates, leisure attractions aren't fairly distributed. Some places have more indoor and outdoor benefits going for them than others. Many of these attractions are doubly important if you want to balance fun and games with the lively arts, and the lively arts with the great outdoors.

COMMON DENOMINATORS

It's lucky geographic circumstances that make clam digging, hang gliding, alpine skiing, river rafting, or growing good tomatoes better in some parts of the country than in others.

But geography has little to do with more conventional activities: golfing at a public course on a week-day morning when the greens fees are cheaper; team bowling in the din at a local tenpin center; catching a movie at a showcase cinema in a shopping mall off the interstate; or dining out in a quality restaurant.

You might call these familiar activities "common denominators." They are everywhere. On a per-person basis, though, their supply varies from place to place.

Counting Stars: Good Restaurants

The most common service establishment in this country is the one where you walk in, sit down, and order something to eat. If you enjoy an occasional dinner splurge you might as well go to a worthwhile eatery instead of a diner or a portion-controlled Casa de la Maison House where distantly prepared frozen packs of beef Wellington and veal *cordon bleu* are microwaved, dished out, and "menued" at 10 times what the chef paid for them.

To learn which places have restaurants more than just a cut or two above average, *Retirement Places Rated* consulted the seven-volume *Mobil Travel Guide*, which since 1958 has rated restaurants across the country.

The Mobil ratings come from two sources: customer comments and inspection reports of field representatives who dine anonymously at establishments throughout the year. Restaurants are judged by the quality of their food, service, and ambience. Ratings range from one star for a "good, better than average" restaurant to five stars for "one of the best in the country."

Retirement Places Rated divides the local population by the number of quality stars awarded establishments in each place. Three two-star restaurants and four three-star restaurants, for example, would yield 18 quality stars.

Counting Holes: Public Golf Courses

On a gray winter day in the Arkansas Ozarks, a group of older men and women who've challenged each other to play once a day throughout the year—rain, sleet, or

Dry Places

Travel writers note that good places to eat are seldom found in countiesd where the sale of liquor is prohibited. This may explain why three have few or no Mobil-rated restaurants.

Blairsville, GA
Hiawassee, GA
Kentucky Lake, KY

Eighteen Places for Dining Out

Though small places have fewer good restaurants than larger, glitzier places, many can still claim at least one Mobil quality star for every 2,000 people.

Place	Residents per star
Northern Door Peninsula, WI	236
St. Simons–Jekyll Islands, GA	503
Southern Berkshire County, MA	734
East End Long Island, NY	800
Taos, NM	866
Carmel–Monterey–Pebble Beach, CA	1,247
Ocean City, MD	1,361
Williamsburg, VA	1,467
Ketchum–Sun Valley, ID	1,515
Hilton Head Island, SC	1,531
Bar Harbor, ME	1,548
Santa Fe, NM	1,573
Cape Cod, MA	1,653
Woodstock, VT	1,673
Dare Outer Banks, NC	1,861
San Juan Islands, WA	1,937
Hanover, NH	1,972
Key West–Key Largo–Marathon, FL	1,980

Source: Derived from *Mobile Travel Guide* and Woods & Poole Economics, Inc., population forecasts.

Twelve Places for Public Golf

Listed below are places with fewer than 250 residents per public golf hole.

Place	Residents per hole
Hilton Head Island, SC	85
Myrtle Beach, SC	98
Northern Door Peninsula, WI	108
St. Simons–Jekyll Islands, GA	147
Southport–Brunswick Islands, NC	148
Charlevoix–Boyne City–East Jordan, MI	197
Ketchum–Sun Valley, ID	210
Houghton Lake, MI	214
Southern Pines–Pinehurst, NC	216
Pagosa Springs, CO	225
Bend, OR	226
Eagle River, WI	242

Source: Derived from National Golf Foundation, unpublished data, and Woods & Poole Economics, Inc., population forecasts.

Still, because public regulation golf is an excellent indicator of other leisure options in any place, *Retirement Places Rated* counts not the number of municipal and daily-fee courses but their total number of holes per capita. Durango, Colorado, and Beaver Lake, Arkansas, each have one municipal course, for example. But there are 36 holes at the course in the Rocky Mountain resort, and only nine at the one in the Ozarks.

Counting Lanes: Tenpin Bowling

The sound of a hardwood ball striking hardwood pins was sometimes mistaken for a thunderclap in early 19th-century America. The sport has been around a long, long time indeed, and along with all its variations —skittles, fivepins, ninepins, tenpins, candlepins, duckpins, and bocce—is probably played by more people in the world than any other game.

In the United States, the dominant variation is tenpins, and nearly 71 million people take a turn at it once or twice a year. But if the 8,100 bowling centers had to depend solely on this kind of casual participation, many might quickly convert to exercise studios or oil-change shops for a steadier income. The credit for keeping the alleys in business goes to the American Bowling Congress (ABC), to which 3.2 million men belong, and the Women's International Bowling Congress (WIBC), with 3 million women members, which promote tournaments throughout the country.

Forget the notion that it's only a blue-collar, indoor sport. Doctors are prescribing it. Besides relieving the postural backache that comes from sitting too long, the physical exercise and the challenge of making the ball knock down all those pins produce better coordination of vision and mind with practically all the muscles of the body.

Another plus for newcomers is the ready-made social contacts that are part of formal bowling competition. Whether you're in Chapel Hill, Charleston, or

shine—are duffing away in their parkas on the Bella Vista Golf Course. Everywhere, surveys show, the portion of persons of their age who play golf regularly is greater than that of any other group.

You've got three options if you're searching for golf on an idle, sunny weekend: the private course, typically part of a country club or leisure-living community open only to members and guests; a private, daily-fee operation open to all players for a fee; and a municipal course operated by a tax-supported agency such as a city, county, school, or park district.

If you can afford to join a private country club with an 18-hole course, the dues you pay buy more than valet parking and the use of the swimming pool and tennis courts. You belong to the 14 percent of golfers who don't have to kill time waiting to tee off at crowded public courses. On the other hand, if you're one of 23 million golfers in the country who regularly play a round at a daily-fee or municipal course, only six of every 10 of the nation's courses are open to you.

Fourteen Places for Tenpin Bowling

A weather-exempt pastime, bowling is thought by some to be just a blue-collar excuse for an evening out of the house. But the sound of balls hitting pins is heard in resorts around the country. Listed below are places with fewer than 1,000 residents per lane.

Place	Residents per lane
Northern Door Peninsula, WI	335
Annapolis, MD	492
Myrtle Beach, SC	584
Lake Havasu City, AZ	624
Pahrump Valley, NV	680
Ruidoso, NM	723
Wickenburg, TX	743
McCall–Cascade–Payette Valley, ID	786
Eagle River, WI	818
Blairsville, GA	881
Rehoboth Bay–Indian River Bay, DE	913
Payson, AZ	941
Southern Berkshire County, MA	986
Beaufort, SC	992

Source: Derived from American Bowling Congress, unpublished data, and Woods & Poole Economics, Inc., population forecasts.

Charlottesville, you'll find team bowling. With 1.5 million teams in 117,469 leagues around the country, what better odds can there be for meeting a group that's right for you?

Counting Screens: The Movies

The number of people over 55 who regularly caught a commercial film doubled during the 1980s. This may seem odd since the studios rarely think that older adults are part of audience demographics when new picture ideas are pitched for playability in Peoria, Pittsburgh, and Portland. Aside from there being more people over 55 each year, another reason for increased attendance is the afternoon discount at cinemas in suburban shopping malls.

You may recall the 1940s when moviegoing was a routine family activity. Remember when John Huston won two Academy Awards—best director and best screenplay—for *The Treasure of Sierra Madre?* And his father, Walter, was named best supporting actor for his portrayal of the old prospector in the same film? Jane Wyman won an Oscar for her role in *Johnny Belinda;* *Hamlet* was best picture, and its star, Laurence Olivier, best actor.

The year was 1948, a time when moviegoing was the American thing to do in the evening, any evening. Popcorn was regularly swept up from the aisles between shows, the next John Wayne or Spencer Tracy film was announced on a large easel in the lobby, usherettes took you to your seat with a red-lensed flashlight, and you always got a MovieTone or Warner-Pathé newsreel with the show. There were 18,631 movie houses back then.

Most were neighborhood establishments with a few downtown palaces for premieres and first-run screenings. Never again would there be so many.

Retirement Places Rated divides the local population by the number of commercial four-wall (as opposed to drive-in) theater screens to figure access to movies. Most are in multiplex cinemas run by exhibitors like United Artists, Loews, and Cineplex Odeon at shopping malls. But the single-screen or twin Bijou or Strand kind of neighborhood theater is still alive in many places.

THE LIVELY ARTS

How do you measure the cultural goings-on in another place? If you loved your hometown's symphony, will you, after surfacing somewhere, have to settle for shaded seats at the annual outdoor Country Harmonica Blow-off?

Put it another way: if you exchange a big place for a smaller one, dirty air for clean, cold seasons for warm sun, the costly for the economical, do you also risk trading the lively arts for a cultural desert?

The Lively Arts Calendar

Long before a touring pianist, European boys choir, or visiting New York contemporary dance troupe comes to town for a date at the local performing arts center, it is booked by a nonprofit college or community concert association.

Does this mean you'll find the performing arts only in a big city blessed with an expensive concert hall and a nonprofit community concert association bankrolled by philanthropists, managed by paid professionals, and attended by season member-subscribers? Not necessarily.

The attendance growth at fine arts concerts is due not to turning up the volume and variety of performances in big cities but to popular interest in smaller cities and towns. And a good part of the interest comes from older fans. Among the 183 places in this guide, 113 benefit from 318 college and community arts series that regularly book touring artists.

Resident Ensembles

Besides taking in the touring attractions, people in some places have the additional option of attending performances of resident ensembles.

Opera. The image of horned helmets, silvery shields, and unintelligible singing is a low-brow cliché. Fans boast that operatic stagecraft is the most demanding of the performing arts because of the unique commingling of instruments and voice with theater and dance; if you're introduced to a good production, they say, you'll be hooked for life. Twenty-nine places have live opera. Brevard, Las Vegas, and Santa Fe may have little else in common but they all belong to this group.

Symphony Orchestras. Orchestras are more common than opera companies. Seventy-two places have at least one. Their music is heard in woodsy state parks, high-school auditoriums, philharmonic halls, impressive new civic arts centers, and small-town bandboxes and pavilions. Phoenix, San Antonio, and San Diego support "major" symphonies; that is, orchestras with budgets over $5 million.

OUTDOOR RECREATION ASSETS

For many, the great outdoors is one "destination pull" outweighing all the "origin push" factors associated with urban crime, traffic, and high costs of living. It takes in a wide range of possibilities. It might mean lying on a Gulf Coast beach, tramping the Appalachian Trail, flycasting for Rocky Mountain rainbow, daysailing on Chesapeake Bay, or just getting away from it all to a cabin on the edge of a Pacific Northwest wilderness area.

Well before the time comes for shedding job obligations, many people have already identified from past family vacations the places where, when they retire, their own ideal of the great outdoors will be right outside their door.

The Water Draw

Maryland watermen tell mainland tourists who come to Chesapeake Bay fishing villages for the oysters and soft-shell crabs that the true length of estuarine shore reached by the Bay's tide would total more than 8,000 miles if all the kinks and bends were flattened out.

They say in Michigan's Roscommon County that the locals tend to live away from Houghton Lake, the state's biggest inland body of water, while the transplanted retired folks who've migrated up from Detroit or Cleveland or Chicago unerringly light on the shore like loons there for the duration.

And Oklahomans vaunt the state's collection of Corps of Engineer lakes. If you could tip the state a bit to the south, they say, the water would flow out and flood Texas for a good while.

There's not much connection between the migration of retired people on the one hand and the sight of water on the other, however. Water didn't play nearly as great a part in attracting older adults during the 1980s as did a mild climate and resort development. In fact, certain Arizona, Nevada, and New Mexico counties that are desert-dry attracted retired people at a faster rate than wet counties in other parts of the country.

For all that, you'll spot lakes, ponds, and marine bays in nine out of 10 of the 183 *Retirement Places Rated* locations. Aside from being a basic necessity for supporting life, water is regarded by most people as a scenic amenity; many regard it as a recreational amenity—as long as there is enough of it to fish in, boat on, or swim in without enduring snowmelt-cold temperatures. What's Petoskey without the Straits of Mackinac?

Protected Land

In the 13 places listed below, more than half the land is set aside for state parks, national forests, national parks, and national wildlife refuges.

Place	Percentage of specially designated land
McCall–Cascade–Payette Valley, ID	85%
Wenatchee, WA	75
Hamilton–Bitterroot Valley, MT	73
Kalispell–Flathead Valley, MT	72
Sonora–Groveland–Twain Harte, CA	72
Clayton, GA	63
Bellingham, WA	61
Brookings–Gold Beach, OR	60
Port Townsend, WA	59
Payson, AZ	56
Hiawassee, GA	53
Bend, OR	50
Pagosa Springs, CO	50

Source: Places Rated Partnership survey.

Or Cape Cod minus the Atlantic Ocean? Four out of five Americans today live within 100 miles of a coastline; in another 10 years the Department of the Interior predicts three out of four will live within 50 miles. Not surprisingly, 76 *Retirement Places Rated* havens have an ocean or Great Lakes coastline.

Counting Acres: The Public Lands

Of all the outdoor activities that older adults take to most frequently, the leading ones—pleasure driving, walking, picnicking, sightseeing, bird-watching, nature walking, and fishing—might arguably be more fun in the country's splendid system of federal- and state-run public recreation areas.

National Forests. "Clear-Cutting Turns Off Tourists" say the bumper stickers in northwest Arkansas. So do rumbling, 18-wheel loggers' trucks. Although various parts of the national forests are classified as "wilderness," "primitive," "scenic," "historic," or "recreation" areas, the main purpose of the system is silviculture: growing wood, harvesting it carefully, and preserving naturally beautiful areas from the depredations of amateur chain saws, burger palaces, miniature golf, and time-share condos.

In rainy Deschutes National Forest near Bend, Oregon, the harvest is Douglas fir. Among the widespread components of Mark Twain National Forest in the southern Missouri Ozarks, the crop is local hardwoods of blackjack oak and hickory. Within Pisgah National Forest in western North Carolina the trees are virgin oak, beech, and black walnut.

But also within the forest system are more than a quarter of a million miles of paved roads, built not just for logging crews but for everyone. They lead to a wide variety of recreation developments: some 400 privately operated resorts, marinas, and ski lodges, plus fishing lakes and streams, campgrounds, and hiking trails. In 89 places profiled in the following pages, more than 3.5 million acres are national forest lands.

National Parks. Where multiple use is the philosophy behind national forests, the National Park System preserves irreplaceable geographic and historic treasures for public recreation. This has been its mission ever since Congress created Yellowstone National Park in adjacent western corners of the old Montana and Wyoming territories "as a public park or pleasuring ground for the benefit and enjoyment of the people" back in 1872.

The collection of national parks, preserves, monuments, memorials, battlefields, seashores, riverways, and trails makes up the oldest and largest national park system in the world. Twelve and a half million of the National Park System's 79 million acres are found in *Retirement Places Rated* areas.

National Wildlife Refuges. Wildlife refuges protect native flora and fauna from people. This purpose hasn't changed since 1903, when Theodore Roosevelt created the first refuge, Pelican Island near Vero Beach, Florida,

to save the mangrove-nesting egrets from poachers scrounging for plumage to adorn women's hats.

Most of the country's 498 refuges are open for wildlife activities, particularly photography and nature observation. In certain of the refuges and at irregular times, fishing and hunting are permitted, depending on the size of the refuge's wild populations. You don't have to move to the sticks to be close to nature. One-third of the land area of Clark County, Nevada (where Las Vegas is the seat of government), is dedicated to wildlife refuges. Fort Myers–Cape Coral, Florida, has four refuges on 5,648 acres—Caloosahatchee, J.N. "Ding" Darling, Matlacha Pass, and Pine Island.

State Recreation Areas. The 10 million acres of state-run recreation areas are often equal in quality to the federal public lands, and in most states older visitors get a break on entrance fees. They range from small day-use parks in wooded areas or on beaches, offering little more than picnic tables and rest rooms, to large rugged parks and forests with developed hiking trails and campsites, and big-time destination resorts complete with golf courses, swimming pools, tennis courts, and full-time recreation staffs.

GRADING: Leisure Living

Ranking places for leisure attractions, let's admit, can't be done fairly. A Florida bass fisherman, hauling out his smoky outboard motor for a tune-up, may care less for the announced dates of a local civic concert series. A Cape Cod couple lolling on the beach may never know the joys of Wisconsin ice fishing, nor would they ever regret the loss.

There are too many differences in taste for a rating system to suit everyone. Yet it's still possible to measure the supply of specific amenities. Chamber of Commerce brochures and state tourism promotion kits do it all the time. Travelers make their own comparisons. Hearsay may hold that winter living in the northern Michigan flatwoods is as dull and lonesome today as it was for the natives who quit the area for the city generations ago, or that there's little in the way of peaceful outdoor recreation in sunbaked Boca Raton.

Retirement Places Rated tries a more objective approach. It neither judges the quality of music by local symphonies and opera companies nor pushes the recreation benefits of the desert over seashore or forest environs. It simply indicates the presence of things that most persons agree enhance retirement living.

Each place starts with a base grade of zero, to which grades are added according to the following criteria.

Common Denominators

Places are graded for how accessible four common amenities are to residents. Access is rated AA, A, B, or C (AA indicates the greatest access and C the least), and the place receives a grade: 100 for an AA rating, 90 for an A, 80 for a B, and 70 for a C.

1. *Good restaurants.*

A place receives a rating of . . .	If there is one Mobil star for every . . .
AA	4,000 or fewer people
A	4,001 to 10,000 people
B	10,001 to 20,000 people
C	20,001 or more people

2. *Public golf courses.*

A place receives a rating of . . .	If there is one public golf hole for every . . .
AA	700 or fewer people
A	801 to 1,300 people
B	1,301 to 2,750 people
C	2,751 or more people

3. *Bowling lanes.*

A place receives a rating of . . .	If there is one certified lane for every . . .
AA	1,500 or fewer people
A	1,501 to 2,000 people
B	2,001 to 3,000 people
C	3,001 or more people

4. *Movie theaters.*

A place receives a rating of . . .	If there is one theater screen for every . . .
AA	6,500 or fewer people
A	6,501 to 10,000 people
B	10,001 to 15,000 people
C	15,001 or more people

The Lively Arts Calendar

In the calendar year, the number of dates booked for touring fine arts groups to perform at local campus and civic auditoriums is added to the number of performance dates for local opera companies and symphony orchestras. The result is then scaled against a standard where 26 dates or more receives a grade of 100 and no dates gets a 0.

Outdoor Assets

In the United States, a total of 18.63 percent of the land area is classified as inland or coastal water, federal protected land, or state recreation area.

Each place's own area percentage total for these four kinds of outdoor recreation assets is scaled against a standard where more than twice the national average gets a perfect 100 and none gets a 0.

RANKINGS: Leisure Living

Ten factors are used to derive the grade for a place's leisure-living assets: (1) good *restaurants,* (2) holes of *public golf,* (3) certified lanes of tenpin *bowling,* (4) movie *theater screens,* (5) campus and civic auditorium touring *artist bookings,* (6) resident *opera companies and symphony orchestras,* (7) ocean and Great Lakes *coastal water areas,* (8) *inland water areas,* (9) federal *protected lands,* and (10) state *recreation areas.*

Grades are rounded two decimal places. Locations that are tied get the same rank and are listed alphabetically.

Retirement Places from First to Last

Rank	Grade	Rank	Grade	Rank	Grade
1. Cape Cod, MA	897.50	26. Northern Door Peninsula, WI	83.33	47. Virginia Beach, VA	75.33
1. East End Long Island, NY	97.50	27. Hot Springs, AR	82.57	48. Sarasota, FL	75.19
3. Naples, FL	95.83	28. Yuma, AZ	82.39	49. Brevard, NC	74.40
4. Fort Collins–Loveland, CO	95.00	29. Savannah, GA	81.96	50. Boca Raton–Delray Beach, FL	72.17
5. Coeur d'Alene, ID	93.67	30. Palm Springs–Coachella Valley, CA	81.30		
6. Bellingham, WA	93.33			51. Gainesville, FL	71.73
7. St. Petersburg–Clearwater, FL	93.28	30. Southern Berkshire County, MA	81.30	52. Easton–St. Michaels–Oxford, MD	71.33
8. Santa Barbara, CA	92.50	32. Ketchum–Sun Valley, ID	81.01	53. Phoenix–Mesa–Scottsdale, AZ	71.00
9. Camden, ME	91.83	33. Grand Junction, CO	80.77	54. Woodstock, VT	70.98
10. Annapolis, MD	90.01	34. Key West–Key Largo–Marathon, FL	80.17	55. Litchfield Hills, CT	70.72
11. Kalispell–Flathead Valley, MT	89.50	35. Daytona Beach, FL	80.04	56. Redding, CA	69.67
12. Taos, NM	89.01	36. Carmel–Monterey–Pebble Beach, CA	80.03	57. Reno–Sparks, NV	69.50
13. Las Vegas, NV	87.61	37. St. George–Zion, UT	79.89	58. Albuquerque, NM	69.48
14. San Diego, CA	87.60	38. Tucson, AZ	79.80	59. San Juan Islands, WA	69.33
15. Lower Cape May, NJ	87.33	39. Santa Fe, NM	79.75	59. Grants Pass, OR	69.33
16. Newport–Lincoln City, OR	87.23	40. Toms River–Barnegat Bay, NJ	79.10	61. Fairhope–Gulf Shores, AL	69.24
17. Hanover, NH	86.98			62. Durango, CO	69.17
18. Melbourne, FL	86.76			63. Port Angeles–Sequim, WA	68.50
19. Charleston Sea Islands, SC	86.47	41. Lake Havasu City, AZ	78.33	64. Hilton Head Island, SC	68.33
20. Burlington, VT	86.31	42. Prescott–Prescott Valley, AZ	78.17	65. San Luis Obispo, CA	68.00
21. Traverse City, MI	86.13	43. Carson City–Carson Valley, NV	77.48	66. Lakeland–Winter Haven, FL	67.81
22. Lake Winnipesaukee, NH	85.68	44. Oxford, MS	76.00	67. Colorado Springs, CO	67.56
23. Williamsburg, VA	85.59	45. Petoskey–Harbor Springs, MI	75.84	68. Charlottesville, VA	67.54
24. Fort Myers–Cape Coral, FL	85.14			69. Boone–Blowing Rock, NC	67.14
25. Medford–Ashland, OR	83.86	46. Wenatchee, WA	75.67	70. Sandpoint–Priest River, ID	67.00

Rank	Grade
71. Port Charlotte–Punta Gorda, FL	66.71
72. Amherst–Northampton, MA	65.72
73. Maui, HI	65.13
74. Laguna Beach–Dana Point, CA	65.07
74. Santa Rosa–Sonoma, CA	65.07
76. Bar Harbor, ME	65.02
77. Fayetteville, AR	64.86
78. Dare Outer Banks, NC	64.17
79. Placerville–Shingle Springs, CA	63.83
80. Panama City, FL	63.71
81. Oscoda–Tawas–Huron Shore, MI	63.33
82. Hesperia–Apple Valley–Victorville, CA	62.97
83. Beaufort, SC	62.83
84. Bend, OR	62.50
84. Payson, AZ	62.50
86. State College, PA	62.45
87. Silver City, NM	62.32
88. Austin, TX	62.12
89. Pompano Beach, FL	61.68
90. Brookings–Gold Beach, OR	61.67
90. Sonora–Groveland–Twain Harte, CA	61.67
92. Asheville, NC	61.18
93. Lake Conroe, TX	60.80
94. Las Cruces, NM	60.71
95. Leesburg–Lady Lake, FL	60.39
96. Cottonwood–Clarkdale, AZ	60.17
97. Port Townsend, WA	60.00
97. Whidbey Island, WA	60.00
99. San Antonio, TX	59.90
100. Eagle River, WI	59.06
101. Houghton Lake, MI	58.59
102. Western St. Tammany Parish, LA	58.53
103. McCall–Cascade–Payette Valley, ID	58.33
104. Oakhurst–Coarsegold, CA	57.95
105. St. Augustine, FL	57.25
106. Bay St. Louis–Pass Christian, MS	57.05
107. Ocean City, MD	57.04

Rank	Grade
108. Florence, OR	56.67
109. Charles Town–Harpers Ferry–Shepherdstown, WV	56.23
110. Hamilton–Bitterroot Valley, MT	55.83
111. St. Jay–Northeast Kingdom, VT	55.76
112. Ocala, FL	54.77
113. Paradise–Magalia, CA	54.71
114. Northern Neck, VA	53.97
115. Charlevoix–Boyne City–East Jordan, MI	53.44
116. Grass Valley–Nevada City, CA	51.84
117. Maryville, TN	51.24
118. Montrose, CO	50.76
119. Pagosa Springs, CO	50.00
120. Clemson–Pendleton District, SC	49.45
121. Blairsville, GA	49.17
122. Amador County, CA	48.96
123. Chapel Hill, NC	48.64
124. Branson, MO	48.07
125. Sedona, AZ	47.58
126. New Bern, NC	47.36
127. Polson–Mission Valley, MT	47.12
128. Myrtle Beach, SC	46.96
129. Rockport–Aransas Pass, TX	45.83
130. Inverness, FL	45.80
131. Sebring–Avon Park, FL	45.41
132. Delta–Cedaredge, CO	44.76
133. Rehoboth Bay–Indian River Bay, DE	43.66
134. New Port Richey, FL	43.17
135. Alamogordo, NM	42.99
136. Wickenburg, AZ	41.83
137. Kingman, AZ	41.67
137. Riviera–Bullhead City, AZ	41.67
137. Clayton, GA	41.67
140. Norfork Lake, AR	40.97
141. Kentucky Lake, KY	40.22
142. Bradenton, FL	40.10
143. Vero Beach–Sebastian, FL	39.90
144. Lake of the Ozarks, MO	39.13
145. Aiken, SC	38.80

Rank	Grade
146. Mission–McAllen–Alamo, TX	38.34
147. Fredericksburg–Spotsylvania, VA	38.14
148. Southern Pines–Pinehurst, NC	37.25
149. Thomasville, GA	35.88
150. Ruidoso, NM	35.71
151. Athens, GA	35.51
152. Hendersonville–East Flat Rock, NC	34.65
153. Fredericksburg, TX	34.55
154. Chewelah, WA	34.38
155. Alpine–Big Bend, TX	33.73
156. Hiawassee, GA	33.33
157. Kauai, HI	33.18
158. Southport–Brunswick Islands, NC	32.12
159. Lake Martin, AL	32.09
160. Cedar Creek Lake, TX	31.29
161. New Braunfels, TX	31.18
162. Pahrump Valley, NV	31.13
163. Edenton, NC	30.76
164. Lake Granbury, TX	29.78
165. Crossville, TN	29.60
166. St. Simons–Jekyll Islands, GA	29.36
167. Guntersville, AL	29.30
168. Kissimmee–St. Cloud, FL	29.29
169. Beaver Lake, AR	28.82
170. Winchester, VA	28.52
171. Brooksville–Spring Hill, FL	28.35
172. Table Rock Lake, MO	26.90
173. Kerrville, TX	26.85
174. Wimberly–San Marcos, TX	26.59
175. Smith Mountain Lake, VA	25.94
176. York Beaches, ME	25.77
177. Lake Livingston, TX	25.53
178. Lake Buchanan–Lake LBJ, TX	24.35
179. Pike County, PA	22.13
180. Lake of the Cherokees, OK	20.02
181. Tryon, NC	18.61
182. Conway, SC	16.79
183. Madison, MS	11.98

Place Profiles: Leisure Living

The following profiles are a selective catalogue of leisure-living assets in each place.

The profiles begin with the category **Common Denominators,** which are everyday options that ought to be available everywhere. The access rating for each item is shown in the right-hand column (AA indicates the greatest access and C the least). The Restaurants entry, besides showing the total number of local eating establishments, also tells how many of them were awarded quality stars (4 ** means, for example, that the place has four two-star restaurants).

The second category, **Performing Arts Calendar,** counts the annual number of dates booked at local campus and civic auditoriums for touring arts groups as reported by Musical America's latest survey. The number of dates for resident opera and symphony performances is also counted.

The third category, **Outdoor Recreation Assets,**

counts each place's square miles of ocean or Great Lakes coastal water, its square miles of inland water, and the acreage for all its state parks and national forests, national parks, and wildlife refuges.

The figures for inland water include ponds and lakes if their surface areas are 40 acres or more; streams, canals, and rivers are also counted if their width is one-eighth mile or more. The water area along irregular Great Lakes and ocean coastlines is counted, too, if the bays, inlets, and estuaries are between one and 10 miles in width.

A list of units of the National Park System, national forests, and national wildlife refuges is included. The following abbreviations are used in this section:

NF	National Forest	NWR	National Wildlife Refuge
NP	National Park	SB	State Beach
NHP	National Historic Park	SF	State Forest
NRA	National Recreation Area	SHP	State Historic Park
NHS	National Historic Site	SHS	State Historic Site
NSR	National Scenic River	SP	State Park
NMP	National Military Park	SR	State Reserve or Refuge
NS	National Seashore	SRA	State Recreation Area
NM	National Monument		

A place's grade is the average of the grades in parentheses to the right of the **Common Denominators,** **Lively Arts Calendar,** and **Outdoor Assets** headings. A check mark (✓) preceding a place's name highlights it as one of the top 18 places for leisure living.

Information comes from these sources: ABC Leisure Magazines, *Musical America: 1995 International Directory of the Performing Arts,* 1995; American Bowling Congress, unpublished zip code data, 1995; American Symphony Orchestra League, *Orchestra and Business Directory,* 1994; National Golf Foundation, unpublished zip code data, 1994; Places Rated Partnership survey of state parks and recreation departments, 1994; Macmillan Travel, *Mobil Travel Guide* (7 volumes), 1994; Quigley Publishing Company, *Motion Picture Almanac,* 1994; U.S. Department of Agriculture, *Land Areas of the National Forest System,* 1994; U.S. Department of Commerce, Bureau of the Census, unpublished land and water area measurements, 1990, and National Oceanic and Atmospheric Administration, *The Coastline of the United States,* 1975; U.S. Department of the Interior, Fish and Wildlife Service, *Annual Report,* 1994, and unpublished master deed listing, 1994, and National Park Service, *Index to the National Park System and Related Areas,* 1994, and unpublished master deed listing, 1994.

Aiken, SC

	Rating
Common Denominators (60)	
Golf courses: 6 private (99 holes); 6 daily fee (90 holes); 1 municipal (18 holes)	A
Bowling centers: 3 (62 lanes)	B
Movie theaters: 1 single/twin, 1 multiplex; 5 screens	C
Lively Arts Calendar (54)	
Touring artists bookings: 14 dates	
Outdoor Assets (2)	
Inland water: 7.46 square miles	
State recreation areas:	
Aiken SP (1,067 acres)	
Redcliffe SP (350 acres)	
Grade: 39	

Alamogordo, NM

Common Denominators (88)	
Golf courses: 1 private (9 holes); 4 daily fee (45 holes); 1 municipal (18 holes)	A
Bowling centers: 3 (52 lanes)	AA
Good restaurants: 1 **, 1 ***	B
Movie theaters: 1 multiplex; 5 screens	B
Outdoor Assets (41)	
Inland water: 0.90 square miles	
Federal protected areas:	
Lincoln NF (563,712 acres)	
White Sands NM (90,955 acres)	
State recreation area:	
Oliver Lee Memorial SP (200 acres)	
Grade: 43	

Albuquerque, NM

Common Denominators (80)	
Golf courses: 5 private (81 holes); 3 daily fee (45 holes); 5 municipal (72 holes)	C
Bowling centers: 7 (216 lanes)	B
Good restaurants: 13 *, 13 **, 4 ***	B
Movie theaters: 1 single/twin, 11 multiplex; 71 screens	A
Lively Arts Calendar (100)	
Touring artists bookings: 20 dates	
Resident ensembles:	
Albuquerque Civic Light Opera (42 dates)	
New Mexico Symphony Orchestra (280 dates)	
Opera Southwest (12 dates)	

	Rating
Outdoor Assets (28)	
Inland water: 2.61 square miles	
Federal protected areas:	
Cibola NF (75,951 acres)	
Petroglyph NM (1,241 acres)	
State recreation areas:	
Coronado SP (218 acres)	
Rio Grande Nature Center SP (170 acres)	
Grade: 69	

Alpine–Big Bend, TX

Common Denominators (48)	
Golf courses: 1 daily fee (9 holes)	A
Movie theaters: 1 single/twin; 2 screens	AA
Outdoor Assets (54)	
Inland water: 0.18 square miles	
Federal protected areas:	
Big Bend NP (774,940 acres)	
Rio Grande Wild and Scenic River	
State recreation areas:	
Big Bend Ranch SNA (18,000 acres)	
Elephant Mountain SP (200 acres)	
Grade: 34	

Amador County, CA

Common Denominators (88)	
Golf courses: 2 daily fee (36 holes); 1 municipal (18 holes)	A
Bowling centers: 1 (24 lanes)	A
Good restaurants: 1 **	B
Movie theaters: 1 multiplex; 4 screens	A
Outdoor Assets (59)	
Inland water: 11.70 square miles	
Federal protected area:	
Eldorado NF (77,955 acres)	
State recreation area:	
Indian Grinding Rock SHP (135 acres)	
Grade: 49	

Amherst–Northampton, MA

Common Denominators (83)	
Golf courses: 2 private (18 holes); 8 daily fee (108 holes); 1 municipal (18 holes)	A
Bowling centers: 1 (32 lanes)	C

	Rating
Good restaurants: 4 **	B
Movie theaters: 3 single/twin, 2 multiplex; 18 screens	A

Lively Arts Calendar (100)
Touring artists bookings: 33 dates
Resident ensemble:
Commonwealth Opera (6 dates)
Outdoor Assets (15)
Inland water: 16.44 square miles
State recreation areas:
C.M. Gardner SP (29 acres)
D.A.R. SF (1,517 acres)
Deer Hill SP (259 acres)
East Branch SF (2,000 acres)
Holyoke Range SP (2,252 acres)
Krug Sugarbush SNA (77 acres)
Middlefield SF (1,849 acres)
Skinner SP (390 acres)
Worthington SF (175 acres)
Grade: 66

✓ Annapolis, MD

	Rating
Common Denominators (90)	
Golf courses: 9 private (144 holes); 1 daily fee (36 holes); 2 municipal (27 holes)	B
Bowling centers: 11 (342 lanes)	AA
Good restaurants: 2 *, 6 **, 5 ***	A
Movie theaters: 3 multiplex; 18 screens	A

Lively Arts Calendar (100)
Touring artists bookings: 3 dates
Resident ensembles:
Annapolis Opera (5 dates)
Annapolis Symphony Orchestra (14 dates)
Outdoor Assets (80)
Chesapeake coastal water: 134.02 square miles
Inland water: 37.87 square miles
Federal protected area:
National Capital Parks (432 acres)
State recreation areas:
Patapsco Valley SP (986 acres)
Sandy Point SP (786 acres)
Grade: 90

Asheville, NC

	Rating
Common Denominators (78)	
Golf courses: 4 private (72 holes); 3 daily fee (45 holes); 2 municipal (36 holes)	B
Bowling centers: 2 (48 lanes)	C
Good restaurants: 2 *, 4 **, 2 ***	B
Movie theaters: 8 single/twin; 16 screens	B

Lively Arts Calendar (81)
Touring artists bookings: 11 dates
Resident ensemble:
Asheville Symphony Orchestra (10 dates)
Outdoor Assets (25)
Inland water: 3.77 square miles
Federal protected areas:
Pisgah NF (31,464 acres)
Blue Ridge Parkway (5,552 acres)
Grade: 61

Athens, GA

	Rating
Common Denominators (83)	
Golf courses: 2 private (27 holes); 2 daily fee (36 holes)	B
Bowling centers: 1 (32 lanes)	B
Good restaurants: 1 **	C
Movie theaters: 1 single/twin, 2 multiplex; 18 screens	AA

Lively Arts Calendar (23)
Touring artists bookings: 6 dates
Outdoor Assets (1)
Inland water: 0.46 square miles
Grade: 36

Austin, TX

	Rating
Common Denominators (78)	
Golf courses: 13 private (225 holes); 7 daily fee (126 holes); 4 municipal (81 holes)	C

	Rating
Bowling centers: 7 (214 lanes)	C
Good restaurants: 3 *, 6 **, 4 ***	C
Movie theaters: 1 single/twin, 16 multiplex; 104 screens	AA

Lively Arts Calendar (100)
Touring artists bookings: 67 dates
Resident ensembles:
Austin Civic Orchestra Society (8 dates)
Austin Lyric Opera (9 dates)
Outdoor Assets (9)
Inland water: 32.78 square miles
State recreation area:
McKinney Falls SP (641 acres)
Grade: 62

Bar Harbor, ME

	Rating
Common Denominators (73)	
Golf courses: 2 private (18 holes); 8 daily fee (90 holes)	AA
Good restaurants: 6 *, 10 **, 2 ***	AA
Movie theaters: 5 single/twin; 6 screens	A

Lively Arts Calendar (46)
Touring artists bookings: 12 dates
Outdoor Assets (77)
Atlantic coastal water: 166 square miles
Inland water: 299.01 square miles
Federal protected area:
Acadia NP (36,641 acres)
State recreation areas:
Duck Lake SNA (25,000 acres)
Four Ponds SNA (4,500 acres)
Holbrook Island Sanctuary SP (1,345 acres)
Lamoine SP (55 acres)
Scraggly Lake SNA (10,000 acres)
Grade: 65

Bay St. Louis–Pass Christian, MS

	Rating
Common Denominators (58)	
Golf courses: 1 private (18 holes); 2 daily fee (36 holes)	B
Good restaurants: 1 **	C
Movie theaters: 1 single/twin, 1 multiplex; 5 screens	B

Lively Arts Calendar (15)
Touring artists bookings: 4 dates
Outdoor Assets (99)
Gulf coastal water: 386.96 square miles
Inland water: 23.16 square miles
Federal protected areas:
Desoto NF (62,516 acres)
Gulf Islands Seashore (19,997 acres)
State recreation area:
Buccaneer SP (393 acres)
Grade: 57

Beaufort, SC

	Rating
Common Denominators (88)	
Golf courses: 5 private (81 holes); 4 daily fee (72 holes)	A
Bowling centers: 3 (56 lanes)	AA
Good restaurants: 1 *	C
Movie theaters: 2 multiplex; 8 screens	A

Lively Arts Calendar (38)
Touring artists bookings: 10 dates
Outdoor Assets (63)
Atlantic coastal water: 55.81 square miles
Inland water: 109.66 square miles
Federal protected areas:
Ace Basin NWR (833 acres)
Pinckney Island NWR (1,325 acres)
State recreation area:
Hunting Island SP (5,000 acres)
Grade: 63

Beaver Lake, AR

	Rating
Common Denominators (83)	
Golf courses: 1 private (18 holes); 1 municipal (9 holes)	B
Bowling centers: 1 (10 lanes)	B
Good restaurants: 1 *, 3 **	AA
Movie theaters: 1 single/twin; 1 screen	C

Rating   Rating

Outdoor Assets (4)
Inland water: 8.54 square miles
State recreation areas:
Beaver Lake SP (619 acres)
Old Carrollton SP (3 acres)
Grade: 29

✓ **Bellingham, WA**
Common Denominators (80)
Golf courses: 3 private (36 holes); 8 daily fee (117   **A**
holes); 1 municipal (54 holes)
Bowling centers: 4 (76 lanes)   **A**
Good restaurants: 2 **, 1 ***   **C**
Movie theaters: 2 single/twin; 4 screens   **C**
Lively Arts Calendar (100)
Touring artists bookings: 27 dates
Outdoor Assets (100)
Puget Sound coastal water: 328.16 square miles
Inland water: 55.43 square miles
Federal protected areas:
Mt. Baker NF (452,736 acres)
North Cascades NP (281,690 acres)
Ross Lake NRA (107,067 acres)
San Juan Islands NWR (3 acres)
State recreation areas:
Birch Bay SP (193 acres)
Larrabee SP (1,687 acres)
Peace Arch SP (20 acres)
Grade: 93

Bend, OR
Common Denominators (88)
Golf courses: 4 private (63 holes); 16 daily fee (297   **AA**
holes)
Bowling centers: 3 (34 lanes)   **B**
Good restaurants: 3 *, 2 **, 1 ***, 1 ****   **A**
Movie theaters: 2 single/twin, 1 multiplex; 7 screens   **B**
Outdoor Assets (100)
Inland water: 36.64 square miles
Federal protected area:
Deschutes NF (980,193 acres)
State recreation areas:
Cline Falls SP (9 acres)
Lapine SRA (2,333 acres)
Pilot Butte SP (101 acres)
Roger Sawyer SP (1 acre)
Sisters SP (28 acres)
Smith Rock SP (624 acres)
Tumalo SP (330 acres)
Grade: 63

Blairsville, GA
Common Denominators (48)
Golf courses: 2 municipal (18 holes)   **A**
Bowling centers: 1 (16 lanes)   **AA**
Outdoor Assets (100)
Inland water: 6.47 square miles
Federal protected areas:
Chattahoochee NF (97,647 acres)
Appalachian National Trail (642 acres)
State recreation area:
Vogel SP (280 acres)
Grade: 49

Boca Raton–Delray Beach, FL
Common Denominators (85)
Golf courses: 56 private (972 holes); 7 daily fee   **B**
(144 holes); 4 municipal (72 holes)
Bowling centers: 5 (236 lanes)   **A**
Good restaurants: 4 *, 14 **, 11 ***, 1 *****   **A**
Movie theaters: 5 multiplex; 46 screens   **B**
Lively Arts Calendar (100)
Touring artists bookings: 603 dates
Resident ensemble:
Florida Symphonic Pops (40 dates)

Outdoor Assets (32)
Atlantic coastal water: 9.59 square miles
Inland water: 256.27 square miles
Federal protected area:
Loxahatchee NWR (2,550 acres)
State recreation area:
Macarthur Beach SP (225 acres)
Grade: 72

Boone–Blowing Rock, NC
Common Denominators (88)
Golf courses: 2 private (36 holes); 1 daily fee (18 holes)   **B**
Bowling centers: 1 (16 lanes)   **B**
Good restaurants: 2 *, 2 **   **A**
Movie theaters: 2 single/twin, 2 multiplex; 14 screens   **AA**
Lively Arts Calendar (100)
Touring artists bookings: 30 dates
Outdoor Assets (14)
Inland water: 0.20 square miles
Federal protected areas:
Blue Ridge Parkway (9,873 acres)
Pisgah NF (393 acres)
Grade: 67

Bradenton, FL
Common Denominators (83)
Golf courses: 8 private (144 holes); 7 daily fee   **B**
(126 holes); 3 municipal (54 holes)
Bowling centers: 3 (128 lanes)   **B**
Good restaurants: 5 *, 11 **, 3 ***   **A**
Movie theaters: 1 single/twin, 3 multiplex; 24 screens   **B**
Outdoor Assets (38)
Gulf coastal water: 46.73 square miles
Inland water: 55.15 square miles
Federal protected areas:
De Soto NMem (25 acres)
Passage Key NWR (36 acres)
State recreation areas:
Benjamin Memorial SHS (17 acres)
Bickel Mound SHS (10 acres)
Lake Manatee SRA (556 acres)
Myakka River SP (10,150 acres)
Grade: 40

Branson, MO
Common Denominators (95)
Golf courses: 1 private (18 holes); 2 daily fee (27 holes)   **A**
Bowling centers: 1 (16 lanes)   **A**
Good restaurants: 8 *, 1 **   **AA**
Movie theaters: 1 single/twin, 1 multiplex; 5 screens   **AA**
Outdoor Assets (49)
Inland water: 19.12 square miles
Federal protected area:
Mark Twain NF (63,941 acres)
State recreation area:
Table Rock SP (294 acres)
Grade: 48

Brevard, NC
Common Denominators (25)
Golf courses: 2 private (36 holes); 3 daily fee (54 holes)   **AA**
Lively Arts Calendar (100)
Resident ensembles:
Brevard Music Center & Opera Workshop (6 dates)
Brevard Chamber Orchestra (4 dates)
Outdoor Assets (98)
Inland water: 2.21 square miles
Federal protected areas:
Nantahala NF (4,533 acres)
Pisgah NF (82,154 acres)
Blue Ridge Parkway (1,031 acres)
Grade: 74

Brookings–Gold Beach, OR
Common Denominators (85)
Golf courses: 1 daily fee (9 holes)   **B**

	Rating
Bowling centers: 1 (16 lanes)	AA
Good restaurants: 1 *, 1 **	A
Movie theaters: 1 single/twin; 1 screen	C

Outdoor Assets (100)
- Pacific coastal water: 35.41 square miles
- Inland water: 7.07 square miles
- Federal protected areas:
  - Oregon Islands NWR (368 acres)
  - Siskiyou NF (617,356 acres)
- State recreation areas:
  - Azalia SP (36 acres)
  - Cape Blanco SP (1,880 acres)
  - Cape Sebastian SP (1,104 acres)
  - Floras Lake SP (1,371 acres)
  - Harris Beach SP (173 acres)
  - Humbug Mountain SP (1,842 acres)
  - Loeb SP (320 acres)
  - Pistol River SP (440 acres)
  - Samuel Boardman SP (1,471 acres)

Grade: 62

Brooksville–Spring Hill, FL
Common Denominators (63)

	Rating
Golf courses: 5 private (90 holes); 6 daily fee (162 holes)	A
Bowling centers: 2 (76 lanes)	A
Movie theaters: 1 single/twin, 2 multiplex; 8 screens	C

Outdoor Assets (23)
- Gulf coastal water: 8.71 square miles
- Inland water: 23.72 square miles
- Federal protected area:
  - Chassahowitzka NWR (6,707 acres)

Grade: 28

Burlington, VT
Common Denominators (95)

	Rating
Golf courses: 1 private (18 holes); 9 daily fee (135 holes); 1 municipal (9 holes)	A
Bowling centers: 6 (118 lanes)	AA
Good restaurants: 3 *, 4 **, 4 ***	A
Movie theaters: 10 multiplex; 54 screens	AA

Lively Arts Calendar (100)
- Touring artists bookings: 72 dates
- Resident ensemble:
  - Vermont Symphony Orchestra (25 dates)

Outdoor Assets (64)
- Inland water: 192.7 square miles
- State recreation areas:
  - Grand Isle SP (226 acres)
  - Knight Point SP (54 acres)
  - North Hero SP (399 acres)
  - Sand Bar SP (20 acres)
  - Underhill SP (150 acres)

Grade: 86

✓ Camden, ME
Common Denominators (88)

	Rating
Golf courses: 1 private (9 holes); 4 daily fee (54 holes)	A
Bowling centers: 1 (4 lanes)	C
Good restaurants: 2 *, 4 **, 1 ***	AA
Movie theaters: 1 multiplex; 4 screens	A

Lively Arts Calendar (88)
- Touring artists bookings: 23 dates

Outdoor Assets (100)
- Atlantic coastal water: 159.36 square miles
- Inland water: 74.51 square miles
- Federal protected areas:
  - Acadia NP (4,144 acres)
  - Franklin Island NWR (12 acres)
  - Seal Island NWR (65 acres)
- State recreation areas:
  - Camden Hills SP (5,474 acres)
  - Montpelier SHS (7 acres)
  - Rocky Lake SNA (8,800 acres)

Grade: 92

✓ Cape Cod, MA
Common Denominators (93)

	Rating
Golf courses: 12 private (207 holes); 13 daily fee (207 holes); 9 municipal (153 holes)	AA
Bowling centers: 3 (33 lanes)	C
Good restaurants: 28 *, 28 **, 10 ***, 1 ****	AA
Movie theaters: 3 single/twin, 6 multiplex; 47 screens	AA

Lively Arts Calendar (100)
- Touring artists bookings: 15 dates
- Resident ensemble:
  - Cape Cod Symphony Orchestra (20 dates)

Outdoor Assets (100)
- Atlantic coastal water: 465.55 square miles
- Inland water: 60.05 square miles
- Federal protected areas:
  - Cape Cod Seashore (27,398 acres)
  - Monomoy NWR (2,702 acres)
- State recreation areas:
  - Hawksnest SP (218 acres)
  - Nickerson SP (1,779 acres)
  - Scusset Beach State Reservation (380 acres)
  - Shawne-Crowell SF (2,756 acres)
  - South Cape Beach SP (790 acres)
  - Washburn Island SNA (355 acres)

Grade: 98

Carmel–Monterey–Pebble Beach, CA
Common Denominators (90)

	Rating
Golf courses: 6 private (108 holes); 8 daily fee (144 holes); 1 municipal (18 holes)	A
Bowling centers: 2 (48 lanes)	B
Good restaurants: 17 *, 17 **, 18 ***, 1 ****	AA
Movie theaters: 2 single/twin, 3 multiplex; 17 screens	A

Lively Arts Calendar (100)
- Touring artists bookings: 11 dates
- Resident ensembles:
  - Hidden Valley Opera Ensemble (25 dates)
  - Monterey County Symphony Orchestra (27 dates)

Outdoor Assets (50)
- Pacific coastal water: 132.49 square miles
- Inland water: 12.72 square miles
- Federal protected areas:
  - Los Padres NF (305,072 acres)
  - Pinnacles NM (1,283 acres)
  - Salinas River NWR (364 acres)
- State recreation areas:
  - Andrew Molera SP (4,749 acres)
  - Asilomar Conference and SB (106 acres)
  - Carmel River SB (297 acres)
  - Fremont Peak SP (54 acres)
  - Garrapata SP (2,939 acres)
  - John Little SR (21 acres)
  - Julia Pfeiffer Burns SP (3,642 acres)
  - Marina SB (171 acres)
  - Monterey SHP (10 acres)
  - Moss Landing SB (60 acres)
  - Pfeiffer Big Sur SP (802 acres)
  - Point Lobos SR (1,325 acres)
  - Point Sur SHP (33 acres)
  - Salinas River SB (246 acres)
  - Zmudowski SB (156 acres)

Grade: 80

Carson City–Carson Valley, NV
Common Denominators (85)

	Rating
Golf courses: 3 daily fee (45 holes); 2 municipal (36 holes)	A
Bowling centers: 1 (44 lanes)	A
Good restaurants: 1 *, 3 ** 1 ***	A
Movie theaters: 2 single/twin; 3 screens	C

Lively Arts Calendar (100)
- Touring artists bookings: 42 dates
- Resident ensemble:
  - Carson City Chamber Orchestra (6 dates)

Outdoor Assets (47)
- Inland water: 40.11 square miles

Rating

Federal protected areas:
    Eldorado NF (53 acres)
    Toiyabe NF (71,669 acres)
State recreation areas:
    Lake Tahoe SP (3,690 acres)
    Mormon Station SHS (2 acres)
Grade: 77

Cedar Creek Lake, TX
Common Denominators (73)
Golf courses: 2 private (36 holes); 1 daily fee (18 holes)   C
Bowling centers: 1 (22 lanes)   B
Good restaurants: 1 *   C
Movie theaters: 1 multiplex; 4 screens   C
Outdoor Assets (21)
Inland water: 74.72 square miles
State recreation area:
    Purtis Creek SRA (566 acres)
Grade: 31

Chapel Hill, NC
Common Denominators (45)
Golf courses: 3 private (54 holes); 3 daily fee (45 holes)   B
Movie theaters: 1 single/twin, 4 multiplex; 17 screens   AA
Lively Arts Calendar (100)
Touring artists bookings: 157 dates
Outdoor Assets (1)
Inland water: 1.36 square miles
Grade: 49

Charles Town–Harpers Ferry–Shepherdstown, WV
Common Denominators (85)
Golf courses: 2 private (27 holes); 3 daily fee   A
    (36 holes); 1 municipal (9 holes)
Bowling centers: 1 (24 lanes)   A
Good restaurants: 2 *, 1 ***   A
Movie theaters: 1 single/twin; 1 screen   C
Lively Arts Calendar (77)
Touring artists bookings: 14 dates
Outdoor Assets (7)
Inland water: 2.03 square miles
Federal protected areas:
    Appalachian National Trail (1,050 acres)
    Harpers Ferry NHP (1,024 acres)
Grade: 56

Charleston Sea Islands, SC
Common Denominators (90)
Golf courses: 10 private (180 holes); 10 daily fee   A
    (198 holes); 2 municipal (36 holes)
Bowling centers: 8 (186 lanes)   A
Good restaurants: 1 *, 15 **, 7 ***   A
Movie theaters: 7 multiplex; 39 screens   A
Lively Arts Calendar (100)
Touring artists bookings: 8 dates
Resident ensemble:
    Charleston Symphony Orchestra (90 dates)
Outdoor Assets (69)
Atlantic coastal water: 35.06 square miles
Inland water: 119.13 square miles
Federal protected areas:
    Cape Romain NWR (34,049 acres)
    Charles Pinckney NHS (29 acres)
    Fort Sumter NM (28 acres)
    Francis Marion NF (59,525 acres)
State recreation areas:
    Charles Towne Landing SP (664 acres)
    Drayton Hall SP (550 acres)
    Hampton Plantation SP (322 acres)
Grade: 86

Charlevoix–Boyne City–East Jordan, MI
Common Denominators (93)
Golf courses: 2 private (36 holes); 6 daily fee   AA
    (108 holes); 1 municipal (9 holes)
Bowling centers: 2 (22 lanes)   AA

Rating

Good restaurants: 1 *, 2 **, 2 ***   AA
Movie theaters: 1 single/twin; 1 screen   C
Outdoor Assets (68)
Great Lakes coastal water: 93 square miles
Inland water: 39.77 square miles
Federal protected area:
    Michigan Islands NWR (233 acres)
State recreation areas:
    Fisherman's Island SP (2,919 acres)
    Young SP (563 acres)
Grade: 53

Charlottesville, VA
Common Denominators (93)
Golf courses: 4 private (54 holes); 2 daily fee   A
    (54 holes); 3 municipal (45 holes)
Bowling centers: 2 (76 lanes)   A
Good restaurants: 1 *, 3 **, 2 ***   A
Movie theaters: 3 single/twin, 3 multiplex; 18 screens   AA
Lively Arts Calendar (100)
Touring artists bookings: 56 dates
Resident ensembles:
    Ash Lawn–Highland Opera Company (27 dates)
    Charlottesville & University Symphony Orchestra (10
    dates)
    Ash Lawn–Highland Opera Company (27 dates)
    Charlottesville & University Symphony Orchestra (10
    dates)
Outdoor Assets (10)
Inland water: 3.49 square miles
Federal protected areas:
    Appalachian National Trail (692 acres)
    Blue Ridge Parkway
    Shenandoah NP (14,861 acres)
Grade: 68

Chewelah, WA
Common Denominators (48)
Golf courses: 1 municipal (18 holes)   AA
Bowling centers: 1 (6 lanes)   A
Outdoor Assets (56)
Inland water: 62.33 square miles
Federal protected areas:
    Colville NF (209,085 acres)
    Coulee Dam NRA (36,215 acres)
    Kaniksu NF (11,774 acres)
    Little Pend Oreille NWR (39,979 acres)
State recreation area:
    Crystal Falls SP (156 acres)
Grade: 34

Clayton, GA
Common Denominators (25)
Golf courses: 1 daily fee (18 holes); 1 municipal (9 holes)   AA
Outdoor Assets (100)
Inland water: 5.94 square miles
Federal protected areas:
    Appalachian National Trail (190 acres)
    Chattahoochee NF (149,652 acres)
State recreation areas:
    Black Rock Mountain SP (1,502 acres)
    Moccasin Creek SP (32 acres)
Grade: 42

Clemson–Pendleton District, SC
Common Denominators (58)
Golf courses: 2 private (36 holes); 6 daily fee   A
    (99 holes); 1 municipal (18 holes)
Bowling centers: 1 (24 lanes)   C
Movie theaters: 1 multiplex; 3 screens   C
Lively Arts Calendar (58)
Touring artists bookings: 15 dates
Outdoor Assets (33)
Inland water: 102.91 square miles
Federal protected area:
    Sumter NF (79,856 acres)

Rating

Rating

State recreation areas:
    Keowee Toxaway SP (1,000 acres)
    Lake Hartwell SP (681 acres)
    Oconee SP (1,165 acres)
    Oconee Station SP (211 acres)
    Sadlers Creek SP (395 acres)
    Table Rock SP (3,068 acres)
Grade: 49

✓ **Coeur d'Alene, ID**
Common Denominators (88)
    Golf courses: 2 private (36 holes); 5 daily fee (108 holes) **A**
    Bowling centers: 3 (56 lanes) **AA**
    Good restaurants: 1 *, 2 **, 1 *** **B**
    Movie theaters: 1 single/twin, 1 multiplex; 6 screens **B**
Lively Arts Calendar (100)
    Touring artists bookings: 30 dates
Outdoor Assets (94)
    Inland water: 70.57 square miles
    Federal protected areas:
        Coeur d'Alene NF (241,545 acres)
        Kaniksu NF (3,602 acres)
    State recreation areas:
        Farragut SP (2,688 acres)
        Heyburn SP (7,825 acres)
        Mowry SP (329 acres)
        Old Mission SP (114 acres)
Grade: 94

Colorado Springs, CO
Common Denominators (83)
    Golf courses: 11 private (198 holes); 3 daily fee **C**
    (45 holes); 3 municipal (45 holes)
    Bowling centers: 11 (282 lanes) **A**
    Good restaurants: 4 *, 9 **, 2 ***, 1 **** **B**
    Movie theaters: 3 single/twin, 7 multiplex; 47 screens **A**
Lively Arts Calendar (100)
    Touring artists bookings: 22 dates
    Resident ensembles:
        Colorado Opera Festival (4 dates)
        Colorado Springs Symphony (80 dates)
Outdoor Assets (20)
    Inland water: 3.02 square miles
    Federal protected area:
        Pike NF (100,597 acres)
Grade: 68

Conway, SC
Common Denominators (48)
    Golf courses: 5 daily fee (81 holes) **AA**
    Movie theaters: 1 multiplex; 6 screens **A**
Outdoor Assets (3)
    Inland water: 11.78 square miles
    State recreation area:
        Myrtle Beach SP (312 acres)
Grade: 17

Cottonwood–Verde Valley, AZ
Common Denominators (58)
    Bowling centers: 1 (10 lanes) **C**
    Good restaurants: 2 *, 2 ** **A**
    Movie theaters: 1 single/twin; 1 screen **C**
Lively Arts Calendar (23)
    Touring artists bookings: 6 dates
Outdoor Assets (100)
    Inland water: 4.79 square miles
    Federal protected areas:
        Coconino NF (427,107 acres)
        Kaibab NF (25,119 acres)
        Montezuma Castle NM (841 acres)
        Prescott NF (1,194,459 acres)
        Tonto NF (316,997 acres)
        Tuzigoot NM (58 acres)
    State recreation areas:
        Dead Horse Ranch SP (320 acres)

    Fort Verde SHS (11 acres)
    Jerome SHS (3 acres)
    Red Rock SP (286 acres)
Grade: 60

Crossville, TN
Common Denominators (68)
    Golf courses: 5 private (81 holes); 4 daily fee (72 holes) **AA**
    Bowling centers: 2 (26 lanes) **AA**
    Movie theaters: 1 single/twin; 2 screens **C**
Lively Arts Calendar (19)
    Touring artists bookings: 5 dates
Outdoor Assets (2)
    Inland water: 3.34 square miles
    Federal protected area:
        Obed Wild and Scenic River (50 acres)
    State recreation area:
        Cumberland Mountain SP (1,562 acres)
Grade: 30

Dare Outer Banks, NC
Common Denominators (93)
    Golf courses: 3 daily fee (54 holes) **AA**
    Bowling centers: 1 (24 lanes) **AA**
    Good restaurants: 1 *, 7 ** **AA**
    Movie theaters: 1 single/twin; 1 screen **C**
Outdoor Assets (100)
    Atlantic coastal water: 31.23 square miles
    Inland water: 867.65 square miles
    Federal protected areas:
        Alligator River NWR (124,353 acres)
        Cape Hatteras Seashore (24,704 acres)
        Fort Raleigh NHS (279 acres)
        Pea Island NWR (5,823 acres)
        Wright Brothers NM (425 acres)
    State recreation area:
        Jockey's Ridge (385 acres)
Grade: 64

Daytona Beach, FL
Common Denominators (85)
    Golf courses: 3 private (54 holes); 9 daily fee **B**
    (171 holes); 3 municipal (54 holes)
    Bowling centers: 8 (228 lanes) **A**
    Good restaurants: 1 *, 8 **, 3 *** **B**
    Movie theaters: 5 single/twin, 8 multiplex; 59 screens **A**
Lively Arts Calendar (100)
    Touring artists bookings: 82 dates
Outdoor Assets (55)
    Atlantic coastal water: 16.77 square miles
    Inland water: 158.97 square miles
    Federal protected areas:
        Canaveral Seashore (28,148 acres)
        Lake Woodruff NWR (18,225 acres)
    State recreation areas:
        Addison Blockhouse SHS (5 acres)
        Blue Spring SP (2,192 acres)
        Bulow Creek SP (2,198 acres)
        De Leon Springs SRA (401 acres)
        Green Mound SHS (6 acres)
        Haw Creek SNA (1,756 acres)
        Hontoon Island SP (1,051 acres)
        New Smyrna Sugar Mill Ruins SHS (17 acres)
        North Peninsula SRA (442 acres)
        Spruce Creek SRA (610 acres)
        Tomoka SP (998 acres)
Grade: 80

Delta–Cedaredge, CO
Common Denominators (63)
    Golf courses: 1 daily fee (9 holes) **B**
    Bowling centers: 1 (12 lanes) **A**
    Movie theaters: 2 single/twin; 2 screens **B**
Outdoor Assets (72)
    Inland water: 6.40 square miles

Rating

Federal protected areas:
 Grand Mesa NF (91,529 acres)
 Gunnison NF (100,141 acres)
State recreation areas:
 Crawford SRA (821 acres)
 Sweitzer Lake SRA (73 acres)
Grade: 45

Durango, CO
Common Denominators (93)
Golf courses: 2 daily fee (36 holes); 1 municipal (36 holes) — **AA**
Bowling centers: 1 (18 lanes) — **A**
Good restaurants: 2 *, 3 **, 1 *** — **AA**
Movie theaters: 2 single/twin; 3 screens — **B**
Lively Arts Calendar (15)
Resident ensemble:
 San Juan Symphony (4 dates)
Outdoor Assets (100)
Inland water: 7.74 square miles
Federal protected area:
 San Juan NF (402,555 acres)
State recreation area:
 Mancos Lake SRA (338 acres)
Grade: 69

Eagle River, WI
Common Denominators (98)
Golf courses: 2 private (27 holes); 4 daily fee (45 holes); 2 municipal (36 holes) — **AA**
Bowling centers: 3 (24 lanes) — **AA**
Good restaurants: 5 *, 1 ** — **AA**
Movie theaters: 1 single/twin; 2 screens — **A**
Lively Arts Calendar (19)
Touring artists bookings: 5 dates
Outdoor Assets (61)
Inland water: 145.12 square miles
Federal protected areas:
 Chequamegon NF (6,459 acres)
 Nicolet NF (48,010 acres)
Grade: 59

✓ East End Long Island, NY
Common Denominators (93)
Golf courses: 13 private (198 holes); 2 daily fee (45 holes); 2 municipal (27 holes) — **A**
Bowling centers: 3 (24 lanes) — **B**
Good restaurants: 10 *, 18 **, 7 *** — **AA**
Movie theaters: 2 single/twin, 4 multiplex; 22 screens — **AA**
Lively Arts Calendar (100)
Touring artists bookings: 106 dates
Outdoor Assets (100)
Atlantic coastal water: 838.45 square miles
Inland water: 248.41 square miles
Federal protected areas:
 Amagansett NWR (36 acres)
 Conscience Point NWR (60 acres)
 Elizabeth A. Morton NWR (187 acres)
 Fire Island Seashore (6,235 acres)
 Lake Woodruff NWR (18,225 acres)
 Seatuck NWR (183 acres)
 Target Rock NWR (80 acres)
 Wertheim NWR (2,398 acres)
State recreation areas:
 Bayard Cutting Arboretum SP (690 acres)
 Belmont Lake SP (459 acres)
 Bethpage SP (1,475 acres)
 Brookhaven SP (2,137 acres)
 Caleb Smith SP (543 acres)
 Camp Hero SP (415 acres)
 Cannetoquot River SP (3,473 acres)
 Captree SP (298 acres)
 Caumsett SP (1,486 acres)
 Gilgo SP (1,223 acres)
 Heckscher SP (1,657 acres)
 Hither Hills SP (1,755 acres)

Rating

Montauk Downs SP (171 acres)
Montauk Point SP (861 acres)
Napeague SP (1,364 acres)
Orient Beach SP (363 acres)
Robert Moses SP (875 acres)
Sunken Meadow SP (1,266 acres)
Walt Whitman SHS (1 acre)
Wildwood SP (767 acres)
Grade: 98

Easton–St. Michaels–Oxford, MD
Common Denominators (95)
Golf courses: 2 private (36 holes); 1 municipal (18 holes) — **B**
Bowling centers: 1 (24 lanes) — **AA**
Good restaurants: 2 *, 1 **, 2 *** — **AA**
Movie theaters: 1 single/twin, 1 multiplex; 5 screens — **AA**
Lively Arts Calendar (19)
Touring artists bookings: 5 dates
Outdoor Assets (100)
Chesapeake coastal water: 150.46 square miles
Inland water: 57.17 square miles
State recreation areas:
 Seth SF (125 acres)
 Wye Oak SP (29 acres)
Grade: 71

Edenton, NC
Common Denominators (23)
Golf courses: 1 private (18 holes)
Good restaurants: 1 ** — **A**
Outdoor Assets (70)
Inland water: 60.68 square miles
Grade: 31

Fairhope–Gulf Shores, AL
Common Denominators (83)
Golf courses: 2 private (27 holes); 7 daily fee (126 holes); 2 municipal (72 holes) — **AA**
Bowling centers: 2 (28 lanes) — **C**
Good restaurants: 6 *, 2 ** — **B**
Movie theaters: 1 single/twin, 2 multiplex; 11 screens — **B**
Lively Arts Calendar (77)
Touring artists bookings: 20 dates
Outdoor Assets (48)
Gulf coastal water: 234.52 square miles
Inland water: 98.08 square miles
Federal protected area:
 Bon Secour NWR (3,066 acres)
State recreation area:
 Gulf SP (6,000 acres)
Grade: 69

Fayetteville, AR
Common Denominators (83)
Golf courses: 3 private (45 holes); 1 daily fee (18 holes) — **C**
Bowling centers: 2 (68 lanes) — **A**
Good restaurants: 2 *, 1 *** — **C**
Movie theaters: 4 single/twin, 2 multiplex; 22 screens — **AA**
Lively Arts Calendar (100)
Touring artists bookings: 56 dates
Resident ensemble:
 North Arkansas Symphony Orchestra (20 dates)
Outdoor Assets (12)
Inland water: 5.83 square miles
Federal protected area:
 Ozark NF (21,762 acres)
State recreation areas:
 Devil's Den SP (1,927 acres)
 Prairie Grove SP (130 acres)
Grade: 65

Florence, OR
Common Denominators (70)
Golf courses: 3 daily fee (45 holes); 1 municipal (18 holes) — **AA**
Bowling centers: 1 (12 lanes) — **A**
Good restaurants: 2 ** — **A**

Rating

Outdoor Assets (100)
Pacific coastal water: 10.36 square miles
Inland water: 64.22 square miles
Federal protected areas:
Oregon Islands NWR (12 acres)
Siuslaw NF (245,576 acres)
Umpqua NF (151,249 acres)
Willamette NF (1,032,247 acres)
State recreation areas:
Alderwood State Wayside (76 acres)
Armitage SP (5,776 acres)
Ben and Kay Dorris SP (92 acres)
Blachly Mountain Forest Wayside (69 acres)
Carl Washburne Memorial SP (1,089 acres)
Darlingtonia State Wayside (18 acres)
Devil's Elbow SP (547 acres)
Elijah Bristow SP (848 acres)
Howard Morton Memorial SP (24 acres)
Jessie Honeyman Memorial SP (522 acres)
Neptune SP (303 acres)
Willamette River Greenway (925 acres)
Grade: 57

✓ **Fort Collins–Loveland, CO**
Common Denominators (85)
Golf courses: 2 private (36 holes); 4 daily fee (63 holes);   A
5 municipal (108 holes)
Bowling centers: 7 (120 lanes)   A
Good restaurants: 4 *, 2 **   C
Movie theaters: 4 single/twin, 4 multiplex; 22 screens   A
Lively Arts Calendar (100)
Touring artists bookings: 92 dates
Resident ensemble:
Fort Collins Symphony Orchestra (25 dates)
Outdoor Assets (100)
Inland water: 32.56 square miles
Federal protected areas:
Rocky Mountain NP (144,315 acres)
Roosevelt NF (624,049 acres)
State recreation areas:
Boyd Lake SRA (197 acres)
Lory SP (2,479 acres)
Picnic Rock SP (10 acres)
Grade: 95

Fort Myers–Cape Coral, FL
Common Denominators (90)
Golf courses: 20 private (351 holes); 21 daily fee   A
(396 holes); 3 municipal (108 holes)
Bowling centers: 9 (228 lanes)   A
Good restaurants: 7 *, 21 **, 3 ***   A
Movie theaters: 2 single/twin, 6 multiplex; 50 screens   A
Lively Arts Calendar (100)
Touring artists bookings: 190 dates
Resident ensemble:
Southwest Florida Symphony Orchestra & Chorus (17
dates)
Outdoor Assets (65)
Gulf coastal water: 6.05 square miles
Inland water: 236.47 square miles
Federal protected areas:
Caloosahatchee NWR (40 acres)
J.N. Darling NWR (4,976 acres)
Matlacha Pass NWR (244 acres)
Pine Island NWR (404 acres)
State recreation areas:
Cayo Cosia SP (1,629 acres)
Gasparilla Island SRA (125 acres)
Koreshan SHS (156 acres)
Lovers Key SRA (434 acres)
Grade: 85

Fredericksburg, TX
Common Denominators (68)
Golf courses: 2 municipal (18 holes)   A

Rating

Bowling centers: 1 (10 lanes)   A
Good restaurants: 1 *, 1 **   A
Lively Arts Calendar (35)
Touring artists bookings: 9 dates
Outdoor Assets (1)
Inland water: 0.42 square miles
Federal protected areas:
Lyndon B. Johnson NHP (504 acres)
State recreation areas:
Admiral Nimitz Museum SHS (5 acres)
Enchanted Rock SNA (1,424 acres)
Lyndon Johnson SHS (733 acres)
Grade: 35

Fredericksburg–Spotsylvania, VA
Common Denominators (85)
Golf courses: 1 private (18 holes); 1 daily fee (18 holes)   C
Bowling centers: 1 (50 lanes)   A
Good restaurants: 2 **, 1 ***   B
Movie theaters: 3 multiplex; 18 screens   AA
Lively Arts Calendar (15)
Resident ensemble:
Mary Washington College–Community Symphony (4
dates)
Outdoor Assets (14)
Inland water: 11.41 square miles
Federal protected area:
Fredericksburg and Spotsylvania NMP (5,235 acres)
Fredericksburg National Cemetery (12 acres)
State recreation area:
Lake Anna SP (2,000 acres)
Grade: 38

Gainesville, FL
Common Denominators (78)
Golf courses: 2 private (36 holes); 2 daily fee   C
(36 holes); 1 municipal (18 holes)
Bowling centers: 3 (80 lanes)   B
Good restaurants: 2 **, 1 ***   C
Movie theaters: 1 single/twin, 4 multiplex; 28 screens   A
Lively Arts Calendar (100)
Touring artists bookings: 69 dates
Resident ensemble:
Gainesville Chamber Orchestra (6 dates)
Outdoor Assets (38)
Inland water: 94.88 square miles
State recreation areas:
Devil's Millhopper Geological SHS (63 acres)
Marjorie Rawlings SHS (12 acres)
O'Leno SP (169 acres)
Paynes Prairie State Preserve (18,400 acres)
River Rise SNA (1,706 acres)
San Felasco Hammock SNA (6,034 acres)
Grade: 72

Grand Junction, CO
Common Denominators (85)
Golf courses: 1 private (18 holes); 1 daily fee   B
(18 holes); 2 municipal (45 holes)
Bowling centers: 2 (76 lanes)   AA
Good restaurants: 1 *, 2 **   C
Movie theaters: 2 single/twin, 2 multiplex; 14 screens   A
Lively Arts Calendar (85)
Touring artists bookings: 5 dates
Resident ensemble:
Grand Junction Symphony Orchestra (17 dates)
Outdoor Assets (72)
Inland water: 13.36 square miles
Federal protected areas:
Colorado NM (20,454 acres)
Grand Mesa NF (252,647 acres)
Manti-La Sal NF (4,542 acres)
Uncompahgre NF (207,256 acres)
White River NF (31,236 acres)
State recreation areas:
Highline SRA (570 acres)

Rating

Rating

Island Acres SRA (130 acres)
Vega SRA (898 acres)
Grade: 81

Grants Pass, OR
Common Denominators (85)
Golf courses: 3 daily fee (45 holes); 1 municipal (18 holes)   **A**
Bowling centers: 2 (56 lanes)   **AA**
Good restaurants: 1 **   **C**
Movie theaters: 3 single/twin; 5 screens   **B**
Lively Arts Calendar (23)
Touring artists bookings: 6 dates
Outdoor Assets (100)
Inland water: 2.04 square miles
Federal protected areas:
Oregon Caves NM (484 acres)
Rogue River NF (31,236 acres)
Siskiyou NF (373,949 acres)
State recreation areas:
Gateway State Wayside (272 acres)
Illinois River SP (368 acres)
Rogue River Scenic Waterway (76 acres)
Grade: 69

Grass Valley–Nevada City, CA
Common Denominators (75)
Golf courses: 1 private (18 holes); 2 daily fee (27 holes)   **C**
Bowling centers: 1 (10 lanes)   **C**
Good restaurants: 1 *, 4 **, 1 ***   **A**
Movie theaters: 2 single/twin, 1 multiplex; 6 screens   **C**
Outdoor Assets (81)
Inland water: 16.88 square miles
Federal protected areas:
Tahoe NF (169,686 acres)
Toiyabe NF (2,574 acres)
State recreation areas:
Donner Memorial SP (342 acres)
Empire Mine SHP (801 acres)
Malakoff Diggins SHP (2,963 acres)
Grade: 52

Guntersville, AL
Common Denominators (60)
Golf courses: 3 private (45 holes); 5 daily fee (90 holes); 1 municipal (27 holes)   **AA**
Good restaurants: 1 *   **C**
Movie theaters: 1 single/twin; 2 screens   **C**
Outdoor Assets (28)
Inland water: 56.11 square miles
State recreation area:
Lake Guntersville SP (5,559 acres)
Grade: 29

Hamilton–Bitterroot Valley, MT
Common Denominators (68)
Golf courses: 1 private (9 holes); 1 municipal (18 holes)   **B**
Bowling centers: 2 (20 lanes)   **AA**
Good restaurants: 2 **   **A**
Outdoor Assets (100)
Inland water: 6.09 square miles
Federal protected areas:
Beaverhead NF (1,107,828 acres)
Lee Metcalf NWR (2,792 acres)
Lolo NF (8,131 acres)
State recreation area:
Painted Rocks SP (263 acres)
Grade: 56

✓ Hanover, NH
Common Denominators (70)
Golf courses: 1 private (9 holes); 8 daily fee (108 holes); 1 municipal (18 holes)   **AA**
Good restaurants: 6 *, 13 **, 3 ***   **AA**
Movie theaters: 2 single/twin, 1 multiplex; 8 screens   **B**

Lively Arts Calendar (100)
Touring artists bookings: 75 dates
Resident ensemble:
Opera North (12 dates)
Outdoor Assets (91)
Inland water: 36.79 square miles
Federal protected areas:
Appalachian National Trail (6,330 acres)
White Mountain NF (342,449 acres)
State recreation areas:
Bedell Bridge SHS (71 acres)
Crawford Notch SP (25 acres)
Franconia Notch SP (6,692 acres)
George Pond Lot SNA (9 acres)
Plummer Ledge SNA (3 acres)
Sculptured Rocks SNA (272 acres)
Wellington SP (205 acres)
Grade: 87

Hendersonville–East Flat Rock, NC
Common Denominators (60)
Golf courses: 2 private (36 holes); 6 daily fee (90 holes)   **A**
Bowling centers: 1 (32 lanes)   **B**
Movie theaters: 1 multiplex; 4 screens   **C**
Lively Arts Calendar (23)
Resident ensemble:
Hendersonville Symphony Orchestra (6 dates)
Outdoor Assets (21)
Inland water: 1.01 square miles
Federal protected areas:
Blue Ridge Parkway (523 acres)
Carl Sandburg Home NHS (264 acres)
Pisgah NF (17,295 acres)
Grade: 35

Hesperia–Apple Valley–Victorville, CA
Common Denominators (75)
Golf courses: 3 private (45 holes); 3 daily fee (45 holes); 1 municipal (18 holes)   **C**
Bowling centers: 2 (56 lanes)   **C**
Good restaurants: 1 **   **C**
Movie theaters: 3 multiplex; 27 screens   **A**
Lively Arts Calendar (100)
Touring artists bookings: 40 dates
Resident ensemble:
Desert Sinfonia (4 dates)
Outdoor Assets (14)
Inland water: 44.61 square miles
Federal protected areas:
Angeles NF (10,289 acres)
Death Valley NM (81,152 acres)
Joshua Tree NM (74,426 acres)
San Bernardino NF (457,872 acres)
State recreation areas:
Chino Hills SP (6,775 acres)
Providence Mountains SRA (5,891 acres)
Seccombe Lake SRA (50 acres)
Silverwood Lake SRA (2,201 acres)
Grade: 63

Hiawassee, GA
Outdoor Assets (100)
Inland water: 5.35 square miles
Federal protected areas:
Appalachian National Trail (350 acres)
Chattahoochee NF (57,503 acres)
Grade: 33

Hilton Head Island, SC
Common Denominators (100)
Golf courses: 15 private (252 holes); 20 daily fee (396 holes); 1 municipal (18 holes)   **AA**
Bowling centers: 1 (24 lanes)   **AA**
Good restaurants: 2 *, 6 **, 3 ***   **AA**
Movie theaters: 1 single/twin, 2 multiplex; 9 screens   **AA**

Rating | Rating

Lively Arts Calendar (42)
Resident ensemble:
Hilton Head Orchestra (11 dates)
Outdoor Assets (63)
Atlantic coastal water: 55.81 square miles
Inland water: 109.66 square miles
Federal protected areas:
Ace Basin NWR (833 acres)
Pinckney Island NWR (1,325 acres)
State recreation area:
Hunting Island SP (5,000 acres)
Grade: 68

Hot Springs, AR
Common Denominators (83)
Golf courses: 2 private (36 holes); 1 daily fee (9 holes) — C
Bowling centers: 2 (48 lanes) — A
Good restaurants: 5 *, 5 ** — A
Movie theaters: 2 multiplex; 6 screens — B
Lively Arts Calendar (77)
Touring artists bookings: 20 dates
Outdoor Assets (88)
Inland water: 56.56 square miles
Federal protected areas:
Hot Springs NP (4,564 acres)
Ouachita NF (113,412 acres)
State recreation areas:
Lake Ouachita SP (370 acres)
Mid-America Museum (21 acres)
Grade: 83

Houghton Lake, MI
Common Denominators (90)
Golf courses: 6 daily fee (81 holes); 1 municipal (18 holes) — AA
Bowling centers: 2 (20 lanes) — AA
Good restaurants: 1 *, 1 ** — A
Movie theaters: 1 single/twin; 1 screen — C
Lively Arts Calendar (58)
Touring artists bookings: 15 dates
Outdoor Assets (28)
Inland water: 58.45 square miles
Federal protected area:
Kirtlands Warbler NWR (40 acres)
State recreation area:
South Higgins Lake SP (962 acres)
Grade: 59

Inverness, FL
Common Denominators (85)
Golf courses: 4 private (63 holes); 8 daily fee (135 holes) — A
Bowling centers: 4 (78 lanes) — AA
Good restaurants: 2 *** — B
Movie theaters: 1 multiplex; 6 screens — C
Outdoor Assets (52)
Gulf coastal water: 10.98 square miles
Inland water: 79.80 square miles
Federal protected areas:
Chassahowitzka NWR (23,730 acres)
Crystal River NWR (46 acres)
State recreation areas:
Crystal River Archaeological SHS (15 acres)
Fort Cooper SP (545 acres)
Homosassa Springs SP (150 acres)
Lake Rousseau SRA (1,684 acres)
Yulee Sugar Mill Ruins SHS (6 acres)
Grade: 46

✓ Kalispell–Flathead Valley, MT
Common Denominators (88)
Golf courses: 7 daily fee (108 holes); 3 municipal (72 holes) — AA
Bowling centers: 4 (38 lanes) — A
Good restaurants: 1 *, 5 **, 1 *** — A
Movie theaters: 1 single/twin; 2 screens — C

Lively Arts Calendar (81)
Touring artists bookings: 10 dates
Resident ensemble:
Glacier Orchestra & Chorale (11 dates)
Outdoor Assets (100)
Inland water: 158.00 square miles
Federal protected areas:
Flathead NF (1,717,996 acres)
Glacier NP (642,749 acres)
Kootenai NF (51,829 acres)
Lolo NF (18,324 acres)
State recreation areas:
Les Mason SP (8 acres)
Logan SP (18 acres)
Lone Pine SP (182 acres)
Wayfarers SP (68 acres)
West Shore SP (146 acres)
Whitefish Lake SP (10 acres)
Grade: 90

Kauai, HI
Common Denominators (63)
Golf courses: 9 daily fee (144 holes); 1 municipal (36 holes) — AA
Bowling centers: 1 (28 lanes) — B
Movie theaters: 1 multiplex; 4 screens — C
Outdoor Assets (37)
Pacific coastal water: 63.51 square miles
Inland water: 8.86 square miles
Federal protected areas:
Hanalei NWR (917 acres)
Huleia NWR (240 acres)
Kilauea Point NWR (160 acres)
State recreation areas:
Ahukini State Recreation Pier (1 acre)
Fort Elizabeth SHS (17 acres)
Haena SP (62 acres)
Hanalei State Recreation Pier (1 acre)
Kokee SP (4,345 acres)
Na Pali Coast SP (6,175 acres)
Polihale SP (138 acres)
Wailua River SP (1,126 acres)
Waimea Canyon SP (1,866 acres)
Waimea State Recreation Pier (1 acre)
Grade: 33

Kentucky Lake, KY
Common Denominators (83)
Golf courses: 2 private (27 holes); 4 daily fee (72 holes) — A
Bowling centers: 2 (34 lanes) — A
Good restaurants: 1 *, 1 ** — C
Movie theaters: 1 single/twin, 1 multiplex; 5 screens — B
Lively Arts Calendar (15)
Touring artists bookings: 4 dates
Outdoor Assets (23)
Inland water: 59.94 square miles
State recreation areas:
Kenlake State Resort Park (1,795 acres)
Kentucky Dam Village State Resort Park (1,351 acres)
Grade: 40

Kerrville, TX
Common Denominators (80)
Golf courses: 1 private (18 holes); 1 municipal (18 holes) — B
Bowling centers: 1 (16 lanes) — B
Good restaurants: 1 * — C
Movie theaters: 2 multiplex; 6 screens — A
Outdoor Assets (1)
Inland water: 1.49 square miles
State recreation area:
Kerrville-Schreiner SRA (517 acres)
Grade: 27

Rating

Ketchum–Sun Valley, ID
Common Denominators (93)
- Golf courses: 1 private (18 holes); 4 daily fee (72 holes) — **AA**
- Bowling centers: 1 (12 lanes) — **AA**
- Good restaurants: 1 *, 3 **, 1 *** — **AA**
- Movie theaters: 1 single/twin; 1 screen — **C**

Lively Arts Calendar (69)
- Touring artists bookings: 18 dates

Outdoor Assets (82)
- Inland water: 16.24 square miles
- Federal protected areas:
  - Challis NF (2,449 acres)
  - Craters of the Moon NM (13,587 acres)
  - Minidoka NWR (2,304 acres)
  - Sawtooth NF (488,667 acres)

Grade: 81

Key West–Key Largo–Marathon, FL
Common Denominators (83)
- Golf courses: 4 private (72 holes); 1 daily fee (18 holes) — **C**
- Bowling centers: 2 (34 lanes) — **B**
- Good restaurants: 7 *, 16 **, 2 *** — **AA**
- Movie theaters: 1 single/twin, 1 multiplex; 7 screens — **B**

Lively Arts Calendar (58)
- Touring artists bookings: 15 dates

Outdoor Assets (100)
- Atlantic coastal water: 540.56 square miles
- Inland water: 406.81 square miles
- Federal protected areas:
  - Big Cypress N Preserve (126,268 acres)
  - Crocodile Lake NWR (4,206 acres)
  - Dry Tortugas NP (61,480 acres)
  - Everglades NP (943,635 acres)
  - Great White Heron NWR (6,206 acres)
  - Key West NWR (1,865 acres)
  - National Key Deer NWR (8,000 acres)
- State recreation areas:
  - Bahia Honda SP (325 acres)
  - Coral Reef SP (2,350 acres)
  - Fort Zachary Taylor SHS (51 acres)
  - Indian Key SHS (17 acres)
  - Key Largo Hammock State Botanical Site (1,039 acres)
  - Lignumvitae Key Botanical Site (486 acres)
  - Long Key SRA (850 acres)
  - Windley Key Geological SHS (28 acres)

Grade: 80

Kingman, AZ
Common Denominators (80)
- Golf courses: 1 daily fee (18 holes); 1 municipal (9 holes) — **B**
- Bowling centers: 1 (16 lanes) — **B**
- Good restaurants: 1 * — **C**
- Movie theaters: 1 multiplex; 4 screens — **A**

Outdoor Assets (45)
- Inland water: 158.08 square miles
- Federal protected areas:
  - Grand Canyon NP (517,156 acres)
  - Havasu NWR (12,248 acres)
  - Kaibab NF (5,468 acres)
  - Lake Mead NRA (796,812 acres)
  - Pipe Spring NM (40 acres)
- State recreation area:
  - Lake Havasu SP (13,072 acres)

Grade: 42

Kissimmee–St. Cloud, FL
Common Denominators (55)
- Golf courses: 2 daily fee (36 holes) — **C**
- Good restaurants: 1 *, 1 ** — **C**
- Movie theaters: 2 multiplex; 12 screens — **B**

Outdoor Assets (33)
- Inland water: 184.47 square miles

Grade: 29

Laguna Beach–Dana Point, CA
Common Denominators (55)
- Golf courses: 3 private (45 holes); 1 daily fee (18 holes) — **C**
- Good restaurants: 2 *, 2 ** — **C**
- Movie theaters: 6 single/twin, 1 multiplex; 15 screens — **B**

Lively Arts Calendar (100)
- Touring artists bookings: 73 dates
- Resident ensemble:
  - Saddleback Chamber Players (8 dates)

Outdoor Assets (40)
- Pacific coastal water: 14.8 square miles
- Inland water: 10.23 square miles
- Federal protected area:
  - Cleveland NF (21,720 acres)
- State recreation areas:
  - Bolsa Chica SB (170 acres)
  - Chino Hills SP (3,115 acres)
  - Corona Del Mar SB (30 acres)
  - Crystal Cove SP (3,940 acres)
  - Doheny SB (274 acres)
  - Huntington SB (129 acres)
  - San Clemente SB (117 acres)

Grade: 65

Lake Buchanan–Lake LBJ, TX
Common Denominators (65)
- Golf courses: 3 private (54 holes); 6 daily fee (81 holes); 2 municipal (36 holes) — **AA**
- Bowling centers: 1 (20 lanes) — **A**
- Movie theaters: 1 single/twin; 1 screen — **C**

Outdoor Assets (8)
- Inland water: 56.27 square miles
- State recreation areas:
  - Enchanted Rock SNA (219 acres)
  - Inks Lake SP (1,202 acres)
  - Longhorn Cavern SP (639 acres)

Grade: 24

Lake Conroe, TX
Common Denominators (55)
- Golf courses: 14 private (216 holes); 3 daily fee (72 holes) — **C**
- Bowling centers: 2 (76 lanes) — **B**
- Movie theaters: 2 multiplex; 10 screens — **C**

Lively Arts Calendar (100)
- Touring artists bookings: 50 dates

Outdoor Assets (27)
- Inland water: 32.58 square miles
- Federal protected area:
  - Sam Houston NF (47,609 acres)
- State recreation area:
  - Lake Houston SP (1,912 acres)

Grade: 61

Lake Granbury, TX
Common Denominators (80)
- Golf courses: 3 private (54 holes); 1 daily fee (9 holes) — **C**
- Bowling centers: 1 (24 lanes) — **AA**
- Good restaurants: 2 * — **B**
- Movie theaters: 1 single/twin; 1 screen — **C**

Outdoor Assets (9)
- Inland water: 15.19 square miles
- State recreation area:
  - Acton SHS (1 acre)

Grade: 30

Lake Havasu City, AZ
Common Denominators (90)
- Golf courses: 2 daily fee (36 holes) — **A**
- Bowling centers: 3 (60 lanes) — **AA**
- Good restaurants: 1 ** — **B**
- Movie theaters: 1 single/twin, 1 multiplex; 5 screens — **A**

Lively Arts Calendar (100)
- Touring artists bookings: 27 dates

Outdoor Assets (45)
- Inland water: 158.08 square miles

Rating

Federal protected areas:
Grand Canyon NP (517,156 acres)
Havasu NWR (12,248 acres)
Kaibab NF (5,468 acres)
Lake Mead NRA (796,812 acres)
Pipe Spring NM (40 acres)
State recreation area:
Lake Havasu SP (13,072 acres)
Grade: 78

Lake Livingston, TX
Common Denominators (38)
Golf courses: 1 daily fee (18 holes); 1 municipal (9 holes)   B
Bowling centers: 1 (12 lanes)   C
Outdoor Assets (39)
Inland water: 130.96 square miles
Federal protected areas:
Big Thicket N Preserve (16,798 acres)
Davy Crockett NF (67,679 acres)
Sam Houston NF (59,683 acres)
State recreation area:
Lake Livingston SRA (636 acres)
Grade: 26

Lake Martin, AL
Common Denominators (78)
Golf courses: 1 private (18 holes); 1 daily fee (18 holes);   A
1 municipal (18 holes)
Bowling centers: 1 (12 lanes)   C
Good restaurants: 1 **   C
Movie theaters: 2 single/twin; 3 screens   B
Outdoor Assets (19)
Inland water: 48.26 square miles
Federal protected area:
Horseshoe Bend NMP (2,040 acres)
State recreation area:
Wind Creek SP (1,400 acres)
Grade: 32

Lake of the Cherokees, OK
Common Denominators (43)
Golf courses: 3 private (45 holes); 1 daily fee (9 holes)   C
Bowling centers: 2 (22 lanes)   AA
Outdoor Assets (18)
Inland water: 51.63 square miles
State recreation areas:
Bernice SP (88 acres)
Honey Creek SP (30 acres)
Upper Spavinah SP (51 acres)
Grade: 20

Lake of the Ozarks, MO
Common Denominators (90)
Golf courses: 2 private (36 holes); 3 daily fee (63 holes)   AA
Bowling centers: 1 (10 lanes)   C
Good restaurants: 8 *, 3 **   AA
Movie theaters: 1 multiplex; 4 screens   A
Outdoor Assets (27)
Inland water: 53.71 square miles
State recreation areas:
Ha Ha Tonka SP (2,696 acres)
Lake of the Ozarks SP (9,253 acres)
Grade: 39

Lake Winnipesaukee, NH
Common Denominators (90)
Golf courses: 2 private (36 holes); 13 daily fee   AA
(189 holes); 1 municipal (9 holes)
Bowling centers: 1 (24 lanes)   C
Good restaurants: 4 *, 8 **, 5 ***   AA
Movie theaters: 1 single/twin, 2 multiplex; 11 screens   A
Lively Arts Calendar (100)
Touring artists bookings: 150 dates
Resident ensemble:
New Hampshire Music Festival Orchestra (25 dates)

Rating

Outdoor Assets (67)
Inland water: 125.68 square miles
Federal protected area:
White Mountain NF (145,005 acres)
State recreation areas:
Cathedral Ledge SP (280 acres)
Crawford Notch SP (5,925 acres)
Echo Lake SP (118 acres)
Ellacoya SP (107 acres)
Endicott Rock SHS (1 acre)
Governor Wentworth SHS (96 acres)
Heath Pond Bog SNA (250 acres)
Humphrey Ledge SNA (36 acres)
Madison Boulder SNA (17 acres)
Ossipee Lake SNA (400 acres)
Wentworth Beach SRA (51 acres)
White Lake SP (903 acres)
Grade: 86

Lakeland–Winter Haven, FL
Common Denominators (83)
Golf courses: 10 private (171 holes); 17 daily fee   A
(279 holes); 4 municipal (63 holes)
Bowling centers: 7 (240 lanes)   A
Good restaurants: 3 *, 1 **, 2 ***, 1 ****   C
Movie theaters: 4 single/twin, 5 multiplex; 42 screens   B
Lively Arts Calendar (100)
Touring artists bookings: 55 dates
Resident ensemble:
Imperial Symphony Orchestra (7 dates)
Outdoor Assets (21)
Inland water: 135.26 square miles
State recreation areas:
Lake Arbuckle SP (2,813 acres)
Lake Kissimmee SP (5,030 acres)
Tonoroc SRA (5,989 acres)
Grade: 68

Las Cruces, NM
Common Denominators (78)
Golf courses: 4 private (63 holes); 4 daily fee (63 holes)   B
Bowling centers: 2 (42 lanes)   C
Good restaurants: 2 *, 2 **, 1 ***   B
Movie theaters: 2 single/twin, 2 multiplex; 15 screens   B
Lively Arts Calendar (92)
Touring artists bookings: 12 dates
Resident ensemble:
Las Cruces Symphony at NMSU (12 dates)
Outdoor Assets (13)
Inland water: 7.44 square miles
Federal protected areas:
San Andres NWR (57,217 acres)
White Sands NM (52,779 acres)
State recreation area:
Leasburg Dam SP (140 acres)
Grade: 61

✓ Las Vegas, NV
Common Denominators (78)
Golf courses: 8 private (135 holes); 13 daily fee   C
(225 holes); 5 municipal (90 holes)
Bowling centers: 11 (428 lanes)   B
Good restaurants: 10 *, 6 **, 6 ***, 3 ****   B
Movie theaters: 2 single/twin, 9 multiplex; 71 screens   B
Lively Arts Calendar (100)
Touring artists bookings: 146 dates
Resident ensembles:
Nevada Opera Theater (12 dates)
Las Vegas Civic Symphony (5 dates)
Outdoor Assets (85)
Inland water: 180.34 square miles
Federal protected areas:
Desert NWR (828,794 acres)
Lake Mead NRA (589,024 acres)
Toiyabe NF (59,218 acres)

Rating   Rating

State recreation areas:
  Floyd Lamb SP (2,041 acres)
  Old Las Vegas Mormon Fort (3 acres)
  Spring Mountain Ranch SP (17,600 acres)
  Valley of Fire SP (34,880 acres)
Grade: 88

Leesburg–Lady Lake, FL
Common Denominators (83)
Golf courses: 4 private (72 holes);13 daily fee (234   **A**
  holes)
Bowling centers: 6 (136 lanes)   **AA**
Good restaurants: 2 *, 1 **, 1 ***   **C**
Movie theaters: 1 single/twin, 1 multiplex; 7 screens   **C**
Lively Arts Calendar (19)
Touring artists bookings: 5 dates
Outdoor Assets (80)
Inland water: 203.40 square miles
Federal protected areas:
  Lake Woodruff NWR (280 acres)
  Ocala NF (84,081 acres)
State recreation areas:
  Hontoon Island SP (599 acres)
  Lake Griffin SRA (255 acres)
  Lake Louisa SP (1,790 acres)
  Lower Wekiva River SNA (2,580 acres)
Grade: 60

Litchfield Hills, CT
Common Denominators (85)
Golf courses: 7 private (81 holes); 7 daily fee (81 holes);   **B**
  1 municipal (18 holes)
Bowling centers: 3 (100 lanes)   **A**
Good restaurants: 1 *, 4 **, 7 ***   **A**
Movie theaters: 3 multiplex; 18 screens   **B**
Lively Arts Calendar (100)
Touring artists bookings: 74 dates
Outdoor Assets (27)
Inland water: 24.63 square miles
Federal protected area:
  Appalachian National Trail (5,635 acres)
State recreation areas:
  American Legion SF (782 acres)
  Black Rock SP (443 acres)
  Burr Pond SP (436 acres)
  Dennis Hill SP (240 acres)
  Haystack Mountain SP (224 acres)
  Housatonic Meadows SP (451 acres)
  John A. Minetto SP (678 acres)
  Kent Falls SP (275 acres)
  Lake Waramaug SP (95 acres)
  Macedonia Brook SP (2,300 acres)
  Mohawk Mountain SP (260 acres)
  Mohawk SF (3,351 acres)
  Mt. Tom SP (223 acres)
  Peoples SF (29,544 acres)
  Topsmead SF (514 acres)
Grade: 71

✓ Lower Cape May, NJ
Common Denominators (70)
Golf courses: 2 private (36 holes); 2 daily fee (36 holes)   **B**
Good restaurants: 2 *, 12 **, 1 ***   **AA**
Movie theaters: 1 single/twin, 3 multiplex; 20 screens   **AA**
Lively Arts Calendar (92)
Touring artists bookings: 24 dates
Outdoor Assets (100)
Atlantic coastal water: 172.5 square miles
Inland water: 29.99 square miles
Federal protected area:
  Cape May NWR (2,587 acres)
State recreation areas:
  Cape May Point SP (190 acres)
  Corson's Inlet SP (341 acres)
  Great Sound SP (217 acres)
Grade: 87

Madison, MS
Common Denominators (25)
Golf courses: 2 private (36 holes)
Movie theaters: 1 multiplex; 10 screens   **AA**
Outdoor Assets (11)
Inland water: 22.89 square miles
Federal protected area:
  Natchez Trace National Trail (4,703 acres)
Grade: 12

Maryville, TN
Common Denominators (78)
Golf courses: 2 private (36 holes); 6 daily fee   **A**
  (108 holes); 1 municipal (9 holes)
Bowling centers: 1 (16 lanes)   **C**
Good restaurants: 1 **   **C**
Movie theaters: 1 multiplex; 8 screens   **B**
Outdoor Assets (76)
Inland water: 8.09 square miles
Federal protected areas:
  Appalachian National Trail (115 acres)
  Great Smokey Mountains NP (97,741 acres)
Grade: 51

Maui, HI
Common Denominators (60)
Golf courses: 2 private (27 holes); 16 daily fee   **AA**
  (270 holes); 1 municipal (36 holes)
Bowling centers: 1 (10 lanes)   **C**
Movie theaters: 1 single/twin, 1 multiplex; 6 screens   **C**
Lively Arts Calendar (100)
Touring artists bookings: 42 dates
Resident ensemble:
  Maui Symphony Orchestra (20 dates)
Outdoor Assets (35)
Pacific coastal water: 123.6 square miles
Inland water: 3.60 square miles
Federal protected areas:
  Haleakala NP (26,911 acres)
  Kakahaia NWR (45 acres)
  Kalaupapa NHP (23 acres)
State recreation areas:
  Halekii-Pihana Heiaus State Monument (10 acres)
  Iao Valley State Monument (6 acres)
  Kaumahina State Wayside (8 acres)
  Launiupoko State Wayside (6 acres)
  Papalaua State Wayside (7 acres)
  Polipoli Spring SRA (10 acres)
  Puaa Kaa State Wayside (3 acres)
  Wahikuli State Wayside (8 acres)
  Waianapanapa SP (120 acres)
  Wailua Valley State Wayside (2 acres)
Grade: 65

McCall–Cascade–Payette Valley, ID
Common Denominators (75)
Golf courses: 2 municipal (27 holes)   **AA**
Bowling centers: 1 (10 lanes)   **AA**
Good restaurants: 1 **   **AA**
Movie theaters: 1 single/twin; 1 screen   **A**
Outdoor Assets (100)
Inland water: 55.65 square miles
Federal protected areas:
  Boise NF (1,073,921 acres)
  Payette NF (884,187 acres
  Salmon NF (71,616 acres)
State recreation area:
  Ponderosa SP (1,281 acres)
Grade: 58

Medford–Ashland, OR
Common Denominators (83)
Golf courses: 2 private (27 holes); 2 daily fee (36   **B**
  holes); 1 municipal (27 holes)
Bowling centers: 3 (74 lanes)   **B**

Rating

	Rating
Good restaurants: 3 **, 1 ***	B
Movie theaters: 1 single/twin, 3 multiplex; 16 screens	A

Lively Arts Calendar (100)
Touring artists bookings: 8 dates
Resident ensembles:
Rogue Opera (10 dates)
Rogue Valley Symphony (22 dates)
Outdoor Assets (69)
Inland water: 16.58 square miles
Federal protected areas:
Crater Lake NP (944 acres)
Klamath NF (26,334 acres)
Rogue River NF (411,681 acres)
Umpqua NF (10,628 acres)
State recreation areas:
Casey SP (80 acres)
Joseph Stewart SP (911 acres)
Prospect State Wayside (11 acres)
Tou Velle SP (51 acres)
Valley of the Rogue SP (278 acres)
Grade: 84

✓ **Melbourne, FL**
Common Denominators (88)

Golf courses: 5 private (90 holes); 3 municipal (54 holes)	C
Bowling centers: 7 (204 lanes)	AA
Good restaurants: 1 *, 7 **, 2 ***	B
Movie theaters: 6 multiplex; 50 screens	AA

Lively Arts Calendar (100)
Touring artists bookings: 52 dates
Resident ensemble:
Brevard Symphony Orchestra Inc. (20 dates)
Outdoor Assets (73)
Atlantic coastal water: 26.28 square miles
Inland water: 275.96 square miles
Federal protected areas:
Canaveral Seashore (29,479 acres)
St. Johns NWR (6,255 acres)
State recreation area:
Sebastian Inlet SRA (121 acres)
Grade: 87

Mission–McAllen–Alamo, TX
Common Denominators (70)

Golf courses: 4 private (63 holes); 2 daily fee (36 holes); 5 municipal (72 holes)	C
Bowling centers: 2 (64 lanes)	C
Good restaurants: 2 *	C
Movie theaters: 2 single/twin, 3 multiplex; 27 screens	C

Lively Arts Calendar (38)
Touring artists bookings: 4 dates
Resident ensemble:
Valley Symphony Orchestra & Chorale (6 dates)
Outdoor Assets (7)
Inland water: 13.71 square miles
Federal protected areas:
Lower Rio Grande Valley NWR (15,002 acres)
Santa Ana NWR (2,087 acres)
State recreation area:
Bentsen–Rio Grande Valley SP (588 acres)
Grade: 38

Montrose, CO
Common Denominators (85)

Golf courses: 1 daily fee (18 holes)	B
Bowling centers: 2 (26 lanes)	AA
Good restaurants: 1 *, 1 **	A
Movie theaters: 1 single/twin; 1 screen	C

Outdoor Assets (67)
Inland water: 1.96 square miles
Federal protected areas:
Black Canyon of the Gunnision NM (20,646 acres)
Curecanti NRA (10,833 acres)
Gunnison NF (11,610 acres)
Manti–La Sal NF (22,563 acres)
Uncompahgre NF (292,997 acres)

State recreation area:
Ute Indian Museum SHS (9 acres)
Grade: 51

Myrtle Beach, SC
Common Denominators (98)

Golf courses: 5 private (81 holes); 41 daily fee (729 holes); 2 municipal (36 holes)	AA
Bowling centers: 4 (128 lanes)	AA
Good restaurants: 2 *, 4 **, 1 ***	A
Movie theaters: 6 multiplex; 32 screens	AA

Lively Arts Calendar (38)
Touring artists bookings: 5 dates
Resident ensemble:
Long Bay Symphony Orchestra (5 dates)
Outdoor Assets (5)
Atlantic coastal water: 10.95 square miles
Inland water: 11.78 square miles
State recreation area:
Myrtle Beach SP (312 acres)
Grade: 47

✓ **Naples, FL**
Common Denominators (88)

Golf courses: 28 private (486 holes); 9 daily fee (180 holes)	A
Bowling centers: 3 (80 lanes)	B
Good restaurants: 10 *, 13 **, 11 ***	AA
Movie theaters: 1 single/twin, 2 multiplex; 17 screens	B

Lively Arts Calendar (100)
Touring artists bookings: 104 dates
Resident ensemble:
Naples Philharmonic (80 dates)
Outdoor Assets (100)
Gulf coastal water: 18.88 square miles
Inland water: 90.97 square miles
Federal protected areas:
Big Cypress N Preserve (405,745 acres)
Everglades NP (39,262 acres)
Florida Panther NWR (24,310 acres)
State recreation areas:
Collier–Seminole SP (6,423 acres)
Delnor–Wiggins Pass SRA (166 acres)
Fakahatchee Strand SNA (58,548 acres)
Grade: 96

New Bern, NC
Common Denominators (85)

Golf courses: 3 private (54 holes); 5 daily fee (90 holes)	A
Bowling centers: 2 (40 lanes)	B
Good restaurants: 1 *, 1 **, 1 ***	B
Movie theaters: 2 multiplex; 9 screens	A

Outdoor Assets (57)
Inland water: 66.26 square miles
Federal protected area:
Croatan NF (61,296 acres)
Grade: 47

New Braunfels, TX
Common Denominators (85)

Golf courses: 1 daily fee (18 holes); 1 municipal (18 holes)	B
Bowling centers: 1 (24 lanes)	B
Good restaurants: 2 *, 1 ***	B
Movie theaters: 2 multiplex; 10 screens	AA

Outdoor Assets (9)
Inland water: 13.15 square miles
State recreation areas:
Guadalupe River SP (1,000 acres)
Honey Creek SNA (2,294 acres)
Grade: 31

New Port Richey, FL
Common Denominators (80)

Golf courses: 6 daily fee (90 holes)	B
Bowling centers: 5 (162 lanes)	A

	Rating
Good restaurants: 1 *, 1 **	C
Movie theaters: 2 single/twin, 2 multiplex; 19 screens	B

Lively Arts Calendar (38)
  Touring artists bookings: 10 dates
Outdoor Assets (12)
  Gulf coastal water: 9.99 square miles
  Inland water: 23.13 square miles
  State recreation area:
    Anclote Key SNA (160 acres)
Grade: 43

✓ **Newport–Lincoln City, OR**

Common Denominators (85)	
Golf courses: 4 daily fee (45 holes)	A
Bowling centers: 2 (20 lanes)	B
Good restaurants: 2 *, 2 **, 1 ***, 1 ****	AA
Movie theaters: 1 single/twin; 1 screen	C

Lively Arts Calendar (96)
  Touring artists bookings: 25 dates
Outdoor Assets (81)
  Pacific coastal water: 20.12 square miles
  Inland water: 13 square miles
  Federal protected areas:
    Oregon Islands NWR (38 acres)
    Siuslaw NF (171,652 acres)
  State recreation areas:
    Beachside SP (17 acres)
    Beverly Beach SP (130 acres)
    Depoe Bay SP (1 acre)
    Devil's Lake SP (109 acres)
    Devil's Punchbowl SP (8 acres)
    Ellmaker SP (76 acres)
    Fogarty Creek SP (142 acres)
    Lost Creek SP (34 acres)
    Nelson SP (2 acres)
    Ona Beach SP (237 acres)
    Patterson Memorial SP (10 acres)
    South Beach SP (434 acres)
    Yachats SP (94 acres)
    Yaquina Bay SP (32 acres)
Grade: 87

Norfork Lake, AR

Common Denominators (63)	
Golf courses: 1 daily fee (18 holes)	B
Bowling centers: 2 (34 lanes)	AA
Good restaurants: 1 *	C

Outdoor Assets (60)
  Inland water: 32.37 square miles
  Federal protected areas:
    Buffalo NR (991 acres)
    Ozark NF (62,830 acres)
Grade: 41

Northern Door Peninsula, WI

Common Denominators (100)	
Golf courses: 5 daily fee (63 holes); 1 municipal (18 holes)	AA
Bowling centers: 3 (26 lanes)	AA
Good restaurants: 18 *, 8 **, 1 ***	AA
Movie theaters: 2 single/twin, 1 multiplex; 6 screens	AA

Lively Arts Calendar (50)
  Touring artists bookings: 13 dates
Outdoor Assets (100)
  Great Lakes coastal water: 186 square miles
  Inland water: 24.71 square miles
  Federal protected areas:
    Gravel Island NWR (27 acres)
    Green Bay NWR (2 acres)
  State recreation areas:
    Newport SP (2,368 acres)
    Peninsula SP (3,763 acres)
    Potawatomi SP (1,226 acres)
    Rock Island SP (912 acres)
    Whitefish Dunes SP (863 acres)
Grade: 83

Northern Neck, VA

Common Denominators (63)	
Golf courses: 1 private (18 holes); 3 daily fee (45 holes)	AA
Good restaurants: 1 **	B
Movie theaters: 1 single/twin; 1 screen	C

Outdoor Assets (99)
  Atlantic coastal water: 150.86 square miles
  Inland water: 40.71 square miles
Grade: 54

Oakhurst–Coarsegold, CA

Common Denominators (78)	
Golf courses: 1 private (18 holes); 4 daily fee (63 holes); 1 municipal (54 holes)	A
Bowling centers: 2 (38 lanes)	B
Good restaurants: 1 *	C
Movie theaters: 1 single/twin; 1 screen	C

Outdoor Assets (96)
  Inland water: 14.96 square miles
  Federal protected areas:
    Devils Postpile NM (799 acres)
    Inyo NF (52,241 acres)
    Sierra NF (362,049 acres)
    Yosemite NP (66,886 acres)
  State recreation areas:
    Millerton Lake SRA (3,296 acres)
    Wassama Round House SHP (27 acres)
Grade: 58

Ocala, FL

Common Denominators (80)	
Golf courses: 3 private (45 holes); 7 daily fee (117 holes); 3 municipal (45 holes)	B
Bowling centers: 4 (120 lanes)	A
Good restaurants: 1 *, 2 **, 1 ***	C
Movie theaters: 2 single/twin, 3 multiplex; 17 screens	B

Outdoor Assets (84)
  Inland water: 84.11 square miles
  Federal protected area:
    Ocala NF (275,473 acres)
  State recreation areas:
    Lake Rousseau SRA (696 acres)
    Silver River SP (4,432 acres)
Grade: 55

Ocean City, MD

Common Denominators (100)	
Golf courses: 2 private (36 holes); 5 daily fee (90 holes); 2 municipal (27 holes)	AA
Bowling centers: 2 (28 lanes)	AA
Good restaurants: 5 *, 9 **, 2 ***	AA
Movie theaters: 2 single/twin, 3 multiplex; 20 screens	AA

Outdoor Assets (71)
  Atlantic coastal water: 11 square miles
  Inland water: 111.46 square miles
  Federal protected areas:
    Assateague Island Seashore (7,295 acres)
    Chincoteague NWR (418 acres)
  State recreation areas:
    Assateague SP (756 acres)
    Pocomoke River SP (914 acres)
    Pocomoke SF (13,276 acres)
Grade: 57

Oscoda–Tawas–Huron Shore, MI

Common Denominators (90)	
Golf courses: 1 private (18 holes); 3 daily fee (45 holes); 1 municipal (18 holes)	AA
Bowling centers: 3 (30 lanes)	AA
Good restaurants: 1 *	C
Movie theaters: 2 single/twin; 4 screens	A

Outdoor Assets (100)
  Great Lakes coastal water: 132 square miles
  Inland water: 17.42 square miles
  Federal protected area:
    Huron NF (111,749 acres)

Rating

State recreation area:
  Tawas Point SP (175 acres)
Grade: 63

Oxford, MS
Common Denominators (85)
  Golf courses: 1 private (9 holes); 1 municipal (18 holes)   **B**
  Bowling centers: 1 (16 lanes)   **B**
  Good restaurants: 2 **   **A**
  Movie theaters: 1 single/twin, 1 multiplex; 5 screens   **A**
Lively Arts Calendar (100)
  Touring artists bookings: 66 dates
Outdoor Assets (43)
  Inland water: 48.18 square miles
  Federal protected area:
    Holly Springs NF (38,840 acres)
Grade: 76

Pagosa Springs, CO
Common Denominators (50)
  Golf courses: 2 daily fee (27 holes)   **AA**
  Movie theaters: 1 single/twin; 1 screen   **AA**
Outdoor Assets (100)
  Inland water: 5.26 square miles
  Federal protected areas:
    Rio Grande NF (22,792 acres)
    San Juan NF (406,424 acres)
  State recreation area:
    Navajo SRA (2,000 acres)
Grade: 50

Pahrump Valley, NV
Common Denominators (50)
  Golf courses: 1 daily fee (18 holes)   **AA**
  Bowling centers: 2 (14 lanes)   **AA**
Outdoor Assets (43)
  Inland water: 12.47 square miles
  Federal protected areas:
    Ashe Meadows NWR (12,849 acres)
    Death Valley NM (107,616 acres)
    Humboldt NF (248,321 acres)
    Toiyabe NF (1,501,601 acres)
  State recreation areas:
    Belmont Courthouse SHS (1 acre)
    Berlin–Ichthyosaur SP (1,248 acres)
Grade: 31

Palm Springs–Coachella Valley, CA
Common Denominators (93)
  Golf courses: 39 private (648 holes); 28 daily fee   **AA**
    (477 holes); 1 municipal (18 holes)
  Bowling centers: 2 (52 lanes)   **C**
  Good restaurants: 9 *, 25 **, 12 ***   **AA**
  Movie theaters: 1 single/twin, 6 multiplex; 51 screens   **AA**
Lively Arts Calendar (100)
  Touring artists bookings: 150 dates
Outdoor Assets (51)
  Inland water: 95.66 square miles
  Federal protected areas:
    Cleveland NF (78,133 acres)
    Coachella Valley NWR (2,589 acres)
    Joshua Tree NM (474,110 acres)
    San Bernardino NF (212,871 acres)
  State recreation areas:
    Anza-Borrego Desert SP (35,177 acres)
    California Citrus SHP (247 acres)
    Chino Hills SP (296 acres)
    Lake Elsinore SRA (2,976 acres)
    Lake Perris SRA (5,240 acres)
    Mount San Jacinto SP (13,718 acres)
    Salton Sea SRA (9,000 acres)
Grade: 81

Panama City, FL
Common Denominators (93)
  Golf courses: 2 private (36 holes); 7 daily fee (117 holes)   **A**

Rating

  Bowling centers: 5 (82 lanes)   **A**
  Good restaurants: 5 *, 5 **   **A**
  Movie theaters: 1 single/twin, 5 multiplex; 30 screens   **AA**
Lively Arts Calendar (58)
  Touring artists bookings: 15 dates
Outdoor Assets (41)
  Gulf coastal water: 15.07 square miles
  Inland water: 118.91 square miles
  State recreation area:
    St. Andrews SRA (1,268 acres)
Grade: 64

Paradise–Magalia, CA
Common Denominators (83)
  Golf courses: 2 daily fee (18 holes)   **B**
  Bowling centers: 1 (24 lanes)   **A**
  Good restaurants: 1 **   **C**
  Movie theaters: 1 multiplex; 6 screens   **A**
Lively Arts Calendar (35)
  Touring artists bookings: 4 dates
  Resident ensemble:
    Paradise Symphony Orchestra (5 dates)
Outdoor Assets (47)
  Inland water: 37.62 square miles
  Federal protected areas:
    Lassen NF (51,178 acres)
    Plumas NF (82,299 acres)
  State recreation areas:
    Bidwell–Sacramento River SP (181 acres)
    Lake Oroville SRA (28,753 acres)
    Mansion SHP (5 acres)
Grade: 55

Payson, AZ
Common Denominators (88)
  Golf courses: 1 daily fee (18 holes)   **A**
  Bowling centers: 1 (16 lanes)   **AA**
  Good restaurants: 3 *   **A**
  Movie theaters: 1 single/twin; 1 screen   **C**
Outdoor Assets (100)
  Inland water: 28.03 square miles
  Federal protected areas:
    Coconino NF (3,352 acres)
    Tonto NF (1,700,390 acres)
    Tonto NM (1,120 acres)
  State recreation area:
    Tonto Natural Bridge SP (160 acres)
Grade: 63

Petoskey–Harbor Springs, MI
Common Denominators (93)
  Golf courses: 3 private (54 holes); 5 daily fee (81 holes)   **AA**
  Bowling centers: 1 (24 lanes)   **AA**
  Good restaurants: 4 *, 4 **   **AA**
  Movie theaters: 1 single/twin; 1 screen   **C**
Lively Arts Calendar (100)
  Touring artists bookings: 35 dates
Outdoor Assets (35)
  Great Lakes coastal water: 39.8 square miles
  Inland water: 16.25 square miles
  State recreation areas:
    Petoskey SP (298 acres)
    Wilderness SP (7,579 acres)
Grade: 76

Phoenix–Mesa–Scottsdale, AZ
Common Denominators (83)
  Golf courses: 36 private (639 holes); 53 daily fee   **B**
    (927 holes); 8 municipal (153 holes)
  Bowling centers: 32 (918 lanes)   **B**
  Good restaurants: 29 *, 32 **, 15 ***, 4 ****   **B**
  Movie theaters: 7 single/twin, 41 multiplex; 298 screens   **A**
Lively Arts Calendar (100)
  Touring artists bookings: 600 dates

Resident ensembles:
    Arizona Opera Company (13 dates)
    Metro Pops Orchestra (14 dates)
Outdoor Assets (30)
  Inland water: 20.81 square miles
  Federal protected area:
    Tonto NF (657,695 acres)
Grade: 71

Pike County, PA
Common Denominators (40)
  Golf courses: 2 private (27 holes); 2 daily fee (36 holes)   A
  Movie theaters: 1 single/twin; 2 screens   C
Outdoor Assets (26)
  Inland water: 19.59 square miles
  Federal protected areas:
    Delaware Water Gap NRA (17,380 acres)
    Upper Delaware Scenic River (1 acre)
  State recreation area:
    Promised Land SP (5,736 acres)
Grade: 22

Placerville–Shingle Springs, CA
Common Denominators (73)
  Golf courses: 2 private (36 holes); 1 daily fee (9 holes)   C
  Bowling centers: 2 (28 lanes)   C
  Good restaurants: 4 *, 2 **, 2 ***   B
  Movie theaters: 1 single/twin, 1 multiplex; 6 screens   C
Lively Arts Calendar (19)
  Touring artists bookings: 5 dates
Outdoor Assets (100)
  Inland water: 79.81 square miles
  Federal protected area:
    Eldorado NF (496,086 acres)
  State recreation areas:
    Auburn SRA (12,000 acres)
    D.L. Bliss SP (2,219 acres)
    Emerald Bay SP (1,463 acres)
    Folsom Lake SRA (10,000 acres)
    Lake Valley SRA (150 acres)
    Marshall Gold Discovery SHP (275 acres)
    Sugar Pine Point SP (2,011 acres)
    Washoe Meadows SP (628 acres)
Grade: 64

Polson–Mission Valley, MT
Common Denominators (73)
  Golf courses: 3 daily fee (36 holes)   AA
  Bowling centers: 3 (22 lanes)   AA
  Movie theaters: 2 single/twin; 3 screens   A
Outdoor Assets (69)
  Inland water: 159.94 square miles
  Federal protected areas:
    Dungeness NWR (245 acres)
    Flathead NF (156,602 acres)
    National Bison Range NWR (8,694 acres)
    Swan River NWR (1,569 acres)
  State recreation areas:
    Big Arm SP (55 acres)
    Elmo SP (40 acres)
    Finley Point SP (24 acres)
    Lambeth SP (76 acres)
    Wild Horse Island SP (2,163 acres)
    Yellow Bay SP (10 acres)
Grade: 47

Pompano Beach, FL
Common Denominators (80)
  Golf courses: 17 private (306 holes); 7 daily fee   C
    (126 holes); 2 municipal (36 holes)
  Bowling centers: 7 (296 lanes)   B
  Good restaurants: 2 *, 24 **, 17 ***   A
  Movie theaters: 1 single/twin, 6 multiplex; 50 screens   B
Lively Arts Calendar (100)
  Touring artists bookings: 30 dates

Outdoor Assets (5)
  Atlantic coastal water: 9.82 square miles
  Inland water: 12.67 square miles
  State recreation areas:
    Birch SRA (180 acres)
    Lloyd Beach SRA (251 acres)
Grade: 62

Port Angeles–Seqium, WA
Common Denominators (83)
  Golf courses: 1 private (18 holes); 2 daily fee (36 holes)   B
  Bowling centers: 3 (40 lanes)   A
  Good restaurants: 1 *, 3 **, 1 ***   A
  Movie theaters: 1 single/twin; 1 screen   C
Lively Arts Calendar (23)
  Resident ensemble:
    Port Angeles Symphony Orchestra (6 dates)
Outdoor Assets (100)
  Pacific coastal water: 702.17 square miles
  Inland water: 35.41 square miles
  Federal protected areas:
    Dungeness NWR (245 acres)
    Flattery Rocks NWR (125 acres)
    Olympic NF (199,333 acres)
    Olympic NP (865,967 acres)
    Protection Island NWR (3 acres)
    Quillayute Needles NWR (104 acres)
  State recreation areas:
    Bogachiel SP (123 acres)
    Clallam Bay SP (36 acres)
    Dungeness SP (1 acre)
    Hoko River SP (33 acres)
    Point of Arches SP (21 acres)
    Sequim Bay SP (92 acres)
Grade: 69

Port Charlotte–Punta Gorda, FL
Common Denominators (78)
  Golf courses: 5 private (81 holes); 7 daily fee (117 holes)   A
  Bowling centers: 2 (48 lanes)   B
  Good restaurants: 3 *   C
  Movie theaters: 1 multiplex; 8 screens   C
Lively Arts Calendar (81)
  Touring artists bookings: 21 dates
Outdoor Assets (42)
  Gulf coastal water: 4.32 square miles
  Inland water: 122.38 square miles
  Federal protected area:
    Island Bay NWR (20 acres)
  State recreation areas:
    Don Pedro Island SRA (133 acres)
    Port Charlotte Beach SRA (213 acres)
Grade: 67

Port Townsend, WA
Common Denominators (80)
  Golf courses: 4 daily fee (45 holes); 1 municipal (9 holes)   AA
  Bowling centers: 1 (12 lanes)   B
  Good restaurants: 1 *   C
  Movie theaters: 1 single/twin; 1 screen   C
Outdoor Assets (100)
  Puget Sound coastal water: 168.99 square miles
  Inland water: 62.57 square miles
  Federal protected areas:
    Olympic NF (166,961 acres)
    Olympic NP (540,167 acres)
    Protection Island NWR (317 acres)
    Quillayute Needles NWR (196 acres)
  State recreation areas:
    Anderson Lake SP (410 acres)
    Dosewallips SP (425 acres)
    Fort Flagler SP (783 acres)
    Fort Worden SP (434 acres)
    Kinney Point SP (76 acres)
    Mystery Bay SP (10 acres)
    Old Fort Townsend SP (377 acres)

Rating

Pleasant Harbor (1 acre)
Right Smart Cove (1 acre)
Rothschild House SP (1 acre)
Triton Cove SP (28 acres)
Grade: 60

Prescott–Prescott Valley, AZ
Common Denominators (58)
Golf courses: 2 municipal (36 holes)   B
Good restaurants: 2 *, 2 **   B
Movie theaters: 2 single/twin; 4 screens   C
Lively Arts Calendar (77)
Touring artists bookings: 20 dates
Outdoor Assets (100)
Inland water: 4.79 square miles
Federal protected areas:
Coconino NF (427,107 acres)
Kaibab NF (25,119 acres)
Montezuma Castle NM (841 acres)
Prescott NF (1,194,459 acres)
Tonto NF (316,997 acres)
Tuzigoot NM (58 acres)
State recreation areas:
Dead Horse Ranch SP (320 acres)
Fort Verde SHS (11 acres)
Jerome SHS (3 acres)
Red Rock SP (286 acres)
Grade: 78

Redding, CA
Common Denominators (60)
Golf courses: 2 private (36 holes); 4 daily fee (45 holes)   C
Bowling centers: 4 (62 lanes)   B
Movie theaters: 2 single/twin, 3 multiplex; 18 screens   A
Lively Arts Calendar (50)
Touring artists bookings: 9 dates
Resident ensemble:
Shasta Symphony Orchestra (4 dates)
Outdoor Assets (99)
Inland water: 61.95 square miles
Federal protected areas:
Lassen NF (248,007 acres)
Lassen Volcanic NP (66,862 acres)
Shasta FN (470,018 acres)
Trinity NF (30,626 acres)
Whiskeytown–Shasta–Trinity NRA (42,459 acres)
State recreation areas:
Ahjumawi Lava Springs SP (5,890 acres)
Castle Crags SP (4,383 acres)
McArthur–Burney Falls Memorial SP (761 acres)
Shasta SHP (23 acres)
Grade: 70

Rehoboth Bay–Indian River Bay, DE
Common Denominators (85)
Golf courses: 6 private (99 holes); 1 daily fee (18 holes)   C
Bowling centers: 5 (132 lanes)   AA
Good restaurants: 9 *, 14 **, 1 ***   AA
Movie theaters: 1 multiplex; 8 screens   C
Outdoor Assets (46)
Atlantic coastal water: 123.48 square miles
Inland water: 41.34 square miles
Federal protected area:
Prime Hook NWR (8,818 acres)
State recreation areas:
Cape Henlopen SP (3,270 acres)
Delaware Seashore SP (1,851 acres)
Fenwick Island SP (208 acres)
Holts Landing SP (301 acres)
Trap Pond SP (966 acres)
Grade: 44

Reno–Sparks, NV
Common Denominators (83)
Golf courses: 1 private (18 holes); 4 daily fee (63 holes);   B
5 municipal (81 holes)

Rating

Bowling centers: 6 (166 lanes)   A
Good restaurants: 1 *, 5 **, 2 ***, 1 ****   B
Movie theaters: 2 single/twin, 4 multiplex; 25 screens   B
Lively Arts Calendar (100)
Touring artists bookings: 8 dates
Resident ensembles:
Nevada Opera (7 dates)
Reno Philharmonic (18 dates)
Outdoor Assets (26)
Inland water: 209.01 square miles
Federal protected areas:
Anaho Island NWR (248 acres)
Sheldon NWR (187,240 acres)
Toiyabe NF (66,742 acres)
State recreation areas:
Lake Tahoe SP (10,552 acres)
Washoe Lake SRA (7,778 acres)
Grade: 70

Riviera–Bullhead City, AZ
Common Denominators (80)
Golf courses: 1 daily fee (18 holes)   B
Bowling centers: 1 (24 lanes)   A
Good restaurants: 2 *   C
Movie theaters: 1 multiplex; 4 screens   B
Outdoor Assets (45)
Inland water: 158.08 square miles
Federal protected areas:
Grand Canyon NP (517,156 acres)
Havasu NWR (12,248 acres)
Kaibab NF (5,468 acres)
Lake Mead NRA (796,812 acres)
Pipe Spring NM (40 acres)
State recreation area:
Lake Havasu SP (13,072 acres)
Grade: 42

Rockport–Aransas Pass, TX
Common Denominators (38)
Golf courses: 1 private (18 holes)
Good restaurants: 1 *   B
Movie theaters: 1 single/twin; 1 screen   C
Outdoor Assets (100)
Gulf coastal water: 6.87 square miles
Inland water: 207.36 square miles
Federal protected area:
Aransas NWR (52,461 acres)
State recreation areas:
Copano Bay Fishing Pier SP (6 acres)
Fulton Mansion SHS (2 acres)
Goose Island SRA (314 acres)
Grade: 46

Ruidoso, NM
Common Denominators (73)
Golf courses: 1 private (18 holes); 1 daily fee (18 holes);   AA
2 municipal (27 holes)
Bowling centers: 2 (18 lanes)   AA
Good restaurants: 1 **   A
Outdoor Assets (35)
Inland water: 0.19 square miles
Federal protected areas:
Cibola NF (34,336 acres)
Lincoln NF (364,579 acres)
State recreation area:
Smokey Bear SP (3 acres)
Grade: 36

St. Augustine, FL
Common Denominators (80)
Golf courses: 11 private (189 holes); 3 daily fee   B
(45 holes); 1 municipal (27 holes)
Bowling centers: 1 (24 lanes)   C
Good restaurants: 7 *, 7 **, 1 ***   AA
Movie theaters: 1 multiplex; 6 screens   C

Rating

Lively Arts Calendar (58)
Touring artists bookings: 15 dates
Outdoor Assets (34)
Atlantic coastal water: 14.84 square miles
Inland water: 63.99 square miles
Federal protected areas:
Castillo de San Marcos NM (20 acres)
Fort Matanzas NM (228 acres)
State recreation areas:
Anastasia SRA (1,522 acres)
Faver–Dykes SP (752 acres)
Guana River SP (2,398 acres)
Grade: 57

St. George–Zion, UT
Common Denominators (85)
Golf courses: 1 private (18 holes); 1 daily fee (9 holes);   A
5 municipal (81 holes)
Bowling centers: 3 (40 lanes)   A
Good restaurants: 1 *, 1 **, 1 ***   B
Movie theaters: 2 multiplex; 6 screens   B
Lively Arts Calendar (62)
Touring artists bookings: 10 dates
Resident ensemble:
Southwest Symphony Orchestra (6 dates)
Outdoor Assets (93)
Inland water: 2.87 square miles
Federal protected areas:
Dixie NF (394,556 acres)
Zion NP (130,798 acres)
State recreation areas:
Gunlock Lake SP (548 acres)
Quail Creek SP (3,677 acres)
Snow Canyon SP (5,740 acres)
Grade: 80

St. Jay–Northeast Kingdom, VT
Common Denominators (88)
Golf courses: 2 daily fee (18 holes); 1 municipal (9 holes)   A
Bowling centers: 1 (16 lanes)   A
Good restaurants: 1 *, 2 **, 1 ***   AA
Movie theaters: 1 single/twin; 1 screen   C
Lively Arts Calendar (77)
Touring artists bookings: 20 dates
Outdoor Assets (3)
Inland water: 6.78 square miles
Grade: 56

✓ St. Petersburg–Clearwater, FL
Common Denominators (80)
Golf courses: 20 private (342 holes); 6 daily fee   C
(108 holes); 3 municipal (54 holes)
Bowling centers: 13 (426 lanes)   B
Good restaurants: 20 *, 22 **, 7 ***   B
Movie theaters: 5 single/twin, 15 multiplex; 110 screens   A
Lively Arts Calendar (100)
Touring artists bookings: 315 dates
Resident ensembles:
Florida Lyric Opera (12 dates)
Tampa Bay Opera (20 dates)
Outdoor Assets (100)
Gulf coastal water: 94.92 square miles
Inland water: 65.37 square miles
Federal protected area:
Pinellas NWR (15 acres)
State recreation areas:
Anclote Key SNA (35 acres)
Caladesi Island SP (632 acres)
Honeymoon Island SRA (408 acres)
Weedon Island SNA (602 acres)
Grade: 93

St. Simons–Jekyll Islands, GA
Common Denominators (50)
Golf courses: 6 daily fee (99 holes)   AA
Good restaurants: 7 *, 5 **, 4 ***   AA

Rating

Outdoor Assets (38)
Atlantic coastal water: 6.43 square miles
Inland water: 60.66 square miles
Federal protected area:
Fort Frederica NM (239 acres)
State recreation area:
Hofwyl–Broadfield Plantation SHS (1,268 acres)
Grade: 29

San Antonio, TX
Common Denominators (78)
Golf courses: 14 private (234 holes); 3 daily fee   C
(54 holes); 6 municipal (144 holes)
Bowling centers: 18 (534 lanes)   B
Good restaurants: 16 *, 8 **, 5 ***, 1 ****   C
Movie theaters: 18 multiplex; 148 screens   A
Lively Arts Calendar (100)
Touring artists bookings: 66 dates
Resident ensemble:
San Antonio Symphony (100 dates)
Outdoor Assets (2)
Inland water: 9.83 square miles
Federal protected area:
San Antonio Missions NHP (258 acres)
State recreation area:
Jose Antonio Navarro SHS (1 acre)
Grade: 60

✓ San Diego, CA
Common Denominators (75)
Golf courses: 29 private (513 holes); 27 daily fee   C
(477 holes); 5 municipal (126 holes)
Bowling centers: 24 (896 lanes)   C
Good restaurants: 13 *, 39 **, 23 ***   B
Movie theaters: 18 single/twin, 26 multiplex; 194   B
screens
Lively Arts Calendar (100)
Touring artists bookings: 301 dates
Resident ensembles:
San Diego Chamber Orchestra (14 dates)
San Diego Civic Light Opera Association (75 dates)
San Diego Comic Opera Company (18 dates)
San Diego Opera (25 dates)
Outdoor Assets (88)
Pacific coastal water: 26.7 square miles
Inland water: 54.43 square miles
Federal protected areas:
Cleveland NF (289,498 acres)
Cabrillo NM (137 acres)
Sweetwater Marsh NWR (316 acres)
Tijuana Slough NWR (407 acres)
State recreation areas:
Anza–Borrego Desert SP (522,097 acres)
Border Field SP (397 acres)
Cardiff SB (505 acres)
Carlsbad SB (28 acres)
Cuyamaca Rancho SP (24,614 acres)
Leucadia SB (11 acres)
Moonlight SB (13 acres)
Old Town San Diego SHP (27 acres)
Palomar Mountain SP (1,909 acres)
San Elijo SB (587 acres)
San Onofre SB (3,036 acres)
San Pasqual Battlefield SHP (50 acres)
Silver Strand SB (363 acres)
South Carlsbad SB (118 acres)
Torrey Pines SB (61 acres)
Torrey Pines SR (1,494 acres)
Grade: 88

San Juan Islands, WA
Common Denominators (50)
Golf courses: 3 daily fee (27 holes)   AA
Good restaurants: 3 **   AA
Lively Arts Calendar (58)
Touring artists bookings: 15 dates

Outdoor Assets (100)
Puget Sound coastal water: 361.99 square miles
Inland water: 81.16 square miles
Federal protected areas:
San Juan Islands NWR (379 acres)
San Juan NHS (1,726 acres)
State recreation areas:
Blind Island SP (3 acres)
Castle Island SP (2 acres)
Clark Island SP (55 acres)
Doe Island SP (6 acres)
Dot Rock SP (1 acre)
Freeman Island SP (1 acre)
Iceberg Island SP (3 acres)
James Island SP (114 acres)
Jones Island SP (188 acres)
Lime Kiln Point SP (36 acres)
Lopez Island Tidelands SP (1 acre)
Matia Island SP (5 acres)
Moran SP (5,176 acres)
Mud Bay Tidelands SP (1 acre)
Northwest McConnel Rock SP (3 acres)
Olga SP (1 acre)
Park Bay Island SP (3 acres)
Patos Island SP (207 acres)
Posey Island SP (1 acre)
Skull Island SP (1 acre)
Spencer Spit SP (130 acres)
Stuart Island SP (148 acres)
Sucia Island SP (564 acres)
Turn Island SP (35 acres)
Twin Rocks SP (1 acre)
Unnamed Islands SP (8 acres)
Victim Island SP (5 acres)
Grade: 69

San Luis Obispo, CA
Common Denominators (75)
Golf courses: 2 private (36 holes); 3 daily fee (54 holes);   **C**
  2 municipal (27 holes)
Bowling centers: 4 (74 lanes)   **C**
Good restaurants: 3 *, 7 **, 1 ***   **B**
Movie theaters: 8 single/twin, 1 multiplex; 23 screens   **B**
Lively Arts Calendar (100)
Touring artists bookings: 51 dates
Resident ensembles:
Pacific Repertory Opera (7 dates)
San Luis Obispo County Symphony (11 dates)
Outdoor Assets (29)
Pacific coastal water: 29.25 square miles
Inland water: 18.75 square miles
Federal protected area:
Los Padres NF (7,335 acres)
State recreation areas:
Cayuccos SB (16 acres)
Hearst San Simeon SHM (160 acres)
Los Osos Oaks SR (85 acres)
Montana De Oro SP (8,227 acres)
Morro Bay SP (1,987 acres)
Morro Strand SB (159 acres)
Pismo SB (1,055 acres)
San Simeon SP (543 acres)
William Randolph Hearst SB (8 acres)
Grade: 68

Sandpoint–Priest River, ID
Common Denominators (70)
Golf courses: 4 daily fee (54 holes)   **AA**
Bowling centers: 1 (16 lanes)   **A**
Good restaurants: 1 ***   **A**
Lively Arts Calendar (31)
Touring artists bookings: 8 dates
Outdoor Assets (100)
Inland water: 182.00 square miles
Federal protected areas:
Coeur d'Alene NF (14,027 acres)

Kaniksu NF (425,691 acres)
Kootenai NF (35,909 acres)
State recreation areas:
Priest Lake SP (756 acres)
Round Lake SP (142 acres)
Grade: 67

✓ **Santa Barbara, CA**
Common Denominators (78)
Golf courses: 7 private (126 holes); 5 daily fee (72   **C**
  holes); 1 municipal (18 holes)
Bowling centers: 6 (172 lanes)   **B**
Good restaurants: 2 *, 6 **, 5 ***   **B**
Movie theaters: 11 single/twin, 5 multiplex; 38 screens   **B**
Lively Arts Calendar (100)
Touring artists bookings: 59 dates
Resident ensembles:
Santa Barbara Civic Light Opera (28 dates)
Santa Barbara Chamber Orchestra (9 dates)
Outdoor Assets (100)
Pacific coastal water: 103.81 square miles
Inland water: 13.03 square miles
Federal protected areas:
Channel Islands NP (63,552 acres)
Los Padres NF (629,118 acres)
State recreation areas:
Carpinteria SB (57 acres)
Chumash Painted Cave SHP (8 acres)
El Capitan SB (134 acres)
El Presidio de Santa Barbara SHP (4 acres)
Gaviota SP (2,756 acres)
La Purisima Mission SHP (966 acres)
Point Sal SB (84 acres)
Refugio SB (155 acres)
Grade: 93

Santa Fe, NM
Common Denominators (85)
Golf courses: 3 private (45 holes); 1 daily fee (54 holes)   **B**
Bowling centers: 1 (32 lanes)   **C**
Good restaurants: 10 *, 13 **, 11 ***, 1 ****   **AA**
Movie theaters: 4 single/twin, 1 multiplex; 12 screens   **A**
Lively Arts Calendar (100)
Touring artists bookings: 40 dates
Resident ensembles:
Santa Fe Opera (38 dates)
Santa Fe Symphony Orchestra & Chorus Inc. (9
dates)
Outdoor Assets (54)
Inland water: 1.60 square miles
Federal protected areas:
Bandelier NM (826 acres)
Pecos NM (87 acres)
Santa Fe NF (245,005 acres)
State recreation areas:
Hyde Memorial SP (350 acres)
Santa Fe River SP (5 acres)
Grade: 80

Santa Rosa–Sonoma, CA
Common Denominators (80)
Golf courses: 1 private (18 holes); 8 daily fee   **B**
  (117 holes); 4 municipal (72 holes)
Bowling centers: 8 (184 lanes)   **B**
Good restaurants: 8 *, 9 **, 1 ***   **B**
Movie theaters: 2 single/twin, 6 multiplex; 33 screens   **B**
Lively Arts Calendar (100)
Touring artists bookings: 20 dates
Resident ensemble:
New West Chamber Orchestra (16 dates)
Outdoor Assets (15)
Pacific coastal water: 16.29 square miles
Inland water: 29.21 square miles
Federal protected area:
San Pablo Bay NWR (249 acres)

Rating   Rating

State recreation areas:
  Annadel SP (4,916 acres)
  Armstrong Redwoods SR (752 acres)
  Austin Creek SRA (4,234 acres)
  Bothe–Napa Valley SP (144 acres)
  Fort Ross SHP (3,276 acres)
  Jack London SHP (983 acres)
  Kruse Rhododendron SR (317 acres)
  Petaluma Adobe SHP (41 acres)
  Robert Louis Stevenson SP (1,538 acres)
  Salt Point SP (5,676 acres)
  Sonoma Coast SB (5,054 acres)
  Sonoma SHP (64 acres)
  Sugarloaf Ridge SP (2,514 acres)

Grade: 65

Sarasota, FL
Common Denominators (93)

Golf courses: 13 private (225 holes); 18 daily fee (306 holes); 4 municipal (63 holes)	A
Bowling centers: 5 (152 lanes)	A
Good restaurants: 4 *, 6 **, 12 ***	A
Movie theaters: 1 single/twin, 7 multiplex; 55 screens	AA

Lively Arts Calendar (100)
Touring artists bookings: 119 dates
Resident ensembles:
  Sarasota Opera Association (36 dates)
  Florida West Coast Symphoy Orchestra (27 dates)

Outdoor Assets (33)
Gulf coastal water: 11.93 square miles
Inland water: 34.21 square miles
State recreation areas:
  Myakka River SP (18,725 acres)
  Oscar Scherer SRA (462 acres)

Grade: 75

Savannah, GA
Common Denominators (83)

Golf courses: 9 private (153 holes); 3 daily fee (45 holes); 2 municipal (27 holes)	C
Bowling centers: 4 (112 lanes)	B
Good restaurants: 2 *, 9 **, 3 ***	A
Movie theaters: 1 single/twin, 4 multiplex; 30 screens	A

Lively Arts Calendar (100)
Resident ensemble:
  Savannah Symphony Orchestra (55 dates)

Outdoor Assets (63)
Atlantic coastal water: 19.06 square miles
Inland water: 56.43 square miles
Federal protected areas:
  Fort Pulaski NM (5,365 acres)
  Savannah Coastal NWR (5,527 acres)
  Wassaw NWR (10,050 acres)
State recreation areas:
  Skidaway Island SP (506 acres)
  Wormsloe SHS (8,222 acres)

Grade: 82

Sebring–Avon Park, FL
Common Denominators (70)

Golf courses: 1 private (9 holes); 10 daily fee (162 holes); 2 municipal (36 holes)	AA
Bowling centers: 1 (32 lanes)	B
Movie theaters: 2 multiplex; 12 screens	AA

Lively Arts Calendar (46)
Touring artists bookings: 12 dates

Outdoor Assets (20)
Inland water: 77.88 square miles
State recreation area:
  Highlands Hammock SP (3,520 acres)

Grade: 45

Sedona, AZ
Common Denominators (50)

Golf courses: 2 private (36 holes); 2 daily fee (36 holes)	AA
Movie theaters: 1 multiplex; 6 screens	AA

Outdoor Assets (93)
Inland water: 4.79 square miles
Federal protected areas:
  Coconino NF (427,107 acres)
  Glen Canyon NRA (44,953 acres)
  Grand Canyon NP (662,038 acres)
  Kaibab NF (1,526,993 acres)
  Lake Mead NRA (83,116 acres)
  Montezuma Castle NM (841 acres)
  Navajo NM (40 acres)
  Prescott NF (43,695 acres)
  Sitgreaves NF (284,325 acres)
  Sunset Crater NM (3,040 acres)
  Walnut Canyon NM (2,012 acres)
  Wupatki NM (35,253 acres)
State recreation areas:
  Dead Horse Ranch SP (320 acres)
  Riordan SHS (5 acres)
  Slide Rock SP (43 acres)

Grade: 48

Silver City, NM
Common Denominators (63)

Golf courses: 1 municipal (18 holes)	B
Bowling centers: 1 (16 lanes)	A
Movie theaters: 1 single/twin; 2 screens	B

Lively Arts Calendar (31)
Touring artists bookings: 8 dates

Outdoor Assets (93)
Inland water: 1.62 square miles
Federal protected area:
  Gila NF (883,394 acres)

Grade: 62

Smith Mountain Lake, VA
Common Denominators (58)

Golf courses: 4 private (54 holes); 6 daily fee (90 holes); 1 municipal (9 holes)	A
Bowling centers: 1 (24 lanes)	C
Good restaurants: 1 ***	C

Outdoor Assets (20)
Inland water: 34 square miles
Federal protected areas:
  Appalachian National Trail (120 acres)
  Blue Ridge Parkway (9,328 acres)
  Booker T. Washington NM (224 acres)
  Jefferson NF (18,810 acres)
State recreation area:
  Smith Mountain Lake SP (21,506 acres)

Grade: 26

Sonora–Groveland–Twain Harte, CA
Common Denominators (85)

Golf courses: 4 daily fee (63 holes)	A
Bowling centers: 1 (16 lanes)	C
Good restaurants: 3 ***	A
Movie theaters: 1 single/twin, 1 multiplex; 6 screens	A

Outdoor Assets (100)
Inland water: 38.87 square miles
Federal protected areas:
  Calaveras Bigtree NF (380 acres)
  Stanislaus NF (612,324 acres)
  Yosemite NP (428,605 acres)
State recreation areas:
  Calaveras Big Trees SP (2,683 acres)
  Columbia SHP (263 acres)
  Railtown 1897 SHP (20 acres)

Grade: 62

Southern Berkshire County, MA
Common Denominators (98)

Golf courses: 2 private (36 holes); 3 daily fee (45 holes)	A
Bowling centers: 2 (32 lanes)	AA
Good restaurants: 4 *, 13 **, 3 ***, 1 ****	AA
Movie theaters: 1 single/twin, 2 multiplex; 10 screens	AA

Rating

Lively Arts Calendar (100)
Touring artists bookings: 41 dates
Resident ensembles:
Berkshire Opera Company (10 dates)
Berkshire Symphony (4 dates)
Outdoor Assets (46)
Inland water: 14.95 square miles
Federal protected area:
Appalachian National Trail (4,734 acres)
State recreation areas:
Bash Bish Falls SP (417 acres)
Beartown SF (10,555 acres)
Becket SF (656 acres)
Campbell's Falls SP (5 acres)
Clarksburg SP (3,250 acres)
Cookson SF (2,385 acres)
East Mountain SP (375 acres)
Mt. Everett SR (1,100 acres)
Mt. Greylock SR (10,327 acres)
Mt. Washington SF (1 acre)
Natural Bridge SP (17 acres)
October Mountain SF (15,710 acres)
Otis SF (3,861 acres)
Peru SF (3,150 acres)
Pittsfield SF (9,695 acres)
Sandisfield SF (7,785 acres)
Savoy Mountain SF (10,500 acres)
Taconic Trail SP (930 acres)
Tolland SF (8,000 acres)
Wahconah Falls SP (53 acres)
Western Gateway Heritage SP (1 acre)
Windsor SF (1,626 acres)
Grade: 81

Southern Pines–Pinehurst, NC
Common Denominators (63)
Golf courses: 14 private (243 holes); 17 daily fee — AA
(297 holes)
Good restaurants: 3 * — C
Movie theaters: 1 single/twin, 1 multiplex; 6 screens — B
Lively Arts Calendar (46)
Touring artists bookings: 12 dates
Outdoor Assets (3)
Inland water: 7.54 square miles
State recreation area:
Weymouth Woods (628 acres)
Grade: 37

Southport–Brunswick Islands, NC
Common Denominators (80)
Golf courses: 22 daily fee (387 holes); 2 municipal — AA
(36 holes)
Bowling centers: 1 (20 lanes) — C
Good restaurants: 1 *, 1 ** — C
Movie theaters: 1 multiplex; 6 screens — B
Outdoor Assets (16)
Atlantic coastal water: 15.52 square miles
Inland water: 39.97 square miles
Grade: 32

State College, PA
Common Denominators (83)
Golf courses: 2 private (27 holes); 5 daily fee (81 holes) — B
Bowling centers: 3 (62 lanes) — B
Good restaurants: 2 **, 1 *** — B
Movie theaters: 3 single/twin, 2 multiplex; 16 screens — A
Lively Arts Calendar (100)
Touring artists bookings: 30 dates
Resident ensemble:
Nittany Valley Symphony (6 dates)
Outdoor Assets (5)
Inland water: 4.32 square miles
State recreation areas:
Bald Eagle SP (5,900 acres)
Black Moshannon SP (3,481 acres)
McCall Dam SP (8 acres)

Rating

Penn Roosevelt SP (100 acres)
Poe Paddy SP (10 acres)
Poe Valley (620 acres)
Grade: 62

Table Rock Lake, MO
Common Denominators (43)
Golf courses: 1 daily fee (9 holes) — B
Bowling centers: 1 (12 lanes) — A
Outdoor Assets (38)
Inland water: 47.68 square miles
Federal protected area:
Mark Twain NF (15,960 acres)
State recreation area:
Table Rock SP (62 acres)
Grade: 27

✓ **Taos, NM**
Common Denominators (75)
Golf courses: 4 daily fee (63 holes); 1 municipal (18 — AA
holes)
Good restaurants: 2 *, 9 **, 3 *** — AA
Movie theaters: 1 multiplex; 4 screens — AA
Lively Arts Calendar (100)
Touring artists bookings: 41 dates
Outdoor Assets (92)
Inland water: 1.46 square miles
Federal protected area:
Carson NF (483,026 acres)
Grade: 89

Thomasville, GA
Common Denominators (83)
Golf courses: 1 private (18 holes); 1 municipal (18 holes) — B
Bowling centers: 1 (20 lanes) — A
Good restaurants: 1 ** — B
Movie theaters: 1 multiplex; 3 screens — B
Lively Arts Calendar (23)
Touring artists bookings: 6 dates
Outdoor Assets (2)
Inland water: 3.69 square miles
State recreation area:
Lapham–Patterson House SHS (1 acre)
Grade: 36

Toms River–Barnegat Bay, NJ
Common Denominators (78)
Golf courses: 3 private (36 holes); 3 daily fee (63 holes); — C
5 municipal (81 holes)
Bowling centers: 8 (234 lanes) — A
Good restaurants: 2 *, 2 ** — C
Movie theaters: 4 single/twin, 6 multiplex; 39 screens — B
Lively Arts Calendar (100)
Touring artists bookings: 42 dates
Resident ensemble:
Garden State Philharmonic Symphony Orchestra (7
dates)
Outdoor Assets (60)
Atlantic coastal water: 15.86 square miles
Inland water: 120.99 square miles
Federal protected area:
Edwin B. Forsythe NWR (13,015 acres)
State recreation areas:
Barnegat Lighthouse SP (32 acres)
Double Trouble SP (5,118 acres)
Island Beach SP (3,002 acres)
Manasquan Canal SRA (5 acres)
Monmouth Battlefield SP (1,520 acres)
Veterans of All Wars Memorial SHS (1 acre)
Grade: 79

Traverse City, MI
Common Denominators (98)
Golf courses: 1 private (18 holes); 8 daily fee — AA
(117 holes); 1 municipal (9 holes)
Bowling centers: 2 (72 lanes) — AA

Good restaurants: 3 *, 2 **, 3 ***   **A**
Movie theaters: 2 single/twin, 1 multiplex; 12 screens   **AA**
Lively Arts Calendar (100)
Touring artists bookings: 180 dates
Resident ensemble:
Traverse Symphony Orchestra (12 dates)
Outdoor Assets (61)
Great Lakes coastal water: 11 square miles
Inland water: 26.21 square miles
Federal protected area:
Manistee NF (2 acres)
State recreation areas:
Interlochen SP (187 acres)
Traverse City SP (45 acres)
Grade: 86

Tryon, NC
Common Denominators (40)
Golf courses: 2 private (27 holes)
Good restaurants: 1 ***   **A**
Movie theaters: 1 single/twin; 1 screen   **C**
Lively Arts Calendar (15)
Touring artists bookings: 4 dates
Outdoor Assets (1)
Inland water: 0.75 square miles
Grade: 19

Tucson, AZ
Common Denominators (83)
Golf courses: 16 private (279 holes); 10 daily fee   **C**
(153 holes); 6 municipal (108 holes)
Bowling centers: 11 (324 lanes)   **B**
Good restaurants: 7 *, 14 **, 12 ***, 1 ****, 1 *****   **A**
Movie theaters: 1 single/twin, 12 multiplex; 80 screens   **A**
Lively Arts Calendar (100)
Touring artists bookings: 214 dates
Resident ensembles:
Arizona Opera Company (13 dates)
Tucson Philharmonia Youth Orchestra (3 dates)
Outdoor Assets (57)
Inland water: 2.43 square miles
Federal protected areas:
Buenos Aires NWR (21,977 acres)
Cabeza Prieta NWR (416,211 acres)
Coronado NF (390,474 acres)
Organ Pipe Cactus NM (329,316 acres)
Saguaro NM (82,035 acres)
State recreation area:
Catalina SP (5,511 acres)
Grade: 80

Vero Beach–Sebastian, FL
Common Denominators (83)
Golf courses: 12 private (207 holes); 3 daily fee   **A**
(45 holes); 3 municipal (54 holes)
Bowling centers: 3 (68 lanes)   **A**
Good restaurants: 1 *, 2 **, 1 ***   **B**
Movie theaters: 1 multiplex; 6 screens   **C**
Lively Arts Calendar (15)
Touring artists bookings: 4 dates
Outdoor Assets (22)
Atlantic coastal water: 7.69 square miles
Inland water: 36.79 square miles
Federal protected area:
Pelican Island NWR (43 acres)
State recreation area:
Sebastian Inlet SRA (457 acres)
Grade: 40

Virginia Beach, VA
Common Denominators (80)
Golf courses: 5 private (90 holes); 3 daily fee (54 holes);   **C**
3 municipal (54 holes)
Bowling centers: 7 (206 lanes)   **B**
Good restaurants: 6 *, 10 **, 1 ***   **B**
Movie theaters: 6 multiplex; 42 screens   **A**

Lively Arts Calendar (46)
Resident ensemble:
Virginia Beach Symphony Orchestra (12 dates)
Outdoor Assets (100)
Atlantic coastal water: 70.83 square miles
Inland water: 58.33 square miles
Federal protected areas:
Back Bay NWR (4,589 acres)
Mackay Island NWR (874 acres)
State recreation areas:
False Cape SP (4,321 acres)
Seashore SP (2,770 acres)
Grade: 75

Wenatchee, WA
Common Denominators (85)
Golf courses: 1 private (18 holes); 3 daily fee (36 holes);   **A**
2 municipal (45 holes)
Bowling centers: 1 (10 lanes)   **C**
Good restaurants: 2 *, 1 **   **B**
Movie theaters: 2 multiplex; 10 screens   **AA**
Lively Arts Calendar (42)
Touring artists bookings: 7 dates
Resident ensemble:
Wenatchee Valley Symphony (4 dates)
Outdoor Assets (100)
Inland water: 72.24 square miles
Federal protected areas:
Lake Chelan NRA (59,307 acres)
North Cascades NP (66,751 acres)
Wenatchee NF (1,311,949 acres)
State recreation areas:
Ice Caves SP (160 acres)
Lake Chelan SP (127 acres)
Lake Wenatchee SP (473 acres)
Squilchuck SP (293 acres)
Twenty-Five Mile Creek SP (235 acres)
Grade: 76

Western St. Tammany Parish, LA
Common Denominators (83)
Golf courses: 2 private (36 holes); 2 daily fee (27 holes)   **C**
Bowling centers: 1 (32 lanes)   **B**
Good restaurants: 1 **, 2 ***   **B**
Movie theaters: 1 single/twin, 2 multiplex; 15 screens   **AA**
Lively Arts Calendar (19)
Touring artists bookings: 5 dates
Outdoor Assets (74)
Inland water: 259.80 square miles
Federal protected area:
Bogue Chitto NWR (23,112 acres)
State recreation areas:
Fairview-Riverside SP (99 acres)
Fontainebleau SP (2,809 acres)
Slidell SP (71 acres)
Grade: 59

Whidbey Island, WA
Common Denominators (80)
Golf courses: 2 private (36 holes); 1 daily fee (18 holes)   **C**
Bowling centers: 4 (62 lanes)   **AA**
Good restaurants: 2 **   **B**
Movie theaters: 1 single/twin, 1 multiplex; 4 screens   **C**
Outdoor Assets (100)
Pacific coastal water: 295.43 square miles
Inland water: 13.36 square miles
Federal protected areas:
Ebey's Landing NH Res (1,379 acres)
San Juan Islands NWR (65 acres)
State recreation areas:
Camano Island SP (134 acres)
Deception Pass SP (1,249 acres)
Ebey's Landing SP (46 acres)
Fort Casey SP (417 acres)
Fort Ebey SP (644 acres)

Rating

Joseph Whidbey SP (112 acres)
South Whidbey SP (85 acres)
Grade: 60

Wickenburg, AZ
Common Denominators (95)
Golf courses: 1 private (18 holes); 1 daily fee (18 holes)   AA
Bowling centers: 1 (12 lanes)   AA
Good restaurants: 1 *   A
Movie theaters: 1 single/twin; 1 screen   A
Outdoor Assets (30)
Inland water: 20.81 square miles
Federal protected area:
Tonto NF (657,695 acres)
Grade: 42

Williamsburg, VA
Common Denominators (100)
Golf courses: 2 private (36 holes); 6 daily fee (126 holes)   AA
Bowling centers: 2 (46 lanes)   AA
Good restaurants: 3 *, 11 **, 2 ***, 1 ****   AA
Movie theaters: 1 single/twin, 2 multiplex; 12 screens   AA
Lively Arts Calendar (92)
Touring artists bookings: 12 dates
Resident ensemble:
Williamsburg Symphonia (12 dates)
Outdoor Assets (65)
Atlantic coastal water: 14.82 square miles
Inland water: 22.12 square miles
Federal protected area:
Colonial NHP (2,972 acres)
State recreation area:
York River SP (2,505 acres)
Grade: 86

Wimberly–San Marcos, TX
Common Denominators (60)
Golf courses: 3 daily fee (45 holes)   B
Bowling centers: 1 (24 lanes)   C
Movie theaters: 2 multiplex; 10 screens   A
Lively Arts Calendar (19)
Touring artists bookings: 5 dates
Outdoor Assets (1)
Inland water: 1.92 square miles
Grade: 27

Winchester, VA
Common Denominators (80)
Golf courses: 1 private (18 holes); 2 daily fee (27 holes)   C
Bowling centers: 1 (40 lanes)   A
Good restaurants: 1 **   C
Movie theaters: 2 single/twin, 1 multiplex; 10 screens   A
Outdoor Assets (6)
Inland water: 1.08 square miles
Federal protected area:
George Washington NF (4,931 acres)
Grade: 29

Rating

Woodstock, VT
Common Denominators (93)
Golf courses: 3 private (45 holes); 5 daily fee (63 holes)   A
Bowling centers: 2 (40 lanes)   AA
Good restaurants: 1 *, 6 **, 7 ***   AA
Movie theaters: 3 single/twin; 4 screens   B
Lively Arts Calendar (100)
Touring artists bookings: 56 dates
Outdoor Assets (20)
Inland water: 4.77 square miles
Federal protected areas:
Appalachian National Trail (3,300 acres)
Green Mountain NF (22,008 acres)
Marsh-Billings NHP
State recreation areas:
Ascutney SP (1,984 acres)
Camp Plymouth SP (300 acres)
Coolidge SP (16,165 acres)
Quechee Gorge SP (612 acres)
Silver Lake SP (34 acres)
Wilgus SP (100 acres)
Grade: 71

York Beaches, ME
Common Denominators (63)
Golf courses: 4 private (54 holes); 6 daily fee (81 holes)   B
Good restaurants: 4 *, 8 **, 4 ***   A
Movie theaters: 4 single/twin, 1 multiplex; 13 screens   B
Outdoor Assets (15)
Atlantic coastal water: 20.11 square miles
Inland water: 31.65 square miles
Federal protected area:
Rachel Carson NWR (3,287 acres)
State recreation areas:
Ferry Beach SP (117 acres)
Fort McClary SHS (27 acres)
John Paul Jones SHS (2 acres)
Vaughan Woods SHS (250 acres)
Grade: 26

Yuma, AZ
Common Denominators (78)
Golf courses: 1 private (18 holes); 3 daily fee (36 holes);   B
1 municipal (18 holes)
Bowling centers: 4 (86 lanes)   A
Good restaurants: 1 *, 2 **   C
Movie theaters: 1 multiplex; 4 screens   C
Lively Arts Calendar (96)
Touring artists bookings: 20 dates
Resident ensemble:
Yuma Community Orchestra (5 dates)
Outdoor Assets (74)
Inland water: 4.89 square miles
Federal protected areas:
Cabeza Prieta NWR (443,800 acres)
Kofa NWR (523,040 acres)
State recreation area:
Territorial Prison SHS (9 acres)
Grade: 82

ET CETERA: Leisure Living

RETIREMENT PLACES WITH THE BEST BASS FISHING

Black bass, the premier gamefish in North America, are found in lakes and rivers in every state but Alaska. They aren't abundant in all areas, however, and some regions do not have the large bass-holding waters that can withstand extensive public attention. *Field & Stream* recently named the 50 best fishing spots in the United States and Canada, and one or more of these are within the following retirement places.

Amherst–Northampton, Massachusetts

Located in a wilderness setting just east of Amherst, the 25,000-acre Quabbin Reservoir is the largest body of water in Massachusetts and a principal source of Boston's water supply. In addition to trout and salmon, it sports a good fishery for bass, particularly smallmouth, and is tightly managed for fishing and boating.

Boca Raton–Delray Beach, Florida

Lake Okeechobee, at the western edge of this retirement place, is the most renowned of Florida's largemouth bass factories. It has over 200,000 acres of shallow, grass-filled water and is often the least affected Florida bass lake during late winter and early spring, offering phenomenal fishing when the weather is stable.

Burlington, Vermont

With the Green Mountains on the east and the Adirondack Mountains on the west, 120-mile-long Lake Champlain, a natural lake on the Vermont–New York border, is nestled in the midst of some outstanding country. The premier gamefish is smallmouth bass, especially in the northern sector. Largemouth bass are abundant, too, particularly in weedy bays. In addition, walleye, trout, salmon, and perch fishing is excellent.

Hot Springs, Arkansas

Lake Ouachita, a Corps of Engineers lake about 35 miles from Hot Springs, is part of the Ouachita National Forest and is known for a variety of good fishing. Largemouth and spotted (locally called "Kentucky") bass are plentiful here. Stripers, too, are abundant among the rotting timber left standing in this lake when it was flooded.

Kentucky Lake, Kentucky

Kentucky Lake and Barkley Lake are magnets for warm-water anglers throughout the Midwest. Combined, they are the second-largest manmade water system in America, and their 3,500 miles of shoreline provide countless coves, bays, finders, and hideaways for bass. Largemouth and spotted (Kentucky) bass are plentiful, and smallmouth bass have become especially prominent in recent years.

Kissimmee–St. Cloud, Florida

There are numbers of shallow, grassy lakes in Florida's Kissimmee River chain. Lake Kissimmee (the largest) and East and West Tohopekaliga are among the most prominent. West Toho is rated one of the best places for trophy bass, which is high praise in a state that has many trophy largemouth waters.

Lake Havasu City, Arizona

Lake Mohave, an impoundment on the Colorado River downstream from Lake Mead (see Las Vegas, Nevada), is an excellent largemouth bass lake, providing good fishing on points, cliffs, brush, and other habitats that

---

Inland Water

Aside from ocean or Great Lakes coastal bays and river estuaries, big lakes in the interior are a recreation draw for miles around. In the 19 locations below, more than five percent of the surface area is big-lake water.

Place	Percentage surface-area big-lake water
Burlington, VT	23.7%
Eagle River, WI	14.3
Polson–Mission Valley, MT	9.7
Sandpoint–Priest River, ID	9.5
Table Rock Lake, MO	9.3
Guntersville, AL	9.0
Kentucky Lake, KY	8.0
Cedar Creek Lake, TX	7.9
Hot Springs, AR	7.7
Lake of the Ozarks, MO	7.6
Oxford, MS	7.1
Sebring–Avon Park, FL	7.0
Lake of the Cherokees, OK	6.5
Lake Martin, AL	6.3
Lake Winnipesaukee, NH	5.9
Norfork Lake, AR	5.5
Coeur d'Alene, ID	5.4
Clemson–Pendleton District, SC	5.3
Lake Livingston, TX	5.3

Source: Bureau of the Census, unpublished area measurements.

---

are typical of these weedless desert lakes. Cold water issuing from Hoover Dam makes the upper 15 miles more suitable for trout, but the rest of the 67-mile-long lake offers plenty of bass fishing opportunities.

Lake Winnipesaukee, New Hampshire

Squam Lake, location for the movie *On Golden Pond*, is noted for its smallmouth bass fishing. Its 44,000-acre neighbor, Lake Winnipesaukee, is the largest of New Hampshire's many lakes. Here, trout and landlocked salmon are the locally preferred fish, but many smallmouth and largemouth bass are caught as well.

Lakeland–Winter Haven, Florida

The Florida Phosphate Pits, which are flooded, reclaimed phosphate-mining areas of varying size, possess an abundance of chunky largemouth bass, including plenty of trophy-size fish. There are lots of pits in the south-central mining country, and the newest publicly accessible ones are in the Tenoroc State Reserve outside of Lakeland.

Las Vegas, Nevada

Near Las Vegas and backed by the Hoover Dam, Lake Mead has lots of good bass cover, resulting in an abundance of 1- to 3-pound largemouth bass. Stripers, too, benefit from the expanded forage base and are popular on this lake, with small fish up to 10 pounds being plentiful.

Norfork Lake, Arkansas

Norfork Lake and nearby Bull Shoals are among the best largemouth bass waters in the Ozarks, have excellent spring and fall fishing, and provide good angling throughout the year for a variety of species, including white bass and crappies. Trout and smallmouth bass are also present.

Ocala, Florida

Good largemouth fishing can be had in many areas of Florida's lengthy and renowned St. Johns River, particularly Rodman Reservoir at the northern edge of the Ocala National Forest and Lake George, upriver yet south of Rodman Reservoir.

San Diego, California

San Diego's water supply lakes are small and intensively fished. Fifteen of these San Diego County Lakes are open to the public for fishing, and they have some of the best catch rates in California, including record-size Florida-strain largemouth bass.

Table Rock Lake, Missouri

Table Rock Lake, an impoundment of the White River in southeastern Missouri, is surrounded by the Mark Twain National Forest. Its 43,100 acres are spread out in a meandering, mazelike configuration of coves and creeks that hide many bass.

PUTTING IT ALL TOGETHER

Is there really an ideal place for retirement in America? Various Chambers of Commerce, real-estate promoters, and state tourism and economic development agencies may claim the title for their own locales. After all, with 12 million persons due to turn 65 over the rest of this decade, attracting footloose people to the Leisure Villages, Palm Shores, and Mountain Homes of this country is a highly promising growth industry.

You might even nominate your own neighborhood. The distant haven may exist somewhere for you, but living there is either unaffordable, inconvenient, or not much better than where you are now.

By this book's criteria, however, the ideal place would have the climate of Maui, Hawaii, where a southerly latitude and the Pacific Ocean keeps the air temperature from ever dropping below 65 degrees or from topping 90 degrees much of the time.

It would have to be a rural place if it were to match the low crime of Hiawassee in the northeast Georgia mountains, or the inexpensive housing around Guntersville and Lake Martin in Alabama.

Yet the ideal spot would also have to be a large college town to duplicate Gainesville's or Chapel Hill's full range of health-care facilities, public transportation, and continuing education opportunities.

For variety in recreation, you might choose a place like Cape Cod, which not only has good restaurants and a calendar of symphony orchestra performances and guest artist dates but excellent opportunities for public golf and other outdoor activities as well.

For finding part-time work, the place should have Las Vegas's prospects for job growth in the retail trade, services, and finance, insurance, and real estate industries.

Finally, the ideal place should offer retired persons the low living costs of Mission–McAllen–Alamo on the north bank of the Rio Grande in southernmost Texas.

Obviously this ideal haven is a fiction. You can explore the geography long and hard, but you will never find the single place that combines all the firsts according to this book's criteria. Moreover, because one person's haven can often be another's purgatory, and your rural retreat someone else's boondocks, one can argue that there really is no such thing as the ideal place.

Your active retirement years can now amount to one-quarter of your life. Choosing where to spend these years isn't easy. The first tactic is to focus on *your* preferences and needs. The section "Making the Chapters Work for You," at the front of the book, can help you identify what these preferences and needs might be.

Having said all this, one can still try to discover which of the 183 places come close to the ideal.

America's Top Retirement Places

Place	Average Grade
1. Las Vegas, NV	84.47
2. St. Petersburg–Clearwater, FL	83.88
3. Bellingham, WA	83.25
4. Fort Collins–Loveland, CO	83.09
5. Medford–Ashland, OR	82.37
6. Tucson, AZ	82.26
7. Coeur d'Alene, ID	82.12
8. Traverse City, MI	81.77
9. Phoenix–Mesa–Scottsdale, AZ	81.66
10. Melbourne, FL	81.38
11. Savannah, GA	80.95
12. Daytona Beach, FL	80.73
13. Fort Myers–Cape Coral, FL	80.54
14. Fayetteville, AR	80.18
15. Gainesville, FL	80.08
16. San Diego, CA	79.96
17. San Antonio, TX	79.78
18. Camden, ME	79.33
19. Austin, TX	79.26
20. Port Angeles–Seqium, WA	79.09
21. Hanover, NH	79.05
22. Colorado Springs, CO	78.91
23. Boca Raton–Delray Beach, FL	78.82
24. Grand Junction, CO	78.58
25. Fairhope–Gulf Shores, AL	78.53
26. Albuquerque, NM	78.52
27. Kalispell–Flathead Valley, MT	78.50
28. State College, PA	78.44
29. Hot Springs, AR	78.42
30. Burlington, VT	78.31

FINDING THE BEST ALL-AROUND PLACES

The method for determining America's best all-around places is quite simple: The grades of every place for each of the seven factors—money matters, housing, climate, personal safety, services, working, and leisure living—are averaged for a final grade.

The list at the start of the following column highlights the places that rise to the top as the better spots for retirement in America. In some respects, the list of the top 30 in this edition of *Retirement Places Rated* resembles that of the previous 1990 edition. Although their rankings have changed somewhat, 10 of the places were in the top 30 before.

By no means are these places untarnished. Fifteen rank near the bottom in one or more of the seven categories. Moreover, not one of the 183 places ranks in the upper half in all of them. Back to the point: there isn't an ideal haven in America. In spite of a blot or two, many come close through a combination of strengths. Whether their strengths are vital or unimportant or whether their blots are knockout factors or trivial is for you to decide.

RANKINGS: Putting It All Together

The following chart gives each place's grade in each of *Retirement Places Rated*'s seven chapters. On the right-hand side, the average of these seven grades, rounded two decimal places, is also shown as is the overall rank.

For example, Asheville's average grade of 77.75 places it 32nd overall among 183 locations. The best possible final grade is 100, meaning perfection in all seven categories.

Retirement Place	Money Matters	Housing	Climate	Personal Safety	Services	Working	Leisure Living	Final Grade	Rank
Aiken, SC	92	96	78	81	62	72	39	74.24	78
Alamogordo, NM	93	93	77	87	64	27	43	69.25	131
Albuquerque, NM	83	89	75	63	95	74	69	78.52	26
Alpine–Big Bend, TX	93	90	82	87	69	12	34	66.61	164
Amador County, CA	76	69	80	93	68	55	49	69.98	120
Amherst–Northampton, MA	71	72	69	93	85	52	66	72.42	100
Annapolis, MD	62	70	76	86	80	79	90	77.57	35
Asheville, NC	83	90	76	87	81	66	61	77.75	32
Athens, GA	86	83	78	79	93	48	36	71.74	107
Austin, TX	80	83	78	75	94	83	62	79.26	19
Bar Harbor, ME	77	86	66	94	82	53	65	74.76	70
Bay St. Louis–Pass Christian, MS	88	90	78	87	70	44	57	73.50	90
Beaufort, SC	85	84	79	75	75	60	63	74.26	77
Beaver Lake, AR	93	96	74	89	49	49	29	68.42	147
Bellingham, WA	85	80	83	87	89	66	93	83.25	3
Bend, OR	87	88	74	88	66	68	63	76.22	47
Blairsville, GA	95	87	77	96	46	38	49	69.86	123
Boca Raton–Delray Beach, FL	71	84	75	76	79	94	72	78.82	23
Boone–Blowing Rock, NC	79	74	72	93	85	57	67	75.13	62
Bradenton, FL	84	87	75	71	74	83	40	73.40	91
Branson, MO	94	96	72	82	60	62	48	73.57	89
Brevard, NC	81	83	76	94	61	42	74	73.19	94
Brookings–Gold Beach, OR	91	76	89	91	47	44	62	71.43	110
Brooksville–Spring Hill, FL	88	84	76	81	47	76	28	68.46	145
Burlington, VT	75	80	63	87	95	63	86	78.31	30
Camden, ME	80	81	68	93	92	50	92	79.33	18
Cape Cod, MA	58	66	76	81	83	60	98	74.43	75
Carmel–Monterey–Pebble Beach, CA	28	39	94	89	72	68	80	67.26	159
Carson City–Carson Valley, NV	76	84	76	85	67	50	77	73.62	86
Cedar Creek Lake, TX	92	85	77	86	58	45	31	67.66	155
Chapel Hill, NC	72	77	76	83	97	64	49	74.05	80
Charles Town–Harpers Ferry–Shepherdstown, WV	88	83	72	93	75	44	56	73.04	95
Charleston Sea Islands, SC	87	79	79	70	89	51	86	77.25	38
Charlevoix–Boyne City–East Jordan, MI	89	94	61	93	49	54	53	70.43	118
Charlottesville, VA	73	81	74	87	91	54	68	75.52	56
Chewelah, WA	96	96	70	93	53	33	34	67.83	154
Clayton, GA	91	78	78	94	48	42	42	67.39	158
Clemson–Pendleton District, SC	93	91	77	89	71	72	49	77.64	33

Retirement Place	Money Matters	Housing	Climate	Personal Safety	Services	Working	Leisure Living	Final Grade	Rank
Coeur d'Alene, ID	90	88	69	86	83	65	94	82.12	7
Colorado Springs, CO	88	89	70	84	84	71	68	78.91	22
Conway, SC	93	87	77	79	81	82	17	73.72	85
Cottonwood-Verde Valley, AZ	87	78	76	92	68	72	60	76.01	49
Crossville, TN	96	93	75	92	45	51	30	68.77	137
Dare Outer Banks, NC	75	66	82	83	32	69	64	67.13	160
Daytona Beach, FL	89	87	78	77	80	75	80	80.73	12
Delta-Cedaredge, CO	97	93	72	92	50	0	45	64.14	175
Durango, CO	87	85	64	87	86	34	69	73.21	93
Eagle River, WI	83	84	67	92	51	46	59	68.96	135
East End Long Island, NY	38	64	77	89	71	73	98	72.60	99
Easton-St. Michaels-Oxford, MD	67	77	76	86	55	20	71	64.63	174
Edenton, NC	86	86	79	87	53	13	31	61.97	179
Fairhope-Gulf Shores, AL	90	91	77	90	61	71	69	78.53	25
Fayetteville, AR	91	95	73	89	87	60	65	80.18	14
Florence, OR	95	90	88	85	53	62	57	75.78	53
Fort Collins-Loveland, CO	88	87	69	89	84	69	95	83.09	4
Fort Myers-Cape Coral, FL	79	83	74	80	76	87	85	80.54	13
Fredericksburg, TX	89	91	78	95	49	38	35	68.00	151
Fredericksburg-Spotsylvania, VA	78	80	73	90	68	59	38	69.44	127
Gainesville, FL	90	91	76	66	99	68	72	80.08	15
Grand Junction, CO	92	92	71	88	71	56	81	78.58	24
Grants Pass, OR	90	82	81	90	60	50	69	74.81	69
Grass Valley-Nevada City, CA	66	59	79	90	62	70	52	68.24	149
Guntersville, AL	96	98	75	91	55	55	29	71.39	111
Hamilton-Bitterroot Valley, MT	97	89	71	96	49	23	56	68.68	140
Hanover, NH	77	79	64	93	95	58	87	79.05	21
Hendersonville-East Flat Rock, NC	84	85	76	91	64	55	35	69.90	122
Hesperia-Apple Valley-Victorville, CA	72	82	81	74	74	84	63	75.94	50
Hiawassee, GA	92	77	77	98	59	10	33	63.87	177
Hilton Head Island, SC	52	66	80	77	79	60	68	68.92	136
Hot Springs, AR	87	95	75	85	82	43	83	78.42	29
Houghton Lake, MI	93	94	63	83	49	17	59	65.33	171
Inverness, FL	90	84	75	91	48	69	46	71.90	104
Kalispell-Flathead Valley, MT	94	90	70	87	67	52	90	78.50	27
Kauai, HI	61	60	87	89	65	65	33	65.64	168
Kentucky Lake, KY	96	97	73	94	86	41	40	75.21	61
Kerrville, TX	88	89	77	89	64	52	27	69.18	132
Ketchum-Sun Valley, ID	66	69	71	86	75	41	81	69.84	124

Retirement Place	Money Matters	Housing	Climate	Personal Safety	Services	Working	Leisure Living	Final Grade	Rank
Key West–Key Largo–Marathon, FL	57	55	78	60	73	66	80	67.04	161
Kingman, AZ	89	83	81	82	59	80	42	73.60	87
Kissimmee–St. Cloud, FL	85	93	75	72	54	85	29	70.46	117
Laguna Beach–Dana Point, CA	27	46	93	87	62	99	65	68.58	142
Lake Buchanan–Lake LBJ, TX	86	88	78	92	48	41	24	65.35	170
Lake Conroe, TX	83	89	76	85	47	75	61	73.60	87
Lake Granbury, TX	86	91	76	92	41	56	30	67.49	157
Lake Havasu City, AZ	82	76	78	87	59	80	78	77.19	40
Lake Livingston, TX	94	94	75	89	40	43	26	65.90	167
Lake Martin, AL	96	99	77	88	60	27	32	68.46	145
Lake of the Cherokees, OK	96	90	74	94	43	39	20	65.21	173
Lake of the Ozarks, MO	88	85	71	94	50	56	39	69.17	133
Lake Winnipesaukee, NH	77	79	66	91	65	54	86	73.82	83
Lakeland–Winter Haven, FL	90	92	74	69	76	69	68	76.87	43
Las Cruces, NM	90	87	78	82	81	60	61	76.98	42
Las Vegas, NV	81	86	79	78	86	95	88	84.47	1
Leesburg–Lady Lake, FL	87	89	75	82	58	75	60	75.13	62
Litchfield Hills, CT	54	69	67	93	75	49	71	68.15	150
Lower Cape May, NJ	67	83	79	81	69	59	87	74.87	68
Madison, MS	90	91	75	89	54	56	12	66.90	163
Maryville, TN	94	93	76	88	58	57	51	74.02	81
Maui, HI	56	61	86	83	63	80	65	70.76	114
McCall–Cascade–Payette Valley, ID	83	85	52	85	51	45	58	65.47	169
Medford–Ashland, OR	92	86	79	86	87	63	84	82.37	5
Melbourne, FL	84	87	77	78	83	74	87	81.38	10
Mission–McAllen–Alamo, TX	96	96	78	82	75	78	38	77.50	36
Montrose, CO	94	93	71	91	51	46	51	70.91	113
Myrtle Beach, SC	80	78	80	76	86	82	47	75.50	57
Naples, FL	67	78	74	78	52	77	96	74.54	72
New Bern, NC	83	85	78	82	76	53	47	71.97	103
New Braunfels, TX	86	91	77	82	47	65	31	68.52	144
New Port Richey, FL	91	87	76	87	65	85	43	76.18	48
Newport–Lincoln City, OR	92	88	88	85	52	36	87	75.70	54
Norfork Lake, AR	93	95	73	96	50	49	41	71.09	112
Northern Door Peninsula, WI	78	81	69	96	53	51	83	73.03	96
Northern Neck, VA	77	86	75	95	51	37	54	67.89	153
Oakhurst–Coarsegold, CA	80	87	80	80	46	56	58	69.46	125
Ocala, FL	90	89	74	73	61	69	55	72.82	97
Ocean City, MD	80	83	77	74	54	55	57	68.61	141

Retirement Place	Money Matters	Housing	Climate	Personal Safety	Services	Working	Leisure Living	Final Grade	Rank
Oscoda–Tawas–Huron Shore, MI	94	95	67	91	49	22	63	68.71	138
Oxford, MS	94	90	76	79	70	48	76	75.89	52
Pagosa Springs, CO	90	77	57	88	35	35	50	61.67	180
Pahrump Valley, NV	86	86	80	83	49	65	31	68.69	139
Palm Springs–Coachella Valley, CA	61	75	78	71	82	87	81	76.41	46
Panama City, FL	91	91	79	78	64	53	64	74.19	79
Paradise–Magalia, CA	77	76	85	85	87	63	55	75.29	60
Payson, AZ	81	72	75	90	51	55	63	69.44	127
Petoskey–Harbor Springs, MI	85	91	62	89	70	55	76	75.36	58
Phoenix–Mesa–Scottsdale, AZ	77	86	77	74	88	99	71	81.66	9
Pike County, PA	76	79	69	91	30	27	22	56.13	183
Placerville–Shingle Springs, CA	68	71	82	88	68	66	64	72.36	101
Polson–Mission Valley, MT	94	85	70	93	64	26	47	68.54	143
Pompano Beach, FL	77	87	75	59	82	88	62	75.58	55
Port Angeles–Seqium, WA	87	80	86	90	89	53	69	79.09	20
Port Charlotte–Punta Gorda, FL	84	83	73	92	51	73	67	74.58	71
Port Townsend, WA	86	76	86	90	73	54	60	74.94	67
Prescott–Prescott Valley, AZ	80	77	76	89	68	72	78	77.21	39
Redding, CA	77	83	80	83	75	67	70	76.52	45
Rehoboth Bay–Indian River Bay, DE	82	85	76	82	66	69	44	72.15	102
Reno–Sparks, NV	76	82	75	79	93	69	70	77.61	34
Riviera–Bullhead City, AZ	76	60	78	83	59	80	42	68.38	148
Rockport–Aransas Pass, TX	86	84	79	77	30	10	46	58.77	182
Ruidoso, NM	87	87	77	83	54	26	36	64.09	176
St. Augustine, FL	81	85	78	78	61	70	57	72.79	98
St. George–Zion, UT	78	74	77	91	65	71	80	76.68	44
St. Jay–Northeast Kingdom, VT	87	89	62	91	67	21	56	67.55	156
St. Petersburg–Clearwater, FL	85	91	75	71	85	86	93	83.88	2
St. Simons–Jekyll Islands, GA	65	59	80	67	66	67	29	61.99	178
San Antonio, TX	88	92	78	73	89	78	60	79.78	17
San Diego, CA	57	57	91	76	90	100	88	79.96	16
San Juan Islands, WA	63	65	86	93	40	47	69	66.08	166
San Luis Obispo, CA	51	43	93	89	84	68	68	70.67	115
Sandpoint–Priest River, ID	88	86	63	87	47	45	67	69.10	134
Santa Barbara, CA	44	53	93	85	90	69	93	75.12	64
Santa Fe, NM	73	74	74	83	70	67	80	74.32	76
Santa Rosa–Sonoma, CA	53	60	88	86	81	80	65	73.26	92
Sarasota, FL	80	88	76	80	68	79	75	77.94	31
Savannah, GA	84	90	78	76	88	69	82	80.95	11

Retirement Place	Money Matters	Housing	Climate	Personal Safety	Services	Working	Leisure Living	Final Grade	Rank
Sebring–Avon Park, FL	91	94	73	81	60	57	45	71.54	109
Sedona, AZ	67	72	75	92	73	68	48	70.51	116
Silver City, NM	95	95	79	77	69	48	62	75.03	65
Smith Mountain Lake, VA	89	91	76	96	56	52	26	69.46	125
Sonora–Groveland–Twain Harte, CA	76	65	81	91	72	56	62	71.76	106
Southern Berkshire County, MA	70	72	68	95	87	48	81	74.49	74
Southern Pines–Pinehurst, NC	77	85	75	89	70	53	37	69.42	129
Southport–Brunswick Islands, NC	82	78	80	93	54	71	32	70.11	119
State College, PA	86	91	69	92	91	58	62	78.44	28
Table Rock Lake, MO	93	93	73	94	29	48	27	65.26	172
Taos, NM	84	78	71	86	50	59	89	73.86	82
Thomasville, GA	97	98	75	80	63	14	36	66.24	165
Toms River–Barnegat Bay, NJ	67	76	76	90	75	62	79	74.95	66
Traverse City, MI	87	91	61	90	90	67	86	81.77	8
Tryon, NC	82	93	77	94	49	9	19	60.47	181
Tucson, AZ	81	84	78	75	92	86	80	82.26	6
Vero Beach–Sebastian, FL	78	85	78	82	54	72	40	69.95	121
Virginia Beach, VA	78	80	78	87	68	60	75	75.31	59
Wenatchee, WA	92	93	74	85	67	56	76	77.39	37
Western St. Tammany Parish, LA	88	90	76	88	55	62	59	73.81	84
Whidbey Island, WA	82	74	86	94	51	56	60	71.86	105
Wickenburg, AZ	81	81	77	89	52	99	42	74.52	73
Williamsburg, VA	73	88	77	88	94	35	86	77.19	40
Wimberly–San Marcos, TX	84	80	77	93	67	48	27	67.96	152
Winchester, VA	85	85	73	88	67	58	29	69.32	130
Woodstock, VT	74	82	61	93	74	47	71	71.67	108
York Beaches, ME	76	73	67	93	71	65	26	67.04	161
Yuma, AZ	84	91	78	76	62	58	82	75.90	51

RETIREMENT REGIONS

If your sights are set on southwestern desert retirement, parts of five states make up that target. If you're tending toward mountain living, even more states fill the bill. Why not think of regions?

Here are 17 that look, feel, talk, and act differently from one another, yet the places within them share a number of characteristics. Few of their boundaries match the political borders you'll find in your road atlas; most of them embrace parts of more than one state and some states are apportioned among more than one region.

On the following pages *Retirement Places Rated* describes these regions into which the 183 places seem to fall. Some have been resort country for well over a century. Some have unsophisticated, small-town manners. Others are relatively new and heavily promoted. One—the Florida Interior—is nationally synonymous with retirement.

Still others aren't associated with retirement by anyone but savvy residents of nearby metropolitan areas. The North Woods country of Michigan and Wisconsin is such a place for Chicagoans, Milwaukeeans, and Detroiters. So are some of the New England locations of coastal Maine and rural New Hampshire and Vermont to Bostonians and New Yorkers.

Each regional heading is accompanied by a list of places in the region along with their overall ranks. Thirteen of the regions include one or more of the 30 best all-around retirement places. A check mark (✓) indicates these.

Whether you decide to move or end up staying right where you are, Retirement Places Rated hopes that your later years will rank among your best.

CALIFORNIA COAST

Carmel–Monterey–Pebble Beach, CA (#159)

Laguna Beach–Dana Point, CA (#142)

✓ San Diego, CA (#16)

San Luis Obispo, CA (#115)

Santa Barbara, CA (#64)

Santa Rosa–Sonoma, CA (#92)

For all its troubles—earthquakes, fires, flooding, and an economic slump after two decades of flush times—California still has long-term strengths. For some, it is also a fine state for retirement; ask the many older adults who've returned after a disappointing period elsewhere.

Its coast certainly isn't a homogeneous area, stretching as it does from the Border Beach on the Mexican boundary all the way up to the wine country north of San Francisco. About the only natural features these six California Coast places have in common is a Pacific shoreline and a mild Mediterranean climate.

All six in this region rank high, not just for their mild climates, but also for their available services and long-term prospects for job growth. In spite of price drops, all six rank near the bottom in costs of housing and how far typical retirement income will stretch.

For all that, these locations have been popular for retirement since the end of World War II. One in seven retired Navy officers lives somewhere within San Diego County, as does one in 50 retired physicians. San Luis Obispo County is one of the most populous areas in the country without a large central city, and much of its growth comes from attracting older persons.

Nonetheless, because of the high cost of living, a limited supply of water, and restrictions on development, population growth along the California Coast is slowing during the last years of this century. Indeed, some experts predict the area will lose more retired persons than it will attract. The living may be easy, but it is not cheap.

DESERT SOUTHWEST

Cottonwood–Clarkdale, AZ (#49)

Hesperia–Apple Valley–Victorville, CA (#50)

Kingman, AZ (#87)

Lake Havasu City, AZ (#40)

✓ Las Vegas, NV (#1)

Pahrump Valley, NV (#139)

Palm Springs–Coachella Valley, CA (#46)

Payson, AZ (#127)

✓ Phoenix–Mesa–Scottsdale, AZ (#9)

Prescott–Prescott Valley, AZ (#39)

Riviera–Bullhead City, AZ (#148)

St. George–Zion, UT (#44)

Sedona, AZ (#116)

Silver City, NM (#65)

✓ Tucson, AZ (#6)

Wickenburg, AZ (#73)

Yuma, AZ (#51)

The Desert Southwest, in the southern end of the Great Basin, lies between the country's two highest mountain ranges, the Rockies to the east and the Sierra Nevadas to the west. The two mountain ranges not only add beauty, grandeur, and ruggedness to the region, they also block moist air coming from either the Pacific Ocean or the Gulf of Mexico. The entire region is high, mountainous, and dry; the valleys are dusty, with scant vegetation. The mountains and cliffsides, eroded by wind and sand, are jagged, angular, and knife-sharp.

If it's sun you're after, this is the place. Yuma is officially designated America's sunniest spot. Hot, sunny, cloudless days followed by cool, even chilly, nights are the rule here. This means you can enjoy outdoor activities in the daytime and still get a good night's rest . . . under a blanket or two.

Rapidly growing Arizona is the prototypical Sun Belt state. Tucson, a leading retirement area, has an excellent supply of health care and public transportation facilities. Metropolitan Phoenix is home to the world's largest planned retirement development, Sun City.

Many parts of the Desert Southwest, however, suffer from high crime rates (Las Vegas ranks 154th and Yuma 163rd in that category), and the supply of health-care facilities varies greatly from location to location. Indeed, newcomers to Prescott–Prescott Valley and Cottonwood–Clarkedale report difficulties finding a physician.

Despite its rapid population growth (the seventeen places profiled above gained nearly a million persons since 1990, for example), this is thinly settled land. There is so much space here, with such great distances even between small towns, that people who have lived in thickly populated regions like the Great Lakes or the Northeast might find it difficult to adjust to the feeling of isolation.

FLORIDA INTERIOR

Brooksville–Spring Hill, FL (#145)

✓ Gainesville, FL (#15)

Inverness, FL (#104)

Kissimmee–St. Cloud, FL (#117)

Lakeland–Winter Haven, FL (#43)

Leesburg–Lady Lake, FL (#62)

Ocala, FL (#97)

Sebring–Avon Park, FL (#109)

Perhaps because they so recently hailed from other places, few of Florida's residents are aware of the state's long and fascinating history. The land was first claimed by Spain in the 16th century, wrested away by the British, taken back by Spain, declared an independent republic by a group of ragtag Americans, and finally turned over by Spain to the United States in 1819. Very little happened in this remote, mosquito infested outpost until the real-estate boom of the 1920s. Then, dream cities sprouted up everywhere as the pitch of the real estate promoter was heard in the land. Property values increased from hour to hour, and thousands of persons bought unseen acres, many under salt water. It took three disasters—the hurricanes of 1926 and 1928 and the crash of 1929—to burst the bubble. But by then, the lure of Florida had been implanted in the American soul.

Today Florida constitutes America's tropics. The state's first tourist, Juan Ponce de Leon, didn't find his fountain of youth when he stepped ashore near St. Augustine in 1513, but modern-day retired persons, who are moving here at the rate of one thousand per week, are still trying. Whether beside a Fort Lauderdale beach, at a Fort Myers condo swimming pool, at a Miami jai alai fronton, or on a St. Petersburg park bench, they look for rejuvenation.

Florida has been elevated to its so-called "mega-state" niche by a migration unique in American history. In 1950, the state had two million people; when 1995 figures are tallied, the number will top 14 million, nearly all of the increase coming from people moving in from other states. The state's population exceeded Ohio in 1984, Illinois in 1986, and Pennsylvania in 1987. It is now the fourth largest state, behind California, Texas, and New York.

Peter Dickinson, a well-known authority on retirement, once said that if you're determined to find whatever it is you're searching for in retirement, you'll find it somewhere in Florida. Florida is the number-one tourist destination in the world. It has nine distinct media markets, two coasts, snow, perpetual sunshine, swamps, islands, new no-down-payment homes for $65,000, and houses you can't afford if you have to ask their price. If there are two factors that account for the numbers of highly rated places here, they are climate and the near-term outlook for employment. One factor that mars their ratings, however, is unquestionably crime.

HAWAII

Kauai, HI (#168)   Maui, HI (#114)

The last state to join the Union (1959), Hawaii is also the southernmost state. Just below 22 degrees of latitude, Honolulu, the capital, is as far south as middle Mexico. The state of 120 islands is 2,400 airline miles from mainland United States. Let's use the word paradise only once to note where it sits in the American mind. The word aptly fits; and then, again, it doesn't.

This is the only state in the tropical climate zone, officially defined as anywhere temperatures never fall below 64 degrees. Orchids grow wild here; the sun shines most of the time; the Pacific trade winds keep the islands temperate; the beaches are superb; the water deep and blue.

The cost of living, however, is so high that this is the only state to discourage mainland persons from moving in for retirement. From the Commission on Aging on down to professionals selling condominiums, you're going to hear the discouraging word. Though the islands are relatively inexpensive to visit, they are unaffordable for year-round living for most retired persons.

Still, they come. Honolulu, like San Diego and San Antonio, is extremely popular with ex-military. Apropos of its size, it ranks high in services, prospects for employment growth, and leisure living. It also experiences a surprisingly modest level of crime. Maui, Kauai, and the Big Island of Hawaii are now drawing older newcomers at a faster rate than Honolulu.

MID-ATLANTIC METRO BELT

Annapolis, MD (#35)

Chapel Hill, NC (#80)

Charles Town–Harpers Ferry–Shepherdstown, WV (#95)

Charlottesville, VA (#56)

East End Long Island, NY (#99)

Easton–St. Michaels–Oxford, MD (#174)

Fredericksburg–Spotsylvania, VA (#127)

Lower Cape May, NJ (#68)

Northern Neck, VA (#153)

Ocean City, MD (#141)

Pike County, PA (#183)

Rehoboth Bay–Indian River Bay, DE (#102)

✓ State College, PA (#28)

Toms River–Barnegat Bay, NJ (#66)

Virginia Beach, VA (#59)

Williamsburg, VA (#40)

The area south from New York City to Washington and through the northern Virginia suburbs to Richmond is the most densely settled in America. Many cities in this region—notably Newark, Trenton, Philadelphia, Wilmington, and Baltimore—have been losing population for years.

In the midst of stagnation, however, one can easily overlook the pockets of retirement growth not visible from the Amtrak rails or I-95: the Atlantic beach counties, Chesapeake Bay, the Catskills, and small-scale metro areas like State College and Charlottesville, home of major state universities.

The 127 miles of New Jersey's sandy Atlantic coastline, particularly from the tip of Cape May north to Toms River, is rebounding after years of decline. One in five residents of Ocean County is over 65, compared with the U.S. average of one in nine.

The retired newcomers among them didn't have to come far; they are often New Yorkers and Philadelphians, some returning after a disappointing stint in Florida. Many planned retirement communities have been built or are being developed here, though people who want less structure can find many small seaside towns, particularly south of Atlantic City and west of the Garden State Parkway.

Farther south, you'll find retirement destinations within hailing distance of Washington and Baltimore on the Delmarva Peninsula and the shores of Chesapeake Bay. Many of the bigger summer resorts resemble Miami Beach rather than the charming, small seaside communities they once were before the opening of the Chesapeake Bay Bridge in 1952. Delaware's Rehoboth Beach, which has a winter population of 2,040 and a summer population of 50,000, calls itself the nation's summer capital because so many federal workers crowd its beaches. Ocean City, just over the border in Maryland, is also a popular resort among Washington and Baltimore residents.

MID-SOUTH

Aiken, SC (#78)	Madison, MS (#163)
Athens, GA (#107)	Oxford, MS (#52)
Crossville, TN (#137)	Southern Pines–Pinehurst, NC (#129)
Guntersville, AL (#111)	
Kentucky Lake, KY (#61)	Thomasville, GA (#165)
Lake Martin, AL (#145)	

This region is neither north nor, with the exception of Thomasville, Georgia, too far south to be thoroughly Dixie. It's mainly in the center of the country's eastern half and includes North Carolina's and Georgia's Piedmont (but not their mountains—they are part of Southern Highlands) and most of Kentucky and Tennessee.

Middle Tennessee, hemmed in by the looping Tennessee River, is gently rolling bluegrass country: fertile, well watered, and famous for its fine livestock. The heart of the state, it is rich in tradition and history and its rural people keep up southern folkways.

Kentucky encompasses mountains in its sandstone area, deep gorges and caves in its limestone region, and swampy flats and oxbow lagoons in the far western part of the state. This end of Kentucky is called the Purchase, after the Jackson Purchase, which bought 8,500 square miles in Kentucky and Tennessee from the Chickasaw Indians. Although Kentucky always had plenty of navigable rivers, it wasn't until the TVA projects of the 1930s and 1940s that it had a large number of lakes. These impoundments, created by dams on the Tennessee River and its tributaries, have transformed both Kentucky and Tennessee into frontrunners for fishing and water recreation.

Why is the mid-South such an attractive retirement region? For one thing, the region lies north of more established retirement areas of the Sun Belt. Although the Sun Belt still remains a big drawing card for older adults, the Retirement Belt seems to be widening north.

People are discovering the benefits of being closer to their former homes in the Midwest or Northeast, the desirability of mild, four-season climates as opposed to the monotony of the semitropical varieties, and the great advantages of low costs and low crime rates compared with many retirement areas farther south.

Furthermore, the gently rolling terrain with its pleasant scenery, the unhurried pace of life (far less manic than in many parts of Florida), the outdoor recreational options and the weather to enjoy them make the mid-South a winner.

NEW ENGLAND

Amherst–Northampton, MA (#100)	Litchfield Hills, CT (#150)
Bar Harbor, ME (#70)	St. Jay–Northeast Kingdom, VT (#156)
✓ Burlington, VT (#30)	Southern Berkshire County, MA (#74)
✓ Camden, ME (#18)	
Cape Cod, MA (#75)	Woodstock, VT (#108)
✓ Hanover, NH (#21)	York Beaches, ME (#161)
Lake Winnipesaukee, NH (#83)	

In New England, the preferred retirement destinations aren't in heavily urbanized Connecticut, Massachusetts, or Rhode Island. One big exception is Massachusetts' Barnstable County (Cape Cod), where one in three residents over the past 15 years has been a newcomer and where one in five is now over age 65. A future exception may be in Hampshire County (Amherst–Northampton) in western Massachusetts. To find the most popular retirement spots in New England, however, look in the countryside pockets of the north, in Maine, New Hampshire, and Vermont.

In the decades since 1970, Maine's population has jumped 21 percent. By Sun Belt standards, such growth may seem paltry. For the Pine Tree State, though, it's been the fastest upsurge since the mid-19th century.

Most retired newcomers choose the rocky Atlantic coast over the hard-going farm areas and rough-cut paper- and lumber-mill towns in Maine's interior. Within the seascape counties—Hancock, Knox, Lincoln, and York—the places that draw retired people are the small lobster ports and summer resort towns off old U.S. Highway 1, places with names like Camden, Bar Harbor, Ellsworth, Wiscasset, and Rockland.

New Hampshire, too, is growing. Indeed, it is growing the most quickly of all the northeastern states— mainly at the expense of Massachusetts, its heavily taxed neighbor. You'll pay no income or sales taxes here (the only other state where this is still possible is Alaska). But you will pay handsomely for real estate along huge Lake Winnipesaukee's shoreline and around Hanover (home of Dartmouth College) and in the environs of North Conway, a resort town.

For all its attraction for disaffected New Yorkers and Pennsylvanians who come to live year 'round, Vermont remains the most rural state in America according to the Census Bureau. Two of every three residents here live beyond the built-up limits of cities. Much of the state unmistakably is a 19th-century Currier & Ives landscape of sugar maples, dairy farms, and steepled white Congregational churches that dominate every green town common. In early October, the brilliant fall foliage draws busloads of weekenders from Boston and New York.

NORTH WOODS

Charlevoix–Boyne City–East Jordan, MI (#118)

Eagle River, WI (#135)

Houghton Lake, MI (#171)

Northern Door Peninsula, WI (#96)

Oscoda–Tawas–Huron Shore, MI (#138)

Petoskey–Harbor Springs, MI (#58)

✓ Traverse City, MI (#8)

One region violating the "Law of Thermodemographics" (warm bodies eventually head south to the Sun Belt and stay there) has got to be that which includes the northern counties of Michigan's Lower Peninsula and the Wisconsin counties in Packer country near Green Bay. Winters here are long and cold. Spring, summer, and fall are lovely seasons but are all too short.

During the 1970s, this area saw a population increase unequaled since waves of Finns, Germans, Czechs, and Poles arrived 80 years previously. Growth continues, but at a slower pace. On any summer weekend, campers, RVs, and boat-trailing cars crowd the northbound lanes of I-75 out of Detroit, I-94 out of Chicago, and I-43 out of Milwaukee. The traffic offers a clue to why the formerly depressed North Woods, forested with hemlock and Norway pine, have come back.

The area's pull is strong for many vacationers from the big industrial cities of the Great Lakes. Many of these people decide to winterize their rural lakefront or flatwoods second home and retire for year-round residency.

This is recreation land with a rugged, Paul Bunyan flavor, not only in the summer months when the population doubles, but during the fall deer-hunting and winter skiing season, too. Most of Michigan's 11,000 and Wisconsin's 15,000 lakes are up here. "In some lakes," the *New York Times* reported in a profile of Eagle River and its environs, "the fishermen can see thirty feet down in waters forest green, or black, or blue, depending on the time of day or the perspective, and can retrieve dropped eyeglasses or snagged fishing lures."

In spite of high personal income and property taxes in these two North Woods states, the cost of living is still lower than in most other retirement regions. Except for small cities like Sturgeon Bay in Wisconsin and Traverse City and Petoskey in Michigan, though, you won't find much in the way of structured retirement activities or a full range of health-care facilities. Nor will you find expanding job prospects. Do expect to drive a good

distance for retail shopping; this is rough, beautiful, but sparsely settled, country.

OZARKS AND OUACHITAS

Beaver Lake, AR (#147)

Branson, MO (#89)

✓ Fayetteville, AR (#14)

✓ Hot Springs, AR (#29)

Lake of the Cherokees, OK (#173)

Lake of the Ozarks, MO (#133)

Norfork Lake, AR (#112)

Table Rock Lake, MO (#172)

Like the Southern Highlands, the Ozarks and Ouachitas of southern Missouri, northern and western Arkansas, and eastern Oklahoma are a highland area with distinct folkways and geology that are undergoing rapid changes. In both areas, country craft galleries and bluegrass music festivals abound, and the mountain roads that wind through small towns also wind through some of the nation's prettiest countryside. Here, an automobile is a virtual necessity. Many Ozark and Ouachita natives can trace their family names all the way back to Carolina and Virginia mountain roots.

Nearly two million people live in these hilly plateaus (the Ozarks) and ridge-and-valley mountains (the Ouachitas). Mention this region and you evoke an image of small-scale subsistence farming, chickens roosting in the hickory tree out back, shoeless springs and summers, moonshining, poverty, and isolation. Applied to the rural counties, the image was accurate until the 1960s.

When the public utilities built hydroelectric dams, they produced a series of large impounded lakes in hardwood forests, which in turn produced resorts and a steady migration of retired people from Des Moines, Omaha, Tulsa, Oklahoma City, Memphis, Kansas City, St. Louis, and especially Chicago.

Some of the newcomers are what demographer Calvin Beale calls the new gentry-professional people with good incomes who can see themselves doing a bit of farming on a small section of land. Others he describes as the new peasantry, back-to-the-land types interested in raising their own food, promoting conservation, maintaining rural values, and using alternative fuel sources.

Lately, this region has been waking up to the problems that come with growth. Concerns about the loss of a special way of life are increasingly voiced; some locals say it may have already passed from the scene, never to be revived, despite local folk culture institutes and craft schools. The areas outside the biggest cities—Fayetteville and Fort Smith, Arkansas, and Springfield and Joplin, Missouri—aren't densely populated, yet some of the lakes are having pollution problems, and some of the better-known resorts are acquiring a tacky patina of liquor stores, fast-food outlets, tourist attractions, and New Age crystal shops.

PACIFIC NORTHWEST

✓ Bellingham, WA (#3)
Bend, OR (#47)
Brookings–Gold Beach, OR (#110)
Florence, OR (#53)
Grants Pass, OR (#69)
✓ Medford–Ashland, OR (#5)

Newport–Lincoln City, OR (#54)
✓ Port Angeles–Seqium, WA (#20)
Port Townsend, WA (#67)
San Juan Islands, WA (#166)
Whidbey Island, WA (#105)

In the 1970s, no other state made so clear its desire to discourage immigration as did Oregon when its popular governor, Tom McCall, urged tourists to give the state a try. "But for heaven's sake," he quickly added, "don't come to live here." This awareness of the harm that rapid population growth can bring to beautiful, pristine land is commonly felt elsewhere in the Pacific Northwest.

Nevertheless, the near collapse of the lumber industry in Oregon and Washington in the early 1980s has caused local planners to behave like their counterparts in other states and compete for industrial development and population growth.

Certain rural areas are being pitched as retirement havens—ironic, because older adults from the Great Lakes, the distant Northeast, and even sun-baked Southern California have been coming to this area for years to enjoy the clear air, quiet, and uncrowded space.

In Washington state, their destinations are most often the islands reached by bridge or ferry from downtown Seattle, and places like Olympia, Port Angeles, Port Townsend, Sequim, and Bellingham with saltwater frontages. The area, with the tall Cascades and Olympic mountains in view, has a somewhat wet marine climate, low crime rates, and outstanding outdoor recreation endowments.

In Oregon, retired persons settle along the spectacular but damp Pacific Coast and in the forested cities and towns along I-5 between Portland and the California border.

Calvin Beale, a well-known demographer, observed not long ago that the popularity of the Pacific Northwest Cloud Belt just goes to show that " 'Sun Belt' is a very imperfect synonym for population growth."

During the 1970s, for example, Bend and the surrounding forested environs in Deschutes County, Oregon, made up one of the fastest-growing places west of Florida. Of more than 300 metropolitan areas in the United States, Olympia, Washington's parklike state capital, ranked in the top 10 in rate of growth over the same period, along with the Florida metro areas of Ocala and Fort Myers–Cape Coral.

RIO GRANDE COUNTRY

Alamogordo, NM (#131)
✓ Albuquerque, NM (#26)

Alpine–Big Bend, TX (#164)
Las Cruces, NM (#42)

Mission–McAllen–Alamo, TX (#36)
Ruidoso, NM (#176)

Santa Fe, NM (#76)
Taos, NM (#82)

The Rio Grande rises in the Rocky Mountains in southwestern Colorado, flows south through the center of New Mexico west of Santa Fe, through Albuquerque and Las Cruces, and serves as a 1,240-mile boundary between Texas and Mexico before emptying into the Gulf of Mexico some 60 miles downriver from Brownsville.

Like the Delta South, this area has a large ethnic population. Two of every five persons are Mexican American, and one in 10 is American Indian. Like the Delta South, too, Rio Grande Country is distinguished by low incomes, large families, poor housing, joblessness, low levels of education, and other social problems.

Along the river's southward progress are a few pockets of phenomenal retirement growth. Not only Albuquerque but also Las Cruces and the settled areas around them have all seen their number of residents over age 65 jump at three or more times the average national rate. Even with the well-publicized growth that most of and semiarid New Mexico has experienced, there are still fewer than eight persons per square mile. The desert-mesa vastness is imposing, the distances between towns great, and the loneliness outside city limits a little scary to retired persons hailing from large cities.

The lower valley in southmost Texas isn't lonely at all. This is the number-one winter tourist destination in all of Texas. Since 1990, Cameron County (Brownsville) and Hidalgo County (Mission–McAllen–Alamo) have together gained 130,000 people, many of them retired Midwesterners who found a climate as mild as Florida's and living costs nearly as low as Mexico's.

ROCKY MOUNTAIN

Chewelah, WA (#154)
✓ Coeur d'Alene, ID (#7)
✓ Colorado Springs, CO (#22)
Delta–Cedaredge, CO (#175)
Durango, CO (#93)
✓ Fort Collins–Loveland, CO (#4)
✓ Grand Junction, CO (#24)
Hamilton–Bitterroot Valley, MT (#140)
✓ Kalispell–Flathead Valley, MT (#27)

Ketchum–Sun Valley, ID (#124)
McCall–Cascade–Payette Valley, ID (#169)
Montrose, CO (#113)
Pagosa Springs, CO (#180)
Polson–Mission Valley, MT (#143)
Sandpoint–Priest River, ID (#134)
Wenatchee, WA (#37)

What does green and rugged Coeur d'Alene in Idaho's panhandle have in common with sun-baked Silver City in southwestern New Mexico? Very little. Yet the Census Bureau lumps them together in a region it labels Mountain. By better reasoning, Silver City with its desert flavor more properly belongs in Rio Grande Country. When it comes to certain foothill-and-mountain counties in Arizona, Colorado, Idaho, and Montana, however, the feel is definitely high-country, definitely Rocky Mountains.

In spite of the reservations many older adults have about high altitudes and cold winters, the Rockies are emerging from their vacation-only status, becoming an area where older adults are moving for year-round living.

In Colorado, one can easily distinguish between the Eastern Slope and Western Slope areas. Large cities like Colorado Springs (in a setting that reminds many of Asheville in the North Carolina mountains) and Fort Collins are Eastern Slope. Grand Junction, near the Utah border, is the population center of the Western Slope. The two slopes have different political orientations (conservative Western Slope versus Pat Schroeder liberalism) and different growth rates.

In Idaho, where the population rose by more than one third in the last 15 years, retired newcomers head for the city of Coeur d'Alene, within commuting distance of Spokane, Washington, or they settle near metropolitan Boise. In Montana, the spectacular but sparsely settled western counties—particularly Flathead, Lake, Missoula, and Ravalli—are the ones drawing older newcomers.

SOUTH ATLANTIC COAST

Beaufort, SC (#77)

✓ Boca Raton, FL (#23)

Charleston Sea Islands, SC (#38)

Conway, SC (#85)

Dare Outer Banks, NC (#160)

✓ Daytona Beach, FL (#12)

Edenton, NC (#179)

Hilton Head Island, SC (#136)

Key West–Key Largo–Marathon, FL (#161)

✓ Melbourne, FL (#10)

Myrtle Beach–North Myrtle Beach, SC (#57)

New Bern, NC (#103)

Pompano Beach, FL (#55)

St. Augustine, FL (#98)

St. Simons–Jekyll Islands, GA (#178)

✓ Savannah, GA (#11)

Southport–Brunswick Islands, NC (#119)

Vero Beach–Sebastian, FL (#121)

The retirement places in the South Atlantic Coast region have a special appeal and flavor. Although the coastline is dotted with many very old cities, such as Charleston, Galveston, and Savannah, it experienced rapid growth during the 1970s.

Most of these resort-retirement areas lie in low, marshy land either on the mainland itself or on nearby barrier islands. Palmetto palms, scrub oak, dune grass, and Spanish moss swaying in the sea breezes impart a languid, relaxed mood. Fishing shanties lie scattered near the piers where shrimpers, crabbers, and trawlers moor, Stately planter style cottages set back from the narrow street are almost hidden behind tall hedges and are surrounded by massive live oaks. Streets paved with old oyster and clam shells; small gift shops, boutiques, and shops offering seafood, gumbo, and chicory coffee;

taverns and inns of all ages and sizes—these are what you'll find in every metro area, town, and village of the coastal islands.

The South Atlantic and Gulf Coast resorts are less crowded and have lower living costs than most comparable places on the Florida peninsula. Furthermore, their summer months, while sometimes uncomfortable, are less rugged than those farther south. You are likely to find newer buildings and younger people here than in some older retirement havens.

On the minus side, crime rates are high. Of the 12 retirement places in this region, only four—Edenton Albemarle Sound, Fairhope–Gulf Shores, New Bern, and Southport—have above-average ratings for personal safety. Health-care facilities can be inadequate, and while housing costs are generally low for the region, some places (such as Hilton Head and Beaufort in South Carolina) are expensive. Finally, these low-lying oceanside locations are subject to damage from severe tropical storms.

SOUTHERN HIGHLANDS

Asheville, NC (#32)

Blairsville, GA (#123)

Boone–Blowing Rock, NC (#62)

Brevard, NC (#94)

Clayton, GA (#158)

Clemson–Pendleton District, SC (#33)

Hendersonville–East Flat Rock, NC (#122)

Hiawassee, GA (#177)

Maryville, TN (#81)

Smith Mountain Lake, VA (#125)

Tryon, NC (#181)

Winchester, VA (#130)

There is a 600-mile stretch of Appalachian Mountains from Frederick County in Virginia to Hall County, Georgia, that absorbed a good deal of antipoverty money during the 1960s and 1970s. Much of the area is still poor. Much of it, too, is as scenic as any place in the nation.

This is a land of peaks and ridges, rushing streams and thundering waterfalls. In the earliest spring days, the hillsides burst with flowering trees and shrubs: rhododendron, azalea, dogwood, and magnolia. The George Washington, Pisgah, and Chattahoochee national forests stand tall with black walnut, pine, beech, poplar, birch, and oak. The mountain vistas, especially along the Blue Ridge Parkway, show row after spectacular row of parallel mountain ridges. Distant parts of what you see from the road are so inaccessible that it's unlikely humans have regularly hiked more than 10 percent of the topography.

Because the area is bookended, so to speak, by Atlanta in the south and Washington in the north, it isn't at all unusual to encounter ex-urbanites from these major cities among the retired persons in places like Clayton in north Georgia, Asheville and Hendersonville in western North Carolina, and Smith Mountain Lake in Virginia. What is unusual are the new "Florida Clubs" formed by retired persons who settle here after a disappointing stint in the Sunshine State.

The Southern Highlands are becoming a major destination for retired persons. Many of the region's communities are ideal for retirement living, offering a wide range of special services for older residents. The Appalachian counties generally combine low costs of living and housing, low crime rates, adequate health-care facilities in most places, and some of the country's mildest four-season climates.

You're going to need a car to get around comfortably in much of this region, though. It is a rough wilderness area abundant in natural beauty, yet it is located within reach of major eastern population centers, which eliminates the feeling of isolation so often associated with wilderness areas.

TAHOE BASIN AND THE OTHER CALIFORNIA

Amador County, CA (#120)
Carson City–Carson Valley, NV (#86)
Grass Valley–Nevada City, CA (#149)
Oakhurst–Coarsegold, CA (#125)
Paradise–Magalia, CA (#60)
Placerville–Shingle Springs, CA (#101)
Redding, CA (#45)
Reno–Sparks, NV (#34)
Sonora–Groveland–Twain Harte, CA (#106)

In California, three out of four residents live either in the Los Angeles basin or in metropolitan San Francisco–Oakland–San Jose. Everyone else lives in a part of the state the Beach Boys seem never to have sung about.

You might call it the Other California. Parts of it—the Mother Lode Country and the northern Sacramento Valley—are seeing a growing number of retired newcomers, most of whom are Californians.

Mother Lode Country, the mountainous interior, with alpine meadows, blizzard-filled passes, clear lakes, trout streams, and magnificent scenery, was once a hard-worked mining area. Now it is a tourist haven. Donner Lake, a popular summer beach resort, also doubles as a winter ski area. Even in midsummer, this high mountain lake tends to be on the chilly side. Tuolumne County, roughly 100 miles to the south, contains spectacular Yosemite National Park, with all of the opportunities for outstanding outdoor recreation. Although the gold rush is over, these areas continue to attract people with scenery, mountain climate, and open spaces. Places like Grass Valley, Nevada City, Truckee, and Twain Harte are seeing higher living costs, especially those associated with owning a home.

TEXAS INTERIOR

✓ Austin, TX (#19)
Cedar Creek Lake, TX (#155)
Fredericksburg, TX (#151)
Kerrville, TX (#132)
Lake Buchanan–Lake LBJ, TX (#170)
Lake Conroe, TX (#87)
Lake Granbury, TX (#157)
Lake Livingston, TX (#167)
New Braunfels, TX (#144)
✓ San Antonio, TX (#17)
Wimberly–San Marcos, TX (#152)

Of all the states, Texas perhaps occupies the most distinctive place in the American mind. To paraphrase a guidebook published by the state during the depression, Texas is so large that if it could be folded up and over, using its northernmost boundary as a hinge, McAllen would be plunked down in the middle of North Dakota; and if it were folded eastward, El Paso would lie just off the coast of Florida.

Out in the country, there are more internally sharp contrasts here than in any other state. Northeast Texas looks like Arkansas. East Texas is deeply southern with small farms bringing in sugar cane, cotton, and rice. Southwest Texas is mainly lonely open-range cattle country. Northwest Texas is dry and mountainous and resembles parts of New Mexico.

You'll find contrasting retirement regions, too. The lower Rio Grande valley is distinctly Hispanic and has winters as mild as Florida's. So do the Gulf Coast beaches, from South Padre Island up to just above Corpus Christi. Then there's an area in the middle of the state encompassing the lovely cedar-scented Hill Country along with Austin and San Antonio.

According to visitors, Austin, state capital and home of the University of Texas, seems to have the same terrain and natural vegetation as New England. Metropolitan Austin is growing so quickly that its population by the year 2000 is projected to be double what it was 10 years previously. The negative housing price appreciation due to the slumping Texas economy is over. Housing costs here are somewhat high. Austin is a "books and bureaucrats" city, drawing a good many retired University of Texas alumni from all over the nation along with Texas government employees.

San Antonio's appeal as a retirement destination, on the other hand, has four causes: Brooks, Kelly, Lackland, and Randolph. These are big Air Force bases. Many veterans who were posted to them during the 1940s and 1950s have returned for the mild San Antonio winters, low living costs, and pleasant Hispanic atmosphere.

West of Austin and northwest of San Antonio, the Hill Country towns (Fredericksburg and Kerrville) have spic-and-span layouts in their old sections. These are towns settled by Germans who fled their homeland in the mid-19th century. So attractive is this area that much of it is experiencing second-home development by prosperous Texans and others from outside the state.

APPENDICES

RELOCATION RESOURCES

No single book can satisfy every reader. If you feel *Retirement Places Rated* didn't give you what you wanted or needed, here are some others that might.

Consumer Digest, *Best-Rated Retirement Cities & Towns,* New York, 1988. A review of 100 attractive places in 16 southern and western states.

Dickinson, Peter, *Sunbelt Retirement,* Potomac, MD, Philips Publishing International, 1991. This book, by a pioneer writer on retirement relocation, first appeared in the 1970s and has been revised ever since. It concentrates on desirable locations in 13 southern and western states.

Dickinson, Peter, *Retirement Edens Outside the Sunbelt,* Glenview, IL, Scott, Foresman and Company, 1987. An alternative to the author's guide described above, this one focusing on places in 37 states north of the sunbelt.

Ford, Norman, *The Fifty Healthiest Places to Live & Retire in the United States,* New York, Ballantine, 1991.

Howells, John, *Where To Retire,* Oakland, CA, Gateway Books, 1994. Written with humor and humanity by a former journalist who prefers lifestyles over statistics. Covers the Sun Belt and Oregon.

Rosenberg, Lee and Saralee, *Fifty Fabulous Places to Retire in America,* Hawthorne, NJ, Career Press, 1991.

It may be that while *Retirement Places Rated* helped you, there are still some areas where you need more information or want to do your own research. Here are some resources. A good library will have many, but you'll have to write for others.

How places present themselves. There are 710 separate Chamber of Commerce organizations promoting the benefits of living and doing business somewhere within the 183 places profiled in this book (see the "Retirement Place Finder" that follows in this Appendix for their address listings). That should give you an idea of how competitive the market is for attracting new residents, especially ones with large net worths.

Writing to Chambers of Commerce for their "newcomer's pack" produces a collection of promotional brochures, maps, business statistics, cost-of-living data, and events calendars and may also trigger mail and telephone calls from real estate brokers. The annual *World Chamber of Commerce Directory* lists the chamber name, address, and telephone number, as well as the name of the chamber's contact person, for over 4,000 locations in the United States. It is available in larger libraries.

Be aware that some chambers promptly respond to your inquiry with useful materials; others do not respond at all. Frequently you'll receive more material if you identify yourself as a prospective new resident than you will if you say you're retired.

Multimedia views. You'll be surprised at the number of communities that have videotapes. These are short, quality-of-life promotion pieces for a general audience —tourists, footloose industry, and families—with the cost of production underwritten by a state grant or by the local bank or electric power company.

Community videos are either free of charge, loaned with a box for prepaid return, or sent out at nominal cost by the chamber of commerce or economic development board. You have to ask if one is available and how you can obtain a copy. One firm that produces promotion videos has tape collections for different Sun Belt states available for sale or subscription.

> Leisure Living, Inc.
> P.O. Box 890
> Springfield, MO 65806
> (800) 755-6555

What really goes on in other places. If you've identified a few likely locations, a short-term subscription to their local newspapers is invaluable (see the "Place Finder" in this book's Appendix for address listings). After reading a month's worth, you'll have an excellent idea of consumer prices, political issues, and other matters on the mind of residents.

For the name, address, telephone number, monthly subscription cost, special features, and politics (typically independent) of each of the country's 1,635 daily newspapers, the best source is *Editor & Publisher's International Yearbook.*

Note: You'll learn that one or two newspapers arriving in the mail every day becomes quickly overwhelming. A weekend edition is adequate for keeping up with local happenings. Most dailies publish Sunday editions and will fill "Sunday Only" subscriptions. Whether you want a daily or just a Sunday subscription, be sure to tell the circulation department that you want to receive the classified sections and shopping inserts. To save postage, newspapers omit these sections in mail subscriptions.

For similar information on the 6,890 semiweekly and weekly newspapers (often the only publications covering rural areas), *Gale's Directory of Publications* is an alternative source.

A vacation can lead to migration. Free, quality travel guides abound. Attracting tourists is a competitive aspect of state government, and more than a few realize that capturing new residents is a happy consequence of strong travel promotion. You'll find many of the contacts listed below can send you information on local retirement, in addition to a state travel guide.

Alabama Bureau of Tourism and Travel
401 Adams Ave., Montgomery 36104
(800) 242-4169

Alaska Division of Tourism
P.O. Box 110801, Juneau 99811
(907) 465-2010

Arizona Office of Tourism
1100 W. Washington St., Phoenix 85007
(602) 542-8687

Arkansas Department of Parks & Tourism
One Capitol Mall, Little Rock 72201
(501) 682-1088

California Office of Tourism
801 K St., Sacramento 95814
(800) 462-2543

Colorado Tourism Board
1675 Broadway, Denver 80238
(303) 592-5510

Connecticut Board of Tourism
865 Brook St., Rocky Hill 06067
(203) 258-4355

Delaware Tourism Office
99 Kings Highway, Box 1401, Dover 19903
(800) 441-8846

Florida Division of Tourism
107 W. Gaines, Tallahassee 32399
(904) 487-1462

Tour Georgia
P.O. Box 1776, Atlanta 30301
(404) 656-3590

Hawaii Visitors Bureau
2270 Kalakaua Ave., Honolulu 96815
(808) 923-1811

Idaho Travel Council
707 W. State St., Boise 83720
(800) 635-7820

Illinois Board of Tourism
100 W. Randolph St., Chicago 60604
(800) 223-0121

Indiana Board of Tourism
One N. Capitol St., Indianapolis 46204
(800) 289-6646

Iowa Department of Tourism
200 E. Grand Ave., Des Moines 50309
(800) 345-IOWA

Kansas Board of Tourism
700 SW Harrison, Topeka 66603
(800) 2 KANSAS

Kentucky Department of Tourism
2200 Capital Plaza Tower, Frankfort 40601
(800) 225-TRIP

Louisiana Office of Tourism
P.O. Box 94291, Baton Rouge 70804
(800) 33 GUMBO

Maine Publicity Bureau
P.O. Box 2300, Hallowell 04347
(207) 623-0363

Maryland Office of Tourism
217 E. Redwood St., Baltimore 21202
(800) 543-1036

Massachusetts Office of Tourism
100 Cambridge St., Boston 02202
(617) 727-3201

Michigan Travel Bureau
P.O. Box 30226, Lansing 48909
(800) 543-2937

Minnesota Travel Information Center
375 Jackson St., St. Paul 55101
(800) 657-3700

Mississippi Division of Tourism
P.O. Box 849, Jackson 39205
(800) 647-2290

Missouri Division of Tourism
Truman Bldg., Jefferson City 65102
(800) 877-1234

Travel Montana
1424 9th Ave., Helena 59620
(800) 541-1447

Nebraska Tourism Division
P.O. Box 94666, Lincoln 68509
(800) 228-4307

Nevada Commission on Tourism
Capitol Complex, Carson City 89710
(800) NEVADA 8

New Hampshire Vacation Center
Box 1856, Concord 03301
(603) 271-2666

New Jersey Tourism Division
20 W. State St., Trenton 08625
(800) JERSEY 7

New Mexico Travel Division
491 Old Santa Fe Trail, Santa Fe 87503
(800) 545-2040

New York State Board of Tourism
1515 Broadway, New York 12245
(800) CALL NYS

North Carolina Board of Tourism
430 N. Salisbury St., Raleigh 27603
(800) VISIT-NC

North Dakota Tourism Promotion
Liberty Memorial Bldg., Bismarck 58505
(701) 224-2525

Ohio Office of Travel & Tourism
P.O. Box 1001, Columbus 43216
(800) BUCKEYE

Oklahoma Tourism & Recreation Department
215 N.E. 28th St., Oklahoma City 73105
(405) 521-2409

Oregon Tourism Division
595 Cottage St. NE, Salem 97310
(800) 547-7842

Pennsylvania Office of Travel Marketing
453 Forum Bldg., Harrisburg 17120
(800) VISIT PA

Rhode Island Tourism Promotion
7 Jackson Walkway, Providence 02903
(800) 556-2484

South Carolina Division of Tourism
Box 71, Columbia 29202
(803) 734-0122

South Dakota Division of Tourism
711 E. Wells Ave., Pierre 57501
(800) S DAKOTA

Tennessee Department of Tourist Development
320 6th Ave., Nashville 37202
(800) TENN 200

Texas Tourism Division
Box 12728, Austin 78701
(800) 8888 TEX

Utah Travel Council
Capitol Hill, Salt Lake City 84114
(801) 538-1030

Vermont Travel Division
134 State St., Montpelier 05602
(802) 828-3236

Virginia Division of Tourism
1021 E. Cary St., Richmond 23219
(800) VISIT VA

Washington Tourism Division
P.O. Box 42500, Olympia 98504
(800) 544-1800

Wisconsin Division of Tourism
P.O. Box 7970, Madison 53707
(800) 432-TRIP

Wyoming Travel Commission
College Dr., Cheyenne 82002
(800) CALL WYO

General living costs. For some who live in high-cost areas, the only way to afford retirement is to move away. Living costs vary enormously around the country, but so do household budgeting skills. While it isn't possible to settle anywhere you wish if your retirement income is typical, you can settle in most places in differing degrees of comfort.

Every three months, the American Chamber of Commerce Researchers Association (ACCRA) surveys the costs of housing, food, services, transportation, and health care in nearly 300 locations around the United States. While the ACCRA survey is modeled on what a young family of four buys, and hence isn't meant for retirement purposes, it is still useful for making comparisons.

You can order a four-quarter subscription for $110, or the latest quarter's survey for $55 from:

ACCRA
Box 6749
Louisville, KY 40206
(502) 897-2890

Better yet, save your money. If you're thinking of only one or two destinations, call your local Chamber of Commerce. If it belongs to ACCRA, it can readily give you cost comparisons over the telephone.

State income taxes. After housing prices, the biggest cost difference between places in differing states is taxes. The best way to learn what your income tax will be in a new state is to write for its *resident* (not its *out of state*) income tax form and instructions, fill it out, and compare the bottom line with that of your current state income tax return.

New Hampshire and Tennessee do not tax earned income, but both have tax forms for interest and dividend income. Seven others—Alaska, Florida, Nevada, South Dakota, Texas, Washington, and Wyoming—don't tax personal income, but their revenue departments can send you information on intangible, inheritance, and sales taxes residents pay. Telephone numbers listed below are "taxpayer assistance" lines.

Alabama Department of Revenue
P.O. Box 327470, Montgomery 36132
(205) 242-1175

Alaska Department of Revenue
State Office Bldg., Juneau 99811
(907) 465-2300

Arizona Department of Revenue
1600 W. Monroe St., Phoenix 85007
(602) 255-3381

Arkansas Department of Revenue
P.O. Box 3628, Little Rock 72201
(501) 682-7255

California Franchise Tax Board
1020 N St., Rancho Cordova 95741
(800) 852-5711

Colorado Department of Revenue
1375 Sherman St., Denver 80261
(303) 534-1209

Connecticut Department of Revenue
92 Farmington Ave., Hartford 06105
(203) 297-4907

Delaware Department of Finance
820 N. French St., Wilmington 19801
(302) 577-3300

Government of District of Columbia
300 Indiana Ave., NW, Washington 20001
(202) 727-6104

Florida Department of Revenue
5050 W. Tennessee St., Tallahassee 32399
(800) 352-3671

Georgia Department of Revenue
Trinity-Washington Bldg., Atlanta 30334
(404) 656-4071

Hawaii First Taxation District
P.O. Box 259, Honolulu 96809
(800) 222-3229

Idaho State Tax Commission
P.O. Box 36, Boise 83722
(208) 334-7660

Illinois Department of Revenue
P.O. Box 19010, Springfield 62794
(217) 782-3128

Indiana Department of Revenue
100 N. Senate Ave., Indianapolis 46204
(317) 232-2240

Iowa Department of Revenue & Finance
Hoover Office Bldg., Des Moines 50306
(515) 281-3114

Kansas Department of Revenue
P.O. Box 12001, Topeka 66625
(913) 296-2430

Kentucky Revenue Cabinet
200 Fair Oaks, Frankfort 40620
(502) 564-4581

Louisiana Department of Revenue
P.O. Box 201, Baton Rouge 70821
(504) 925-7532

Maine Bureau of Taxation
State House Station 24, Augusta 04333
(207) 287-3695

Maryland Income Tax Division
110 Carroll St., Annapolis 21411
(410) 974-3029

Massachusetts Department of Revenue
100 Cambridge St., Boston 02204
(617) 727-4545

Michigan Department of Treasury
430 W. Allegan St., Lansing 48922
(800) 487-7000

Minnesota Department of Revenue
Mail Station 7131, St. Paul 55146
(612) 296-3781

Mississippi State Tax Commission
P.O. Box 1033, Jackson 39205
(601) 359-1141

Missouri Department of Revenue
P.O. Box 3022, Jefferson City 65105
(314) 751-5337

Montana Department of Revenue
P.O. Box 5808, Helena 59604
(406) 444-0291

Nebraska Department of Revenue
P.O. Box 94818, Lincoln 68509
(402) 471-5729

Nevada Department of Taxation
1340 S. Curry St., Carson City 89710
(702) 687-4820

New Hampshire Department of Revenue
P.O. Box 637, Concord 03302
(603) 271-2191

New Jersey Division of Taxation
50 Barrack Street—CN269, Trenton 08646
(609) 588-2200

New Mexico Department of Revenue
P.O. Box 630, Santa Fe 87509
(505) 827-0827

New York Department of Taxation & Finance
State Campus Bldg. 8, Albany 12227
(518) 438-1073

North Carolina Department of Revenue
P.O. Box 25000, Raleigh 27640
(919) 733-4682

North Dakota Tax Commissioner
600 E. Boulevard Ave., Bismarck 58505
(701) 224-3450

Ohio Department of Taxation
P.O. Box 2476, Columbus 43266
(614) 433-7750

Oklahoma Tax Commission
2501 Lincoln Blvd., Oklahoma City 73194
(405) 521-3108

Oregon Department of Revenue
955 Center Street, NE, Salem 97310
(503) 378-4988

Pennsylvania Department of Revenue
Income Tax Forms, Harrisburg 17128
(717) 787-8201

Rhode Island Division of Taxation
1 Capitol Hill, Providence 02908
(401) 277-2905

South Carolina Department of Revenue
P.O. Box 125, Columbia 29214
(803) 737-5085

South Dakota Department of Revenue
700 Governors Drive, Pierre 57501
(605) 773-3311

Tennessee Department of Revenue
Andrew Jackson Bldg., Nashville 37242
(615) 741-2594

Texas Comptroller of Public Accountants
Capitol Stn., Austin 78774
(800) 252-5555

Utah State Tax Commission
210 N. 195 W., Salt Lake City 84134
(801) 297-2200

Vermont Department of Taxes
109 State St., Montpelier 05609
(802) 828-2865

Virginia Department of Taxation
P.O. Box 1115, Richmond 23208
(804) 367-2062

Washington Department of Revenue
General Administration Bldg., Olympia 98504
(800) 233-6349

West Virginia Tax Department
P.O. Box 3784, Charleston 25337
(304) 558-3333

Wisconsin Department of Revenue
P.O. Box 8903, Madison 53708
(608) 266-1961

Wyoming Department of Revenue
The Capitol, Cheyenne 82002
(307) 777-5200

Planned retirement communities. *Retirement Places Rated* typically profiles housing options and costs in countywide areas. Many of these areas have planned retirement communities located within them. These can be age-segregated or not, and typically are developed by one firm with built-in amenities and architectural controls. The national retirement magazines refer to them as "neighborhoods." Here are a few selected titles to give you some background on a lifestyle many find appealing.

Fitzgerald, Frances, *Cities on a Hill*, New York, Simon & Schuster, 1986. A Pulitzer–prize winning author profiles a large retirement community in Florida in a long, perceptive chapter. Couples driving about in golf carts with Rolls Royce grills, she thinks, seem like "unsupervised children."

Lee, Fred and Alice, *The 50 Best Retirement Communities in America*, New York, St. Martin's Press, 1994.

Schoenstein, Ralph, *Every Day is Sunday*, Boston, Little, Brown & Co., 1986. A humorous account of one man's quest for the best community for his own retirement, with some acerbic observations along the way.

Among the tour guides, flyers, brochures, and broadsides picked up at Visitor Information Centers, the catalog of homes for sale is probably the most common item. The real estate industry, it seems, is the driving force behind promotions to attract retired persons to local environs. A call or a note to the Chamber of Commerce always produces a useful collection of this literature. So also does a call to the newspaper, the major printer and distributor of local home catalogs. Here are some other resources to help you price the local market at long distance.

What would it cost to build your house elsewhere? Do you know a professional appraiser? Ask him or her to do an analysis, using *Marshall and Swift's Residential Cost Handbook*, of what building your home would cost in, say, Albuquerque or Austin. The handbook is a standard among appraisers and insurance adjusters and is updated every three months. Using a "Current Cost Multiplier" and a "Local Cost Multiplier," the appraiser can give you a good idea of how construction costs differ in over 500 locations around the country.

Local home markets; an initial look. Selling residential real estate has gotten so competitive that many brokers now show homes on cable television, ship videotapes to newcomers who are qualified buyers, and advertise their listings in major out-of-state daily newspapers.

The biggest franchiser of slick, local home sales catalogs is Homes & Land. You can preview any of 40 rental markets and 500 home sales markets in their magazines. Remember, you are under no obligation when you request copies. If you don't wish to be contacted by a local broker, say so to the person who takes your order.

Homes & Land Publishing Corporation
P.O. Box 5018
Tallahassee, FL 32314
(800) 874-8163

Finding and buying rural land. Pricing rural land isn't at all the same as pricing a house in the suburbs. Often there aren't enough recent sales of nearby parcels of similar size, topography, and quality to provide a basis for value. This is especially true of sloping acreage that's good for nothing but enjoying the view. For these reasons, many parcels are advertised nationally in the United Farm catalog to attract buyers who may value scenic land or agricultural acreage differently than the locals do.

Many would-be land buyers have found the prices in these catalogs are high. Nevertheless, they offer some idea of what you may be up against if your goal is a small farm or a hideaway in the mountains. Certainly the photographs and capsule descriptions will feed a daydream or two. The semiannual *United Farm* catalog is $4.95 (for delivery in three weeks) or $7.45 (for delivery in one week) from:

United National Real Estate
4700 Belleview
Kansas City, MO 64112
(800) 999-1020

Buying subdivided lots. The federal government's Office of Interstate Lands Sales Registration (OILSR) maintains records of 17,000 multilot developments that are promoted in interstate commerce. If you want to do a little homework on real estate investment before making any commitment, OILSR publishes a booklet, "Buying Lots for Development," available free by writing:

Office of Interstate Lands Sales Registration
451 Seventh Street, S.W., Room 9160
Washington, DC 20410
(202) 708-2716

OILSR can also tell you if a particular development is registered and if there have been any complaints filed against the developer.

Exchange trial. Living in a new community before selling your house back home is a good way to evaluate the new area at your own pace before burning bridges. It's possible to swap houses with someone in the area you're interested for a trial period. Here are three major home-exchange clubs where you can list your home in their directories for a fee of $15 to $35. You are then free to exchange letters and make appropriate arrangements. Deadlines for listings are about six months in advance of the time you might want to swap. For details, write:

Vacation Exchange Club
12006 111th Ave.
Youngtown, AZ 85363
(602) 972-2186

Loan-a-Home
Two Park Lane, Apt. 6E
Mt. Vernon, NY 10552
(914) 664-7640

International Home Exchange Service
P.O. Box 190070
San Francisco, CA 94119
(415) 435-3497

How climate hits you. Good books about climate's sway over health and personality are few. Here are two, plus a valuable sourcebook that steers you to professional-level articles in the field of bioclimatology.

Gallagher, Winifred, *The Power of Place*, New York, Poseidon Press, 1993. While some psychologists put down relocation as "running away from your problems," many people who purposely move do end up feeling much better. A book about seasonal affective disorders (SAD), bipolar personalities, and a lot else about how we thrive and suffer by where we live.

Landsberg, H.E., *Weather and Health*, Garden City, Anchor Books, 1969. Deliberate climate selection can lead to improved physical health. Alas, the perfect climate in the United States may be an illusion. A small classic, now out of print, by an eminent bioclimatologist.

How does your climate compare? Beware of chamber of commerce blandishments about a place's annual average temperature. San Francisco's is 57°F. So is St. Louis's. But San Francisco's climate is cool and remarkably stable year 'round. St. Louis's is neither. The most comprehensive source for day-by-day climate data is located in Asheville, NC.

Meteorologists at the National Climatic Data Center can take your order for comparative data that the center publishes for any of thousands of locations in this country.

The center's bestseller is the annual *Comparative Climatic Data for the United States*, a collection of month-by-month and annual summaries for normal daily maximum and minimum temperature, average and maximum wind speed, percent of possible sunshine, rainfall, snowfall, and morning and afternoon humidity at each of 300 "first order" weather stations in this country. The cost is $3.

If the place you have in mind doesn't have a first order weather station, it may yet be one of more than 5,000 locations with a "cooperative" weather station. Their data are Climatography of the United States, Series 20, a two-page publication for each location containing freeze and precipitation probability data; tables of long-term monthly and annual mean maximum, mean minimum, and average temperature; and tables of monthly and annual total precipitation and total snowfall. The cost is $1 for each location.

All orders carry a $5 shipping and handling fee and must be prepaid by check, MasterCard, Visa, or American Express. Call or write:

National Climatic Data Center
Federal Building
Asheville, NC 28801
(704) 271-4871

Finding local crime rates. In most instances, *Retirement Places Rated* uses counties to define places. One caveat: just as crime rates vary from one county to another, so do crime rates vary among towns within a *single* county. Though a retirement place may end up with a personal safety grade that makes it look as dangerous as the rough-cut 19th-century frontier, certain towns within its county boundaries are havens of rectitude and serenity.

Two examples are Phoenix (Maricopa County), Arizona, and Daytona Beach (Volusia County), Florida. With respective rankings of 169 and 159 out of 183 places, these two are among the more crime-ridden in this book. Yet despite these poor grades, both counties contain suburban towns that contrast sharply with their more dangerous surroundings. Within metropolitan Phoenix, the towns of Avondale, Buckeye, El Mirage, and Paradise Valley are extremely safe. So are Edgewater, Lake Helen, Ponce Inlet, and Port Orange within metropolitan Daytona Beach.

How safe are Phoenix and Daytona Beach? There, as elsewhere, it all depends on where you live within the county. One popular source that helps you determine the relative safety of hundreds of places is the FBI's annual *Crime in the United States*. It is available in most libraries, or for $24 you can order it postpaid from:

Superintendent of Documents
U.S. Government Printing Office
Washington, DC 20402
(202) 512-1800

A more detailed report, *Crime by County*, shows reported crime figures in each of nearly 16,000 law-enforcement jurisdictions throughout the country. In unbound, laser-printed form, it is obtainable for $40 from:

Uniform Crime Reporting Section
Federal Bureau of Investigation, HQ
Washington, DC 20535
(202) 324-2614

If you're interested only in spots within specific states, the FBI's Uniform Crime Reporting Section will photocopy one or more state segments from its *Crime by County* report for a minimum fee of $10.

Better yet, directly contact any of the 42 states that have uniform crime reporting programs of their own. While supplies last, the state reports in quotation marks are revised annually and are free.

"Crime in Alabama"
Alabama Criminal Justice Information Center
770 Washington Ave., Montgomery 36130
(205) 242-4900

"Crime Reported in Alaska"
Alaska Public Safety Information
5700 E. Tudor Road, Anchorage 99507
(907) 269-5659

"Arizona Uniform Crime Report"
Department of Public Safety
P.O. Box 6638, Phoenix 85005
(602) 223-2263

"Crime in Arkansas"
Arkansas Crime Information Center
One Capitol Mall, Little Rock 72201
(501) 682-2222

"Crime and Delinquency in California"
California Department of Justice
P.O. Box 903427, Sacramento 94203
(916) 739-5593

"Crime in Colorado"
Colorado Bureau of Investigation
690 Kipling St., Denver 80215
(303) 239-4300

"Crime in Connecticut"
Uniform Crime Reporting Program
294 Colony St., Meriden 06450
(203) 238-6653

"Crime in Delaware"
Delaware Bureau of Identification
P.O. Box 430, Dover 19903
(302) 739-5875

"Crime in Florida"
Florida Department of Law Enforcement
P.O. Box 1489, Tallahassee 32302
(904) 487-1179

"Summary Report"
Georgia Bureau of Investigation
P.O. Box 370748, Decatur 30037
(404) 244-2614

"Crime in Hawaii"
Department of the Attorney General
810 Richards St., Honolulu 96813
(808) 586-1416

"Crime in Idaho"
Department of Law Enforcement
6064 Corporal Lane, Boise 83704
(208) 327-7130

"Crime in Illinois"
Department of State Police
726 S. College St., Springfield 62704
(217) 782-8263

"Iowa Uniform Crime Report"
Department of Public Safety
Wallace Office Bldg., Des Moines 50319
(515) 281-8422

"Crime in Kansas"
Kansas Bureau of Investigation
1620 S.W. Tyler St., Topeka 66612
(913) 232-6000

"Crime in Kentucky"
Kentucky State Police
1250 Louisville Road, Frankfort 40601
(502) 227-8717

"Crime in Maine"
Department of Public Safety
36 Hospital St., Augusta 04333
(207) 624-7004

"Maryland Uniform Crime Report"
State Police Department
1711 Belmont Ave., Baltimore 21244
(410) 298-3883

"Uniform Crime Report"
Michigan State Police
7150 Harris Drive, Lansing 48913
(517) 322-5542

"Minnesota Crime Information"
Department of Public Safety
395 John Ireland Blvd., St. Paul 55155
(612) 296-7589

"Missouri Crime and Arrest Report"
Department of Public Safety
1510 E. Elm St., Jefferson City 65101
(314) 751-4905

"Crime in Montana"
Montana Board of Crime Control
303 N. Roberts, Helena 59620
(406) 444-3604

"Crime in Nebraska"
Nebraska Commission on Law Enforcement
P.O. Box 94946, Lincoln 68509
(402) 471-3982

"Crime in New Hampshire"
New Hampshire State Police
10 Hazen Drive, Concord 03305
(603) 271-2509

"Uniform Crime Report"
New Jersey State Police
P.O. Box 7068, West Trenton 08628
(609) 882-2000

"Crime and Justice Annual Report"
New York Division of Criminal Justice
Stuyvesant Plaza, Albany 12203
(518) 457-8381

"North Carolina Uniform Crime Report"
North Carolina Bureau of Investigation
407 N. Blount St., Raleigh 27601
(919) 733-3171

"Crime in North Dakota"
Bureau of Criminal Investigation
P.O. Box 1054, Bismarck 58502
(701) 221-5500

"Uniform Crime Report"
Oklahoma Bureau of Investigation
6600 N. Harvey, Oklahoma City 73116
(405) 848-6724

"Report of Criminal Offenses and Arrests"
Oregon Executive Department
155 Cottage Street, NE, Salem 97310
(503) 378-3057

"Uniform Crime Report"
Pennsylvania State Police
1800 Elmerton Ave., Harrisburg 17120
(717) 783-5536

"Crime in Rhode Island"
Rhode Island State Police
311 Danielson Pike, North Scituate 02857
(401) 444-1000

"Crime in South Carolina"
South Carolina Division of Law Enforcement
P.O. Box 21398, Columbia 29221
(803) 896-7162

"Crime in South Dakota"
Statistical Analysis Center
500 E. Capitol Ave., Pierre 57501
(605) 773-6310

"Crime in Texas"
Department of Public Safety
P.O. Box 4143, Austin 78765
(512) 465-2091

"Crime in Utah"
Department of Public Safety
4501 S. 2700 W., Salt Lake City 84119
(801) 965-4445

"Uniform Crime Report"
Vermont Department of Public Safety
P.O. Box 189, Waterbury 05676
(802) 244-8786

"Crime in Virginia"
Virginia State Police
P.O. Box 27472, Richmond 23261
(804) 674-2023

"Crime in Washington State"
Association of Sheriffs and Police Chiefs
P.O. Box 826, Olympia 98507
(206) 586-3221

"Crime in West Virginia"
Uniform Crime Reporting Program
725 Jefferson Rd., South Charleston 25309
(304) 746-2159

"Wisconsin Crime and Arrests"
Office of Justice Assistance
222 State St., Madison 53703
(608) 266-3323

"Crime in Wyoming"
Division of Criminal Investigation
316 W. 22nd St., Cheyenne 82002
(307) 777-7625

Finding specialized hospital services. Health-care guides are expensive, but they usually sit on reference shelves in major public libraries, in libraries at colleges with health science programs, and also in hospitals. Your doctor's guess is as good as yours when it comes to what's available in distant, unfamiliar locations. The best source for that purpose is the American Hospital Association's annual *Guide to the Health-Care Field.*

Organized by state and by city, the guide has data on every hospital in the United States, including address and telephone number, control (public, private, investor-owned, federal, city, state), length of stay (short term, long term), and which ones are certified for Medicare participation and accredited by the joint Commission on Accreditation of Health-Care Organizations.

More important, the guide details which of 85 specialized facilities are available in each hospital. Cardiac intensive care, physical therapy, hemodialysis, oncology services, psychiatric outpatient service, blood bank, home care, and health promotion, for example, are several important facilities not obtainable everywhere.

Finding better hospitals. The federal government's Bureau of Health Standards and Quality tracks several factors for each of America's 5,500 short-term, acute-care hospitals. Three of these factors can help you compare hospitals: (1) death rates for Medicare patients, (2) percent of doctors who are board-certified, and (3) teaching programs.

A nonprofit group publishes these data in *The Consumer Guide to Hospitals* for $12, including postage and handling. Call or write:

Center for the Study of Services
733 15th Street NW
Washington, DC 20005
(202) 347-7283

The Joint Commission on Accreditation of Health-Care Organizations (JCAHO), the main accrediting body for U.S. hospitals, has also started selling report cards on individual hospitals, nursing homes, ambulatory-care facilities, and other institutions. Each report costs $30 and includes an overall score plus individual scores on areas such as medication and staff qualifications.

JCAHO
875 North Michigan Ave.
Chicago, IL 60611
(708) 916-5600

Verifying medical credentials. It is up to the states to license and regulate professions. Kentucky licenses watchmakers and auctioneers but not psychologists; Maine certifies tree surgeons and movie projectionists but not occupational therapists; Arkansas licenses insect exterminators but not opticians. Fortunately, physicians and dentists must be certified before they can practice in any state.

Check a dentist's background in the *American Dental Directory.* Check a doctor's background in the *Directory of Board-Certified Medical Specialists* and *Directory of Physicians in the United States.* The three sources are updated each year, and are organized by state and by city. What to look for: medical or dental school attended, year graduated (you're not looking for a health-care professional who is about to retire), specializations, and board certifications.

Contact hospitals in distant places that interest you for their directory of physicians with admitting privileges. These Dr. Finders, as they're called, can be better sources of information on local M.D.s than any national publications.

Quacks operate everywhere, however, because credentials that look impressive aren't difficult to obtain. One California firm, recently shut down by the Postal Service, furnished a medical degree complete with transcript, diploma, and letters of recommendation to anyone for $28,000. For $5, another firm mailed out "Outstanding Service" citations.

Experts testifying in a recent House of Representatives hearing estimated that one out of 50 "doctors" is doing a thriving business with fraudulent credentials, and that three out of five of their patients are over 65.

The Public Citizen Health Research Group can send you a list of doctors disciplined for negligence, substance abuse, or other misconduct by state or federal authorities. The cost is $15 per state. Call or write:

Public Citizen Health Research Group
2000 P Street, NW
Washington, DC 20036
(202) 833-3000

Note that there are big differences in the way states discipline physicians. An M.D. not on the list may never have had disciplinary action brought against him or her yet still be regarded as questionable.

State Aging Commissions. Don't be put off by the bureaucratic titles. State aging offices are gold mines of information on government services, job openings, self-employment opportunities, volunteer activities and programs, and taxes. They also put you in touch with other local public and private organizations for retired persons.

Alaska Division of Senior Services
3601 C St., Anchorage 99503
(907) 563-5654

Alabama Commission on Aging
770 Washington Ave., Montgomery 36130
(205) 242-5743

Arizona Aging and Adult Administration
1789 W. Jefferson St., Phoenix 85007
(602) 542-4446

Arkansas Office of Aging and Adult Services
P.O. Box 1437, Little Rock 72201
(501) 682-2441

California Department of Aging
1600 K St., Sacramento 95814
(916) 322-5290

Colorado Aging and Adult Services
1575 Sherman St., Denver 80203
(303) 866-3851

Connecticut Elderly Services
25 Sigourney St., Hartford 06106
(203) 424-5281

Delaware Division of Aging
1901 N. DuPont Hwy., New Castle 19720
(302) 577-4791

Florida Department of Elder Services
1321 Winewood Blvd., Tallahassee 32399
(904) 922-5297

Georgia Office of Aging
2 Peachtree St., NE, Atlanta 30303
(404) 657-5258

Hawaii Executive Office on Aging
335 Merchant St., Honolulu 96813
(808) 586-0100

Idaho Office on Aging
Statehouse, Boise 83720
(208) 334-3833

Illinois Department on Aging
421 E. Capitol Ave., Springfield 62701
(217) 785-2870

Indiana Aging Division
402 W. Washington St., Indianapolis 46207
(317) 232-7020

Iowa Department of Elder Affairs
914 Grand Ave., Des Moines 50309
(515) 281-5187

Kansas Department on Aging
915 S.W. Harrison St., Topeka 66612
(913) 296-4986

Kentucky Division for Aging Services
275 E. Main St., Frankfort 40621
(502) 564-6930

Louisiana Office of Elder Affairs
4550 N. Blvd., Baton Rouge 70806
(504) 925-1700

Maine Bureau of Elder and Adult Services
Statehouse, Station 11, Augusta 04333
(207) 624-5335

Maryland Office on Aging
301 W. Preston St., Baltimore 21201
(301) 225-1100

Massachusetts Office of Elder Affairs
1 Ashburton Pl., Boston 02108
(617) 727-7750

Michigan Office of Services to the Aging
P.O. Box 30026, Lansing 48909
(517) 373-8230

Minnesota Board on Aging
444 Lafayette Rd., St. Paul 55155
(612) 296-2770

Mississippi Council on Aging
750 N. State St., Jackson 39202
(601) 359-4929

Missouri Division on Aging
P.O. Box 1337, Jefferson City 65102
(314) 751-3082

Montana Office on Aging
State Capitol, Helena 59620
(406) 444-3111

Nebraska Department on Aging
301 Centennial Mall S., Lincoln 68509
(402) 471-2306

Nevada Division for Aging Services
State Mail Room, Las Vegas 89158
(702) 486-3545

New Hampshire Division of Adult Services
115 Pleasant St., Concord 03301
(603) 271-4680

New Jersey Division on Aging
S. Broad and Front Streets, Trenton 08625
(609) 292-4833

New Mexico State Agency on Aging
224 E. Palace Ave., Santa Fe 87501
(505) 827-7640

New York Office for the Aging
Empire State Plaza, Albany 12223
(518) 474-4425

North Carolina Division on Aging
693 Palmer Dr., Raleigh 27626
(919) 733-3983

North Dakota Aging Services
State Capitol, Bismarck 58507
(701) 224-2577

Ohio Department of Aging
50 W. Broad St., Columbus 43266
(614) 466-5500

Oklahoma Aging Services
312 NE 28th St., Oklahoma City 73125
(405) 521-2327

Oregon Senior Services
500 Summer St. NE, Salem 97310
(503) 378-4728

Pennsylvania Department of Aging
400 Market St., Harrisburg 17101
(717) 783-1550

Rhode Island Department of Elderly Affairs
160 Pine St., Providence 02903
(401) 277-2858

South Carolina Division on Aging
202 Arbor Lake Dr., Columbia 29223
(803) 737-7500

South Dakota Office of Adult Services
700 Governors Dr., Pierre 57501
(605) 773-3656

Tennessee Commission on Aging
500 Deaderick Bldg., Nashville 37243
(615) 741-2056

Texas Department on Aging
P.O. Box 12786, Capitol Stn., Austin 78741
(512) 444-2727

Utah Division on Aging
P.O. Box 45500, Salt Lake City 84145
(801) 538-3910

Vermont Office on Aging
103 S. Main St., Waterbury 05676
(802) 241-2400

Virginia Department for the Aging
700 E. Franklin St., Richmond 23219
(804) 225-2271

Washington Adult Services Administration
P.O. Box 45050, Olympia 98504
(206) 586-3768

West Virginia Commission on Aging
State Capitol, Charleston 25305
(304) 348-3317

Wisconsin Bureau on Aging
217 S. Hamilton St., Madison 53707
(608) 266-2536

Wyoming Commission on Aging
Hathaway Bldg., Cheyenne 82002
(307) 777-7986

RETIREMENT PLACE FINDER

The following listing, organized alphabetically by state, presents the 183 retirement places, their county definitions, and all cities, towns, and unincorporated areas with populations over 500 within their boundaries.

A boldface **Z** with five digits next to a location's name is the zip code for Visitor Bureaus, Chambers of Commerce, and newspaper addresses listed immediately underneath. Chambers of Commerce are indicated by "C/C." Newspaper names are in italics; a boldface **D** indicates daily publication, and a boldface **W** indicates weekly.

ALABAMA
Fairhope–Gulf Shores (Baldwin county)
Bay Minette (7,168) **Z** 36507
Bay Minette Area C/C, 301 McMeans Ave.
W *The Baldwin Times*, P.O. Box 571
Daphne (11,290)
Fairhope (8,485) **Z** 36532
Eastern Shore C/C, 327 Fairhope Ave.
W *Eastern Shore Courier*, 325 Fairhope Ave.
Foley (4,937) **Z** 36535
South Baldwin C/C, 100 N. McKenzie St.
Gulf Shores (3,261) **Z** 36542
Alabama Gulf Coast C/C, 3150 Gulf Shores Pkwy.
Loxley (1,161)
Orange Beach (2,253) **Z** 36561
Orange Beach C/C, P.O. Drawer 399
Point Clear (2,125)
Robertsdale (2,401) **Z** 36567
Central Baldwin C/C, 22765 Milwaukee Rd.
Robertsdale (2,401)
Silverhill (556)
Spanish Fort (3,732)
Summerdale (559)
Guntersville (Marshall county)
Albertville (14,507) **Z** 35950
Albertville C/C, 316 Sand Mountain Dr.
Arab (6,299) **Z** 35016
Arab C/C, P.O. Box 626
Boaz (6,336)
Grant (638)
Guntersville (7,038) **Z** 35976
Lake Guntersville C/C, 200 Gunter Ave.
W *The Advertiser-Gleam*, P.O. Box 190
Lake Martin (Tallapoosa county)
Alexander City (14,917) **Z** 35010
Alexander City Area C/C, 100 Tallapoosa St.
D *Outlook*, 139 Church St.
Camp Hill (1,415)
Dadeville (3,276) **Z** 36853
Dadeville Area C/C, P.O. Box 483

Jacksons' Gap (789)
New Site (669)
Tallassee (1,802)

ARIZONA
Cottonwood–Verde Valley (part of Yavapai county)
Camp Verde (6,243) **Z** 86322
Camp Verde C/C, 435 Main St.
Clarkdale (2,144) **Z** 86324
Clarkdale C/C, P.O. Box 161
Cornville (2,089)
Cottonwood (5,918) **Z** 86326
Cottonwood/Verde Valley C/C, 1010 S. Main St.
Jerome (403) **Z** 86331
Jerome C/C, P.O. Drawer K
Kingman (part of Mohave county)
Kingman (12,722) **Z** 86401
Kingman Area C/C, 333 W. Andy Devine Ave.
D *Miner*, P.O. Box 3909
Lake Havasu City (part of Mohave county)
Lake Havasu City (24,363) **Z** 86403
Lake Havasu Area C/C, 1930 Mesquite Ave.
D *Today's Daily News*, 1890 W. Acoma Blvd.
Payson (part of Gila county)
Payson (8,377) **Z** 85541
Payson C/C, 100 W. Main St.
W *The Payson Roundup*, P.O. Box 2520
Phoenix–Mesa–Scottsdale (part of Maricopa county)
Avondale (16,169) **Z** 85323
Tri-City West C/C, 501 W. Van Buren
Buckeye (5,038) **Z** 85326
Buckeye Valley C/C, 904 Monroe Ave.
Carefree (1,666)
Cave Creek (2,925) **Z** 85331
Carefree–Cave Creek C/C, 748 Easy St.
Chandler (90,533) **Z** 85224
Chandler C/C, 218 N. Arizona Ave.
D *Chandler Arizonian Tribune*, 25 S. Arizona Place
El Mirage (5,001)
Fountain Hills (10,030)

Gila Bend (1,747) **Z** 85337
Gila Bend C/C, P.O. Box 507
Gilbert (29,188) **Z** 85234
Gilbert C/C, 1111 N. Gilbert Rd.
Glendale (148,134) **Z** 85301
Glendale C/C, 7105 N. 59th Ave.
Goodyear (6,258)
Guadalupe (5,458)
Komatke (1,116)
Litchfield Park (3,303)
Mesa (288,091) **Z** 85201
Mesa C/C, 120 N. Center St.
D *Mesa Tribune*, 120 W. 1st Ave.
Paradise Valley (11,671)
Peoria (50,618) **Z** 85345
Peoria C/C, 8322 W. Washington St.
Phoenix (983,403) **Z** 85004
Arizona Black C/C, P.O. Box 20191
Arizona C/C, 1221 E. Osborn Rd.
Arizona Chinese C/C, 626 W. Indian School
Arizona Hispanic C/C, 2400 N. Central Ave.
Arizona Mexican C/C, 6330 N. Central Ave.
Greater Paradise Valley C/C, 3135 E. Cactus Rd.
Phoenix & Valley Visitors Bureau, One Arizona Center
Phoenix C/C, 34 W. Monroe St.
South Mountain C/C, P.O. Box 8172
D *Arizonia Republic*, 120 E. Van Burne
Queen Creek (2,667) **Z** 85242
Queen Creek C/C, 22350 S. Ellsworth
Scottsdale (130,069) **Z** 85250
Fountain Hills C/C, 16838 Palisades
Scottsdale C/C, 7343 Scottsdale Mall
D *Progress*, P.O. Box 1150
Sun City (38,126) **Z** 85351
Northwest Valley C/C, 12211 W. Bell Rd.

D *News-Sun,* 10102 Santa Fe Dr.
Sun City West (15,997)
Sun Lakes (6,578)
Surprise (7,122)
Tempe (141,865) **Z** 85281
Tempe C/C, 60 E. Fifth St.
D *Tempe Daily News Tribune,* 120 W. 1st Ave.
Tolleson (4,434) **Z** 85353
Tolleson C/C, 9555 W. Van Buren
Youngtown (2,542)
Prescott–Prescott Valley (part of Yavapai county)
Bagdad (1,858)
Prescott (26,455) **Z** 86301
Prescott C/C, 117 W. Goodwin
D *Courier,* P.O. Box 312
Prescott Valley (8,858) **Z** 86314
Prescott Valley C/C, 8307 E. Hwy. 69
Riviera–Bullhead City (part of Mohave county)
Bullhead City (21,951) **Z** 86430
Bullhead Area C/C, P.O. Box 66
D *Mohave Valley Daily News,* 2075 Miracle Mile
Mohave Valley (6,962) **Z** 86440
Sedona (part of Coconino and Yavapai counties)
Rimrock (340)
Sedona (8,500)
Williams (2,532) **Z** 86046
Williams–Grand Canyon C/C, P.O. Box 235
Tucson (Pima county)
Ajo (2,919) **Z** 85321
Ajo Dist. C/C, 321 Taladro St.
Avra Valley (3,403)
Catalina (4,864)
Flowing Wells (14,013)
Green Valley (13,231) **Z** 85614
Green Valley C/C, 180 W. Continental Rd.
W *Green Valley News & Sun,* P.O. Box 567
Marana (2,187) **Z** 85653
Greater Marana–Arva Valley C/C, 13418 N. Sandario Rd.
Oro Valley (6,670)
Picture Rocks (4,026)
Sells (2,750)
South Tucson (5,093)
Three Points (2,175)
Tucson (405,390) **Z** 85701
Metropolitan Tucson Visitors Bureau, 130 S. Scott Ave.
Tucson Metropolitan C/C, 465 W. St. Mary's Rd.
D *Citizen,* **D** *Star,* 4850 S. Park Ave.
W *Tucson Weekly,* P.O. Box 2429
Tucson Estates (2,662)
Valencia West (3,277)
Wickenburg (part of Maricopa county)
Wickenburg (4,515) **Z** 85390
Wickenburg C/C, P.O. Drawer CC
Yuma (Yuma county)
Fortuna Foothills (7,737)
San Luis (4,212)

Somerton (5,282)
Wellton (1,066)
Yuma (54,923) **Z** 85364
Yuma County C/C, 377 S. Main St.
D *Daily Sun,* P.O. Box 271
W *Bajo El Sol,* 2055 Arizona Ave.

ARKANSAS

Beaver Lake (Carroll county)
Berryville (3,212) **Z** 72616
Berryville C/C, P.O. Box 402
Eureka Springs (1,900) **Z** 72632
Eureka Springs C/C, 81 Kingshighway
Green Forest (2,050) **Z** 72638
Green Forest C/C, P.O. Box 376
W *Green Forest Tribune,* P.O. Box 1390
Fayetteville (Washington county)
Elkins (692)
Elm Springs (893)
Farmington (1,322)
Fayetteville (42,099) **Z** 72701
Fayetteville C/C, 123 W. Mountain St.
D *Northwest Arkansas Times,* 212 N. East St.
Goshen (589)
Greenland (757)
Johnson (599)
Lincoln (1,460)
Prairie Grove (1,761) **Z** 72753
Prairie Grove C/C, P.O. Box 23
Springdale (29,034)
Springdale C/C, 700 W. Emma St.
D *Morning News,* 514 E. Emma Ave.
West Fork (1,607)
Hot Springs (Garland county)
Hot Springs (32,462) **Z** 71902
Greater Hot Springs C/C, 659 Ouachita
Hot Springs Women's C/C, P.O. Box 1865
Hot Springs Visitors Bureau, 134 Convention Blvd.
D *Sentinel-Record,* 300 Spring St.
Hot Springs Village (5,259)
Lake Hamilton (1,331)
Mountain Pine (866)
Piney (2,500)
Rockwell (2,514)
Norfork Lake (Baxter county)
Cotter (867) **Z** 72626
Cotter C/C, P.O. Drawer G
Gassville (1,167)
Mountain Home (9,027) **Z** 72653
Mountain Home Area C/C, 1023 Hwy. 62 E.
D *Baxter Bulletin,* P.O. Box Drawer A
W *North Arkansas View,* P.O. Box 1087

CALIFORNIA

Amador County (Amador county)
Amador City (196) **Z** 95601

W *Amador Ledger/Record,* 10776 Argonaut Lane
W *Lode Monitor,* 1500 S. Highway 49
Ione (6,516)
Jackson (3,545) **Z** 95642
Amador County C/C, 125 Peek St.
Plymouth (811)
Sutter Creek (1,835)
Carmel–Pebble Beach (part of Monterey county)
Carmel Valley Village (4,407)
Carmel-by-the-Sea (4,239) **Z** 93923
Carmel Valley C/C, 71 W. Carmel Valley Rd.
W *Carmel Pine Cone–Valley Outlook,* P.O. Box G-1
Monterey (31,954) **Z** 93940
Monterey Peninsula C/C, 380 Alvarado St.
D *The Herald,* Pacific & Jefferson Sts.
Pacific Grove (16,117) **Z** 93950
Pacific Grove C/C, P.O. Box 167
W *Pacific Grove Monarch,* P.O. Box 667
Seaside (38,901) **Z** 93955
Seaside–Sand City C/C, 505 Broadway Ave.
W *Coast Weekly,* 668 Williams Ave.
Grass Valley–Nevada City (Nevada county)
Alta Sierra (5,709)
Glenshire–Devonshire (2,133)
Grass Valley (9,048) **Z** 95945
Grass Valley & Nevada County C/C, 248 Mill St.
D *Union,* 11464 Sutton Way
W *Nevada County Nugget,* 11464 Sutton Way
Lake of The Pines (3,890)
Nevada City (2,855) **Z** 95959
Nevada City C/C, 132 Main St.
Penn Valley (1,242)
Truckee (3,484) **Z** 96161
Truckee–Donner C/C, P.O. Box 2757
W *Sierra Sun,* P.O. Box 2973
Hesperia–Apple Valley–Victorville (part of San Bernardino county)
Apple Valley (46,079) **Z** 92307
Apple Valley C/C, 21812 Hwy. 18
W *The Valley News,* P.O. Box 1147
Hesperia (50,418) **Z** 92345
Hesperia C/C, P.O. Box 403656
W *Hesperia Valley Wide Reporter,* 1692 S. Main St.
Twentynine Palms (11,821) **Z** 92277
Twentynine Palms C/C, 6136 Adobe Rd.
W *Desert Trail,* 6396 Adobe Rd.
Upland (63,374) **Z** 91786
W *The Upland News,* P.O. Box 4000
Victorville (40,674) **Z** 92392

Victorville C/C, 14174
Greentree Blvd.
D *Press,* P.O. Box 1389
Laguna Beach–Dana Point (part
of Orange county)
Aliso Viejo (7,612)
Dana Point (31,896) **Z** 92629
Dana Point C/C, 24681 La
Plaza
Laguna Beach (23,170)
Z 92652
Laguna Beach C/C, 357
Glenneyre Ave.
Laguna Niguel (44,400)
Z 92677
Laguna Niguel C/C, 30110
Crown Valley Pkwy.
W *Laguna Niguel News,*
23811 Via Fabricante
Oakhurst–Coarsegold (Madera
county)
Bonadelle Ranchos–Madera
Ranchos (5,705)
Chowchilla (5,930) **Z** 93610
Chowchilla Dist. C/C, 115 S.
2nd St.
Madera (29,281) **Z** 93637
Madera Dist. C/C, 131 W.
Yosemite Ave.
D *Tribune,* 100 E. 7th St.
W *The Ranchos News,* 37221
Ave. 12
Madera Acres (5,245)
Oakhurst (2,602) **Z** 93644
Eastern Madera County C/C,
49074 Civic Cir.
Parksdale (1,911)
Parkwood (1,659)
Yosemite Lakes (2,367)
Palm Springs–Coachella Valley
(part of Riverside county)
Cathedral City (30,085)
Z 92234
Cathedral City C/C, 68845
Perez Rd.
Coachella (16,896) **Z** 92236
Desert Hot Springs (11,668)
Z 92240
Desert Hot Springs C/C,
11711 West Dr.
W *Desert Sentinel,* P.O. Box
338
Idyllwild–Pine Cove (2,853)
Indian Wells (2,647)
Indio (36,793) **Z** 92201
Indio C/C, 82-503 Hwy. 111
La Quinta (11,215) **Z** 92253
La Quinta C/C, 51-351
Avenida Bermudas
Moreno Valley (118,779)
Z 92553
Moreno Valley C/C, 22620
Golden Crest Dr.
W *The Valley Times,* 25873
Alessandro Blvd.
Palm Desert (23,252) **Z** 92260
Palm Desert C/C, 72-990
Hwy. 111
W *Palm Desert Post,* 74405
Highway 111
Palm Springs (40,181) **Z** 92262
Palm Springs C/C, 190 W.
Amado Rd.
D *Desert Sun,* 750 N. Gene
Autry Trail
W *Desert Weekly,* 333 N.
Palm Canyon Dr.

Rancho Mirage (9,778)
Z 92270
Palm Springs Visitors
Bureau, 69930 Hwy. 111
Rancho Mirage, 42-464
Rancho Mirage Lane
Thousand Palms (4,122)
Z 92276
Thousand Palms C/C, P.O.
Box 365
Paradise–Magalia (part of Butte
county)
Magalia (8,987)
Paradise (25,408) **Z** 95969
Paradise C/C, 5587
Scottwood
W *Paradise Post,* P.O. Box
Drawer 70
Placerville–Shingle Springs (El
Dorado county)
Cameron Park (11,897)
Diamond Springs (2,872)
El Dorado Hills (6,395) **Z** 95360
W *The Reporter,* P.O. Box
1028
Placerville (8,355) **Z** 95667
El Dorado County C/C, 542
Main St.
D *Mountain Democrat,* 1360
Broadway
Pollock Pines (4,291) **Z** 95726
Pollock Pines–Camino C/C,
6532-C Pony Express Trail
Shingle Springs (2,049)
Z 95682
Shingle Springs–Cameron
Park C/C, 4065 Mother
Lode Dr.
South Lake Tahoe (21,586)
Z 96150
South Lake Tahoe C/C, 3066
Lake Tahoe Blvd.
D *Tahoe Tribune,* 3079
Harrison Ave.
Redding (Shasta county)
Anderson (8,299) **Z** 96007
Anderson C/C, 1856 Hwy.
273 & Deschutes Rd., P.O.
Box 1144
W *Valley Post,* P.O. Box 1148
Burney (3,423) **Z** 96013
Burney C/C, 37477 Main St.
W *Intermountain News,* P.O.
Box 1030
Central Valley (4,340)
Cottonwood (1,747) **Z** 96022
Cottonwood C/C, P.O. Box
584
Redding (66,462) **Z** 96001
Greater Redding C/C, 747
Auditorium Dr.
D *Record Searchlight,* P.O.
Box 492397
San Diego (San Diego county)
Alpine (9,695) **Z** 91901
Alpine C/C, 2157 Alpine Blvd.
Bonita (12,542)
Bonsall (1,881) **Z** 92003
W *North County Messenger,*
P.O. Box 304
Borrego Springs (2,244)
Z 92004
Borrego Springs C/C, 622
Palm Canyon Dr.
Bostonia (13,670)
Carlsbad (63,126) **Z** 92008

Carlsbad C/C, 5411 Avenida
Encinas
W *Carlsbad Journal,* P.O.
Box 248
Casa de Oro–Mount Helix
(30,727)
Chula Vista (135,163) **Z** 91910
Chula Vista C/C, 233 Fourth
Ave.
W *Chula Vista Star-News,* 835
Third Ave.
Coronado (26,540) **Z** 92118
Coronado C/C, 1009 C Ave.
W *Coronado Journal,* 1224
10th St.
Del Mar (4,860) **Z** 92014
Greater Del Mar C/C, 1442
Camino Del Mar
W *Del Mar Surfcomber,* P.O.
Box 878
W *The Del Mar Citizen,* 341
S. Cedros
El Cajon (88,693) **Z** 92020
El Cajon C/C, 109 Rea Ave.
D *Californian,* 1000 Pioneer
Way
Encinitas (55,386) **Z** 92024
Encinitas C/C, 345 First St.
W *Coast Dispatch,* P.O. Box
878
Escondido (108,635) **Z** 92025
Escondido C/C, 720 N.
Broadway
D *Times Advocate,* 207 E.
Pennsylvania Ave.
Fallbrook (22,095) **Z** 92028
Fallbrook C/C, 233-A E.
Mission Rd. 92088
W *The Enterprise,* 232 S.
Main St.
Granite Hills (3,157)
Harbison Canyon (2,122)
Hidden Meadows (2,371)
Imperial Beach (26,512)
Z 91932
Imperial Beach C/C, 600
Palm Ave.
W *Imperial Beach Times,* P.O.
Box 1208
Jamul (2,258)
Julian (1,284) **Z** 92036
Julian C/C, P.O. Box 413
La Mesa (52,931) **Z** 91941
La Mesa C/C, 8155
University Ave.
Lake San Marcos (3,802)
Lakeside (39,412) **Z** 92040
Lakeside C/C, 9760 Winter
Gardens Blvd.
Lemon Grove (23,984) **Z** 91945
Lemon Grove C/C, 3443
Main St.
W *Lemon Grove Review,*
3439 Grove St.
National City (54,249) **Z** 91950
National City C/C, 711 A Ave.
91951
Oceanside (128,398) **Z** 92054
Oceanside C/C, 928 N. Hill
St.
D *Blade Citizen,* 1722 S. Hill
W *Oceanside Breeze,* P.O.
Box 878
Pine Valley (1,297)
Poway (43,516) **Z** 92064
Poway C/C, 12709 Poway
Rd.

W *Poway News Chieftain,*
13247 Poway Rd.
Rainbow (2,006)
Ramona (13,040) **Z** 92065
Ramona C/C, 1306 Main St.
W *Ramona Sentinel,* 611
Main St.
Rancho San Diego (6,977)
San Diego (1,110,549) **Z** 92101
Diamong Gateway C/C, P.O.
Box 720082
Golden Triangle C/C, 4350
Executive Dr.
Greater San Diego C/C, 402
W. Broadway
Mid City C/C, P.O. Box 5044
Mira Mesa–Scripps Ranch
C/C, P.O. Box 26174
Old Town C/C, 2461 San
Diego Ave.
Peninsula C/C, P.O. Box
7018
Rancho Bernardo C/C, 11650
Iberia Pl.
San Diego Visitors Bureau,
1200 Third Ave.
San Diego County Hispanic
C/C, P.O. Box 85152
D *Union Tribune,* 350 Camino
De La Reina
San Diego Country Estates
(6,874)
San Marcos (38,974) **Z** 92069
San Marcos C/C, 144 W.
Mission Rd.
W *San Marcos Courier,* 321
S. Rancho Santa Fe Rd.
Santee (52,902) **Z** 92071
Santee C/C, 10315 Mission
Gorge Rd.
Solana Beach (12,962) **Z** 92075
Greater Solana Beach C/C,
210 W. Plaza St.
W *Solana Beach Sun,* P.O.
Box 878
Spring Valley (55,331) **Z** 91977
Spring Valley C/C, P.O. Box
1211
W *Spring Valley Bulletin,* P.O.
Box 127
Valley Center (1,711) **Z** 92082
Valley Center C/C, 28714
Valley Center Rd.
W *Valley Roadrunner,* P.O.
Box 1529
Vista (71,872) **Z** 92084
San Luis Obispo (San Luis
Obispo county)
Arroyo Grande (14,378)
Z 93420
Arroyo Grande C/C, 800-A
W. Branch St.
Atascadero (23,138) **Z** 93422
Atascadero C/C, 6550 El
Camino Real
W *Atascadero News,* P.O.
Box 6068
Baywood–Los Osos (14,377)
Cambria (5,382) **Z** 93428
Cambria C/C, 767 Main St.
W *The Cambrian,* 2442 Main
St.
Cayucos (2,960) **Z** 93430
Cayucos C/C, 80 N. Ocean
Ave.
El Paso de Robles (18,583)

Grover City (11,656) **Z** 93433
Grover City C/C, 177 S. 8th
St.
Lake Nacimiento (1,556)
Morro Bay (9,664) **Z** 93442
Morro Bay C/C, 895 Napa
Ave.
W *Central Coast Sun-Bulletin,*
1149 Market St.
Nipomo (7,109) **Z** 93444
Nipomo C/C, P.O. Box 386
Oceano (6,169)
Pismo Beach (7,669) **Z** 93449
Pismo Beach C/C, 581
Dolliver St.
San Luis Obispo (41,958)
Z 93401
San Luis Obispo C/C, 1039
Chorro St.
D *County Telegram Tribune,*
3825 S. Higuera St.
W *Central Coast Sun-Bulletin,*
1149 Market St.
W *New Times,* 738 Higuera
St.
San Miguel (1,123)
Templeton (2,887) **Z** 93465
Templeton C/C, P.O. Box 701
Santa Barbara (Santa Barbara
county)
Buellton (3,506) **Z** 93427
Buellton C/C, 376 Ave. of
Flags
Carpinteria (13,747) **Z** 93013
Carpinteria Valley C/C, 5036
Carpinteria Ave.
Guadalupe (5,479) **Z** 93434
Guadalupe C/C, P.O. Box
417
Isla Vista (20,395)
Lompoc (37,649) **Z** 93436
Lompoc Valley C/C, 111 S. I
St.
D *Record,* 115 North H St.
Mission Hills (3,112)
Santa Barbara (85,571)
Z 93101
Santa Barbara County C/C,
504 State St.
D *News-Press,* De La Guerra
Plaza
W *Santa Barbara
Independent,* 607 State St.
Santa Maria (61,284) **Z** 93454
Santa Maria Valley C/C, 614
S. Broadway
D *Times,* 3200 Skyway Dr.
Santa Ynez (4,200)
Solvang (4,741) **Z** 93463
Solvang C/C, 1593 Mission
Dr.
W *Santa Ynez Valley News,*
P.O. Box 647
Vandenberg Village (5,971)
Santa Rosa–Sonoma (Sonoma
county)
Bodega Bay (1,127) **Z** 94923
Bodega Bay Area C/C, 850
Hwy. One
W *Bodega Bay Navigator,*
P.O. Box 865
Boyes Hot Springs (5,973)
Cloverdale (4,924) **Z** 95425
Cloverdale C/C, 132 S.
Cloverdale Blvd.
W *Cloverdale Reveille Inc.,*
207 N. Cloverdale Blvd.

Cotati (5,714) **Z** 94931
Cotati C/C, 8000 Old
Redwood Hwy.
El Verano (3,498)
Eldridge (1,144)
Fetters Hot Springs–Agua
Calient (2,024)
Forestville (2,443) **Z** 95436
Forestville C/C, Westside
Center
Glen Ellen (1,191) **Z** 95442
Graton (1,409) **Z** 95444
Guerneville (1,966) **Z** 95446
Russian River C/C, 16200
First St.
W *The Russian River News,*
14065 Armstrong Woods
Rd.
Healdsburg (9,469) **Z** 95448
Healdsburg Area C/C, 217
Healdsburg Ave.
Larkfield–Wikiup (6,779)
Monte Rio (1,058) **Z** 95462
Monte Rio C/C, P.O. Box 220
Occidental (1,300) **Z** 95465
Occidental C/C, P.O. Box
159
Petaluma (43,184) **Z** 94952
Petaluma Area C/C, 215
Howard St.
Rohnert Park (36,326) **Z** 94928
Rohnert Park C/C, 6020
Commerce Blvd.
W *The Rohnert Park–Cotati
Clarion,* P.O. Box 2508
Roseland (8,779)
Santa Rosa (113,313) **Z** 95401
Hispanic C/C of Sonoma
County, P.O. Box 11392
Santa Rosa C/C, 637 First
St.
Sonoma County Visitors
Bureau, 10 4th St.
D *Press Democrat,* 427
Mendocino Ave.
W *The Sonoma County Paper,*
P.O. Box 12065
W *The Sonoma Index-Tribune,*
117 W. Napa St.
Sebastopol (7,004) **Z** 95472
Sebastopol Area C/C, 265 S.
Main St.
Sonoma (8,121) **Z** 95476
Sonoma Valley C/C, 645
Broadway
South Santa Rosa (4,128)
Temelec (1,594)
Windsor (13,371) **Z** 95492
Windsor C/C, 8499 Old
Redwood Hwy.
W *The Times,* P.O. Box 799
Sonora–Groveland–Twain Harte
(Tuolumne county)
Columbia (1,799)
East Sonora (1,675)
Groveland–Big Oak Flat (2,753)
Jamestown (2,178)
Mi-Wuk Village (1,175)
Mono Vista (2,599)
Phoenix Lake–Cedar Ridge
(3,569)
Sonora (4,153) **Z** 95370
Tuolumne County C/C, 55
Stockton St.
D *Union Democrat,* 84 S.
Washington St.

Soulsbyville (1,732)
Tuolumne City (1,686)
Twain Harte (2,170) **Z** 95383
Twain Harte C/C, Joaquin
Gully Rd.

COLORADO
Colorado Springs (El Paso
county)
Black Forest (8,143)
Calhan (562)
Cascade–Chipita Park (1,479)
Cimarron Hills (11,160)
Colorado Springs (281,140)
Z 80903
Colorado Springs Visitors
Bureau, 104 S. Cascade
Colorado Springs C/C, 2 N.
Cascade
D *Gazette-Telegraph*, 30 S.
Prospect St.
Fountain (9,984) **Z** 80817
Fountain C/C, P.O. Box 201
Gleneagle (1,661)
Green Mountain Falls (634)
Manitou Springs (4,535)
Z 80829
Manitou Springs C/C, 354
Manitou Ave.
W *Pikes Peak Journal*, 22
Ruxton
Monument (1,020) **Z** 80132
Tri-Lakes C/C, 212
Washington St.
W *The Tribune*, P.O. Box 488
Palmer Lake (1,480)
Ramah (94)
Security–Widefield (23,822)
Stratmoor (5,854)
Woodmoor (3,858)
Delta–Cedaredge (Delta county)
Cedaredge (1,380)
Crawford (221) **Z** 81415
Crawford Area C/C, P.O. Box
56
Delta (3,789) **Z** 81416
Delta Area C/C, 301 Main St.
W *Delta County Independent*,
353 Main St.
Hotchkiss (744) **Z** 81419
Hotchkiss Community C/C,
P.O. Box 158
Orchard City (2,218)
Paonia (1,403) **Z** 81428
Paonia C/C, P.O. Box 366
Durango (La Plata county)
Bayfield (1,090) **Z** 81122
Vallecito Lake C/C, P.O. Box
804
W *Pine River Times*, P.O. Box
830
Durango (12,430) **Z** 81301
Durango Area C/C, 111 S.
Camino del Rio
D *Herald*, 1275 Main Ave.
Ignacio (720)
Fort Collins–Loveland (Larimer
county)
Berthoud (2,990) **Z** 80513
Berthoud Area C/C, P.O.
Box 1709
W *The Old Berthoud
Recorder*, P.O. Box J
Campion (1,692)
Estes Park (3,184) **Z** 80517
Estes Park C/C, 500 Big
Thompson Hwy.

W *Estes Park Trail-Gazette*,
P.O. Box 1707
Fort Collins (87,758) **Z** 80521
Fort Collins Visitors Bureau,
420 S. Howes St.
Fort Collins Area C/C, 225 S.
Meldrum St.
D *Coloradoan*, P.O. Box 1577
W *The Fort Collins Triangle
Review*, P.O. Box 2063
Loveland (37,352) **Z** 80538
Loveland Info C/C, 926
Logan Ct.
Loveland C/C, 114 E. 5th St.
D *Reporter-Herald*, 450
Cleveland
Wellington (1,340)
Grand Junction (Mesa county)
Clifton (12,671)
Fruita (4,045) **Z** 81521
Fruita C/C, P.O. Box 117
Fruitvale (5,222)
Grand Junction (29,034)
Z 81501
Grand Junction Area C/C,
360 Grand Ave.
D *The Daily Sentinel*, 734 7th
St.
Orchard Mesa (5,977)
Palisade (1,871) **Z** 81526
Palisade C/C, P.O. Box 729
W *The Palisade Tribune*, 124
W. 3rd St.
Redlands (9,355)
Montrose (Montrose county)
Montrose (8,854) **Z** 81401
Montrose Visitors Bureau,
550 N. Townsend
Montrose C/C, 1519 E. Main
St.
D *Press*, 5355 1st St.
Nucla (656) **Z** 81424
Nucla–Naturita C/C, P.O.
Box 104
W *San Miguel Basin Forum*,
P.O. Box 9
Olathe (1,263) **Z** 81425
Olathe C/C, P.O. Box 117
Pagosa Springs (Archuleta
county)
Pagosa Springs (1,207)
Z 81147
Pagosa Springs Area C/C,
402 San Juan St.
W *The Pagosa Springs Sun*,
466 Pagosa St.

CONNECTICUT
Litchfield Hills (part of Litchfield
county)
Canaan (1,057)
Cornwall (1,414)
Goshen (2,329)
Kent (2,918) **Z** 06757
Kent C/C, P.O. Box 124
W *Kent Good Times Dispatch*,
14 N. Main St.
Litchfield (8,365)
W *Litchfield Enquirer*, 132
Danbury Rd.
Salisbury (4,090)
Sharon (2,928)

DELAWARE
Rehoboth Bay–Indian River Bay
(Sussex county)

Bethany Beach (326) **Z** 19930
Bethany–Fenwick Area C/C,
P.O. Box 1450
W *The Wave*, P.O. Box 1420
Blades (834)
Bridgeville (1,210)
Delmar (962)
Frankford (591)
Georgetown (3,732) **Z** 19947
Greater Georgetown C/C,
P.O. Box 1
W *The Sussex Countian*, 115
N. Race St.
Greenwood (578)
Laurel (3,226)
Lewes (2,295) **Z** 19958
Lewes C/C, 120 Kings Hwy.
D *Daily Whale*, Rte 1, Midway
Shopping Center
Long Neck (886)
Milford (3,564) **Z** 19963
C/C for Greater Milford 11 S.
Dupont Blvd.
Millsboro (1,643)
Milton (1,417)
Ocean View (606)
Rehoboth Beach (1,234)
Z 19971
Rehoboth Beach–Dewey
Beach C/C, 501 Rehoboth
Ave.
W *Delaware Coast Press*,
3719 Highway One
Seaford (5,689) **Z** 19973
Greater Seaford C/C, 400
High St.
Selbyville (1,335) **Z** 19975
Selbyville C/C, P.O. Box
1150

FLORIDA
Boca Raton (part of Palm Beach
county)
Boca Raton (61,492) **Z** 33434
Boca Raton West C/C, 9817
W. Glades Rd.
Greater Boca Raton C/C,
1800 N. Dixie Hwy.
D *News*, 33 S.E. Third St.
Boynton Beach (46,194)
Z 33435
Greater Boynton Beach C/C,
639 E. Ocean Ave.
Delray Beach (47,181) **Z** 33483
Greater Delray Beach C/C,
64 S.E. 5th Ave.
Lake Worth (28,564) **Z** 33462
Greater Lake Worth C/C,
1702 Lake Worth Rd.
Greater Lantana C/C, 212 Iris
St.
Bradenton (Manatee county)
Anna Maria (1,744)
Bayshore Gardens (17,062)
Bradenton (43,779) **Z** 34202
Manatee C/C, 222 10th St.
W.
D *Herald*, 102 Manatee Ave.
West
Bradenton Beach (1,657)
Z 34217
Anna Maria Island C/C, P.O.
Box 1892
Cortez (4,509)
Ellenton (2,573) **Z** 34222
Manatee County Tourist
Center, 5030 U.S. 301 N.

Holmes Beach (4,810)
Longboat Key (2,544)
Memphis (6,760)
Palmetto (9,268)
Samoset (3,119)
South Bradenton (20,398)
West Bradenton (4,528)
West Samoset (3,819)
Whitfield (3,152)
Brooksville–Spring Hill (Hernando county)
Brookridge (2,805)
Brooksville (7,440) **Z** 34601
  Greater Hernando C/C, 101 E. Fort Dade Ave.
  W *Hernando Today*, 15299 Cortez Blvd.
Hernando Beach (1,767)
High Point (2,814)
North Brooksville (1,459)
Ridge Manor (1,947)
South Brooksville (1,586)
Spring Hill (31,117) **Z** 34606
  Greater Hernando C/C, 3563 Commercial Way
Timber Pines (3,182)
Weeki Wachee Acres (1,394)
Weeki Wachee Gardens (1,170)
Daytona Beach (Volusia county)
Daytona Beach (61,921) **Z** 32114
  Daytona Beach–Halifax Area C/C, 126 E. Orange Ave.
  Daytona Beach Shores C/C, 3048 S. Atlantic Ave.
  Holly Hill C/C, 1056 Ridgewood Ave.
  Port Orange–South Daytona C/C, 3431 Ridgewood Ave.
  D *News-Journal*, 901 Sixth St.
Daytona Beach Shores (2,335)
De Bary (7,176) **Z** 32713
  De Bary Area C/C, 133 S. US 17-92
De Land (16,491) **Z** 32720
  De Land Area C/C, 336 N. Woodland Blvd.
De Land Southwest (1,249)
De Leon Springs (1,481)
Deltona (50,828) **Z** 32725
  Deltona C/C, 682 Deltona Blvd.
Edgewater (15,337)
Glencoe (2,282)
Holly Hill (11,141)
Lake Helen (2,344)
New Smyrna Beach (16,543) **Z** 32169
  New Smyrna Beach–Edgewater–Oak Hill C/C, 115 Canal St.
  D *Observer*, 823 S. Dixie Freeway
North De Land (1,493)
Oak Hill (917)
Orange City (5,347) **Z** 32763
  Greater Orange City Area C/C, 520 N. Volusia Ave.
Ormond Beach (29,721) **Z** 32174
  Ormond Beach C/C, 165 W. Granada Blvd.
Ormond Beach (29,721)
Ormond-By-The-Sea (8,157)
Pierson (2,988)
Ponce Inlet (1,704)
Port Orange (35,317)

Samsula-Spruce Creek (3,404)
South Daytona (12,482)
West De Land (3,389)
Fort Myers–Cape Coral (Lee county)
Alva (1,036)
Bonita Springs (13,600) **Z** 33923
  Bonita Springs Area C/C, 8801 W. Terry St.
Cape Coral (74,991) **Z** 33909
  Cape Coral C/C, 1625 Cape Coral Pkwy. E.
  Southwest Florida C/C-Welcome Center, 2051 Cape Coral Pkwy.
  D *Daily Breeze*, P.O. Box 846
Cypress Lake (10,491)
Estero (3,177)
Forest Island Park (5,988)
Fort Myers (45,206) **Z** 33901
  C/C of Southwest Florida, 8191 College Pkwy.
  Greater Fort Myers C/C, 2310 Edwards Dr.
  Lee County Visitors Bureau, 2180 W. First St.
  North Fort Myers C/C, 3405 Hancock Brdg. Pkwy.
  D *News Press*, 2442 Martin Luther King Blvd.
Fort Myers Beach (9,284) **Z** 33931
  Greater Fort Myers Beach Area C/C, 1661 Estero Blvd.
Fort Myers Shores (5,460)
Iona (9,565)
Lehigh Acres (13,611) **Z** 33971
  Lehigh Acres C/C, 1110 Homestead Rd., P.O. Box 757
Lochmoor Waterway Estates (4,091)
McGregor (6,504)
Morse Shores (3,771)
North Fort Myers (30,027)
Page Park–Pine Manor (5,116)
Punta Rassa (1,493)
San Carlos Park (11,785)
Sanibel (5,468) **Z** 33957
  Sanibel-Captiva Islands C/C, P.O. Box 166
St. James City (1,904)
Suncoast Estates (4,483)
Tice (3,971)
Villas (9,898)
Whiskey Creek (5,061)
Gainesville (Alachua county)
Alachua (4,529) **Z** 32615
  Alachua C/C, P.O. Box 387
Archer (1,372)
Gainesville (84,770) **Z** 32601
  Gainesville Area C/C, 300 E. University Ave.
  D *Gainesville Sun* 2700 SW 13th St.
Hawthorne (1,305) **Z** 32640
  Hawthorne C/C, P.O. Box 125
High Springs (3,144) **Z** 32643
  High Springs C/C, P.O. Box 863
Micanopy (612)
Newberry (1,644) **Z** 32669
  Newberry Area C/C, P.O. Box 929
Waldo (1,017)

Inverness (Citrus county)
Beverly Hills (6,163)
Citrus Springs (2,213)
Crystal River (4,044) **Z** 34428
  Crystal River C/C, 28 N.W. Hwy. 19
  D *Citrus County Chronicle*, 1624 N. Meadowcrest Blvd.
Floral City (2,609)
Hernando (2,103)
Homosassa (2,113)
Homosassa Springs (6,271) **Z** 34447
  Homosassa Springs Area C/C, 3495 S. Suncoast Blvd.
Inverness (5,797) **Z** 34450
  Citrus County C/C, 208 W. Main St.
Lecanto (1,243)
Sugarmill Woods (4,073)
Key West–Key Largo–Marathon (Monroe county)
Big Coppitt Key (2,388)
Big Pine Key (4,206) **Z** 33043
  Lower Keys C/C, U.S. Hwy. 1, MM 31
Cudjoe Key (1,714)
Islamorada (1,220) **Z** 33036
  Islamorada C/C, P.O. Box 915
Key Colony Beach (977)
Key Largo (11,336) **Z** 33037
  Key Largo C/C, 105950 Overseas Hwy.
Key West (24,832) **Z** 33040
  Greater Key West C/C, 402 Wall St.
  D *Citizen*, 3420 N. Side Drive
Layton (183)
Marathon (8,857) **Z** 33050
  Greater Marathon C/C, 3330 Overseas Hwy.
North Key Largo (1,490)
Plantation Key (4,405)
Stock Island (3,613)
Tavernier (2,433)
Kissimmee–St. Cloud (Osceola county)
Buena Ventura Lakes (14,148)
Campbell (3,884)
Kissimmee (30,050) **Z** 34741
  Kissimmee–Osceola County C/C, 1425 E. Vine St.
Poinciana Place (3,618)
St. Cloud (12,453) **Z** 34769
  Saint Cloud Area C/C, 1200 New York Ave.
Lakeland–Winter Haven (Polk county)
Auburndale (8,858) **Z** 33823
  Auburndale C/C, 111 E. Park St.
Babson Park (1,125)
Bartow (14,716) **Z** 33830
  Greater Bartow C/C, 510 N. Broadway Ave.
Combee Settlement (5,463)
Crooked Lake Park (1,575)
Crystal Lake (5,300)
Cypress Gardens (9,188)
Davenport (1,529) **Z** 33837
  Greater Davenport C/C, 5 Allapaha St.
Dundee (2,335) **Z** 33838
  Dundee Area C/C, 310 Main St.

Eagle Lake (1,758) **Z** 33839
Eagle Lake Area C/C, 45 Fourth St.
Fort Meade (4,976) **Z** 33841
Fort Meade C/C, 315 N. Charleston Ave.
Frostproof (2,808) **Z** 33843
Frostproof C/C, 118 E. Wall St.
Fussels Corner (3,840)
Gibsonia (5,168)
Haines City (11,683) **Z** 33844
Haines City C/C, P.O. Box 986
Highland City (1,919)
Inwood (6,824)
Jan Phyl Village (5,308)
Kathleen (2,743)
Lake Alfred (3,622) **Z** 33850
Greater Lake Placid C/C, 10 E. Interlake Blvd.
Lake Alfred C/C, 685 S. Lake Shore Way
Lake Hamilton (1,128)
Lake Wales (9,670) **Z** 33853
Lake Wales Area C/C, 340 W. Central Ave. 33859
Lakeland (70,576) **Z** 33801
Lakeland Area C/C, 35 Lake Morton Dr.
D *Ledger,* P.O. Box 408
Lakeland Highlands (9,972)
Loughman (1,214)
Medulla (3,977)
Mulberry (2,988) **Z** 33860
Greater Mulberry C/C, 400 N. Church Ave.
Polk City (1,439)
Wahneta (4,024)
Waverly (2,071)
Willow Oak (4,017)
Winston (9,118)
Winter Haven (24,725) **Z** 33880
Winter Haven Area C/C, 401 Ave. B N.W.
D *News-Chief,* P.O. Box 1440
Leesburg–Lady Lake (Lake county)
Astatula (981)
Astor (1,273)
Bassville Park (2,752)
Clermont (6,910)
Eustis (12,967) **Z** 32726
Eustis C/C, #1 W. Orange Ave.
Fruitland Park (2,754)
Groveland (2,300) **Z** 34736
Groveland/Mascotte C/C, P.O. Box 115
Hawthorne (1,804)
Howey-in-the-Hills (724)
Lady Lake (8,071)
W *The Village Tri-County Sun,* 1200 Aventida Central
Leesburg (14,903) **Z** 34748
Leesburg Area C/C, P.O. Box 490309
Mascotte (1,761)
Mid Florida Lakes (2,776)
Minneola (1,515)
Montverde (890)
Mount Dora (7,196) **Z** 32757
Mount Dora C/C, 341 N. Alexander St.
Mount Plymouth (1,752)
Oakland Park (1,743)
Silver Lake (1,573)

Sunnyside (1,008)
Tavares (7,383) **Z** 32778
Tavares C/C, 912 Sinclair Ave.
Umatilla (2,350) **Z** 32784
Umatilla C/C, 23 S. Central Ave.
Yalaha (1,168)
Melbourne (part of Brevard county)
Malabar (1,977)
Melbourne (59,646) **Z** 32901
Melbourne–Palm Bay Area C/C, 1005 E. Strawbridge Ave.
D *Florida Today,* P.O. Box 419000
Melbourne Beach (3,021)
Merritt Island (32,886) **Z** 32952
Cocoa Beach Area C/C, 400 Fortenberry Rd.
Satellite Beach (9,889)
Naples (Collier county)
East Naples (22,951)
Everglades (321)
Everglades Area C/C, P.O. Box 130
Golden Gate (14,148)
Immokalee (14,120) **Z** 33934
Immokalee C/C, 907 Roberts Ave.
Lely (3,014)
Marco (9,493) **Z** 33969
Marco Island Area C/C, 1102 N. Collier Blvd.
Naples (19,505) **Z** 33940
Naples Area C/C, 3620 Tamiami Trail North
D *News,* 1075 Central Ave.
Naples Manor (4,574)
Naples Park (8,002)
North Naples (13,422)
Palm River (3,507)
New Port Richey (part of Pasco county)
Elfers (12,356)
Holiday (19,360)
Land O' Lakes (7,892) **Z** 34639
Land O'Lakes C/C, 6221 Land O'Lakes Blvd. (US 41)
Pasco County Tourist Info. Center, 6221 Land O'Lakes Blvd.
New Port Richey (14,044) **Z** 34652
West Pasco C/C, 5443 Main St.
W *The Suncoast News,* 6241 U.S. Hwy 19, P.O. Box 663
W *West Pasco Press,* 5744 Missouri, P.O. Box 785
Port Richey (2,523)
Ocala (Marion county)
Belleview (2,666) **Z** 34420
Belleview-South Marion C/C, 5301 S.E. Abshier Blvd.
Dunnellon (1,624) **Z** 34431
Dunnellon Area C/C, 20500 E. Pennsylvania Ave.
Ocala (42,045) **Z** 34473
Marion Oaks Area C/C, 128 Marion Oaks Blvd.
Ocala–Marion County C/C, 110 E. Silver Springs Blvd.
D *Star-Banner,* 2121 S.W. 19th Ave.

Reddick (554)
Silver Springs Shores (6,421)
Panama City (Bay county)
Callaway (12,253)
Cedar Grove (1,479)
Hiland Park (3,865)
Laguna Beach (1,876)
Lower Grand Lagoon (3,329)
Lynn Haven (9,298) **Z** 32444
Lynn Haven C/C, 825 Ohio Ave.
Mexico Beach (992) **Z** 32410
Mexico Beach C/C, P.O. Box 13382
Panama City (34,378) **Z** 32401
Bay County C/C, 235 W. 5th St.
D *The News-Herald,* 501 W. 11th St.
Panama City Beach (4,051)
Parker (4,598)
Pretty Bayou (3,839)
Springfield (8,715)
Upper Grand Lagoon (7,855)
Pompano Beach (Broward county)
Coral Springs (79,443)
Deerfield Beach (46,325) **Z** 33441
Greater Deerfield Beach C/C, 1601 E. Hillsboro Blvd.
Fort Lauderdale (149,377) **Z** 33326
Davie–Cooper City C/C, 4185 S.W. 64th Ave.
Greater Fort Lauderdale C/C, 512 N.E. Third Ave.
Greater Plantation C/C, 7401 N.W. 4th St.
Lauderdale By The Sea C/C, 4201 Ocean Dr.
Sunrise C/C, 3832 N. University Dr.
Tamarac C/C, 8043 W. McNab Rd.
Weston Area C/C, 1290 Weston Rd.
D *Sun-Sentinel,* 200 East Las Olas Blvd.
Lighthouse Point (10,378)
Oakland Park (26,326)
Plantation (66,692)
Pompano Beach (72,411) **Z** 33063
Coral Springs C/C, 9801 W. Sample Rd.
Greater Pompano Beach C/C, 2200 E. Atlantic Blvd.
Tri-City C/C, Cocoa Gate Plaza
W *Pompano Beach Tribune,* 601 Fairway Dr.
W *The Pompano Ledger,* 660 S. Federal Hwy.
Tamarac (44,822)
Port Charlotte–Punta Gorda (Charlotte county)
Charlotte Harbor (3,327)
D *Charlotte Sun Herald,* 23170 Harbor View Rd.
Charlotte Park (2,225)
Cleveland (2,896)
Englewood (4,946)
Grove City (2,374)
Harbour Heights (2,523)
Manasota Key (1,395)

Port Charlotte (41,535)
Z 33952
Charlotte County C/C, 2702
Tamiami Trail
Punta Gorda (10,747) **Z** 33950
Charlotte County C/C, 326
W. Marion
Rotonda (3,576)
Solana (1,128)
Sarasota (Sarasota county)
Bee Ridge (6,406)
Desoto Lakes (2,807)
Englewood (10,079) **Z** 34223
Englewood Area C/C, 601 S.
Indiana Ave.
Fruitville (9,808)
Gulf Gate Estates (11,622)
Kensington Park (3,026)
Lake Sarasota (4,117)
Laurel (8,245)
Longboat Key (3,393) **Z** 34228
Longboat Key C/C, 5360 Gulf
of Mexico Dr.
Nokomis (3,448)
North Port (11,973)
North Sarasota (6,702)
Osprey (2,597)
Plantation (1,885)
Ridge Wood Heights (4,851)
Sarasota (50,961) **Z** 34236
Sarasota Visitors Bureau,
655 N. Tamiami Trail
Sarasota C/C, 1819 Main St.
D *Herald-Tribune,* 801 S.
Tamiami Trail
Sarasota Springs (16,088)
Siesta Key (7,772)
Siesta Key C/C, 5263 Ocean
Blvd.
South Gate Ridge (5,924)
South Sarasota (5,298)
South Venice (11,951)
Southgate (7,324)
The Meadows (3,437)
Vamo (3,325)
Venice (16,922) **Z** 34287
North Port Area C/C, 12705
S. Tamiami Trail
Venice Area C/C, 257
Tamiami Trail N.
Venice Gardens (7,701)
Warm Mineral Springs (4,041)
Sebring–Avon Park (Highlands
county)
Avon Park (8,042) **Z** 33825
Avon Park C/C, 28 E. Main
St.
W *The News-Sun/Avon Park*
Lake Placid (1,158)
W *Lake Placid Journal,* 232
N. Main St.
Placid Lakes (2,045)
Sebring (8,900) **Z** 33870
Greater Sebring C/C, 309 S.
Circle
W *The News-Sun,* 2227 U.S.
27 South
Sylvan Shores (2,155)
St. Augustine (St. Johns county)
Butler Beach (3,377)
Crescent Beach (1,081)
Fruit Cove (5,904)
Hastings (595)
Palm Valley (9,960)
Sawgrass (2,999)
St. Augustine (11,692) **Z** 32084

St. Augustine/St. Johns
County C/C, One Riberia
St.
D *Record,* P.O. Box 1630
St. Augustine Beach (3,657)
St. Augustine Shores (4,411)
St. Augustine South (4,218)
Villano Beach (1,867)
St. Petersburg–Clearwater
(Pinellas county)
Baskin (3,834)
Bay Pines (4,171)
Belleair (3,968)
Belleair Beach (2,070)
Belleair Bluffs (2,128)
Clearwater (98,784) **Z** 34615
Greater Clearwater C/C, 128
N. Osceola Ave.
Dunedin (34,012) **Z** 34698
Dunedin C/C, 301 Main St.
Feather Sound (2,690)
Gandy (3,164)
Gulfport (11,727)
Harbor Bluffs (2,659)
Highpoint (13,818)
Indian Rocks Beach (3,963)
Z 34635
Gulf Beaches C/C, 105 5th
Ave.
Indian Shores (1,405)
Kenneth City (4,462)
Largo (65,674) **Z** 34640
Greater Largo C/C, 395 1st
Ave. S.W.
Lealman (21,748)
Madeira Beach (4,225)
North Redington Beach (1,135)
Oldsmar (8,361) **Z** 34677
Oldsmar C/C, 101 E. State
St.
Palm Harbor (50,256) **Z** 34684
Greater Palm Harbor Area
C/C, 33451 U.S. 19 N.
Pinellas Park (43,426) **Z** 34665
Pinellas Park C/C, 5851 Park
Blvd.
Redington Beach (1,626)
Redington Shores (2,366)
Safety Harbor (15,124)
Z 34695
Safety Harbor C/C, 200 Main
St.
Seminole (9,251) **Z** 34645
Greater Seminole Area C/C,
8400 113th St. North
South Pasadena (5,644)
St. Petersburg (238,629)
Z 33706
Gulf Beaches on Sand Key
C/C, 501 150th Ave.
St. Petersburg Area C/C, 100
Second Ave. N.
Treasure Island C/C,
152-108th Ave.
D *St. Petersburg Times,* P.O.
Box 1121
St. Petersburg Beach (9,200)
Z 33706
St. Petersburg Beach Area
C/C, 6990 Gulf Blvd.
Tarpon Springs (17,906)
Z 34689
Tarpon Springs C/C, 210 S.
Pinellas Ave.
Treasure Island (7,266)
Vero Beach–Sebastian (Indian
River county)

Fellsmere (2,179)
Florida Ridge (12,218)
Gifford (6,278)
Indian River Shores (2,278)
Roseland (1,379)
Sebastian (10,205) **Z** 32958
Sebastian River Area C/C,
1302 U.S. Hwy. 1
South Beach (2,754)
Vero Beach (17,350) **Z** 32960
Vero Beach-Indian River C/C,
1216 21st St.
D *Press-Journal,* P.O. Box
1268
Vero Beach South (16,973)
Wabasso (1,145)

GEORGIA

Athens (Clarke county)
Athens (45,734) **Z** 30601
Athens Area C/C, 220
College Ave.
D *Banner-Herald-News,* P.O.
Box 912
Gaines School (11,354)
Winterville (876)
Blairsville (Union county)
Blairsville (564) **Z** 30512
Blairsville/Union County C/C,
385 Blue Ridge Hwy.
W *North Georgia News,*
Cleveland St.
Clayton (Rabun county)
Clayton (1,613) **Z** 30525
Rabun County C/C, Hwy. 441
N.
Mountain City (784)
Hiawassee (Towns county)
Hiawassee (547) **Z** 30546
Towns County C/C, U.S.
Hwy. 76
W *Towns County Herald,* P.O.
Box 365
Young Harris (604)
Savannah (Chatham county)
Bloomingdale (2,271)
Garden City (7,410)
Georgetown (5,554)
Isle Of Hope–Dutch Island
(2,637)
Montgomery (4,327)
Pooler (4,453) **Z** 31322
Pooler Area C/C, 301
Governor Treutlan Dr.
Port Wentworth (4,012)
Savannah (137,560) **Z** 31401
Savannah Area C/C, 222 W.
Oglethorpe Ave.
D *Morning News,* **D** *Evening
Press,* 105-111 W. Bay St.
Skidaway Island (4,495)
Thunderbolt (2,786)
Tybee Island (2,842) **Z** 31328
Tybee Island Visitors Center,
209 Butler Ave.
Whitemarsh Island (2,824)
Wilmington Island (11,230)
St. Simons–Jekyll Islands (part of
Glynn county)
St. Simons (12,026) **Z** 31522
St. Simons Island C/C, 530B
Beachview Dr. West
W *The Islander,* P.O. Box 539
Thomasville (Thomas county)
Boston (1,395)
Coolidge (610)
Meigs (1,067)

Ochlocknee (588)
Thomasville (17,457) **Z** 31792
Thomasville–Thomas County
C/C, 401 S. Broad St.
D *Times-Enterprise,* P.O. Box
650

HAWAII
Kauai (Kauai county)
Anahola (1,181)
Eleele (1,489)
Hanamaulu (3,611)
Hanapepe (1,395)
Kalaheo (3,592)
Kapaa (8,149)
Kaumakani (803)
Kekaha (3,506)
Kilauea (1,685)
Koloa (1,791)
Lawai (1,787)
Lihue (5,536) **Z** 96766
Kauai C/C, P.O. Box 1969
D *The Garden Island,* P.O.
Box 231
Omao (1,142)
Pakala Village (565)
Poipu (975)
Princeville (1,244)
Puhi (1,210)
Wailua (2,018)
Wailua Homesteads (3,870)
Waimea (1,840)
Maui (Maui county)
Haiku–Pauwela (4,509)
Haliimaile (841)
Hana (683)
Kaanapali (579)
Kahului (16,889) **Z** 96732
Maui C/C, 26 N. Puunene
Ave.
Kaunakakai (2,658) **Z** 96748
Molokai C/C, P.O. Box 515
Kihei (11,107)
Kualapuu (1,661)
Lahaina (9,073)
Lanai City (2,400)
Makawao (5,405)
Napili–Honokowai (4,332)
Paia (2,091)
Pukalani (5,879)
Waihee–Waiehue (4,004)
Waikapu (729)
Wailea–Makena (3,799)
Wailuku (10,688) **Z** 96793
D *Maui News,* P.O. Box 550

IDAHO
Coeur d'Alene (Kootenai county)
Coeur d'Alene (24,563)
Z 83814
Coeur d'Alene Area C/C,
1621 N. Third St.
D *The Press,* 201 Second
Ave.
Dalton Gardens (1,951)
Hayden (3,744)
Post Falls (7,349) **Z** 83854
Post Falls C/C, 510 E. 6th
Ave.
Rathdrum (2,000)
Spirit Lake (790)
Ketchum–Sun Valley (Blaine
county)
Bellevue (1,275)
Hailey (3,687) **Z** 83333
Hailey C/C, P.O. Box 100

W *Wood River Journal,* 112 S.
Main St.
Ketchum (2,523)
W *Idaho Mountain Express,*
591 First Ave. N. Rd.
Sun Valley (938) **Z** 83353
Sun Valley–Ketchum C/C,
P.O. Box 2420
McCall–Cascade–Payette Valley
(Valley county)
Cascade (877) **Z** 83611
Cascade C/C, P.O. Box 571
McCall (2,005) **Z** 83638
McCall Area Visitors Bureau,
116 N. 3rd
McCall Area C/C, 1001 State
St.
W *The Star-News,* P.O. Box
985
Sandpoint–Priest River (Bonner
county)
Priest River (1,560) **Z** 83856
W *Priest River Times,*
Cottonwood Village
Sandpoint (5,203) **Z** 83864
Greater Sandpoint C/C, Hwy.
95 N.
D *Bee,* P.O. Box 159

KENTUCKY
Kentucky Lake (Calloway and
Marshall counties)
Benton (3,899) **Z** 42025
Marshall County C/C, Rt. 7
Box 145
W *Tribune-Courier,* 308 E.
12th St.
Calvert City (2,531)
Hardin (595)
Murray (14,439) **Z** 42071
Murray–Calloway County
C/C, 805 N. 12th St.
D *Ledger & Times,* 1001
Whitnell Ave.

LOUISANA
Western St. Tammany Parish
(part of St. Tammany Parish)
Abita Springs (1,296)
Covington (7,691) **Z** 70433
St. Tammany Tourism
Commission, 600 N. Hwy.
190
St. Tammany–West C/C, 832
E. Boston St.
W *St. Tammany Farmer,* 321
N. New Hampshire St.
W *St. Tammany News-Banner,*
P.O. Box 90
Lacombe (6,523) **Z** 70445
Bayou Lacombe C/C, P.O.
Box 889
Mandeville (7,083) **Z** 70448
Mandeville Greater C/C, 122
Lisa Lane
Pearl River (1,507)

MAINE
Bar Harbor (Hancock county)
Bar Harbor (4,443) **Z** 04609
Bar Harbor C/C, 93 Cottage
St.
Blue Hill (1,941)
Brooklin (785)
Brooksville (760)

Bucksport (4,825) **Z** 04416
Bucksport Bay Area C/C,
P.O. Box 1880
Castine (1,161)
Dedham (1,229)
Deer Isle (1,829)
Ellsworth (5,975) **Z** 04605
Ellsworth Area C/C, High St.
W *The Ellsworth American,* 63
Main St.
Franklin (1,141)
Gouldsboro (1,986)
Hancock (1,757)
Lamoine (1,311)
Mount Desert (1,899) **Z** 04660
Mount Desert C/C, Sea St.
Orland (1,805)
Penobscot (1,131)
Sedgwick (905)
Southwest Harbor (1,952)
Stonington (1,252) **Z** 04681
Deer Isle–Stonington C/C,
P.O. Box 459
W *Island Ad-Vantages,* P.O.
Box 36
Sullivan (1,118)
Surry (1,004)
Tremont (1,324)
Trenton (1,060)
Verona (515)
Winter Harbor (1,157) **Z** 04693
Schoadic Peninsula C/C,
P.O. Box 327
Camden (Knox county)
Appleton (1,069)
Camden (5,060) **Z** 04843
Rockport–Camden–Lincolnville
C/C, Public Landing
W *The Camden Herald,* P.O.
Box 248
Cushing (988)
Friendship (1,099)
Hope (1,017)
Owls Head (1,574)
Rockland (7,972) **Z** 04841
Rockland–Thomaston Area
C/C, Harbor Park
W *The Courier-Gazette,* P.O.
Box 249
Rockport (2,854)
South Thomaston (1,227)
St. George (2,261)
Thomaston (3,306)
Union (1,989) **Z** 04862
Union C/C, P.O. Box 839
Vinalhaven (1,072)
Warren (3,192)
Washington (1,185)
York Beaches (York county)
Acton (1,727)
Alfred (2,238)
Arundel (2,669)
Berwick (5,995)
Biddeford (20,710) **Z** 04005
Biddeford–Saco C/C & Ind.,
170 Main St.
Buxton (6,494)
Cornish (1,178)
Dayton (1,197)
Eliot (5,329)
Hollis (3,573)
Kennebunk (8,004) **Z** 04043
W *York County Coast Star,*
U.S. Route 1 South
Kennebunkport (3,356)
Z 04046

Kennebunk–Kennebunkport
C/C, P.O. Box 740
Kittery (9,372) **Z** 03904
Kittery–Eliot C/C, P.O. Box
526
Lebanon (4,263)
Limerick (1,688)
Limington (2,796)
Lyman (3,390)
Newfield (1,042)
North Berwick (3,793)
Ogunquit (974) **Z** 03907
Ogunquit C/C, Route 1 &
Obed's Lane
Old Orchard Beach (7,789)
Z 04064
Old Orchard Beach C/C, First
St.
Parsonsfield (1,472)
Saco (15,181)
Sanford (20,463) **Z** 04073
Sanford–Springvale C/C, 261
Main St.
Shapleigh (1,911)
South Berwick (5,877)
Waterboro (4,510)
Wells (7,778) **Z** 04090
Wells C/C, Route 1 at
Kimball Lane
York (9,818) **Z** 03909
Yorks C/C, P.O. Box 417
W *York Weekly,* 17
Woodbridge Rd.

MARYLAND

Annapolis (part of Anne Arundel
county)
Annapolis (33,187) **Z** 21401
Greater Annapolis C/C, One
Annapolis St.
D *Capital,* 2000 Capital Dr.
Arden-on-the-Severn (2,427)
Arnold (20,261) **Z** 21012
Anne Arundel County C/C,
1460 Ritchie Hwy.
Cape St. Claire (7,878)
Crofton (12,781) **Z** 21114
Crofton C/C, 2135 Defense
Hwy.
Crownsville (1,514)
Herald Harbor (1,707)
Mayo (2,537)
Riva (3,438)
Riviera Beach (11,376)
Selby-on-the-Bay (3,101)
Severn (24,499)
Severna Park (25,879) **Z** 21146
Severna Park C/C, P.O. Box
93
Easton–St. Michaels–Oxford
(Talbot county)
Easton (9,372) **Z** 21601
Talbot County C/C, 805
Goldsborough St.
D *Star-Democrat,* 1 Airpack
Dr.
Oxford (699)
St. Michaels (1,301)
Trappe (974)
Ocean City (Worcester county)
Berlin (2,616)
W *Maryland Coast-Dispatch,*
P.O. Box 467
Ocean City (5,146) **Z** 21842
Ocean City Visitors Bureau,
4001 Coastal Hwy.

Ocean City C/C, 12320
Ocean Gateway
W *Maryland Times-Press,*
3316 Coastal Hwy.
Ocean Pines (4,251)
Pocomoke City (3,922) **Z** 21851
Pocomoke City C/C, City
Hall, Clarke Ave.
Snow Hill (2,217) **Z** 21863
Snow Hill C/C, P.O. Box 176
West Ocean City (1,928)

MASSACHUSETTS

Amherst–Northampton
(Hampshire county)
Amherst (35,228) **Z** 01002
Amherst C/C, 11 Spring St.
W *Amherst Bulletin,* 55
University Dr.
Belchertown (10,579)
Chesterfield (1,048)
Cummington (785)
Easthampton (15,537) **Z** 01027
Easthampton C/C, 33 Union
St.
Goshen (830)
Granby (5,565)
Hadley (4,231)
Hatfield (3,184)
Huntington (1,987)
Northampton (29,289) **Z** 01060
Greater Northampton C/C,
62 State St.
D *Daily Hampshire Gazette,*
115 Conz St.
Pelham (1,373)
Plainfield (571)
South Hadley (16,685) **Z** 01075
South Hadley C/C, 10
Harwich Place
Southampton (4,478)
Ware (9,808)
Westhampton (1,327)
Williamsburg (2,515)
Worthington (1,156)
Cape Cod (Barnstable county)
Barnstable (40,949)
Bourne (16,064)
Brewster (8,440)
Chatham (6,579) **Z** 02633
Chatham C/C, P.O. Box 793
Dennis (13,864) **Z** 02638
Dennis C/C, 242 Swan River
Rd., West Dennis
Eastham (4,462) **Z** 02642
Eastham C/C, P.O. Box 1329
Falmouth (27,960) **Z** 02540
Falmouth C/C, Academy Ln.
02541
Harwich (10,275) **Z** 02645
Harwich C/C, P.O. Box 34
02646
Hyannis (13,000) **Z** 02601
Hyannis Area C/C, 319
Barnstable Rd.
Cape Cod C/C, P.O. Box 16
D *Cape Cod Times,*
319 Main St.
Mashpee (7,884)
Orleans (5,838)
Provincetown (3,561) **Z** 02657
Provincetown C/C, 307
Commerical St.
Sandwich (15,489)
Truro (1,573)
Wellfleet (2,493) **Z** 02667
Wellfleet C/C, Off Rte. 6

Yarmouth (21,174) **Z** 02664
Yarmouth Area C/C, 657 Rt.
28
W *Cape Cod Newspapers,*
495 Station Ave.
Southern Berkshire County (part
of Berkshire county)
Great Barrington (7,725)
Z 01230
Southern Berkshire C/C, 362
Main St.
W *The Berkshire Courier,* 268
Main St.
W *The Berkshire Record,* 272
Main St.
Lee (5,849)
Lenox (5,069) **Z** 01240
Lenox C/C, Lenox Academy,
75 Main St.
Monterey (805)
Otis (1,073)
Sandisfield (667)
Sheffield (2,910)
Stockbridge (2,408) **Z** 01262
Stockbridge C/C, Main St.
West Stockbridge (1,483)

MICHIGAN

Charlevoix–Boyne City–East
Jordan (Charlevoix county)
Boyne City (3,478) **Z** 49712
Boyne City C/C, 28 S. Lake
St.
W *Charlevoix County Press,*
108 Groveland
Charlevoix (3,116) **Z** 49720
Charlevoix Area C/C, 408
Bridge St.
W *Charlevoix Courier,* 405
Bridge St.
East Jordan (2,240) **Z** 49727
East Jordan Area C/C, 118
N. Lake St.
Houghton Lake (Roscommon
county)
Houghton Lake (3,353)
Z 48629
Houghton Lake C/C, 1625 W.
Houghton Lake Dr.
W *The Houghton Lake
Resorter,* 4049 W.
Houghton Lake Dr.
Prudenville (1,513)
Roscommon (858) **Z** 48653
W *The Roscommon County
Herald,* P.O. Box 8
St. Helen (2,390) **Z** 48656
Saint Helen C/C, P.O. Box
642
Oscoda–Tawas–Huron Shore
(Iosco county)
Au Sable (1,542)
East Tawas (2,887)
W *Iosco County News Herald,*
101 W. State St.
Oscoda (1,061) **Z** 48750
Oscoda–Au Sable C/C, 4440
N. U.S. 23
Tawas City (2,009) **Z** 48763
Tawas Bay Tourist Bureau,
P.O. Box 10
Tawas Area C/C, 402 E. Lake
St.
Petoskey–Harbor Springs
(Emmet county)
Alanson (677)

Harbor Springs (1,540)
Z 49740
Harbor Springs C/C, P.O. Box 37
Pellston (583)
Petoskey (6,056) **Z** 49770
Petoskey Regional C/C, 401 E. Mitchell St.
D *News-Review,* 319 State St.
Traverse City (Grand Traverse county)
Kingsley (738)
Traverse City (15,116) **Z** 49684
Grand Traverse Visitors Bureau, 415 Munson Ave.
Traverse City Area C/C, 202 E. Grandview Pkwy.
D *Record-Eagle,* 120 W. Front St.

MISSISSIPPI

Bay St. Louis–Pass Christian (parts of Hancock and Harrison counties)
Bay St. Louis (8,063) **Z** 39520
Hancock C/C, 412 Hwy. 90
W *Sea Coast Echo,* 124 Court St.
Kiln (1,262)
Pearlington (1,603)
Long Beach (15,804)
Pass Christian (5,557)
W *Tarpon Beacon,* 226 Davis Ave.
Madison (Madison county)
Canton (10,062) **Z** 39046
Canton Visitors Bureau, 226 E. Pearl St.
Madison County C/C, P.O. Box 544
W *Madison County Herald,* 159 E. Center St.
W *Madison County Journal,* P.O. Box 219
Flora (1,482)
Madison (7,471) **Z** 39110
Madison C/C, P.O. Box 544
Ridgeland (11,714)
Oxford (Lafayette county)
Oxford (9,984) **Z** 38655
Oxford–Lafayette County C/C, 299 W. Jackson
Oxford Tourism Council, P.O. Box 965
D *Eagle,* 916 Jackson Ave.

MISSOURI

Branson (Taney county)
Branson (3,706) **Z** 65616
Branson/Lakes Area C/C, P.O. Box 220
D *Branson Tri-Lakes Daily News,* P.O. Box 1900
Forsyth (1,175) **Z** 65653
Forsyth C/C, US Hwy. 160, P.O. Box 777
Hollister (2,628)
Merriam Woods (601)
Lake of the Ozarks (Camden county)
Camdenton (2,561) **Z** 65020
Camdenton Area C/C, N. Hwy. 5 at Ryland Center
D *Lake Sun Leader,* 114 N. Highway 5
Osage Beach (2,511) **Z** 65065

Lake Area C/C, #7 Kings Plaza, P.O. Box 193
Sunrise Beach (112) **Z** 65079
Lake of the Ozarks West C/C, Hwy. 5
Village of Four Seasons (805)
Table Rock Lake (Stone county)
Crane (1,218) **Z** 65633
Crane C/C, P.O. Box 23
W *The Stone County Republican,* 108 Main St.
Kimberling City (1,590) **Z** 65686
Table Rock Lake–Kimberling City Area C/C, N. Hwy. 13
W *Kimberling City-Table Rock Gazette,* P.O. Box 432

MONTANA

Hamilton–Bitterroot Valley (Ravalli county)
Darby (625)
Hamilton (2,737) **Z** 59840
Bitterroot Valley C/C, 105 E. Main St.
D *Ravalli Republic,* 232 Main St.
Pinesdale (670)
Stevensville (1,221)
Kalispell–Flathead Valley (Flathead county)
Columbia Falls (2,942) **Z** 59912
Columbia Falls Area C/C, 233 13th Street East
W *Hungry Horse News,* P.O. Box 189
Evergreen (4,109)
Kalispell (11,917) **Z** 59901
Kalispell Area C/C, 15 Depot Park
D *Inter Lake,* 727 E. Idaho
Whitefish (4,368) **Z** 59937
Whitefish Area C/C, Burlington Northern Depot
Polson–Mission Valley (Lake county)
Pablo (1,298)
Polson (3,283) **Z** 59860
Polson Area C/C, 302 Main St.
W *Lake County Leader,* 213 Main St.
Ronan (1,547) **Z** 59864
Ronan C/C, 214 Main S.W.
St. Ignatius (778) **Z** 59865
Saint Ignatius C/C, P.O. Box 396

NEVADA

Carson City–Carson Valley (Carson City independent city and Douglas county)
Carson City (40,443) **Z** 89701
Carson City C/C, 1900 S. Carson St.
D *Nevada Appeal,* 200 Bath St.
Gardnerville (2,177) **Z** 89410
Carson Valley C/C & Visitors Auth., 1524 Hwy. 395 N. #1
W *The Record-Courier,* 1218 Eddy St.
Gardnerville Ranchos (7,455)
Indian Hills (2,544)
Johnson Lane (2,551)
Kingsbury (2,238)

Minden (1,441)
Stateline (1,379) **Z** 89449
Tahoe–Douglas C/C, 195 Hwy. 50-Round Hill Mall
Zephyr Cove–Round Hill Village (1,434)
Las Vegas (Clark county)
Boulder City (12,567) **Z** 89005
Boulder City C/C, 1497 Nevada Hwy.
W *Boulder City News,* 1227 Arizona St.
East Las Vegas (11,087)
D *Review-Journal,* **D** *Las Vegas Sun,* 111 W. Bonanza
Enterprise (6,412)
Henderson (64,942)
Indian Springs (1,164) **Z** 89018
Henderson C/C, 100 E. Lake Mead Dr.
Las Vegas (258,295) **Z** 89109
Las Vegas Visitors Bureau, 3150 Paradise Rd.
Las Vegas C/C, 711 E. Desert Inn Rd.
Latin C/C, 829 S. Sixth St.
Nevada Black C/C, 1048 W. Owens Ave.
North Las Vegas C/C, 1023 E. Lake Mead Blvd.
Laughlin (4,791) **Z** 89029
Laughlin C/C, 1725 Casino Dr.
Mesquite (1,871)
Moapa Valley (3,444)
North Las Vegas (47,707)
Paradise (124,682)
Spring Valley (51,726)
Sunrise Manor (95,362)
Winchester (23,365)
Pahrump Valley (part of Nye county)
Pahrump (7,424) **Z** 89041
Pahrump Valley C/C, Hwy. 160 at Pahrump Station
Reno–Sparks (Washoe county)
Incline Village–Crystal Bay (7,119) **Z** 89451
Incline Village–Crystal Bay C/C, 969 Tahoe Blvd.
W *North Lake Tahoe Bonanza,* 917 Tahoe Blvd.
New Washoe City (2,875)
Reno (133,850) **Z** 89501
Greater Reno–Sparks C/C, 405 Marsh Ave.
Nevada State C/C, P.O. Box 3499
Reno–Sparks Visitors Bureau, P.O. Box 837
D *Reno Gazette-Journal,* 955 Kuenzli Lane
Sparks (53,367) **Z** 89431
Sparks Community C/C, 831 Victorian Ave.
D *Daily Tribune,* 1002 C St.
Sun Valley (11,391)
Wadsworth (640)

NEW HAMPSHIRE

Hanover (Grafton county)
Alexandria (1,190)
Ashland (1,915)
Bath (784)
Bethlehem (2,033) **Z** 03574
Bethlehem C/C, Maple St.

Bridgewater (796)
Bristol (2,537) **Z** 03222
  Newfound Region C/C, P.O.
    Box 454
Campton (2,377) **Z** 03223
  Waterville Valley Region C/C,
    RFD 1, Box 1067
Canaan (3,045)
Enfield (3,979)
Franconia (811) **Z** 03580
  Franconia-Sugar Hill-Easton
    C/C, 1 Main St.
Grafton (923)
Hanover (9,212) **Z** 03755
  Hanover C/C, 37 S. Main St.
Haverhill (4,164)
Holderness (1,694)
Lebanon (12,183) **Z** 03766
  Greater Lebanon C/C, 2
    Whipple Pl.
Lincoln (1,229) **Z** 03251
  Lincoln-Woodstock C/C,
    Route 112, P.O. Box 358
Lisbon (1,664) **Z** 03585
  Lisbon Area C/C, P.O. Box
    77
Littleton (5,827) **Z** 03561
  Littleton Area C/C, 141 Main
    St.
  W *The Courier,* 146 Union St.
Lyme (1,496)
Monroe (746)
Orford (1,008)
Piermont (624)
Plymouth (5,811)
Rumney (1,446)
Thornton (1,505)
Warren (820)
Wentworth (630)
Woodstock (1,167)
Lake Winnipesaukee (Belknap
  and Carroll counties)
Alton (3,286) **Z** 03809
  Alton/Alton Bay C/C, P.O.
    Box 550
Barnstead (3,100)
Belmont (5,796)
Center Harbor (996) **Z** 03226
  Center Harbor-Moultonboro
    C/C, P.O. Box 824
Gilford (5,867)
Gilmanton (2,609)
Laconia (15,743) **Z** 03246
  Greater Laconia-Weirs
    Beach C/C, 11 Veterans
    Sq.
Meredith (4,837) **Z** 03253
  Meredith C/C, P.O. Box 732
Freedom (935)
Moultonborough (2,956)
Ossipee (3,309)
Tamworth (2,165)
Wolfeboro (4,807) **Z** 03894
  Wolfeboro C/C, Railroad
    Square
  W *The Granite State News,*
    Endicott St.

NEW JERSEY

Lower Cape May (part of Cape
  May county)
Avalon (1,809) **Z** 08202
  Avalon C/C, 30th & Ocean
    Dr.
Cape May (4,668) **Z** 08204
  C/C of Greater Cape May,
    609 Lafayette St.

Cape May County C/C, Crest
  Haven Rd. & Garden State
  Pkwy.
Cape May County Dept. of
  Tourism, P.O. Box 365
W *Cape May Star And Wave,*
  513 Washington Mall
Stone Harbor (1,025)
Wildwood (4,484) **Z** 08260
  Greater Wildwood C/C,
    Schellenger on the
    Boardwalk
  W *Cape May County Gazette
    Leader,* 1212 Atlantic Ave.
Toms River-Barnegat Bay
  (Ocean county)
Barnegat (12,235)
Barnegat Light (675)
Bay Head (1,226)
Beach Haven (1,475)
Beachwood (9,324)
Berkeley (37,319)
Brick (66,473) **Z** 08723
  Brick Twp. C/C, 909 Cedar
    Bridge Ave.
Brick (66,473)
Dover (76,371)
Eagleswood (1,476)
Island Heights (1,470)
Jackson (33,233)
Lacey (22,141)
Lakehurst (3,078) **Z** 08733
  W *Advance News,* 2048
    Route 37 West Road 1
Lakewood (45,048) **Z** 08701
  Lakewood C/C, 200 Clifton
    Ave.
Lavallette (2,299)
Little Egg Harbor (13,333)
Long Beach (3,407) **Z** 08008
  Southern Ocean County C/C,
    265 W. 9th St.
Manchester (35,976)
Ocean (5,416)
Ocean Gate (2,078)
Pine Beach (1,954)
Plumsted (6,005)
Point Pleasant (18,177)
  Z 08742
  Greater Point Pleasant Area
    C/C, 517A Arnold Ave.
Point Pleasant Beach (5,112)
Seaside Heights (2,366)
Seaside Park (1,871)
Ship Bottom (1,352)
South Toms River (3,869)
  Z 08757
Stafford (13,325)
Surf City (1,375)
Toms River (15,680) **Z** 08753
  Toms River-Ocean County
    C/C, 1200 Hooper Ave.
  D *Observer,* 8 Robbins St.
Tuckerton (3,048)

NEW MEXICO

Alamogordo (Otero county)
Alamogordo (27,596) **Z** 88310
  Alamogordo C/C, 1301 White
    Sands Blvd.
  D *Alamogordo Daily News,*
    P.O. Box 870
Boles Acres (1,409)
Cloudcroft (636) **Z** 88317
  Cloudcroft C/C, Zenith Park
La Luz (1,625)

Mescalero (1,159)
Tularosa (2,615) **Z** 88352
  Tularosa C/C, 301 Central
Albuquerque (Bernalillo county)
Albuquerque (384,736) **Z** 87102
  Albuquerque Visitors Bureau,
    121 Tijeras N.E.
  Greater Albuquerque C/C,
    401 Second St. N.W.
  South Valley C/C, 4323 Isleta
    Blvd. S.W.
  D *Albuquerque Journal,*
    7777 Jefferson, N.E.
Corrales (535)
Isleta Pueblo (1,355)
Los Ranchos de Albuquerque
  (3,955)
North Valley (12,507)
Paradise Hills (5,513)
Sandia (6,742)
Sandia Heights (3,519)
South Valley (35,701)
Las Cruces (Dona Ana county)
Anthony (5,160) **Z** 88021
  Anthony C/C, P.O. Box 1086
Chaparral (2,962)
Dona Ana (1,202)
Hatch (1,136) **Z** 87937
  Hatch Valley C/C, 224 Elm
    St.
Las Cruces (62,126) **Z** 88001
  Las Cruces Visitors Bureau,
    311 N. Downtown Mall
  Las Cruces C/C, 760 W.
    Picacho
  D *Sun-News,* 256 W. Las
    Cruces Ave.
Mesilla (1,975)
Sunland Park (8,179)
University Park (4,520)
White Sands (2,616)
Ruidoso (Lincoln county)
Capitan (842) **Z** 88316
  Capitan C/C, Hwy. 380
Carrizozo (1,075) **Z** 88301
  Carrizozo C/C, P.O. Box 567
Ruidoso (4,600) **Z** 88345
  Ruidoso Visitors Bureau, 111
    Sierra Blanca Dr.
  Ruidoso Valley C/C, 720
    Sudderth Dr.
  W *The Ruidoso News,* 104
    Park Ave.
Ruidoso Downs (920)
Santa Fe (Santa Fe county)
Agua Fria (3,717)
Chimayo (639)
Edgewood (2,880)
Eldorado at Santa Fe (2,260)
Espanola (2,179)
La Cienega (1,066)
Nambe (1,246)
Pojoaque (1,037)
Santa Cruz (2,504)
Santa Fe (55,859) **Z** 87501
  Santa Fe Visitors Bureau,
    P.O. Box 909
  Santa Fe County C/C, P.O.
    Box 1928
  D *New Mexican,* 202 E.
    Marcy
  W *Santa Fe Reporter,* P.O.
    Box 2306
Tesuque (1,490)
Silver City (Grant county)
Bayard (2,598)

Central (1,835)
Hurley (1,534)
Silver City (10,683) **Z** 88061
　Silver City–Grant County
　　C/C, 1103 N. Hudson St.
　D *Press & Independent,* 300
　　W. Market St.
Taos (Taos county)
　Penasco (648)
　Questa (1,707)
　Ranchos De Taos (1,779)
　Red River (387) **Z** 87558
　　Red River C/C, P.O. Box 870
　Taos (4,065) **Z** 87571
　　Taos County C/C, 1139
　　　Paseo del Pueblo Sur
　　W *The Taos News,* 120
　　　Camino De La Placita
　Taos Pueblo (1,187)

NEW YORK

East End Long Island (part of
　Suffolk county)
　East Hampton (1,402) **Z** 11937
　　East Hampton C/C, 4 Main
　　　St.
　Greenport (2,070)
　Sag Harbor (2,134) **Z** 11963
　　Sag Harbor C/C, 459 Main
　　　St.
　　W *Sag Harbor Express,* Main
　　　St.
　Shelter Island (2,263)
　　W *Shelter Island Reporter,*
　　　Drawer 3020
　Southampton (44,976) **Z** 11968
　　Southampton C/C, 76 Main
　　　St.
　Southold (19,836)
　　W *The Traveler-Watchman,*
　　　Traveler St.

NORTH CAROLINA

Asheville (Buncombe county)
　Asheville (61,607) **Z** 28801
　　Asheville Area C/C, 151
　　　Haywood St.
　　D *Citizen-Times,* 14 O'Henry
　　　Ave.
　Avery Creek (1,144)
　Bent Creek (1,487)
　Biltmore Forest (1,327)
　Black Mountain (5,418)
　　Z 28711
　　Black Mountain–Swannanoa
　　　C/C, 102 E. State St.
　Fairview (1,830)
　Montreat (693)
　Royal Pines (4,418)
　Swannanoa (3,538)
　Weaverville (2,107)
　Woodfin (2,736)
Boone–Blowing Rock (Watauga
　county)
　Blowing Rock (1,213) **Z** 28605
　　Blowing Rock C/C, Main St.
　　W *The Blowing Rocket,*
　　　Sunset Dr.
　Boone (12,915) **Z** 28607
　　Boone Area C/C, 112 W.
　　　Howard St.
　　North Carolina High Country
　　　Host, 701 Blowing Rock
　　　Rd.
　　W *Watuga Democrat,* 300 W.
　　　King St.

Brevard (Transylvania county)
　Brevard (5,388) **Z** 28712
　　Brevard–Transylvania C/C,
　　　35 W. Main St.
Chapel Hill (Orange county)
　Carrboro (11,553)
　Chapel Hill (37,604) **Z** 27515
　　Chapel Hill–Carrboro C/C,
　　　104 S. Estes Dr.
　　D *Herald,* 106 Mallette St.
　Hillsborough (4,263) **Z** 27278
　　Hillsborough Area C/C, 150
　　　E. King St.
Dare Outer Banks (Dare county)
　Kill Devil Hills (4,238) **Z** 27948
　　Outer Banks C/C, Ocean Bay
　　　Blvd. & Mustian St.
　Kitty Hawk (1,937)
　Manteo (991)
　Nags Head (1,838)
　Southern Shores (1,447)
　Wanchese (1,380)
Edenton (Chowan county)
　Edenton (5,268) **Z** 27932
　　Edenton–Chowan C/C, 116
　　　E. King St.
Hendersonville–East Flat Rock
　(Henderson county)
　Balfour (1,118)
　Barker Heights (1,137)
　East Flat Rock (3,218)
　Etowah (1,997)
　Fletcher (2,787)
　Hendersonville (7,284) **Z** 28793
　　Greater Hendersonville C/C,
　　　330 N. King St.
　　Henderson County Travel &
　　　Tourism, 739 N. Main St.
　　D *Times-News,* 1717 Four
　　　Seasons Blvd.
　Laurel Park (1,322)
　Mountain Home (1,898)
　Valley Hill (1,802)
New Bern (Craven county)
　Havelock (20,268) **Z** 28532
　　Havelock C/C, P.O. Box 21
　James City (4,279)
　Neuse Forest (1,110)
　New Bern (17,363) **Z** 28560
　　New Bern Area C/C, 233
　　　Middle St.
　　D *Sun Journal,* 226 Pollock
　　　St.
　River Bend (2,408)
　Trent Woods (2,366)
　Vanceboro (946)
Southern Pines–Pinehurst (Moore
　county)
　Aberdeen (2,700)
　　D *Citizen News-Record,* 206
　　　N. Sandhills Blvd.
　Carthage (976)
　Pinebluff (876)
　Pinehurst (5,103)
　Robbins (970)
　Seven Lakes (2,049)
　Southern Pines (9,129)
　　Z 28387
　　Sandhills Area C/C, 1480
　　　Hwy. 15-501 N.
　　W *The Pilot,* 145
　　　Pennsylvania Ave.
　Vass (670)
　Whispering Pines (1,243)
Southport–Brunswick Islands
　(Brunswick county)
　Boiling Spring Lakes (1,650)

Calabash (1,210)
Holden Beach (626)
Leland (1,801)
Long Beach (3,816)
Ocean Isle Beach (523)
Shallotte (965) **Z** 28459
　South Brunswick Islands
　　C/C, 4948 Main St.
　W *The Brunswick Beacon,*
　　4709 Main St.
Southport (2,369) **Z** 28461
　Southport–Oak Island C/C,
　　4848 Long Beach Rd. S.E.
　W *The State Port Pilot,* 105 S.
　　Howe St.
Yaupon Beach (734)
Tryon (Polk county)
　Columbus (812)
　Tryon (1,680) **Z** 28782
　　Tryon Thermal Belt C/C, 401
　　　N. Trade St.
　　D *Bulletin,* 106 N. Trade St.

OKLAHOMA

Lake of the Cherokees (Delaware
　county)
　Colcord (628)
　Grove (4,020) **Z** 74344
　　Grove Area C/C, 104 W. 3rd
　　　St.
　Jay (2,220) **Z** 74346
　　Jay C/C, P.O. Box 806
　　W *Delaware County Journal,*
　　　P.O. Box 1050
　Kansas (556)
　West Siloam Springs (539)

OREGON

Bend (Deschutes county)
　Bend (20,469) **Z** 97701
　　Bend C/C, 63085 N. Hwy. 97
　　Sunriver Area C/C, P.O. Box
　　　3246
　　D *Bulletin,* 1526 N.W. Hill St.
　Deschutes River Woods (2,373)
　Redmond (7,163) **Z** 97756
　　Redmond C/C, 106 S.W. 7th
　　　St.
　Sisters (679) **Z** 97759
　　Sisters Area C/C, 151 N.
　　　Spruce St.
　Terrebonne (1,143)
　Three Rivers (1,268)
Brookings–Gold Beach (Curry
　county)
　Brookings (4,400) **Z** 97415
　　Brookings–Harbor C/C,
　　　16330 Lower Harbor Rd.
　Gold Beach (1,546) **Z** 97444
　　Gold Beach C/C, 1225 S.
　　　Ellensburg Ave.
　　W *Curry County Reporter,*
　　　510 N. Ellensburg Ave
　Harbor (2,143)
　Port Orford (1,025) **Z** 97465
　　Port Orford C/C, P.O. Box
　　　637
Florence (part of Lane county)
　Florence (5,162) **Z** 97439
　　Florence Area C/C, 270 Hwy.
　　　101
　　W *The Siuslaw News,* 148
　　　Maple
Grants Pass (Josephine county)
　Cave Junction (1,126) **Z** 97523
　　Illinois Valley C/C, 201 Caves
　　　Hwy.

Grants Pass (17,488) **Z** 97526
Grants Pass/Josephine
County C/C, 1501 N.E. 6th
St.
D *Courier,* P.O. Box 1468
Harbeck–Fruitdale (3,982)
Redwood (3,702)
Medford–Ashland (Jackson
county)
Ashland (16,234) **Z** 97520
Ashland C/C, 110 E. Main St.
D *Tidings,* 1661 Siskiyou
Blvd.
Central Point (7,509) **Z** 97502
Central Point C/C, 714 E.
Pine St.
Eagle Point (3,008)
Gold Hill (964)
Jacksonville (1,896) **Z** 97530
Jacksonville C/C & Visitors
Info., P.O. Box 33
Medford (46,951) **Z** 97501
C/C of Medford/Jackson
County, 101 W. 8th
Medford Visitors Bureau, 304
S. Central Ave.
D *Mail Tribune,* 33 North First
St.
Phoenix (3,239)
Rogue River (1,759) **Z** 97537
Rogue River Area C/C, 111
E. Main St.
W *Rogue River Press,* P.O.
Box 1485
Shady Cove (1,351)
Talent (3,274)
White City (5,891)
Newport–Lincoln City (Lincoln
county)
Depoe Bay (870) **Z** 97341
Depoe Bay C/C, 630 S.E.
Hwy. 101
Lincoln Beach (1,507)
Lincoln City (5,892) **Z** 97367
Lincoln City C/C, 801 S.W.
Hwy. 101
W *The News Guard,* 930 S.E.
Hwy 101
Newport (8,437) **Z** 97365
Newport C/C, 555 S.W.
Coast Hwy.
W *News-Times,* P.O. Box 965
Rose Lodge (1,257)
Toledo (3,174)
Waldport (1,595)
Yachats (533) **Z** 97498
Yachats Area C/C, P.O. Box
728

PENNSYLVANIA

Pike County (Pike county)
Blooming Grove (2,022)
Delaware (3,527)
Dingman (4,591)
Greene (2,097)
Lackawaxen (2,832)
Lehman (3,055)
Matamoras (1,934)
Milford (1,013) **Z** 18337
Pike County C/C, 305 Broad
St.
W *Pike County Dispatch,* 105
W. Catharine St.
Palmyra (1,976)
Shohola (1,586)
Westfall (2,106)
State College (Centre county)

Bellefonte (6,358) **Z** 16823
Bellefonte Area C/C, Train
Station
Benner (5,085)
Boggs (2,686)
Centre Hall (1,203)
College (6,709)
Curtin (516)
Ferguson (9,368)
Gregg (1,805)
Haines (1,315)
Halfmoon (1,469)
Harris (4,167)
Howard (1,004)
Howard (749)
Huston (1,282)
Liberty (1,747)
Marion (730)
Miles (1,494)
Milesburg (1,144)
Millheim (847)
Patton (9,971)
Penn (935)
Philipsburg (3,048) **Z** 16866
Port Matilda (669)
Potter (3,020)
Rush (3,411)
Snow Shoe (1,756)
South Philipsburg (438)
Spring (5,344)
State College (38,923) **Z** 16801
Centre County Visitors
Bureau, 1402 S. Atherton
St.
State College Area C/C, 131
S. Fraser St.
D *Centre Daily Times,* 3400
E. College Ave.
Taylor (714)
Union (895)
Walker (2,801)
Worth (709)

SOUTH CAROLINA

Aiken (Aiken county)
Aiken (19,872) **Z** 29801
Greater Aiken C/C, 400
Laurens St. N.W.
D *The Standard,* 124 Rutland
Dr.
Belvedere (6,133)
Clearwater (4,731)
Gloverville (2,753)
Jackson (1,681)
New Ellenton (2,515)
North Augusta (15,344)
Z 29841
Greater North Augusta C/C,
235 Georgia Ave.
Wagener (731)
Beaufort (part of Beaufort county)
Beaufort (9,576) **Z** 29902
Greater Beaufort C/C, 1006
Bay St.
D *Beaufort Gazette,*
1556 Salem Rd.
Port Royal (2,985)
Charleston Sea Islands
(Charleston county)
Charleston (80,414) **Z** 29401
Charleston Trident Visitors
Bureau, P.O. Box 975
Charleston Trident C/C, 81
Mary St.
D *Post & Courier,* 134
Columbus St.
Folly Beach (1,398)

Hollywood (2,094)
Isle of Palms (3,680)
Kiawah Island (718)
Ladson (3,046)
Lincolnville (716)
Meggett (787)
Mount Pleasant (30,108)
North Charleston (69,111)
Ravenel (2,165)
Seabrook Island (948)
Sullivan's Island (1,623)
Clemson–Pendleton District
(parts of Anderson, Oconee,
and Pickens counties)
Central (2,438)
Clemson (11,064) **Z** 29633
Clemson Area C/C, 103
Clemson St.
Liberty (3,228) **Z** 29657
Greater Liberty C/C, P.O.
Box 123
Norris (884)
Pendleton (3,314)
Seneca (7,726)
Six Mile (562)
Westminster (3,120)
Conway (part of Horry county)
Conway (9,819) **Z** 29526
Conway Area C/C, 203 Main
St.
Hilton Head Island (part of
Beaufort county)
Bluffton (738)
Hilton Head Island (23,694)
Z 29926
Hilton Head Island Visitors
Bureau, P.O. Box 5647
Hilton Head Island C/C, One
Chamber of Commerce Dr.
D *Island Packet,*
1 Pope Ave.
Myrtle Beach–North Myrtle
Beach (part of Horry county)
Little River (3,470) **Z** 29566
Little River C/C, P.O. Box
400
Myrtle Beach (24,848) **Z** 29577
Myrtle Beach Area Visitors
Bureau, 710 21st Ave. N.
Myrtle Beach Area C/C, 1301
N. Kings Hwy. 29578
D *Sun News*
914 Frontage Rd.
North Myrtle Beach (8,636)
Z 29582
North Myrtle Beach, P.O.
Box 754
Surfside Beach (3,845)

TENNESSEE

Crossville (Cumberland county)
Crab Orchard (876)
Crossville (6,930) **Z** 38555
Greater Cumberland County
C/C, 108 S. Main St.
W *Crossville Chronicle,* 312
S. Main St.
W *Cumberland Times,* P.O.
Box 745
Fairfield Glade (2,209)
Pleasant Hill (494)
Maryville (Blount county)
Alcoa (6,400)
Eagleton Village (5,169)
Friendsville (792)
Maryville (19,208) **Z** 37801

Blount County C/C, 309 S.
Washington St.
D *Times,* P.O. Box 9740
Rockford (646)
Seymour (1,922)
Townsend (329) **Z** 37882
Townsend in the Smokies
C/C, 7906 Lamar
Alexander Pkwy.

TEXAS

Alpine–Big Bend (Brewster
county)
Alpine (5,637) **Z** 79830
Alpine C/C, 106 N. 3rd St.
W *Alpine Avalanche,* P.O.
Box 719
Austin (Travis county)
Austin (463,178) **Z** 78767
Austin Visitors Bureau, 201A
E. 2nd St.
Austin Women's C/C of
Texas, P.O. Box 26051
Austin/Travis County
Hispanic C/C, 221 E. 9th
St.
Greater Austin C/C, 111
Congress Ave.
Texas State C/C, 900
Congress Ave.
D *American-Statesman,* 305
S. Congress
Garfield (1,233)
Jollyville (1,112)
Jonestown (1,250)
Lago Vista (2,199)
Lakeway (4,044)
Lost Creek (4,095)
Manor (1,041)
Onion Creek (1,544)
Pflugerville (4,444)
Rollingwood (1,388)
Tanglewood Forest (2,941)
Wells Branch (7,094)
West Lake Hills (2,542)
Windemere (3,207)
Cedar Creek Lake (Henderson
county)
Athens (10,967) **Z** 75751
Athens C/C, 1206 S.
Palestine
D *Review,* 201 S. Prairieville
Berryville (749)
Brownsboro (545)
Chandler (1,630)
Eustace (662) **Z** 75124
Eustace Area C/C, P.O. Box
333
Gun Barrel City (3,526)
Malakoff (2,038) **Z** 75148
Malakoff C/C, City Hall
W *The Malakoff News,* 107 W.
Main St.
Murchison (510)
Payne Springs (606)
Seven Points (723)
Tool (1,712)
Trinidad (1,056)
Fredericksburg (Gillespie county)
Fredericksburg (6,934) **Z** 78624
Fredericksburg C/C, 106 N.
Adams
W *Standard Radio Post,* P.O.
Box 473
Kerrville (Kerr county)
Ingram (1,408)

Kerrville (17,384) **Z** 78028
Kerrville Area C/C, 1700
Sidney Baker St.
D *The Times,* 429 Jefferson
St.
Lake Buchanan–Lake LBJ
(Burnet and Llano counties)
Bertram (849)
Burnet (3,423)
W *Burnet Bulletin,* P.O. Box
160
Cottonwood Shores (548)
Granite Shoals (1,378)
Marble Falls (4,007)
Meadowlakes (514)
Buchanan Dam (1,099)
Z 78609
Lake Buchanan C/C, Hwy. 29
Horseshoe Bay (1,222)
Kingsland (2,725) **Z** 78639
Kingsland/Lake LBJ C/C,
Hwy. 1431, P.O. Box 465
Llano (2,962) **Z** 78643
Llano County C/C, 700
Bessemer
W *The Llano News,* P.O. Box
187
Lake Conroe (part of
Montgomery county)
Conroe (27,610) **Z** 77301
Greater Conroe C/C, 101 W.
Phillips St.
D *The Courier,* 100 Ave. A
Magnolia (940)
Montgomery (356) **Z** 77356
Lake Conroe Area C/C, P.O.
Box 1
Pinehurst (3,284)
Willis (2,764)
Lake Granbury (Hood county)
Granbury (4,045) **Z** 76048
Lake Granbury Area C/C,
108 N. Crockett St.
W *Hood County News,* 1419
S. Morgan St.
Oak Trail Shores (1,750)
Tolar (523)
Lake Livingston (parts of Polk,
San Jacinto, and Trinity
counties)
Coldspring (538) **Z** 77331
Coldspring C/C, P.O. Box
980
Corrigan (1,764)
Groveton (1,071) **Z** 75845
Groveton C/C, 106 Main
Livingston (5,019) **Z** 77351
Polk County C/C, 516 W.
Church
W *Polk County Enterprise,*
100 Calhoun St.
Onalaska (728) **Z** 77360
Onalaska C/C, P.O. Box 880
Shepherd (1,812) **Z** 77371
Greater Shepherd C/C, W.
Hwy. 150
Mission–McAllen–Alamo (Hidalgo
county)
Alamo (8,210)
Donna (12,652) **Z** 78537
Donna C/C, 210 N. D.
Salinas Blvd.
Freer C/C, 154 E. Hwy. 44
Edinburg (29,885) **Z** 78539
Edinburg C/C, 521 S. 12th
Hidalgo (3,292) **Z** 78557
Hidalgo C/C, 611 E. Coma

La Joya (2,604)
McAllen (84,021)
D *The Monitor,* 1101 Ash St.
Mission (28,653) **Z** 78572
Mission C/C, 220 E. Ninth St.
Penitas (1,077)
Pharr (32,921) **Z** 78577
Pharr C/C, P.O. Box 1341
San Juan (10,815) **Z** 78589
San Juan C/C, 125 W. 5th
New Braunfels (Comal county)
Canyon Lake (9,975) **Z** 78130
W *Times Guardian-Chronicle,*
P.O. Box 2098
Garden Ridge (1,450)
New Braunfels (27,091)
Z 78131
New Braunfels C/C, 390 S.
Seguin St.
D *Herald-Zeitung,* 707 Landa
St.
Rockport–Aransas Pass (Aransas
county)
Aransas Pass (912) **Z** 78336
W *Aransas Pass Progress,*
346 S. Houston St.
Fulton (763)
Rockport (4,753) **Z** 78382
Rockport–Fulton Area C/C,
404 Broadway
W *Rockport Pilot,* 1200 Wharf
St.
W *The Herald,* P.O. Box 1448
San Antonio (Bexar county)
Alamo Heights (6,502)
Balcones Heights (3,022)
Castle Hills (4,198)
China Grove (872)
Converse (8,887)
Cross Mountain (1,112)
Dominion (1,196)
Elmendorf (568)
Fair Oaks Ranch (1,640)
Helotes (1,535)
Hill Country Village (1,038)
Hollywood Park (2,841)
Kirby (8,326)
Leon Valley (9,581)
Live Oak (10,023)
Olmos Park (2,161)
San Antonio (935,933) **Z** 78201
Greater San Antonio C/C,
602 E. Commerce
North San Antonio C/C, 45
N.E. Loop 410
Randolph Metrocom C/C,
12702 Toepperwein Rd.
San Antonio Visitors Bureau,
P.O. Box 2277
San Antonio Hispanic C/C,
110 Broadway
SouthSide C/C, 908
McCreless Mall
D *Express-News,* Ave. E &
3rd St.
Scenic Oaks (2,352)
Shavano Park (1,708)
Somerset (1,144)
St. Hedwig (1,443)
Terrell Hills (4,592)
Timberwood Park (2,578)
Universal City (13,057)
Windcrest (5,331)
Wimberly–San Marcos (Hays
county)
Buda (1,795)

W *Hays County Free Press,*
 P.O. Box 339
Dripping Springs (1,033)
 Z 78620
 W *Dripping Springs Dispatch,*
 P.O. Box 426
Kyle (2,225)
San Marcos (28,743) **Z** 78666
 San Marcos Visitors Bureau,
 P.O. Box 2310
 San Marcos C/C, 202 N.
 C.M. Allen Pkwy.
 D *Daily Record,*
 1910 I-35 South
Wimberley (2,403) **Z** 78676
 Wimberley C/C, P.O. Box 12
 W *The Wimberley View,* P.O.
 Box 49
Woodcreek (889)

UTAH

St. George–Zion (Washington
 county)
 Enterprise (936)
 Hildale (1,325)
 Hurricane (3,915) **Z** 84737
 Hurricane Valley C/C, P.O.
 Box 101
 Ivins (1,630)
 La Verkin (1,771)
 Santa Clara (2,322)
 St. George (28,502) **Z** 84770
 Saint George Area C/C, 97 E.
 St. George Blvd.
 Washington County Visitors
 Bureau, 425 S. 700 E.
 D *Spectrum,* P.O. Box 1630
 Washington (4,198)

VERMONT

Burlington (Chittenden county)
 Alburg (1,362)
 Bolton (971)
 Burlington (39,127) **Z** 05401
 Lake Champlain Reg. C/C,
 209 Battery St.
 D *Free Press,* 191 College St.
 Charlotte (3,148)
 Colchester (14,731)
 Essex (16,498)
 Grand Isle (1,642)
 Hinesburg (3,780)
 Huntington (1,609)
 Jericho (4,302)
 Milton (8,404)
 North Hero (502) **Z** 05474
 Lake Champlain Islands C/C,
 P.O. Box 213
 Richmond (3,729)
 Shelburne (5,871)
 South Burlington (12,809)
 South Hero (1,404)
 St. George (705)
 Underhill (2,799)
 Westford (1,740)
 Williston (4,887)
 Winooski (6,649)
St. Jay–Northeast Kingdom
 (Caledonia county)
 Barnet (1,415)
 Burke (1,406)
 Danville (1,917)
 Groton (862)
 Hardwick (2,964) **Z** 05843
 Hardwick Area C/C, P.O. Box
 111

Lyndon (5,371) **Z** 05849
 Lyndon Area C/C, P.O. Box
 886
Peacham (627)
Ryegate (1,058)
Sheffield (541)
St. Johnsbury (7,608) **Z** 05819
 Northeast Kingdom C/C, 30
 Western Ave.
 D *Caledonian-Record,* 25
 Federal St.
Sutton (854)
Walden (703)
Waterford (1,190)
Woodstock (Windsor county)
 Barnard (872)
 Bethel (1,866)
 Bridgewater (895)
 Cavendish (1,323)
 Chester (2,832) **Z** 05143
 Chester C/C, P.O. Box 623
 Hartford (9,404)
 Hartland (2,988)
 Ludlow (2,302) **Z** 05149
 Ludlow Area C/C, Lemere
 Square
 Norwich (3,093)
 Pomfret (874)
 Reading (614)
 Rochester (1,181) **Z** 05767
 Rochester Valley C/C,
 General Delivery
 Royalton (2,389)
 Sharon (1,211)
 Springfield (9,579) **Z** 05156
 Springfield C/C, 14 Clinton
 St.
 Stockbridge (618)
 Weathersfield (2,674)
 West Windsor (923)
 Weston (488)
 Windsor (3,714) **Z** 05089
 Windsor Area C/C, Main St.
 Woodstock (3,212) **Z** 05091
 Woodstock Area C/C, 18
 Central St.
 W *Vermont Standard,* P.O.
 Box 88

VIRGINIA

Charlottesville (Charlottesville
 independent city and
 Albemarle County)
 Barracks (4,710)
 Commonwealth (5,538)
 Charlottesville (40,341)
 Z 22902
 Charlottesville–Albemarle
 County C/C, Fifth & E.
 Market St.
 D *Daily Progress,* 685 W. Rio
 Rd.
 Crozet (2,256)
 Hollymead (2,628)
 Rio (5,133)
 Scottsville (220) **Z** 24590
 Scottsville C/C, Route 4, Box
 57
 University Heights (6,900)
Fredericksburg–Spotsylvania
 (Fredericksburg independent
 city and Spotsylvania county)
 Fredericksburg (19,027) **Z**
 22401
 Fredericksburg–Stafford–
 Spotsylvania C/C,
 4201 Plank Rd.

D *Free Lance-Star,* 616
 Amelia St.
 Spotsylvania Courthouse
 (2,694)
Northern Neck (Lancaster and
 Northumberland counties)
 Irvington (496) **Z** 22480
 Irvington C/C, P.O. Box 282
 Kilmarnock (1,053) **Z** 22482
 Kilmarnock C/C, P.O. Box
 1357
Smith Mountain Lake (Bedford
 and Franklin counties)
 Forest (5,624)
 Ferrum (1,514)
 Moneta (11,000) **Z** 24121
 Smith Mountain Lake C/C, 2
 Bridgewater Plaza
 Rocky Mount (4,098) **Z** 24151
 Franklin County C/C, E.
 Court St.
Virginia Beach (Virginia Beach
 independent city)
 Virginia Beach (393,069)
 Z 23451
 Hampton Roads C/C-Virginia
 Beach, 4512 Virginia Beach
 Blvd.
 Virginia Beach Visitors
 Bureau, 2101 Parks Ave.
 W *The Virginia Beach Sun,*
 138 S. Rosemont Rd.
Williamsburg (Williamsburg
 independent city and James
 City County)
 Williamsburg (11,530) **Z** 23187
 Williamsburg Area C/C, 201
 Penniman Rd.
 W *The Virginia Gazette,* 213
 Ironbound Rd.
Winchester (Frederick County and
 Winchester independent city)
 Winchester (21,947) **Z** 22601
 Winchester-Frederick Co.
 Visitor Center, 1360 S.
 Pleasant Rd.
 D *Winchester Star,* 2 N. Kent
 St.
 Middletown (1,061)
 Stephens City (1,186)

WASHINGTON

Bellingham (Whatcom county)
 Bellingham (52,179) **Z** 98225
 Bellingham/Whatcom C/C &
 Ind., 1801 Roeder Ave.
 D *Bellingham Herald,* 1155
 State St.
 Birch Bay (2,656)
 Blaine (2,489) **Z** 98230
 Birch Bay C/C, 7387 Jackson
 Rd.
 Everson (1,490)
 Ferndale (5,398) **Z** 98248
 Ferndale C/C, 5640 Riverside
 Dr.
 Lynden (5,709) **Z** 98264
 Lynden C/C, 444 Front St.
 Marietta–Alderwood (2,766)
 Nooksack (584)
 Sudden Valley (2,615)
 Sumas (744)
Chewelah (part of Stevens
 county)
 Chewelah (1,945) **Z** 99109
 Chewelah C/C, 110 E. Main
 St.

W *The Chewelah Independent,* P.O. Box 5
Port Angeles–Seqium (Clallam county)
Port Angeles (17,710) **Z** 98362
Port Angeles C/C, 121 E. Railroad Ave.
D *Penninsula Daily News,* 305 W. 1st Ave.
Port Angeles East (2,672)
Sequim (3,616) **Z** 98382
Sequim–Dungeness Valley C/C, 1192 E. Washington
W *Sequim Gazette,* 147 W. Washington
Port Townsend (Jefferson county)
Hadlock–Irondale (2,742)
Port Townsend (7,001) **Z** 98368
Port Townsend C/C, 2437 E. Sims Way
W *Port Townsend–Jefferson County Leader,* P.O. Box 552
San Juan Islands (San Juan county)
Friday Harbor (1,492) **Z** 98250
San Juan Island C/C, P.O. Box 98
Wenatchee (Chelan county)
Cashmere (2,544) **Z** 98815
Cashmere C/C, P.O. Box 834
Chelan (2,969) **Z** 98816

Lake Chelan C/C, P.O. Box 216
W *Lake Chelan Mirror,* 315 E. Woodin Ave.
Leavenworth (1,692) **Z** 98826
Leavenworth C/C, 894 Hwy. 2
South Wenatchee (1,207)
Sunnyslope (1,907)
Wenatchee (21,756) **Z** 98801
Wenatchee Area C/C, 2 S. Chelan
D *Wenatchee World,* 14 N. Mission St.
West Wenatchee (2,220)
Whidbey Island (Island county)
Ault Field (3,795)
Clinton (1,564)
Coupeville (1,377) **Z** 98239
Central Whidbey C/C, P.O. Box 152
Freeland (1,278) **Z** 98249
Freeland Community C/C, P.O. Box 361
Langley (845) **Z** 98260
Langley C/C, 124 1/2 2nd St.
W *South Whidbey Record,* 201 2nd & Athens Ave.
Oak Harbor (17,176) **Z** 98277
Greater Oak Harbor C/C, 5506 Hwy. 20
W *Whidbey News Times,* 3098-300 Ave. West

WEST VIRGINIA
Charles Town–Harpers Ferry–Shepherdstown (Jefferson county)
Bolivar (1,013)
Charles Town (3,122) **Z** 25414
Jefferson County C/C, 200 E. Washington St.
W *Spirit Of Jefferson Advocate,* P.O. Box 966
Harpers Ferry (308)
Ranson (2,890)
Shepherdstown (1,287)

WISCONSIN
Eagle River (Vilas county)
Eagle River (1,374) **Z** 54521
Vilas County C/C, Courthouse
W *Vilas County News Review,* P.O. Box 1929
Lac du Flambeau (1,423) **Z** 54538
Lac du Flambeau C/C, P.O. Box 158
Northern Door Peninsula (part of Door county)
Bailey's Harbor (1,098)
Egg Harbor (183)
Ephraim (502)
Sister Bay (675)
Sturgeon Bay (9,176) **Z** 54235
Door County C/C, 1015 Green Bay Rd.

ABOUT THE AUTHOR

Since 1982, **David Savageau** has traveled throughout the country visiting locations that attract older adults. He writes the "Tale of Two-Cities" column for *Expansion Management* magazine and is a featured speaker at the U.S. Department of State's quarterly seminar on retirement.

He would appreciate comments, criticisms, and suggestions for improving the next edition of *Retirement Places Rated.* Write to:

Places Rated Partnership
P. O. Box 1327
Gloucester, MA 01931